Using QuickC®

Using QuickC®

Werner Feibel

Osborne **McGraw-Hill**
Berkeley, California

Osborne **McGraw-Hill**
2600 Tenth Street
Berkeley, California 94710
U.S.A.

For information on translations and book distributors outside of the U.S.A., write to Osborne **McGraw-Hill** at the above address.
A complete list of trademarks appears on page 595.

Using QuickC®

1234567890 DODO 8987

ISBN 0-07-881292-5

For my parents, with love and thanks
for all they've done for me

Contents

Introduction   xiii

1   Introducing C   1
C Features   2
An Example of C Programming   3
The Nature of C   5
Using C   7
Why QuickC   11

2   A Quick Look at Quick C   13
Hands-on QuickC   14
Exploring Program Execution   28
QuickC Commands   38
Summary   72

3   Simple Types and Operators   73
C Program Structure   74
Statements   80
Identifiers   81
Variable Definition: Making Room   84
Simple Data Types   88
Variants on Simple Type   99
Constants   101
Arithmetic Operators   107
print( ) Once More   113
Summary   114

4   Preprocessors and Programs   115
Program Structure   115
The C Preprocessor   119

Preprocessor Commands   122
Library Functions   135
Macros That Look Like Functions   141
Header and Other Include Files   143
Summary   144

5   Reading and Writing in C   145
Reading Characters   146
More About printf( )   153
Values and Variables: The Address Operator   158
Summary   165

6   Controlling C   167
Relational and Equality Operators   168
Logical Operators   170
The if-else Construct   172
The switch Statement   178
More Operators   182
Loops in C   186
Components of the while Loop   188
The do-while Loop   191
The for Loop   193
break and continue   201
Summary   204

7   Functioning in C   205
C Functions   206
Flow of Control   207
Function Returns   213
Formal and Actual Parameters   217
Summary   225

8   Function Prototypes   227
Influence of Prototypes on Syntax for Formal Parameters   231
Syntax: Old and New   237
Functions: Miscellaneous Points   237
Summary   238

9   Scope, Lifetime, and Storage Class   239
Scope and Visibility   239
Duration of Variables   249
Storage Class   251
Default Storage Classes and Storage Durations   259
Summary   261

10 **Pointers** **263**

Objects, Lvalues, Values 264
Pointers 267
Pointers as Function Parameters 274
Pointer Arithmetic 280
Miscellaneous Points 284
Pointer Pitfalls 285
Summary 287

11 **Arrays and Strings** **289**

Array Basics 290
Arrays and Pointers 293
Array Parameters 298
Strings 303
Multidimensional Arrays 315
Pointer Arrays 322
Summary 327

12 **More on Functions and More Functions** **329**

Functions Returning Pointers 330
Error Handling and stderr 338
Adding to Your Function Collection 344
Recursion 359
Summary 368

13 **Command Line Arguments** **369**

main( ) as Program and as Function 370
What Are Command Line Arguments? 371
Command Line Arguments in DOS 372
Arguments to main( ) 376
A Program to Exercise Command Line Arguments 382
Summary 390

14 **Files and Memory** **391**

Files 392
Dynamic Memory Allocation 403
Summary 420

15 **Bit and Other Operators** **421**

Bitwise Operators 421
The Conditional Operator 451
Summary 455

16   **Structures, Unions, and Other Types**   **457**

Structures   458
Bit-Fields   492
Unions   497
Enumeration Types   500
Summary   502

17   **QuickC Library Functions**   **505**

stdio.h   506
stdlib.h   515
string.h   525
ctype.h   536
dos.h   541
io.h   548
math.h   551
Other Files   555
Summary   556

A   **ASCII Codes**   **557**

B   **Building Libraries in QuickC**   **559**

Building Quick Libraries   560
Building Stand-Alone Libraries   564
Summary   569

C   **QuickC Command Summary**   **571**

Commands for Calling QuickC   572
Useful Commands in the QuickC Environment   573
Editing Commands   573
Menu Commands   576
Compiling and Linking Outside of QuickC   584
Controlling the Linker   586

D   **Features of QuickC and Microsoft C 5.0**   **589**

Environment and Performance   589
Memory Models and Libraries   590
Debugging   592
Miscellaneous   593
Similarities   593

Index   597

Acknowledgments

Many people deserve thanks for making this book possible. The following people were particularly helpful and encouraging throughout the project.

Kris Jamsa deserves thanks for his technical review and very helpful suggestions. Many of the book's good features are there because of his suggestions and corrections; the book's defects are there because I didn't listen to Kris's objections.

I also wish to thank the people at Osborne/McGraw-Hill who are always helpful, friendly, and accommodating; it has been a pleasure to work with them. Jeff Pepper deserves special thanks for getting this project started and for keeping it on the smoothest course possible. Liz Fisher and Lyn Cordell helped keep me on course, and dealt gracefully and efficiently with ambiguous materials and last minute changes, for which I thank them. Thanks also to the unsung heroes in the art and production departments at Osborne/McGraw-Hill. They had to work extra hard (on a tight schedule made even tighter by changes required late in the production process) to turn the manuscript into a real book.

Finally, I owe my friends many thanks for putting up with me and keeping me going during the past few months. In particular, I want to thank Luanne Panarotti, Scott Barnes, Alexa Beiser, Dan Kiely, and little Dylan Beiser Kiely, whose favorite part of the project was the printer cable.

This book may have gotten done without these people, but it would have been a lot less fun.

Introduction

Welcome to C and to the QuickC environment! You can use this book to learn about both the C language and the QuickC implementation.

C is a small but extremely powerful language that is becoming the language of choice for all sorts of software development projects. Programs written in C range from simple utilities through data base management systems to compilers (including C compilers!) and operating systems. QuickC is an interactive, easy-to-use, programming environment that provides all the necessary components to create, compile, test, and run C programs.

QuickC is an ideal environment for learning C because it enables your editor, compiler, and debugger to support each other. This makes the program development process much faster and more convenient. For example, the QuickC compiler can keep a record of the errors it finds while compiling your program and put you back in the editor at the location of the first error when the compiling is done. The QuickC editor lets you jump from one compiler error to the next, and make all your corrections in one session. Then, with a single keystroke, you can compile and run your program again. If you're familiar with other compilers that require you to make corrections one at a time (leaving the compiler and starting the editor as a separate program each time), you will appreciate this feature. If you haven't worked with compilers before, you'll learn from the start how convenient programming in C can be.

This book introduces you to the C programming language and shows you how to use Quick C to write programs quickly and effectively. My purpose has been to explain the advantages of C and the features of the QuickC programming environment. In later chapters, you'll find sections that illustrate how to use various QuickC features as part of the discussion of particular C constructs. I've also included advice on some pitfalls you may encounter when writing C programs and on how to avoid them.

The book focuses on the version of C implemented in QuickC and in the Microsoft C version 5.0 compiler. This version of C conforms to the official language definition currently being drafted, so you can also use this book to learn C with other compilers.

The text contains lots of examples, since these usually illustrate a point better than several paragraphs of description. You'll also find suggested modifications and variations to try. The programs are designed to let you experiment easily, and many of them will report on their own actions.

The best way to learn a programming language is to use it. Whether your main interest is in C or QuickC, you'll get a lot more out of this book—and enjoy it much more—if you enter the programs and examples and try them out yourself. Once you've done that, experiment with the examples; change some of the functions or the input. One of the best ways to deepen your understanding of a language is to experiment with it. Then, once you feel comfortable with the material covered here, work on projects that interest *you*.

You'll find it is helpful, though not essential, to have some familiarity with programming—perhaps with a language such as Pascal or BASIC. If you have used either or both of these languages, you'll find that C differs in important, and sometimes in very subtle, ways. If you have no programming experience, don't worry. You'll still be able to use this book, but you may need to put in some extra effort to be sure you understand some of the terms and concepts.

Program Source Files

This book contains dozens of programs that illustrate C concepts. Many of these programs are designed for experimentation and exploration, and some are quite entertaining to use, such as the trivial-fact generating programs in Chapter 2. Throughout the book, I encourage you to play with the programs—to enter, compile, and run them—and to observe the effects when you modify them.

The complete source code for all the programs is included here, so you can simply type them in from the book. However, if you want to save yourself the demands of that task, the source code for all the programs in this book (as well as some additional programs and functions) can be purchased on two 360K diskettes, for $22 ($20 plus $2 for postage and handling). The diskettes contain about 450K of source files. In addition to the programs from the book, these files include a quick and dirty program for testing functions during development, a simple daily reminder program that you can tailor to your needs, and several others.

To order the diskette, use the form that follows this introduction.

To order the source code diskettes for *Using QuickC,* please provide the following information and a check or money order for the appropriate amount:

$25 per copy ($20 + $5 shipping and handling) for foreign orders

$23 per copy ($20 + $2 shipping and handling + $1 sales tax) for Massachusetts residents

$22 per copy ($20 + $2 shipping and handling) for other orders

Number of copies: _____   Amount enclosed: _____

Name _____

Company (if applicable)_____

Street Address _____

City _____ State _____ ZIP Code _____

Please send this information, along with your check or money order to:

Werner Feibel
P.O. Box 2499
Cambridge, MA 02238

Osborne/McGraw-Hill assumes no responsibility for this offer. This is solely the offer of Werner Feibel, and not of Osborne/McGraw-Hill.

Introducing C

C is an elegantly simple language; it is also a challenge to programmers. At times, you will love C; at other times, you'll hate it.

There is much to like about C: it is small, powerful, and when used properly, C is fast, efficient and portable, meaning that it's moved easily from one computer or operating system to another.

C lets you do marvelous things, such as building compilers, operating systems, and editors. C can also turn nasty — overwriting compilers, operating systems, editors, or whatever else you may have stored in your system's memory.

C gives you the power and potential portability of high-level languages such as Pascal or Modula-2 along with the flexibility and destructive potential of low-level languages, such as assembly language. C lets you build complex data structures found in other high-level languages and enables you to manipulate individual bits of that data structure in ways normally possible only with assembly language.

However, C will not protect your programs from themselves, and will let them destroy your data if you are not careful.

1

On balance, you'll be able to do all sorts of things with C, without getting yourself into any more trouble than with another programming language — as long as you don't get too fancy or too sloppy.

Every language — whether English or C — has a set of rules that defines the language. For example, in English, a period ends a sentence. Such a set of rules is known as a *syntax* for the language. Learning the syntax is the easy part of C; learning how to use the language to its fullest is your real challenge. Your rewards, which include programming power and a better understanding of your computer, are definitely worth the effort.

Microsoft Corporation's QuickC makes C available and accessible by providing a complete, easy-to-use language implementation. QuickC is an enhanced compiler (it converts programs into object code), a linker (it produces executable files), a shell (it serves as a command interpreter), and a rich programming environment. With the help of this book, you'll be able to take advantage of QuickC's special features, and make C work for you.

C Features

Several features make C a very attractive programming language for projects large and small. These include performance features, such as speed and efficiency of your executable program, and also features relating to the transportability and modularity of programs. Modularity lets you break a large program into small, manageable pieces, which you may be able to reuse in other programs. Of course, the extent to which a particular program takes advantage of these features of C depends on how well the program is written. The examples in this text provide a solid foundation for you to develop good C programs.

Performance Features

C is smaller than Pascal, Modula-2, or even BASIC. C has only about 30 *keywords* or *reserved words*. Because many of C's actions are close to assembly-level activity, using C can increase the speed of your program and make it easier to create concise, "optimized" expressions.

C gives you a complete set of tools. It's your job to maximize its potential. Because C lets you get very close to the actual memory cells and registers in your computer, you can do just about anything in a C program. This capability makes C very powerful—ideal for complex projects, or programs that need to take full advantage of the system on which they are running.

Portability

C can be very portable. One reason for C's portability is the preprocessor, which makes it possible to substitute information specific to a particular machine when compiling or running a program. As you'll see in later chapters, you can use the preprocessor to help make your programs run faster.

Modularity

One feature that helps make C portable is its capacity to build programs out of small functions and library modules that have already been compiled. The library modules can contain C functions specific to a particular machine. Because you can build and compile independent function libraries, C allows you to write programs in a modular fashion. You can break large programs into smaller units, which contain functions that can be used together in other applications. Because individual modules are built and modified separately, you can use a strategy that makes it easier to move programs to other machines.

An Example of C Programming

The following listing shows one way of incorporating information from other files into a program, and illustrates one way of increasing program portability.

```
/* Program showing the use of an include file containing program specific
   messages. Each program can have its own system or program
   specific include file.
*/
```

```
#include "proginfo.h"  /*  a file containing various definitions. */

main ()  /* the main C program */
{
        /* write value of PROG_MESSAGE to screen */
        printf ( "%s\n", PROG_MESSAGE);
}
```

The main program, the C function **main( )**, simply writes something to the screen: the value of something named PROG—MESSAGE.

The writing is done by the function **printf( )**, which is predefined for you in QuickC and other C implementations. The function **printf( )** writes whatever you tell it to. In this case, the program tells it to write the value of PROG—MESSAGE.

When it encounters the \ **n**, **printf( )** writes a carriage return and a line feed, which puts the cursor at the leftmost column of the next line.

The % begins a placeholder for a particular type of information, whose value is substituted when **printf( )** writes the material; the **s** indicates that a string is to be written. In our example, **%s** is the placeholder for PROG— MESSAGE, which contains a string. In C, a string is a sequence of characters terminated by a special character, which we'll discuss later.

The escape code **\n** is a compact way of moving the cursor in a particular way. Later, we'll study the syntax for **printf( )** in more detail, including how to write other types of information (such as integers and real numbers), and there will be more about escape codes, such as **\n**.

The structure of function **main( )** illustrates the format of functions in C. A function starts with a name (in this case, **main**), followed by parentheses (which may have something between them). The main body of a function is enclosed in braces.

Within the body of the function, individual statements end with a semicolon. Comments may appear anywhere in a program, and are enclosed between /* and */.

Note that PROG—MESSAGE is not defined anywhere in the program file. Rather, this value is specified in the header file, **proginfo.h**, which the compiler reads when processing the file containing the main program. Such header files are common in C. Each system or program may have its own header files. These files contain program or operating system specific values and definitions. For example, when running under QuickC, the program's message would read "QuickC Version 1.0"; running under Microsoft C Version 5.0, the message might be "Microsoft C Version 5.0." These messages are stored in a file such as **proginfo.h**.

Most C compilers provide a file called **stdio.h**, which contains system-and implementation-specific information, and which associates specific values, such as "QuickC Version 1.0" with names, such as PROG—MESSAGE. Search your QuickC directories for files with the extension .h. These are the header files provided with your compiler.

The Nature of C

C can be described as a middle-level language, having characteristics and capabilities of both high- and low-level languages. This is one reason for its apparently contradictory properties. C lets you create complex data structures, as do other high-level languages. However, unlike such languages, C does minimal range and type checking when you use such variables. At the other extreme, C lets you look at the contents of specific address locations in memory; C even lets you do arithmetic with addresses. Such capabilities are available in assembly languages, but rarely in high-level languages.

There are several reasons for C's contrasting features. It was designed to be flexible, permissive, fast, and portable. Dennis Ritchie, who developed C, and Brian Kernighan, who was involved in much of the early work with C, intended C to be useful for writing systems (such as operating systems) as well as application programs (such as editors). Therefore, the developers gave C the speed and flexibility of assembly language, but the data structures and control constructs (such as **if-then**, **for**, **while**) of high-level languages.

Table 1-1 lists some properties of high- and low-level languages, and indicates where C stands with respect to these properties. Note that C has almost every property listed.

A Small Language

C has a very small vocabulary — only about 30 keywords. Although the words are few, you can say a great deal with them. A small vocabulary does not mean

Table 1-1. C Measured Against the Properties of High- and Low-level Languages

High-level Languages	C		Low-level Languages
Structured	yes	yes	Fast
Easy to use	yes	yes	Compact
Safeguards	yes/no	yes	(Can be) efficient
Complex data structures	yes	yes	Address and bit manipulation

a weak language: some linguists claim that fewer than 900 words are needed to communicate effectively in English.

On the other hand, C has lots of operators or symbols that cause specific actions. In fact, C has more operators than keywords! This combination of a small vocabulary and many operators lets you use C as a "construction set." You can easily create individual statements or functions to do just the right amount of work. As you'll see, C programs are usually built of small functions that perform specific tasks. These functions are collected in modules and used as needed.

The Power of C

Despite its small size, C is being used for a huge range of programs. Large parts of the powerful UNIX and DOS operating systems are written in C. Similarly, C has been used to write compilers (including C compilers), editors, typesetting programs (such as **troff** and **TeX**), and such programs as dBaseIII and Microsoft Windows.

At the other end of the spectrum, you will find many C programs that perform specific tasks, such as display a calendar for any month or year, count the number of words in a file, list the contents of a directory, find a particular word or other expression in specified files, compute the interest payments on a loan under various conditions, and so on. Source code for many of these programs is available on electronic bulletin boards, from user groups, or in inexpensive utility packages. You may want to look at (or use) some of these programs, to study and play with the code. In later chapters we'll look at a few programs of this sort.

Standard Versions

There is as yet no official standard for C. Although C is used everywhere, it is only now being officially defined. There has been a *de facto* standard version of the language, summarized in *The C Programming Language* by Brian Kernighan and Dennis Ritchie (Englewood Cliffs, New Jersey: Prentice-Hall, 1978). This version of C is known as "K&R C," with compilers often claiming that they implement "full K&R C," or "K&R C, with extensions."

After several years, however, a standards committee is about to complete its work on an official definition of the language. The working name for this version is "Draft Proposed ANSI Standard C." Eventually, C's official name will be "ANSI Standard C." (ANSI stands for American National Standards Institute.)

The committee's task is to resolve ambiguities and to make it easier to port C programs. Also, without sacrificing any of C's power, the committee has added some of the high-level language features that help protect programmers from the consequences of their errors. The version of C emerging from the deliberations of this committee will be more powerful than ever.

This book, QuickC itself, and most new C compilers will conform to the draft version of the ANSI standard.

Using C

Getting a C program from idea to completion takes several steps, with each step modifying or extending your program. In the next chapter you'll learn how to write C programs and get them to run using QuickC. This section summarizes the main components of a C program and the major tasks involved in getting from your text file to a running program. We'll see that QuickC puts the tools for accomplishing various tasks under one program "shell." This makes it easy to move from one phase of the program creation process to another.

When you create a C program, various types of files are created and used. These include: source and header files created with a text editor; library and other object files, linked with the compiled version of your main program file; and an executable file that runs the program.

The first step is to create the program in text form—this is the source file. The following listing is an example of a source file for a C program:

```
/* Sample C source file.
   This program adds two numbers and writes the sum to the screen.
*/

#include "proginfo.h"  /* file containing program specific information */

main ()                /* main program function */
{
        int result;   /* definition of an integer variable, named result */

        printf ( "%s\n", PROG_MESSAGE);
        i1 = 7 + 9;                         /* add 7 + 9, assign sum to result */
        printf ( "sum = %d\n", result);  /* write result to screen */
}
```

The output from this program is

```
QuickC version 1.0
sum = 16
```

The file contains the main program, **main( )**, which calls **printf( )**, as did our first example. There is also an instruction (**#include "proginfo.h"**) to read the contents of a header file, **proginfo.h.**

There are several new features. Notice that this program also writes numerical information, the value of variable **i1**. The **%d** (for decimal) placeholder indicates this fact. In the second call to **printf( )**, the value to be substituted is the value of **i1**, which is 16 after the addition is carried out.

The second argument, information passed to **printf( )**, is substituted for the placeholder in the function's first argument. This simple replacement strategy extends to handle additional arguments, as you'll soon see.

The program also illustrates how to define a variable in C, that is, how to associate a data type with a variable name. (If you're not used to working with data types, and are not sure what they are, don't worry. Data types are explained in Chapter 3.) The variable **i1** is defined to be of type **int**, for integer.

Finally, the statement,

```
i1 = 7 + 9;
```

assigns the result of adding 7 and 9 to the variable **i1**. You'll learn about variable definition and assignments in Chapter 3.

Compiling and Linking

The source file containing the listing is processed by the QuickC compiler, which creates another version of the file by translating your program into another form. During compilation, QuickC reads the header file **proginfo.h** and makes the requested substitutions and definitions.

Source files include definitions for the functions you need in your program, and may include definitions of variables used by multiple functions in your program. There may also be instructions to read additional header or other files. Your program will have one main source file, and may have additional include files.

Header files are ordinary text files either written by you or provided with the compiler. These files generally contain information needed for specific tasks on a particular machine or with a particular compiler. Associated with this information are mnemonic names, which are easier to remember than obscure numerical values. When you use these names, the compiler substitutes the values it finds for each name in the header files. For example, the header file, **proginfo.h**, may contain the following:

```
/* Partial contents of file, proginfo.h. */

#define PROG_NAME  "QuickC version 1.0"  /* C version name */
#define MAX_INT  32767              /* largest integer value in system */
#define FALSE  0                    /* value to substitute when test is false */
```

The second statement provides a name for the largest integer represented on the system. This name is much more meaningful than the actual number, which may vary from machine to machine. When the compiler sees MAX__INT in the source file, it substitutes the value 32767. In the third instance, the compiler substitutes the numerical value 0 when you use **false** in your program. (Later, you will see how C represents true and false.)

Such substitutions work out well for you and your program. You can use meaningful and easy-to-remember names. The compiler substitutes actual values, so it need not look up the value associated with the name you used, as would be necessary with variables. This makes your program run faster.

The compiler produces an object file that contains your program (as well as other information) in a form more readily understood by the machine on which the program runs. Your program may use functions that have already been defined for you, or that you have defined elsewhere, compiled, and saved in a separate file. A linker program combines the recently compiled object file with function library files and other precompiled (object) files. The outcome of this linking process is the program itself, often known as an *executable file*.

Library Files

It is common among C programmers to build and use precompiled library files containing commonly used functions. These functions are linked with a program only if they are needed. This approach has several advantages. When writing the program, you need not write the functions because they are already written and available. When compiling, you need not compile the functions each time because they are already compiled. This saves time, since the compiled source file being composed is shorter.

Function libraries or modules make it easier to build portable programs because system-dependent functions can be collected in modules isolated from system-independent functions. To move to a new system, only the modules containing system-dependent functions need to be rewritten or replaced. The new version can then be linked into your program after it has been recompiled for the new system. Later, we will discuss library files and look at some of the most commonly supplied functions. To summarize, a C program consists of the following basic components:

1. Source files created with an editor and processed by the compiler. One of these files contains the main program function, **main( )**. Every C program must have at least one source file.

2. Optional header files, which may contain various values and definitions for the program or the environment.

3. Library files and other object files, which are linked with your com-

piled program files at the appropriate point in the program development process.

4. An executable file.

▶**REMEMBER**

- There must be at least one source file—otherwise you have nothing to compile or run.

- There must also be a function called **main( )** somewhere in the source files.

- The program starts executing at **main( )**.

All files other than source files—headers, libraries, and so forth—are optional. Whether you need such files, and how you add them, depends on the C compiler you are using and the tasks you are trying to accomplish in your program.

If all goes well, and the compilation and linking processes take place without error, your program will be ready to run. Of course, that's often when the real fun begins, when you discover the surprising things you've unintentionally instructed your program to do.

▶**REMEMBER**   There are three steps in creating a C program:

1. Creating source file(s)

2. Compiling the source file(s)

3. Linking the resulting object file with whatever libraries and additional modules are needed

Why QuickC?

QuickC makes it easy to carry out the steps required for C programming in a flexible manner, within a tightly integrated and powerful environment. The QuickC system provides a shell within which you can easily move from one step to another when creating and testing your program.

You can edit, compile, link, debug (watch your program as it runs, looking for errors, or bugs), and execute your program, all within QuickC. Moreover, QuickC lets you specify options for any of these phases. This is very easy to do with QuickC. For example, it takes just a single keystroke to tell QuickC to optimize the program for speed (at the cost of program size); or you can ask it to warn you about any questionable programming practices, such as constructs that violate the official language definition.

If you are used to writing programs, you know the tedium involved in fixing small errors as the compiler encounters them. You must stop the compilation, call up your editor, change your file, save it, call up the compiler, find the next error, and so on.

In QuickC, all of this can be done within one program. After you have created your source file, QuickC lets you compile, link, and run it in just a few keystrokes. If there are any problems with the program, QuickC puts you back in the source file at the appropriate place. You can edit the file, then tell QuickC to continue. The system then recompiles, relinks, and reruns the revised program.

QuickC's integrated environment is also convenient for debugging. You can trace the program's execution using the debugging facility. If a change is needed, simply make it, then tell QuickC to continue. Again, a few keystrokes will get the system to reprocess your program and run it again, but this time in debugging mode.

QuickC comes "preloaded" with many functions defined in separate libraries by other C implementations. This gives you access to a more powerful C without forcing you to link in separate libraries to get this power.

Best of all, QuickC does its work *quickly*. In the next chapter, we will look at the QuickC environment and explore it with a few sample programs. Throughout the book, you will learn ways of taking particular advantage of QuickC's environment.

2

A Quick Look
at QuickC

Microsoft's QuickC is a very powerful integrated program development environment, which includes an editor (for creating your program files), a compiler (for translating your programs into a form understandable to the computer), and a debugger (for tracing the execution of your program to identify errors in it). These components are all accessible within the QuickC shell, so you can switch between them quickly. A linker is also available for use by QuickC and as a separate program. There are many additional features, such as on-line help, that make QuickC even nicer to use.

This chapter provides two kinds of information. The first half presents an informal introduction to some of QuickC's features. You'll learn how to use QuickC to create, compile, watch, and run your programs. This section is designed to give you a chance to explore the most commonly used features of

QuickC. It is by no means an exhaustive discussion. Its purpose is to give you a feel for what's involved in building C programs with QuickC. You may want to use the QuickC command summary in Appendix C as a supplement to this introduction.

The second half of the chapter is a more systematic summary of the most common QuickC commands for the editor, compiler, and debugger.

Hands-on QuickC

Although QuickC includes dozens of options and commands in its collection, the chances are very good that a large proportion of the things you'll need to do in most applications will involve only a dozen or so commands. In this part of the chapter, we'll focus on some of these.

By becoming familiar with these commands, you can acquire enough experience to use QuickC comfortably. This experience will provide a base to which you can add other commands as you need them.

Since you haven't learned much about C yet, you'll have to do some typing, trusting that the programs work without being told how they work. The only way to learn something is to do it. So, you are *strongly* encouraged to type in the programs and try the suggested activities.

To make this process somewhat more enjoyable, we'll build programs that you can modify easily. This will enable you to play with the programs a bit to add to your knowledge of QuickC and should also provide a bit of entertainment. The programs will be as short as possible, while still producing an interesting result. To keep them short, we've skipped many of the niceties and checks that a sound program should have. If you find any of the programs interesting, you may want to return to them later and make them more to your liking.

So, let's get started. We'll assume you have QuickC installed on your hard disk or on floppy disks and that you are currently in a directory or on a disk from which you can access the **qc.exe** program. We'll also assume that you are familiar with your keyboard, and that you know where keys such as the RETURN, ALT, CTRL, DEL, INS, HOME, SHIFT, TAB, and BACKSPACE are located.

A Quick Introduction

As you try things, you'll get a better feel for the command structure of QuickC. You'll notice that commands generally tend to be either single keystrokes or a combination of the ALT, CTRL, or SHIFT key with a letter key.

Also, as you spend more time in the QuickC environment, you'll notice that it includes several menus, which provide you with access to QuickC's components. To select a menu, you will need to press the ALT key together with a letter key (the first letter of the menu's name). Once in a menu, you can select an option by pressing a letter key or highlighting the option and then pressing RETURN. The default option is always highlighted when you get into a menu. You can also call many commands directly—that is, without going through a menu. In the first half of this chapter we will give commands directly and with a menu, depending on the command. In the second half of the chapter, you'll learn the alternative ways of giving commands.

Selection of an option inside a menu generally brings you to a dialog box, in which QuickC shows you the values it has for the options, and gives you a chance to change some of these values. For these options, the default values will generally be highlighted, and will be in effect if you just press RETURN.

Finally, if you ever find yourself in a position where you don't know the command to accomplish something, just press the F1 function key, to call up the on-line Help facility.

To get you started with QuickC, let's create a small C program. This will give you an opportunity to use the editor and the compiler. The sequence of steps described below will get you started. As you follow these steps, keep in mind that you sometimes need to press RETURN (also called ENTER) after completing a command or a line. We'll mention this explicitly at first, but will eventually stop reminding you. At other times, however, you should *not* press RETURN.

To get QuickC to a point where you can start entering a program, type **qc**, then press RETURN. Once QuickC has started up, your screen should appear as shown in Figure 2-1. You are now ready to start writing a program. Type in the following program:

```
#define DIST  93000000.0

main()
```

```
{
        printf ( "The sun is %lf miles from the earth.\n", DIST);
}
```

To do this, just start typing. When you get to the end of the first line, press RETURN twice in succession to end the first line and to add a blank second line. Type things exactly the way you find them in the listing; make sure to observe the case of the characters. If you make a mistake, use the BACKSPACE key to delete the error. Pressing BACKSPACE deletes the last character you typed.

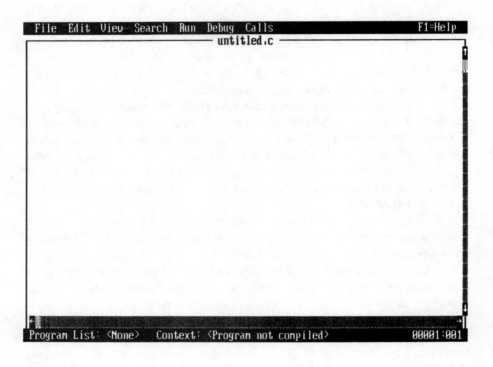

Figure 2-1. The initial Quick C screen

To get the indentation in the fifth line (the one beginning with **printf**), press the TAB key before starting to type the line. When you press RETURN at the end of this line, you'll find the cursor directly under the *p* in **printf** — that is, indented. Type the right curly brace. Then, to move it back to the leftmost column, press the SHIFT and TAB keys simultaneously to get a "reverse tab."

When you've finished typing in the program, it's time to compile and run it. To do so:

1. Press ALT-R (press the ALT and R keys simultaneously).

2. Press RETURN.

QuickC will quickly compile and run your program. You should get the following output from the program:

```
The sun is 93000000.000000 miles from the earth.
```

This will be followed by a QuickC message telling you to press any key.

Congratulations, you've just finished running a QuickC program! To save the program to disk,

1. Press any key, as instructed by QuickC.

2. Press ALT-F, but *do not* press RETURN.

3. Then press X (for Exit) or S (for Save), but *do not* press RETURN.

After verifying that you want to save the changes, QuickC will ask you for a file name. Press the BACKSPACE key until you've erased the default name, **untitled.c**. Type in the name under which you want to save the program. For this discussion we'll use **first.c**. (Actually, all you need to type here is **first**. QuickC adds the extension **.c** by default.) If you press ALT-F X, QuickC will save your program under the name you specify and will return you to the DOS prompt; if you press ALT-F S, QuickC will return you to the file after saving it. To quit, press ALT-F X.

Modifying the Program

Now, let's modify the file to make it do something more interesting. You can start QuickC with your program file preloaded by including the file name on the DOS command line when you call QuickC as shown here:

```
qc first
```

Notice that we did not include the file extension **.c** when telling QuickC about the file. Unless you tell it otherwise, QuickC assumes you want to work with a file ending in **.c**. You can, of course, include the **.c** extension when you type your file name on the preceding command line.

You're going to add several new lines to the program, and also delete one line. Once you're in the QuickC environment, and have the **first.c** file open, move the cursor to the line immediately below the #**define** line.

Start entering the additional #**define** statements in the following version of the program. Make sure all the uppercase names are entered *exactly* as in the listing, and make sure the #**define** is always in lowercase.

```
#define DIST        93000000.0
#define PTA         "sun"
#define PTB         "earth"
#define DIST_MESS   "Distance between"
#define DIST_UNIT   "miles"

#define SPEED       3.5
#define SPEED_MESS  "Average human walking speed: "
#define SPEED_UNIT  "mph"

#define TIME_MESS   "Time required to cover "
#define TIME_UNIT   "years"

#define MAGIC_NR    8766  /* hours per year */

#define FORMULA     DIST / SPEED / MAGIC_NR

main()
{
        printf ( "%s %s and %s: %lf %s\n",
                DIST_MESS, PTA, PTB, DIST, DIST_UNIT);
        printf ( "%s %lf %s\n", SPEED_MESS, SPEED, SPEED_UNIT);
        printf ( "%s %lf %s = %lf %s\n",
                TIME_MESS, DIST, DIST_UNIT, FORMULA, TIME_UNIT);
}
```

Once you've added all the new #**define** lines, move the cursor down to the line beginning with **printf**. When you're on that line, press CTRL-Y, to delete the entire line. Enter the replacement lines from the preceding program.

Then press ALT-R and RETURN to run the new version of the program. You may get a message asking whether to rebuild your program. If you get this message, press RETURN to respond "yes."

The program now produces the following output:

```
Distance between sun and earth: 93000000.000000 miles
Average human walking speed:  3.500000 mph
Time required to cover  93000000.000000 miles = 3031.191895 years
```

To see what happens when you get a compiler error, let's go back into the file and change something. Press the PGDN key to move near the end of the file. Then use the arrow keys to move to the line, beginning with **printf**, that contains references to SPEED—MESS, SPEED, and SPEED—UNIT. In each of these three names, delete one of the *E*'s, to give SPED—MESS, SPED, and SPED—UNIT. To do this, use the CTRL-RIGHT ARROW keys to move the cursor to SPEED—MESS. Then move to one of the *E*'s in this word, using the RIGHT ARROW key. Press DEL to delete this *E*. Then move to SPEED and do the same thing. Finally, delete an *E* from SPEED—UNIT. To recompile and try to run, press ALT-R RETURN again. This time the compiler gives you an error message, as shown in Figure 2-2.

The compiler tells you that SPED—MESS is undefined, and that the error is the first of three. Use the arrow keys to move to the *E* in SPED— MESS. Once there, simply type *E* again.

Then press SHIFT-F3, that is, the SHIFT key and the function key F3 simultaneously. QuickC will leave you on the same line, and will give you the same error message, but will tell you that this is error two of three. Make the correction to SPED, and press SHIFT-F3 again. You will see the third error message. Correct this, then press ALT-R RETURN to recompile. This time things should work as they did earlier.

What the compiler did was process your entire file, cataloging the errors. Since none was fatal, it was able to do so successfully. When the compilation process was finished, the compiler put you back into the editing mode, at the approximate location of the first error. The SHIFT-F3 command lets you move from one error to the next in your file, making it easy to correct compiler errors.

This program provides some moderately interesting trivia. Let's change

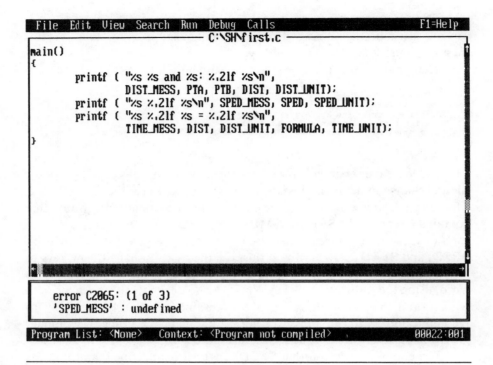

Figure 2-2.   Work file after compiler errors have been detected

the program once again to clean up the output somewhat. You'll format the output, so that the numbers are displayed only to two decimal places, using QuickC's Search facility.

Once you've got the **first.c** file open, press ALT-S, immediately followed by C. Do not press RETURN.

You will get the dialog box shown in Figure 2-3:

In the top box, labeled **Find What**, type %lf. Then type ALT-T to move the cursor to the **Change To** box. In this box, type %.2lf. Then press RETURN.

Because the default setting is to ask you to verify each change, QuickC will highlight each occurrence of %lf in your file. Press RETURN to accept the default; that is, to verify that each occurrence is to be changed.

```
 File  Edit  View  Search  Run  Debug  Calls                    F1=Help
┌─────────────────────────── C:\SH\first.c ───────────────────────────┐
│#define DIST      93000000.0                                         ▯│
│#define PTA       "sun"                                              ░│
│#define PTB     ┌───────────────────────────────────────────────┐   ░│
│#define DIST    │                                               │   ░│
│#define DIST    │ Find What: ┌────────────────────────────────┐ │   ░│
│                │            └────────────────────────────────┘ │   ░│
│#define SPEE    │                                               │   ░│
│#define SPEE    │ Change To: ┌────────────────────────────────┐ │   ░│
│#define SPEE    │            └────────────────────────────────┘ │   ░│
│                │                                               │   ░│
│#define TIME    │    [ ] Whole Word                             │   ░│
│#define TIME    │    [ ] Match Upper/Lowercase                  │   ░│
│                │    [ ] Regular Expression                     │   ░│
│#define MAGI    │                                               │   ░│
│                │ ┌─────────────────┐  ┌────────────┐  ┌──────┐ │   ░│
│#define FORM    │ │ Find and Verify │  │ Change All │  │Cancel│ │   ░│
│                │ └─────────────────┘  └────────────┘  └──────┘ │   ░│
│main()          └───────────────────────────────────────────────┘   ░│
│{                                                                    ░│
│        printf ( "%s %s and %s: %.2lf %s\n",                         ░│
│              DIST_MESS, PTA, PTB, DIST, DIST_UNIT);                 ▯│
└──────────────────────────────────────────────────────────────────────┘
 Program List: <None>   Context: <Program not compiled>       00001:001
```

Figure 2-3.   Dialog box for changing text

When all the changes have been made, press ALT-R RETURN — that is, the ALT and R keys simultaneously, followed by a RETURN — to start the compiler. The program will run and will display the information in the two decimal place format, as follows:

```
Distance between sun and earth: 93000000.00 miles
Average human walking speed:  3.50 mph
Time required to cover  93000000.00 miles = 3031.19 years
```

Before we modify the program to display some different trivia, let's look at what's going on. Essentially, the program displays its information by displaying exactly what it's told at the appropriate point. By using the #**define** statements (see Chapter 4), you are providing information for the compiler to substitute when it creates your program.

Thus, when the compiler sees DIST in your program, it substitutes 93000000.0; when it sees DIST__UNIT, the compiler substitutes "miles" and so forth. The second line beginning with **printf** actually displays the following:

```
SPEED_MESS SPEED SPEED_UNIT
```

This becomes "Average human walking speed: 3.50 mph" when the substitutions are made. So, all you've done is provided canned phrases for the program to display.

Two definitions are worth looking at more closely. The MAGIC__NR in this case represents the number of hours in a year. The material between /* and */ is a comment that indicates this fact to a reader of the source code.

The FORMULA is the expression used to compute the amount of time it would take a human to walk to the sun. Dividing DIST by SPEED (93000000.0 / 3.5) gives you the number of hours this walk would take. Dividing this result by MAGIC__NR (8766) tells you how many years these hours represent. The compiler substitutes exactly what you have specified when it encounters FORMULA in your program, then substitutes the values and messages for DIST, SPEED, and MAGIC__NR. What is finally displayed is the result of 93000000.0 / 3.5 / 8766.

Separating Program Components

To make this program display a different set of distance and speed facts, you can change the details of the terms you've defined. For example, to specify how long it would take a giant tortoise to walk from Earth to Mars, you need to make these changes:

- 93000000.0 to 35000000.0

- "sun" to "mars"

- 3.5 to .124

- "Average human walking speed:" to "Average giant tortoise walking speed:"

If you make the changes directly in your program file, you'll lose your original example about walking to the sun. Instead of writing it directly into **first.c**, write this information to a separate file. In this way, you'll be able to change the program to enable you to create as many distance files as you wish.

To accomplish this, use the following strategy:

1. Copy the definition lines from **first.c** to another file, **mars.h**, which will contain the new set of information. This is the file you will modify.

2. Copy these same lines to a file, **sun.h**, which will contain the information from the original example.

3. Delete these lines from **first.c**.

4. Modify the beginning of **first.c**.

To do this, start QuickC with **first.c** as your work file. If you aren't already working on this file, type

```
qc first
```

and press RETURN.

Inside **first.c**, move the cursor to the top of the file if it's not there already. Press CTRL-HOME or CTRL-Q R (CTRL and Q keys, followed by the R key) to accomplish this.

To move something from one place to another, you first need to mark the text you want to move. To do so, keep pressing SHIFT-DOWN ARROW until all the definition lines have been highlighted. When all these lines have been marked, press ALT-E (no RETURN) to get to the Edit menu. During the following session, whenever you are asked whether to save a file before moving on, press RETURN to indicate "yes."

1. Press C to copy the marked text.

2. Press ALT-F N to create a new file.

3. Name this file **mars.h** in the text box.

4. Once inside **mars.h**, press ALT-E P to paste the marked lines into this file.

5. Press ALT-F N to create another new file.

6. Name this file **sun.h** in the text box.

7. Once inside **sun.h**, press ALT-E P to paste the marked lines into this file as well.

8. Press ALT-F O to *open* an existing file.

9. Specify **first** as the file you want to open.

10. Use the SHIFT-DOWN ARROW keys to mark the definition lines again.

11. When these are all marked, press ALT-E T to cut these lines from **first.c**.

After doing all this, you'll have three files instead of your original one: **first.c**, **mars.h**, and **sun.h**.

Before leaving **first.c** again, add the following line at the top of the file. Make sure to include the quotes this time:

```
#include "mars.h"
```

Now go back to the **mars.h** file to make the required changes in that file. To do this, press ALT-F O and enter **mars.h** in the resulting text box.

To change 93000000.0 to 35000000.0, press CTRL-RIGHT ARROW twice. The cursor should then be on the 9 in 93000000.0. Press the DEL key twice, to delete the 93. Then type 35 to insert these two digits.

To change "sun" to "mars" use the Search menu again. Type CTRL-S C to change text. Type **sun** (no quotes) as the **Find What** text. Then press ALT-T to move to the **Change To** box. Type **mars** (again, no quotes) here, then press RETURN. You can use the same method to change 3.5 to .124 and "human" to "giant tortoise" (once again, no quotes) in the file.

Then press ALT-F F to reopen the last file, which was **first.c**. Once back in this file, press ALT-R R to Restart the compiler. This time the program will produce the following output:

```
Distance between mars and earth: 35000000.00 miles
Average giant tortoise walking speed:  0.12 mph
Time required to cover  35000000.00 miles = 32199.19 years
```

To have the program display information about walking to the sun again, just change the file name on the first line of **first.c** to **sun.h** from **mars.h**. (The **.h** extension stands for *header file*. Chapter 4 includes more information about header files.)

Here's one more sample file you can use. This one provides the information needed to determine how long it would take sound to travel from New York City to Peking, China. Use the commands you've learned so far to create this file.

```
#define DIST        11000.0
#define PTA         "New York"
#define PTB         "Peking"
#define DIST_MESS   "Distance between"
#define DIST_UNIT   "miles"

#define SPEED       760.0
#define SPEED_MESS  "Average sound speed: "
#define SPEED_UNIT  "mph"

#define TIME_MESS   "Time required to cover "
#define TIME_UNIT   "hours"

#define MAGIC_NR    1  /* hours per hour */

#define FORMULA     DIST / SPEED / MAGIC_NR
```

If you find this program amusing, you can use the following listing to build more files. The next program (called **builder.c**) will create a file with the name you specify, and will write the values you enter to this file. Once **builder** has written your file, you can make **first** use this file by substituting the new file's name for **sun.h** at the beginning of **first**. (Leave the quotes in this case.) To compile and run **first** after making these changes, just press ALT-R RETURN.

```
/* Program to generate files for trivial facts program. */

#include <stdio.h>
#include <string.h>
#include <stdlib.h>
#define MAX_STR  80

void str_info ( char *message, FILE *fptr)
{
        char str [ MAX_STR];

        printf ( "%s? ", message);
        gets ( str);
        fprintf ( fptr, "#define %s  \"%s\"\n", message, str);
}

void val_info ( char *message, FILE *fptr)
{
        char str [ MAX_STR];
        double value;

        printf ( "%s? ", message);
        gets ( str);
        value = atof ( str);
```

```
              fprintf ( fptr, "#define %s  %lf\n", message, value);
      }


      main()
      {
              char    str [ MAX_STR];
              void    val_info ( char *, FILE *), str_info ( char *, FILE *);
              FILE    *fp;

              printf ( "Complete file name? ");
              gets ( str);
              fp = fopen ( str, "w");

              if ( fp != NULL)
              {
              val_info ( "DIST", fp);
              str_info ( "PTA", fp);
              str_info ( "PTB", fp);
              str_info ( "DIST_MESS", fp);
              str_info ( "DIST_UNIT", fp);
              val_info ( "SPEED", fp);
              str_info ( "SPEED_MESS", fp);
              str_info ( "SPEED_UNIT", fp);
              str_info ( "TIME_MESS", fp);
              str_info ( "TIME_UNIT", fp);
              val_info ( "MAGIC_NR", fp);

              printf ( "FORMULA? ");
              gets ( str);
              fprintf ( fp, "#define FORMULA  %s\n", strupr (str));

              fclose ( fp);
      }
      else
              printf ( "File not opened.\n");
}
```

To make this program more useful, you should compile this program to an executable file. To do this:

1. Type **qc builder** and press RETURN , to start QuickC with **builder.c** as your work file. If you're already in QuickC and are working on this file, then this step is unnecessary.

2. Select the Compile option from the Run menu, by typing ALT-R C.

3. In the Compile dialog box, use the arrow keys to set the **Warning Levels** to Level 1. This will keep QuickC from displaying messages that would just be distracting now.

4. Type X to select the Exe output option.

5. Then press RETURN to compile and link the program to an executable file, named **builder.exe**.

6. Exit from QuickC by typing ALT-F X.

You should now have a file called **builder.exe** on your disk. To run this program, just type **builder** at the DOS prompt, and answer the questions the program asks you. Be forewarned that the program does not check whether you already have a file with the name you specify. If you give the name of an existing file, the program will create a new file with that name and your original file will be lost. So be careful.

Review

Let's summarize the things you've done so far, and the commands to accomplish these things.

- Creating a program source file: To create a file, you start QuickC, using the **qc** command, and start typing the contents of your file. To save the file, select the Save option on the File menu (ALT-F S). QuickC will ask you for a name under which to save the file.

- Editing an existing source file: Once you've created a file, you can work with it in QuickC. To specify the file, you can either type the file name on the command line when you call QuickC (for example, **qc first**), or you can start QuickC, then select Open on the File menu (ALT-F O), and type the name of the file you want to open in the resulting dialog box.

- Compiling and running a program within QuickC: Once you've got the program file in the shape you want, you can select the Start option on the Run menu by typing ALT-R S or ALT-R RETURN. This will run the program.

- Compiling a program and creating an executable (self-standing) program file: Select the Compile option on the Run menu (ALT-R C), then select X for an Exe output file, then press RETURN to accept the default action of building the program (that is, compiling and linking it, in this case).

- Moving around from file to file: Use the ALT-F to get the File menu and select the Open, New, or Last File options (O, N, and F keys, respectively).

- Marking text to be copied or cut: Use the SHIFT-DOWN ARROW keys.

- Copying text into a clipboard: Use the Copy option in the Edit menu (ALT-E C).

- Cutting text from a file: Use the Cut option in the Edit menu (ALT-E T).

- Pasting the contents of the clipboard in another file or at another location in the same file: Use the Paste option in the Edit menu (ALT-E P).

Exploring Program Execution

Often, you'll want to know what's happening while your program is executing. This information can be very useful if your program isn't doing what it's supposed to be doing. The information can also help you better understand the behavior of an algorithm (which is a well-defined solution process) in your program.

Debuggers are programs that let you execute a program step by step, and check the values of key variables at various points in the program. By determining where your program "went wrong," you should be able to find a way of fixing it. In this section, you'll learn how to use QuickC's built-in debugger to look inside your program while it's executing.

We won't try to fix program bugs, however. Rather, we'll use the debugger to see how a particular algorithm works as it tries to reach a certain value. The program applies the algorithm over and over, until a satisfactory solution is found. You can watch how values change as the algorithm converges on the "correct" answer.

The algorithm we'll use is a simple one, involving only whole numbers. Ironically, it turns out to be an unanswered question whether the algorithm will eventually stop for any starting value. The algorithm is often known as the

3A + 1 algorithm, and works as follows:

1. Start with an arbitrary whole number, A.

2. If A = 1, stop.

3. If A is even, replace A with A / 2 and go back to step 2.

4. If A is odd, replace A with 3A + 1 and go back to step 2.

The question is whether the algorithm will always end at 1 for any starting value. (It's known that the algorithm stops for all values less than 536870912, or 2^{29}.)

The following program implements this algorithm, and also computes and displays some information about the solution process. In particular, the program keeps track of the number of times **val**, the current number, is odd and even.

```
#include <stdio.h>
#include <stdlib.h>
#define MAX_STR  80

main ()
{
        long val, count = 0, even = 0, odd = 0;
        char str [ MAX_STR];

        printf ( "Starting value? ");
        gets ( str);
        val = atol ( str);

        do
        {
                count++;
                if ( val == 1)
                        odd++;
                else if ( !(val % 2))   /* if val is even */
                {
                        even++;
                        val /= 2;
                }
                else /* if val is odd, but not 1 */
                {
                        odd++;
                        val = 3 * val + 1;
                }
                printf ( "val = %ld; odd = %ld; even = %ld\n",val,odd,even);
                if ( !(count % 23))
                {
                        printf ( "Press a key to go on.");
                        getch ();
                        printf ( "\n");
```

```
                }
        }
        while ( val != 1);
        printf ( "After %ld iterations, result = 1.\n", count);
        printf ( "# even values = %ld; # odd values = %ld.\n", even, odd);
}
```

The program, which we'll call **algor.c**, does not show you the intermediate values created while applying the algorithm. You could get this information by adding the appropriate instructions to the program. Or you can use the debugger to peek at the values of specific variables as the program is running. We'll use the debugger to watch the program execute.

Setting Up for Debugging

When using the QuickC debugger, you can specify the variables whose values you want to watch and the program lines at which you would like to see these values. The debugger will then stop whenever it reaches one of these lines, called *breakpoints,* and will let you see the most recent values of the variables you asked to watch.

To use the debugger with a program, you must first compile the program in a way that will enable the debugger to get the information it needs. Assume **algor.c** is your current work file and you are ready to compile.

1. Type ALT-R C to select the Compile option on the Run menu.

2. In the dialog box you get, make sure the Debug option is marked with an X. If it is, just press RETURN. If the Debug option does not have an X, type D to set this option. Then press RETURN.

The compiler will compile your program to memory, with the "hooks" needed for the debugger to tell you what you want to know. After this is done, you'll be back in your program file.

To set things for the debugger, you'll want to do two things: specify the variables you want to watch, and set the breakpoints at which you want to see the values of these variables.

In this case, let's set three watch variables, **val**, **even**, and **odd**. To look at these variables, we'll set a breakpoint at the following line in the **algor** program:

```
printf ( "val = %ld; odd = %ld; even = %ld\n", val, odd, even);
```

To set the watch variables,

1. Type ALT-D C to clear all current breakpoints (just to be on the safe side).

2. Type ALT-D L to clear all current watch variables (again, as a precaution).

3. Type ALT-D RETURN to get the Add Watch variable dialog box.

4. Type **val; even; odd;** in the box to specify that you want three watch variables. The semicolons are necessary. After you type this, but before you press RETURN, the dialog box should look like Figure 2-4.

5. Move your cursor to the **printf()** statement at which you want to set your breakpoint.

6. Type ALT-D B to set a breakpoint at this line.

7. Type ALT-R RETURN to start executing the program.

The program's source code will be displayed as the program executes. When the program reaches the breakpoint, execution will stop temporarily, and you can look at the values of the watch variables (shown at the top of the screen). Figure 2-5 shows the first time the program stops at the breakpoint when executing with a starting value of 21. When you're ready to let the program move on, press the function key, F5.

The program will execute in this mode until it reaches its normal end — that is, until **val** becomes 1. To avoid starting values requiring a large number of trials before **val** reaches 1, you may want to try one or more of the following starting values: 5, 8, 10, 16, 20, or 21. (If you get caught in a run that is taking too long for you, you can use the file menu to get out. Type ALT-F X.)

One More Example

Let's look at another example, which will show you how to use run-time program options, and will also help increase your familiarity with the QuickC commands you've learned so far.

The following program displays unusual facts, just as an earlier program did. This time, however, the program generates the information to present at random, from a predefined list of facts. You provide the program with a **seed** value, which the program uses to select an object or entity at random from a

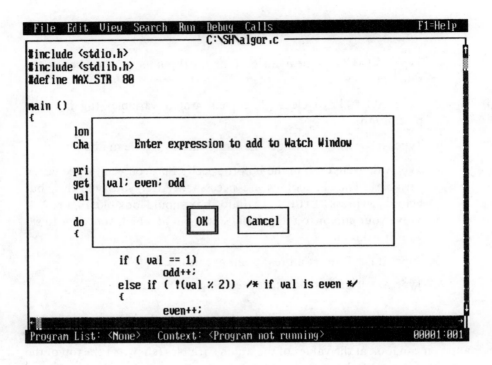

```
  File  Edit  View  Search  Run  Debug  Calls                    F1=Help
 ─────────────────────────── C:\SH\algor.c ────────────────────────────┐
 #include <stdio.h>                                                     ↑
 #include <stdlib.h>
 #define MAX_STR  80

 main ()
 {
     lon┌──────────────────────────────────────────────────────────┐
     cha│        Enter expression to add to Watch Window           │
        │                                                          │
     pri│ ┌──────────────────────────────────────────────────────┐│
     get│ │val; even; odd                                        ││
     val│ └──────────────────────────────────────────────────────┘│
        │                                                          │
     do │         ┌──────┐      ┌────────┐                         │
     {  │         │  OK  │      │ Cancel │                         │
        └─────────┴──────┴──────┴────────┴─────────────────────────┘

         if ( val == 1)
                 odd++;
         else if ( !(val % 2))   /* if val is even */
         {
             even++;                                               ↓
 ─────────────────────────────────────────────────────────────────→
 Program List: <None>   Context: <Program not running>       00001:001
```

Figure 2-4.   The dialog box with three watch variables entered

collection. The program determines the weight associated with this object, then selects another such object or entity at random, and determines its weight. Finally, the program provides information about the relative weights of these two selected objects.

```
#include <stdio.h>
#include <dos.h>
#include <stdlib.h>
#define MAX_STR      80
#define CYCLE        1024

#define UNIT         "kg"
#define MAX_ENTRY    11

char *obj [ MAX_ENTRY] = { "water molecule", "wasp", "chicken", "person",
                  "blue whale", "747", "moon", "Jupiter",
                  "Milky Way", "Universe", "car"};
```

```
 File  Edit  View  Search  Run  Debug  Calls                    F1=Help
val: 64
even: 0
odd: 1
                        ┌─ C:\SH\algor.c ─┐
            else if ( !(val % 2))  /* if val is even */
            {
                    even++;
                    val /= 2;
            }
            else /* if val is odd, but not 1 */
            {
                    odd++;
                    val = 3 * val + 1;
            }
            printf ( "val = %ld; odd = %ld; even = %ld\n", val, odd, even)
            if ( !(count % 23))
            {
                    printf ( "Press a key to go on.");
                    getch ();
                    printf ( "\n");
            }
    }

 Program List: <None>   Context: algor.c:main              00029:001
```

Figure 2-5.   Program execution stopped at a breakpoint

```
double data [ MAX_ENTRY] = { 7.99e-26, 5e-9, 3.15, 67.3, 1.38e5, 3.51e5,
                        7.5e22, 1.9e27, 2.2e41, 1e51, 1900.0};

int my_rand ( int *seed)
{
        *seed = (29 * (*seed) + 1) % 1024;
        return ( *seed);
}

main ( int argc, char *argv [ ])
{
        int     ch, index1, index2, my_rand ( int *), seed;
        char    str [ MAX_STR];
        double  data1, data2, nr;
        void    nice_print ( double, char *, char *);

        if ( argc == 2)
                seed = atoi ( argv [ 1]);
        else
        {
```

```
                  printf ( "Seed? ");
                  gets ( str);
                  seed = atoi ( str);
          }
          seed %= CYCLE;

          do
          {
                  index1 = my_rand( &seed) % MAX_ENTRY;
                  do
                  {
                          index2 = my_rand ( &seed) % MAX_ENTRY;
                  }
                  while ( index1 == index2);

                  data1 = data [ index1];
                  data2 = data [ index2];
                  if ( data1 > data2)
                          nr = data1 / data2;
                  else
                          nr = data2 / data1;
                  if ( data1 > data2)
                          nice_print ( nr, obj [ index2], obj [ index1]);
                  else
                          nice_print ( nr, obj [ index1], obj [ index2]);
                  printf ( "\nA %s is %.21g %s\n",
                          obj [ index1], data [ index1], UNIT);
                  printf ( "A %s is %.21g %s\n",
                          obj [ index2], data [ index2], UNIT);
                  printf ( "\n\n Press ! to stop. ");
                  ch = getche ();
          }
          while ( ch != '!');
}

void nice_print ( double num, char *str1, char *str2)
{
#define  CUTOFF  1e12

if ( num <= CUTOFF)
        printf ( "It would take %.21f %ss to make 1 %s.\n", num, str1, str2);
else
        printf ( "It would take %.21g %ss to make 1 %s.\n", num, str1, str2);
}
```

Enter the program, and give it a name. We'll call it **game.c** here. When you compile the program within QuickC—that is, when you use the ALT-R RETURN option, the program prompts you for a **seed**. After you provide this, the program generates random facts, based on the information available to it. The program keeps generating facts as long as you press any key other than the exclamation point (!), which ends the program.

The following listing was produced using a **seed** of 235:

```
It would take 6.3e+016 water molecules to make 1 wasp.

A wasp is 5e-009 kg
A water molecule is 8e-026 kg

 Press ! to stop.

It would take 13460000000.00 wasps to make 1 person.
```

```
A wasp is 5e-009 kg
A person is 67 kg

 Press ! to stop.
It would take 4.4e+049 wasps to make 1 Milky Way.

A Milky Way is 2.2e+041 kg
A wasp is 5e-009 kg

 Press ! to stop.
It would take 43809.52 chickens to make 1 blue whale.

A blue whale is 1.4e+005 kg
A chicken is 3.2 kg

 Press ! to stop. !
```

This program is actually different from the previous ones you've built. To see the difference most clearly, compile the program to an executable file. To do this,

1. Type ALT-R C to get the Compile options in the Run menu.

2. Use the arrow keys to set **Warning Levels** to 1, if it's not already at that value.

3. Type X to compile to an Exe output file, if this isn't already the default output file.

4. Then press RETURN.

Once you have an executable version of the program, you can simply type **game** at the DOS command line, and the program will start executing. Try this. You'll find that the program asks you for a **seed**, just as it did earlier.

Now, run the program again but this time type:

```
game 271
```

On this run, the program does *not* ask you for a **seed**, because the program takes the 271 as the **seed**. The effect is the same as if you had typed 271 in response to the program's earlier prompt.

Typing 271 when you start **game** is similar to what you do when you call QuickC with the name of the file you want to edit. The ability to specify certain information when calling a program can be very useful, as you'll see later.

You can accomplish the same thing even if you just compile the program to memory. A Run-Time option in the Run menu lets you specify the information you would type in addition to the program name.

To see how this works, select the Run-Time option in the Run menu, by typing ALT-R O (for Options). You will get a text box with the label, **Command Line**. Type 271 in this box, then press RETURN. Then type ALT-R RETURN to compile and run **game** in memory. This time, the program will not ask for a **seed**, and will behave just as it did in the executable version.

To close this part of the chapter, here's a program to generate fact collections for use with the **game.c** program.

```
/* Program to generate files for trivial facts program. */

#include <stdio.h>
#include <string.h>
#include <stdlib.h>
#define MAX_STR   80
#define MAX_ENTRY 100

main( int argc, char *argv [])
{
        char    str [ MAX_STR];
        void    val_info ( char *, FILE *), str_info ( char *, FILE *);
        void    nice_print ( int, char *, FILE *);
        void    nice_val ( int, double, FILE *);
        FILE    *fp;
        double data [ MAX_ENTRY];
        int count, nr_in;

        if ( argc == 2)
                fp = fopen ( argv [ 1], "w");
        else
        {
                printf ( "Complete file name? ");
                gets ( str);
                fp = fopen ( str, "w");
        }
        if ( fp != NULL)
        {
                printf ( "How many entries? ");
                gets ( str);
                nr_in = atoi ( str);
                fprintf (fp, "#define MAX_ENTRY %d\n", nr_in);
                printf ( "UNIT? ");
                gets ( str);
                fprintf (fp, "#define UNIT \"%s\"\n", str);

                fprintf ( fp, "\n\nchar *obj [ MAX_ENTRY] = \n{ ");
                for ( count = 0; count < nr_in; count++)
                {
                        printf ( "Object? ");
                        gets ( str);
                        if ( count < (nr_in - 1))
                                nice_print ( count, str, fp);
                        else
                                fprintf ( fp, "\"%s\"};\n", str);
                        printf ( "Value? ");
                        gets ( str);
                        data [ count] = atof ( str);
                }

                fprintf ( fp, "\n\ndouble data [ MAX_ENTRY] = \n{ ");
                for ( count = 0; count < nr_in; count++)
```

```
              {
                    if ( count < ( nr_in - 1))
                            nice_val ( count, data [ count], fp);
                    else
                            fprintf ( fp, "%lf};\n", data [ count]);
              }
              fclose ( fp);
        }
        else
              printf ( "File not opened.\n");
}

void  nice_print ( int nr, char *str, FILE *fptr)
{
        if ( (nr % 4) != 3)
              fprintf ( fptr, " \"%s\", ", str);
        else
              fprintf ( fptr, " \"%s\", \n  ", str);
}

void  nice_val ( int nr, double val, FILE *fptr)
{
        if ( (nr % 6) != 5)
              fprintf ( fptr, " %lg, ", val);
        else
              fprintf ( fptr, " %lg, \n  ", val);
}
```

Again, you should compile this program to an executable file to make it as useful as possible. Recall that to do this, you just need to select the Exe Output option in the Compile options under the Run menu. Let's use **makefact.c** and **makefact.exe** for this program's source and executable files, respectively.

With this program, you can specify a file name when you invoke the program. For example, if you typed

```
makefact myfacts.h
```

and entered object names and values, the program would write this information to a file named **myfacts.h**. To use this collection of facts, you would need to cut the top part of the **game.c** file as you did earlier with **first.c**. That is, you would need to cut everything beginning with the line

```
#define UNIT "kg"
```

through the end of the values entered for **data[MAX_ ENTRY]**. You would also need to add the following line near the beginning of **game**, probably right after the definition line for CYCLE:

```
#include "myfacts.h"
```

This program wrote the following listing into a file called **area.h**.

```
#define MAX_ENTRY 13
#define UNIT "square km"

char *obj [ MAX_ENTRY] =
{ "New York City", "Earth", "Jupiter", "Asia",
   "Pacific Ocean", "Sun", "Vatican City", "USSR",
   "USA", "Austria", "Pentagon", "Creat Pyramid at Cheops",
  "Florence"};

double data [ MAX_ENTRY] =
{ 830, 5.1e+008, 6.4e+010, 4.425e+007, 1.65e+008, 6e+012,
   0.44, 2.24e+007, 9500000, 84000, 0.12, 0.053,
  102.000000};
```

These data can be used by the **game** program if you include the following line between the definition line for CYCLE and the first line of the **my—rand( )** function:

```
#include "area.h"
```

As you become more familiar with C, you can come back and modify these programs if you wish. If you have become more comfortable moving around in the QuickC environment as a result of working with these programs, then they have served their purpose. If you also found them interesting to play with or if you picked up some information you didn't know before, all the better.

QuickC Commands

In the remainder of this chapter, we'll look more closely at the QuickC features and commands you're most likely to use in ordinary applications. The *QuickC Programmer's Guide* provides additional information about many of these commands and also describes features and commands not discussed here. This discussion will be largely a catalog of commands and features. Our main intent is to gather in one place brief summaries of the most common QuickC features and commands, although we will suggest things for you to try and you are strongly encouraged to experiment. This section lays the foundation for your use of QuickC throughout this book. To get the most from this chapter and from QuickC, try the things suggested and, by all means, experiment.

On-Line Help

The first command to learn is for the on-line help available in the QuickC environment. If you're ever uncertain of the command to do something, press function key F1. This gives you a dialog box, the first of several help screens, that contains summaries of the major commands. The box also contains several choices for action. The default is to display the next screen of help information, which is a summary of C operator precedence. Press P to see the previous help screen, and also to make backwards paging the default action.

If you want a summary of C keywords or of QuickC library functions, press K while in the Help dialog box. Use the arrow keys to select the label that best describes the general topic about which you want information. Press RETURN to get a complete list of keywords for which help is available in that topic.

▶**REMEMBER**   To get on-line help, press function key F1.

Creating and Editing Files

When you start QuickC, the program immediately loads a work file. This will be either a file you have specified on the command line, as you saw earlier in this chapter, or a file named **untitled.c**.

As soon as QuickC has loaded your file into memory, you can start inserting text into the file. Thus, to create a file, just start typing. To do other things, such as move around in the text or switch to an overwrite mode from the default insert mode, you need to use the QuickC commands described in this section.

In the following discussion, notice that many of the commands are available in two different contexts: as a command sequence while you're editing or as options on a menu. Ultimately, you'll probably find it more convenient to use the command sequences, so you won't have to leave the editor. Initially, however, you may find it easier to let the menus serve as your memory.

Editing Modes   QuickC's editor operates in one of two modes: *insert mode* (the default) and *overtype mode*. In insert mode, text is inserted at the current cursor position. Any text at or to the right of the cursor is moved to the right. Thus, if the cursor is sitting on top of a character (let's say, *a* in the following listing), when you insert a different character (let's say *z*), the original character (*a*) will not be lost. Rather, it and all subsequent characters on the line will be moved to the right.

The following listing shows the result of inserting *z* into the word *maybe* on the first line when the cursor is on the *a* in that word. The second line in the listing shows the result.

```
maybe not
mzaybe not
```

In overtype mode, on the other hand, any character at the current cursor position is overwritten when you type a new character. Surrounding characters are not affected. Essentially, typing in overtype mode amounts to crossing out text and substituting new text. The cursor changes from a small blinking line to a large block when you go into overtype mode.

The following two lines show the result of typing a *z* when the cursor is on the *a* in the string.

```
maybe not
mzybe not
```

When you first start QuickC, the editor is in insert mode. To switch to overtype mode, press the INS key or press CTRL-V. The editor toggles between these two modes, so to return to insert mode, just press INS again. Remember, the cursor is larger when you are in overtype mode, so you can always tell what mode you're in.

Moving in Your File   To move around in your file, you need to decide how far to move, and also the direction in which to move. The QuickC editor has a rich set of movement commands, so it may take a while to become familiar with all of them. Many of the commands are the same as those in WordStar, so if you've used that program you'll find the task somewhat easier.

When moving in your file, you can either move the cursor through the file or you can scroll the file past the cursor. We'll look at the cursor movement commands first.

The smallest vertical movement you can make is up or down one line, and the smallest horizontal movement is left or right one character. The QuickC editor has two ways of accomplishing each of these four moves. The most intuitive way is with the arrow keys. The UP ARROW key moves you up one line, the DOWN ARROW key moves you down one line, and the LEFT ARROW and RIGHT ARROW keys move you left and right one character, respectively.

You can also use commands involving the CTRL key to accomplish these moves. The four keys, S, E, D, and X, form a cross on the keyboard. Each of these keys, in conjunction with the CTRL key, moves you in one of the four directions. Thus, CTRL-E moves you up one line, and its counterpart CTRL-X moves you down one line. Similarly, the other pair of keys, CTRL-S and CTRL-D move you left and right one character, respectively. Table 2-1 summarizes these movement commands.

All of these moves are nondestructive. That is, the commands simply move the cursor; they do not delete or insert any text, regardless of the mode you're in.

You can also make larger moves. To move to the right or left one *word*, use the RIGHT and LEFT ARROW keys together with the CTRL key. That is, to move one word to the right, press CTRL-RIGHT ARROW; to move one word to the left, press CTRL-LEFT ARROW. You can also use CTRL-F and CTRL-A to move right and left by one word, respectively. (It may help to remember the latter two commands if you think of them as more extreme versions of the single character moves, CTRL-D and CTRL-S, based on the relative locations of the F and A keys on the keyboard.) Table 2-2 summarizes the commands for moving by words.

Table 2-1.   Single Character Cursor Movement

Key(s)	Effect
UP ARROW	Move cursor up one line
CTRL-E	Move cursor up one line
DOWN ARROW	Move cursor down one line
CTRL-X	Move cursor down one line
LEFT ARROW	Move cursor left one character
CTRL-S	Move cursor left one character
RIGHT ARROW	Move cursor right one character
CTRL-D	Move cursor right one character

Table 2-2.   Single Word Cursor Movement

Key(s)	Effect
CTRL-LEFT ARROW	Move cursor left one word
CTRL-A	Move cursor left one word
CTRL-RIGHT ARROW	Move cursor right one word
CTRL-F	Move cursor right one word

Before we look at more editing commands, let's look at some general properties of the commands. At a general level, there are three types of keys involved in editor commands:

- Ordinary character keys, such as E, D, X, and S
- "Special keys," such as the arrow keys, BACKSPACE, HOME, TAB, and the function keys
- "Modifier keys," such as the CTRL, ALT, and SHIFT keys

Ordinary characters cannot be used alone as commands because the editor will interpret these as part of the text for your file. To use these keys in editor commands, you need to modify them, as you've seen in commands such as CTRL-S and CTRL-A, for example. Thus, the minimal requirement for using an ordinary character in a command is the use of a modifier key with it.

Special keys *can* be used by themselves as commands, as you've seen in the UP ARROW and RIGHT ARROW commands, for example. You don't need any additional keys to use special keys as commands.

One strategy for organizing commands is to add modifiers to existing commands when these commands are intended to apply to different-sized units. You've seen an example of this: a RIGHT ARROW moves right one *character,* but a RIGHT ARROW modified by a CTRL moves right one *word.* This strategy is common in the QuickC editor commands; being aware of it will make it easier to learn what may seem like a lot of arbitrary commands.

To move on the entire screen, you need to modify the E and the X keys for moving vertically. Thus, to move to the top of the screen, press CTRL-Q E. That is, press CTRL-Q then the E key. The CTRL-Q sequence tells the editor to interpret the next character as part of a command, rather than as an ordinary text character for your file. Similarly, press CTRL-Q X to move to the bottom of the screen. Table 2-3 summarizes the commands for moving a screen at a time.

To move to the beginning or end of a line, press CTRL-Q S or CTRL-Q D, respectively. Note that these are the lateral movement characters (S and D), modified by CTRL-Q. You can also use the special keys, HOME and END to get to the beginning and end of the line, respectively, as summarized in Table 2-4.

To get to the beginning or end of the *file,* modify the HOME and END keys, as shown in Table 2-5. Thus, CTRL-HOME moves the cursor to the beginning of the file, and CTRL-END moves it to the end of the file. (CTRL-Q R and CTRL-Q C will also move the cursor to the beginning and end of the file, respectively.)

Table 2-3.   Cursor Movement by Screen

Key(s)	Effect
CTRL-Q E	Move to the top of the screen
CTRL-Q X	Move to the bottom of the screen

Table 2-4.   Cursor Movement by Line

Key(s)	Effect
HOME	Move to the beginning of the line
CTRL-Q S	Move to the beginning of the line
END	Move to the end of the line
CTRL-Q D	Move to the end of the line

Table 2-5.   Cursor Movement by File

Key(s)	Effect
CTRL-HOME	Move to the beginning of the file
CTRL-Q R	Move to the beginning of the file
CTRL-END	Move to the end of the file
CTRL-Q C	Move to the end of the file

The QuickC compiler will keep trying to compile your file as long as possible. Sometimes, the compiler will have to stop because of a fatal compiler error, such as being unable to open a specified file. In other cases, the compiler may be able to process your file completely—finding and cataloging errors, but not producing a compiled file. In that case, the compiler will return you to the editor at the approximate spot where the first error was found. The compiler will give you a message telling you the nature of the error and also the number of errors it encountered, as shown in Figure 2-2, earlier in this chapter.

You can move to errors that the QuickC compiler has found in your file, as shown in Table 2-6. To move to the next error in your file, press SHIFT-F3, that is, the SHIFT key and function key F3 simultaneously. To move to the previous error, press SHIFT-F4.

All the movement commands we've just summarized move the cursor through the file. You can also move the file in relation to the cursor, however. This is known as *scrolling*. You can scroll up and down one line at a time or one screen at a time. To scroll up one line, press CTRL-W; to scroll down one line, press CTRL-Z. These two keys are right next to the E and X keys, respectively, so you may find it helpful to use those keys for orientation in remembering the scrolling commands.

Similarly, to scroll up one screen, or window, at a time, press CTRL-R; to scroll down one screen at a time, press CTRL-C. These two keys are on the other side of E and X, respectively. You can also use the special keys, PGUP and PGDN, to scroll up and down one screen. Scrolling commands are summarized in Table 2-7.

Table 2-6.   Cursor Movement Between Errors

Key(s)	Effect
SHIFT-F3	Move to next error in file
SHIFT-F4	Move to previous error in file

Table 2-7.   Scrolling Commands

Key(s)	Effect
CTRL-W	Scroll up one line
CTRL-Z	Scroll down one line
PGUP	Scroll up one screen
CTRL-R	Scroll up one screen
PGDN	Scroll down one screen
CTRL-C	Scroll down one screen

Marking and Moving Text   You can easily move text from one part of your file to another, or even to another file, simply by marking the section of text you want to move and then specifying where you want to move it. You've already used some of these commands in the first part of this chapter.

The first step in moving or deleting a chunk of text is to mark it. Once you mark the text, you can use the Edit menu to place the text on the Clipboard, a buffer where you can temporarily place text in order to move it to a new location, without necessarily deleting your original text. All commands for marking text involve the SHIFT key.

As with cursor movement, you can specify text units of different sizes to mark. The smallest unit is a single character, and the largest is an entire file. To mark characters to the left of the cursor, press SHIFT-LEFT ARROW once for each character you want to mark. This command does *not* mark the character (if any) at the current cursor position. To mark characters to the right of the current cursor position, press SHIFT-RIGHT ARROW once for each character you want to mark. This command *does* mark the character at the current cursor position.

To mark individual words, you need to use both SHIFT and CTRL as modifiers. That is, you will need to press three keys simultaneously: SHIFT, CTRL and an arrow key. To mark *words* to the left of the current cursor position, press SHIFT-CTRL-LEFT ARROW once for each word you want to mark. Notice that this command will also mark portions of words. For example, if you have the cursor on the *r* in *careful,* and you press SHIFT-CTRL-LEFT ARROW, the first "word" to be marked will be the *ca* to the left of the current cursor position. Thus, this command will mark words or partial words to the left of the current cursor position; the command does not mark the character (if any) *at* the current cursor position. To mark words to the right of the current cursor position, type SHIFT-CTRL-RIGHT ARROW. This command also marks partial words, and it also marks the character (if any) at the current cursor position. Thus, if your cursor is on the *r* in *careful* again, pressing SHIFT-CTRL-RIGHT ARROW would mark the *reful* from the cursor to the end of the word.

To mark an entire line of text, use the SHIFT key in conjunction with the UP ARROW and DOWN ARROW keys. To mark lines above the current one, press SHIFT-UP ARROW once for each line you want to mark. Notice that this command does *not* mark the current line. To mark lines below the current one, press SHIFT-DOWN ARROW once for each line you want to mark. This command *does* mark the current line. Figure 2-6 shows an example of marked text in a file.

To mark from your current cursor position to the beginning of the file, press SHIFT-CTRL-PGUP; to mark from your current position to the end of the file, press SHIFT-CTRL-PGDN.

Table 2-8 summarizes the commands for marking text.

Once you've marked text, you can copy it to the Clipboard by pressing CTRL-INS. This is equivalent to calling up the Edit menu (press ALT-E to do this) and selecting the Copy option. You can accomplish this by pressing C when you have the Edit menu selected, or by using the DOWN ARROW key to highlight the Copy option and then pressing RETURN.

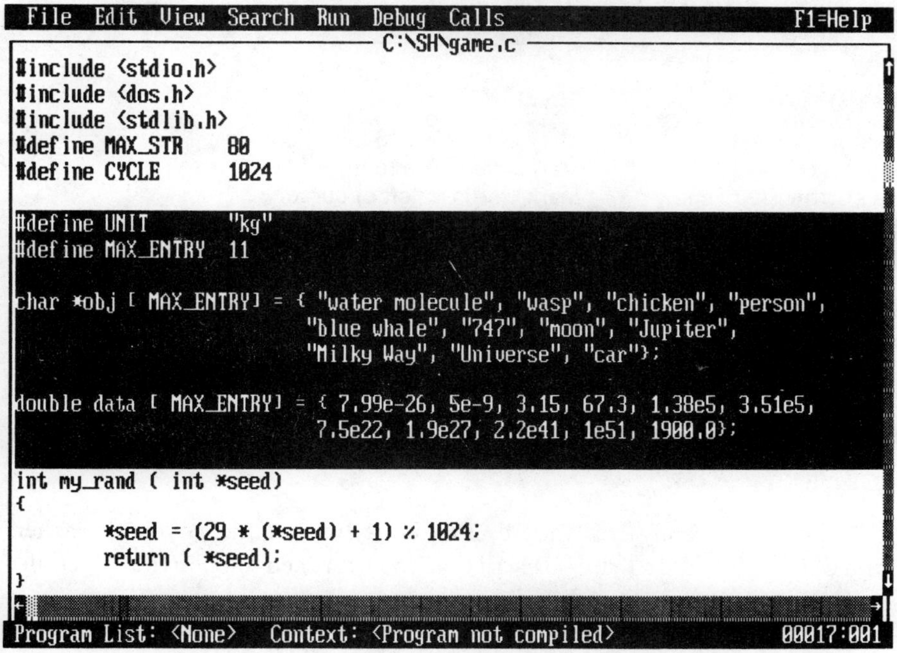

```
 File  Edit  View  Search  Run  Debug  Calls                    F1=Help
                           C:\SH\game.c
#include <stdio.h>                                                          ↑
#include <dos.h>
#include <stdlib.h>
#define MAX_STR     80
#define CYCLE       1024

#define UNIT        "kg"
#define MAX_ENTRY   11

char *obj [ MAX_ENTRY] = { "water molecule", "wasp", "chicken", "person",
                "blue whale", "747", "moon", "Jupiter",
                "Milky Way", "Universe", "car"};

double data [ MAX_ENTRY] = { 7.99e-26, 5e-9, 3.15, 67.3, 1.38e5, 3.51e5,
                7.5e22, 1.9e27, 2.2e41, 1e51, 1900.0};

int my_rand ( int *seed)
{
        *seed = (29 * (*seed) + 1) % 1024;
        return ( *seed);                                                    ↓
}
Program List: <None>    Context: <Program not compiled>            00017:001
```

Figure 2-6.   Screen showing marked text

Once text has been copied to the Clipboard, you can paste the text into other files or at other locations in the current file. To paste the text at a different location in the same file,

1. Move the cursor to the target location.

2. Select the Edit menu, by pressing ALT-E.

3. Select the Paste option by pressing P. You can also use the arrow keys to highlight the Paste option, and then press RETURN to select the option.

Table 2-8.   Text Marking Commands

Key(s)	Effect
SHIFT-LEFT ARROW	Mark characters to left of cursor
SHIFT-RIGHT ARROW	Mark characters to right of cursor
SHIFT-CTRL-LEFT ARROW	Mark words to left of cursor
SHIFT-CTRL-RIGHT ARROW	Mark words to right of cursor
SHIFT-UP ARROW	Mark lines above cursor line
SHIFT-DOWN ARROW	Mark lines below cursor line
SHIFT-CTRL-PGUP	Mark to beginning of file
SHIFT-CTRL-PGDN	Mark to end of file

You can also copy from the Clipboard to a different file, as you did earlier. (You did try that, didn't you?) Recall that you first need to open the target file:

1. Press ALT-F O to select the File menu and the Open option in that menu.

2. Enter the name of the file in the dialog box.

3. Once in the new file, move the cursor to the desired location.

4. Press ALT-E to select the Edit menu again.

5. Select the Paste option by pressing P.

Actually, if you have just copied the text to the Clipboard, you will be able to carry out steps 4 and 5 (that is, call Edit menu and select Paste option) much more easily. You can simply move the cursor to the desired location and press SHIFT-INS while editing. This will paste the text from the Clipboard to the file at the current cursor position, which is equivalent to pressing ALT-E P after you've moved the cursor. This command sequence will paste the desired text. The reason the ALT-E P command sequence works here is because the Paste option is accessible as a single letter command if you have just copied material to the Clipboard.

To see what's going on here, look at the Edit menu. The menu includes six options. Some of these options have single characters underlined. If you type an underlined character, that option will be selected. The Edit menu you get after copying to the Clipboard has the *P* in *Paste* underlined. That's why you can select the option in a shorter command sequence. (It's also why ALT-F O lets you open a file.)

The options available at a given time depend on the actions you've just carried out. For example, the Paste option is available only if something is on the Clipboard. Options that have a character underlined in the menu are available.

There is another way of moving material from one place to another. The Merge option in the File menu (ALT-F M) copies the contents of an entire file to your current file, inserting them at the current cursor position. Note that the entire file is merged with your current file.

To use the Merge capability:

1. Move the cursor to the location in the current file where you want to add the material.

2. Press ALT-F M to select the Merge option on the File menu.

3. In the resulting dialog box, specify the file whose contents you want to merge with your current file.

4. Press RETURN.

Once you've successfully pasted your text, you'll probably want to delete the text from its original location. To do this, mark the text you want to delete, then press DEL. This deletes the text without copying it to the Clipboard. Pressing DEL while editing your file is equivalent to pressing ALT-E E, to call the Edit menu and select the Clear option. (Notice that in this case the *e* in *Clear* is underlined in the Edit menu.)

It is possible, but not advisable, to delete text and copy it to the Clipboard in one step using the SHIFT-DEL key while editing or the Cut option in the Edit menu. This essentially combines the copying before pasting and the subsequent deletion. If you get into the habit of using this lazy way to move text you will almost certainly regret it at some point when you accidentally lose something vital.

Table 2-9 summarizes the operations that are possible when you have selected text using the commands listed in Table 2-8. You can also use the commands shown in Tables 2-10 through 2-12 to insert and delete text while editing — that is, without going to the Edit menu. You don't need to select the text before invoking the commands listed in those tables. To delete the character at the current cursor position, use the DEL key or press CTRL-G. The DEL command is also used to delete marked text, as you've just seen. The editor will know what to do from the context. To delete the character to the left of the current cursor position, use the BACKSPACE key or press CTRL-H. When editing, press RETURN any time you want to end a line or insert a blank line.

Table 2-9.   Commands for Deleting and Copying Text

Key(s)	Effect
CTRL-INS	Copy selected text to Clipboard
ALT-E C	Copy selected text to Clipboard
SHIFT-INS	Paste text to specified location
ALT-E P	Paste text to specified location
ALT-F M	Merge file to be specified into current file
DEL	Delete text without copying to Clipboard
ALT-E E	Delete text without copying to Clipboard
SHIFT-DEL	Delete text and copy to Clipboard
ALT-E T	Delete text and copy to Clipboard

Table 2-10.   Character Deletion Commands

Key(s)	Effect
DEL	Delete current character
CTRL-G	Delete current character
BACKSPACE	Delete preceding character
CTRL-H	Delete preceding character

Table 2-11.   Word Deletion and Undo Commands

Key(s)	Effect
CTRL-T	Delete to end of current word
ALT-BACKSPACE	Undo action on current line
CTRL-E U	Undo action on current line

Table 2-12.   Line Deletion and Undo Commands

Key(s)	Effect
CTRL-Y	Delete entire line
CTRL-Q Y	Delete to end of line
SHIFT-INS	Undo line deletion

To delete a word (actually, the part of the word to the right of the current cursor position, including the current character), press CTRL-T. If you decide that this deletion was not a good idea, immediately press ALT-BACKSPACE or select the Edit menu and press RETURN. These commands select the Undo option on the Edit menu, which restores a line to its status before your last action. Undo works only for the current line, and only if you have not yet moved the cursor from the current line. Table 2-11 summarizes these commands.

You can delete an entire line or the portion of the line to the right of the cursor. To delete the entire line, press CTRL-Y. To delete just to the end of the line, press CTRL-Q Y. *Line* here refers to a line on the screen, not to a sentence. You can undo either of these actions by pressing SHIFT-INS. This command will restore only the last line deleted.

If you want to look at your file but don't want to make any changes, especially inadvertent ones, you can make your work file read-only. This prevents accidental changes. Press ALT-E R to set this option. Pressing the same keys again turns the option off. When your file is read-only, an *R* appears on the status line at the bottom of your file.

To insert tabs, use the TAB key or press CTRL-I, as shown in Table 2-13. As you saw earlier, you can also move left to a tabspace by pressing SHIFT-TAB. If you have marked several lines of text and you press TAB or SHIFT-TAB , the selected lines will jump to the next tabspace in the appropriate direction.

More QuickC Features Sometimes you will want to return to certain portions of your file frequently. For example, while writing one of the programs in the first part of this chapter, you may have needed to check the definition lines while writing various parts of the program. Getting to a particular location can be tedious, especially if it is not at the beginning or end of the file, which can be reached with short command sequences.

Never fear, QuickC has an easy solution. You can mark up to four locations in your file, associating them with the numbers 0, 1, 2, and 3. To mark such locations,

1. Move your cursor to the desired location.

2. Press CTRL-K followed by 0, 1, 2, or 3.

Later, when you want to jump quickly to one of those locations, just press CTRL-Q followed by the number associated with the targeted text. Table 2-14 summarizes the commands for setting and jumping to markers.

Table 2-13. Miscellaneous Edit Commands

Key(s)	Effect
ALT-E R	Turn read-only format on/off
TAB	Move to next tabspace
SHIFT-TAB	Move to preceding tabspace

Table 2-14.   Commands for Marking and Finding Text

Key(s)	Effect
CTRL-K	0, 1, 2, or 3 Set marker 0, 1, 2, 3, respectively
CTRL-Q	0, 1, 2, or 3 Jump to marker 0, 1, 2, or 3, respectively

C relies heavily on braces and parentheses to block off sections of text. You can get into real difficulties if you mismatch braces or parentheses. To help minimize the chance of this happening, QuickC lets you find matching braces or parentheses. To find the left brace that matches a right brace you recently typed,

1. Move the cursor to the right brace whose counterpart you want to find.

2. Press CTRL-{ to find the matching left brace. (To find a right brace matching a left brace, you would type CTRL-} after moving the cursor to the appropriate location.)

Table 2-15 shows the commands for locating matching braces.

File Manipulation with the File Menu   The File menu provides the commands for opening and saving files. You've already used several of these commands, so the discussion here will be brief.

Press ALT-F N to create a new file. You will be asked to provide a name for this file. QuickC checks for duplicate file names, and will allow you to choose another name if you are accidentally about to overwrite an existing file with the same name as the one you want to create.

The Open and Open Last File options let you open existing files for editing. The Open option (ALT-F O) lets you specify the file to edit. The Open Last File option (F2 or ALT-F F) opens the file you had open just before switching to your current work file. For example, suppose you edited **game.c**

Table 2-15. Commands for Finding Matching Braces

Key(s)	Effect
CTRL-{	Find matching left brace
CTRL-}	FInd matching right brace

then used the Open option to start editing another file, **area.h**. If you press F2 at that point, QuickC will automatically return you to **game.c**, since that was the last file open before **area.h**.

Finally, you can write a file to disk using the Save option. If the file has no official name (that is, if it is named **untitled.c**), QuickC asks you to provide a name. If the file exists, QuickC will prompt you to verify that you really intend to overwrite the existing version of the file.

The Save As option lets you specify the name under which to store the current working file. This can be handy if you need to revise a program temporarily. For example, suppose you want to modify **game.c** in some way. Knowing that the current version of the program works fairly well, you want to keep that source code from accidental destruction. After making many changes to **game.c**, you are reluctant to overwrite the file since your new version may have unanticipated bugs, in which case you will need to go back to the original.

To handle this situation, you can create a new file "on the way out." You can tell QuickC to save the current file under a new name, let's say **game2.c**. The original version of the work file will be unchanged, and **game2.c** will contain the altered version of **game.c**. To accomplish this, press ALT-F A, then specify a file name and press RETURN.

Table 2-16 summarizes the first set of File menu commands. We'll discuss the File menu options relating to program lists later in this chapter.

The Search Menu   The Search Menu lets you move through and modify your file based on textual rather than physical criteria. The options you've seen so far have involved physical units, such as current character, word, or line.

Table 2-16.   File Manipulation Commands

Key(s)	Effect
ALT-F N	Create a new file
ALT-F O	Open a file to be specified
F2	Open file edited before current file
ALT-F F	Open file edited before current file
ALT-F S	Save current file
ALT-F A	Save current file under new name

The Search menu lets you specify a character, word, or phrase to find or replace. As was the case with the Edit menu, several of the options on the Search menu are available as commands while editing, as you'll see.

To find a specific instance of text, such as a phrase, press CTRL-Q F. Then type the phrase you want to find in the resulting **Find What** text box. You can also accomplish this by pressing CTRL-S to select the Search menu, then pressing RETURN or F to select the Find option. QuickC will search the file for the next occurrence of the specified phrase. The search begins at the current cursor position and proceeds to the end of the file. If the phrase is not found, the search continues at the beginning of the file, and proceeds until the phrase is found or the current cursor position is reached again.

When one occurrence of the phrase is found, you can tell QuickC to search for the next occurrence by pressing the F3 function key. Or you can select the Repeat option on the Search menu by pressing ALT-S R.

You can also mark text on a given line, and tell QuickC to find this selected text. To mark the text, use the SHIFT and arrow keys as described above. Once you've selected the text to search for (note that the text must all be on a single line), press CTRL-\ —that is, the CTRL and backslash keys simultaneously.

If you want to change text in your file, you can press CTRL-Q A. In the resulting dialog box, enter the text to be changed in the **Find What** text box, then press ALT-T to move to the **Change To** box. Specify the new text there. Table 2-17 summarizes the commands for finding and changing text.

Table 2-17.   Commands to Find and Change Text

Key(s)	Effect
CTRL-Q F	Find text to be specified
ALT-S F	Find text to be specified
F3	Find next occurrence of specified text
ALT-S R	Find next occurrence of specified text
CTRL-\	Find selected text
CTRL-Q A	Change text to be specified
ALT-S C	Change text to be specified
ALT-T (in Change dialog box)	Move to Change To box

Find Options   When finding and replacing text, you can put constraints on the actions or make your commands even more general, as summarized in Table 2-18. The dialog boxes for the Find and Change options allow you to specify whether QuickC is to consider something found only if it is surrounded by space or punctuation — that is, if the text is a word, rather than simply part of a word. To make this stipulation, press ALT-W. This command toggles, so you can cancel the restriction by pressing ALT-W again.

Similarly, you can specify that the case of the characters in the text found should match the case in the text you're looking for. For example, if you ask QuickC to find MAX__ENTRY, and press CTRL-M to select the Match Upper/Lowercase option, QuickC will not find Max__Entry.

You can also generalize the text QuickC is to find by creating a *regular expression*. Regular expressions consist of text that includes certain characters that are given particular interpretations. To get QuickC to accept your **Find What** text as a regular expression (as opposed to a *literal expression*), you must select the Regular Expression option, by pressing ALT-R in the dialog box. The following characters have special significance in regular expressions:

. * $ ^ \ [ ] [-] [^]

You can put a period (.) in the **Find What** text you specify. This tells QuickC to accept any single character in that position. For example, suppose

Table 2-18.   Options When Finding Text

Key(s)	Effect
ALT-W	Require word match
ALT-M	Require letter case match
ALT-R	Text to find is a regular expression

you specify the following in the **Find What** dialog box:

```
do.r
```

QuickC would match any of the following words if they appeared in your file:

```
doer
door
dour
```

The search would not match *dollar,* however, since the period can represent only a single character. Characters that are used to stand for other characters in this way are called *wild cards.*

You can also tell QuickC to accept one or more consecutive occurrences of a particular character. To do this, put an asterisk (*) immediately after the character you want to handle in this way. For example, specifying

```
fur*y
```

matches *fury* as well as *furry.*

If you put a dollar sign ($) at the end of your **Find What** text, QuickC will report only those occurrences of the text that come at the end of a line in the file. For example, suppose you specify the following as your **Find What** text:

```
are you?$
```

QuickC would match the first of the following lines, but not the second.

```
Hello there. How are you?
/* not acceptable */ Hello there. How are you? That's good.
```

Similarly, you can *begin* your text with a caret ($^\wedge$) to tell QuickC to search only for text at the start of a line. For example,

```
^void
```

finds the first, but not the second of the following lines.

```
void beep_user ();
    void beep_user ();  /* Leading blanks are characters too! */
```

Sometimes you may want to search for the occurrence of any of a number of characters. For example, suppose you wanted to search for the first occurrence of any digit. Both of the following **Find What** strings would specify this:

```
[0123456789]
```

If you put square brackets around text in the **Find What** string, QuickC will search for the first occurrence of any of the characters specified between the brackets. The first string explicitly lists each of the digits you are seeking. The second string uses one of the two special characters allowed within these brackets.

If you put a hyphen (-) between two characters in this context, QuickC will search for any occurrence of an ASCII character with a value between the values of the two characters surrounding the hyphen. It turns out that the digits are represented as consecutive characters in the ASCII character set (see Appendix A). Therefore, the second **Find What** string simply says to match any ASCII character between 0 and 9 inclusive — that is, between ASCII values 48 and 57, inclusive.

The other special character is a caret ($^\wedge$) again. In this context, the caret must be the first character after the left bracket. The caret tells QuickC to match any characters *except* those within the brackets. Thus, the following expressions both tell QuickC to match anything except a digit:

```
[^0123456789]

[^0-9]
```

Suppose you actually wanted to search for a dollar sign, a period, or a caret. The backslash character (\ ) tells QuickC to treat the next character literally, rather than as a special character. The following three strings would tell QuickC to search for a dollar sign, a period, and a backslash, respectively:

```
\$

\.

\\
```

Table 2-19 summarizes the options and characters used in regular expressions.

Table 2-19.   Special Characters in Regelar Expressions

Key(s)	Effect
.	Match any single character
*	Match one or more occurrences of preceding character
$	Match only at end of line
^	Match only at start of line
\	Treat following character literally
[ ]	Match any characters within brackets
\ (in [ ])	Match any ASCII values between two characters
^ (in [ ])	Match any characters except those specified

Change Options   There are also several options available if your are replacing text. By default, QuickC verifies each replacement before making it. This means that QuickC stops at each occurrence of the string to be replaced, and waits for you to press RETURN to verify that the change should be made.

When QuickC finds the text, it pauses and you are able to specify whether to change that occurrence or to skip it. To change it, simply press RETURN; to skip it, press S first. This changes the default setting to Skip, rather than Change. Now if you want to skip something you must press RETURN. If you want to change something, press C. This restores Change as the default action. Notice that these actions merely change the default; they do not affect the current text occurrence. To do that, you need to press RETURN to verify the appropriate action. In such a context, pressing RETURN accepts the current setting, whatever it is at the time.

If you do not want QuickC to verify each change, you can press ALT-C in the Change dialog box. This tells QuickC to change all occurrences of the specified text, without verifying. You had better be sure of this one, because QuickC makes the changes *very* quickly.

Table 2-20 summarizes the options you have when changing text.

Two other options on the Search menu are commands to find the next and the previous error found by the compiler. You learned how to do this earlier. Such jumps can be very handy if you want to quickly correct the errors the compiler has found. You can compile your entire file, let the compiler find all the things to correct, work through the file making the required changes, then simply compile the program again.

Table 2-20.   Options When Changing Text

Key(s)	Effect
ALT-C	Change each occurrence without verifying
S (when text is found)	Change default action to skip
C (when text is found)	Change default action to change

The Run Menu

The Run menu lets you compile and execute your programs.

Starting and Continuing Programs   Once you've finished editing your program file, press ALT-R for the Run menu and press RETURN or S to select the Start option. This option compiles the program to memory and runs it if the compilation is successful. This is the option you will usually select while creating your programs.

The Continue option lets you resume execution of a stopped program. A program may be stopped because the compiler found an error, or because you were running the debugger and the program had stopped at a breakpoint. For example, if the compiler finds an error while compiling your program, it will put you back in the program source file. You can make the correction and tell Quick C to Continue by pressing the F5 function key or CTRL-R N. The compiler will let you recompile before resuming the program. Table 2-21 summarizes the Run menu options.

Compiling a Program   When you compile your program, you may want to specify various things to the compiler. The Compile option on the Run menu gives you access to a dialog box containing several possible instructions for the compiler. Figure 2-7 shows the dialog box for the Compile option.

Table 2-21.   Run Menu Options

Key(s)	Effect
ALT-R S	Start compiling and running
F5	Continue halted program execution
ALT-R N	Continue halted program execution
ALT-R R	Restart program execution
ALT-R C	Set compile options
ALT-R O	Set Run-Time options

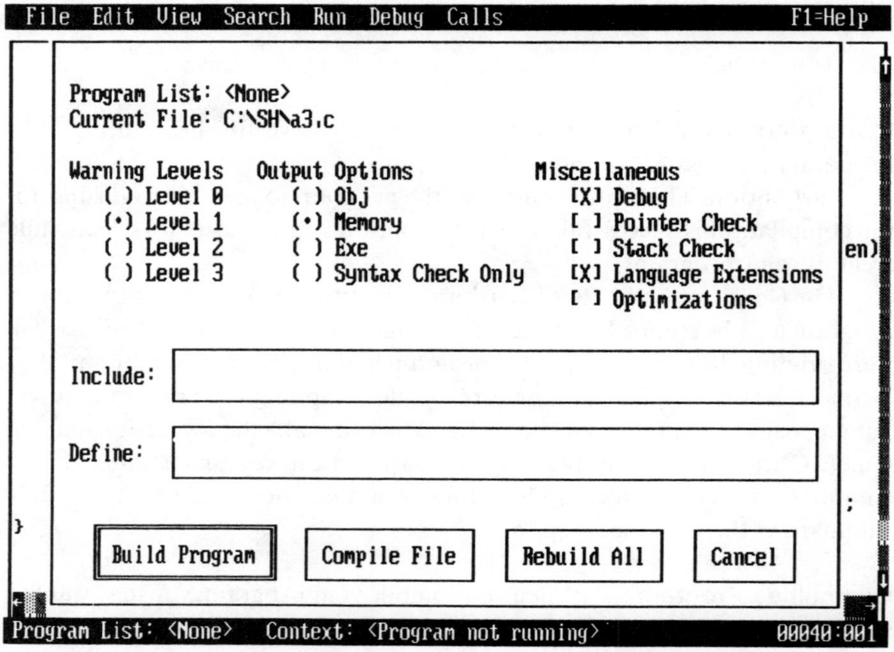

```
 File  Edit  View  Search  Run  Debug  Calls                    F1=Help

   Program List: <None>
   Current File: C:\SH\a3.c

   Warning Levels     Output Options        Miscellaneous
       ( ) Level 0        ( ) Obj              [X] Debug
       (•) Level 1        (•) Memory           [ ] Pointer Check
       ( ) Level 2        ( ) Exe              [ ] Stack Check          en)
       ( ) Level 3        ( ) Syntax Check Only [X] Language Extensions
                                               [ ] Optimizations


   Include: [                                                      ]


   Define:  [                                                      ]

 }
      | Build Program |   | Compile File |   | Rebuild All |   | Cancel |


 Program List: <None>   Context: <Program not running>       00040:001
```

Figure 2-7.   Compile option dialog box

One thing you can tell the compiler is how broad a range of warnings it is to give you during the compilation process. In the C world, compilers are able to warn you about things in your program that are not syntax errors, but that may affect program results, execution, or portability. Experiment with some programs compiling them at different **Warning Levels**.

Level 0 is completely silent. At this level, the compiler tells you only about errors, not about questionable practices. Level 1 is moderate, and tells you about such things as incorrect use of pointers. Level 2 is considerably noisier; in particular, this level complains about possibly discrepant function declarations and calls. Finally, Level 3 complains about the largest number of things, including deviations from the Draft Proposed ANSI Standard definition of the C language. Appendix E in the *QuickC Programmer's Guide* shows you the **Warning Level** required for the compiler warning messages summarized there. (Compiler warnings are the errors with numbers in the 4000s and with the prefix C, such as C4056.) In this book, we'll compile with the **Warning Level** set to Level 1. The UP ARROW and DOWN ARROW keys let you move among the levels.

The QuickC compiler can create various compiled output versions of your program. For any compilation, you can have only one of these ouput options set. If you are just trying to compile and run the program in the QuickC environment, the Memory option is the appropriate one. This is also the default option. With this option, no permanent compiled version of your program is created. To select this option if a different one is checked, press M while in the Compile option dialog box.

If you are building libraries, as described in Appendix B, you will want to create an object (**.obj**) file. This is a compiled version of the file that can be linked with other files when building programs or libraries. To select this type of output file, press O in the dialog box. To build an executable version of the program (an **.exe** file), as you did in the first part of the chapter, press X.

Finally, you can have QuickC check your program only for syntactic errors, without running the program and without producing either an **.exe** or an **.obj** file. Press Y for the Syntax Check option in the dialog box for this type of compilation.

The remaining compiler options instruct the compiler to provide various types of information for use when debugging or running your program. These option settings toggle. That is, if you select the option to turn the setting on, you can turn it off by selecting the same option again.

The Debug option tells the compiler to prepare the information needed for the debugger to let you step through your program, watching what lines are executed and what happens to variable values as the program executes. Press D to set this option.

The Pointer Check option tells the compiler to run portions of your program during compilation, to make sure you are not using pointers in a way that could destroy things you want to keep. To select this option, press P in the dialog box.

Pointer checks are a very good idea when you are first learning C, because they help protect you against common errors and careless use of pointers. When you select this option, the resulting program may run much more slowly then otherwise, however. To make the program faster, you can tell the compiler do such checking only for certain pointers. See the *Programmer's Guide* for information on how to do this.

The Stack Check option (S in the dialog box) provides another check on your program's performance. In this case, the compiler tries to make sure that there will be enough of the required (stack) memory available to load functions and their variables when running the program. This check is also recommended when you first start developing your program. As with the Pointer Check option, you can tell the compiler to do Stack Checks on portions of your program. See the *Programmer's Guide* for details.

Microsoft's implementation of C provides the constructs and syntax specified by the Draft Proposed ANSI Standards committee. However, Microsoft has provided some language extensions in their C version 5.0 and QuickC compilers. When writing QuickC or Microsoft C 5.0 programs, you need to decide whether you will want to compile them under non-Microsoft compilers. If so, you should not choose the Language Extensions option — that is, the box for this option should be blank. If you decide to choose the option, press L.

Finally, you can ask the compiler to generate the fastest code it can, at the price of making the resulting program file somewhat larger. To select this option, press Z.

As you'll find out in Chapter 4, C programs often use header files that contain special definitions or other information. Ordinarily, QuickC has certain default places where it searches for such files. Two places are the current directory and the **include** directory (if you installed QuickC with the default directory structure).

You may want QuickC to search other directories as well when compiling a particular program. In that case, write the paths to all these directories in the Include text box. These paths should be separated by commas, and the names must conform to DOS conventions. To get into the Include text box, press I if you are in the dialog box for the Compile options. Press ALT-I if you are in the Define text box.

The Define text box lets you specify definitions that are to be used with the current program file. Press F in the dialog box or ALT-F if you're in the Include text box. This facility is useful if you want to compile your program differently under different circumstances. You are unlikely to need this facility very much when you first start programming in C. See the *Programmer's Guide* for more details about the Define text box.

Once you've set everything the way you want it, you can tell QuickC what to compile by selecting one of the boxes at the bottom of the Compile option dialog box. The Build Program option compiles only those source files used in the program that have been changed since the last compile, and links these with the unchanged object files. Press RETURN to select this option.

To compile just the source file you're editing, press C, to select the Compile File option. Finally, to compile all source files used in the program, regardless of whether they have changed, press R to select the Rebuild All option.

Table 2-22 summarizes the compiler options.

Table 2-22.   Compiler Instructions

Key(s)	Effect
UP ARROW	Change **warning Level** setting
DOWN ARROW	Change **warning Level** setting
M	Compile to memory
O	Compile to object file
X	Compile to executable file
Y	Just check syntax, do not create a compiled file
D	Turn Debug on/off
P	Turn Pointer Checks on/off
S	Turn Stack Checks on/off
L	Turn Language Extensions on/off
Z	Turn optimization for speed on/off
I	Search in paths to be specified for include files
ALT-I	Search in paths to be specified for include files
D	Include definitions to be specified
ALT-D	Include definitions to be specified
B	Compile only changed source files
C	Compile only current source file
R	Recompile and relink all source files

Run-Time Options   Sometimes you will want to specify certain things when *running* (rather than compiling) the program. The Run-Time option on the Run menu lets you specify such information. Earlier you saw how to specify additional information to be passed to the program before it starts. You specified a **seed** to be used in generating random facts. To specify such information, type the information in the **Command Line** text box.

The only other Run-Time option you might use when you first start out is the Stack Size option. If the Stack Check compiler instruction indicates that there is not enough stack space to run your program, increase the value currently specified for this option, by pressing ALT-S and specifying the amount of stack space to allocate. The largest amount of stack space you can allocate is 65,536 bytes (64K).

Table 2-23 shows the Run-Time options. These options are available only in the dialog box for Run-Time options.

The Debug Menu

In the first part of the chapter, you learned how to step through a program, watching the changes in values of specified variables at certain lines in the program. You used the QuickC debugger to do this. To make use of the QuickC debugger, you first need to compile your program with the Debug Compile option on (with an *X* in the Debug option box), as you did earlier.

Table 2-23.   Run-Time Options

Key(s)	Effect
ALT-N	Specify space to be allocated for global variables
ALT-S	Specify stack space to be allocated for local variables

Once this is done, you can specify the variables and expressions you want to watch while running the program. To do so, select the Add Watch option in the Debug menu (ALT-D RETURN), and write the variables or expressions you want to watch into the text box that appears when you select this option. If you want to watch more than one variable or expression, they must be separated by semicolons.

You can ask to see the values of the watch variables in a variety of output formats, including octal (base 8) and hexadecimal (base 16). These are described in the *Programmer's Guide,* and Appendix C. They are similar to the formats you can use to display information in C programs, as described in Chapter 5.

You can delete all currently set watch variables by selecting the Delete All Watch option in the Debug menu (press ALT-D L to do this). Or you can delete the most recently specified watch variable by selecting the Delete Last Watch option (press SHIFT-F2 or ALT-D E).

If you select the Trace option in the debugger, the program will execute from breakpoint to breakpoint. In the process, each statement will be highlighted as it executes. If this option is off, only the breakpoint statements will be highlighted during execution. This option toggles. The default setting is off. To turn this option on, press ALT-D T. When tracing is turned on, a check will appear next to the option in the Debug menu.

Finally, you can set breakpoints as you did earlier in the chapter. To set a breakpoint, move the cursor to the desired line in the file. Then press the function key F9 or press ALT-D B to set a breakpoint at that line. This command also toggles. To clear all breakpoints, press ALT-D C.

Table 2-24 summarizes the Debug menu options.

Searching for Functions

The Search menu includes a Function option that we haven't yet discussed, but that can help make program editing easier. The Function option lets you jump to the beginning of a function's definition in the file.

That is, this command essentially serves to find something. However, it doesn't simply find an occurrence of a particular phrase (here, a function name). Rather, it finds a *particular* occurrence of this phrase — namely, the occurrence that begins the definition of the function itself.

Table 2-24. Debug Options

Key(s)	Effect
ALT-D A	Add watch variables
SHIFT-F2	Delete last watch variable set
ALT-D E	Delete last watch variable set
ALT-D L	Delete all watch variables currently set
ALT-D T	Turn tracing on/off
ALT-D S	Turn screen swapping on/off
F9	Turn breakpoint on/off
ALT-D B	Turn breakpoint on/off
ALT-D C	Clear all breakpoints

For example, **nice_print** is the name of a function in the **game.c** program. This name occurs at several points in the file. If you search for this name using the Find option in the Search menu, the first occurrence will be near the beginning of the function **main( )**, since this is the first time the phrase **nice_print** is used in the file.

If you search for this same name using the Function option — that is, by pressing ALT-S U — the cursor will be moved to the left brace that starts the main body of the function, near the end of the **game.c** file. This is convenient when you have large files, or when you are trying to find a function that is called frequently in the program.

To make it possible for QuickC to find this particular occurrence of a function name, you first need to compile the program with the Debug compiler option selected. Again, this provides the information needed to determine which occurrence of the name in a file represents the beginning of the function's definition.

Table 2-25 shows the command for finding a function's definition.

Program Lists

Many C environments have utilities that will let you keep track of changes made to different files that make up a larger program. This is important when you have large programs that take very long to compile.

Instead of compiling the entire program each time, it is often possible to recompile only those component files that have changed since the last time the program was compiled. These new **.obj** (object) files can be linked with object versions of the unchanged files that did not need to be recompiled.

A *program list* specifies all the source files that are used in a program. You can create a program list for a program by using the Set Program List option on the File menu. Press ALT-F S to get a dialog box that will let you specify the files to be included in the program list. For each file, or program *module,* you want to include in the program list, type the name and press RETURN. If the file is not yet on the list, QuickC adds it; if the name is already on the list, QuickC removes it. That is, the Add/Remove option in the dialog box toggles. When you have finished entering all the file names, press ALT-S to save the file.

QuickC will create a file with the same name as your program, but with the extension **.mak**. This file will contain the information the compiler needs to determine what files to recompile.

To discard a program list associated with a program, use the Clear option in the File menu after you've called up the program source file. To edit an existing program list, press ALT-F E.

Table 2-25.   Commands to Find a Function's Definition

Key(s)	Effect
ALT-S U	Find start of function to be specified

You probably won't need program lists when you first start programming in C, but you'll find this facility extremely useful when you start writing long programs. See the *QuickC Programmer's Guide* for more details about program lists.

Table 2-26 summarizes the File menu options for working with program lists.

Other Features

QuickC includes two additional features that can be very helpful on occasion.

Sometimes it can be useful to have a printed version of your file. You can print your file, or portions of it, while in QuickC. To do this, press ALT-F P to call up a dialog box for printing. Specify whether you want to print the entire file or just the text you have marked. The Print option sends your file to the printer attached to LPT1.

QuickC also lets you go back, temporarily, to the DOS command line. This command suspends (but saves) your current session with QuickC, and temporarily transfers control back to DOS. QuickC remains in memory, however, because you will return to the QuickC environment. To specify this command, select the DOS Shell option on the File menu (press ALT-F D).

Table 2-26.   Commands for Program Lists

Key(s)	Effect
ALT-F L	Create a program list file
ALT-F E	Edit existing program list file
ALT-F C	Clear program list associated with file

Once on the DOS command line, you can run other programs or do whatever you need, within limits. Be very careful when deleting files during such a side trip. In particular, do not delete any **.mak** files, source files, or files included in your current program list. See the *Programmer's Guide* for more information. When you're finished with DOS, type

```
exit
```

to return to QuickC. Table 2-27 summarizes these commands.

We have not covered all the features and commands available in QuickC, since that would take us beyond what we can cover in this book. As you become more proficient in C, you may find a need for these other features. At that point, with a solid grasp of the more common commands and features that you'll gain by working through this book, you can learn about these additional capabilities.

One topic about which you may want more information is compiling and linking programs outside the QuickC environment — that is, using the compiler and linker separately for greater flexibility. A brief introduction to this topic is included in Appendix B.

You'll also find more information about QuickC in Appendixes C and D, which provide a QuickC command summary and a comparison of QuickC and Microsoft C 5.0, respectively.

Table 2-27.   Miscellaneous File Menu Commands

Key(s)	Effect
ALT-F P	Print current file
ALT-F D	Exit temporarily to DOS shell

Summary

In this chapter, you've had an informal introduction to QuickC and how to use it; you've also read a brief discussion of the most common commands and features. There's much more to learn about QuickC, but there's little point in doing so until you've learned more about C, which is what you're about to do.

The following chapters will tell you about C and will give you an opportunity to consolidate your understanding of the features and capabilities of QuickC so that you can take advantage of this powerful environment from the start of your C programming career. Happy learning!

3

Simple Types
and Operators

In this chapter, we'll look at some of the data types available in C, and how to define variables in a program. We'll look at some of the operators C provides for working with data. In the process of exploring these topics, you'll learn the rules and conventions for naming things in C. You'll see that there's more than one way to write a number or a letter.

Before jumping into these topics, let's look quickly at some of the general characteristics and components of a C program—the program itself, functions, and statements. You'll find enough information about these elements to provide a foundation for the other constructs in this chapter.

C Program Structure

C programs consist of functions (similar to subroutines in other programming languages); functions consist of statements. Statements serve to define or express something, or to carry out some action. The following program illustrates each of these:

```
/* Sample C program to illustrate three components of a program:
   program; functions; statements.
*/

main()  /* the main program */
{
        first_message ();    /* call function first_message */
        second_message ();   /* call function second_message */
}

first_message ()      /* a simple function; writes a word on screen. */
{
        printf ( "hello,");
}

second_message ()    /* another simple function; write to screen. */
{
        printf ( " world\n");
}
```

This program is similar to prior examples in Chapter 1. This time, however, let's focus on the components of the program, rather than on what the program does.

First, all information in this listing is contained in the same source file. The program contains three functions: **first_message( )**, **second_message( )**, and **main( )**. The actual program starts executing with **main( )**.

The **main( )** function contains two simple statements, each a function call (the command to execute a function) and each ending with a semicolon (;). The function calls have a format similar to the **printf( )** calls in the Chapter 1 examples. This time, however, calls are to functions already defined in the program.

Note that parentheses are used when **main( )** calls the functions, even though there are no arguments (values or variables) to be passed to the functions. In C, these parentheses are necessary when calling any function.

The two "message" functions, **first_message( )** and **second_message( )**, each call **printf( )**. This time, calls to **printf( )** have only one argument. Everything to be written is contained in the first arguments ("hello," and "world \n"); there are no placeholders to be replaced when actually writing.

This is not an efficient program because the job could have been done by **main( )** alone, calling **printf( )** directly. However, the purpose here is not to write an efficient program, but to illustrate functions, function calls, and statements.

Comments

Program comments make it possible to include remarks and reminders within program listings. This, in turn, makes it easier for other people to read your code, and help you to understand your own code six months after you wrote it. Comment your code thoroughly. The next time you need the code you will thank yourself.

Program comments in C begin with /* and end with */. The compiler ignores all material between the comment start characters (/*) and the comment finish characters (*/). Comments may occupy multiple lines, but you may not nest comments, as shown in this (incorrect) example:

/* Nested comments, such as /* followed by */ are not allowed. */

because the compiler takes the first */ encountered as the end of the comment, leaving "are not allowed.*/" as uncompilable text after the comment.

▶**CAUTION**   Beware of accidentally commenting out code (inadvertently including code between comment start and finish characters). If you do that, you may lose lots of hair, sleep, or both, trying to find your programming error.

C's main( ) Rule

C programs are built of functions. For now, think of a function as consisting of a name or identifier (such as **main**), followed by a pair of parentheses ( ), which may be filled under certain conditions. These two components (identifier and parentheses) make up the function's interface. The actual body of the function is contained between the left curly brace following the function interface and the matching right brace. Figure 3-1 shows a function's major components.

The **main( )** function is special in C. A C program starts executing in **main( )**, and the function's closing brace marks the end of the program. All other function calls are made (directly or indirectly) from **main( )**. Put simply, **main( )** *is* the program.

Although a program begins and ends with **main( )**, you can place this function anywhere in your program file. You may not have more than one **main( )** in a program. If you do, you'd have two programs.

▶**REMEMBER**   C programs must have the **main( )** function since the program starts and finishes executing in this function.

The printf( ) Function

The **printf( )** function serves to write information to the screen. It is predefined in QuickC and in other implementations of C. To call **printf( )**, type the function name, putting any arguments to the function within the parentheses. (An argument is information passed to a function; the function is generally expected to use or modify the information. Functions may have more than one argument.)

The following is a call to **printf( )** with one argument:

```
printf ( "a string argument for printf()");
```

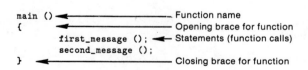

Figure 3-1.   Major components of a C function

This function call writes the sentence within the double quotes to the screen.

Writing to the screen can be a simple task or it can involve various substitutions by **printf( )**. The string argument to **printf( )** may contain special character sequences, beginning with %, that serve as placeholders for other information. When **printf( )** does its work, it replaces each placeholder by a value of a specific type. The following program illustrates placeholders and some other features of **printf( )**.

```
/* Program to illustrate some features of function printf(). */
#include "strings.h"    /* Read file containing string definitions. */

main ()
{
        int i1, i2;      /* define two variables */

        i1 = 37;
        i2 = 73;
        printf ( "one string,\n but written on two lines\n\n");
        printf ( "one placeholder, for a string: %s\n\n", PF_EXAMPLE);
        printf ( "one placeholder, for an integer: %d\n\n", i1);
        printf ( "two placeholders, both for integers: %d and %d\n\n", i1, 8);
        printf ( "two placeholders, a string: %s, and an integer: %d\n\n",
                PF_EXAMPLE2, i1);
        printf ( "four integer placeholders, note spacing: %d %d%d %d\n\n",
                i1, i2, i1, i2);
}
```

This produces the following result:

```
one string,
 but written on two lines

one placeholder, for a string: THE SUBSTITUTED STRING.

one placeholder, for an integer: 37

two placeholders, both for integers: 37 and 8

two placeholders, a string: THE STRING PORTION, and an integer: 37

four integer placeholders, note spacing: 37 7337 73
```

Again, this program has many aspects in common with the examples you've seen. There is a header file, which contains the values substituted for PF—EXAMPLE and PF—EXAMPLE2; there is a variable definition; and the calls to **printf( )** write things similar to what you've seen in earlier examples.

A feature of **printf( )** that has not been explored in previous examples is that it can be called with a varying number of arguments. The first call contains only a string (contained within quotation marks), without placeholders. Don't be misled by the fact that the output appears on two different lines. This is because the **\n** (for *newline*) escape code was placed in the middle of the string. (The two newline commands at the end of the string terminate the second line and force a blank line in the output.) Calling **printf( )** with just a string is probably the simplest call you will ever make to the function.

Each of the next two calls has two arguments. In both cases, the first argument has a placeholder in it (**%s** and **%d**, respectively). The **printf( )** function replaces each placeholder with the information contained in the second argument. In one case, the second argument has a string value; in the other, the argument is an integer variable. In each case, the placeholders (**%s** and **%d**) will be replaced by the current values of the second argument.

The next two calls have three arguments each: a string argument and two additional arguments. In each case, there are two placeholders in the string argument (which is always the first one). The number of placeholders in the first argument must always equal the number of additional arguments to **printf( )**.

Look at the output for these calls, particularly the spacing. In the call that writes a string and an integer, notice that the comma comes immediately after the substituted string, without space. Also, there is no space between **%s** and the comma in the string argument to **printf( )** for that example.

Finally, the last call to **printf( )** has five arguments. This statement is intended to clarify some points about spacing in the output. Notice in the output that the middle two numbers are "fused." There is no space between the 73 and the 37. Now look at the function call that generated this output. There is no space between the middle two placeholders; hence, there is no space between the numbers substituted for them in the output.

Later, we'll look at other placeholders and at additional format commands available when using **printf( )**. For now, there are three aspects of the function to keep in mind:

- The **printf( )** function generally has at least one argument, a string (enclosed in quotation marks). This may be followed by additional arguments, separated by commas. Each additional argument consists of a variable or expression.

- Portions of the string argument that begin with % are placeholders that specify where particular values are to be placed, and the type (integer, string, etc.) of variable to be written at that spot in the output.

- You must have exactly as many placeholders in the first argument to

printf( ) as there are additional arguments.

▶**REMEMBER**   If there are multiple arguments to **printf( )**, the string argument *must* be first.

Escape Codes

You have already seen the use of the newline character, **\n**, to move to the next line in the output. Newline is an example of an *escape code* or *escape sequence*. You may put escape codes anywhere in your string argument to **printf( )**. Escape codes consist of two characters: a backslash (\) followed immediately by a single character. For example:

\n (newline)

\t (tab)

\b (backspace)

**** (backslash character)

are all escape sequences. Escape codes are two characters long (with one group of exceptions, which we'll see later). Any characters after the escape code are considered part of the regular string, rather than of the escape sequence:

```
printf ( "line 1 \nand line 2\n");
```

produces the following output:

```
line 1
and line 2
```

Because the escape code for a new line ended with **\n**, the character **a** was treated as the next character in the string.

Table 3-1 summarizes some of the more common escape sequences. Given the information in this table, how would you write a single quote (')? Try it. What do you suppose will happen if you write **\r**, followed immediately by **\b**? Also, can you predict the output from the following **printf( )** call?

```
printf ( "a \bn historic occasion\no?");
```

Table 3-1.   Common Escape Sequences

Escape Code	Meaning	Description
\b	backspace	Move cursor one space to the left
\n	newline	Move cursor to start of next line
\r	CR	Return cursor to start of current line
\t	tab	Move cursor to next tab position
\\	\	Write the backslash character
\"	"	Write the double quote character

Statements

Statements are the main components of functions, instructions, or definitions. C allows simple and compound statements. Statements can be used in various contexts (for example, if-then tests and loops) and can serve many purposes, such as writing expressions, assigning a value, returning from a function, or continuing a loop. In this section, you will find some basic information about statements and their use.

Simple Statements

The following are all *simple statements* in C:

```
printf ( "this is a simple statement in C\n");
curr_int = 7;
return ( 8.5);
continue;
```

Each simple statement ends with a semicolon. Semicolons are important characters in C, as they are in languages such as Pascal. Their use is different, however. In Pascal, semicolons *separate* statements, meaning that you need to put a semicolon after a statement only if there is another statement after it. In C, semicolons *terminate* statements, meaning that you *must* put a semicolon after a statement, whether another statement follows or not.

▶REMEMBER   Every simple statement in C must end with a semicolon.

Compound Statements

You can "collect your thoughts," by grouping several statements together and treating them as a single, extended statement, known as a *compound statement*. A compound statement consists of zero or more statements (simple or compound), with the statement collection being bounded by left and right curly braces ({ and }), respectively. Compound statements are often called *blocks*. Thus, the { and } symbols correspond to BEGIN and END, respectively, in languages such as Pascal.

The following are two compound statements:

```
{
  printf ( "this is not");
  printf ( " a simple statement,\n");
  printf ( "since it consists of several simple statements");
  printf ( " followed by a right brace.\n");
  printf ( "The entire collection of statements makes up a");
  printf ( " compound statement.\n");
}
{
  ;
}
```

In Pascal, some programmers omit the semicolon between the last statement in a block and the END that terminates the block. However, they must usually put a semicolon after the END, since another statement is likely to follow. In C, the semicolon rules are just the reverse: you must end the last statement before the right brace with a semicolon, but you need not put a semicolon after the right brace.

▶**REMEMBER**   Compound statements in C consist of simple or compound statements bracketed by { and }.

We'll examine certain types of statements (such as assignment statements) later in this chapter. For now, just remember when and where you need semicolons. (Incidentally, what do you suppose will happen if you change the compound statement {;} to {} ?)

Identifiers

So far, we've discussed two functions, namely **main( )** and **printf( )**; we have used some variables (**i1** and **i2**); and we've used names for values specified in header files: PROG_MESSAGE, PF_EXAMPLE, PF_EXAMPLE2, and FALSE. In this section, you'll learn what constitutes a valid name, or identifier, in C, and also learn about some naming and spelling conventions among C programmers.

Naming Rules in C

The naming rules for C variables and functions are similar to the rules in other languages. An identifier, or name, consists of some combination of valid characters. The only real trick is remembering what characters are valid and when each is valid. Valid characters for C identifiers are:

- The letters 'A' through 'Z', 'a' through 'z' (letters);
- The underscore characters, '_' (underscore);
- The characters '0' through '9' (digits);

Identifiers *must* begin with a letter or an underscore. Digits are *not* allowed as the first character of an identifier.

▶**REMEMBER**   Identifiers must begin with a letter or an underscore; this starting character may be followed by any combination of letters, digits, or underscores. Identifiers may not begin with a digit.

Table 3-2 shows examples of valid and invalid identifiers. The table also contains a column of identifiers on which to test your understanding of the naming rules for C. If you're unsure whether an identifier in the third column is valid, try it in a short program. Even if you are sure, it's sometimes interesting to test your certainty; after all, surprises do happen.

By convention, library variables and functions (which we'll discuss later) often have names beginning with an underscore. Don't start your identifiers with an underscore. For example, try to keep from using names such as **_my_identifier** for your variables and functions.

In C, the case of the characters in a name *does* matter. Thus, **hello**, **Hello**, and **HELLO** are different names. If you are used to languages (such as Pascal) where case does not matter, you'll need to be extra careful.

Table 3-2.   Identifiers — Good, Bad, and for You to Decide

Valid Identifiers	Invalid Identifiers	? Identifiers
HelLo	h*llo	hello__
valid	8inValid	__WhIch
VALID__identifier	__not__valid	__
Also__valid__this	But__NOT__this	And?this
And__ __ __THIS	But__not-this	Or__ __this

▶**REMEMBER**   Case matters in C names.

You are free to use whatever case you want in your identifiers, but be consistent. Many C programmers use only lowercase letters and underscores for their identifiers. In general, you are asking for trouble if you use identifiers that differ only in the case of their characters.

By convention, identifiers containing only uppercase characters indicate that the name is used in a header file. You've seen examples of such identifiers in earlier listings, such as PF__EXAMPLE and PF__EXAMPLE2.

▶**REMEMBER**   Avoid using names that differ only in the case of some of the characters.

How long can a name be? Older compilers often read only the first few characters of a name to identify the variable or function. This number was usually 8; however, the proposed ANSI standard requires compilers to use up to 31 characters for a name. QuickC reads your entire identifier, up to 31 characters, as required by the ANSI standard.

You can, of course, make the name even longer than 31 characters, if you're so inclined. Even if you are feeling verbose, keep in mind that compilers are not required to read beyond the 31st character of a name. This means that if, for some strange reason, you used two names that were identical through their 32nd characters, the compiler would very probably treat them as the same variable.

No Keywords for Identifiers

As you read in Chapter 1, C is a small programming language, with only about 30 keywords. Although the list is small, C is very serious about these words being reserved. Compilers will not let you use any of the keywords as identifiers. Table 3-3 lists C's keywords.

▶**REMEMBER**   You *may* not use reserved words as identifiers.

Keywords in parentheses in Table 3-3 have been added in the proposed ANSI standard version. Some older compilers also include the following reserved words: **asm**, **entry**, **fortran**.

Variable Definition:
Making Room

C programs generally manipulate information stored in specific memory locations in your computer. When writing a program, you'll use variables to store the information. A *variable* is essentially a slot capable of holding information.

A memory address is associated with a variable, and the variable's value is stored at that address. To use variables in C, you must give the compiler a list of variables names that you'll be using in your program. For each variable identifier, you must also tell the compiler what kind of information you want to store in that variable; that is, you must associate *a type* with each variable name.

A variable's type tells the compiler something about how the information is to be stored, what operations can be performed on the information, and also how much storage space must be allocated to store the variable's value.

When you provide both a variable name and a type specifier, you are

Table 3-3.   Key Words

auto	double	int	struct
break	else	long	switch
case	enum	register	typedef
char	extern	return	union
(const)	float	short	unsigned
continue	for	(signed)	void
default	goto	sizeof	(volatile)
do	if	static	while

defining the variable. When a variable is defined:

- A particular data type is associated with the name.
- Storage is allocated for the variable, to hold values of the specified type.

You've already seen several examples of the variable definition process. Earlier, we had the following line in a listing:

```
int i1, i2;
```

This statement tells the compiler that two variables, **i1** and **i2**, will be used in the program. The type component of this statement also indicates that whole numbers, or integers, will be stored in these variables.

The syntax for variable definitions uses the keyword for the variable's type (in this case, **int**), followed by one or more identifiers, separated by commas. A definition statement ends in a semicolon, as do other types of statements.

▶**REMEMBER**   A variable definition has the following form:
 <*variable type*>   <*variable identifier*>{, <*variable identifier*>};

Terms in the braces may be repeated; the semicolon is required.

Terminology for variable definition is inconsistent and may be a bit confusing. Sometimes you'll see a related term, *variable declaration*, used to represent the process of specifying variable identifiers and types. However, variable declaration differs in subtle ways from the definition process described above. Until we get to the differences, don't worry about it; just try to get into the habit of using "definition" in this context.

Assignment Statements

Values are stored in variables by means of *assignment statements*. This process puts the value found on one side of the assignment statement into the variable specified on the other side. Assignments are made using the *assignment operator* (=). For example, the following listing shows how to assign a number to a variable.

```
main ()
{
        int i1, i2;

        i1 = 37;
        i2 = 27 + 10;
        printf ( "after assignment, i1 has the value %d\n", i1);
        printf ( "after assignment, i2 has the value %d\n", i2);
}
```

This program does three things:

1. Defines variables **i1** and **i2**

2. Assigns 37 as the value to both **i1** and **i2**

3. Writes values of variables to the screen along with messages

The variable definition has set aside space for two variables of type **int**. The first assignment operator, =, stores the value on the right side of the assignment operator (37) in the variable specified on the left side (**i1**). The result is that the memory location associated with **i1** now contains the value 37.

In the second instance, the system first evaluates the expression to the right of the assignment operator (27 + 10), then assigns the result of the evaluation to the variable, **i2**.

In the first assignment, the right hand side of the assignment statement contains a single number. The right hand side can also be a more complex expression, which evaluates to a specific value, as in the second assignment statement. In that case, the system first evaluates the expression, then assigns the result to the variable on the left.

▶**REMEMBER**   C assumes that you are assigning values of an appropriate type to a variable.

C gives you great flexibility in the expressions you can put on the right side of the assignment operator. The expressions can actually contain assignments under certain conditions. Such assignments "within" assignments are unnecessary and potentially troublesome.

If you want to explore complex assignment statements on your own, begin with a statement such as this:

```
i3 = i2 = i1;
```

Make sure you have defined all three variables to be of the same type. What are the values of **i2** and **i3** when all the assignments are completed? What, if anything, does this tell you about the order in which QuickC evaluates assignments? Use **printf( )** to answer these questions.

Initialization During Variable Definition

There is a special form of assignment that can be used under certain circumstances. Essentially, a variable can be initialized when it is first defined. Look carefully at the following program:

```
main ()
{
        int i1 = 45, i2 = 23;
```

```
        printf ( "the initialized i1 has the value %d\n", i1);
        printf ( "the initialized i2 has the value %d\n", i2);
}
```

This program writes the values of the two variables, **i1** and **i2**. While basically the same as the previous program, this version does not have the two assignment statements of the earlier listing.

This time, the assignments are made when the variables are defined. In this program, the system immediately stores the value 45 in the memory location reserved for **i1** when that variable is defined; in the same way, the system stores the value 23 in **i2**.

C will let you assign initial values to variables when you first define them. Because variables are separated by commas in a definition statement, all you need to do is add the assignment operator and the initial value before the comma.

You cannot nest *initialization* assignments in QuickC. The following is invalid:

```
int i1 = i2 = i3 = 45;
```

This is only one way in which the initialization rules differ from those of regular assignment in C; you'll learn about other restrictions later.

▶**REMEMBER**   You may not initialize multiple variables with nested assignment statements.

Simple Data Types

After the brief discussion above of the structure of C programs and functions, let's find out about some of the data types C provides for programmers.

Variables may contain simple pieces of information (such as a character or a number) or multiple pieces of information (such as a string of characters or an array of numbers).

In the following discussion, we'll concentrate on variables that contain a single piece of information. Such variables belong to a *simple data type*.

C has the "usual" simple data types: characters, integers, and numbers with fractional components. In addition, C allows variants on some of these types, and lets you convert some simple types into others. Simple types include **char**, **int**, **float**, and **double**. These types differ in the sort of information they contain and in the amount of storage space allocated to them on different systems, ranging from 1 to 8 bytes.

The *char* Type

C's character type is known as **char**. C allocates 1 byte for storing a character. This means you can have at most 256 character values. Generally, the byte used to store a character variable is interpreted as having values ranging from −128 to 127. QuickC represents characters this way.

Depending on the character encoding scheme used, positive values of a character variable correspond to particular characters. For example, a character value of 100 corresponds to the character **d** in the ASCII character set used on most systems. (See Appendix A for a list of ASCII codes.)

Negative values generally do not have a "useful" interpretation; however, the values themselves can be used in operations, as we'll see.

The *int* Type

The integer type (**int**) is used to represent whole numbers within a specified range of values. Variables of type **int** are usually stored in a 16-bit area of memory on PCs. This lets you store 65536 different values. QuickC uses the 16 bits allocated for **int** variables to represent values ranging from −32768 to 32767 (-2^{15} to $2^{15} - 1$).

On larger systems, 32 bits may be allocated for an integer, with possible values ranging from −2,147,483,648 to 2,147,483,647 (-2^{31} to $2^{31} - 1$).)

Suppose you try to represent a number larger than the maximum possible? If you try to store such a number, you will get odd results. For example, if you try to add 1 to 32767 on a computer with 16-bit integers, you will not get 32768. Try it. Because of the way integer values are represented, the system ends up reading this new value as a very large *negative* number. This result is due to overflow in the representation of the integer; overflow simply means you have exceeded the possible range of values.

▶**REMEMBER**   Beware of overflow when doing computations using integers.

What do you suppose will happen if you try to use a negative number beyond the allowable range? For example, what does the following program return?

```
/* Sample program to illustrate the consequences of trying to use
   values beyond the permissible range of integers.
*/

main ()
{
        int i1, i2;

        i1 = -32770;  /* exceeding negative range limit by 2 */
        printf ( "instead of -32770, i1 has the value %d\n", i1);

        i2 = 32769;  /* exceeding positive range limit by 2 */
        printf ( "instead of 32769, i2 has the value %d\n", i2);
}
```

Hint: think of the integer values as being on a giant wheel, with 0 at the top, and the maximum positive and negative values next to each other at the bottom, as shown in Figure 3-2. Then think of overflow conditions as arising when you continue counting in the same direction, but past the maximum value.

The *float* Type

This type represents what is known as a *floating point* or *real* number. A real number is one that may have a fractional part, as opposed to an integer, which is a whole number.

Such numbers are called floating point numbers because a value is usually represented in three parts: a sign, a numerical value, and an exponent that tells how to move the "decimal" point separating the fractional from the whole number part. For example, you can represent the number 500.250 in each of the following ways: 500.250e0, 50.0250e1, or 50025.0e−2. These representations tell you to move the decimal point 0 places, 1 place to the right, and 2 places to the left, respectively.

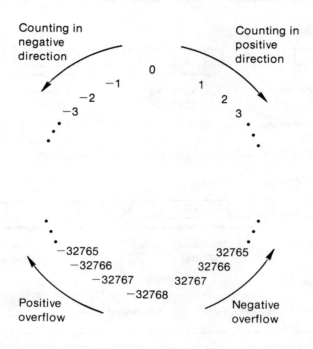

Figure 3-2.   Representation of overflow conditions

Internally, *float* values also are stored in three components: a sign bit, some number of bits to store a fractional component of the number (called the *mantissa*), and the remaining bits to store an exponent (see Figure 3-3). These components correspond to the three parts of a floating point representation. The only difference between the actual representation of floats and our discussion is that the internal values are all in terms of binary values. (That is, the exponent in an internal representation tells how many "binary" places to move the point.)

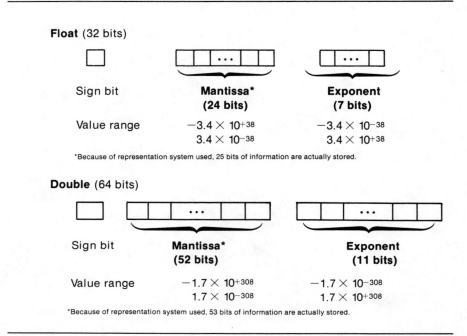

Figure 3-3.   Representation of floating point type in QuickC

QuickC allocates four bytes (32 bits) to variables of **float**. By using some clever arithmetic when storing the information about a number, QuickC gives you a range of roughly $3.4e^{-38}$ to $3.4e^{+38}$ for **float** values. (Because of the sign bit, you can represent the same range of negative values.)

The *double* Type

The **double** type is for double precision floating point numbers. **double** values are stored in a fashion similar to float values — sign, mantissa, and exponent. For **doubles**, QuickC allocates 8 bytes (64 bits). The information in double variables is of the same sort as in **floats**; however, the range and number of possible values is much greater for **doubles**, because more bits are allocated for representing this type.

As with **floats**, arithmetic makes the range of possible values larger than it might have been. A **double** allows representation of values ranging from $1.7 * 10^{-308}$ to $1.7 * 10^{+308}$, with the same range of values possible for negative numbers.

The main difference between **floats** and **doubles** is the amount of space allocated for these numbers. Be careful about assuming that two variables have *exactly* the same values. Because of the way **floats** and **doubles** are represented, not all possible values within the permissible range can be represented. Also, intermediate computations in an expression may introduce rounding errors that could change the value of a particular variable slightly. This means that such values may only be approximately correct, or nearly equal. (For most calculations, you won't need to worry about the effects of such errors. Just remember they can occur.)

The following listing and output illustrate some of the ways in which values can differ because of limited representation accuracy and because of factors such as rounding when computing results.

```
/* Program to illustrate that
    1) floating point representations are only approximate, that
    2) rounding errors in computations can lead to different values, and that
    3) double representations are more accurate than float representations.
*/

main ()
{
        /* define float and double variables;
           initialize to arbitrary starting values.
        */
        float f1 = 230.6,
            f2 = 230.6, f3 = 1.0,
                f_dv = 11.0;                /* float DiVisor */
        double d1 = 230.6,
            d2 = 230.6, d3 = 1.0,
                d_dv = 11.0;                /* double DiVisor */

        /* display initial values. */
        printf ( "STARTING VALUES\nf1 = %20.17f\nd1 = %20.17lf\n\n", f1, d1);

        /* compute quotients, using REPEATED DIVISION */
        f1 = f1 / f_dv / f_dv / f_dv / f_dv / f_dv / f_dv / f_dv;
        d1 = d1 / d_dv / d_dv / d_dv / d_dv / d_dv / d_dv / d_dv;

        /* compute new divisors, using REPEATED MULTIPLICATION */
        f3 = f3 * f_dv * f_dv * f_dv * f_dv * f_dv * f_dv * f_dv;
        d3 = d3 * d_dv * d_dv * d_dv * d_dv * d_dv * d_dv * d_dv;

        /* compute "same" quotients, using SINGLE DIVISION */
        f2 = f2 / f3;
        d2= d2 / d3;

        /* display new results */
        printf ( "RESULTS\nf2 = %20.17f\nd2 = %20.17lf\n\n", f2, d2);

        /* display the DIVISORS used */
        printf ( "DIVISORS\nf3 = %20.17f\nd3 = %20.17lf\n\n", f3, d3);
```

```
        /* report outcome */
        printf ( "%20.17f (f1) does NOT equal\n%20.17f (f2)\n\n\n", f1, f2);
        printf ( "%19.17lf (d1) equals\n%19.17lf (d2)\n", d1, d2);
}


/* Output for listing */

STARTING VALUES
f1 = 230.60000000000000000
d1 = 230.60000000000000000

RESULTS
f2 =   0.00001183342556033
d2 =   0.00001183342620640

DIVISORS
f3 = 19487172.00000000000000000
d3 = 19487171.00000000000000000

 0.00001183342646982 (f1) does NOT equal
 0.00001183342556033 (f2)


0.00001183342620640 (d1) equals
0.00001183342620640 (d2)
```

This program computes the "same value" in two different ways, and displays the results of the two computational methods. The program does this with variables of type **float** as well as **double**. The results for the two types are different.

The first method computes the quotient by repeatedly dividing the current value by the same divisor, until the division has been carried out far enough. Each division may introduce approximation errors.

The second method first multiplies the divisor by itself as often as needed to get the "appropriate" quotient. Then the program carries out the division. Each multiplication may introduce approximation errors, but these will be different from those introduced by repeated division.

Mathematically, these two methods produce the same results. Therefore, any differences are due to representation or computational "approximations." There are three differences in the output; there is also one important result where there is *no* difference.

The difference between **f1** and **f2** is the result of computation error. The difference is very small, less than one part in 10 billion. You won't have to worry about such errors in most of your work, since they will probably be too small to make any practical difference for your answer.

If the two answers are not identical, which is more accurate, which is closer to the "true" result? Such questions are studied (and sometimes even answered) by analyzing algorithms (computational methods). Keep in mind that sometimes the manner in which you compute a result might make a difference in the outcome.

Notice that the two **double** results are identical. That's because the precision used to represent **double** values is great enough to be accurate within 17 decimal places for this problem. If you did enough computations, you would get differences even in the **double** representation.

The differences between **f3** and **d3** and between **f2** and **d2** are also due in part to the effects of rounding during computations. The differences between the divisors (**f3** and **d3**) show that such errors arise even when dealing with large numbers.

The last point to notice concerns the output format specifications. Notice that the **float** results (**f1** versus **f2**) are indented one column, unlike the **double** results, because of the field widths for the two outputs. The **float** information is to be written in 20 columns, the double information in 19. The format specifies 17 decimal digits, the decimal point takes one place, and the 0 takes another. This makes 19 places, and leaves one empty column in the **float** output. In such a case, the function puts any empty columns to the left of the output.

Integral and Floating Point Types

So far we have seen four of C's simple data types. **char** and **int** variables are called *integral types,* and **float** and **double** are *floating point* types. The reason for including **char** as an integral type will become clear soon.

Exploring Simple Types

The following program shows how to define and write simple types. The program is fairly long, and contains lots of new features. We'll go through it in detail in the following pages.

```
/* Sample program to illustrate properties of simple data types
   and certain syntactic rules and conventions for using these types.
*/

main ()
{
        char c1, c2, c3;    /* define three variables of type char */
        int i1, i2, i3;     /* ...                 type int */
        float f1, f2;       /* ...                 type float */
        double d1, d2;      /* ...                 type double */
```

```
/* assignment statements involving chars; note the different uses. */
        c1 = 'a';       /* assign character constant 'a' to variable c1 */
        c2 = 97;        /* substitute 353 (255 + 98); what's happening? */
        c3 = c1 + 3;    /* what are the types in this "addition" expression? */

/* display the information; note the differences between the 2 lines */
        printf ( "char as char: c1 = %c; c2 = %c; c3 = %c\n", c1, c2, c3);
        printf ( "char as int : c1 = %d; c2 = %d; c3 = %d\n\n", c1, c2, c3);

/* assignment statements for ints; note the types in third assignment */
        i1 = 23;
        i2 = i1 + 3;
        i3 = i2 + c1;   /* note types being added. */

/* write the int values */
        printf ( "ints: i1 = %d; i2 = %d; i3 = %d\n\n", i1, i2, i3);

/* assignment statements for floats. */
        f1 = 23.000000000000001;
        f2 = f1 + 3.00000000000000;    /* see result of this addition. */

/* write float results; note use of formatting */
        printf ( "float : f1 = %f; f2 = %40.37f\n\n", f1, f2);

/* assignment statements for doubles. */
        d1 = 23.00000000000001;
        d2 = d1 + 3.00000000000000;    /* see result of this addition. */

/* write double results; compare output with that for float. */
        printf ( "double: d1 = %lf; d2 = %40.37lf\n", d1, d2);

/* write double results AS INTEGERS; compare output with above. */
        printf ( "\nThe following is INVALID OUTPUT, incorrect results.\n");
        printf ( "double as int: d1 = %d; d2 = %40d\n", d1, d2);
}
```

This program produces the following output:

```
char as char: c1 = a; c2 = a; c3 = d
char as int : c1 = 97; c2 = 97; c3 = 100

ints: i1 = 23; i2 = 26; i3 = 123

float : f1 = 23.000000; f2 = 26.0000000000000000000000000000000000000

double: d1 = 23.000000; d2 = 26.00000000000001000000000000000000000000

The following is INVALID OUTPUT, incorrect results.
double as int: d1 = 3; d2 =                                          0
```

In addition to illustrating topics discussed above, this program shows some new features of **printf( )** and of some variable types. Essentially, the program does some manipulations using each of the four simple types we've seen so far, then it writes the result to the screen. Altogether, the program defines 10 variables: three **char**, three **int**, two **float**, and two **double**.

The first two **char** assignment statements show that you can assign a value to a **char** variable in more than one way: by actually specifying the character to be stored there or by assigning the ASCII value associated with the character to the variable. In the first assignment, the system translates your character (written within the *single* quotes) into its ASCII code, and stores this code in binary form. You can assign 97 to **c2** because characters are stored in a byte capable of holding values between −128 and 127, and 97 falls within this range. (Note what happens if you add a larger number, as the program suggests.)

The third assignment actually adds an integer to a character. While this may seem odd, it is allowed in C because, internally, C actually represents **char** variables as integers anyway. Essentially, you are adding 3 to a numerical (ASCII) value. Since 100 is still a valid character, the system handles the result in the same way as if you had simply assigned the value 100 to **c3**. This assignment also illustrates the use of the addition operator (+). You'll learn more about other operators later is this chapter.

The first call to **printf( )** has four arguments: the string argument (containing three placeholders) and three **char** variables, whose values will be substituted for the placeholders. This call to **printf( )** also illustrates how to get the function to write a **char**: by using the %c (for character) placeholder.

Notice that the values written for **c2** and **c3** are actual characters, rather than numerical codes, despite the fact that we had assigned numerical values to the variables. Using %c tells the function to translate the numerical code into the actual character before writing it.

The second call to **printf( )** seems to violate a rule we saw earlier — that the placeholder type should match the types of the variables passed as the additional arguments to **printf( )**. That is, the %d does not match the **char** variables whose values will be written. This is allowed for the same reason that adding characters and integers was valid: because **char** variables are actually represented as integers internally.

The third integer assignment statement (**i3 = i2 + c1**) also illustrates that **int** and **char** variables can be used together in an expression. The result can be assigned to an integer variable.

The **float** assignments actually use values too small for the system to handle completely as a **float**. That's why the output doesn't include the 1 in the rightmost digit of **f1**.

To write a **float**, use the %f placeholder. The **printf( )** that writes the **floats** uses two different forms of the placeholder. To write **f1**, the function uses the system defaults for the number of decimal digits shown; for **f2**, we told the system how to write the result. The first number (40) tells the the system the *field width*—how many places to allocate for the entire value. The second format parameter specifies the number of decimal places to write. The period between these two formatting parameters is not a decimal point; it's just the character used to separate the two values.

▶**REMEMBER**   Formatting parameters must appear between the % and the variable type indicator (in this case, **f**).

The assignments and output for the double variables had the same goal as for the **float** values. This time, however, the **1** *does* show up in the output— because a **double** can represent more numbers within its range than the single precision **float** can. Notice the syntax for placeholders for **double** variables: %**lf** (for **long float**, which is essentially what a **double** is). The %**lf** is not available as a placeholder in all implementations of C. In some cases, you would use %**f** to write either a **float** or a **double**.

The Draft Proposed ANSI Standard uses %**f** for float and %**lf** for **double** variables. The system recognizes know the variable's type from its definition.

▶**REMEMBER**   Make sure that the variable type on the left side of an assignment statement is able to store information of the type which the right hand side evaluates.

The last call to **printf( )** illustrates an error that will get you into all sorts of trouble. Trying to substitute a floating point value for an integral placeholder leads to unpredictable results, just about guaranteed to be wrong. Notice that the system writes seemingly arbitrary values; it does not simply leave off the fractional part of the number. The reason for this concerns the way the bits are organized for integral and for floating point types.

The second integral placeholder also contains a format command. You can specify the field width for integers as well as floating point types. Since there are no decimal places, you need only one number to specify the format for integers. Check the QuickC documentation for even more ways to specify formats.

The last thing to notice is the use of the newline escape code (**\n**) at the beginning of the string argument. We've already seen the trick of using two consecutive newlines to produce a blank line between entries. The introductory sentence in the next-to-last **printf( )** shows that you can put the newlines codes anywhere in your string argument.

Variants on Simple Types

In addition to simple types, C provides other types, which are variations on **char** and **int**. These types are essentially requests for a different range of values or for different amounts of memory to be allocated for storing a value.

Signed types, where numbers can be positive or negative, are standard in most languages. C also lets you declare integers as unsigned, so the sign bit is used as part of the number rather than as a sign indicator.

For example, **unsigned char** and **unsigned int** are requests to allow only positive values and zero. This roughly doubles the size of the largest possible positive **char** or **int** value by taking away negative values entirely. An **unsigned char** can take on values from 0 to 255. In QuickC, an **unsigned int** can take on values between 0 and 65535. There are also **signed char** and **signed int** types in the proposed ANSI standard. These types do what the base types **char** and **int** do already, in most implementations. There are no unsigned floating point types.

The following program illustrates how to define variables of these new types.

```
/* Program to illustrate how to define signed and unsigned variable types. */
main ()
{
        signed char sc1;
        signed int si1;
        unsigned char uc1;
        unsigned int ui1;

        printf ( "Just a filler line.\n");
}
```

Short and long are requests for versions of the **int** type for which different amounts of storage may be allocated, depending on implementation. You can also define variables of types **unsigned short**, **unsigned long**, **signed short**, and **signed long**. The syntax for defining such variable types is the same as for the other simple types. For example:

```
short si1;
long li1;
```

These two definitions allocate space for variables of type **short** (integer) and **long** (integer). The amount of space allocated for these variants depends on the implementation. For example, QuickC allocates the same amount of space to

int and **short** (two bytes), but more to **long** (four bytes). Regarding storage allocation, the only guarantees are:

1. The same amount of storage will be allocated to **int** and **unsigned int** variables.

2. The storage for a **short int** will be $\leq$ the storage allocated for an **int**.

3. The storage for a **long** will be $\geq$ the storage allocated for an **int**.

C also requires **char** variables to be stored in 1 byte, and insists that a **double variable** be allocated at least as much space as a **float**. The following program will show you how much space QuickC allocates for each simple type.

```
/* Program to show the amount of storage allocated for each of C's
   simple types.
   NOTE : sizeof() is an operator that returns an integer
          indicating the number of bytes of storage allocated to
          for the base type of the variable passed as an argument.
*/

main ()
{
        printf ( "TYPE      SIZE (in Bytes)\n\n");
        printf ( "char      %d bytes\n", sizeof ( char));
        printf ( "short     %d bytes\n", sizeof ( short));
        printf ( "int       %d bytes\n", sizeof ( int));
        printf ( "unsigned %d bytes\n", sizeof ( unsigned));
        printf ( "signed    %d bytes\n", sizeof ( signed));
        printf ( "long      %d bytes\n", sizeof ( long));
        printf ( "float     %d bytes\n", sizeof ( float));
        printf ( "double    %d bytes\n", sizeof ( double));
}
```

This produces the following output:

```
TYPE      SIZE (in Bytes)

char      1 bytes
short     2 bytes
int       2 bytes
unsigned  2 bytes
signed    2 bytes
long      4 bytes
float     4 bytes
double    8 bytes
```

This program includes calls to **sizeof( )**, a built-in function (actually an operator) that returns an integer representing the number of bytes allocated to store a variable of the type it is asked about. You need not ask about the actual variable type identifier (i.e., **char**, **int**). We could just as easily have passed in a **char** variable (e.g., **c1**) to get the same information.

▶**CAUTION**   The types whose storage sizes are most likely to differ from system to system include **short int**, **int**, and **long int**. Such differences may affect the portability of your program.

Table 3-4 summarizes information about simple data types. Notice that some of the variants on a type have the same range of values. For the floating point types, note that both extremes have very large positive exponents. This amounts to saying that **float** and **double** values range from very large negative to very large positive numbers. Remember, a positive number with an exponent such as -38 (e.g., 5e-38) is a very tiny number, but still positive, and therefore larger than a number such as -1e25.

Constants

You may find the need for a specific value at some point in a program. This may be the only place you need the value; or you may need it in lots of places, but the value never changes. Such unchanging values are called *constants*. Specific values—as opposed to variable names—that are used in assignment statements or other expressions are also called constants.

Depending on its value, a constant will be interpreted as being of a particular type. For example, the letter **q** is a character constant, **hello** is a

Table 3-4.   Summary of Simple Data Types

Type	Range of Values in QuickC
char	$-128..127$
signed char	$-128..127$
unsigned char	$0..255$
int	$-32768..32767$
signed int	$-32768..32767$
unsigned int	$0..65535$
short	$-32768..32767$
long	$-2147483648..2147483647$
float	$-3.4e+48..3.4e+48$
double	$-1.7e+308..1.7e+308$

string constant, the number **8** is an integer constant, and the number **2.78** is a floating point constant. As we'll see, C is quite flexible in how it lets you write constants for the various types.

Integer Constants

C facilitates representation of integers in various ways. To write a decimal integer, write the digits of the number. For example, **32254** is a decimal integer; so is **−32254**. Note that there are no commas in the number; commas are not allowed in an integer.

C also makes it easy for you to write integers in number bases other than base 10. In particular, it is sometimes convenient to write a number in base 8 (octal form) or base 16 (hexadecimal form). Such alternate bases can be more convenient because it is easier to translate a binary representation into one of these bases than into base 10.

The following program writes the same number (32254) in three different bases: 10, 8, and 16. We'll discuss these alternate number bases after we analyze some of the program's new constructs.

```
/* Program to write a number in decimal, octal, and hexadecimal format. */

main ()
{
        int i1 = 32254;   /* initialize variable during definition */

        /* Write the number 3 different ways.
           Note that the same variable is substituted each time.
        */
        printf ( "decimal %d;\toctal %o;\thexadecimal %x\n", i1, i1, i1);
}
```

This program produces the following output. Each value represents the same number (the decimal 32254).

```
decimal 32254;  octal 76776;    hexadecimal 7dfe
```

This program simply writes numbers. It uses the initialization during definition that we have already seen. It also introduces two new placeholders and uses an escape code we haven't tried yet.

The %o placeholder tells the system to write the value substituted in octal form. This means that the value stored in variable **i1** is transformed before it is written to the screen. Similarly, the %x specifies that the value is to be written in base 16.

The \t escape code is a tab, and tells the system to move to the next tabstop before continuing with the writing. Notice that there is no space between \t and the following word. This is because everything after the **t** in \t is interpreted as part of the string argument.

The decimal numbering system uses powers of 10 for its place values. For example, the number 32254 consists of 4 ones, 5 tens, 2 hundreds, 2 thousands, and 3 ten thousands. If you add $(3 * 10000) + (2 * 1000) + (2 * 100) + (5 * 10) + (4 * 1)$, you will get 32254. Each place value is ten times the power of the place value to its right. Thus, the third column from the right (hundreds) is ten times the second column from the right (tens).

The octal numbering system uses the same principle of increasing powers going from right to left. However, in this case, powers of eight are used. Thus, each place value is eight times the place value to its right. The octal representation for this number is 76776: 6 ones, 7 eights, 7 sixty-fours, 6 five hundred twelves $(512 = 64 * 8)$, and 7 four thousand ninety-sixes $(4096 = 512 * 8)$. (With names such as four thousand ninety-sixes, aren't you glad we use decimal numbering?) Check this by computing $(7 * 4096) + (6 * 512) + (7 * 64) + (7 * 8) + (6 * 1)$.

In base 16, the same principle applies, but this time the powers are based on 16, so that each place value is 16 times the place value to its right. The hexadecimal value for our number is 7dfe. This translates into: e ones, f sixteens, d two hundred fifty-sixes $(16 * 16)$, and 7 four thousand ninety-sixes $(256 * 16)$. If you don't know what these strange numbers — d, e, f — are, check the next paragraph.

In base 10, you use 10 digits: 0 through 9. The next number is $10 - 1$ ten and 0 ones. In base eight, there are eight digits: 0 through 7. The next octal number is 10: 1 *eight* and 0 ones. Not surprisingly, you need 16 digits to count in hexadecimal. There aren't enough digits to count in base 16. Therefore, the first six letters of the alphabet—a through f—are used to represent the "digits" 10 through 15 in hexadecimal. So, the hexadecimal digits are 0 through 9, a through f. The next hexadecimal number is 10: 1 *sixteen* and 0 ones. Thus, the hexadecimal representation translates into: $(7 * 4096) + (13 * 256) + (15 * 16) + (14 * 1)$.

You will find hexadecimal and octal representations in many C programs. The nice thing about hexadecimal representations is that every "digit" in base 16 corresponds to 4 bits in binary. This makes it easy to represent a binary pattern in hexadecimal form. A 16-bit number will have 4 hexadecimal digits. Similarly, every octal digit corresponds to 3 binary digits.

When you write an integer, the system has to know whether you are writing it in decimal, octal, or hexadecimal. We've already seen that the decimal representation is just the number itself. If you are writing an octal number, write **0** (the digit 0, not the letter O) immediately before the octal representation of the number. To write 32254 in octal, write 076776. Notice that the program does not write a zero before an octal number when it writes the number. Presumably you know what kind of representation you've asked for, so the system sees no need to preface the value in any way.

Finally, to represent a number as a hexadecimal constant, write **0x** or **0X** immediately before the hexadecimal representation: 0x7DFE. Case does not matter when writing hexadecimal values. To write the negative form of this number, write −0x7DFE, not 0x−7DFE.

▶**CAUTION**   Decimal integers are written as you would normally write them. Octal integers start with the digit 0. Hexadecimal integers start with 0x or 0X. Signs must come first in any representation of a negative integer.

Constants of Character

Character constants are written within single quotes. For example, 'Q' is a **char** constant. You can also specify a character constant in other ways, however. For example, the letter 'Q' has ASCII code 81 (121 in octal). C lets you specify a character by writing its ASCII code. Because of this, 'Q' and 81 are equivalent ways of writing the value of the character constant. When discussing integers, we learned that integers could be written in bases other than base ten. Thus, you could just as well write 0121 to represent this **char** constant. (Remember, the 0 indicates the number is an octal.)

Finally, you can write a character by specifying an octal escape code (\121) corresponding to the character's ASCII value. Note the following about this representation: a backslash starts the escape code; the use of octal, rather than decimal, and the absence of the 0 before the octal representation when writing the character as an escape code.

The following program illustrates these different ways of writing a character value.

```
/* Program to illustrate four ways of writing a character value. */
main ()
{
        char c1 = 'A', c2 = 65, c3 = '\101', c4 = 0101;
        printf ( "%c\t%c\012%c\t%c\n", c1, c2, c3, c4);
}
```

This produces the following output:

```
A       A
A       A
```

The program writes the same character value, 'A', based on four different initial representations. In all instances, the same numerical value is being stored, but different representations are used.

Notice that the output is on two lines, split between the second and third characters. The reason is that **\012** immediately follows the second **char** placeholder. This is another way of writing a newline command, using the ASCII line feed character (decimal 10, octal 012).

The **\012** to move to the next line is an escape code, like the **\n**, you used previously. Such an octal escape code is the exception to the one character limit on escape codes that was mentioned in a previous section.

String Constants

String constants consist of a sequence of characters. We've already seen examples of string constants, such as the first argument to **printf( )**. String constants begin and end with double quotes. For example,

"this is a string constant. \n"

is a string constant. On the other hand, the following is *not* a string constant because it is not within double quotes.

'this is NOT a string constant. \n'

▶REMEMBER   String constants begin and end with double quotes.

Float and Double Constants

C is remarkably flexible in how it lets you write **float** or **double** values. For example, the following are all valid:

$$-.5 \qquad -5.0e-1 \qquad -.05E+1 \qquad 50e-2 \qquad 1.$$

When writing constants, the only difference between a **float** and a **double** is in the possible range of values. You may get an error if you try to assign a value to a float that is too large for the allocated storage. Except for size, **float** and **double** values are written in exactly the same way.

Basically, a real number can be written in most of the ways you would think. The number must have a number portion; this may be preceded by a sign and may be followed by an exponent portion.

The number portion has one of the following forms:

&.54   Decimal point followed by 1 or more digits

54.   One or more digits followed by a decimal point

54.54   One or more digits followed by a decimal point, followed by 1 or more digits

The sign is optional, and must be either $-$ or $+$. Most older implementations will not let you use a unary $+$ operator. The Draft Proposed ANSII Standard includes a unary plus operator, which would make a number such as $+54.54$ legal. The exponent portion is also optional; the exponent starts with **e** or **E**, and is followed by an integer. The integer may be preceded by a sign, for example, $7.5E+5$.

There is one other way of writing a real number: as one or more digits, with no decimal point or portion following. In this case, the number *must* have an exponent portion. For example, 1e5 is a valid **float**, but 10 is not. Ten is an **int**, no matter what you intended. This is how the system distinguishes **floats** from **ints**. Be careful when writing floats without fractional components. Write 1.0 rather than 1 because the latter is an **int**.

▶**REMEMBER**   Float and **double** constants can be written using three components: an optional minus $(-)$ sign, a numerical part, and an exponent part. The sign and exponent portion are optional (with one exception, as described in the text). Parts must be included in the order listed.

Arithmetic Operators

C provides arithmetic operators you know:

$$+ \qquad - \qquad * \qquad /$$

Each of these works with integral as well as floating point types. Some of the operators produce different results, depending on the type on which the operations are being carried out. In this section, we'll look at some of the properties of the arithmetic operators, and will discuss them in terms of operator precedence, or evaluation priority.

Operators with Floating Point Types

When applied to floating point types, these operators do the obvious: add, subtract, multiply, divide. The only quirk here is the danger of exceeding the range for the variable type. If the result of an operation is a value outside the floating point type's range, you will get an error message.

The result of operations with floating point variables and values should be stored in a floating point variable. Thus, if you are adding two **float** values and want to assign the results to another **float**, the system will assign a **float** result to the variable. If you are assigning the results to a **double**, the system will return a **double**.

Operators with Integer Types

Again, arithmetic operators do what you expect them to do—in most instances. A frequent problem in doing arithmetic with integers is overflow. If an integer computation overflows, the system returns an incorrect value, but no error message.

For example, the following program produces an incorrect result, but you get no error message from the system.

```
/* program to illustrate integer overflow. */
main ()
{
        int i1 = 32000;

        i1 = i1 * 3;
        printf ( "value after overflow: %d\n", i1);
}
```

This program returns 30464, rather than the 96000 you would expect, because 96000 exceeds the largest integer value possible. There is no error message.

▶**CAUTION**   Avoid overflow when doing integer arithmetic.

When applied to integers, the operators will return integers. This means that certain operators must work differently with integers than they do with floating point types. For example, if you divide 7.0 by 2.0, the result is 3.5. On the other hand, if you divide the integer 7 by the integer 2, the result cannot be 3.5 because 3.5 is not an integer. The result will actually be 3, which is what you get if you divide 7 by 2 and throw away the remainder. The C compiler decides what kind of division (integer or floating point) it is doing, based on the types of the variables or numbers involved.

In addition to the four common operators already mentioned, there is another operator—%—available for **int** variables. This modulus operator returns the remainder when dividing one integer by another. Thus, in the previous example, where 7 / 2 returned 3, 7 % 2 would return 1, which is the remainder when 7 is divided by 2.

Be careful when doing division or when using the modulo operator with negative numbers. When doing division, the sign of the result depends on the sign of the numbers involved in the division. Specifically, if both the first and second values involved are positive *or* both are negative (that is, if the values before and after the division operator (/) have the same sign), the result is a positive number. If the numbers involved have different signs, the result is a negative number. For example, 36.0 / 12.0 = 3.0, as does −36.0 / −12.0. On the other hand, 36.0 / −12.0 = 3.0, as does −36.0 / 12.0.

For the modulus operator, the first of the numbers determines the sign. If the first number (i.e., the number from which the remainder will be computed) is positive, the result is positive; if the first number is negative, the result is negative. These are the rules for the modulus operator in QuickC; other implementations may handle this operator differently.

Binary and Unary Operators

All of the preceding operators (+, −, ∗, /, %) are *binary operators*. This means

they take two values, and return a single value as their result. For example, 7 %
4 takes the two values 7 and 4, and returns the single value, 3.

There is also an important *unary operator* that you already know about.
Earlier, −31000 was mentioned as a valid integer value. This is actually the
number 31000, modified by the unary operator, −, known as arithmetic
negation. This is *not* the same as subtraction.

▶**REMEMBER**   Arithmetic negation, a unary operator, is not the same as
subtraction, a binary operator.

In most older implementations there is no unary plus operator. The Draft
Proposed ANSI Standard does provide for such an operator, however. This is
why you may find that a number such as +32254 is not valid, if you have an
older compiler. Because there is a unary minus operator, −32254 is valid in any
implementation. QuickC does include a unary plus operator.

Operator Precedence

The relative precedence of two operators tells you which of the operators to
apply first in an expression. For example, 3 + 5 * 4 could equal 32 or 23,
depending on the order in which the computations are carried out. In algebra,
we learned that the answer should be 23, because multiplication takes precedence over addition: 5 * 4 is computed first. On the other hand, (3 + 5) * 4
does equal 32, because the parentheses tell you to add 3 and 5 before multiplying the result by 4. The parentheses override the existing operator precedence
hierarchy.

The operators we have seen so far also fall into a precedence hierarchy,
summarized in Table 3-5. The topmost operators have the highest precedence
in the table.

Operators on the same level have the same precedence. In this case,
operators are evaluated in the order in which they are encountered, usually left
to right. In the case of the arithmetic binary operators, expressions are
evaluated left to right. This means the leftmost operator is evaluated first,
provided all operators are at the same level.

Table 3-5.   Precedence Hierarchy for Operators

Operator	Unary or Binary	Comments
+, −, sizeof( )	unary	− is arithmetic negation
*, /, %	binary	
+, −	binary	− is subtraction
=	binary	assignment operator

Yes, assignment is an operation, so we have an assignment operator. This operator has very low precedence, at least compared to the operators we've seen so far. The consequence of this is that the assignment to a variable is made only after the entire expression to the right of the operator is evaluated. Notice that the **sizeof( )** we used earlier is actually an operator. It has the same high precedence level as the unary minus operator. The **sizeof( )** operator returns an integer value, as we saw earlier.

Operations on Mixed Types

Earlier we said that a number such as 35 would be treated as an integer, even if you had meant to write a **float**, and that an expression such as 35 / 7 produces an integer result. But what happens to an expression such as 35 / 7.0?

In C, variables in expressions with multiple types undergo something called *type promotion*. This means that, for the purposes of evaluating the expression, variables of a "lower" type are promoted to, or treated as, variables of the highest type appearing in the expression. In general, integral types are lower than floating point types. More specifically, **char** is lower than **int**, which is lower than **float**; and **float** is lower than **double**.

In the case of the example above, 35 would be "promoted" to a **float**, that is, it would be treated as 35.0. (On the other hand, 35 / 7 would involve only integers because both variables are at the same level, so there is no need to do any type promotion.) The rules for type promotion (or coercion, as it is sometimes called) are as follows.

The **char** and **short** variables are *automatically* promoted to **int**. (Characters are essentially treated as integers internally. This is why we are able to do addition using chars.It is also why we can **printf( )** the char variables using %**d**, or decimal, format.)

unsigned char and **unsigned short** variables are automatically promoted to **unsigned int**.

After any of the above conversions have been made, additional promotions are made, as needed, up the following hierarchy (from lowest to highest): **int** to **unsigned** to **long** to **float** to **double**.

This means that the value of an **int** in an expression containing a **float** is first promoted to **float**; then the expression is evaluated and the result is of type **float**. The following program contains some examples of type promotions. The program also illustrates the importance of being careful when dealing with mixed expressions.

```
/* Program to illustrate some of the rules and subtleties of
   mixing variable types in expressions.
*/

main ()
{
        int i1 = -12, i2 = 3, i3 = 4;
        unsigned u1 = 10, u2;  /* define some unsigned integers. */
        float f1, f2 = 3.0, f3 = 4.0;

        u2 = u1 + i1;  /* add an unsigned and an int */
        /* a new output type is introduced, u for unsigned */
        printf ( "unsigned result %u\n", u2);

        /* float gets assigned result of operating on ints */
        f1 = i2 / i3;  /* is division result int or float? */
        printf ( "\ni1 / i3 (3 / 4) --> float, written as float: %f\n", f1);

        f1 = i2 / f3;  /* is division result int or float? */
        printf ( "i1 / f3 (3 / 4.0) --> float, written as float: %f\n", f1);

        f1 = i3 / i2;
        printf ( "\ni3 / i2 (4 / 3) --> float, written as float: %f\n", f1);

        f1 = i3 / f2;
        printf ( "i3 / f2 (4 / 3) --> float, written as float: %f\n", f1);

        /* write int result as float type : BEWARE of doing such things */
        printf ( "\nBAD: 4 / 3 as float: %f\n", i3 / i2);
        /* write int result as int type : this is OK */
        printf ( "OK: 4 / 3 as int: %d\n", i3 / i2);

        /* write float result as int type : BEWARE of doing such things */
        printf ( "\nBAD: 4.0 / 3.0 as int: %d\n", f3 / f2);
        /* write float result as float type : this is OK */
        printf ( "OK: 4.0 / 3.0 as float: %f\n", f3 / f2);
}
```

This program produces the following output:

```
unsigned result 65534

i1 / i3 (3 / 4) --> float, written as float: 0.000000
i1 / f3 (3 / 4.0) --> float, written as float: 0.750000

i3 / i2 (4 / 3) --> float, written as float: 1.000000
i3 / f2 (4 / 3) --> float, written as float: 1.333333
```

```
BAD: 4 / 3 as float: 0.000000
OK: 4 / 3 as int: 1

BAD: 4.0 / 3.0 as int: 21845
OK: 4.0 / 3.0 as float: 1.333333
```

The program again shows how to initialize variables when defining them. It also shows how to define an unsigned integer variable. The remaining points concern the process of evaluating expressions and the transformations when writing information.

One important point can be made using the last four **printf( )** calls. The information to be substituted for placeholders in those functions calls is actually an expression, rather than a variable name. This means that the expression is first evaluated, and its result is substituted for the placeholder. The examples in the listing show what happens under good and bad conditions.

Note that when the result of $(-12 +10)$, an expression that we would evaluate to -2, is stored in an **unsigned int**, the result is a very large positive number. This is because the sign bit (the high order, or leftmost, bit) is 1 for negative numbers, but is used to help represent magnitude for an **unsigned int**. Be careful when working with different combinations of signed and unsigned values.

The next few assignment/output couples show what happens when your expressions involve different types. Note that the result of evaluating the *integer* expression, 3 / 4 (which yields 0 by integer division) returns 0.00 as the value assigned to the **float**. Remember, division has a higher precedence than assignment. The system first carries out an integer division, producing 0 in this case; the (integer) result is then promoted in the process of being assigned to the float variable. Thus, the relative precedence of the assignment and division operators influenced the value assigned to the **float**.

The same thing happens in the second division. 4 / 3. This example also shows that promotion in this case happens *after* the division is evaluated, not before the expression is even touched.

The next two couples show that things work smoothly if either of the elements in the division expression is a **float**. Type promotion occurs during division here, rather than upon assignment.

The final couples illustrate how to write information correctly and incorrectly. Earlier, we found that the placeholder and the argument to be substituted had to be of the same type. Later we learned that **char** values were exempt, to a certain extent, from this requirement. Here, we'll find out what happens if you really violate this restriction.

The first of these function calls is expected to substitute the results of an integer operation for a **float** placeholder. This substitution process is not an operator, so type promotion doesn't apply. Instead, you get odd answers, such as 0.000000. Similarly, trying to substitute the result of two **float** values into an **int** placeholder also produces bizarre values, such as 21485.

▶**CAUTION**   Be very careful when computing expressions containing mixed types, especially if the types include both an integral and a floating point type. The order in which operators are applied may make a difference. When writing out the results of expressions containing mixed types, make sure the resulting type and the type specified in your string argument to **printf( )** match.

printf( ) Once More

You have learned most of the placeholders and a few of the formatting options possible with **printf( )**. Table 3-6 summarizes the types you can write with **printf( )**.

Notice the %**ld** placeholder command. This says that the information coming is a **long** and should be written as such. Similarly, %**lf** is intended for a double in the Draft Proposed ANSI Standard (and, hence, also in QuickC),

Table 3-6.   Placeholder Types for **printf( )**

Command	Type	Comments
%c	char	
%d	int	
%f	float	
%f	double	non-ANSI implementations
%ld	long int	l usable with integral types
%lf	double	ANSI Standard implementations
%o	octal	integral types only
%u	unsigned	
%x	hexadecimal	integral type only

but is not used in all implementations. Some systems make no distinction between **float** and **double** in placeholder specifiers. They simply write the variable passed as required by the variable's data type.

Summary

In this chapter, you've learned something about the makeup of a C program: the structure of a program, of functions, and of statements (simple and compound). Two functions that are particularly important in C—**main( )** and **printf( )**—were also discussed. You've also seen how to put comments into your program, and how to define variables of different types.

The chapter also introduced you to C's simple data types and their variants. In the process, you learned how to represent these types and how to carry out certain operations using variables and constants.

In the next chapter, you'll find out more about the structure of C programs and about the files that make up such programs. You'll also learn ways to make your files cleaner and easier to read.

4

Preprocessors and Programs

In this chapter you'll find out more about C programs. In the last chapter, we saw a very simple program—made up of a few functions defined in a single source file. In this chapter, we'll elaborate a bit on that barebones program structure. You learn about the C preprocessor and the directives you can give it. You'll also learn how to write macros to do certain things, and how to declare library functions you want to use.

In Chapter 1 you learned about program source and header files, and in Chapter 3 you learned that programs consist of functions. Now, we'll look more closely at program files, and at how to use definitions in programs.

Program Structure

In addition to functions, a program can contain instructions on the contents of a file, or it can contain variable definitions. You can hide many detailed definitions or environment-specific information in header files. You can also create variables that are accessible to more than just one function.

The following listing provides a more extensive example of a program's structure and features. Below the listing is the output the program will produce.

```
/* Program to illustrate instructions for header files, and
   global definitions.
*/

#include "proginfo.h"    /* contains various substitutions */

int line_number;         /* a global variable definition */

/* write a greeting to screen. Add to line counter for each line written. */
write_message ()
{
        line_number = line_number + 1;  /* increment line counter. */
        printf ( "%2d\t%s\n%2d\t\t%s\n%2d\t\t %s\n",
                 line_number, GREETING,
                 line_number + 1, CLOSING,
                 line_number + 2, SENDER);
        line_number = line_number + 2;  /* increment line counter. */
}


/* display information about program. Add to line counter. */
write_program_info ()
{
        line_number = line_number + 1;  /* increment line counter. */
        printf ( "%2d\t%s Version %5.1f\n",
                 line_number, PROGRAM, VERSION_NR);
}


main()
{
        /* no variable definitions this time. */

        line_number = 0;            /* initialize line counter */
        write_program_info ();      /* start calling other functions */
        write_message ();
        empty_line ();

        write_program_info ();
        write_message ();
```

```
        empty_line ();
        fake_empty ();
        empty_line ();

        write_program_info ();
        write_message ();
        printf ( "\n\n%2d lines written\n", line_number);
}


/* write an empty (but numbered) line on screen. */
empty_line ()
{
        line_number = line_number + 1;
        printf ( "%2d\n", line_number);
}


/* write an empty line with message to screen */
fake_empty ()
{
        line_number = line_number + 1;
        printf ( "%2d\t %s\n", line_number, BLANK_MESSAGE);
}



/* Output from Program */

 1 QuickC Version   1.0
 2 Hello,
 3 Sincerely,
 4  World
 5
 6 QuickC Version   1.0
 7 Hello,
 8 Sincerely,
 9  World
10
11  <this line intentionally left blank>
12
13 QuickC Version   1.0
14 Hello,
15 Sincerely,
16  World


16 lines written
```

The next listing shows the header file read by the program.

```
/* PROGINFO.H : header file for QuickC listings. (5.20.87) */

/* one-line version */
#define PROG_MESSAGE  "QuickC version 1.0"

/* two components to program information */
#define PROGRAM  "QuickC"        /* program being used */
#define VERSION_NR  1.0          /* product version number */

#define GREETING "Hello, "
#define CLOSING "Sincerely,"
#define SENDER "World"

#define BLANK_MESSAGE  "<this line intentionally left blank>"
```

The program writes the same messages to the screen. In addition, it counts the number of lines being written and gives you a total at the end.

The program above uses substitutions defined in the **proginfo.h** file. When QuickC encounters a name defined in **proginfo.h** in the source file, it replaces the identifier with the information associated with the name in **proginfo.h**.

If you could read function **write_program_info ( )** after it has been compiled, it would look like the following listing:

```
write_program_info ()
{
        line_number = line_number + 1;
        printf ( "%2d\t%s Version %5.1f\n", line_number, "QuickC", 1.0);
}
```

The difference between this and the original, pre-compiled version is that the references to identifiers found in file **proginfo.h** have been replaced by their string or numerical equivalents. For example, instead of PROGRAM, the function now has "QuickC." Note, however, that you never actually see the substituted text in your source code. Instead, QuickC places the substituted value into the executable code. The substitutions are literal—exact replicas of what you wrote in the header file are reproduced in the function. Later, you'll learn how to make more complex substitutions that will actually perform a task.

The version number (1.0) is being written in five columns, with one decimal place. Although "1.0" is an exact substitution from **proginfo.h**, you must specify the format if you want control over the output. This is because the substituted value is treated like any other value of the type specified by the placeholder. Thus, the identifier VERSION—NR was replaced by the floating point value 1.0; this value was then sent to the output processes in **printf( )**.

The variable **line—number** is intended for use by several functions in the program. Each function must be able to change its value. The **main( )** function writes the current value of the variable at the end of the program.

A variable defined within a function is accessible only to that function, unless the variable is defined globally—that is, outside of any particular function. In the preceding program, **line—number** is an example of such an **external** variable. For now, we'll just make any external definitions at the beginning of the main source file, after any **#include** instructions, but before any function definitions. Later, you'll learn how to position and define variables to make them accessible only to certain functions.

The C Preprocessor

The C preprocessor provides a means of modifying a C source file in various ways before the actual compilation. This capability lets you extend the C language to make it easier or more useful for particular purposes. The preprocessor is conceptually distinct from the compiler, but it isn't necessarily a separate program. The important distinction is that the compiler treats your source as if you had actually typed the material the preprocessor substitutes for the appropriate identifiers.

For example, the #**define** directive enables you to use mnemonic names (such as FALSE or VERSION—NR) instead of the arbitrary numerical values needed in your program. In such cases, the preprocessor replaces the identifiers with the actual values you've associated with those names. After the substitution, the compiler never knows that the source file ever contained anything but the actual values.

In this section, you'll learn how to use some of the preprocessor commands, or directives, available in QuickC. You'll see that the preprocessor commands provide a sort of "mini-language," which lets you do some fairly extensive modification of your program before compilation.

Table 4-1 contains the C preprocessor commands, according to the Draft Proposed ANSI Standard. Notice that you've already used two of the commands in previous programs.

Table 4-1. C Preprocessor Commands

#define	#elif	#else
#endif	#error	#if
#ifdef	#ifndef	#include
#line	#pragma	#undef

One of the preprocessor's major functions is handling simple substitutions, where the replacement is just a single value, such as a number or a string constant. The identifiers replaced by the values are known as *manifest constants.* The **#define** commands we have used so far have all been manifest constants.

The preprocessor also handles *macros.* A macro is a name that will be replaced by other material, such as a statement or an expression. The replacement text is called the *macro body.* Later, we'll look at such macros, in which you can even use arguments to specify what substitutions are to be made. Such macros are sometimes called function-like macros because they can be used instead of C functions. We'll see how macros and functions differ when used in a C program.

An example of a function-like macro will help make the discussion clearer. Suppose you had the following in your program:

```
#define SQUARE(x)  (x) * (x)      /* sample function-like macro */

main ()
{
   printf ( "%f\n", SQUARE(3.5));
}
```

The preprocessor substitutes (3.5) * (3.5) when the line calling **printf( )** is encountered. This is actually two replacements: (x) * (x) for SQUARE(x), and (3.5) for (x).

When the preprocessor encounters a macro identifier, it replaces the identifier with the macro body you have specified. For manifest constants, a direct substitution is all that is needed. For macros with arguments, the actual information included as the argument must also be put into the text (as in the listing above). Then the substitution text replaces the macro. This process of exchanging the macro call for the information it represents is known as *macro expansion*.

General Preprocessor Rules

All preprocessor commands or directives begin with #. Most C compilers — including QuickC and Microsoft C 5.0 — will let you start your preprocessor command anywhere on the line, provided there is only blank space before the #. Some older compilers make you start preprocessor commands in the first column of a line. The Draft Proposed ANSI Standard lets you put a space between the # and the command name. Both QuickC and C 5.0 will let you do this. However, some older compilers will not allow this, so check your compiler for the exact form a preprocessor command must take.

▶**REMEMBER**   All preprocessor commands begin with #. There may be blank space (but nothing else) before the # on the line. The ANSI Standard will also let you put space between the # and the command name.

After the directive name, the command includes the constant or macro name and the replacement text for the macro or constant, each separated by one or more blanks, as shown here:

```
#define        NAME           "Quick C"
   ↑             ↑                ↑

Directive     Manifest        Replacement
              constant        text
```

If your entire command won't fit on one line, or if you want to make the command easier to read, you can tell the preprocessor that the command continues on the next line. To do this, end the current line with a \ (backslash). When the preprocessor sees the backslash, it will keep reading the next line. For example:

```
#define SQUARE(x) \
        (x) * (x)    /* multiple line command --- for readability. */
```

```
#define TOO_LONG   "I made this too long to fit on one preprocessor \
                   line."

main ()
{
        printf ( "%f\n\n", SQUARE (2.5));
        printf ("%s\n", TOO_LONG);
}

/* Output from Program */

6.250000

I made this too long to fit on one preprocessor                line.
```

This program writes the results of processing two definitions. One value is the result of a simple substitution for a manifest constant (TOO__LONG); the other is the result of expanding a macro (SQUARE(x)).

The two #**define** commands each extend over two lines. Notice that the output for the TOO__LONG constant has a large blank space in it — because the original command has blank space before the text on the second line. The preprocessor takes the replacement text literally, blank space and all.

This also explains why preprocessor commands don't have semicolons at the end. Any semicolon at the end of the string would show up inside the parentheses for the **printf( )** call, which is not acceptable to the compiler.

The use of space in the string replacement text for TOO__LONG has had an effect. By putting the space at the beginning of the second line, a gap was introduced in the output text. On the other hand, the SQUARE(x) macro was called with a space between the name and the argument list (in parentheses), despite the fact that the original macro name had no such space. This is allowed by most compilers — including QuickC, and in the Draft Proposed ANSI Standard — because the system ignores any spaces between names and argument lists for functions or macros.

In other words, the SQUARE (2.5) is processed just as if it had read SQUARE(2.5). This means you can use spaces to help make your source file easier to read. You may not leave spaces in the middle of a name, however.

Preprocessor Commands

There are many preprocessor commands, which serve various purposes. In this section, you will find information about these commands, constants, and macros.

The #include Command

This command tells the preprocessor to substitute the contents of the file named at the spot in the source file where the **#include** command is found. For example,

```
#include "proginfo.h"
```

causes the contents of the file **proginfo.h** to be written in the source file location where the command was found. You could have achieved the same thing by actually typing the contents of #**proginfo.h** directly into your source file.

There are two forms of the **#include** command. In one case (used in the examples so far), the file name is specified as a string constant, between double quotes (e.g., "proginfo.h"). The system searches for the file in the current directory. Some implementations may also search in other places, if the file is not found in the current directory. This form of the command is most useful for including header files you've created.

In the other form of the command, the file name is written, *without quotes*, between < and >. For example,

```
#include <proginfo.h>
```

tells the preprocessor to search for the file in a directory specified for the implementation. Usually, this directory will be where the particular implementation keeps its header files. For example, QuickC looks for such header files in a directory named **\include**. Again, if the file is not found in that directory, the system may look in other places specified by the implementation. This form of the **#include** command is primarily for including files created by the developers of QuickC or whatever C compiler you're using.

▶**REMEMBER**   The two main ways to specify what file to include:

1. Within quote marks (" ") for files in the current directory.

2. Within angle brackets (< >) for files in a default "include file" directory.

In QuickC, you can have **#include** commands inside include files. That is, you can nest include files. Most implementations of C let you do this; however, they differ in the number of nesting levels you can use. QuickC and Microsoft C 5.0 let you nest up to 10 levels deep. Check your compiler to see how many levels of nesting it allows.

The #define Command

Most of your preprocessor commands are likely to be definitions, using the **#define** command, which we used in most of the header files discussed so far. In this section we'll look more closely at this command.

Manifest Constants

A manifest constant is an identifier without arguments. The preprocessor substitutes the replacement text exactly as written for the constant name at the appropriate points in the program file. The substitution text begins right after the name, although there must usually be at least one blank between the name and replacement value. For example, the following are all valid preprocessor definitions. (All but the macro FL—BYTES are manifest constants.)

```
/* Program to print out number of bytes on a double sided DOS floppy disk.
   Disk capacity is computed using several preprocessor definitions.

   Note use of L at end of DOS_SECTOR_SIZE macro body
   --- to indicate long.
   Remove the L, then run the program. What happens? Why?
   Hint: Display the information in long hexadecimal format (%lx).
*/

#define DOS_SECTOR_SIZE  0x200L  /* size of a DOS sector, 512 bytes */
#define FL_SIDES 2L              /* number of sides on a floppy disk */
#define FL_TRACKS  40L           /* number of tracks on a floppy disk */
#define FL_SEC_PER_TRACK  9L     /* sectors per track on a floppy disk */

/* Number of bytes on a floppy disk; split over two lines */
#define FL_BYTES  FL_SIDES * FL_SEC_PER_TRACK * FL_TRACKS * \
        DOS_SECTOR_SIZE

main()
{
        printf ( "decimal\t\t %ld\n", FL_BYTES);
        printf ( "octal\t\t %lo\n", FL_BYTES);
        printf ( "hexadecimal\t %lx\n", FL_BYTES);
}
```

This program produces the following output:

```
decimal         368640
octal           1320000
hexadecimal     5a000
```

This program writes the same information in three different formats, illustrating some new points about the **printf( )** function, and shows some features of preprocessor command definitions.

First, note the three placeholders in the call to **printf( )**. You've already seen the use of %**ld** to specify **long int** output. In Table 3-6, I mentioned that **L** (or **l**) could be used with integral types to specify a long value. The %**lx** and %**lo** are the natural extensions to the %**ld**. Essentially, the **L** tells the system to look for its information in a memory location the size of a **long** (4 bytes in QuickC); the **x** tells the system to convert the information to hexadecimal form before writing it.

Now let's look at the preprocessor commands. The first manifest constant, **DOS_SECTOR_SIZE**, is defined as a hexadecimal constant (**0x**), equal to 2 * 256, or 512 decimal. The **L** (or **l**) at the end of the replacement text tells the C compiler that the value is to be treated as a **long**. (We'll see why these values need to be treated as **long** later.)

The next three manifest constants have the same format, except that they are written in decimal form. In preprocessor commands, the only difference between decimal, octal, or hexadecimal representations is their convenience for reading. As you'll notice, powers of 16, such as 256, are "round" numbers when represented in hexadecimal. We'll see other cases where you'll find it convenient to use non-decimal representations.

The FL_BYTES macro is an important example. First, notice that its replacement text is split over two lines.

The more important feature of the definition is the use of manifest constants in the macro body. Let's look at this definition by examining what happens when the preprocessor sees a reference to FL_BYTES in your source file.

The first step is to substitute the macro body for the macro call. Thus, the first call to **printf( )** looks as follows after the substitution:

```
printf ( "decimal\t\t %ld\n",
         FL_SIDES * FL_SEC_PER_TRACK * FL_TRACKS * DOS_SECTOR_SIZE);
```

The preprocessor then sees four new substitutions to make, and makes them, so that the first **printf( )** call looks as follows when all the macro expansion has been carried out:

```
printf ( "decimal\t\t %ld\n", 2L * 9L * 40L * 0x200L);
```

The resulting expression is evaluated before the result is substituted for the **%ld** placeholder in the string argument for **printf( )**.

The preprocessor keeps expanding macros until all required substitutions have been made. There are some limitations on possible substitutions, particularly when it comes to macros with arguments. At that point, there will also be implementation dependent limitations. Check your compiler documentation.

Why do you suppose the manifest constants in the previous listing were defined as **long**? Here is the output for the same program, except that the manifest constants are defined without the L in the replacement text, which makes the system treat them as **int**.

```
decimal        40960
octal          120000
hexadecimal    a000
```

Neither the decimal nor the octal representation seems to provide much information about what might be going on. Look at the hexadecimal result, however. The only difference between this and the earlier listing is that the leftmost digit (5) from the **long** form is missing here. This is exactly what *you* would expect if the system were using only two bytes (four hexadecimal digits) in its computations.

A look at the actual binary representations of this information as an **int** and as a **long** will clarify what is happening. The binary representation of 0xa000 is

1010 0000 0000 0000

where 1010 ($1*8 + 1*2 = 10$) is the binary representation of the hexadecimal digit **a**, and each successive group of four binary digits corresponds to one of the hexadecimal digits — **0** in this case. As an **int**, this would be a negative number, since the sign bit (the leftmost bit) is 1. However, when the system is asked to write the information as a **long**, the following representation is used:

0000 0000 0000 0000 1010 0000 0000 0000

As a **long**, the leftmost bit is 0, so the number is considered positive. By specifying at least one of the manifest constants as a **long**, the computations are done using 4 bytes, so that the correct result is written.

Notice that there is no assignment operator between an identifier and the replacment text. Replacing manifest constants and macro expansion are substitution processes, not assignments. No storage is allocated for variables named FL__SIDES, FL__TRACKS, etc.

The preprocessor will not complain if you do something such as the following:

```
#define FL_SIDES  = 2L
```

The expansion process will simply substitute = **2L** instead of **2L**. Depending on where the macro is being used, this may be acceptable to the compiler. However, the chances are good that the results of this substitution will produce information that may get you into trouble later.

▶ **REMEMBER**   Unless you have a very specific reason for including assignment operators in preprocessor definitions, don't include them.

Similarly, you may inadvertently put a semicolon at the end of the replacement text. Again, there may be times when you actually want to do this. In most cases, however, this will result in a compiler error.

Macros with Parameters

The preprocessor command **#define** can be used with function-like macros to make more complex substitutions. These macros have "slots" into which you can pass specific values when you call the macro in your program. The slots are known as *formal parameters,* and are essentially placeholders. When you call the macro, you pass one argument for each formal parameter in the macro definition. These arguments are also known as *actual parameters*.

For example, the following preprocessor commands define macros with parameters:

```
#define BAD_SQUARE(x)   x * x    /* a definition that can lead to problems. */
#define SQUARE(x)    (x) * (x)   /* a better definition for the square. */
#define SUM(a, b)    (a) + (b)   /* a macro for adding two values. */
```

Each of the "square" macros has one formal parameter, specified by the **x** within the parentheses immediately following the macro name. Any formal parameters in a macro definition must be within the parentheses, and the parentheses must come immediately after the name, with no intervening space. If there were a space, the preprocessor would treat the formal parameter list as part of the macro body.

The SUM(a, b) macro has two formal parameters: **a** and **b**. Formal parameters are separated from each other by commas. You can leave space between formal parameters in your definition because the preprocessor will interpret everything up to the right parenthesis as part of the formal parameter list for the macro.

We've already discussed what happens when macros with parameters are expanded: the macro body replaces the macro call; then all formal parameters are replaced by the arguments, or actual parameters, passed when the macro was called. Let's look at this process in the following listing, which will also show why BAD__SQUARE(x) is not the best way to compute the square of two numbers.

```
/* Program to illustrate macros with parameters. */

#define BAD_SQUARE(x)   x * x  /* a definition that can lead to problems. */
#define SQUARE(x)    (x) * (x)  /* a better definition for the square. */
#define ADD(a, b)    (a) + (b)  /* a macro for adding two values. */

main()
{
        int    good_int_sqr, bad_int_sqr, int_sum;
        double good_dbl_sqr, bad_dbl_sqr, dbl_sum;

        good_int_sqr = SQUARE ( ADD (2, 3));
        bad_int_sqr = BAD_SQUARE ( ADD (2, 3));
        int_sum = ADD (2, 3);

        /* macros can be used with integral or floating point types. */
        good_dbl_sqr = SQUARE (2 + 3.0);
        bad_dbl_sqr = BAD_SQUARE (2 + 3.0);
        dbl_sum = ADD (2.0, 3.0);

        printf ( "Good INT: %d\n", good_int_sqr);
        printf ( "Bad INT: %d\n", bad_int_sqr);
        printf ( "INT Sum: %d\n", int_sum);

        printf ( "Good DOUBLE: %lf\n", good_dbl_sqr);
        printf ( "Bad DOUBLE: %lf\n", bad_dbl_sqr);
        printf ( "DOUBLE Sum: %lf\n", dbl_sum);
}


/* Output from Program */

Good INT: 25
Bad INT: 11
INT Sum: 5
Good DOUBLE: 25.000000
Bad DOUBLE: 11.000000
DOUBLE Sum: 5.000000
```

This program computes a number of things and displays the results. Three function-like macros are defined for the C preprocessor, and are used several times in the main program. Two of the macros, SQUARE(x) and BAD__ SQUARE(x), are supposed to do the same thing; however, they behave quite differently, as shown by the output.

First, notice that the macros are being used with both **int** and **double**. Preprocessor macros can be used with any type of information. The preprocessor will make nonsensical substitutions, if you tell it to, although the compiler would then complain. In the listing, the substitutions result in valid expressions, so all is well syntactically. Although you can use the macros with integral or floating point types, you still need to make certain that the right types are returned and used in other statements, such as the **printf( )** call.

Let's see what happens when the first assignment statement is carried out. The assignment goes through the following versions, as a result of macro expansion:

```
good_int_sqr = SQUARE ( ADD (2, 3));
good_int_sqr = (ADD (2, 3)) * (ADD (2, 3));   /* expand SQUARE(x) */
good_int_sqr = ((2) + (3)) * ((2) + (3));     /* expand ADD(a,b) */
good_int_sqr = (5) * (5);                      /* add terms within ( ) */
good_int_sqr = 25;                             /* multiply 2 sums */
```

The preprocessor expands the first macro it encounters, in this case SQUARE(x). It replaces the macro call with the macro body, substituting the actual argument, ADD (2, 3), wherever the formal parameter, **x**, is used in the macro body. This macro expansion produces the second form of the statement.

The preprocessor then expands the first macro it encounters, ADD(a,b), again substituting arguments for formal parameters. The macro is found twice, so the macro expansion is carried out twice. After all calls to the ADD(a,b) macro have been expanded, the statement involves only numerical expressions and an assignment operator.

Notice all the parentheses appearing as the statement is processed. These are introduced in the macro bodies, for both SQUARE(x) and ADD(a,b).

Let's look at the statement involving **bad__int__sqr**, to see why it produces a different result.

```
bad_int_sqr = BAD_SQUARE ( ADD (2, 3));
bad_int_sqr = ADD (2, 3) * ADD (2, 3);    /* expand BAD_SQUARE(x) */
bad_int_sqr = (2) + (3) * (2) + (3);      /* expand ADD(a,b) */
bad_int_sqr = (2) + (6) + (3);            /* multiply(!!) two middle terms */
bad_int_sqr = 11;                          /* add three terms resulting */
```

The BAD_SQUARE (x) macro does **not** put parentheses around the formal parameter in the macro body. When the argument is substituted in the expansion, no parentheses are included in the expanded version of the statement. The absence of parentheses becomes a factor after the ADD(a,b) macro has also been expanded. Because multiplication has precedence over addition, the two middle elements—(3) and (2)—are multiplied together first. The parentheses in the SQUARE(x) macro override the precedence hierarchy, forcing the two sides of the multiplication operator to be added first.

▶**REMEMBER**   Macros with parameters can be tricky to write. It's generally wise to use parentheses generously when writing macros with parameters.

After seeing how nested macros are expanded, you should have no trouble working through the transformations for the statements involving variables of type double.

Many commands that are already available to you in QuickC are actually macros which are expanded when the preprocessor modifies your program. Some of the "functions" available will actually be macros, which are expanded by the preprocessor.

For our purposes here, there's no difference in how to use the command, except in what happens when a macro or a function is called. When a function is called in a program, the function variable definitions must be loaded into memory (placed on the stack). This takes time. When a macro is expanded, the instructions in the macro body are inserted directly into the source code. This is done either before or during compilation. When compiled, the instructions will be in the compiled program at all the required places; the program will not need to load anything extra into memory.

So, you can sometimes make your program run faster by using macros instead of functions. The trade-off for the speed increase is increased code size. However, macros can be tricky, so it probably won't pay to place too great an emphasis on macros over functions. Still, when used correctly, macros greatly increase the readability and portability of your code.

One danger in using macros with parameters is incorrect results coming about because of operator precedence. The solution is to put parentheses around each parameter in the macro body. It turns out that even this may not be safe enough in certain cases. Often, the safest thing is to put parentheses around the entire macro body. For example, ADD(a,b) would then be defined as follows:

```
#define ADD(a,b)  ((a) + (b)) /* note the extra ( and ) */
```

Decision-making with Preprocessor Macros

You'll probably encounter situations where you may want to make different types of substitutions for the same constant or macro, depending on context. For example, suppose you wanted a program to report the number of bytes on a floppy disk—where the disk could be single- or double-sided, or high-density. The following listing shows how to specify this information using preprocessor commands:

```
#define DOS_SECTOR_SIZE  0x200L  /* size of a DOS sector, 512 bytes */

#define FL_SIDES 2L              /* number of sides on a floppy disk */
/* */
#undef FL_SIDES
/* */

#define FL_TRACKS  40L           /* number of tracks on a floppy disk */

#define QUAD_TRACKS 80L          /* number of tracks on high density disk */
/*
#undef QUAD_TRACKS
*/


/* test whether a particular identifier has been defined.
   if yes, carry out the subsequent actions;
   if not, go to another point in the listing (one starting with #else).
*/
#ifdef FL_SIDES                  /* do following only if FL_SIDES defined */
#define FL_SEC_PER_TRACK  9L     /* sectors per track on a floppy disk */
#define FL_BYTES  FL_SIDES * FL_SEC_PER_TRACK * FL_TRACKS * \
        DOS_SECTOR_SIZE
#else                            /* do following if FL_SIDES not defined */
#ifdef QUAD_TRACKS               /* do following if QUAD_TRACKS defined */
#define QUAD_SIDES 2L
#define FL_SEC_PER_TRACK 15L
#define FL_BYTES  QUAD_SIDES * FL_SEC_PER_TRACK * QUAD_TRACKS * \
        DOS_SECTOR_SIZE
#else                            /* do if QUAD_TRACKS not defined */
#define FL_BYTES  FL_SEC_PER_TRACK * FL_TRACKS * DOS_SECTOR_SIZE
#endif                           /* end the QUAD_TRACKS if-else */
#endif                           /* end the FL_SIDES if-else */

main()
{
        printf ( "decimal\t\t %ld\n", FL_BYTES);
        printf ( "octal\t\t %lo\n", FL_BYTES);
        printf ( "hexadecimal\t %lx\n", FL_BYTES);
}
```

This program computes and displays the capacity, in bytes, of various types of DOS floppy disks: single- or double-sided, or quad density. The preprocessor commands determine what value to display. Currently, the macro FL__BYTES will evaluate to the capacity of a quad density disk used with ATs. Let's see why.

The #undef Command

After defining FL__SIDES, the program removes the definition by "undefining" the constant. After #**undef** FL__SIDES, it is as if the identifier FL__SIDES had not been used. The #**undef** command removes the definition of the constant or macro name following the command.

Notice that #**undef** was not used for QUAD__TRACKS because that preprocessor command is inside a comment. So, by the time the preprocessor gets to:

```
#ifdef FL_SIDES          /* do following only if FL_SIDES defined */
```

we have three new definitions: DOS__SECTOR__SIZE, FL__TRACKS, and QUAD__TRACKS.

The #ifdef and #else Commands

The #**ifdef** FL__SIDES command tells the reprocessor to check whether it has a definition for the identifier FL__SIDES. In this case, no such definition is in effect (because of the #**undef**). If such a definition exists, the preprocessor processes any commands encountered in the file until one of the following commands is encountered:

```
#endif
#else
#elif
```

If FL__SIDES has been defined, then two new definitions are made: FL__TRACKS and FL__BYTES. If FL__SIDES has *not* been defined, then neither of these definitions occurs. Instead, the preprocessor checks the command following the #**else**.

In the example, the next command is another **#ifdef**, this time asking whether QUAD—TRACKS has been defined. If so, all lines until the next **#endif**, **#else**, or **#elif** are read. If the macro has not been defined, the preprocessor skips all lines until the next #endif, #else, or #elif.

In the example, QUAD—TRACKS *has* been defined, so the preprocessor adds three new definitions. Had QUAD—TRACKS not been defined, the next decision point would have been the **#else** following the definition of FL—BYTES. If the preprocessor makes it that far, it means that neither FL—SIDES nor QUAD—TRACKS has been defined. This means that the disk being asked about is single-sided, and is not a high-density disk.

The next two lines tell the preprocessor that an "if" statement has been finished. The first **#endif** signals the end of the **#ifdef** QUAD—TRACKS portion, and the next **#endif** terminates the **#ifdef** FL—SIDES test. Notice that the inner "if" was terminated first. Corresponding **#ifdef** (or **#if**) and **#endif** pairs behave like parentheses, and you should make sure you match them as carefully as you match parentheses.

Although the macro FL—BYTES is defined in three different places, only one of them is processed during any one run of the program. The result to which FL—BYTES evaluates depends on the pattern of definitions in the program. In the current form of the example, the first and third definitions are ignored, since the preprocessor reads only the commands between **#ifdef** QUAD—TRACKS and the next **#else**.

The #if and #endif Commands

Two additional commands deserve mention here. The **#if** command is similar to **#ifdef**, but gives you greater leeway in what you would like to test. The text following the **#if** command must evaluate to an integer. For example:

```
#if 5 > 10
#define ARBITRARY OL
#endif
```

In this case, nothing is defined, because **5 > 10** is false. In C, a false result is indicated by returning the integer 0. Any other numerical value returned is assumed to represent true. Thus, the **5 > 10** evaluates to 0, which means that the definition is not made.

There is considerable flexibility in what follows the **#if** command. We've already seen that the expression must return an integer value. Some implementations, including QuickC, will even let you put macros in the expression.

The **#elif** command is a combination of **#else** followed immediately by an **#if**. You'll find it useful in the middle of a sequence of "if—else" loops.

Another command for conditional actions is **#ifndef**. This macro is similar to **#ifdef**, except that **#ifndef** says to carry out the subsequent actions if the name specified with the **#ifndef** command has **not** been defined.

Other Processor Commands

Some of the remaining preprocessor commands are more specialized, and will be discussed here briefly.

The **#error** command lets you specify an error message that the preprocessor will display if it finds specific situations which it is testing. For example, you may want to ask whether a particular macro has been defined, and display an error message if it has not. You could do this in the following way:

```
#ifndef MY_MACRO
#error "ERROR: MY_MACRO is undefined"
#endif
```

Ordinarily, the compiler counts lines as it processes your program, starting at line 1. The **#line** command lets you specify an arbitrary line number at any point in your source file. The compiler treats the following lines as having numbers continuing from the number you specified. For example:

```
main()                          /* line 1 in source file */
{                               /* line 2 in source file */
        printf ( "Hello,\n");   /* line 3 in source file */
#line 100                       /* specify a new value for current line */
        printf ( "world\n");    /* line 100 in source file */
}                               /* line 101 in source file */
```

This capability is most useful when you are debugging your program, that is, when you are tracing the execution of your program in order to locate errors or incorrect results.

A **#pragma** is a preprocessor command that lets you tell the implementation to behave in certain ways. For example, it lets you tell the implementation that you want to keep a trace of the program's execution — if your implementation supports such a capability. If an action or a declaration specified with a #**pragma** command is not supported by an implementation, the implementation should just ignore the **pragma**.

These commands may not be defined in your particular implementation. QuickC, for example, does not support the #**error** command. See your compiler documentation for more about these preprocessor commands.

Library Functions

We've used the predefined **printf( )** function in many of the programs so far. This is only one of the many functions that have been precompiled, and put into a Run-Time Function Library for use with QuickC.

The Run-Time Library is a compiled module accessible to your C programs. Functions defined in this library are available for use in your programs. Such functions are handy because they save you the trouble of writing instructions to carry out the tasks the library functions are designed to do. Microsoft has put a great deal of work into creating a useful and sound function library; it's to your advantage to make use of the capabilities it provides.

In this section, we'll look at some of the functions available to you through this library, and you'll learn how to tell the compiler you intend to use one of these functions. See the documentation for your Run-Time Library for information about the available functions and macros.

The following program shows how to use predefined functions to compute the absolute value of an **int** or a **long**. (There is also an absolute value function for floating point types, but that requires an additional header file.)

```
main ()
{
        int  pos_start = 357, neg_start = -200;
        int  abs ();
        long pos_long = 357L, neg_long = -50000;
        long labs (), pos_long_result, neg_long_result;

        printf ( "POS INT.   Start = %d\t\tAbsolute value = %d\n",
                pos_start, abs (pos_start));
        printf ( "NEG INT.   Start = %d\t\tAbsolute value = %d\n",
                neg_start, abs (neg_start));

        pos_long_result = labs ( pos_long);
        neg_long_result = labs ( neg_long);
```

```
        printf ( "POS LONG. Start = %ld\t\tAbsolute value = %ld\n",
                 pos_long, pos_long_result);
        printf ( "NEG LONG. Start = %ld\tAbsolute value = %ld\n",
                 neg_long, neg_long_result);
}
```

This program produces the following output:

```
POS INT.   Start = 357        Absolute value = 357
NEG INT.   Start = -200       Absolute value = 200
POS LONG.  Start = 357        Absolute value = 357
NEG LONG.  Start = -50000     Absolute value = 50000
```

This program computes and displays the absolute value of several variables.

The **abs( )** function returns the absolute value of an integer. If the number is positive or zero, the function returns the number itself; if the number is negative, the function returns the positive form of the number (that is, the number without the minus operator). The **labs( )** function operates similarly for **longs**, and the **fabs( )** function returns the absolute value of a floating point variable or value.

There are two important concepts in the preceding program. First, the program shows how to tell the compiler about the functions you want to use. Second, the program shows how to use such functions.

Although the **abs( )** and **labs( )** functions have been predefined, the compiler has no way of knowing whether you are using the functions correctly in your program. One thing the compiler needs to know is what kind of information a particular function is going to return. To tell the compiler this, you **declare** the function before it is used. The declaration for the **labs( )** function is

```
    long labs();
```

This associates a particular identifier (in this case, **labs**) with a data type (in this case, **long**). The double parentheses (after the name) indicate that **labs( )** is a function. Essentially, the function declaration tells the compiler that **labs( )** is a function that evaluates to, or returns, a value of type **long**. The declaration for **abs( )** is similar, except that the declaration specifies that the function returns an **int**.

The program also shows two ways of using function calls in program statements. With some restrictions, you can call a function anyplace you use a value of the sort returned by the function. So, you can call **abs( )** in an argument to **printf( )**, because **abs( )** returns an **int**, which is substituted for the appropriate placeholder in the string argument to **printf( )**.

You can also call a function on the right side of an assignment statement; for example, when the result of computing **labs( )** is assigned to **pos__long__ result** or to **neg__long__result**. Note here that you *cannot* put a function call on the left side of an assignment statement.

A *function declaration* in C does *not* allocate any memory for the variable, unlike a definition, which *does* allocate storage for a function or variable of the specified type.

The general format for a function declaration is data type followed by function name, including parentheses to indicate that it's a function.

▶ **REMEMBER**   The general syntax for a function declaration is

 <data type>   *<function name>*( )

You may be wondering why we haven't declared **printf( )**, even though we've used it in several programs. The reason is that **printf( )** returns the number of characters printed, which is an integer. If the compiler encounters a function for which no declaration has appeared, the compiler assumes the function returns an **int**. Function declarations for library functions that return an **int** are therefore optional.

This is why declaring **printf( )** is unnecessary. It also means that the function declaration for **abs( )** in the program above was actually unnecessary because the compiler would have assumed that the function returned an integer. You may, however, get warnings about this from the compiler — depending on the level of error reporting you have selected when you compile.

Let's look at one more example, to introduce some more library functions. The following listing uses the library functions, **getch( )**, **getche( )**, and **rand( )**, each of which return integers. The program also introduces a new operator, the *equality operator:* ==, as well as providing a first look at a way of making decisions in C.

```
/* Program to illustrate use of library functions.
   Program asks for a user ID, then writes a random integer between
   0 and 100 or between 0 and the maximum integer value,
   depending on the user's input.
*/

main ()
{
#define MY_ID 'w'                   /* user ID; just to show use of getch() */
#define RESTRICT 'r'                /* restrict random range */
#define TOP_RAND_VALUE 100
```

```
#define MAX_INT 32767              /* maximum integer in implementation. */

        int char_read,
            rand_result1, rand_result2;
        int rand(),                /* function returns a random integer */
            getch(),               /* read a character from keyboard; NO echo */
            getche();              /* read a character from keyboard; echo */


        printf ( "Type in your one character ID, please.\nYour character:  ");
        char_read = getch();           /* get user's id */
        if ( char_read == MY_ID)
        {                              /* beginning of a compound statement. */
            printf ( "\nThanks.\n");
            printf ( "Let's try the random number function.\n");
        }                              /* end of compound statement. */
        else                           /* if ID was not recognized */
        {
            printf ( "\nI don't recognize that ID, but\n");
            printf ( "let's try the random number function anyway.\n");
        }

        printf ( "Please type\n\t\t%c\nto restrict range to 0 .. 10.\
                \nYour selection: ", RESTRICT);
        char_read = getche();          /* get character, echo it. */
        if ( char_read == RESTRICT)
        {
            printf ( "\nOK. Number will be between 0 and %d\n",
                    TOP_RAND_VALUE);
            rand_result1 = rand() % TOP_RAND_VALUE;
            rand_result2 = rand() % TOP_RAND_VALUE;
        }
        else            /* if any random integer will do */
        {
            printf ( "\nOK. Number will be between 0 and %d\n",
                    MAX_INT);
            rand_result1 = rand();
            rand_result2 = rand();
        }

        printf ( "Random result 1 = %d\nRandom result 2 = %d\n",
                rand_result1, rand_result2);
}
```

This program produces the following output, when **w** is entered in response to both prompts, for personal ID, and to the question whether to restrict range.

```
Type in your one character ID, please.
Your character:
Thanks.
Let's try the random number function.
Please type
r
to restrict range to 0 .. 10.
Your selection: w
```

```
OK. Number will be between 0 and 32767
Random result 1 = 41
Random result 2 = 18467
```

This program has two major tasks: getting a single-character ID value from the user, and computing two random integers. Upon reading the ID value entered, the program displays one of two messages, depending on whether the value is equal to the predefined MY—ID. The program then computes and returns two random integers — either between 0 and TOP—RAND—VALUE (100) or between 0 and MAX—INT, the maximum integer value defined in the implementation (32767).

The function declarations for the three new functions all have the same format. Functions were declared separately from the **int** variables in **main( )** to make the declarations easier to read.

Look carefully at the output from this program. There are two places where the user is supposed to enter characters. But only one **w** shows up in the output. Why? The program uses two functions to read the two characters: **getch( )** for the first (ID) character, and **getche( )** for the second character. Of these two functions, only **getche( )** echoes the character it has read to the screen. This **w** is displayed in the output, but the character read by **getch( )** is read but not displayed.

Notice that **getch( )** and **getche( )** return **int** values, even though we're looking for character values. Recall that characters are essentially treated as integers in C. Character arguments or returns will almost always be treated as **int**.

The **rand( )** function returns a pseudo-random integer. Pseudo-random refers to the fact that the program will return the same sequence of "random" numbers each time it is run. Thus, you will get the same random numbers each time you run the program in a particular mode. If you asked for the restricted range of random values, the program would return 67 for the second random value. This is just the remainder after applying the modulus operator to the 18467 returned by **rand( )** in non-restricted mode.

The program has some other features worth mentioning. First, notice that the preprocessor definitions occur inside the **main( )** function. Preprocessor commands can appear anywhere in a file, although most programmers place preprocessor commands at the start of a program.

The program introduces a new operator, ==, which evaluates to true (a nonzero value in C) if the elements on either side of the operator have the same value, and to false (0 in C) otherwise. The equality operator has lower precedence than the arithmetic operators we've seen so far, but higher precedence than the assignment operator. (C returns the value 0 if a result or test is false; a nonzero value if the result is true.)

▶**CAUTION**   Do not confuse the equality operator (==) with the assignment operator (=).

This program also includes the first compound statements we've seen in actual programs. There are four of them: after each of the two **if** statements and after each **else**.

Finally, the program shows how do different things depending on a particular value or set of conditions. This construction:

```
if  (some condition holds)
{
...
}
else  /* if the condition does not hold */
{
...
}
```

is the first C control construct we've seen. You'll find out more about it and other constructs in Chapter 6.

The last point to mention about this program concerns the call to **printf( )**, asking about the *RESTRICT* selection. The string argument for this function call actually is split over two lines. To indicate this to the compiler, we've ended the first line with a backslash (\ ), just as we did when a preprocessor definition did not fit on a single line. You need to do this if you split a single string argument over multiple lines; you need not use the backslash if you write additional arguments on a second line.

The important thing to remember about using library functions is that you need to declare the function, that is, associate the function name with a particular type. The type should correspond to the type of value to which the function evaluates. If you don't declare the function, the compiler will assume the function returns an **int**. If you declare it as returning the wrong type, you will get bizarre results. A library function should be declared at the start of whatever function calls it the library function.

Macros That Look Like Functions

In addition to library functions, most implementations provide a large number of predefined macros, many of which you can use just as if they were functions. Just from their usage you would not be able to tell that a particular call was to a preprocessor macro rather than to a true function.

The next program illustrates several such macros which are designed to determine whether the character passed to the macro as an argument has certain properties. For example, **isxdigit( )** returns a 0 (false) if the character is not a hexadecimal digit—that is, if it is not among

0, 1, 2, 3, 4, 5, 6, 7, 8, 9
a, b, c, d, e, f
A, B, C, D, E, F

The function returns true if the character *is* such a digit. Here is the program:

```
/* Program to illustrate the use of predefined ''library" macros.
   Note the inclusion of the file CTYPE.H, which defines the macros used.
*/

#include <ctype.h>

#define TEST_STR "Hello, world.\0"

main(){
        int how_long;                 /* will store length of TEST_STR */
        char alnum_char = 'Q',
            non_alnum_char = '*';
        char hex_char = 'F',
            non_hex_char = 'G';
        int strlen();                 /* actually, a true function */


        how_long = strlen ( TEST_STR);
        printf ( " Length of\n%s\nis %d chars\n\n", TEST_STR, how_long);

        printf ( "%c is an alphanumeric, so function returns %d\n",
                alnum_char, isalnum ( alnum_char));
        printf ( "%c is NOT an alphanumeric, so function returns %d\n\n",
                non_alnum_char, isalnum ( non_alnum_char));
```

```
        printf ( "%c is a hexadecimal digit, so function returns %d\n",
                hex_char, isxdigit ( hex_char));
        printf ( "%c is NOT a hexadecimal digit, so function returns %d\n",
                non_hex_char, isxdigit ( non_hex_char));
}
```

The program produces the following output:

```
 Length of
Hello, world.
is 13 chars

Q is an alphanumeric, so function returns 1
* is NOT an alphanumeric, so function returns 0

F is a hexadecimal digit, so function returns 128
G is NOT a hexadecimal digit, so function returns 0
```

This program writes the results of testing various characters for certain properties. The macros used in this program are defined in the header file, ctype.h, which is found in the implementation's header file directory (**\include** for QuickC). Notice that you need not declare macros. Because the preprocessor just substitutes, the compiler needs to make sure only that the macro expansion is syntactically correct. If the replacement expression has any function calls in it, the same rules about declaration apply as for any other function.

The **isalnum( )** macro returns true if the character argument is a letter or a digit, and returns false otherwise.

The *function* **strlen( )** returns the number of characters in the string argument passed to **strlen( )**. This is a genuine function. You need not declare this particular function because the compiler assumes a function returns **int** if no return type is declared.

You can use preprocessor macros as you would library or other functions. You can put them wherever a value of the appropriate sort is supposed to be returned. Look through your Run-Time Library Documentation to find out what functions and macros are available. Also, take time to look at some of the files with the **.h** extension in the directory **\include**.

Header and Other Include Files

The preprocessor can be a powerful programming tool making your programs cleaner, faster, and easier to develop. By using preprocessor commands, you can sometimes save time when the program is running — because instructions are already in the code, rather than having the overhead for a function call. By creating macros to represent more complex expressions or arbitrary values, you can make your programs more readable and easier to revise. By collecting such definitions, either in one place in the program listing, or in a separate file, you can make it easier to use different sets of definitions and macros.

Such include files are called header files, and are usually recognizable because they have the file name extension, **.h**, as in **proginfo.h**. You need not stick to this convention, but you will probably have an easier time keeping track of your files if you get into the habit of using **.h** for files containing macros and other preprocessor commands.

The use of header files is one step towards program modifiability, because you can create very different versions of a program simply by using different header files when compiling the same program. This is one technique for making your programs more transportable, because specific values are found in the macro definitions rather than in your original source code. When you change the macro definition, you change the text that will be substituted during macro expansion.

So far, we've spoken just about preprocessor commands in separate files. However, you can also collect C functions in separate files, which can also make it easier to read and revise programs. For example, suppose you have a program requiring numerous string manipulations. You might write some functions to do this work for you. If you design them well, these functions may also be useful for other programs.

To make it easy to use your string handling functions in other programs, you might put them all in one file, then include that file in any program that needs the string handling capabilities your functions provide. One approach is to compile the source code for these functions into each new program. This is a straightforward but slow process, since the compiler must process the functions for each new program.

Another way of using these functions in other programs is to compile the file containing the functions, and save the compiled version as a new library file. Then declare the string functions your program needs, just as you've been doing with the library functions. When your program has compiled, you can link in the library file(s) your program needs. Appendix B provides details about how to do this.

The ability to create and compile library files independently of each other is one of C's major advantages, especially because C makes it easy to do. One consequence is the availability of pre-built function libraries for C programmers. There are dozens of library collections available, and there are several books that develop such libraries, such as Kris Jamsa's *The C Library* (Berkeley: Osborne/McGraw-Hill, 1985). These libraries can provide useful tools, and give you good examples of source codes for performing various tasks in C. Reading source code is often a very effective way to get better at a language, especially when you can modify the functions, to try different things or to tailor the functions to your needs.

Summary

In this chapter, you've learned more about the way C programs are put together. You were also introduced to the preprocessor and the kinds of things you can do with it. Finally, we've examined some of the advantages of making your programs modifiable and using separate files to keep distinct portions of your program.

Along the way, you also learned about another operator, equality (==), and about the **if** control construct. There were also two new **printf( )** output formats: %**lo** (**long** in octal format) and %**lx** (**long** in hexadecimal format). Finally, you saw how to indicate that a constant value is to be treated as a **long**.

In the next chapter, we'll discuss how to enter and display information in C programs. This will be helpful for building a useful collection of functions.

5

Reading and
Writing in C

In this chapter, we'll look at some of the functions QuickC provides for *I/O (input/output)*, that is, for getting information into and out of a program. While not part of the C language, these input and output capabilities are provided in libraries or predefined in an implementation. For example, the **printf( )** function is built into the QuickC programming environment. The documentation for your compiler's Run-Time Library has more about the functions described in this chapter.

Input and output can get tricky in C, so we'll look only at some of the ways to do I/O. Some of the I/O functions will have to wait until we've covered certain data types and control constraints more thoroughly.

Reading Characters

You've already seen two functions for reading characters, **getch( )** and **getche( )**. Each of these returns an integer that represents the ASCII code of the character read. The difference is that **getche( )** echoes the character on your screen, but **getch( )** does not.

The **getch( )** and **getche( )** functions actually read their information from a buffer (memory storage area), rather than directly from the keyboard. This turns out to be handy for functions that might read "too much" information.

For example, you may have a function that is supposed to read characters until it encounters a particular character (such as a '—') which is actually intended for another function. Situations such as this can be tricky to handle in most programming languages, since the function doesn't know it wasn't supposed to read the information until it has read it.

C's solution takes advantage of the fact that information can be put into a buffer as well as taken out. The **ungetch( )** function lets you put exactly one character back into this buffer. The buffer being modified is used to store information for the *console*. This "device" is associated with the keyboard for input and with the screen for output.

The following listing illustrates the use of the **ungetch( )** function to put information back into the buffer, thereby making the information usable by another function.

```
#define NEW_VAL 'z'     /* value to assign to ch variable, to "prove"
                           that ungetch really works.
                        */

/* make these definitions and declarations global
   so both first_try() and second_try() can access them.
*/
int ch;
int getch(), ungetch();

main ()
{
        printf ( "Press exactly one key. Do not press z.\n");
        first_try ();
        second_try ();
}

/* Read a character from the console buffer, using getch().
   Put the character back, using ungetch(),
   then assign a new value to ch (a global change).
*/
first_try ()
```

```
{
        ch = getch();
        printf ( "after getch(), ch == %c\n", ch);
        ungetch ( ch);
        ch = NEW_VAL;      /* to give ch a new value before next getch() */
        printf ( "after new assignment, ch == %c\n", ch);
}


/* Display contents of ch before reading console buffer;
   read a character from the console buffer into ch;
   then display contents of ch after rereading console buffer.
*/
second_try ()
{
        printf ( "\n\n\n");
        printf ( "before new getch(), ch == %c\n", ch);
        ch = getch ();
        printf ( "after getch(), ch == %c\n", ch);
}
```

This program produces the following output:

```
Press exactly one key. Do not press z.
after getch(), ch == a
after new assignment, ch == z


before new getch(), ch == z
after getch(), ch == a
```

This program reads some information, then puts the information back, then reads it again. The variable **(ch)**, into which information was read in this program, is assigned a new value between the calls to **getch( )**. The program displays the values stored at various points in the program.

Notice the global definition of the variable **ch**, and declarations of the functions **getch( )** and **ungetch( )**. These are used throughout the program, so the global definition makes them accessible to all the functions.

The function **first—try( )** does the following:

1. Reads a character from the console buffer and stores it in the variable **ch**. This removes the character from the console buffer.

2. Puts the value stored in **ch** back into the console buffer. This merely puts a copy of the value into the console buffer; *it does not* remove the value from **ch**.

3. Assigns a new value to **ch**, overwriting the value stored in **ch** before the

assignment. After this, different character values are stored in **ch** and in the console buffer.

Function **second_try( )** can get a character from the console buffer because **first_try( )** has put one back. Had **ungetch( )** not been called, the program would wait for you to press a key for the **getch( )** in function **second_try( )**.

Unlike **getch( )** or **getche( )**, which take no arguments, **ungetch( )** takes the character you want to put back as its argument. You can call **ungetch( )** only once between reads, otherwise it will fail.

getchar( ) and fgetchar( )

A *stream* is a sequence of characters or bytes depending on the kind of stream under consideration. Certain characters in the stream serve particular functions, such as indicating end-of-line, end-of-input, or end-of-file. We'll consider only *text streams,* which are sequences of characters. Streams are generally associated with files, including devices, such as keyboard or screen. For our purposes, you can think of streams and files as essentially the same.

The **getchar( )** routine reads a character from a predefined stream, the standard input source, **stdin**. This file is opened (made accessible) for you automatically when your C program starts running. Although **stdin** is usually predefined as the keyboard, you can specify another source (such as a text or data file) as **stdin**, using the DOS redirection facility. For now, we'll assume that **stdin** is the keyboard.

In QuickC (and in most other implementations of C), **getchar( )** is defined as a preprocessor macro. To use **getchar( )**, you need to include the file in which this macro is defined. This file is usually called **stdio.h** as in QuickC. So, to use the macro, you need to give the instruction:

```
#include <stdio.h>
```

In your program notice that the instruction uses the $<>$ form of the **#include** preprocessor command. This tells the compiler to look for the header file in predefined locations, such as QuickC's **\include** directory. When you call **getchar( )** in your program, the preprocessor substitutes the macro body for your call.

The **getchar( )** macro returns an **int** representing the character read. If there is an error, or if it has reached the end of input, **getchar( )** returns a predefined value, **EOF**, which is usually defined as (−1). There are library functions that will tell you whether an **EOF** result from **getchar( )** is due to an error or because the end-of-file has been reached. QuickC recognizes CTRL-Z (which you get by typing the letter Z on the CTRL key at the same time) as the end-of-file character. Other implementations may interpret other characters as end-of-file.

Unlike **getche( )**, which returns control to the calling function as soon as it can return a value, **getchar( )** waits until you indicate you are done (usually by pressing the RETURN key) before letting the program continue. Briefly, **get** or ENTER **char( )** reads its character, then ignores anything else until you press Return or indicate end-of-file. (When characters don't echo until the RETURN key is pressed the system is using *buffered input*.) For example, the following program does not end until you press Return:

```
/* Program to illustrate getchar()'s tendency to keep waiting for input. */

#include <stdio.h>              /* file in which getchar() is defined. */

main ()
{
        int ch;

        ch = getchar();         /* Read a character from stdin. */
        printf ( "%d ", ch);
}
```

Implementing **getchar( )** as a macro makes it run more efficiently. Macros differ from functions, however, in the way things are actually read and in the parameter checking that is possible. Sometimes you may need the flexibility of a true function. The **fgetchar( )** function is the function counterpart of **getchar( )**. To use **fgetchar( )** in the preceding program, you could declare the function (although you don't have to because it returns an **int**); you do not need to include **stdio.h**.

getc( ), ungetc( ) and fgetc( )

Sometimes, you need to be able to read characters from specific files, rather than from **stdin**. Character values read into a program using **getchar( )** or **fgetchar( )** come from the same source, **stdin**. As stated, this is usually the keyboard. The **getc( )** macro does the same thing as **getchar( )**, but gets its input from the stream (that is, file) you specify as an argument. Until we discuss files, we'll use **getchar( )** or **fgetchar( )**—instead of **getc( )** and **fgetc( )**—when we need to read individual characters. To give you a feel for how **getc( )** is used, the following example illustrates the format of a **getc( )** call using **stdin** as the stream. (Remember, **stdin** is just another stream. It just happens to be the one for which the system does the work of opening and closing.)

```
/* Program to illustrate use of getc(). */

#include <stdio.h>              /* file in which getchar() is defined. */

main ()
{
        int ch;

        ch = getch ( stdin);    /* Read a character from stdin. */
        printf ( "%d ", ch);
}
```

The only difference between this and the preceding example is in the routine used to get the character. In fact, **getchar( )** is actually defined as **getc(stdin)** in most implementations.

Again, **fgetc( )** is the function equivalent of **getc( )**, and is available in QuickC. Both **fgetc( )** and **getc( )** return either the character read or **EOF**.

The function **ungetc( )** puts the character back into the stream you specify. It takes two arguments: a char, and a stream name. To see how **ungetc( )** works, make the following substitutions in the first listing appearing in this chapter. Note the order of the arguments.

getc(stdin) for **getch( )**

ungetc(ch, stdin) for **ungetch(ch)**

putchar( ) and fputchar( ), putc( ) and fputc( )

It's important to keep in mind that both **ungetch( )** and **ungetc( )** put characters *back*. This means that you must have read a character before trying to put one back. Do not use these functions for output. Rather, these functions serve to restore.

C provides several functions and macros for handling character output. Each of the **getxxx( )** input routines we saw in the previous two sections has an output counterpart.

In most implementations, the macro **putchar( )** and the function **fputchar( )** are the output routines corresponding to **getchar( )** and **fgetchar( )**, respectively. Each of these two output routines takes one argument, the character to output. Both **putchar( )** and **fputchar( )** write the character argument to **stdout**, usually defined as the screen. The routines return the character written or **EOF**, if there is an error. The following listing illustrates the use of these two routines:

```
#include <stdio.h>

main ()
{
        int ch1 = 97, ch2 = 100, test_ch;

        putchar ( ch1);
        fputchar ( ch1);
        test_ch = putchar ( ch1);
}
```

This program writes some characters to **stdout**. Each character is written using either the **putchar( )** macro or the **fputchar( )** function.

The **stdio.h** header file is included because it contains the definition for the **putchar( )** macro. Although it's a macro, **putchar( )** in this program is indistinguishable in its use from the function **fputchar( )**.

Although both routines return an **int**, we make no use of this returned value in either of the first two calls. Rather, the routines are called mainly for the action they perform, not for the value they return. The program does store the value returned by the third call, in the variable **test_ch**. The answer to the question regarding the number of characters displayed hinges on what happens in this third call, to **putchar( )**.

To assign a value to **test_ch**, the expression on the right side of the assignment operator is evaluated. To compute this value, **putchar( )** is expanded, and the replacement body is evaluated. The result is then assigned to **test_ch**. During the evaluation process, however, the statement also writes a character (the contents of **ch2**) to **stdout**. This means that three characters are written, in succession: **aad**.

Although you can call these output routines with or without the returned value, you'll find it useful to check the value returned, especially if you are transferring information from one place to another (such as from the keyboard to a file or from a file to the screen). In such cases, you'll need to check each value to be written to determine when you're done.

The **putc( )** macro and the **fputc( )** functions are available for character output to a file that you specify, just as **getc( )** and **fgetc( )** were for *input from a file*. The **putc( )** and **fputc( )** output routines each take two arguments: the character you want to write and the file to which you want to write that character. As you may have guessed, you can use **putc(ch, stdout)** to accomplish the same thing as with **putchar(ch)**. You can also use **fputc(ch, stdout)** instead of **fputchar(ch)**.

As with **stdin**, the **stdout** file is opened automatically for you at the start of the program, and is closed when the program finishes. You are responsible for opening and closing most other files used in your programs.

The putch( ), getch( ), and getche( ) Commands

The **getch( )** function also has a corresponding output function, **putch( )**. This function writes its character argument directly to the console (screen). The function returns the character written, or **EOF** if not successful.

Think of the **getche( )** function as a combination of **getch( )** and **putch( )**. The following listing illustrates this.

```
/* Program to illustrate use of the complementary functions
   getch() and putch(), to do the work of getche().
*/
main ()
{
        newgetche ();
}

newgetche ()                /* function to mimic getche() */
{
        int ch;

        ch = getch ();      /* read char but don't echo */
        putch ( ch);        /* display char */
}
```

The **newgetche( )** function writes the same information to the console as the predefined **getche( )**. Our function is designed merely to illustrate the use of **getch( )** and **putch( )**, rather than as a substitute for **getche( )**. In general, you're better off using predefined functions when they are available, since these functions have usually been tested quite thoroughly.

More About printf( )

We've already discussed the **printf( )** function, one of the workhorse output routines for C. This function lets you write simple data types, as well as strings, to the screen (actually, to **stdin**), and lets you specify the format this output is to have. In this section, you'll find out more about how to control output with **printf( )**.

Integral Types

The following codes are available in **printf( )** to specify output of an integral type:

```
c   d   i   o   u   x   X
```

When used to form a placeholder, each of these is preceded by a % in the string argument. You've already used most of these codes in earlier examples.

The **%i** also specifies an **int** to be written. This format specifier is not available in most older C implementations, but is included in the Draft Proposed ANSI Standard.

The **%u** indicates an **unsigned int**. The two ways of specifying hexadecimal output actually use different versions of the hexadecimal digits.

If you specify **%x** for your placeholder, your result will use the lowercase digits (**abcdef**); **%X** tells **printf( )** to use uppercase digits (**ABCDEF**).

Each of these format specifiers can be preceded by **l** (lowercase L) or **h** to indicate that the integral type is a long or short version, respectively. For example:

- **%ld** specifies a **long int**
- **%lx** specifies a **long int** written in hexadecimal form
- **%hd** specifies a **short int**
- **%hu** specifies a **short unsigned int**

Floating Point Types

So far, we've used **%f** and **%lf** to specify **float** and **double** variables, respectively. There are two other codes you can use to specify floating point output. Each of these can be written with either lower- or uppercase characters:

e E g G

Specifying **%e** tells **printf( )** to write the value in exponential form. For example:

```
printf ( "%e\n", 1234.587);
```

writes a value of 1.234587e+003. Had we used **%E** instead, the output would also have used an uppercase E: 1.234587E+003. In general, the exponential form writes the value with one digit to the left of the decimal point.

If you specify **%g** or **%G**, the function will use either the "regular" (**%f**) or the exponential format, whichever is more compact, based on the value and the precision you have specified. **%G** uses the uppercase E, if it writes your result in exponential form.

You can use **l** with any of the floating point format specifiers to indicate a double in precision value.

Field Width and Precision

We've seen several examples where the placeholder specification has included digits before the format specifier. Two aspects of the output can be controlled using these numbers. Let's look at a few examples:

```
/* Program to illustrate field width specifiers for output */

main ()
{
        int  i1 = 32, i2 = 29999;

        printf ( ":%5d :%2d\n", i1, i2);
        printf ( ":%10s :%3s\n", "hello", "hello");
}

/* output for listing */

:   32 :29999
:     hello :hello
```

This program writes various values according to different field width specifications. Sometimes the program observes the specifications, and sometimes it overrides them.

The first call to **printf( )** requests an integer to be written in a five-column field. The integer is only two digits, so the function leaves three blanks to the left of the value. The second integer is to be written in only two columns, but the number is five digits long, so **printf( )** ignores the field width specification.

The same thing happens when we ask the function to write string constants: **printf( )** puts five blanks before the first "hello," because we've asked it to write the constant in a ten-column field. As with numbers, **printf( )** ignores field width specifications if the string output requires more space. Field width specifies the **minimum** number of columns to use for the output. By default, any padding is done to the left of the output.

You can also specify *the precision* (essentially the number of decimal places) to be displayed for floating point types. Several examples are shown below:

```
/* Program to illustrate use of precision specifiers for output. */

main ()
{
        double d1 = 3.5, d2 = 12345.67890123;

        printf ( ":%lf :%4.5lf: %.10lf\n", d1, d1, d1);
        printf ( ":%lf :%4.5lf: %.10lf\n", d2, d2, d2);
}

/* output for listing */

:3.500000 :3.50000: 3.5000000000
:12345.678901 :12345.67890: 12345.6789012300
```

This program writes double values with several different precision levels. The first placeholder on each line tells the function to use its defaults for the field width and the precision level. In this case, **printf( )** uses as many columns as it needs to write the value; the default precision is six digits to the right of the decimal point. If the value being written uses fewer decimal digits, the function pads the fractional part with zeros. If the value being written has more decimal digits, **printf( )** truncates the number after the default number of digits.

The second value written by each call to **printf( )** asks for five decimal places, but specifies only a four-column field width. As with integral types, the function overrides the field width specification if it is too small to write the value. Precision is handled in a manner similar to the default: trailing zeros are added if the number has fewer decimal digits, and the number's fractional part is truncated if there are too many digits.

Notice the third placeholders. These indicate that you can specify precision without also specifying a field width. In that case, the function uses its defaults for field width. The decimal point (.) is required, otherwise the function will assume you are trying to specify the field width.

Flags for printf( )

We've seen that **printf( )** right-justifies by default. That is, the function pads any output with blanks to the left of the value, if appropriate. What if you want to left-justify or pad on the right? **printf( )** has flags you can use to do that. The following example illustrates the most common flags:

```
/* Program to illustrate use of flags for controlling output. */

main ()
{
        int  i1 = 32, i2 = -29999;

        printf ( ":%5d :%2d\n", i1, i2);
        printf ( ":%-5d :%-2d\n", i1, i2);
        printf ( ":%+5d :%+2d\n", i1, i2);
        printf ( ":%-+5d :%-+2d\n", i1, i2);
        printf ( ":%10s :%3s\n", "hello", "hello");
        printf ( ":%-10s :%-3s\n", "hello", "hello");
        printf ( ":%+10s :%+3s\n", "hello", "hello");
}

/* output for listing */

:   32 :-29999
:32    :-29999
:  +32 :-29999
:+32   :-29999
:    hello :hello
:hello      :hello
:    hello :hello
```

This program writes the same information four times, using different flags. The first call to **printf( )** does not use any flags, and produces the same output as in our earlier listing. The next call uses the − flag, which tells the function to left-justify the output (as on the second output line). In this case, **printf( )** pads to the *right* of the value.

The third call uses the + flag, which tells the function to include a sign when writing the number. Ordinarily, **printf( )** includes a sign for negative numbers only. The + flag changes this. Notice that the flag does *not* tell the function to write only plus signs (as shown by the −29999).

The fourth call shows that you can use multiple flags in the same placeholder. The two placeholders also show that the order of the flags does not matter. These flags tell the function to left-justify and to include a sign.

The next three calls to **printf( )** output string values. Only the flag to left-justify is relevant, and **printf( )** obeys it in the second line of string output. The sign flag makes no sense with a string variable, so the function ignores it.

One other flag may come in handy at times. The # flag can be used with octal (**o**), hexadecimal (**x, X**), or floating point values. When used with octal or hexadecimal formats (that is, **#o** or **#X**), the flag tells **printf( )** to include the leading **0** or **0X** when writing the value. When used with floating point formats, the flag forces **printf( )** to include a decimal point in the output.

If you are using all the formatting options in **printf( )**, you need to write your placeholder specifications in the following order:

%{*flags*} {*field width*} {*.precision*} {*format*}

Flags, field width, and precision are all optional, but if you use them, they must appear in the order given. The % and the format are required. If you are specifying precision, you need to include the decimal point.

fprintf( )

The **printf( )** function writes its information to the standard output, **stdout**; **fprintf( )** function lets you specify the file to which it should write the information. The only difference between these two functions is that **fprintf( )** takes an argument before the string argument. This argument is the file to which you want to write. The following two statements have the same effect:

```
/* two ways of writing the same information to stdout.
   i1 is a variable of type int.
*/
printf ( "%d", i1);
fprintf ( stdout, "%d", i1);
```

The **fprintf( )** function will become more interesting after we've covered files in more detail.

Values and Variables:
The Address Operator

When you pass a variable as an argument to a function, such as **putchar(ch)**, the variable does not lose its value or become undefined. This is because you are not really passing the actual variable, but a copy of the variable's value. The function is free to do what it needs with this value, without affecting the value stored in the variable itself. In effect, the function never really has access to the actual variable, just to a copy of the value stored there.

What if you *want* a function to change a variable? We've seen one way of doing this: assigning the value returned by the function to the variable you want to change. This has been successful as long as we've been reading one piece of information at a time, as in our character input functions.

However, it can easily become too tedious to read all your information one character at a time. Sometimes you will want to change several variables, possibly of different types with one function. One way of making this possible would be to give the function access to the variables themselves.

Because variables are associated with memory locations, or addresses, you can pass the function addresses, and allow the function to make its changes at those locations. Since the function would then be doing its work in the actual memory location corresponding to the variable passed as an argument, any changes made would remain after the function finishes.

C provides an *address* operator (**&**) to make it easy to pass such information to functions. The address operator returns the *location* of the variable on which **&** operates, rather than returning the value stored at that location.

The next listing illustrates several points about the address operator, and Table 5-1 provides a way of representing how the memory for the variables in the program might be laid out. In the illustration, the actual precision of the values stored in the **double** variables — locations 4858, 4866, and 4874 — will depend on the bit pattern, and will almost certainly differ from the six decimal place precision written by default. Here is the listing:

```
/* Program to illustrate use of address operator. */

main ()
{
        int i1 = 23, i2 = 12345, i3 = 234;
        double d1 = 23.0, d2 = 12345., d3 = .234;
```

```
        printf ( "i1    address: %d, value: %d\n", &i1, i1);
        printf ( "i2    address: %d, value: %d\n", &i2, i2);
        printf ( "i3    address: %d, value: %d\n", &i3, i3);
        printf ( "d1    address: %d, value: %lf\n", &d1, d1);
        printf ( "d2    address: %d, value: %lf\n", &d2, d2);
        printf ( "d3    address: %d, value: %lf\n", &d3, d3);
}

/* output for listing */

i1    address: 4856, value: 23
i2    address: 4854, value: 12345
i3    address: 4852, value: 234
d1    address: 4874, value: 23.000000
d2    address: 4866, value: 12345.000000
d3    address: 4858, value: 0.234000
```

This program writes information about the locations of six different variables and about the values stored there. Three of the variables are integers, and three are of type **double**. The calls to **printf( )** illustrate the notation for the address operator (**&** followed by the variable name).

Notice that the placeholders for addresses are integral values, even if the variable located there is a floating point type. There is no such thing as a fractional address. The distinction between the location and the value of a variable is important, as we'll see in later chapters.

Let's look at the numbers displayed for the addresses. Notice that the addresses of the **int** variables differ by 2 while the addresses of the **double**

Table 5-1.   Memory Layout for Variables

Variable Name	Value	Address
d1	23.000000	4874
d2	12345.000000	4866
d3	0.234000	4858
i1	23	4856
i2	12345	4854
i3	234	4852

variables differ by 8. Recall that C allocates 2 bytes to an **int** and 8 bytes to **double**. For now, this program is intended to illustrate the use of the address operator. Later, you'll see how to do "arithmetic" on address locations.

Incidentally, notice how **d2** and **d3** are initialized (with a trailing and a leading decimal point, respectively). Both of these are valid floating point type representations in C, as we noted in Chapter 3.

Because it takes one element and returns one element, **&** is a unary operator, with the same precedence as the other unary operators we've seen so far: **sizeof( ),** − (arithmetic negation operator), and + (arithmetic plus sign).

scanf( )

The **scanf( )** function is the input counterpart to **printf( )**. It can be a tricky function to use, with many variations, so we'll introduce it now and explain further as we go along. Consult your QuickC Run-Time Library reference manual for more information.

The function **scanf( )** reads data from **stdin**. The data must have your specified format, and **scanf( )** stores the data in locations that you specify. The following line illustrates the structure of a **scanf( )** call:

```
/* this line reads an int, a char, and a double,
   and assigns these data to the variables test_int, test_char, and
   test_double, respectively --- by storing the information at the
   locations of the variable parameters.
*/
scanf ( "%d %c %lf" &test_int, &test_char, &test_double);
```

Notice first that **scanf( )** has a structure just like that of **printf( )**: a string argument, followed by an additional argument for each placeholder in the string argument. Notice also that each of the variable arguments is actually an address. This is necessary for **scanf( )**, since it needs to put the data directly into the variables, so the rest of your program can use the values **scanf( )** read.

When **scanf( )** is called with an argument, the program makes available the memory corresponding to the address of the variable passed as the argument. If **scanf( )** were called, for example, in the program whose variables are depicted in Figure 5-1, the calls would write the information directly into whatever memory locations were passed in that particular call. For example, **scanf ("%d" , &i1)** would call the function with address 4856 (the location of **i1**), so the integer read would be stored in that location.

▶**REMEMBER**   Except for the string argument, you must pass *addresses* as parameters to **scanf( )**.

As with **printf( )**, the string argument can contain regular text, as well as placeholders. However, **scanf( )** is much pickier about what it does with the text in your string argument. It's important to distinguish between *whitespace* (blanks, tabs, and newline characters) and non-whitespace characters. **scanf( )** treats whitespace and non-whitespace characters differently. So, in effect, the string argument to **scanf( )** can have three different kinds of information: placeholders, whitespace, and non-whitespace characters.

If **scanf( )** sees a whitespace character in your string argument, it reads (but doesn't store) any whitespace characters in your input up to the first non-whitespace character. Thus, the following would be valid input for the **scanf( )** statement above, since **scanf( )** would just ignore intervening blanks:

```
17          c       35.6
```

If **scanf( )** sees a non-whitespace character, it reads a matching character in your input. For example, the following statement would require input different from our previous example:

```
/* Line to illustrate effects of non-whitespace characters
   in string argument to scanf(). Note the comma.
*/
scanf ( "%d,%c %lf" &test_int, &test_char, &test_double);
```

For this statement, you'd have to enter something like:

```
17,c        35.6
```

If **scanf( )** *does not* find the character it's looking for, the function terminates. If **scanf( )** does find the character, the function simply discards it and continues processing your input.

▶**CAUTION**   Be careful if you put anything other than placeholders or whitespace in your **scanf( )** calls. You must make sure the non-whitespace characters in the input match those in the string argument to **scanf( )**.

Non-whitespace characters in a string argument exist to tell **scanf( )** what to look for in your input, not to get those characters into your program. This is handy if you have something like a database that has specific words at particular places in a line. If all you really need are the data around these words, you can get **scanf( )** to get just that information by including the words at the appropriate places in your string argument — so **scanf( )** will find and skip over the words.

You can use whitespace to separate the individual items of information in your input, but you cannot use other characters (such as commas) to separate them unless you include those characters at the appropriate place in the string argument. For example, the following **scanf( )** call will fail with the input below it because of the comma in the input:

```
/* this line reads an int, a char, and a double,
   and assigns these data to the variables test_int, test_char, and
   test_double, respectively --- by storing the information at the
   locations of the variable parameters.
*/
scanf ( "%d %c %lf" &test_int, &test_char, &test_double);

/* the function will fail with the following input */
17,c    35.6
```

This is because **scanf( )** is expecting to see a number after reading the comma that is the first **char** encountered after the **int**. Instead, the function sees another character.

You can also specify field widths in your placeholders. These are interpreted as the *maximum* number of places to read for that variable. **scanf( )** will literally stop in midword or midnumber if you specify a field width smaller than the value you expect it to read. Moreover, the function will continue processing from the next character. The following listing illustrates this:

```
/* Program to illustrate use of field width specifications for input. *

main ()
{
        int i1, i2, i3;
        char c1;

        i3 = scanf ( "%1d %c %d", &i1, &c1, &i2);
        printf ( "i1 = %d; c1 = %c; i2 = %d\n", i1, c1, i2);
        printf ( "%d arguments processed\n", i3);
}

/* input to the listing */
123 c 45

/* output from the listing */

i1 = 1; c1 = 2; i2 = 3
3 arguments processed
```

This program reads three pieces of information and writes them out. It also writes out the value returned by **scanf( )**.

The first placeholder in the string argument for **scanf( )** says to read one digit at most, and to store this in variable **i1**. The function does this; then it skips over any intervening whitespace (in this case, none) before reading the next datum. This is a **char**, and **scanf( )** treats the 2 as a character. After assigning 2 to **c1**, **scanf( )** continues processing the input. It starts reading right after the last character it processed, and continues until it reaches a separator (a blank). Because **scanf( )** finds only 3, it assigns this value to the variable **i3**. The other two inputs are ignored, since **scanf( )** has read everything it's been told to read.

The statement containing the call to **scanf( )** also provides information about the type of value returned by **scanf( )**. Whereas **printf( )** returns the number of characters printed, **scanf( )** returns the number of *arguments* processed successfully. You can often use this value to check whether **scanf( )** has at least read the correct number of data.

As with **printf( )**, the number of additional arguments (after the string argument) must equal the number of placeholders in the string argument. There is one important exception to this rule, as we'll see below. You can use the same formats with **scanf( )** as with **printf( )**: %x, %u, %s, %lf, and so on.

▶ **CAUTION**   Be careful when reading character values. A whitespace character in your input is a character just like any other, and **scanf( )** will read it and store it in a character variable, even if you had intended something else.

```
main ()
{
        int i1;
        char c1, c2, c3;

        i1 = scanf ( "%c%c%c", &c1, &c2, &c3);   /* note absence of blank
        printf ( "c1 = %c; c2 = %c; c3 = %c\n", c1, c2, c3);
        printf ( "%d arguments processed\n", i1);
}

/* input to the listing */
a   b   c

/* output from the listing */

c1 = a; c2 =   ; c3 =
3 arguments processed
```

Think carefully about what will happen in the following program—in particular, what **scanf( )** does when it encounters whitespace.

```
main ()
{
        int i1;
        char c1, c2, c3;

        /* note blank at end of string argument */
        i1 = scanf ( "%c%c%c ", &c1, &c2, &c3);
        printf ( "c1 = %c; c2 = %c; c3 = %c\n", c1, c2, c3);
        printf ( "%d arguments processed\n", i1);
}

/* input to the listing */
abc
```

If your program is still waiting, try typing a non-whitespace character, then a **Return**. Remember, when **scanf( )** sees a whitespace character in its string argument, it keeps reading until it finds a non-whitespace character. So, **scanf( )** was waiting for the extra character. **Return** indicates the end of the input line.

Suppressing Values

The ability to include non-whitespace in your string argument to **scanf( )** is handy when you need to "throw away" specific words that might be encountered in the input. But what if different lines have different values to be thrown away? Do you have to write a separate **scanf( )** statement for each line?

Not in C. C allows you to suppress processing of any information in the input string. The following listing illustrates this:

```
/* Program to illustrate how to "skip over," or suppress a
   piece of data during input.
*/

main ()
{
        int i1, i2, i3;

        i3 = scanf ( "%d %*d %d", &i1, &i2);        /* note use of asterisk */
        printf ( "i1 = %d; i2 = %d\n", i1, i2);
        printf ( "%d arguments processed\n", i3);
}

/* input to listing */

1 2 3

/* output from listing */
i1 = 1; i2 = 3
2 arguments processed
```

This program reads three integer values. It processes the first and assigns it to **i1**. The program reads the second integer, but discards it as instructed by the asterisk (*) preceding the format specifier in the second placeholder. The program then processes the third integer and stores it in **i2**.

Notice that only two integer arguments were passed to **scanf( )**, even though there were three placeholders in the string argument. The instruction to suppress tells **scanf( )** not to count the placeholder containing the *. You can also see this in the information concerning the number of arguments processed (the *two* arguments passed in, rather than the three placeholders specified).

There's more to using **scanf( )** than we've covered here. We'll raise other issues in later chapters; we'll also talk about reading strings after we discuss what a string variable is.

The **scanf( )** reads its information from **stdin**. As you might have guessed, based on our discussion of the **getchar( )** and **getc( )** routines, there is a version of **scanf( )** that reads from a specified file. This is the **fscanf( )** function. Its structure and use are just like those of **scanf( )**, except that its first argument is the name of the file. Thus, the following two function calls will do the same thing:

```
scanf ( "%d", i1);
fscanf ( stdin, "%d", i1);
```

Summary

In this chapter, we discussed some of the routines C provides for reading and writing information. We've elaborated on the **printf( )** function that's been so useful throughout, and introduced **scanf( )**, the counterpart for input. In order to discuss **scanf( )**, we also introduced another operator, the address operator (**&**).

In addition, you learned about several functions and macros for reading and writing single characters. In most instances, both macros and functions are available to do the same thing. As you program more in C, you'll develop a feeling for when to use which routines.

We also found that most of the routines in this chapter had versions that used the standard streams (**stdin** and **stdout**) as well as versions where you could specify specific files — for example, **fscanf( )** and **printf( )**.

We'll discuss routines for reading and writing *strings* later, because many of these routines require string *variables* (as opposed to constants). String variables become quite involved, because they rely on pointers.

In the next chapter, we'll look not only at the control constructs C offers, but also at some additional operators than are handy in conjunction with these control constructs. Once you've found out more about the control constructs, we'll be able to start writing more complex functions and programs.

6

Controlling C

In this chapter we will explore the constructs C provides for controlling the flow of your program. These constructs let you specify what your functions and program should do under various conditions. C includes control constructs for selection (taking conditional actions) and for iteration (repeating, or looping actions). These constructs form the core of most C programs.

The behavior of both selection (**if-else**, **switch**) and iteration (**while**, **do-while**, **for**) constructs depends on the results of tests made somewhere in the construct, usually at the start.

In a selection construct, a particular action may be taken *if* a condition holds, or *else* a different action may be taken.

In an iterative construct, a particular action may be taken (possibly with variations) while a condition holds. You will see examples of these constructs in this chapter and throughout the rest of the book.

An important consideration when using control constructs concerns the actions your function takes when a condition you've specified holds. Sometimes, you'll want the function to do exactly one thing if a condition is true; at other times, you'll want it to do several things.

Earlier, we made a distinction between simple and compound statements, the former consisting of one action, the latter including any number of simple or compound statements, placed between curly braces.

The C compiler treats a compound statement as if it were a big simple statement. As you'll see, compound statements, or *blocks,* are important when you use control constructs. Compound statements allow you to specify a group of statements to be performed if a condition holds, or while a condition holds.

Before discussing C's control constructs, let's look at some more operators that will be useful for formulating the conditions tested by the control constructs.

Relational and Equality Operators

The conditions that control selection and iterative constructs are tests that evaluate statements in order to produce a **yes-no** or **true-false** answer. There are, of course, many ways of asking even something as simple as a yes-no question, such as whether one value equals another, whether two values are not equal, whether one value is greater than another, whether it is less than another, and so on.

C provides operators for asking such questions. In this section, you'll learn about two types of operators: relational and equality, both used in asking questions for control constructs.

Relational Operators

The *relational operators* establish the relative magnitude of two elements. For example, 18 is less than 35; you might also say that 35 is greater than 18. In C, you would write these statements as:

```
18 < 35     /* 18 is LESS THAN 35 */
35 > 18     /* 35 is GREATER THAN 18 */
```

Similarly, you might want to be less specific and say something like 24.9999 is less than or equal to 25 or, conversely, 25 is greater than or equal to 24.9999. In C, you would write these as follows:

```
24.9999 <= 25    /* 24.9999 is LESS THAN OR EQUAL TO 25 */
25 >= 24.9999    /* 25 is GREATER THAN OR EQUAL TO 24.9999 */
```

All four relational operators in C have the same precedence, which is lower than that of the arithmetic operators, but higher than that of the assignment operator. Because the arithmetic operators have higher precedence than relational operators, an expression such as the following evaluates to **true**:

```
6.5 < 6 + 1              /* reduces to 6.5 < 7, which is true */
```

Because the addition operator has higher precedence, "6 + 1" is evaluated first. The result, 7, is then compared to the 6.5 on the left side of the less than operator. The expression reads 6.5 < 7.

Equality Operators

We've already seen the *equality operator*, ==, in a previous chapter. The negative counterpart to this operator is the *inequality operator*, !=. The inequality operator lets you test whether two elements are *not equal* to each other. For example, the following expression evaluates to **true**:

```
7 != 8    /* evaluates to true, since it is true that 7 does not equal 8 */
```

because 7 does not equal 8.

Both the equality and inequality operators have the same precedence, and their precedence is immediately below that of the relational operators. This, of course, also puts them below the arithmetic operators. For this reason, the following expression evaluates to **false**:

```
3 + 7 != 6 + 4          /* reduces to 10 != 10 */
```

This is because the additions on either side of the inequality operator are done first, making both sides equal. Since both sides are equal, it is incorrect, or **false**, to say that 10 does not equal 10. Logically, this is just a very complex way of saying that **10 == 10**. When creating your condition tests, try to keep the expression as simple and straightforward as possible.

Logical Operators

When writing a function to accomplish a particular task, you'll often find you need to test several statements at once. For example, a number is divisible by 6 if the number is divisible by 2 *and* divisible by 3. In other cases, you may be satisfied if *any* of several tests comes out **true**. For example, a character is a vowel if it's "a" or "e" or "i" or "o" or "u."

You'll also find cases where you need *exactly one* of several conditions to be **true**. For example, someone filing an income tax return can be *either* single *or* married, but not both, at least not without arousing great suspicions at the IRS.

C provides *logical operators* for combining the results of multiple tests. The *compound expressions* that are created with such operators can be evaluated further, to a single **true** or **false** result.

Binary Logical Operators

Two of C's logical operators are binary, taking two elements and returning a single value based on those two elements and the operator.

The logical *and* operator (**&&**) returns **true** if *both* of the elements it connects are **true**. If either or both of these elements are **false**, the **&&** operator evaluates to **false**. For example:

```
(7 < 12) && (12 > 2.7)     /* evaluates to true: true && true */
(7 > 12) && (12 > 2.7)     /* evaluates to false: false && true */
(7 > 12) && (12 > 23.7)    /* evaluates to false: false && false */
```

The logical *or* operator (||) returns **true** if *either* of the two elements it connects evaluate to **true** or if *both* elements are **true**. Thus, the only time || evaluates to **false** is if both elements it connects are **false**. For example:

```
(7 < 12) || (12 > 2.7)     /* evaluates to true: true || true */
(7 > 12) || (12 > 2.7)     /* evaluates to true: false || true */
(7 > 12) || (12 > 23.7)    /* evaluates to false: false || false */
```

When your program evaluates expressions connected by binary logical operators, it evaluates from left to right. The evaluation stops as soon as the program knows the value that will be returned. For example, a program evaluating:

```
(7 > 12) && (12 > 2.7)     /* evaluates to false: FALSE && (true) */
```

could return **false** as soon as the first element —(7 > 12)—was evaluated. Because this element is **false**, the entire expression must be **false** as the **&&** operator requires *all* components to be **true**. Similarly, you can tell what the following expression will return without evaluating the entire expression:

```
(7 < 12) || (12 > 2.7)     /* evaluates to true: TRUE || (true) */
```

As soon as you see (7 < 12), which is **true**, you know the entire expression will be **true** because it involves only an *or* operator.

These logical operators have fairly low precedence: lower precedence than the equality operators, but higher precedence than the assignment operator. The **&&** operator has higher precedence than the || operator. The *and* operator is sometimes called *logical multiplication,* and the *or* operator *logical addition.* Conveniently, the relative precedence of these two operators is the same as that of the arithmetic multiplication and addition operators. Below, there's a table bringing our operator hierarchy up to date. First, let's look at one more operator, however.

Unary Negation Operator

We've already seen the arithmetic negation operator, which converts a number into its opposite form (for example, positive to negative). C also has a *logical negation* operator, which converts a **true** value into a **false** one and vice versa.

Recall that in C, **false** values are represented as zero, and **true** is any nonzero value. So, the logical negation operator, !, converts any nonzero value (**true**) to zero (**false**) or, conversely, any zero value (**false**) to 1 (**true**), as the following expressions illustrate:

```
!( 7 > 3)                                      /* ---> !( 1) ---> 0 */
!( 7 < 7)                                      /* ---> !( 0) ---> 1 */
/* if the int test_int has the value 13 ... */
!test_int                                      /* ---> !( 13) ---> 0 */
```

The Logical negation operator can also be applied to variables of type **int**. This use is common, showing up often in C statements. In the case of variables, the changes are not made to the actual variable. Rather, the negation is done just for the expression in which the variable is used.

Being a unary operator, logical negation has the same precedence as the other unary operators we've seen so far (the −, +, **&**, and **sizeof( )**). This precedence is higher than those of the arithmetic and relational operators.

Table 6-1 lists the operators covered so far.

The if-else Construct

You've already seen an example of a function that does one thing if a particular condition holds, and something different under other conditions. The **if** construct is used for making decisions within your programs.

There are two major components of an **if** construct: a condition and an action. The condition is an expression that the system evaluates. If the result is a nonzero value (**true**), then C carries out the action specified in the next statement. The action may be simple, or may consist of several actions (compound statement). Sometimes, you may want to specify alternative actions if the condition is not met. In that case, the **if** construct will also include an **else** component. The **else** part is not necessary, however.

Let's look at an example. The following listing computes the absolute value of a number, and shows how to use the **if-else** construct.

```
/* Program to compute the absolute value of an integer entered.
   Program illustrates use of if construct.
*/

main ()
{
        int  val_read, result;

        /* get value */
        printf ( "Please enter an integer: ");
        scanf ( "%d", &val_read);
```

Table 6-1.   Precedence Hierarchy for Selected Operators

Operator	Unary or Binary	Comments
!, &, +, −, sizeof( )	Unary	Unary operators
*, /, %	Binary	Arithmetic (multiplication)
+ −	Binary	Arithemitc (addition)
< <= > >=	Binary	Relational operators
== !=	Binary	Equality operators
&&	Binary	Logical multiplication
‖	Binary	Logical addition
=	Binary	Assignment operator

```
/* compute absolute value */
if ( val_read >= 0)
        result = val_read;
else                    /* if val_read is negative */
{
        printf ( "Changing sign\n");
        result = -val_read;
}

printf ( "result = %d\n", result);        /* display result */
}
```

This program prompts for a whole number, then computes the absolute value of that number. The program informs you if it needs to change the sign of the number when computing the absolute value. The program then prints the result.

Notice the use of the **scanf( )** function to read the number and recall that variable arguments to this function must be addresses—**&val_read**, or "the address of **val_read**," rather than just **val_read**.

The program illustrates the syntax for a simple **if-else** statement. The construct begins with the keyword, **if**, followed by the condition to be tested. This condition, which represents the test for the loop, must be in parentheses. The expression in the test must evaluate to an integer value: 0 if the condition is **false**, and any other value if the condition is **true**.

If the condition is **true** (in this case, if the value stored in **val_read** is greater than or equal to zero), then C carries out the next statement. In the listing, this is a simple statement. If the number is non-negative, the value of **val__read** is assigned to the variable **result**.

If the condition is **false** (**val__read** is negative), the **else** portion of the control construct is carried out. In this case, the program prints a message that the sign is being changed, and assigns −**val__read** to **result**. To make sure that both of these actions are carried out, the two actions are in a compound statement, which the system processes as a single statement. (If the braces were left out around the material for the **else** clause, the function would always return −**val__read**. Why?)

If you are used to programming in a language such as Pascal, note that there is no THEN after the condition being tested, and that you need a semicolon after the **result = val__read** assignment. This is because a statement comes after the **if**, and semicolons terminate simple statements in C.

Let's look at another example to illustrate some other points about the **if** construct.

```
/* Program to determine whether an integer entered is
   positive, negative, or zero.
   Program illustrates if construct.
*/

main ()
{
        int  val_read;

        /* get value */
        printf ( "Please enter an integer: ");
        scanf ( "%d", &val_read);

        /* classify val_read as positive, negative, or zero */
        if ( val_read)
        {
                printf ( "Not zero ...\n");
                if ( val_read < 0)
                        printf ( "Negative\n");
                else
                        printf ( "Positive\n");
        }
        else                            /* if val_read is false, ie == 0 */
                printf ( "Number == zero\n");
}
```

This program reads a number, then tells you whether the number is positive, negative, or zero. The program illustrates a very compact way of writing a condition, and also provides an example of one **if** construct within another. Placing a construct within another construct in this fashion is called *nesting*.

The condition, **if (val__read)**, amounts to asking whether the value of **val__read** is nonzero. If so, the condition evaluates to **true**, and the program carries out the actions in the compound statement.

One of these actions involves another **if-else** construct. This construct is handled in the same way as the outer one. The condition this time is whether **val__read** is negative. If so, the program writes one thing, otherwise the program writes that the value is positive.

Let's look at yet another example to illustrate a somewhat different, but commonly used, form of the **if-else** construct.

```
/* Program to determine whether an integer entered is
   positive, negative, or zero.
   Program illustrates else--if construct.
*/

main ()
{
        int  val_read;

        printf ( "Please enter an integer: ");
        scanf ( "%d", &val_read);

        if ( !val_read)                 /* if val_read == 0 */
                printf ( "Number == zero\n");
        else if ( val_read < 0)
        {
                printf ( "Not zero ...\n");
                printf ( "Negative\n");
        }
        else                            /* if val_read is positive *
        {
                printf ( "Not zero ...\n");
                printf ( "Positive\n");
        }
}
```

This program performs similarly to the preceding program, but in a somewhat different manner. The previous listing first tested whether **val__read** differed from zero, and continued from there. This program first tests whether **val__read** *equals* zero, and continues from there.

Notice the test for the first **if** construct. Remember that **!val__read** is a terse way of asking whether **val__read == 0** because, in that case, **!(val__read)** would evaluate to **true**. In this example, the expression is easy to evaluate, just by looking at it. In other situations, testing the negation of an expression could get very involved. In that case, it's better to write the expression in the less compact form (that is, using the equality operator explicitly).

The program also illustrates a common logical construction:

if A then Z **else if** B then Y **else if** C then X

In this construction, the conditions are tested in order, from top to bottom. As soon as the system finds one that is **true**, the actions associated with that condition are carried out, and the rest of the clauses are bypassed. The program then exits the **if-else** construct.

Notice that there are two **if** and two **else** statements. The first **else** corresponds to the first **if**. If the first condition is not met, the program moves to this **else** portion. The first statement along this path is another **if** construct. The second **else** corresponds to this **if**. This second (and final) **else** catches any states that had not been caught at previous conditions. The only path to this last **else** is to fail the conditions associated with the two **if** statements.

Beware of the Missing *else*

Look at the following listing, and try to determine what the output will be for an input of 0. What is the output for an input of 5?

```
/* Program to illustrate the importance of balancing or grouping
   ifs and elses.
   Program contains an else associated with the "wrong" if.
*/
main ()
{
        int   val_read;

        printf ( "Please enter an integer: ");
        scanf ( "%d", &val_read);

        if ( val_read)                    /* i.e., if val_read != 0 */
                if ( val_read < 0)
                        printf ( "Negative\n");
        else
                printf ( "Number == zero\n");
}
```

This program reads an integer value, and responds differently, depending on whether **val_read** is positive, negative, or zero. The program's indentation indicates the *intended* flow of control.

According to the indentation, the program's goal is to test whether **val_read** is nonzero. If this is **true**, the program should test whether **val_read** is negative. If so, the program writes "Negative." If **val_read** is positive, the program is not supposed to do anything because no **else** construct was included after this inner **if**. According to the indentation, the **if** portion of the outer construct ends here. If the original test was **false** (**val_read** was zero), the program was intended to write "Number == zero."

Unfortunately, the compiler sees this construct somewhat differently. It matches an **else** with the *nearest* **if** that does not have an **else** associated with it. In practice, this is the innermost **if** without an **else**. In this case, the inner **if** has no **else** portion. Therefore, the compiler associates the **else** with this **if**. The result is that the program writes "Number == zero" when **val_read** has the value 5. Because the **else** is associated with the inner **if**, there is no alternative action for the outer **if** (that is, **if (val_read)**). This means the program does nothing when **val_read** has the value 0.

There are two ways around this difficulty. First, you can include an inner **else** that explicitly tells the program to do nothing. The next listing illustrates this.

```
/* Fix for program with the unbalanced if and else.
   This program adds a "dummy," or null, else to match the inner if.
*/

main ()
{
        int  val_read;

        printf ( "Please enter an integer: ");
        scanf ( "%d", &val_read);
        if ( val_read)
                if ( val_read < 0)
                        printf ( "Negative\n");
                else                    /* to close off the inner if */
                        ;               /* do nothing */
        else                            /* if !val_read, i.e., val_read == 0 */
                printf ( "Number == zero\n");
}
```

The semicolon with nothing preceding it is a **null statement** which tells the compiler to do nothing at that point. An **else** containing a null statement provides a matching **else** for the inner **if**.

The second way of dealing with this problem is to use braces to group the statements the way you want, as in the following listing.

```
/* Another fix for the program with unbalanced ifs and elses.
   This program uses braces to enclose the inner if.
*/

main ()
{
        int  val_read;

        printf ( "Please enter an integer: ");
```

```
        scanf ( "%d", &val_read);
        if ( val_read)
        {                               /* put inner if into compound statement */
                if ( val_read < 0)
                        printf ( "Negative\n");
        }                               /* end out if portion. */
        else                            /* if !val_read, i.e. val_read == 0 */
                printf ( "Number == zero\n");
}
```

In this version, the braces tell the compiler that anything within the braces is to be grouped together, and is to be separate from the following material. In this case, the (implicit) effect is to have the compiler do nothing (as originally intended) if **val read** was positive (condition for the inner **if** was **false**). This technique is the preferred method.

▶**CAUTION**   Beware of leaving "dangling" **if** statements when you have **else** clauses following. You and the compiler may disagree on how to match **else** to **if**.

The switch Statement

So far, we've used fairly simple conditions to control a function's actions. In particular, we've only used conditions with a single test, and have avoided compound tests, such as A or B or C or D.

You can use complex expressions when testing for the **if** statement. Sometimes these tests can get lengthy and difficult to follow, however. For example, suppose you wanted to determine whether a particular character was a vowel. You might need an expression with 10 individual tests: 'a,' 'e,' . . . 'O,' 'U.' In this section, you'll learn about the **switch** statement, a selection construct useful when you want to test whether any of several constant values is found.

For example, suppose you want to read a character and determine whether it is a digit or whitespace. The following listing shows how to use the switch construct to make such a decision and how to act accordingly:

```
/* Program to illustrate use of switch construct to determine whether
   a character is a digit, whitespace, or neither.
*/

main ()
{
        char char_read;
```

```
printf ( "Please enter a character: ");
scanf ( "%c", &char_read);

switch ( char_read)
{
        case '0':
        case '1':
        case '2':
        case '3':
        case '4':
        case '5':
        case '6':
        case '7':
        case '8':
        case '9':
                printf ( "Digit\n");
                break;          /* force exit from switch */
        case ' ':
        case '\t':
        case '\n':
                printf ( "Whitespace\n");
                break;          /* force exit from switch */
        default :               /* if neither digit nor whitespace */
                printf ( "Neither\n");
                break;          /* force exit from switch */
}
printf ( "Done\n");
}
```

This program reads a character, then tells you whether the character is a digit, a whitespace character (blank, tab, or newline), or neither type of character. The program uses the **switch** construct to decide what response to give.

The **switch** construct begins with the keyword **switch**, followed by an expression in parentheses. This expression must evaluate to an integer in most implementations. QuickC and Microsoft C 5.0 allow the expression to evaluate to any integral type. The result, however, is converted to an actual **int**. You will get a compiler warning if the expression has evaluated to a **long**. The main body of the **switch** construct is contained in a compound statement, which consists of two types of components: labels (for example, **case '0':**) and statements (for example, **printf ("Whitespace** $\backslash^{n++)=}$**).

Each label represents a possible value for the expression at the top of the **switch** statement. Most labels begin with the **case** keyword. This is followed by a value and a colon. In the preceding listing, the values are characters (treated as integers internally). Notice that each value must get its own label. This means you can't have a label such as case '0,' '1,' '2':. No two labels can represent the same value. This means you can't have case '0': in two different places in the switch.

The **default** keyword represents the case in which none of the other labels applied. In our example, this label captures any characters that are neither digits nor whitespace. You need not include a **default** label in your **switch** statement. If you do, you can have at most one such label.

When the program encounters a **switch** construct, the program evaluates the expression, then searches through the labels in sequence, until it finds the case that corresponds to the current value of the expression. If there are no matches, the program uses the **default** label, if present.

The program starts executing from the first statement it finds after the matching label. For example, for an input of '\t' (a tab key), the program above would start executing at the statement **printf ("Whitespace \n")**. The process continues until it encounters a **break** statement or until it reaches the end of the **switch** construct. The **break** command causes the program to exit from the **switch** construct immediately. Thus, after printing "Whitespace," the program exits from the **switch**, and continues executing from the instruction right after the end of the **switch** body. In our case, the program displays **Done** after exiting from the **switch**.

If there is no **break** after the call to **printf( )**, the program keeps executing any statements it encounters until if finds a break elsewhere or until the end of the **switch** construct. For example, if you removed the first **break** (after the instruction to write "Digit"), and then entered '8' when running the program, the following output would result:

```
Digit
Whitespace
Done
```

Clearly, it's important to include **break** statements in constructs such as the **switch**.

If the program finds no **case** label that matches the current value of the expression at the top of the **switch** construct, the program starts executing from the statement immediately after the **default** label. If the program finds no match and there is no **default** label, the program simply "drops through" the **switch** construct, doing nothing.

Notice the **break** statement even after the **default** label, which ends the **switch** construct in our example. It's good practice to put such a **break** statement in, even at the end because you may add other labels after the **default** at some later point.

You can nest **switch** constructs. The following listing provides such an example.

```
/* Program to illustrate nested switch constructs */

main ()
{
        char char_read;

        printf ( "Please enter a character: ");
        scanf ( "%c", &char_read);

        switch ( char_read)
        {
                case '0':
                case '1':
                case '2':
                case '3':
                case '4':
                case '5':
                case '6':
                case '7':
                case '8':
                case '9':
                        printf ( "Digit\n");
                        /* this will distinguish even from odd digits */
                        switch ( char_read)
                        {
                                case '0':
                                case '2':
                                case '4':
                                case '6':
                                case '8':
                                        printf ( "Even\n");
                                        break;
                                default:
                                        printf ( "Odd\n");
                                        break;
                        }
                        break;
                default :
                        printf ( "Neither\n");
                        break;
                case ' ':
                case '\t':
                case '\n':
                        printf ( "Whitespace\n");
                        break;
        }
}
```

This program prints a message depending on whether the character input is a digit, whitespace, or neither. If the input is a digit, the program's response depends on whether or not it is an even digit. Notice that the same expression can (but need not) be used to control both **switch** statements. The same values are apparently repeated in two **case** labels. This does not contradict the earlier restriction that any value could appear only once in a **switch** construct, because the second occurrence is inside the inner **switch**. In a sense, when the program is in the inner **switch** it doesn't really know that the outer one exists.

Finally, notice the use of the **default** label, instead of five labels for each of the odd digits. This works here, because any character that leads to the inner **switch** construct can only be an even or an odd digit.

▶**REMEMBER**   The expression at the top of a **switch** statement must evaluate to an integral type in QuickC (and to an integer in most other implementations). No **case** label can be repeated and each **case** label can apply to only one value.

More Operators

C provides several operators that make common tasks easy, but are absent from most other languages. The operators are used very frequently in C's control constructs (and elsewhere), so we'll look at them briefly here.

Compound Assignment Operators

If you've done any programming, it is fairly certain that you have written statements in this form:

```
my_int = my_int + another_int;
```

This statement accomplishes the task of adding the value of **another_int** to the value already stored in **my_int**.

To accomplish this, you have to do a lot of typing, and the program has to do some unnecessary computing. The program actually evaluates **my_int** twice, once for the expression to the right of the assignment operator and the second time when storing the result in **my_int**.

C provides *compound assignment operators* to make such statements easier on you and on the program. They are called compound operators because they combine an assignment and an arithmetic operator. For example, you can write the preceding statement as follows in C:

```
my_int += another_int;
```

This accomplishes exactly the same thing as the lengthier assignment statement, but can be evaluated more efficiently by the program. Essentially, the compiler is told to add the value of **another_int** directly to the value stored in **my_int**. This saves one evaluation of **my_int**, and it's easier to type.

There is a compound assignment operator corresponding to each of the five arithmetic operators:

+=
−=
*=
/=
%=

The %= operator can only be used with integral types, as was the case for the simple modulus (%) operator. (You will soon learn about other compound assignment operators that use non-arithmetic operators.) Let's look at some more examples.

```
/* assume my_int has the value 37 */
my_int /= 5;
/* my_int now has the value 7; why? */
my_int %= 7;
/* my_int now has the value 0 */
```

The first of these assignments stores the result of dividing the integer variable **my_int** by 5, using integer division. Remember, for integers, the result of a division operation is the quotient with the remainder discarded: 5 goes into 37 seven times, and the remainder of 2 is discarded. After this assignment, **my_int** has the value 7. The modulus operator returns the remainder upon dividing 7 by 7. This result is 0.

The statements in the previous listing produce exactly the same results as the following versions:

```
/* assume my_int has the value 37 */
my_int = my_int / 5;
my_int = my_int % 7;
```

The only difference is that these versions are less efficient.

Compound assignments store values in a location, just as simple assignment does. Therefore, you must have a variable (you can't have a constant) on the left side of a compound assignment operator. The compound assignment operators all have the same precedence level, which is the same as that of the simple assignment operator.

Increment and Decrement Operators

There is another type of variable change that's common in programs: changing the value of a variable by 1. For example, many loops use some sort of counter whose value is increased or decreased by 1 each time through the loop. C provides operators to make this easy to do.

C provides two forms of the *increment operator* (++) and two forms of the *decrement operator* (−−). The two forms differ in an important way. The operators are useful in loops, and make it possible to control looping conditions compactly. Let's look at an example.

```
/* Program to illustrate use of increment operator, and
   to show different effects of prefix and postfix forms of operator.
*/

main ()
{
        int result, test = 0;

        /* PREFIX increment: increment then use */
        if ( ( result = ++test) == 1)
                printf ( "result == %d\n", result);
        /* else do nothing */
        printf ( "after ++test, value of test == %d\n", test);

        test = 0;                 /* reinitialize test to 0 */

        /* POSTFIX increment: use then increment */
        if ( ( result = test++) == 1)
                printf ( "result == %d\n", result);
        else                      /* if test is still zero at assignment time */
                printf ( "nothing to do, so test must still == 0\n");
        printf ( "after test++, value of test == %d\n", test);
}

/* output from listing */

result == 1
after ++test, value of test == 1
nothing to do, so test must still == 0
after test++, value of test == 1
```

Depending on the value of **test**, which is assigned to **result**, the program writes the value of **result** or a message saying there was nothing to compute. The program also displays the value stored in **test** after its use (and after incrementing): in the first case, **result** == 1, and in the second, **result** == 0. The only difference in the **test** condition is ++**test** versus **test**++.

Let's look carefully at the **test** condition for the **if** construct. Ultimately, expression evaluates as **true** or **false**. The program will assign whatever value is stored in **test** to the variable **result**. After this assignment is made, the program checks whether the value stored in **result** equals 1. The parentheses around the assignment statement ensure that this is the order in which things happen. If there were no parentheses, the equality operator would be applied first, because it has higher precedence than assignment.

The program's actions hinge on the value of **test** at assignment time. This value, in turn, depends on which version of the increment operator is used.

In the first case, ++**test,** the increment operator is applied first — before using **test** in the assignment statement. Thus, the value of **test** is incremented by 1 (from 0), and this result is assigned to the variable **result**. Consequently, the equality test evaluates to **true**, since 1 == 1.

In the case of **test**++, the value of **test** is first used in the assignment, then the value of **test** is incremented to 1. This means that a 0 is stored in **result**. The equality **test** evaluates to **false** in this case, since 0 != 1.

The main purpose of the conditions for the **if** tests is to return a value of **true** or **false**. Assigning a new value to **result** and incrementing **test** occur almost as side effects. As we'll see, however, such "incidental" assignments and changes are used very commonly in C, and make it possible to write compact code.

▶**REMEMBER**   The major difference between the prefix (++**test**) and the postfix (**test**++) forms of the increment operator is that the *prefix form increments first, then uses* the new value in the expression. The *postfix form first uses the current value* in the expression, then increments this value after use.

As with the compound assignment operators, the increment operator can only be applied to variables, that is, entities with memory locations associated with them. Using these operators, you can only increment or decrement by 1 each time.

Because they are unary operators, the increment and decrement operators have very high precedence. Don't confuse the precedence of the operators with the their use in prefix and postfix form. The precedence level only serves to help the compiler properly group the elements in an expression, as the following example shows:

```
main ()
{
        int i1 = 5, i2 = 10, result;
```

```
        result = i1 * i2--;
        printf ( "result == %d;  i2 == %d\n", result, i2);
}

/* output from listing */
result == 50;  i2 == 9
```

The greater precedence of $--$ over $*$ ensures that the compiler does not turn the statement into **result** $= (i1 * i2)--;$. This would be invalid anyway because the expression in parentheses is not a variable.

Using the $--$ in its postfix form just means that the original value (10) of **i2** is used in the multiplication, rather than the lower value (9) after decrementing.

Loops in C

Computers are particularly good at doing something over and over again, perhaps with slight variations. Such repetitions, or iterations, are called loops. The loop construct is very common in programming.

The main type of loop in C is the **while** loop, which comes in two forms and in a more compact variant, called the **for** loop. The following listing illustrates a **while** loop:

```
/* Program to copute and display cubes and sums of cubes
   of first 10 integers.
   Program illustrates use of while loop.
*/

#define CUBE(x)  ((x) * (x) * (x))

main ()
{
        int i1, running_sum = 0;

        i1 = 1;
        while ( i1 <= 10)
        {
                running_sum += CUBE ( i1);
                printf ( "%2d: CUBE == %4d; running_sum == %4d\n",
                        i1, CUBE ( i1), running_sum);
                ++i1;
        }
}
```

This program produces the following output:

```
 1: CUBE ==    1; running_sum ==    1
 2: CUBE ==    8; running_sum ==    9
 3: CUBE ==   27; running_sum ==   36
 4: CUBE ==   64; running_sum ==  100
 5: CUBE ==  125; running_sum ==  225
 6: CUBE ==  216; running_sum ==  441
 7: CUBE ==  343; running_sum ==  784
 8: CUBE ==  512; running_sum == 1296
 9: CUBE ==  729; running_sum == 2025
10: CUBE == 1000; running_sum == 3025
```

This program prints the cubes and the sum of cubes for the first 10 integers. Let's look at the program, to see how the **while** loop works.

The first statement initializes the "counter," or looping, variable, **i1**, to 1. The value of this counter variable is incremented by 1 each time through the loop (++i1), and the loop continues while this counter variable is less than or equal to a particular value (10).

In any kind of looping construct, you need to know whether you can stop or whether you need to keep going. This means that the construct will have some sort of test associated with it. In the case of a **while** loop, this test is called the *continuation condition*. The loop repeats while the continuation condition remains **true**. In our case, the continuation condition is **true** as long as **i1** is less than or equal to 10. The expression representing the continuation condition is in parentheses, just as the test for the **if** statement was. The parentheses are required.

The actions associated with the **while** loop are those in the statement immediately following the continuation condition. As always, this can be a simple or a compound statement. In this case, the program does the following within the main body of the loop:

- Add the cube of the current value of **i1** to **runningsum**.

- Display the values of **i1**, CUBE(**i1**), and **runningsum**.

- Increment the value of **i1** before continuing the loop.

The program carries out each of the actions in the body of the loop. Then the program goes back to the top of the loop, and checks the continuation condition. If this condition is still **true**, the program carries out the actions in the loop once again.

The increment statement, ++**il**, is a common way of modifying the counter variable in a loop because most loops simply change the counter by 1 each time through. In this example, the operator increments **il** by 1. As nothing happens in the loop after the increment, it doesn't really matter whether we use the prefix or the postfix form of the operator. At other times, however, it will make a difference. This increment statement is crucial to the loop. Without it, the value of the counter variable would never change, and the loop would never end, since the continuation condition would always be **true** (1 is always less than or equal to 10).

Components of the while Loop

There are four main components of the **while** loop:

```
i1 = 1;                                     ◄───────  /* Initialization */
while ( i1 <= 10)                           ◄───────  /* Continuation Condition */
{                                           ◄───────  /* Loop Body */
        running_sum += CUBE ( i1);
        printf ( "%2d: CUBE == %4d; running_sum == %4d\n",
                i1, CUBE ( i1), running_sum);
        ++i1;                               ◄───────  /* Change in looping variable */
}
```

The *initialization* refers to the looping variable. It is generally a good idea to initialize the control variable just before starting the loop to make sure you know exactly what value the loop starts with. The *continuation condition* is the test to determine how long the loop continues. Unless you deliberately want to create an infinite loop, make sure your continuation condition can become **false**. The expression in ordinary continuation conditions will always involve the looping variable. The *loop body* contains the actions to be done when executing the loop.

These actions are the main purpose of the loop; the other components are really administrative, to make sure the loop executes the proper number of times, and with the correct values.

Finally, the *change in the looping variable* is designed to ensure that you get closer to making the continuation condition **false** each time you go through the loop. If you are changing the looping variable explicitly in the loop, make sure you change the looping variable in the direction of the continuation condition's boundary, or ending, value (in our case, 10).

▶**REMEMBER**   The four major components of a while loop are: (1) initialization of looping variable; (2) continuation condition; (3) loop body; (4) change in value of looping variable.

In our illustration, the looping variable was changed at the bottom of the main loop body. You can change it anywhere in the body. Be aware, however, that changing it in different places may affect what happens in the loop. The following example moves the change to the top of the loop from the previous example:

```
/* "Sum of cubes" program with looping variable changed at top of loop. */

#define CUBE(x)   ((x) * (x) * (x))

main ()
{
        int i1, running_sum = 0;

        i1 = 1;
        while ( i1 <= 10)
        {
                ++i1;
                running_sum += CUBE ( i1);
                printf ( "%2d: CUBE == %4d; running_sum == %4d\n",
                        i1, CUBE ( i1), running_sum);
        }
}
```

This program produces the following output:

```
 2: CUBE ==    8; running_sum ==    8
 3: CUBE ==   27; running_sum ==   35
 4: CUBE ==   64; running_sum ==   99
 5: CUBE ==  125; running_sum ==  224
 6: CUBE ==  216; running_sum ==  440
 7: CUBE ==  343; running_sum ==  783
 8: CUBE ==  512; running_sum == 1295
 9: CUBE ==  729; running_sum == 2024
10: CUBE == 1000; running_sum == 3024
11: CUBE == 1331; running_sum == 4355
```

This program does the same thing as the previous one (print cubes and sums of cubes) for a different range of values. By moving the change in the looping variable to the top, the value of **i1** is incremented before its cube is computed.

This means that the first cube to be computed is the cube of 2.

Similarly, the value of **i1** is 10, when the program enters the loop for the last time. Before cubing **i1**, however, the program increments it to 11. Thus, this version of the loop displays cubes and sums of cubes for the integers 2 through 11, whereas the previous program displayed for 1 through 10.

Be careful when specifying your loops. The initial value for the looping variable, the form of the continuation condition, and the place where the looping variable is changed can all affect the outcome of the loop. To convince yourself of this, try running this program with each of the variations listed in Table 6-2. The first two cases correspond to the examples we've already done.

Study the behavior of your **while** loop, as you try these variations. They illustrate the issues and problems that might arise in relation to the boundary cases—that is, the first and last times through the loop.

More About the while Loop

The structure illustrated above represents the "vanilla flavored" form of the **while** loop. Sometimes, in actual practice, one or more of these components

Table 6-2.   Suggested Varients on the While Loop

Initial Looping Variable	Continuation Condition	Change in Looping Variable
1	$i1 <= 10$	Bottom
1	$i1 <= 10$	Top
1	$i1 < 10$	Bottom
1	$i1 < 10$	Top
0	$i1 <= 10$	Bottom
0	$i1 <= 10$	Top
0	$i1 < 10$	Bottom
0	$i1 < 10$	Top

might be missing, or might be present only in an implicit form. For example:

```
/* Program to read characters until a blank is entered.
   Program uses while loop with implicit looping variable.
*/

main ()
{
        int ch;

        while ( (ch = getche()) != ' ')
                printf ( "%c", ch);
}
```

If you type the first few letters of the alphabet in order, this program produces the following output:

```
aabbccddeeff
```

The **while** loop in this program has no initialization for the *looping variable* (**ch**, in this case). The looping variable is changed, but not necessarily in a manner that will eventually make the continuation condition **false**. Essentially, this program relies on the fact that the user will eventually get tired and end the input. Later, we'll read information from files, generally using a loop to do so. In those cases, we'll rely on the fact that the loop will eventually encounter an end-of-file character, at which point the loop will stop.

The **while** loop tests the continuation condition at the top of the loop. If the condition is **false** from the start, the loop does not execute. Thus, a **while** loop executes zero or more times. There is a version of the **while** loop that tests its condition at the end of the loop body-after the loop has executed. We'll look at this form of the loop in the next section.

The do-while Loop

Sometimes your program needs to carry out an action at least once. For example, suppose you wanted to get a value between 1 and 10 from the user. The following program will accomplish this.

```
/* Program to prompt user until a value between 1 and 10 has been entered */

main ()
{
        double val;

        do
        {
                printf ( "Please enter a number between 1 and 10 ");
                scanf ( "%lf", &val);
                if ( (val < 1) || ( val > 10))
                        printf ( "Number must be between 1 and 10\n");
        }
        while ( ( val < 1) || ( val > 10));
        printf ( "You entered %lf\n", val);
}
```

This program prompts for a value between 1 and 10, looping until the value entered falls within those bounds. The program then displays the value read.

This loop will always execute at least once because the program will not know what the continuation condition is until the program reaches the **while** statement at the end of the loop body. If the continuation condition still holds (that is, if the value that has been read is *outside* the desired range), the program goes back to the top of the **do-while** loop and tries again.

The syntax for the **while** portion of the **do-while** loop is the same as that of the regular **while** loop: the keyword **while**, followed by a continuation condition in parentheses. This **while** statement is at the *end* of the **do-while** loop unlike its position at the beginning of the regular **while** loop.

Notice the **if** statement nested inside the loop body. This is allowed because control constructs can be nested inside any other. It is just a coincidence that the conditions for the **if** statement and the **while** construct are the same.

Programmers use the **do-while** version of the **while** loop less frequently than the regular form, but, under certain conditions, it is handy.

▶**REMEMBER**   The **while** loop tests at the top and may never execute; the **do-while** loop tests at the bottom, and will execute at least once.

If you are familiar with Pascal, you may recognize the **do-while** loop as comparable to the **REPEAT-UNTIL** construct in that language.

Change the cube-computing program into a **do-while** loop, and see what differences there are in the output for the eight forms of the loop.

The for Loop

As we've already seen, when something is done often, C tends to have a compact way of specifying or doing it. The same is true of loops. C provides a very convenient form of the loop construct, the **for** loop.

Recall that three of the components of a **while** loop were the initialization of the looping variable, the continuation condition, and changing the looping variable's value. The **for** loop lets you gather these components in one place, at the top of the loop, and makes it possible to write the code in a compact but readable manner. Let's look at an example:

```
/* Program to count from 1 to 20.
   Program illustrates for loop syntax and use.
*/

main ()
{
#define TOP_VAL  20        /* highest value in count */

       int index;

       /* start at 1;
          continue while still below maximum value;
          increment index each time through loop
       */
       for ( index = 1; index <= TOP_VAL; index++)
               printf ( "%d\n", index);
}
```

This program uses a **for** loop to display each integer from 1 to 20. Let's look at the **for** loop, to see how it's put together and how it works. The general structure of this loop form is similar to the structure of the **while** loop: a keyword, followed by some material in parentheses, followed by a loop body. The **for** loop is, in fact, equivalent to a **while** loop.

In a **for** loop, the parentheses following the keyword __for__ usually contain three expressions, separated by semicolons. In our example, the first expression, **index** = 1, initializes the looping variable. The second expression, **index** <= TOP__VAL, represents the continuation condition. Finally, the third expression, **index**++, uses the increment operator to change the looping variable each time through the loop. The semicolons are necessary.

Let's look at another example using the **for** loop: a program using the loop to compute Centigrade temperatures corresponding to certain Fahrenheit values. Both temperatures are displayed in a table. The particular temperature values computed depend on the starting and ending values, and on the increment between successive values to be computed.

```
/* Program to list temperatures in degrees Fahrenheit and Centigrade ---
   given starting value, ending value, and increment.
   Program illustrates use of for loop.
*/

#define F_TO_C  (5.0 / 9.0)      /* To convert from Fahrenheit to Centigrade:
                                    subtract 32, then multiply by F_TO_C */
#define OFFSET  32.0

main ()
{
        double cent,            /* current temperature in Centigrade. */
               val,             /* value currently being converted */
               start, ending,   /* starting and ending values to convert */
               increment;       /* amount by which to change current val */

        introduce_program ();           /* describe program and its use */

        /* get information */
        printf ( "Starting value? ");
        scanf ( "%lf", &start);
        printf ( "Ending value? ");
        scanf ( "%lf", &ending);
        printf ( "Increment? ");
        scanf ( "%lf", &increment);

        /* display headings for table */
        printf ( "\nFahrenheit  Centigrade\n");
        printf ( "---------------------\n");

        /* compute and diplay the values */
        for ( val = start; val <= ending; val += increment)
        {
                cent = ( val - OFFSET) * F_TO_C;
                printf ( "%10.5lf  %10.5lf\n", val, cent);
        }
}


introduce_program ()
{
        printf ( "This program displays the temperature ");
        printf ( "in degrees Centigrade and Fahrenheit.\n\n");
        printf ( "Your input: a starting Fahrenheit temperature,\n");
        printf ( "            an ending Fahrenheit temperature,\n");
        printf ( "            an increment.\n\n");
        printf ( "This version does no checking, so it's up to you to ");
        printf ( "make sure your starting,\nending, and increment values ");
        printf ( "produce sensible results.\n\n");
}
```

This program produces the following output:

```
This program displays the temperature in degrees Centigrade and Fahrenheit.

Your input: a starting Fahrenheit temperature,
            an ending Fahrenheit temperature,
            an increment.

This version does no checking, so it's up to you to make sure your starting,
ending, and increment values produce sensible results.

Starting value? 2
Ending value? 212
Increment? 30

Fahrenheit  Centigrade
----------------------
    2.00000    -16.66667
   32.00000      0.00000
   62.00000     16.66667
   92.00000     33.33333
  122.00000     50.00000
  152.00000     66.66667
  182.00000     83.33333
  212.00000    100.00000
```

This **for** loop, again contains three expressions, separated by semicolons. The first expression, **val** = start, initializes the looping variable. The second expression, **val** <= ending, represents the continuation condition. Finally, the third expression, **val** += increment, changes the looping variable each time through the loop.

There are two reasons for using a separate function, **introduceprogram( )**, to write an introductory message. First, to remind you that there are functions other than **main( )**, and not all are Run-Time Library functions. Second, it's generally a good idea (and an important step toward making your programs more modular) to put separate tasks into separate functions. This makes each function easier to read, because it is less cluttered.

The **for** loop in the previous program is equivalent to the following **while** loop:

```
val = start;
while ( val <= ending)
{
        cent = ( val - OFFSET) * F_TO_C;
        printf ( "%10.5lf  %10.5lf\n", val, cent);
        val += increment;
}
```

In a sense, the **for** loop simply takes these three elements from the specific places where they would ordinarily be found and groups them at the top of the loop. This makes it much easier to make sure you've included all three components, and that they are correct. They are far more prominent grouped at the top than if they were distributed in the code.

When the program encounters a **for** loop, the following actions are taken:

1. The first expression is evaluated once, and any initializations are made. This expression is not used again in the loop.

2. The continuation condition (second expression) is evaluated. If it is **false**, the loop terminates, and no further action is taken in the loop body or in the expressions.

3. If the continuation condition is **true**, the loop body is executed.

4. After the loop body has executed, the third expression is processed. This will generally change the looping variable.

5. The program goes back to the top of the **for** loop, and repeats the cycle beginning with step 2 (testing the continuation condition).

Let's look at one more example using the **for** loop, an example that prints a portion of the ASCII table:

```
/* Program to display the printable ASCII characters in a table.
   Program illustrates use of for loop.
*/
/* global, so display function can get at it */
int count;        /* used to decide when to move to next line in output */
int curr_char;    /* contains current ASCII value being processed */

main ()
{
        count = 0;
        for ( curr_char = 32; curr_char < 127; curr_char++)
                display ();
}

/* write ASCII code and corresponding character to the screen.
   Write 5 entries per line.
*/
display ()
{
        printf ( "     %3d  %c", curr_char, curr_char);
        if ( (++count % 5) == 0)
                printf ( "\n");
        else
}
```

This program produces the following partial ASCII table as output.

```
32        33  !     34  "     35  #     36  $
37  %     38  &     39  '     40  (     41  )
42  *     43  +     44  ,     45  -     46  .
47  /     48  0     49  1     50  2     51  3
52  4     53  5     54  6     55  7     56  8
57  9     58  :     59  ;     60  <     61  =
62  >     63  ?     64  @     65  A     66  B
67  C     68  D     69  E     70  F     71  G
72  H     73  I     74  J     75  K     76  L
77  M     78  N     79  O     80  P     81  Q
82  R     83  S     84  T     85  U     86  V
87  W     88  X     89  Y     90  Z     91  [
92  \     93  ]     94  ^     95  _     96  '
97  a     98  b     99  c    100  d    101  e
102  f   103  g    104  h    105  i    106  j
107  k   108  l    109  m    110  n    111  o
112  p   113  q    114  r    115  s    116  t
117  u   118  v    119  w    120  x    121  y
122  z   123  {    124  |    125  }    126  ~
```

The program writes a table of ASCII codes and corresponding characters for the printable portion of the ASCII character set. The program uses a **for** loop to do the work, and relies on an output routine that counts entries to make sure that only five entries are written on a line.

As in the previous example, the expressions at the top of the **for** loop represent the instruction for initializing the looping variable (**curr__char** = 32), the continuation condition (**curr__char** < 127), and the instruction to change the looping variable (**curr__char**++), using the increment operator.

Again, this **for** loop is just a more convenient way of writing the following:

```
curr_char = 32
while ( curr_char < 127)
{
        display ();
        curr_char++;
}
```

Omitting Expressions from the for Loop

So far, all the examples involving a **for** loop have been well-behaved: each contained the three loop components. Sometimes, however, you may want to loop, but with less explicit or less well-defined looping variables. We saw an example of this earlier, when we used a **while** loop to get character input from the user until the user entered a blank character.

Let's look at an example of a "non-standard" **for** loop that illustrates several additional things abou this construct.

```
/* Program to build a long int from character input.
   Program illustrates "non-vanilla" version of for loop.
*/

#define BEEP   '\07'
#define TRUE   1
#define FALSE  0

main ()
{
        int  ch, count = 0;        /* '-' valid for count == 1 */
        int  negative = FALSE;     /* TRUE if value should be negated. */
        long val;

        printf ( "Enter a series of digits; press RETURN when done.\n");
        printf ( "The program will build a number from the digits.\n\n");

        for ( val = 0; ((ch = fgetchar ()) != '\n'); )
        {
                count++;              /* to see whether '-' is first character */
                if ( ( ch >= '0') && ( ch <= '9'))
                {
                        ch -= '0';        /* compute the digit's "value" */
                        val = 10 * val + ch;
                }
                else if ( ( ch == '-') && ( count == 1))
                        negative = TRUE;
                else    /* if not a digit nor a leading '-' */
                {
                        printf ( "%c", BEEP);
                        break;
                }
        }
        if ( negative)
                val *= -1;
        printf ( "\ninteger built == %ld\n", val);
}
```

This program reads character input, and tries to build a **long int** from the input. It displays whatever number it was able to build, and beeps at the user if the input is an invalid character (that is, anything other than a digit, or a '—' in the first position).

The main control loop is a **for** statement. However, this time the first expression initializes the **long int** being built rather than the looping variable. The continuation condition in this example is similar to the one we saw in a **while** loop above where the loop continued until a certain character was encountered. Finally, there is no third expression. Any of the expressions at the top of the **for** loop can be omitted, if the loop's logic allows or requires this; the compiler will not complain.

Let's look at some of the other features of this program. There are some preprocessor definitions, which we haven't been using much in recent listings. The first manifest constant specifies the ASCII code for the beep. It's much easier to understand a piece of code that says to display BEEP than one that calls for " \07." The other two definitions provide mnemonic names for two values that the program will treat as **true** and **false**.

Only two of the variables defined, **ch** and **val**, are used in actually building the number. The others, **count** and **negative**, are used to help control the program's actions. **Count** is used to make sure that a minus sign is considered valid only as the first character read. After the first character, **count** is not really needed anymore. The other, **negative**, is set to TRUE if the character was a minus sign, since this means the resulting value will need to be multiplied by −1.

The **if** construct inside the **for** loop has several features worth noting. First, it provides another example of the **else-if** construct in which conditions are nested inside others. The purpose of the condition for the first **if** is to identify digits. If the character is a digit, then its numerical value must be computed.

We can't simply use the character's ASCII value as the digit's numerical value because values for the digits range from 48 to 57. The expression used to compute the digit's numerical value (**ch** −= '0') takes advantage of the fact that the digits follow each other in order in the ASCII character set. Each digit's value can be found by computing its offset from the ASCII value for '0'. For example, the character '8' has ASCII value 56. If you subtract 48 (the ASCII value for '0') you'll get the digit's numerical value, 8.

The next statement in the **if** construct adds this numerical value to the number that has been built so far, that is, to the current value of **val**. As each new digit is read, it becomes the rightmost digit in the number being built. This means the current number needs to be moved one place to the left—that is, multiplied by 10—before adding the new digit in the 1's place.

If the character read is *not* a digit, the program tests whether it might be a minus sign. The minus sign is acceptable only as the first character. If this is the case, the program sets negative to TRUE.

Finally, the last condition in the **if** construct (neither digit nor leading minus sign) catches invalid characters. As soon as such a character is encountered, the number building process comes to an end. Earlier, we saw that the **break** statement immediately got you out of a **switch** construct. Here, the **break** statement gets you out of the **for** loop, and back to the next level in the **main( )** function.

Here's a list of the main actions performed in building a number from character input. The two major actions are: adding this digit in the proper way to the number (the assignments involving **val**), and determining the digit (the assignments involving **ch**).

```
VAL            CH                           ACTIONS
 0     '1'   ch = ch -'0'          /* compute digit value of ch */
             ch = 49 - 48
             ch = 1
             val = 10 * val + ch   /* add digit to 10 * current value */
             val = 10 * 0 + 1
             val = 0 + 1
             cal = 1
 1     '8'   ch = ch - '0'
             ch = 56 - 48
             ch = 8
             val = 10 * val + ch
             val = 10 * 1 + 8
             val = 10 + 8
             val = 18
18     '5'   ch = ch - '0'
             ch = 53 - 48
             ch = 5
             val = 10 * val + ch
             val = 10 * 18 + 5
             val = 180 + 5
             val = 185
```

The list shows the sequence of steps as the program builds the number 185 from the input characters, '1', '8', and '5'. The actions summarized are intended to provide a conceptual example. The program does not necessarily go through exactly these steps.

As the characters are read left to right, the leftmost part of the number is built each time. When you add a new value, first add a zero in the 1's place (the multiplication by 10) and then add the digit in the 1's place.

Any of the expressions at the top of the **for** loop can be omitted. If the middle expression is left out, the compiler replaces it with a nonzero constant, that is, with a value that is always **true**. In that case, the loop will execute forever. For example, the following program does nothing for a *very* long time, because the compiler replaces the missing middle expression with a nonzero value (e.g., 1). This value remains **true** because there is nothing to change it.

```
/* Infinite loop program, using for loop */

main ()
{
        for ( ; ; )
                ;
}
```

Notice that the semicolons are necessary, even if an expression is omitted.

The Comma Operator

Sometimes your program may need to have several tasks taking place at once in a loop, with each action having its own variables. In such cases, it's convenient to have multiple expressions in the **for** loop. The following example illustrates the *comma operator* (,) that provides such a capability.

```
/* Program to count up from 1 to 20, and down from 20 to 1 at the same time.
   Program illustrates use of the comman operator.
*/

main ()
{
        int up, down;

        for ( up = 1, down = 20; (up <= 20) && ( down >= 1);
              up++, down--)
                printf ( "up %5d; down %5d\n", up, down);
}
```

This program counts up from 1 to 20, and down from 20 to 1 at the same time. The program uses a **for** loop to accomplish this. The approach is to have two counters that are changed and used independently. The comma operator makes it easy to specify multiple steps in each of the expressions at the top of the **for** loop.

In this program two variables are changed in both the first and the third expressions at the top of the **for** loop, with the assignments separated by the comma operator.

The operands for the comma operator are evaluated from left to right: **up = 1** then **down = 20**. Values returned by operands of a comma operator are discarded, except any value returned by the rightmost operand. The only effect of the assignments is to store values in the respective variables. For now, think of the comma operator as a convenient tool for multiple assignments . Later, we'll see some other uses for this operator. The comma operator has the lowest precedence in C, which is why no parentheses were needed in the initializations.

Break and continue

When you need to get out of a loop quickly, before the current iteration of the loop is completed, the **break** statement comes in handy.

For example, in our program to build integers from character input, the algorithm was designed to stop as soon as an invalid character was encountered. The only place to detect an invalid character was inside the **for** loop, so the solution was to use **break** to get out of the loop completely.

The **break** statement terminates the innermost loop or **switch** in which the statement is found. At that point, program control transfers to the next statement in the immediately surrounding block, which may be another loop. The **break** statement can be used only inside a loop or in a **switch** construct.

The **continue** statement is similar to **break** in that both allow exits from a loop. The difference is in what happens after the exit. The **continue** statement exits to the top of the loop in which the statement was found, thus preparing the program to start the next iteration of the loop. The **continue** statement does not apply to **switch** statements.

▶**REMEMBER**   The **break** statement exits from the innermost loop or **switch** in which the statement is found. The **continue** statement exits from the innermost loop (but not **switch**). The **continue** statement transfers control to the top of the loop in which the statement was found. The **break** statement transfers control to the next statement in the immediately surrounding block.

The following example illustrates one instance in which a **continue** statement is useful:

```
/* Program to determine and display all numbers (between 0 and 500)
   that are divisible by each even number between 2 and 12.
   Program illustrates use of continue construct.
*/

main ()
{
        int count;

        for ( count = 0; count <= 500; count++ )
        {
                if ( (count % 2))    /* for odd numbers */
                        continue;
                else if ( (count % 4))
                        continue;
                else if ( (count % 6))
                        continue;
                else if ( (count % 8))
                        continue;
                else if ( (count % 10))
                        continue;
                else if ( (count % 12))
                        continue;
                else
                        printf ( "%d\n", count);
        }
        printf ( "upon exit, count == %d\n", count);
}

/* output from listing */

0
120
240
360
480
upon exit, count == 501
```

This program writes out the values of all numbers divisible by each even number between 2 and 12. The logic is to eliminate a number as soon as one of the divisors leaves a remainder. Thus, if the number is odd, there is no point testing 2, 4, 6, etc. If the number is not divisible by 8, there is no reason to try 10 and 12.

Once a number is eliminated, we want to try the next number in the sequence. That is, we want to go back to the top of the loop and try the next value. This is exactly what the **continue** statement accomplishes.

Notice the expressions being used to test each **if** statement. The tests are asking whether the result of the modulus operation is a nonzero number, whether division by the number leaves a remainder. If it does, then the number does *not* divide the current value of **count**. We could just as easily have phrased the tests more explicitly. For example, **((count % 2) == 1))** tests the same thing, in a manner that is less compact but easier to read.

Contrast the effects of the **continue** statement with the same program, but using a **break** statement instead.

```
/* "Divisibility" program, but using break instead of continue.
   Notice last value checked.
*/

main ()
{
        int count;

        for ( count = 0; count <= 500; count++ )
        {
                if ( (count % 2))      /* for odd numbers */
                        break;
                else if ( (count % 4))
                        break;
                else if ( (count % 6))
                        break;
                else if ( (count % 8))
                        break;
                else if ( (count % 10))
                        break;
                else if ( (count % 12))
                        break;
                else
                        printf ( "%d\n", count);
        }
        printf ( "upon exit, count == %d\n", count);
}

/* output from listing */

0
upon exit, count == 1
```

This program has the same structure as the preceding one. However, the **break** statement exits the **for** loop completely the first time a **break** statement is encountered. Since this happens when **count** takes the first odd value (1), the program ends very quickly.

Summary

In this chapter, you've learned about control constructs in C, and have been introduced to several new operators that are often used in these control constructs. The two major categories of control construct are selection (**if-else** and **switch**) and iteration (**while**, **do-while**, and **for**).

Most of the operators covered in this chapter are commonly used at various points in selection or iteration constructs. For example, the relational ($<, <=, >, >=$) and equality ($==$ and $!=$), and the unary negation operator (!) are often used to create simple tests for an **if** statement or for the continuation condition of an iteration construct.

The logical operators (**&&** and ‖) are used to connect expressions into longer, more complex conditions.

The increment (++), decrement (––) and compound assignment operators (+=, –=, *=, /=, and %=) are used to change looping variables in iteration constructs. Remember, the increment and decrement operators can behave differently, depending on whether you use a prefix or a postfix form of the operator. Finally, the comma operator (,) makes it easier to perform several assignments or to make several changes in one place (such as at the top of a **for** loop).

In the next chapter, we'll look at functions in more detail. You'll find out how to define functions with parameters, and how to return values from functions.

7

Functioning in C

A major advantage C gives you is the ability to create function libraries and then programs using only those library functions needed to accomplish the tasks the program requires. However, so far we've been using functions sparingly. That will change beginning with this chapter.

In previous chapters, we used programs for a range of simple tasks: print ASCII tables, compute sums or sums of cubes, convert temperatures from Fahrenheit to centigrade, and so on. These tasks were done by the **main( )** function, which is actually the program in C.

We've called Run-Time Library functions, such as **printf( )**, **getch( )**, and **scanf( )**. Some of these functions have required arguments, and others have not. We've also written functions to carry out specific tasks in particular programs, for example, **introduce _ program( )** in the temperature conversion program, and **display( )** in the ASCII table program. None of the functions we've defined have involved parameters. So far, we have defined only "bare bones" functions to carry out a task that is independent of variables or values in other parts of the program or that have used global variables accessible to any functions in the program.

In this chapter you'll find out more about functions, and we'll see how to define functions with parameters. You'll also learn how to get information back from a function by returning particular values. Throughout the text, we've been using the values returned by library functions in various ways. For example, the **fgetchar( )** function returns an **int** that represents the character read by the function.

C Functions

Think of C functions as specialists that you call when the need arises. A specialist is someone with a particular collection of skills to perform specific tasks. A function, then, is a collection of instructions (statements) designed to compute a particular value or to accomplish a task.

Just as specialists can save time and effort, functions can save you programming and debugging work. If there is a function available, call it to do the work. If there isn't a function to do what you need, write one. Once written, you can use it over and over again in other C programs.

For example, you might need to alphabetize several lists at different points in a program. You could do this without using functions by writing the instructions in the main program for each separate instance of alphabetization. Suppose it takes 50 lines of instructions to alphabetize, and suppose you need to do this 50 times in the program. That means 2500 lines of instruction in the program. A 2500-plus line function is a clear example of bad programming style. Short functions are much easier to write, understand, and debug than long functions. Keep your functions short and clear.

If you alphabetized the same list each time, you could replicate this code easily by using the copy facility in your editor. Most likely, however, each situation would be slightly different. You might, for example, have to go in and change the variable names, or the number of elements to be sorted, and so on.

At best, accomplishing 50 sorts in the program would require you to copy something 50 times. Things are unlikely to be so simple, however. You will probably have to change some proportion of those lines. Even if you had to change only 30% of the lines, that would be 750 lines — lots of time, and lots of opportunity for making mistakes.

If you had a function for alphabetizing lists, you could simply call the function, give it the list you wanted alphabetized, and the list will be returned in the desired order — you just hand over the job, then get it back when it's done. The great thing about having specialists on call is that they're good at doing their job, and they'll worry about the details of whatever needs to be done.

You don't need to know the details of how a function does its job, only how to ask it to do the work. Again, this is similar to using a specialist: you really need to know just enough about the task to be able to specify correctly what you want done. You also need to know what information you are going to get back from the function. We'll look at both of these issues — how to ask for a function and how to deal with what it gives you — but first, let's look briefly at what happens when you call a function in the program.

Flow of Control

When your program runs, it carries out one instruction after another. The program carries out instructions in the order in which they occur in the source code, unless you specify otherwise, with a selection or iterative construct. Let's look at an example of program execution.

```
/* Program to write the values 1 .. 5 three times.
   Program illustrates flow of control in program execution.
*/
main ()                                  /* function declarator */
{                                        /* start of function body */
        printf ( "Hello, world.\n");                   /* 1 */
```

```
    printf ( "I'm going to count for you\n");           /* 2 */
    printf ( "%d\n", 1);                                 /* 3 */
    printf ( "%d\n", 2);                                 /* 4 */
    printf ( "%d\n", 3);                                 /* 5 */
    printf ( "%d\n", 4);                                 /* 6 */
    printf ( "%d\n", 5);                                 /* 7 */

    printf ( "\nYou didn't catch that?\n");              /* 8 */
    printf ( "Oh, all right, I'll count again.\n");      /* 9 */
    printf ( "%d\n", 1);                                 /* 10 */
    printf ( "%d\n", 2);                                 /* 11 */
    printf ( "%d\n", 3);                                 /* 12 */
    printf ( "%d\n", 4);                                 /* 13 */
    printf ( "%d\n", 5);                                 /* 14 */

    printf ( "\nYou STILL didn't catch that?\n");        /* 15 */
    printf ( "I'll do it one more time.\n");             /* 16 */
    printf ( "But please pay attention this time.\n");   /* 17 */
    printf ( "%d\n", 1);                                 /* 18 */
    printf ( "%d\n", 2);                                 /* 19 */
    printf ( "%d\n", 3);                                 /* 20 */
    printf ( "%d\n", 4);                                 /* 21 */
    printf ( "%d\n", 5);                                 /* 22 */
}                                       /* end of function body */
```

A bit of terminology will make what follows easier to understand.

- The top line of a function is called the *function declarator,* or *function heading.* It contains an identifier (the function name, here, **main( )**) and a set of parentheses that may contain additional information.

- The material in the parentheses is the *formal parameter list,* which we'll discuss in the next section. Notice that there is no semicolon at the end of the function declarator. This tells the compiler that you are defining the function, rather than simply declaring the function (as we've done in earlier chapters). This is done to tell another function what type of value the function is returning.

- The second major component of **main( )** is the *function body,* the actual instructions the function will carry out. The function body is essentially a compound statement, or *block* (hence, the curly braces at top and bottom).

The preceding program prints the first five integers three times. Each time, the list is preceded by a different message. Each statement is numbered to make the discussion easier to follow.

When this program runs, it simply carries out the instructions one after the other. That is, the sequence in which the program executes is from statement 1 through statement 22.

Notice that the same set of five instructions appears three times in the program (statements 3 through 7, 10 through 14, and 18 through 22). The only real inconvenience this repetition caused was having to put statement numbers on each occurrence. The actual statements were easy to copy with the editor.

As the entire program is only about 25 lines long, looking at the source code is not very daunting, nor is the extra work required to number the lines. But suppose we had displayed this information 100 or more times. We would have a very boring program. At first glance, you might feel overwhelmed by the source code listing, which would be well over ten pages long, even though the code would consist of the same lines repeated over and over again. You might, justifiably, be reluctant to *read* such scintillating code; the prospect of *writing* the 800 or so statements required is even less appealing.

The use of a function can help make the task easier. The following example shows how, and will also let us explore the flow of control when functions are called.

```
/* Program to write the values 1 .. 5 three times,
   calling a function to do the writing.
   Program illustrates flow of control when function calls are involved.
*/
main ()
{
        printf ( "Hello, world.\n");                        /* 1 */
        printf ( "I'm going to count for you\n");           /* 2 */
        display ();                                         /* 3 */
                                                            /* 3a */
        printf ( "\nYou didn't catch that?\n");             /* 4 */
        printf ( "Oh, all right, I'll count again.\n");     /* 5 */
        display ();                                         /* 6 */
                                                            /* 6a */
        printf ( "\nYou STILL didn't catch that?\n");       /* 7 */
        printf ( "I'll do it one more time.\n");            /* 8 */
        printf ( "But please pay attention this time.\n");  /* 9 */
        display ();                                         /* 10 */
                                                            /* 10a */
}


display ()
{
        printf ( "%d\n", 1);                                /* 11 */
        printf ( "%d\n", 2);                                /* 12 */
        printf ( "%d\n", 3);                                /* 13 */
        printf ( "%d\n", 4);                                /* 14 */
        printf ( "%d\n", 5);                                /* 15 */
}
```

This program performs exactly the same task as the preceding one. The only difference is that the sequence of instructions to display the numbers has been made into a function, which the **main( )** function calls at the appropriate times.

When this program runs, it starts executing the instructions in sequence. When the program gets to statement 3, however, programs behave differently from the preview version. Essentially, the function name, **display( )**, serves as an indicator that some instructions should be here — namely, those in the body of the function. The program will behave as if the instructions (rather than the function call) had been there, except that the actual instructions are not physically present in the code.

When the program calls **display( )**, control is turned over to that function. The instructions contained in the function body are loaded and executed in succession.

As you already read in Chapter 4, there are differences between a preprocessor macro call (which actually substituted the macro body into the code when the macro call was encountered, before or during compilation) and a function call (for which the code would be loaded when needed by the running program). This loading process, and the time required to accomplish it, is what the discussion there was about.

The flow of control in this program is: 1-3, 11-15. When the function is finished executing, its environment is discarded from working memory, and control returns to the statement immediately after the function call. Think of the control as returning to the empty line, 3a. The rest of the program statements execute in the following sequence: 4-6, 11-15, (6a), 7-10, 11-15, (10a).

Notice that the last "control point" is 10a — the empty line right after the final call to **display( )**. Almost always, functions will return control to the calling functions. Thus, it will almost always be the main program that ends execution, even though it may have nothing more to do after the last statement, if that's a function call.

This entire program is a sequence of function calls. C actually transfers control back and forth between **main( )** and **printf( )**. Because **printf( )** is a library function, and therefore a black box as far as we're concerned, we can think of its activities as a single statement from the point of view of the calling function, **main( )**. A function call temporarily transfers control to the called function. When the function is finished, C transfers control back to the "calling routine."

Often, a function called by the main program will, in turn, call other functions. The same process will be repeated at this inner level. That is, function **display( )** will temporarily transfer control to another function, **printf( )**. When function **printf( )** is done, it will transfer control back to **display( )**. When **display( )** is done, it will, in turn, transfer control back to the main program. The following listing also illustrates nested function calls.

```
/* Program to write the values 1 .. 5 three times,
   calling a function to do the writing.
   The display() function, in turn, calls another function.
   Program illustrates flow of control with nested function calls.
*/
main ()
{
        printf ( "Hello, world.\n");                          /* 1 */
        printf ( "I'm going to count for you\n");             /* 2 */
        display ();                                           /* 3 */
                                                              /* 3a */
        printf ( "\nYou didn't catch that?\n");               /* 4 */
        printf ( "Oh, all right, I'll count again.\n");       /* 5 */
        display ();                                           /* 6 */
                                                              /* 6a */
        printf ( "\nYou STILL didn't catch that?\n");         /* 7 */
        printf ( "I'll do it one more time.\n");              /* 8 */
        printf ( "But please pay attention this time.\n");    /* 9 */
        display ();                                           /* 10 */
                                                              /* 10a */
}


display ()
{
        printf ( "%d\n", 1);                                  /* 11 */
        printf ( "%d\n", 2);                                  /* 12 */
        printf ( "%d\n", 3);                                  /* 13 */
        interruption ();                                      /* 14 */
                                                              /* 14a */
        printf ( "%d\n", 4);                                  /* 15 */
        printf ( "%d\n", 5);                                  /* 16 */
}


interruption ()
{
        printf ( "We interrupt this display to announce:\n"); /* 17 */
        printf ( "The display will continue now.\n");         /* 18 */
}
```

This program displays the numbers, interrupted by two lines of text each time. The output is shown in the next listing:

```
Hello, world.
I'm going to count for you
1
2
3
```

```
We interrupt this display to announce:
The display will continue now.
4
5

You didn't catch that?
Oh, all right, I'll count again.
1
2
3
We interrupt this display to announce:
The display will continue now.
4
5

You STILL didn't catch that?
I'll do it one more time.
But please pay attention this time.
1
2
3
We interrupt this display to announce:
The display will continue now.
4
5
```

The flow of control in this program is as follows: 1-3, 11-14, 17-18, (14a), 15-16, (3a), 4-6, 11-14, 17-18, (14a), 15-16, (6a), 7-10, 11-14, 17-18, (14a), 15-16, (10a).

The **interruption( )** function returns control to **display( )**, rather than to **main( )**. This is because **display( )** (and not **main( )**) called **interruption( )**. In a sense, the main program doesn't really know anything about **interruption( )** because **main( )** has nothing directly to do with that function.

In keeping with the analogy of specialist, you can think of function calls by functions as subcontracting to other specialists. The original contractor need not know anything about these subcontracts, just as the calling function doesn't know anything about the functions called by its specialists.

Function calls are just like other C statements, except that the function call is likely to accomplish the work of several statements. Functions can be used in conjunction with all C's constructs, including the selection and iteration constructs. Let's look at a few examples.

```c
#define MAX_DISPLAY 5

display ()
{
        printf ( "Hello\t");
}


main ()
{
        int index;

        for ( index = 0; index <= MAX_DISPLAY; index++)
                display();
}
```

This program writes hello five times on a line. In the next example, C functions are being used as alternative actions in an **if** construct.

```
#define MAX_SIZE 10
#define LARGE_CUT 1000.0
#define FACTOR 1.9

main()
{
        double start = 2.0;
        int index;

        for ( index = 1; index <= MAX_SIZE; index++)
        {
                if ( start < LARGE_CUT)
                        small_val();
                else
                        large_val();
                start *= FACTOR;
        }
}

large_val ()
{
        printf ( "LARGE\n");
}

small_val ()
{
        printf ( "SMALL\n");
}
```

In this program, the functions **small_val( )** and **large_val( )** just write their size, depending on the value of **start**. Notice that the function calls represent the alternative actions in the **for** loop.

Function Returns

As you've seen already, you can use C functions in two different ways: by doing something with the value returned by the function or by having the function perform some action, but discarding or ignoring the return value, if any. So far, the functions we've *defined* (as opposed to some of the library functions we've used) have all been of the second type — where the program is not counting on any returned value from the function. For example, the **display( )** function in the "counting" programs above just does some work for the calling function.

You will often need or want a function to return a value, for use by other parts of the program. The following listing shows how to define such a function.

```
/* Program to compute as many pseudorandom values as desired
   between 0.0 and 1.0.
   Program illustrates use of functions that return a value,
   including syntax for defining and declaring such a function.
*/

/* Function to return a pseudorandom value between 0.0 and 1.0.
   Note format of function heading:
   <type specifier> <function name> ()
*/

double zero_one_rand ()
{
#define  MAX_VAL  32767.0        /* NOTE: defined as floating point type */
        int  rand ();            /* returns a pseudorandom integer */
        int  rand_result;

        rand_result = rand ();   /* get a pseudorandom integer */
        return ( rand_result / MAX_VAL);
}


main ()
{
#define MAX_COUNT 15       /* maximum number of times through loop. */

        /* function declaration, so main can use it the function properly. */
        double  zero_one_rand ();
        int     count;

        /* main loop. Note how function call to zero_one_rand() is used. */

        for ( count = 1; count <= MAX_COUNT; count++)
              printf ( "%5d: random double == %lf\n",
                        count, zero_one_rand ());
}
```

This program produces the following output. The particular values returned will probably differ when you compile it, depending on the first call to the **rand( )** function.

```
 1: random double == 0.001251
 2: random double == 0.563585
 3: random double == 0.193304
 4: random double == 0.808741
 5: random double == 0.585009
 6: random double == 0.479873
 7: random double == 0.350291
 8: random double == 0.895962
 9: random double == 0.822840
10: random double == 0.746605
11: random double == 0.174108
12: random double == 0.858943
13: random double == 0.710501
14: random double == 0.513535
15: random double == 0.303995
```

This program writes 15 pseudorandom floating point values, between 0.0 and 1.0. The program works by calling a function, **zero — one — rand( )**, we've defined for the purpose. This function returns a value of type **double**, as indicated by the definition of the function and its declaration in **main( )**.

Let's look at how the **zero ―one ―rand( )** function call and return work. When the arguments to **printf( )** are evaluated, the program finds a call to **zero ―one ―rand( )** and transfers control to this function, which computes and returns a **double**. The value returned is substituted for the placeholder in the string argument to **printf( )**.

The function **zero ―one ―rand( )** works in a manner similar to the **rand( )** library function we saw earlier. The library function returned a pseudo-random integer between 0 and 32767 (the largest integer in QuickC). The **zero ―one ―rand( )** calls **rand( )** for such an integer, and then "standardizes" the integer returned by **rand( )** to a **double** value between 0.0 and 1.0. The result is then returned to the calling function.

The **return** statement is the mechanism by which the function result is passed to the calling function. The **return** effects an exit from the function, possibly taking a value out with it. The **return** may include an expression which should evaluate to a value of the type the function returns. The result of the expression is the value returned by the function. Thus, in the example, the **return** was made with the expression, **rand ―result** / MAX ―VAL, which evaluates to a value of type **double**.

The **return** statement has the same effect as the **break** statement we saw earlier, for **switch** and loop constructs. Both types of statements effect an exit from a block. In the case of **break**, this block is a loop or a **switch** statement; in the case of **return**, the block is usually a function. If a function has no **return** statement, or if the **return** statement lacks a value, then the function does not return a value.

If there is no **return**, the function keeps executing until the last statement in the function is done. Then, control reverts to the calling function. If the function includes a **return** statement, but without an accompanying expression, control reverts to the calling function right after the **return**.

You can put **return** statements anywhere in a function. For example, you might want to return different values, depending on the conditions that hold in the function or the results of a computation. Control reverts back to the calling function right after the first **return** statement is evaluated. The value of the function—that is, the value returned by the function—is the result of the expression for the return. C ignores any statements after a **return** in the execution of the function.

The definition for **zero ―one ―rand( )** is more elaborate than the definitions we've seen in previous chapters. First, notice the function declarator for **zero ―one ―rand**. The function name is preceded by a type specifier, **double**.

This specifier indicates the type of value returned by the function. If the type specifier is absent, the function is assumed to return an integer. Functions may return values of any of the types we've seen so far, as well as types we haven't yet covered.

▶**REMEMBER**

- A **return** statement effects an exit from a function, and transfers control to the next statement in the calling function.

- The **return** statement may include an expression that evaluates to the value returned by the function.

- If a function includes no **return** statement, or includes a **return** statement without an associated value, then the function does not return a value.

Sometimes you will want to state explicitly that a function does not return a value. There is a special type specifier, **void**, for this purpose. To indicate that a function does not even return an **int** (the assumed default, if no return type is specified), write **void** before the function name in the function heading. The **display( )** function in the "counting" program would be defined as follows:

```
void display ()
{
        printf ( "%d\n", 1);
        printf ( "%d\n", 2);
        printf ( "%d\n", 3);
        printf ( "%d\n", 4);
        printf ( "%d\n", 5);
}
```

▶**REMEMBER**   To indicate that a function returns a value, specify the type of value returned by a function at the start of the function declarator line. If you do not specify a return type, the compiler assumes the function returns an **int**. If you want to indicate explicitly that the function returns no value, use **void** as the type specifier.

Notice the preprocessor definition at the start of the **zero ▁ one ▁ rand( )** function. This is allowed because preprocessor definitions can appear just about anywhere in a source file. The restriction is that the # must be the first non-whitespace character on the line.

The manifest constant, MAX__VAL, is replaced by a floating point representation of the maximum integer value in QuickC: 32767. The reason for this has to do with types and operator precedence. The value returned by **rand( ), rand __ result,** is an **int.** Had we used the **int** version of 32767 in the example, the result of doing an integer division would always be either 0 or 1 because the only possible values for the numerator would be values between 0 and 32767, none of which is more than the twice 32767 needed to produce a quotient greater than 1.

By dividing with a floating point type, the expression becomes one involving such types, and the division produces a quotient complete with fractional remainder, rather than the 0 or 1 that would result from the integer division.

Formal and Actual Parameters

Earlier, we looked at two versions of a program that counts to five and displays the results on the screen. Suppose you wanted to count to different values each time, again displaying the results. One way to accomplish this would be to go back to the original program, and simply call **printf( )** as often as desired at each point. Again, that could become tedious to do. An alternative would be to modify the definition of the **display( )** function to let you specify how high it should count each time you call it. This solution would use a *parameter* to specify the target value each time you called the function.

Basically, a parameter is a slot through which you can pass information when you actually call the function. This information will let you have some control over how the function executes. Let's look at an example:

```
/* Program to write the values starting at 1 three times.
   Program calls display() to do the writing;
   argument specifies how many values to write in that call.
   Program illustrates use of parameters when defining and using functions.
*/
main ()
{
        printf ( "Hello, world.\n");                        /* 1 */
        printf ( "I'm going to count for you\n");           /* 2 */
        display (5);                                        /* 3 */
                                                            /* 3a */
        printf ( "\nYou didn't catch that?\n");             /* 4 */
        printf ( "Oh, all right, I'll count again.\n");     /* 5 */
        display (3);                                        /* 6 */
                                                            /* 6a */
```

```
        printf ( "\nYou STILL didn't catch that?\n");        /* 7 */
        printf ( "I'll do it one more time.\n");              /* 8 */
        printf ( "But please pay attention this time.\n");    /* 9 */
        display (2);                                          /* 10 */
}


display (how_often)           /* how_often is a formal parameter. */
int  how_often;                      /* declare parameter as an int. */
{
        int  count;

        for ( count = 1; count <= how_often; count++)         /* 11 */
             printf ( "%d\n", count);                         /* 12 */
}
```

This program produces the following outputs:

```
Hello, world.
I'm going to count for you
1
2
3
4
5

You didn't catch that?
Oh, all right, I'll count again.
1
2
3

You STILL didn't catch that?
I'll do it one more time.
But please pay attention this time.
1
2
```

This program counts and displays the results in a manner similar to the earlier programs. The difference is that the program counts to different values each time **display( )** is called. The flow of control in this program, at least inside function **display( )**, also is somewhat different this time.

The calls to **display( )** now include an argument, the value to which the function is to count and display. The definition of function **display( )** also differs from the functions we've seen so far. Corresponding to the argument, or *actual parameter,* we pass when **display( )** is called, the function definition includes a *formal parameter,* **how ___ many**, in the function heading.

The formal parameter represents a slot through which a function call will pass information into the function. The **how ___ often** within parentheses in the function declarator serves to reserve a slot and to provide a local name for that slot. Having done that, you need to declare the formal parameters (in the example, only one) for use in the function. To do this, you need to supply two things: a name to use for the parameter in the function, and information about the parameter's type.

Formal parameters are declared outside the main function body. The storage and the names for the formal parameters exist only while the function is in memory and running. Once the function has finished and is discarded, its variables and parameter slots also disappear. You may use any valid identifier for the formal parameter. This identifier will be the slot's name within the context of the function.

The following illustration identifies the components of a function declarator. The declarator has three main components: a return type, a function name, and a formal parameter list. Each formal parameter included in the list must also be declared as a variable.

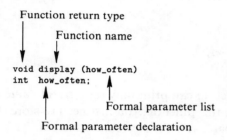

When you call a function with an argument (an *actual* parameter), the program copies the argument value into the storage allocated for the corresponding formal parameter. Thus, the function works with a *copy* of your argument. This means that the function will not change the variables you pass as arguments.

The information flow via the parameter list is one-directional, in what we have seen so far. Because the function only gets a value, rather than an actual variable, such parameter passing is known as *passing by value*. We'll look at bidirectional information passing after we've discussed pointers. In a certain sense, parameters allow functions to use data from the calling function, but protect these data from the function.

To pass information *out* of a function, the function needs to return a value or work with global variables. Using global variables allows the function to bypass parameters and to work directly with variables. The major disadvantage of functions working with global variables is that the function is usable only in programs that include the global variables.

Parameters, on the other hand, set aside generic slots, into which you can pass values from anywhere, provided the values are of the appropriate type. The name you provide in the formal parameter list serves as a name only in the function. The name is not known to the calling function, which means that you can use the same identifier in different contexts. The name you use for the formal parameters need not be the same as the name of any variable in the calling function or in the program. The name and the storage associated with it disappear when the function finishes.

The following example illustrates the difference between using global variables and using parameters.

```
int global_val;

void show_global_val ()
{
        printf ( "%d\n", global_val);
}

void show_any_val ( int val_to_show)
{
        printf ( "%d\n", val_to_show);
}
```

The **show — global — val( )** function can print only the current value of **global — val**. When you want to use this function, you first need to store the value you want to display in **global — val**, then call the function. This is inconvenient at best, and could be a real problem. Suppose the function calling **show — global — val( )** needs to do something with the current value of **global — val** immediately after displaying some other value. To do this you would need to store the current value of **global — val** somewhere, assign the value to be displayed, call **show — global — val( )**, then restore the value you want to use.

With parameters, on the other hand, you can display the contents of **global — val** or any other integer variable, just by calling **show — any — val( )** with the appropriate argument. Because the argument is passed *by value,* the current value of the parameter variable in the calling function will not change. Parameters offer both control and flexibility. We'll use them extensively in the examples in this book.

The function body for **display( )** also contains a local variable definition, for **count**. This definition also associates a type and address with a particular identifier. The storage and name allocated for local variables are known only to the function in which the variable is defined. Both storage and name disappear when the function ends. Local variables cannot directly influence anything outside the function, whereas there are ways of making parameters capable of transferring information back to the calling functions.

For now, think of formal parameters as a way of getting information *into* a function from the calling routine. Think of local variables as a way of storing and manipulating things *within* the function. When the function is called, it is called with one argument for every formal parameter in the function definition. These arguments are known as the *actual parameters* for the function. The calling function, **main( )**, calls **display( )** with an actual parameter of 5. This argument is passed in to tell **display( )** how high to count. The local variable, **count**, serves as the looping variable for the **for** construct.

The flow of control for the first part of the program is: 1-3, 11-12, 11-12, 11-12, 11-12, 11-12, 11, (3a), 4 ... Statements 11 and 12 are each called five times, once for every value from 1 to **how ＿ often**. Notice also that statement 11 is executed one more time than 12. The last time, the continuation condition is false, so the loop (that is, statement 12) is not carried out.

▶**REMEMBER**   In a function definition, the slots through which information will be passed are known as *formal parameters*. In a function call, the items of information passed into the function through these slots are called *arguments*, or *actual parameters*.

Let's look at another example using parameters, to see how to declare such a function when used in another function.

```
/* Program to compute reciprocals of values between -10.0 and 10.0.
   Program illustrates use of parameters.
*/

#define INVALID_VAL -99999.999     /* value to return when result is invalid */


/* Function to return the reciprocal of the argument passed in. */
double reciprocal ( val_to_invert)
double val_to_invert;
{
        if ( val_to_invert != 0.0)
                return ( 1 / val_to_invert);
        else
                return ( INVALID_VAL);
}


main ()
{
#define MAX_COUNT 10
        double   reciprocal ();  /* declare function, so main can use */
        double   count;

        for ( count = -10.0; count <= MAX_COUNT; count++)
                printf ( "%10.2lf: reciprocal == %15.10lf\n",
                        count, reciprocal ( count));
}
```

This program produces the following output:

```
-10.00: reciprocal ==      -0.1000000000
 -9.00: reciprocal ==      -0.1111111111
 -8.00: reciprocal ==      -0.1250000000
 -7.00: reciprocal ==      -0.1428571429
 -6.00: reciprocal ==      -0.1666666667
 -5.00: reciprocal ==      -0.2000000000
 -4.00: reciprocal ==      -0.2500000000
 -3.00: reciprocal ==      -0.3333333333
 -2.00: reciprocal ==      -0.5000000000
 -1.00: reciprocal ==      -1.0000000000
  0.00: reciprocal == -99999.9990000000
  1.00: reciprocal ==       1.0000000000
  2.00: reciprocal ==       0.5000000000
  3.00: reciprocal ==       0.3333333333
  4.00: reciprocal ==       0.2500000000
  5.00: reciprocal ==       0.2000000000
  6.00: reciprocal ==       0.1666666667
  7.00: reciprocal ==       0.1428571429
  8.00: reciprocal ==       0.1250000000
  9.00: reciprocal ==       0.1111111111
 10.00: reciprocal ==       0.1000000000
```

This program displays the reciprocals of values between -10.0 and 10. The **main( )** function calls **reciprocal( )** for this information.

Function **reciprocal( )** has one formal parameter, **val — to — invert**, and returns a value of type **double**. To avoid division by zero, which produces a floating point error, the function checks the actual parameter passed in — that is, the value copied into **val — to — invert**. If this value is 0.0, the function returns a predefined value (INVALID — VAL), which indicates an error.

The definition for this function has the same format as the definition for **display( )** with a parameter. The major difference between the two functions is that **reciprocal( )** returns a value, whereas **display( )** does not.

Notice that the declaration for **reciprocal( )** inside function **main( )** does not provide information about the number and type of parameters that **reciprocal( )** uses. In this declaration format, which we've been using throughout, the compiler just wants to know that you'll be calling a function and what type of value the function is returning; the compiler doesn't require any information about the number and type of parameters function calls should include.

However, because the compiler has minimal information about the function and how it can be used, the compiler can't do any checking for you. For example, the compiler won't tell you whether you've called the function with the wrong number of arguments. If you make such an error, the behavior of the function is undefined. This means you may get incorrect results without ever getting any sort of error message.

The compiler also won't know if you've called the function with the wrong *type* of parameters. Therefore, the compiler will make the substitutions you request, which may cause type incompatibilities when the function being called starts running.

Let's look at one more example, which will also let us see the differences between the prefix and postfix form of the decrement operator.

```
/* Program to illustrate use of function parameters,
   also shows some differences between prefix and postfix forms of the
   operator.
*/

#define MIN_VAL  10

main ()
{
        int  pref, post, index, argument;
        int  leave_alone ();
        int  quadruple (), one_fourth ();  /* for suggested exercise */

        printf ( "Index\tPrefix\tPostfix\n\n");
        for ( index = 20; index >= MIN_VAL; index--)
        {
                argument = index;
                pref = leave_alone ( --argument);
                argument = index;       /* to make sure same value is passed */
                post = leave_alone ( argument--);
                printf ( "%3d\t%4d\t%4d\n", index, pref, post);
        }
}

/* Use this function in conjunction with one_fourth() */
int quadruple ( val)
int val;
{
        return ( 4 * val);
}

/* Use this function in quadruple with one_fourth() */
int one_fourth ( val)
int val;
{
        return ( val % 4);
}

int leave_alone ( val)
int val;
{
        return ( val);
}
```

This program produces the following output:

```
Index   Prefix  Postfix

 20       19      20
 19       18      19
 18       17      18
 17       16      17
 16       15      16
```

```
15        14        15
14        13        14
13        12        13
12        11        12
11        10        11
10         9        10
```

The program writes a series of values and the corresponding value when certain variants on the index are passed to a function that just returns the value it was passed.

Notice that the prefix form of the decrement operator makes its change before the value is passed to the function as an argument. The postfix form makes its change after the value is passed.

This program would compile, but would run incorrectly, if we passed a **double** into **leave_alone( )**. The compiler has no way of knowing that the argument to the function is of the wrong type, because the function declaration did not provide any information about the parameters. Failure to check for such mismatches can cause incorrect results.

▶**CAUTION**   In the current C syntax, function declarations provide no information to the compiler about parameters to the function declared. As a consequence, the compiler is unable to check for function calls with the wrong number or type of arguments.

In the next chapter, you'll find out about a concept designed to provide the compiler with much better checking capabilities in such situations.

Summary

In this chapter we've discussed the fundamental properties and uses of functions. You learned how to return a value from a function, and how to define functions that return such values. You also learned how to use parameters to make functions more flexible. The more flexible a function, the more widely it can be used.

Function libraries are built of functions that perform specific tasks in a variety of contexts. As you program, it's a good idea to design your functions with such uses in mind. As your collection of functions grows, group them in function libraries, to draw on as you need them in other programs. In this chapter, we've created several functions that can be used in your programs: **non＿zero**, **safe＿division( )**, and even **zero＿one＿rand( )**, for some purposes.

In the next chapter we'll look at function prototypes, a concept introduced in the Draft Proposed ANSI Standard. Function prototypes are designed to provide the compiler with the information it needs to do the kinds of checking we mentioned in this chapter.

8

Function
Prototypes

Let's look at the program from the last chapter again. This time, let's see what happens when we pass the functions bad arguments.

```c
/* Program to illustrate consequences of incorrect use of function parameters.
*/

#define MIN_VAL   10


main ()
{
        int    pref, post, index;
        double argument;
        int   leave_alone ();

        printf ( "Index\tPrefix\tPostfix\n\n");
        for ( index = 20; index >= MIN_VAL; index--)
        {
                argument = index;
                pref = leave_alone ( --argument);
                argument = index;
```

```
                    post = leave_alone ( argument--);
                    printf ( "%3d\t%4d\t%4d\n", index, pref, post);
           }

           printf ( "\n\n\nIndex\tPrefix\tPostfix\n\n");
           for ( index = 20; index >= MIN_VAL; index--)
           {
                    argument = index;
                    pref = leave_alone ( --argument, index);
                    argument = index;
                    post = leave_alone ( index, argument--);
                    printf ( "%3d\t%4d\t%4d\n", index, pref, post);
           }
}

int leave_alone ( val)
int val;
{
           return ( val);
}
```

This program produces the following output:

Index	Prefix	Postfix
20	0	0
19	0	0
18	0	0
17	0	0
16	0	0
15	0	0
14	0	0
13	0	0
12	0	0
11	0	0
10	0	0

Index	Prefix	Postfix
20	0	20
19	0	19
18	0	18
17	0	17
16	0	16
15	0	15
14	0	14
13	0	13
12	0	12
11	0	11
10	0	10

In the first part of the program, the call to **leave — alone( )** has the wrong type of argument. The result is clearly incorrect: the compiler has not been told to expect an **int**, so it cannot make any conversions.

In the second part, the call to **leave_alone( )** has the wrong number of arguments. The compiler simply starts processing parameters in its accustomed sequence, and stops as soon as it has the required number of arguments. Because the arguments were passed in different sequences, the results are different.

To avoid such difficulties, the compiler must do a more extensive check of your program's function calls using the Draft Proposed ANSI Standard's *function prototype,* which is essentially a more elaborate function declaration.

The function prototype includes information about the types the function expects as arguments. In a sense, the function prototype provides the same information as the function declarator, except that types rather than identifiers are used to indicate the parameters. For example, the following would be a prototype version of the declaration for **reciprocal( )** within **main( )** in the previous listing:

```
/* function prototype: for use as declaration in main(), in earlier example.
   Note the information regarding parameter type (and number) in declaration.
*/
double   reciprocal ( double);
```

This prototype tells the compiler how many parameters **reciprocal( )** expects, as well as the parameters' type information. If you accidentally call **reciprocal( )** with the wrong number of parameters, the compiler will warn you.

In the preceding program, check what happens when you call the function **reciprocal( )** in **main( )**, with two arguments. Now, modify **main( )** by including a function prototype instead of a simple function declaration for **reciprocal( )**. Then check the result of calling the function with two parameters.

Using a prototype also makes the compiler better at dealing with mismatches between types of the argument and the corresponding formal parameter. For example, if you call **reciprocal( )** with an **int** instead of a **double**, you will get unpredictable results using a simple function declaration. If you use a prototype, however, the compiler will convert the type of your argument to the formal parameter's type, as long as this conversion would be valid in an assignment statement.

Run the following program twice. The first time, run the program as is; the second time, change the function prototype form to a simple declaration of **reciprocal( )**. With the prototype, the compiler knows that the function is expecting a **double**, so it promotes your **int** argument to a double before passing the value to **reciprocal( )**. The second time, you will get garbage, because the compiler does not do the required conversions. (Incidentally, notice the use of the comma operator in the program.)

```
/* Program to compute reciprocals of values between -10.0 and 10.0.
   Program uses an int as looping variable, though parameter is a double.
   Can do this because function was declared using a function prototype.
   Program illustrates advantage of using function prototype.
*/
#define INVALID_VAL -99999.999  /* value to return when result is invalid */


/* Function to return the reciprocal of the argument passed in. */
double reciprocal ( val_to_invert)
double val_to_invert;
{
        if ( val_to_invert != 0.0)
                return ( 1 / val_to_invert);
        else
                return ( INVALID_VAL);
}


main ()
{
#define MAX_COUNT 10
        double  reciprocal (double);
        double  count;
        int test;

        /* Loop to call reciprocal with test, an INT, instead of the
           double expected. Will produce garbage unless reciprocal()
           is declared using a function prototype.
           Note use of comma operator.
        */
        for ( count = -10.0, test = -10; count <= MAX_COUNT; count++, test++)
                printf ( "%10.2lf: reciprocal == %15.10lf\n",
                        count, reciprocal ( test));
}
```

To specify the prototype for a function that takes no parameters, tell the compiler explicitly that a function has no parameters by using the keyword, **void**. For example, the following listing shows the non-prototype and the prototype forms for declaring the parameter-less function, **zero_one_rand( )**, that we used earlier.

```
double zero_one_rand ();        /* NON-prototype form of declaration */
double zero_one_rand (void);    /* Prototype form of declaration */
```

When the compiler sees **void** in this context, it will know that the function you've declared takes no parameters.

The fact that the compiler checks type and number on arguments when you use prototypes should not encourage careless function calls. Rather, you should use prototypes to take advantage of the kind of things compilers are very good at — catching inconsistencies — in order to weed out errors.

The Draft Proposed ANSI Standard is moving the C programming environment toward prototype use. Currently, simple function declarations are used almost exclusively. They are allowed in the Draft Proposed ANSI Standard largely for the sake of existing programs, but are considered obsolescent by most programmers. Simple declarations are expected to disappear from use eventually. In the remainder of this book, we'll use the function prototype form.

Influence of Prototypes on Syntax for Formal Parameters

Prior to discussing function prototypes, we looked at the syntax for defining functions, noting that the function body is preceded by two other components: a function declarator that contains identifiers within parentheses if the function takes formal parameters, and declarations for each of the formal parameters. If the function takes no parameters, the function declarator contains empty parentheses, and the function declaration component is omitted. This "non-prototype" syntax — with separate parameter declarations — is currently used by most C programmers.

However, the Draft Proposed ANSI Standard has declared this syntax only temporarily valid since it will eventually disappear to be replaced by the syntax described in this section. In this new syntax, the function declarator has more similarity to a function prototype.

The intent is to have the following format become the standard way of specifying the formal parameters in the interface between a function and the outside world. The following program illustrates the new syntax, while providing more examples of function prototypes:

```
/* Program to compute ratios of successive pairs of pseudorandom values,
   and to compute a mean_ratio when done.
   Program illustrates use of prototype syntax for specifying formal
   parameters.
*/

#define INVALID_VAL -99999.999  /* value to return when result is invalid */
#define TOLERANCE 1.0e-12
#define TRUE      1
#define FALSE     0


/* Prototype syntax , so no separate parameter declaration. */
int non_zero ( double val)
{
        if ( (( val - 0.0) > TOLERANCE) || ((val - 0.0) < -TOLERANCE))
                return ( TRUE);
        else
                return ( FALSE);
}


double safe_division ( double numer, double denom)
{
        int non_zero ( double);

        if ( non_zero ( denom))
                return ( numer / denom);
        else
                return ( INVALID_VAL);
}


double zero_one_rand ()
{
#define  MAX_VAL 32767.0         /* NOTE: defined as floating point type */
        int  rand (void);        /* returns a pseudorandom integer */
        int  rand_result;

        rand_result = rand ();   /* get a pseudorandom integer */
        return ( rand_result / MAX_VAL);
}


main ()
{
        double safe_division ( double, double);
        double zero_one_rand ( void);

        double val1, val2, ratio, running_sum = 0.0, mean_ratio;
        int    index, how_many;

        printf ( "Compute how many ratios? ");
        scanf ( "%d", &how_many);


        for ( index = 1; index <= how_many; index++)
        {
                val1 = zero_one_rand ();
                val2 = zero_one_rand ();
                ratio = safe_division ( val1, val2);
                running_sum += ratio;
                printf ( "ratio : %10.5lf; running_sum : %10.5lf\n",
                        ratio, running_sum);
        }

        printf ( "after loop, index == %d\n", index);
        mean_ratio = safe_division ( running_sum, --index);
        printf ( "running_sum == %10.5lf; mean ratio == %10.5lf\n",
                running_sum, mean_ratio);
}
```

This program, which was asked to compute ten ratios, produces the following output for a sample run:

```
ratio :      0.00222; running_sum :      0.00222
ratio :      0.23902; running_sum :      0.24124
ratio :      1.21909; running_sum :      1.46033
ratio :      0.39097; running_sum :      1.85130
ratio :      1.10211; running_sum :      2.95341
ratio :      0.20270; running_sum :      3.15611
ratio :      1.38355; running_sum :      4.53966
ratio :     20.28717; running_sum :     24.82683
ratio :      0.25080; running_sum :     25.07762
ratio :      0.88797; running_sum :     25.96559
after loop, index == 11
running_sum ==    25.96559; mean ratio ==       2.59656
```

This program computes ratios of successive pairs of pseudorandom values ranging from 0.0 to 1.0, while keeping a running sum of the ratios as well as of the number of ratios computed. When done, the program computes the mean ratio.

The definitions for **non＿zero( )** and for **zero＿one＿rand( )** illustrate the new form of the function definition syntax termed the *prototype form.* In this form of a function declarator, the identifier and type information for the formal parameters are all included between the parentheses. There are no separate declarations for the formal parameters. Thus, in the prototype form, there are only two components to a function definition: the function declarator and the function body.

▶**REMEMBER**   In the *non-prototype* form, identifiers for formal parameters are included in the function declarator, and the parameters are defined between the function declarator and the function body. In the *prototype* form, parameter identifiers and types are included in the function declarator. There is no separate declaration of the parameters.

Notice that the parameter declarations are separated from each other by commas. Notice also that there are no commas between the type specifier and the identifier. Think of these two pieces of information as belonging together while remaining distinct from the same information for other parameters. Finally, notice that you must list each formal parameter and its type *separately.* Thus, the following function declarator is invalid, and will generate a compiler error:

```
/* INVALID function declarator, because numer and denom are both trying to be
   associated with the same type specifier.
*/
double safe_division ( double numer, denom)
```

The function **zero＿one＿rand( )** takes no parameters. When it was declared in **main( )**, the keyword, **void**, was included to indicate that the declaration was a prototype. To understand why there is no void in the function declarator line for **zero＿one＿rand( )**, we must remember that when the compiler sees a function declarator at the top of a definition (that is, a function declaration without a semicolon at the end), it knows that the function takes as many parameters as are specified between the parentheses. If nothing is specified between the parentheses, the compiler knows that the function takes no parameters; the compiler will not confuse this with an ordinary, non-prototype declaration. That's why you don't need to put **void** here.

In fact, you cannot put **void** between the parentheses for such a function. You will get a compiler error. Essentially, the compiler expects to see either a non-keyword identifier or a type specifier/identifier pair. If it finds just an identifier, the compiler will treat your declarator as being of the non-prototype sort.

▶**REMEMBER**   When using the prototype form of the syntax for specifying formal parameters in the function declarator, a type specifier must be paired with each formal parameter identifier, and multiple type specifier/identifier pairs must be separated by commas. You may not use **void** in a function heading to indicate that the function takes no parameters. You may use **void** to indicate this when declaring the function for use in another function. (You may also use **void** in a function heading to indicate that the function returns to no values.)

Let's look at each of the functions and then work through the program's execution. This will give us a chance to see how the program works and also to raise some additional points about the code. We'll leave the discussion of the **non＿zero( )** function till last, because that function raises additional issues.

The **safe＿division( )** function returns a quotient. The function first calls **non＿zero( )**, to check whether the denominator is too close to zero to allow division. If that is the case, the function returns a predefined error value, INVALID＿VAL.

Keep in mind that the **zero＿one＿rand( )** function returns a pseudorandom value between 0.0 and 1.0.

The **main( )** function does the bulk of the work—calling **zero＿one＿rand( )** and **safe＿division( )** for its values. Notice the statement that assigns a value to **mean＿ratio**. This assignment calls the **safe＿division( )** function. The first argument is a **double**; the second is an **int**. Because we've used a function prototype to declare **safe＿division( )** inside **main( )**, the compiler makes the appropriate type conversion before passing the value of **index** into the function. In addition, the decrement operator (−−) is applied to the value of index *before* it is passed into the function—because we used the prefix form of the operator. The value of **index** must be decreased by one because it is one more than it should be (11 instead of 10).

The other function in the program, **non＿zero( )**, raises some noteworthy issues when using floating point types in programs, especially in loops. The function returns TRUE if the argument that was passed to it differs from zero by more than TOLERANCE. Such a function can be useful when working with floating point types. Because floating point types are subject to rounding and representation inaccuracies, it is often more useful to check whether two values are very close to each other, rather than whether the values are identical—that is, whether their representations have the same bit patterns.

Such a "tolerance" test can be useful if you have a loop where the continuation condition tests strict equality of floating point types. For some values, it's extremely unlikely that you will end up with identical bit patterns in two floating point variables if you compute these values by different means.

Testing whether the variables are equal is, therefore, unlikely to produce an affirmative response. The following program illustrates this. The first **for** loop in the main program uses the **non＿zero( )** function to test for equality. This loop stops after three iterations. The next **for** loop looks for strict equality. This version just keeps going.

Use the QuickC Debugger to watch the value of **test＿val** as the program executes, by setting debug to on in the compiler options before adding **test＿val** as a watch variable. The value is supposedly equal to that of VERY＿TINY at some point, but the loop keeps executing because the zero difference reported was based on the precision you asked for, whereas the actual bit patterns of the two values (that for **test＿val** and the value substituted for VERY＿TINY) are different. Thus, the loop passes the point at which it might have been able to stop, and the program continues until you break out of it.

Notice two things about the way in which **non＿zero( )** is used in the following program.

```
/* Program to compute values until two values are "identical."
   Program illustrates dangers of testing for exact  equality when
   using floating point types, and shows advantages of using a
```

```
        function --- such as non_zero() --- to test for approximate equality.
*/

#define VERY_TINY .00000000027
#define TOLERANCE 1.0e-12
#define TRUE 1
#define FALSE 0

int non_zero ( double val)
{
        if ( (( val - 0.0) > TOLERANCE) || ((val - 0.0) < -TOLERANCE))
                return ( TRUE);
        else
                return ( FALSE);
}

main ()
{
        double test_val;
        double factor = .03;
        int non_zero ( double);

        printf ( "Using non_zero\n");

        for ( test_val = .00001; non_zero ( test_val - VERY_TINY);
                test_val *= factor)
                    printf ( "%20.15lf;  %25.20lf\n",
                             test_val, test_val - VERY_TINY);

        printf ( "Testing for strict equality\n");

        for ( test_val = .00001; test_val != VERY_TINY; test_val *= factor)
                    printf ( "%20.15lf;  %25.20lf\n",
                             test_val, test_val - VERY_TINY);
}
```

First, testing whether the value of **test＿val** VERY＿TINY is non-zero is mathematically equivalent to testing whether the two values differ from each other by less than TOLERANCE. This means you don't need a separate function to test for approximate equality of two arbitrary values.

The second point to notice about the use of the **non＿zero( )** function is its use in the **for** loop's continuation condition. Recall that **non＿zero( )** returns an integer: TRUE if the argument is non-zero, FALSE otherwise. Recall also that the continuation condition is simply a true-false question. As long as the program finds a true value when it tests the result of calling **non＿zero( )**, the loop continues. Once the difference between **text＿val** and VERY＿TINY becomes less than TOLERANCE, the function returns FALSE and the loop stops.

Syntax: Old and New

If you look at existing C programs you will find that the non-prototype syntax is used almost exclusively. It is useful to be familiar with this syntax, because you may very well find yourself reading or revising existing programs.

If you have programmed in C, you are already familiar with this syntax; switching over may be largely a matter of changing your habits. You'll need to decide how quickly, and to what extent, you want to make the switch; I would suggest you at least use prototypes and the corresponding function declarator forms when you work with the programs in this book, to enable you to develop the habit of programming effectively with the new syntax.

Those just learning C should use the prototype syntax right from the start. Compilers that conform to the Draft Proposed ANSI Standard also encourage the use of this syntax, as evidenced by the documentation for QuickC and Microsoft C 5.0.

The prototype form also allows the compiler to do more checking of your program, to catch errors such as incorrect function calls that might otherwise go undetected.

Functions: Miscellaneous Points

If you are used to programming in a language such as Pascal, you may have noticed that we haven't nested any functions inside of others—a practice common among Pascal programmers. There is no nesting of function *definitions* in C. All functions are at the same "level." The most common ways for functions to communicate with each other is by means of

- *Function calls* (possibly with no arguments)
- Parameters, which we've used only to pass information into a function

- Global variables (known and modifiable by the entire program), which allow information to move in or out

- **return** statements, which only allow information to be passed out of the function

Our examples and discussion have been concerned only with **int** and **double** variables, although C functions can also return other types, which will be discussed after we've covered some requisite material.

Summary

In this chapter, we looked at the function prototype, a mechanism provided in the Draft Proposed ANSI Standard. Function prototypes are essentially elaborate function declarations that contain explicit information about number and type of parameters, while specifying a return type or **void**.

By using function prototypes, the compiler is provided with the information it needs to do much more extensive program checking than current compilers provide. The concept of a function prototype is new to C, but it is expected to become the standard style. We'll use the prototype form throughout the rest of this book.

9

Scope, Lifetime, and Storage Class

In this chapter you'll learn about the rules that determine when and how you can use identifiers to refer to particular objects (memory locations) or functions. You'll also learn something about what happens to values stored in a variable when the program moves to a new context, such as a call to a different function.

Scope and Visibility

C recognizes identifiers (such as those for variables, functions, and macros) as valid only in certain parts of a program. Similarly, a memory location may be accessible only in certain functions. The next listing should help raise several key issues as well as provide an introduction to some new terms. Although it's long, the program does little but display a lot of information. Work your way through it, pay attention to the names being used (identifiers) and the values being displayed, along with the *location* of each variable definition. Notice what happens to **int — val** in different parts of the program. Compare this with what happens to **int — val2** in the same program portions.

```
/* Program to print values of several variables at different points in
   the program.
   Program illustrates issues related to scope and visibility.
*/

int int_val = 10;                  /* global definition */
int int_val2;                      /* global definition */


main ()
{
        int  result;               /* local definition */
        int  inner_fn ( void);     /* function declaration */
        void outer_fn ( void);     /* function declaration */

        int_val2 = 20;             /* assignment to global */

        printf ( "in main(), before inner_fn(): int_val == %d\n", int_val);
        printf ( "in main(), before inner_fn(): int_val2 == %d\n", int_val2);

        result = inner_fn ();      /* should see changes in int_val2 */

        printf ( "\in main(), after inner_fn(): result == %d\n", result);
        printf ( "in main(), after inner_fn(): int_val == %d\n", int_val);
        printf ( "in main(), after inner_fn(): int_val2 == %d\n", int_val2);
        outer_fn ();                  /* should see changes in both globals */

        printf ( "\in main(), after outer_fn(): int_val == %d\n", int_val);
        printf ( "in main(), after outer_fn(): int_val2 == %d\n", int_val2);
}


/* show consequences of using same identifier both globally and locally.
   Function name comes from fact that the function uses a local (inner),
   rather than global (outer) object.
*/
int inner_fn ()
{
        int int_val = 5;           /* local definition; hides global name */

        printf ( "\n*** in inner_fn(), (local) int_val == %d\n", int_val);
        printf ( "*** in inner_fn(), before assignment, int_val2 == %d\n",
                int_val2);
        int_val2 = int_val;        /* global gets value of local */
        printf ( "*** in inner_fn(), after assignment, int_val2 == %d\n",
                int_val2);
        return ( int_val);
}
```

```
/* Function name comes from fact that the function uses global (outer),
   rather than local (inner) objects.
*/
void outer_fn ()
{
        printf ( "\n*** in outer_fn(), before assignment, int_val == %d\n",
                int_val);
        printf ( "*** in outer_fn(), before assignment, int_val2 == %d\n",
                int_val2);
        int_val = 30;           /* global variable being changed */
        int_val2 = 60;          /* global variable being changed */
        printf ( "*** in outer_fn(), after assignment, int_val == %d\n",
                int_val);
        printf ( "*** in outer_fn(), after assignment, int_val2 == %d\n",
                int_val2);
}
```

This program produces the following output:

```
in main(), before inner_fn(): int_val == 10
in main(), before inner_fn(): int_val2 == 20

*** in inner_fn(), (local) int_val == 5
*** in inner_fn(), before assignment, int_val2 == 20
*** in inner_fn(), after assignment, int_val2 == 5

in main(), after inner_fn(): result == 5
in main(), after inner_fn(): int_val == 10
in main(), after inner_fn(): int_val2 == 5

*** in outer_fn(), before assignment, int_val == 10
*** in outer_fn(), before assignment, int_val2 == 5
*** in outer_fn(), after assignment, int_val == 30
*** in outer_fn(), after assignment, int_val2 == 60

in main(), after outer_fn(): int_val == 30
in main(), after outer_fn(): int_val2 == 60
```

The program involves four different variables, but only three variable identifiers, because one name (**int — val**) is used for variables in two different places. To distinguish between each use, we need to look at the *scope* and *visibility* of the variables. The *scope* of a variable is the range of contexts in which the variable can be used. The *visibility* of an identifier is the range of contexts over which the identifier is valid and refers to the same object.

Let's look at the variable result first. This local variable is declared in the function body of **main( )**. (Local variables are those defined *within* a function or block, as opposed to the global variables defined *outside* any function.) Within this block, the identifier **result** refers to a particular object, or area of memory. The identifier and its associated area of memory are unknown elsewhere in the program such as within function **inner—fn( )**. Thus, if you tried to use **result** in **inner — fn( )**, you would get an error message about an unidentified variable.

▶**REMEMBER**   The scope of a local variable (that is, one defined within a function or block) is from the declaration point to the end of the function or block.

The variable **int＿val2** has a different scope. This variable is defined globally, that is, outside of any function. Both **main( )** and **inner＿fn( )** can refer to **int＿val2** and can use the value stored in this variable. In fact, both functions change the variable's value.

The scope of a global variable (that is, one defined outside any function) extends from the declaration point to the end of the source file. In this instance, source file refers to both the actual file containing the definition and any files that C reads because of an **#include** preprocessor directive *after* the variable definition.

Now, let's look at the variable **int＿val** defined inside **inner＿fn( )**—a local variable, according to syntax. By our first rule of scope, this variable should be accessible only within function **inner＿fn( )**. This seems to be the case, since the value of 5 for **int＿val** occurs only inside that function.

What about the global **int＿val**—that is, the variable defined at the top of the program? According to our scope rules, this variable should be known throughout the program. A look at **main( )** and **outer＿fn( )** supports this conclusion.

But what happens to the global **int＿val** in **inner＿fn( )**? We just saw that the local **int＿val** rules here. Does this mean the global **int＿val** does not have any scope here? If so, this would violate our second rule.

As it turns out, both **int＿val**s have scope here. However, the two variables differ in *visibility*. The local **int＿val** has greater visibility, meaning that the identifier in **inner＿fnl** is interpreted as referring to the memory location associated with the local variable. Because of this, the local variable's identifier is said to *hide* the outer identifier. This is why the memory location corresponding to the *local* **int＿val**, rather than the location of the global **int＿val**, gets changed in the function.

Let's look at an example in a different context. Suppose your name is Dennis Ritchie. If I were to ask one of your friends, "What language is Dennis Ritchie working on?" they might tell me "English," or "French," or "Latin." Your friends would probably not refer to the Dennis Ritchie who developed C, unless asked explicitly about that Dennis Ritchie.

On the other hand, if I were to ask, "What language is the guy who invented C working on?" they might tell me. "D." Both you and the "guy who invented C" have the same name, and I can get information about both of you.

Both you and the other Dennis Ritchie fall within the scope of my conversation. Locally, among your friends (in your block, so to speak), you have greater visibility, so that when I use the name Dennis Ritchie, people assume I'm asking about you.

Suppose, however, that I were to ask about Dennis Ritchie's new language at AT&T Bell Labs, I would almost certainly get an answer about the Dennis Ritchie who invented C. At AT&T Bell Labs, that Dennis Ritchie has greater visibility than you do. In fact, your scope may not even extend to the labs. Very possibly, people at the labs would not recognize my references to you when I asked about your new language. Thus, at AT&T Bell Labs, the Dennis Ritchie who invented C has greater scope and visibility than you.

In the program example, both **int_val** variables have scope in function **inner_fn( )**, but only the identifier for the local variable has visibility. If you could find a different way of referring to the object associated with the global name **int_val**, you might be able to manipulate its value in function **inner_val( )**.

Parameters and Scope

You've already learned the mechanism for doing this, although we haven't discussed it in these terms. Parameters, as we've seen, provide slots for passing information into a function.

When you specify a formal parameter for a function, the program allocates storage for a value of the specified type, and associates the name you provide with this storage. When you call the function with an actual parameter, the program takes the value you pass (or the value associated with the variable you specify as the argument) and stores this value in the memory allocated for the corresponding formal parameter. Let's look at an example:

```
/* Program to illustrate scope of variables,
   and also to illustrate how to get information from a variable to a
   function by means of parameter values.
*/

int int_val = 10;
int int_val2;

main ()
{
        void  inner_fn ( int);

        int_val2 = 20;
        printf ( "at start of main(), int_val (at %u) == %d\n",
                &int_val, int_val);
```

```
        printf ( "at start of main(), int_val2 (at %u) == %d\n",
                &int_val2, int_val2);

        inner_fn ( int_val);    /* should get changes in int_val2 */

        printf ( "\nin main(), after inner_fn(): int_val (at %u) == %d\n",
                &int_val, int_val);
        printf ( "in main(), after inner_fn(): int_val2 (at %u) == %d\n",
                &int_val2, int_val2);
}

/* change one global and one local variable. */
void inner_fn (int param_val)
{
        int int_val = 5;

        printf ( "\n*** in inner_fn(), param_val (at %u) == %d\n",
                &param_val, param_val);
        printf ( "*** in inner_fn(), int_val (at %u) == %d\n",
                &int_val, int_val);
}
```

This program produces the following output, including address locations for the variables in the program.

```
at start of main(), int_val (at 218) == 10
at start of main(), int_val2 (at 1680) == 20

*** in inner_fn(), param_val (at 4226) == 10
*** in inner_fn(), int_val (at 4220) == 5

in main(), after inner_fn(): int_val (at 218) == 10
in main(), after inner_fn(): int_val2 (at 1680) == 20
```

The program is similar to the preceding one in that it prints the values of several variables to illustrate points about scope and visibility. In addition, the program prints the addresses of the variables involved, to make it easier to see the relationships among value, memory locations, and names.

Notice the value stored in **param_val**, the object associated with the formal parameter of that name. It is the same value as that stored in the global variable, **int_val**. When **inner_fn( )** is called with an actual parameter, the actual parameter is *passed by value.* When **main( )** called **inner_fn( )**, with **int_val** as argument, the program passed the value stored at memory location 218 (in our program run) into the storage area set aside for **param_val** (location 4226, in our run). Because of this call by value, the actual contents of the global **int_val** are not changed in any way by this function call.

We've passed the information contained in **int_val** into the function **inner_fn( )** through the slot created for this purpose. As such, we've taken advantage of the fact that **inner_fn( )** is within the scope of a global variable in order to get information from this variable into the function. Once the value has been passed inside, the function can do what it wants with the value, without the calling routine knowing about it or being affected by it. The same value is now contained in two different objects, as you can see by the addresses of the two objects (218 and 4226, for actual and formal parameters, respectively). Thus, the use of formal parameters is a means of getting around visibility restrictions, at least in one direction.

If you try to use **param_val** in **main( )**, you will get an error message about an undefined variable. This is because the scope of the formal parameter does not extend to other functions.

▶**REMEMBER**   The scope of a formal parameter declaration is from the declaration point to the end of the function's body.

Note also that the global and the local **int_val** identifiers refer to two different memory locations. In the previous program, we saw how visibility influences the use of identifiers when referring to objects. This program provides more information on what is happening, namely, the use of different addresses for different objects having the same name.

Macro names and manifest constant identifiers, both associated with the preprocessor, also have a scope and visibility rule associated with them. These identifiers are active from their declaration point until the end of the source file, or until they are **#undef**d.

▶**REMEMBER**   The scope of a preprocessor identifier (manifest constant or macro name) is from the point of declaration to either the end of the source file or the appearance of an **#undef** instruction for the identifier.

Defining Variables Within Blocks

So far, we've defined variables globally or at the beginning of a function. Recall that the function body is essentially a compound statement, or block. In C, you can actually define a variable at the beginning of any block. The scope of such variables is from their declaration until the end of the block in which they were declared. The following listing illustrates this, and displays the values of the variables at each level of the program:

```
/* Program to illustrate definitions within arbitrary blocks;
   program also illustrates visibility of identifiers.
   Note that each call to printf() is numbered.
   This will make it easier to compare the output with the printf() calls.
*/
int val = 0;                          /* global definition */
int val2 = 0;                         /* global definition */

main ()
{
        int  val = 1;                 /* local to main () */
        void other_fn ( void);

        printf ( "1: val == %d; val2 = %d\n", val, val2);
        other_fn();
        printf ( "6: val == %d; val2 = %d\n", val, val2);
}


void other_fn ()
{
        int  val2 = 2;                /* local to other_fn () */
        void yet_another_fn ( void);

        printf ( "  2: val == %d; val2 = %d\n", val, val2);

        {                             /* arbitrarily defined block */
        int  val = 3;                 /* local to block inside other_fn() */
        printf ( "    3: val == %d; val2 = %d\n", val, val2);
        yet_another_fn ();
        }                             /* end arbitrarily defined block */

        printf ( "  5: val == %d; val2 = %d\n", val, val2);
}                                     /* END of other_fn() */


void yet_another_fn ()
{
        printf ( "      4: val == %d; val2 = %d\n", val, val2);
}
```

This program produces the following output:

```
1: val == 1; val2 = 0
  2: val == 0; val2 = 2
    3: val == 3; val2 = 2
      4: val == 0; val2 = 0
  5: val == 0; val2 = 2
6: val == 1; val2 = 0
```

This program simply displays the values stored in the variables **val** and **val2**. The different values are due to the scope and visibility rules that apply when **printf( )** is called. The indentation in the program indicates the "depth" of the call, while the number at the start of each line indicates the source code line.

There are two cases to look at: what happens with identifiers *within* functions, and what happens with identifiers *across* functions. Let's look at the situation in **other_fn( )** first.

This function includes a local variable, **val2**, whose scope is from the definition to the end of the function. Any reference to **val2** inside **other_fn( )** is a reference to the storage allocated for the local variable. This is why calls 2, 3, and 5 to **printf( )** all have the same value for **val2**. Notice the reference to this variable in call 3 to **printf( )**. This call is just an ordinary statement inside the function, as far as references to **val2** are concerned.

The situation is somewhat different for references to **val**. An arbitrarily defined block inside function **other_fn( )** includes a local definition of **val**. The scope of this variable extends from its definition to the end of the block—right after call 3 to **printf( )**. The three calls to **printf( )** in function **other_fn( )** behave differently, because the identifier **val** has two different visibilities in this function.

An identifier, such as **val**, applies within a function, unless a new variable with the same name is defined, in which case the original variable would be hidden by the new one. Thus, in **other_fn( )**, the global **val** has both scope and visibility in calls 2 and 5—that is, before and after the arbitrarily defined block. Within the block, however, the greater visibility of the local **val** hides the global name.

Notice that call 4 (in **yet_another_fn( )**) uses the global values for both **val** and **val2**. There are no local variables defined in **yet_another_fn( )**. Therefore, when this function is called, it looks for any global objects that might correspond to identifiers used in the function. Even when called by **other_fn( )**, **yet_another_fn( )** does not use the calling function's objects, because the scope of those objects does not extend into other functions. Only global variables can be used directly across functions, although we have seen that passing parameters by value provides a mechanism for using the values of local variables across functions.

Using Debug

A big advantage of QuickC's environment is that you can do many different things with your program file. You can use QuickC's debugging facility to step through the preceding program slowly, in order to study the source code as the program produces its output. QuickC's debugger allows you to look at more than just your selected watch variables. You can, in addition, use this capability to distinguish the different versions of **val** and **val2** — by looking at the values stored immediately after the watch variables. This should work since it's unlikely that two different variables will be followed by the same values. To do this,

1. Call QuickC with the program file.

2. Type CTRL-D, then C, to clear any breakpoints you might have set in the program.

3. Type CTRL-D, then L, to clear any watch variables you might have specified in the program.

4. Type CTRL-R, then C, to get the compiler options.

5. Select the Debug option, if you haven't already done so. Then press RETURN to compile the program with the debugging option on.

6. Type CTRL-D, then RETURN, to add a watch variable. Enter **val,d2d** as the variable to watch. This says to display the value of **val** in decimal format, and also to display the contents of the four bytes following **val**, as **int** values.

7. Type CTRL-D, then RETURN, to add another watch variable. Enter **val2,d2d** as the second variable to watch.

8. Use the CTRL-D, B sequence to set breakpoints at each of the calls to **printf( )**. The cursor must be on the line where you want to set the breakpoint when you select this compiler option. You will set six such breakpoints in all.

9. Type CTRL-R, then RETURN, to start the program.

10. Use the F5 key to move to the next breakpoint when you're ready. Study the changes to **val** and **val2** in relation to the breakpoint's location in the program.

On a sample run, this produced the information in the following illustration, which shows the values of **val** and **val2** as well as the values stored in the four bytes following each of these variables.

printf( )

call	val	next1	next2	val2	next1	next2
1	1	0	1067	0	14897	30240
2	0	0	14897	2	5388	50
3	3	2	5388	0	14897	30240
4	0	0	14897	0	14897	30240
5	0	0	14897	2	5388	50
6	1	0	1067	0	14897	30240

By finding the variables that seem to be at the same memory location (because each is followed by the same two numbers), you can determine the scope of each variable for the six function calls. By connecting the same variables you can get information about their scope and visibility. These groupings should match those in our discussion of the actual program.

Duration of Variables

Scope and visibility determine the rules for accessing and referring to variables. These rules say nothing explicit about what happens to variables when the program is outside their scope. For example, does a local variable retain its value when another function is executing—that is, when the program is outside the variable's scope? Questions such as this relate to the variable's *storage duration,* or *lifetime.* Essentially, the lifetime of a variable determines how long the value stored in the variable endures. C provides two storage durations: automatic and static.

When you define a local variable or a formal parameter for a function, the program allocates space for the variable while the function executes. When the function finishes executing, the program gives back the memory used, including the storage for the local variables and parameters. This storage space can be reused by other parts of the program. Note that anything stored in the memory locations allocated for the function disappears automatically when the memory is used for other purposes. If a variable has *automatic* storage duration, the variable's value disappears at the end of the block within which the variable was defined.

▶**REMEMBER**   Local variables have automatic storage duration, unless you specify otherwise. Formal parameters always have automatic storage duration.

For variables with automatic storage duration, a new area of memory is allocated each time the variable is defined (when the function is called, for example), and this object is discarded after the block ends in any way, whether normally or after a **break** or **return**, for example.

Variables with *static* storage duration are defined and initialized once (essentially, when the program begins executing), and such variables retain their values (unless changed explicitly) while the program is executing. Global variables have static storage duration. Functions (but not necessarily their variables) are also said to have static duration storage, since the information needed to execute a function is always available in a program.

▶**REMEMBER**   Global variables and functions have static storage duration.

Don't confuse storage duration and scope. Scope determines when you can refer to a variable; scope says nothing about whether there is anything stored in the object. Duration determines how long a value will be stored; duration says nothing about whether the variable can be called at a particular point in the program. If a variable has a static lifetime, then, at any point in the program, the memory location allocated for the variable will contain the last value assigned to the variable. You will only be able to access this information if the variable's scope extends to the program portion where you want to access it.

In the following listing, try to determine the identifiers with automatic storage duration and those with static duration.

```
/* Program in which to count the number of local and global identifiers. */
int g1, g2, g3;
main ()
{
        int g1, g2, g3, g4;
        printf ( "hello\n");
}
another ( int p1, int p2)      /* Prototype form of declarator. */
{
        int g1, g2;
        printf ( "another hello\n");
}
```

You should have come up with five identifiers (**g1**, **g2**, **g3**, **main**, and **another**) with static storage duration, and seven (including **p1** and **p2**) with automatic storage duration. The three global **int** variables have the static duration. Remember, functions have static duration and parameters have automatic duration. The fact that the same identifers (for example, **g1**) are used in several places doesn't have any influence on the storage duration. Using the same identifier will only affect the visibility of the identifier.

Storage Class

The lifetime of a variable specifies how long the variable's value will be around. Ordinarily, the values for local variables will simply disappear after the function is done. Sometimes, however, it can be useful to keep a value around for use the next time the function is called. In terms of our discussion so far, such a variable has a somewhat ambiguous status. On the one hand, you want the identifier's scope to be local, which implies an automatic storage duration. On the other hand, you want the variable to retain its value for use the next time around. Thus, you want a local variable with static storage duration.

Another situation that may arise is when a particular variable is used very often (in a loop, for example). If the variable is stored in ordinary memory, it can be time consuming for the program to access the variable each time. C provides a means of suggesting that frequently used variables be put in special registers, for faster access.

C's *storage class specifiers* gives you influence over how and where a variable is to be stored when the program is executing. In this section, we'll look at the storage class specifiers available in C, and you'll learn about some of their properties.

static

The **static** storage class specifier makes it possible to define a local variable whose value continues to exist after the function has finished—so that the most recent value of the variable can be reused the next time the function is called. The following listing shows the syntax for such a specifier:

```
/* Program to count by 2 from 2 to 40.
   Program illustrates use of static storage class specifier to keep
```

```
    a value around even while the function is not active.
*/

/* this function does the actual counting. */
void count_by_two ()
{
        /* NOTE: The static variable i1 is automatically initialized to 0 */
        static int i1;          /* keep this value around, use next time */
                                                            /* line 0 */
        /* get next value when counting by 2 */
        i1 += 2;                                            /* line 1 */
        if ( i1 % 10 == 0)      /* to format output, 5 values per line */
                printf ( "%5d\n", i1);                      /* line 2 */
        else
                printf ( "%5d", i1);                        /* line 3 */
}

main ()
{
#define MAX_COUNT   20
        int   count;
        void count_by_two ( void);

        /* each call to count_by_two() gets the next even number */
        for ( count = 1; count <= MAX_COUNT; count++)
                count_by_two ();                            /* line 4 */
}
```

This program produces the following output:

```
 2    4    6    8   10
12   14   16   18   20
22   24   26   28   30
32   34   36   38   40
```

This program prints the even numbers from 2 through 40, five numbers per line. The main program loop is in **main( )**, but the value being written is local to **count _ by _ two( )**.

The following illustration shows the state of the various program variables during the first few iterations through the loop in **main( )**.

After line	count	i1	if statement
4	1	(0)	(???)
0	(1)	0	true
1	(1)	2	false
3	(1)	2	false
4	2	(2)	(???)
0	(2)	2	false
1	(2)	4	false
3	(2)	4	false
4	3	(4)	(???)
0	(3)	4	false
1	(3)	6	false
3	(3)	6	false

After line	count	i1	if statement
4	4	(6)	(???)
0	(4)	6	false
1	(4)	8	false
3	(4)	8	false
4	5	(8)	(???)
0	(5)	8	false
1	(5)	10	true
2	(5)	10	true
4	6	(10)	(???)
0	(6)	10	true
1	(6)	12	false
3	(6)	12	false

Parentheses indicate that the variable is out of scope in that line. Question marks indicate that a variable is undefined. Notice that **i1** is out of scope at times, but is never undefined — because it has static lifetime. At line 0, when the program enters **count — by — two( )**, **i1** has the same value as the last one written. **i1** is *not* reinitialized to 0, each time **count — by — two( )** executes.

Notice also that **count** retains its value while **count — by — two( )** is executing. This is not because **count** is a static variable, but because the environment for **main( )** is still in existence while **count — by — two( )** executes, since **main( )** called **count — by — two( )**.

Finally, notice that line 2 executes only when **i1** == 10 in the illustration. That is the only value of **i1** for which the **if** condition evaluates to true.

Although the variable **i1** is local to **count — by — two( )**, the variable's current value remains after the function is done. Thus, the variable has static lifetime, but local scope. The static lifetime means that each time it is called, function **count — by — two( )** can pick up where it left off. The local scope of variable **i1** means you could define an **int** called **i1** in **main( )**, without affecting **count — by — two( )**. The storage class specifier, **static**, at the start of the definition of **i1**, gives the variable these properties.

Notice that the program works, even though there is no statement to initialize **i1**. This is because **static** variables are initialized automatically, according to the Draft Proposed ANSI Standard. Such variables are initialized to 0 by default, unless you initialize them to a different value.

▶**REMEMBER**   C automatically initializes variables with **static** storage class to 0.

Local scope and static lifetime are the characteristics of a *local* variable with storage class **static**. You can also use the **static** storage class specifier with global variables. *Global* variables already have static lifetime and global scope, so why would you want to use the **static** specifier? To answer this question let's first consider the ways in which you can incorporate variables and functions into your C programs.

First, you can put an **#include** preprocessor instruction into the program source file and have the compiler read the contents of the file to be included during the compilation process. The other way is to link a precompiled file with your compiled program file, in the process of creating your executable file. You might do this by linking in a function library that you have developed or acquired elsewhere (without source).

When the compiler reads an included file, it makes any functions and needed global variables in that file available throughout the rest of the program. Because you are working with source files, you can easily check whether a global identifier you want to use is also used in the included file — to avoid a duplicate definition error.

When you link a precompiled file into your compiled file, you also make any functions and global variables in the linked file available to the program. In this case, however, you may not be able to check what identifiers are used in the linked file. Since you don't have the source, if your program and the linked file each use the same name for a global variable, you will get a linker error.

To avoid this problem, you must use the **static** storage class specifier with the global variables in the linked file. By defining these variables as having a **static** storage class, you make them inaccessible to the linker. This means the variables become "local" to the linked file. Whenever functions from the linked file are called, they use the values specified in their file for these variables; whenever your functions are called, they use the values specified for your global variables.

For example, suppose I have two files, **utils.c** and **prog.c**. The main program and the functions unique to a particular program are in **prog.c**. The file **utils.c** contains general utility functions that may be used by various programs.

Suppose I have the following definition at the top of **utils.c**:

```
int test_count = 300;
```

Similarly, suppose I have the following definition at the top of **prog.c**:

```
int test_count = 10;
```

If the compiler reads the contents of **utils.c** while compiling **prog.c**, the duplicate definition causes a compiler error — regardless of whether either definition was specified as having **static** storage class.

If I compile **utils.c** to an object file, and then try to link this with the **prog.obj** object file to create an executable file, the linker will report the redefinition as an error. On the other hand, if I give the definition of **test_count** in **utils.c** **static** storage, and then create a **utils.obj** object file, the linker will not report an error.

You can also use the **static** storage class specifier to modify a function declarator. By specifying that a function definition has **static** storage class, you are making the function inaccessible to the linker. This means your programs cannot use the function directly, but functions in the file containing the function definition can use it. This capability is very useful for making libraries more modular in a process often referred to as information hiding. Your program is aware only of the library routine it needs to access, rather than of each of the smaller functions the library routine uses to perform the task. In this way, you can concentrate on *what* the library routine does, rather than on *how* it does it.

auto storage class

Just as the **static** specifier allowed you to make the lifetime of a local variable static, the **auto** storage class specifier lets you make it automatic. This specifier can only be used in definitions at the top of a block. Thus, you can't specify a global variable with **auto** storage.

If you don't include a storage class specifier for a local variable, the compiler assumes **auto** storage by default. For this reason, you will rarely see the **auto** specifier used explicitly. You might use this specifier when you are deliberately using the same identifier as a global variable, and want to call attention to this fact.

▶**REMEMBER**   In the absence of a storage class specifier for a local variable, the compiler gives the variable *automatic* storage. Variables with **auto** storage class are *not* initialized automatically.

register storage class

The **register** storage class specifier also specifies an automatic storage duration; in addition, this specifier suggests to the compiler that the variable be stored in machine registers for faster access.

Generally, only integer type variables, such as **char** and **int**, can be given register storage. The number of registers and the types that can be given any available register storage will depend on your implementation. QuickC and Microsoft C 5.0 will give a variable register storage, if there is a register available and if the variable is of the appropriate type, **int**.

The **register** storage class is only a request, not a command. If the compiler is unable to comply with the register storage request, the variable becomes an **auto**. Register variables are not initialized automatically. Because there is no way of knowing whether the compiler can give the variable register storage, you cannot use the address operator (**&**) with variables you want stored in registers.

▶**REMEMBER**   You may not use the address operator (**&**) with register variables.

The following listing illustrates the syntax for the **register** storage class:

```
/* Program to test relative speed of functions defined with
   or without the register storage class specifier.
   Program illustrates syntax for register storage class specifier.
*/

main ()
{
        void count1 ( void), count2 ( void);   /* prototype declaration */

        count1 ();
        count2 ();
}

void count1 ()                                  /* No register variables. */
{
        int r_sum = 0;
        int index = 1;

        while ( index++ <= 20000)
                r_sum += 1;
}

void count2 ()                          /* Uses register values. */
{
        register int r_sum = 0;         /* ask for fast-access storage */
        register int index = 1;         /* ask for fast-access storage */

        while ( index++ <= 20000)
                r_sum += 1;
}
```

The two functions perform the same task, but one of them uses register variables. When these two functions were timed, **count2( )** took between one third and two thirds as long as **count1( )** to perform the same task. The differences were due to the faster access to values stored in register variables.

You can also suggest formal parameters for register storage. To do this, simply put the keyword **register** before the type specifier in the function declarator. The following function declarator illustrates the use of **register** storage class specifier with formal parameters:

```
double timing ( register double val, register int how_many)
```

This declarator asks the compiler to store both formal parameters in registers. As with other local variables, the compiler may or may not comply with your request.

extern storage class

When you define a global variable, its storage class is **extern**. This means the identifier and its associated object are accessible to any functions after the declaration, in the same file or in any files read because of an **#include** instruction. Global variables have static storage duration. Such variables are also accessible to the linker, unless you hide them by using the **static** storage class specifier.

You may want to use a global variable — defined in one file — in a function defined in another. If the second file is read after the file in which the global variable is defined, there is no problem. If, however, you want to use a variable before it has been defined, you need to warn the compiler that a global definition will be available somewhere else. If the variable has not been defined, and you have not declared it, the compiler will complain about an undefined variable.

To avoid such an error, use the **extern** storage class specifier. The following listing illustrates this. (Note that this example is not a good one to follow for your own programs. It's generally a bad idea to define your global variables somewhere in the interior of a file. You're much better off, in most cases, just putting the variable definitions before the variable is used.)

```
/* Program to illustrate use of extern storage class specifier to
   "predeclare" a variable. After it sees the extern ... declaration, the
   compiler knows that a definition of the variable will be forthcoming.
   Program sequence is used merely to illustrate the consequences of
   not declaring an external variable that hasn't been define.
   It is generally bad programming practice to put global definitions in
```

```
     the middle or at the end of a source file.
*/

main ()
{
        extern int val;       /* extern needed because val not yet defined */

        printf ( "%d\n", val);
}

int val = 12;                 /* global definition of val */
```

In this program, the variable **val** is declared at the end of the source file, but is used earlier, by the function **main( )**. The first statement in **main( )** is a *variable declaration, not a definition*. The compiler does not allocate any storage for **val** when the compiler sees this line. Rather, the compiler warned that somewhere else there is a *definition* that allocates storage for an **int** variable named **val**.

If **main( )** had consisted only of the **printf( )** statement, with no declarations, the compiler would have generated an undefined variable error. On the other hand, if the keyword, **extern**, were not included in the declaration, the compiler would have treated the line as a local variable definition, and **val** would have been uninitialized.

It is sometimes a good idea to declare global variables at the top of functions that use the variables. The **extern** storage class specifier makes this possible. The explicit declaration is a safeguard, rather than a necessity, if the function falls within the scope of the global variable. The declaration indicates that a global variable is being used and is, therefore, a form of documentation for your code.

Use the **extern** storage specifier if you are using include files that share global variables. Many programmers *define* the global variables at the top of the main source file, and then *declare* the variables at the top of each included file — using the **extern** storage class specifier in each of these declarations. The **extern** specifier prevents the compiler from allocating a second set of storage locations for the variables, and also avoids a duplicate definition error. By declaring the global variables in this way, you again provide a certain amount of documentation by making explicit the fact that your code uses variables defined elsewhere.

Default Storage Classes
and Storage Durations

If you don't specify a storage class for an identifier, the compiler makes default decisions depending on where the variable is defined. There is a general correspondence between storage class and default storage duration. Certain storage classes are also restricted in the scope they can have.

Local variables and formal parameters are, by default, assumed to have storage class **auto**, and automatic storage duration. You can give local variables (but not formal parameters) static storage duration by using the **static** storage class specifier. Global variables and all functions are assumed to have storage class **extern** and static storage duration. Functions cannot have an automatic storage.

Variables with **register** or **auto** storage classes always have automatic lifetimes. Such variables are always local to a function or to a block within a function. Variables with **static** and **extern** storage classes have static storage durations. Variables with **extern** storage class are always global. Variables with **static** storage class may be global or local.

Table 9.1 summarizes the relationships among storage class, lifetime, and scope of a variable.

Table 9-1.   Storage Class, Lifetime, and Scope of a Variable

Storage Class	Lifetime	Scope
register	Automatic	Local
auto	Automatic	Local
static	Static	Local or Global
extern	Static	Global

The typedef Storage Class

The **typedef** specifier differs from the other storage class specifiers in that it does not explicitly specify a storage class. Instead it is grouped with the storage class specifiers largely for syntactic convenience, according to the Draft Proposed ANSI Standard.

Also the **typedef** specifier does not actually define a new information type, as its name might suggest. No storage is allocated when you create a **typedef**. Rather, the specifier lets you provide a synonym for an existing type identifier. This can be useful when you're writing programs for specific applications, where specific vocabulary may make things clearer. The following examples illustrate the use of the **typedef** specifier:

```
/* Examples of typedef specifications.
   In no case is a completely new type actually defined.
*/

typedef double distance;          /* make distance synonymous with double */
typedef double profit;            /* make z_score synonymous with double */
typedef int    whole_nr, integer; /* make these synonymous with int */
```

To create a synonym for an existing type, you need to preface the definition with the keyword **typedef**, then the type you want your new type to represent (for example, **double**), and finally the new type identifier (for example, **progit**). Note that the **typedef** simply associates a type identifier with an existing type. You can use **typedef** to create either global or local types.

The first of these **typedef** specifications defines **distance** as a synonym for **double**. Once you've specified the new type identifier, you may use it in variable definitions such as the following:

```
/* Example variable definitions,
   once new type identifier has been specified.
*/

distance nr_miles, nr_kilometers;  /* declare 2 variables of type distance */
static distance miles_so_far;      /* static variable of type distance */
distance km_per_tank ();           /* function returning distance */
```

The compiler will allocate storage when it sees these definitions. The amount of storage allocated will be the same amount as would be allocated for a variable of the underlying or base type.

Notice that once you have defined a new type identifier, you can use the other storage class specifiers in conjunction with your new type identifier, as in the example declaring a **static distance**, **miles — so — far**. You can even define or declare functions that return a value of the specified type, as in the function declaration, **km — per — tank**, given above.

Thus, the **typedef** specifier allows you to specify new names for existing data types. These names can help make programs easier to understand, by making the program's language fit the content area, rather than imposing the C language's vocabulary on your content.

Although our **typedef** examples so far have involved simple types, you can use **typedef** to create synonyms for more complex types as well, including arrays (groups consisting of elements that are logically related) and other structures. In fact, some of the types that we'll be using later, such as the **FILE** type, are actually names for more abstract types.

Summary

In this chapter, you learned about the concepts related to the use and status of C variables and functions. In particular, you found that scope and visibility rules concern the range of program contexts over which an object or an identifier has meaning. You also learned about the concept of storage duration, which determines the lifetime of a variable value in a program. Finally, you looked at the storage class specifiers C provides, allowing you to influence the lifetime and scope of variables and functions. One of these, the **typedef** specifier, permits you to create identifiers that are synonymous with existing types.

In the next chapter, you'll move into the use of pointers, which are, in many ways, the real core of the C language.

10
Pointers

So far, we've referred to variables directly by name. We've used the variable's identifier to refer to information stored at a particular memory location — the location associated with that variable name. The *location* and the *value* of a variable are *not* the same, as shown in the following program:

```
/* Program to display values and addresses of variables. */

main ()
{
        int    i1 = 100, i2 = 101;
        double d1 = 100.0, d2 = 101.0;
        float  f1 = 100.0, f2 = 101.0;

        printf ( "Name\t      Value\t\tAddress\n\n");

        /* display information about int variables */
        printf ( "i1\t%10d\t\t%7u\n", i1, &i1);
        printf ( "i2\t%10d\t\t%7u\n\n\n", i2, &i2);

        /* display information about float variables */
        printf ( "f1\t%10.5lf\t\t%7u\n", f1, &f1);
        printf ( "f2\t%10.5f\t\t%7u\n\n\n", f2, &f2);

        /* display information about double variables */
        printf ( "d1\t%10.5lf\t\t%7u\n", d1, &d1);
        printf ( "d2\t%10.5lf\t\t%7u\n\n\n", d2, &d2);
}
```

When compiled and run, this program produces the following output on one system:

```
Name        Value           Address

i1          100             4792
i2          101             4790


f1          100.00000       4798
f2          101.00000       4794


d1          100.00000       4810
d2          101.00000       4802
```

This program displays the values of several variables and the addresses associated with the variables. The addresses are the areas of memory that C allocates for the variables while the program is running. (The actual addresses allocated will depend on a number of factors, so you should not place too much weight on the numerical values of addresses.)

Let's look more closely at this program and how it works. To get the *value* of **i1**, we simply passed the variable name as an argument to **printf( )**. In such a context, the variable name, **i1**, is a direct reference to the value stored at the memory location corresponding to **i1**. Think of the variable name as "returning" the current value of the variable.

To get the *address* of the same variable, we passed the variable name in conjunction with the address operator, **&**. This operator returns the address associated with its operand. Thus, as arguments to a function such as **printf( )**, **i1** returns "the value stored in **i1**," whereas **&i1** returns "the address of **i1**."

Objects, Lvalues, Values

Before we discuss the consequences of distinguishing between a variable's value and its memory location, we need to clarify some concepts. In the last chapter, you read about variables as objects. An *object* is just a storage region, whose contents can represent values. Sometimes the object's location is of interest (such as a variable on the left side of an assignment statement); at other times, the contents at the location are desired (such as a variable in an expression on the right side of an assignment statement).

In this section, we'll look at the difference between these two aspects of an object. Let's look at an example where we have statements that use both the location and contents of objects.

```
/* Program to provide examples for discussing difference between a
   variable location and its value.
*/

main ()
{
        unsigned int  i1 = 500, i2 = 300;

        i1 = 100;                                   /* 1 */
        i2 = i1;                                    /* 2 */
        printf ( "i1 = %5u; i2 = %5u\n", i1, i2);   /* 3 */
        i2 = i1 + 2;                                /* 4 */
        i1++;                                       /* 5 */
        printf ( "i1 = %5u; i2 = %5u\n", i1, i2);   /* 6 */
}
```

In the first assignment statement, 1, we are assigning the value 100 to the **int** variable, **i1**. In this instance, we want the location of **i1**, not its value. It doesn't make sense to say that, "500 is assigned the value 100." It does, however, make sense to say, "The value 100 is assigned to (the location of) variable **il**."

Let's look at statement 2, which has two variables. Again, at least **i2** must be interpreted as referring to the variable's location, rather than to the value stored in the variable. In this case, it's meaningless to say, "300 is assigned the value 100."

It makes more sense to say, "The value 100 is assigned to (the location of) variable **i2**," just as in our earlier example. Notice that C treats **i1** as a value. But this means we're treating **i1** and **i2** differently in this statement.

The difference between the two variables in statement 2 is due to the way in which the assignment operator does its work. Essentially, this operator carries out the following actions:

1. Determines the value of the right operand (the right side of the assignment statement). This may be an expression, including a variable.

2. Goes to the location of the left operand (because something is going to be assigned to that location).

3. Stores the value of the right operand in the location of the left operand.

The left operand in statements 2 and 3 must be a location, because of the assignment operator. The right operand, on the other hand, must be a value, since that's what the assignment operator needs to put into the left operand.

Variables whose *locations* are needed, in order to do something at those locations, are known as **lvalues**. Historically, the "l" referred to "left," because **lvalues** often appear on the left side of assignment statements. By the same line of reasoning, the right operand of the assignment statement — whose value, rather than location, was of interest — is sometimes called an **rvalue**. The Draft Proposed ANSI Standard suggests "locator value," instead of "left value" as an elaboration of "**lvalue**." In the proposal, the right operand of an assignment statement is just referred to as the "value of the expression."

Statement 4 is similar to statement 2, except for the constant being added to the value of **i1** before assigning the sum to **i2**.

What about statement 5? There isn't really a left and right operand here because the increment operator only takes one argument. The **i1** in the expression is still an **lvalue**, however, because the operator eventually changes the contents of some location (the location of **i1**). This may be clearer if you think of the increment operator as equivalent to the following assignment

```
i1 = i1 + 1;
```

being made at the proper time (depending on whether the operator is prefix or postfix). In this form, the need for an **lvalue** is clear.

The address operator also needs an **lvalue** as its operand. When the address operator is applied, it essentially does the following:

1. Goes to the "home" of its operand

2. Determines the address of this home

3. Returns this information

While it makes sense to ask about the address of a variable's location, asking for the address of, for example, 100, is meaningless.

Thus, there are three places where **lvalues** are required: left operand to the assignment operator, operand to the increment and decrement operators, and operand to the address operator.

▶**REMEMBER**   An **lvalue** refers to a "locator value." This means that the location of the object, rather than its value, is of interest. The simple and compound assignment operators require an **lvalue** as the left operand. The increment and decrement operators, and the address operator, also require **lvalues** as their operands.

Pointers

A *pointer* is a variable whose value is an address. There, a pointer is a variable that refers indirectly, or points, to another variable. The pointer's "target variable" is the variable at the address stored in the pointer. Let's look at an example. The following listing introduces some notation and syntax, and the diagram after it shows conceptually what the relationship is among pointer and target variables, and the values stored in each.

```
/* Program to illustrate pointers, target variables, and contents of each */

main ()
{
        int target;     /* variable of type int */
        int *ptr;       /* pointer to variable of type int */

        target = 23;            /* store arbitrary value in target */
        ptr = &target;          /* store address of target in ptr. */
        printf ( "address of target = %u; contents of target = %d\n",
                &target, target);
        printf ( "address of ptr = %u; contents of ptr = %u\n",
                &ptr, ptr);
        printf ( "contents of variable to which pointer is pointing = %d\n",
                *ptr);
}
```

This program produces an output similar to the following depending on the system on which the program is run:

```
address of target = 4094; contents of target = 23
address of ptr = 4096; contents of ptr = 4094
contents of variable to which ptr is pointing = 23
```

Before we discuss the notation and syntax, let's summarize the program's actions, and then look at a diagram of what's going on. The program involves two assignments and three calls to **printf( )**. The first assignment, **target = 23**, is just like the other assignments we've seen. On the surface, the second assignment, **ptr** = **&target**, also looks equivalent. The mechanics of the assignment do, in fact, work like the other assignments we've seen. The result is that the *address* corresponding to **target** is stored in **ptr**. There are important differences, however, as we'll see.

The following diagram shows the state of memory after each assignment, and then matches the arguments to the **printf( )** calls with the appropriate component in memory.

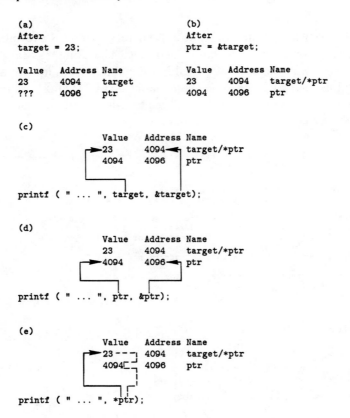

```
(a)                              (b)
After                            After
target = 23;                     ptr = &target;

Value   Address  Name            Value   Address  Name
23      4094     target          23      4094     target/*ptr
???     4096     ptr             4094     4096     ptr


(c)
                Value   Address  Name
              ->23      4094<-  target/*ptr
                4094     4096   ptr

printf ( " ... ", target, &target);


(d)
                Value   Address  Name
                23      4094     target/*ptr
              ->4094    4096<-  ptr

printf ( " ... ", ptr, &ptr);


(e)
                Value   Address  Name
              ->23 ---  4094     target/*ptr
                4094    4096     ptr

printf ( " ... ", *ptr);
```

Parts (a) and (b) simply fill memory according to the assignments. This is straightforward. In parts (c) through (e), the task is to display some numerical information. Parts (c) and (d) are similar, in that one argument refers to a value stored in a particular variable, and the other argument (involving &) refers to the address associated with that variable.

Part (e) is different, however. As you'll notice from the output, the value that is written is 23; this is also the value of **target**. The call to **printf( )** says, essentially, "Write the message, then write the contents of the variable pointed to by **ptr**." Think of the evaluation process for this display as going through steps such as the following:

1. Get to the location of **ptr** (4096, in our case).

2. Determine the contents of this variable (4094, in our case), and interpret those contents as an address.

3. Get to the location specified by this address — that is, to the variable to which **ptr** is pointing.

4. Determine the contents of this variable (23, in our case), and write them.

In the preceding diagram, notice that **target** has two names after assigning the address of **target** to **ptr**. Until now, all the references to variables that we wanted to display have been *direct* references, in which the variable was referred to by name. The variable represented as **∗ptr** is an *indirect* reference to a particular value. **∗ptr** is "the value referred to, or pointed to, by **ptr**." Because it's awkward to speak of "the value pointed to by the pointer" all the time, we'll use "the pointer's target value" to refer to such values.

You can think of a pointer as an address. When you think of **ptr** as an address, **∗ptr** refers to the value associated with that address, or to the contents stored at the specific memory location.

The **∗** in **∗ptr** is C's *indirection operator*. This operator takes a single operand, which must be a pointer, that is, an address. The indirection operator returns a value, namely, the value stored at the address referred to by the pointer. In the call to **printf( )**, the address referred to by the pointer is 4094, and the value stored there (23) is displayed.

The indirection operator is a unary operator. As such, it has very high precedence, the same level as the other unary operators we've seen so far (including the address operator).

Before we look at another example, let's look more carefully at the syntax in the previous listing. The definition of the pointer variable occurs in the statement:

```
int *ptr;
```

This statement defines the variable **ptr** as a *pointer to* an **int**. The * after the type identifier (or before the variable name) indicates that the variable being defined is a pointer to an **int**, rather than just an **int** variable. Strictly speaking, pointers are a separate type, *pointer to*. For our purposes, you can just think of a pointer definition as a way of telling the compiler that it should only expect to find addresses stored in the variable **ptr**.

► **REMEMBER**   When defining or declaring a pointer variable, put * before the variable name.

Once you've defined a pointer variable in a program, you can refer either to the pointer variable itself (a direct reference) or to the pointer's "target" value (an indirect reference). When you refer directly to the pointer in your program, do not include the *. In the previous listing, the first reference to the pointer variable is direct, so only its name is used.

In the following assignment, we store an address in the pointer variable, changing the contents of the pointer variable itself, not of the target value.

```
ptr = &target
```

This assignment looks and happens just like any other assignment. The only difference is that the compiler will check more closely whether you are putting the appropriate kind of information into the variable. Had we tried to put an arbitrary **int** value in here, the compiler would have warned us.

► **REMEMBER**   When referring directly to the pointer variable's value, do not use the * before the pointer's name.

When you want to refer to the pointer's target value, you need to use the indirection operator (*)—to indicate that you want the value to which the pointer is pointing. In the previous program listing, the argument to **printf( )** illustrates this use.

When referring to the pointer's target value, use the indirection operator, *, before the pointer's name.

It may be confusing at first to see the * used in two different ways in relation to pointers—as part of the pointer definition and to specify the pointer's target variable. In program statements, the * is an operator. In definitions or declarations, think of it as telling the compiler that the variable is of type **pointer** to some specified type, and that the compiler should therefore expect to find only addresses stored in the variable.

Let's look at another example, this time using pointers to a different type:

```
/* Program to provide more examples of pointers and their use. */

main ()
{
        double dbl_target, dbl_other; /* variables of type double */
        double *dbl_ptr;                /* pointer to variable of type double */

        dbl_target = 23.0;       /* store arbitrary value in dbl_target */
        dbl_ptr = &dbl_target;   /* store address of dbl_target in dbl_ptr. */

        printf ("address of dbl_target = %u; contents of dbl_target = %lf\n",
                &dbl_target, dbl_target);
        printf ( "address of dbl_ptr = %u; contents of dbl_ptr = %u\n",
                &dbl_ptr, dbl_ptr);
        printf ( "contents of location to which dbl_ptr is pointing = %lf\n",
                *dbl_ptr);

        dbl_other = 46.0;
        *dbl_ptr = dbl_other;  /* assign 46.0 to dbl_ptr's target value */

        printf ("\naddress of dbl_other = %u; contents of dbl_other = %lf\n",
                &dbl_other, dbl_other);
        printf ("address of dbl_target = %u; contents of dbl_target = %lf\n",
                &dbl_target, dbl_target);
        printf ( "address of dbl_ptr = %u; contents of dbl_ptr = %u\n",
                &dbl_ptr, dbl_ptr);
        printf ("contents of location to which dbl_ptr is pointing = %lf\n",
                *dbl_ptr);
}
```

This program produces the following output:

```
address of dbl_target = 5056; contents of dbl_target = 23.000000
address of dbl_ptr = 5064; contents of dbl_ptr = 5056
contents of location to which dbl_ptr is pointing = 23.000000

address of dbl_other = 5066; contents of dbl_other = 46.000000
address of dbl_target = 5056; contents of dbl_target = 46.000000
address of dbl_ptr = 5064; contents of dbl_ptr = 5056
contents of location to which dbl_ptr is pointing = 46.000000
```

A diagram similar to one we used earlier should make some points easier to understand:

```
(a)                                       (b)
After                                     After
dbl_target = 23.0;                        dbl_ptr = &dbl_target;

Value   Address Name                      Value   Address Name
23.0    5056    dbl_target                23.0    5056    dbl_target/*dbl_ptr
???     5064    dbl_ptr                   5056    5064    dbl_ptr
???     5066    dbl_other                 ???     5066    dbl_other

(c)                                       (d)
After                                     After
dbl_other = 46.0;                         *dbl_ptr = dbl_other;

Value   Address Name                      Value   Address Name
23.0    5056    dbl_target/dbl_ptr        46.0    5056    dbl_target/*dbl_ptr
5056    5064    dbl_ptr                   5056    5064    dbl_ptr
46.0    5066    dbl_other                 46.0    5066    dbl_other
```

The first part of this program is just like the previous program, except that this time the statements involve variables of type **double** and pointer to **double**. The storage allocated to the **double** variables is 8 bytes instead of the 2 bytes allocated for an **int**.

The pointer variable, **dbl _ ptr**, is still allocated only two bytes, however. Remember, a pointer contains an address, *not* an ordinary value. The only difference between a pointer to **int** and a pointer to **double** is that the program expects to find a whole number stored at the **int** pointer's target variable, and a floating point value at the **double** pointer's target variable. QuickC always allocates 2 bytes to an ordinary pointer.

Notice that when the contents of the pointer variable are displayed, the information is written as an **unsigned int**, even though we never declared such a value. The output takes this form because an **unsigned int** takes on the range of values possible when using two bytes. This data type is, therefore, useful for displaying possible address values.

The fourth assignment statement (***dbl _ ptr = dbl _ other**) is a construct we haven't seen yet—this is an assignment involving two variables of type **double**: ***dbl _ ptr** refers to the target value of **dbl _ ptr**. Because it is being used as an **lvalue** (as required for the left operand of an assignment), the assignment stores the value of **dbl _ other** (46.0) at the memory location referenced by the pointer. In our example, this location corresponds to the address of the variable **dbl _ target**, as you can see by looking at the output and at part (d) of the diagram.

▶**REMEMBER**   If **ptr _ var** is a pointer to a variable of a particular type (such as **double**), then ***ptr _ var** refers to a value of that target type (**double**). Thus, **ptr _ var** and ***ptr _ type** reference different types.

Pointers and Addresses

We've seen that address operators return a location, and that indirection operators return the value associated with a particular address. In a sense, these two operators are inverses of each other. The following listing illustrates this, and gives you more exposure to pointers. Essentially, the program shows four ways of assigning the value of one variable to another:

```
/* Program to assign variables in 4 different ways.
   Program illustrates pointer use and relationship between address
   and indirection operators.
*/

main ()
{
        double d1 = 3.14, d2, d3, d4;
        double *d_ptr;

        d_ptr = &d1;     /* assign an address to the pointer variable */
        d2 = d1;         /* assign the value of d1 to variable d2 */
        d3 = *d_ptr;     /* assign value of d_ptr's target value to d3 */
        d4 = *&d2;       /* assign value stored at the location returned
                            by &d2 -- i.e., value of d2 --- to variable d4.
                         */

        printf ( "d1 = %lf; d2 = %lf; d3 = %lf; d4 = %lf\n", d1, d2, d3, d4);
}
```

This program produces the following output:

```
d1 = 3.140000; d2 = 3.140000; d3 = 3.140000; d4 = 3.140000
```

The first two assignments are straightforward. The third assignment involves the indirection operator, but should be fairly easy to decipher. Just remember that if **d_ptr** is a pointer to **double**, then ***d_ptr** is a value of type **double**. The last assignment in the program is the most difficult, and it raises several issues regarding pointers and unary operators.

Earlier, we said that the address operator returns an address. Strictly speaking, the operator returns a pointer which, we've seen, has an address as its value. This means **&d2** returns a pointer whose value is the location of **d2**. The indirection operator, in turn, returns the value located at the address stored in the pointer. In this case, the variable is **id2**. The end result is that you assign the value of **d2** to variable **d4**, but in a very roundabout manner.

The mechanics of evaluating the right operand, ***&d2**, illustrate an important difference between the unary operators and most of the other operators. So far we've worked on the assumption that operators were applied in order of precedence, and from left to right when two operators had equal precedence. This is the way things work with the arithmetic and logical operators.

The unary operators, however, are evaluated from right to left when several operators with the same precedence occur in succession. The address operator is applied first, then the indirection operator is applied to the result from the address operator. (The other set of operators that associate from right to left are the simple and compound assignment operators. For example, in an assignment statement, the right operand is evaluated first, then the result is assigned to the left operand.)

Why Pointers?

Pointers operate differently from ordinary assignment and variable definitions because everything is done in an indirect manner. The referents (targets) of an action are often named only in relation to another variable. For example, suppose Pat Smith lives at 79 East 79th Street. You could refer to Pat Smith directly, or you could refer indirectly to Pat Smith as "the person living at the address I have written on my address pad."

Although pointers may sound like a lot of work just to make oblique references to variables, there are several contexts in which pointers are indispensable. First, you will need pointers when working with certain data structures, such as a list whose length is not known in advance. With pointers you can create and manipulate such lists.

A second use of pointers is for manipulating strings. In the next chapter, we'll see that the arrays used to represent strings have a great deal in common with pointers, and that most string manipulations involve pointer operations.

The third major use of pointers is as parameters in function calls, as discussed in the next section.

Pointers as Function Parameters

In Chapter 7, we saw how to get context-specific information into a function, by means of arguments passed in when the function was called. In that discussion, we found that this communication was one-directional—information could get in via parameters, but could not get out that way. So far, the only methods we've seen for passing information out of a function are global variables and the function's return value. In this section, you'll see how to use pointers to get information out of a function.

Suppose you wanted to exchange the values of two variables. The following listing accomplishes this without using pointers. Study the listing to become comfortable with the strategy for swapping, so you'll be able to concentrate on the use of pointers in the next version. Here is the listing:

```
/* Program to swap two values. No pointers used */

main ()
{
        double val1 = 1.0, val2 = 2.0, temp;

        temp = val1;   /* store val 1 temporarily */
        val1 = val2;   /* move val2 to val1 */
        val2 = temp;   /* put the original val1 into val2 */
}
```

This is a straightforward process, and is something done fairly often in certain types of functions, such as sorting routines for ordering data. To swap two values, you need three assignment statements and one temporary variable of the same type as the values you want to swap. The main strategy is to store the value of the first variable (**val1**), then move the second value into the first variable (store value of **val2** in **val1**). Finally, move the original value of the first variable from temporary storage into the second variable (move the contents of **temp** to **val2**).

Now let's look at a program that includes a function to perform this swap. Don't get intimidated by the **swap_dbl( )** function. The actual swapping takes place in just three statements. The rest of the function's statements are calls to **printf( )**, to show you the addresses and contents of the variables involved in the swapping.

```
/* Program to swap two values.
   Program illustrates use of pointers to pass paremeters by reference.
*/

/* Function to actually swap two values. Uses pointer parameters. */
void swap_dbl ( double *first, double *second)
{
        double temp;        /* to store one of the values during swap */

        /* show ADDRESSES of POINTER variables */
        printf ( "address of first = %u; address of second = %u\n",
                &first, &second);
        /* show CONTENTS of POINTER variables */
        printf ( "contents of first = %u; contents of second = %u\n",
                first, second);
        /* show ADDRESS of pointer's TARGET values */
        printf ( "address of *first = %u; address of *second = %u\n",
                *&first, *&second);
        /* show CONTENTS of pointer's TARGET values */
        printf ( "contents of *first = %lf; contents of *second = %lf\n\n",
                *first, *second);
```

```
        /* the next 3 statements are the actual swap routine */
        temp = *first;        /* store *first in safe place, refrigerated */
        *first = *second;     /* move *second */
        *second = temp;       /* restore first to new location */

        printf ( "address of *first = %u; address of *second = %u\n",
                *&first, *&second);
        printf ( "contents of *first = %lf; contents of *second = %lf\n\n",
                *first, *second);
}

main ()
{
        double d1 = 12.3, d2 = 39.5;
        void  swap_dbl ( double *, double *);

        printf ( "address of d1 = %u; address of d2 = %u\n", &d1, &d2);
        printf ( "d1 = %lf; d2 = %lf\n\n", d1, d2);

        swap_dbl ( &d1, &d2);      /* notice use of address operators. */

        printf ( "d1 = %lf; d2 = %lf\n", d1, d2);
}
```

This program produces the following output:

```
address of d1 = 5066; address of d2 = 5058
d1 = 12.300000; d2 = 39.500000

address of first = 5054; address of second = 5056
contents of first = 5066; contents of second = 5058
address of *first = 5066; address of *second = 5058
contents of *first = 12.300000; contents of *second = 39.500000

address of *first = 5066; address of *second = 5058
contents of *first = 39.500000; contents of *second = 12.300000

d1 = 39.500000; d2 = 12.300000
```

Let's look at **main( )** first. This function calls **dbl_swap( )** to swap the values in the two variables. Rather than passing the values themselves as arguments, **main( )** calls **dbl_swap( )** with the *addresses* of the two variables as the actual parameters.

Before we see how **dbl_swap( )** works, look at the prototype declaration for the function in **main( )**. The **double** ∗ indicates that the argument is a *pointer to* **double**, rather than just a **double**. To indicate a **pointer** type in a definition or a declaration, you need to include the ∗, as described above. Generally, this will be immediately before the pointer name; however, for a parameter in a prototype, when you don't need to include an identifier, the indirection indicator is used to specify that the argument is a **pointer** type.

To see how **dbl—swap( )** works, study the following diagram, which shows the program's memory layout after each assignment in **dbl—swap( )**. The identifiers in parentheses are the names associated with particular locations *inside* the function **dbl—swap( )**. The other names (**d1** and **d2**) are the names associated with the same locations in the **main( )** function.

```
(a)                              (b)
After                            After
temp = *first;                   *first = *second;

Value  Address Name              Value  Address Name
5066   5054    (first)           5066   5054    (first)
5058   5056    (second)          5058   5056    (second)
39.5   5058    d2 (*second)      39.5   5058    d2 (*second)
12.3   5066    d1 (*first)       39.5   5066    d1 (*second)


(c)                              (d)
After                            After
*second = temp;                  dbl_swap ( &d1, &d2);

Value  Address Name              Value  Address Name
5066   5054    (first)           ????   5054    ????
5058   5056    (second)          ????   5056    ????
12.3   5058    d2 (*second)      12.3   5058    d2
39.5   5066    d1 (*first)       39.5   5066    d1
```

When **dbl—swap( )** is called, the program sets up the local environment needed for the function. The program allocates space for the formal parameters—in this case, two pointers to **double**—and also for the local variable, **temp**. In the example program above, the two formal parameter variables, **first** and **second**, are stored at addresses 5054 and 5056, respectively. The program copies the values passed in as actual parameters into these two variables. Thus, the address of **d1** (5066) is copied into **first**, then the address of **d2** (5058) is copied into **second**. Because the formal parameters have been defined as pointers, the function treats their contents as addresses. (If we had defined the parameters as just **unsigned int** variables, the information would not be passed out.)

When the function performs the swapping (in the second and third assignment statements), the work done actually affects targets of the two pointer variables, because the assignments include the indirection operator. By passing in the address values, we've managed to get the function to work on a storage location that had been allocated for the *calling* function. This means that any changes made in those locations will stay in effect once the called function's environment and storage disappear.

You can see this in part (d) of the illustration. When control returns to **main( )**, after the call to **dbl‑swap( )**, the storage allocated for **main( )** is still around. Thus, the contents of **d1** and **d2** are still defined; these contents have been changed by the call to **dbl‑swap( )**. Notice, however, that the locations that had been allocated for the two formal parameters to **dbl‑swap( )** are no longer accessible. Those variables had local scope and automatic storage duration, so their storage disappeared when the function ended.

Earlier, we learned that parameters to functions could be passed by value. In that case, the program passed the value of the argument into the function, and this value was stored in the location allocated for the formal parameter. The function worked with a copy of the argument's information.

We've seen one way of passing parameters. Rather than passing the value stored in a particular variable, we pass a reference to the variable itself, in the form of a pointer to the variable's location. This form is known as *passing by reference*. Parameters passed by reference can be changed inside the function; parameters passed by value cannot.

▶**REMEMBER**   To pass a parameter by reference, pass the address of the variable as an argument; inside the function, declare the formal parameter as a pointer to the type of the argument variable.

Let's look at a few more examples of passing parameters by reference. The next program converts a lowercase character to an uppercase one, and converts an uppercase character to a lowercase one.

Notice that the parameter used is a pointer to **int**, rather than a pointer to **char**. You'll see this often in C programs — to avoid unpleasant errors when transporting the program. One reason for this concerns the fact that the high order (leftmost) bit in a character may be handled differently in various implementations. Here is the program:

```
#include <stdio.h>

main ()
{
        int c1;
        void switch_case ( int *);

        printf ( "? " );
        c1 = getchar ();
        printf ( "Before : %c\n", c1);

        switch_case ( &c1);

        printf ( "After  : %c\n", c1);
}
```

```
/* convert lowercase character to uppercase, and
   uppercase character to lowercase.
*/
void switch_case ( int *ch)
{
#define ASCII_OFFSET 32    /* difference between upper and lowercase */

        /* if lowercase, switch to uppercase */
        if ( ( *ch >= 'a') && ( *ch <= 'z'))
                *ch -= ASCII_OFFSET;
        else                           /* if uppercase, switch to lowercase */
                if ( ( *ch >= 'A') && ( *ch <= 'Z'))
                        *ch += ASCII_OFFSET;
}
```

This program reads a character, then calls **switch_case( )** to convert uppercase characters to lowercase and lowercase characters to uppercase. Other characters are left alone.

The **switch_case( )** function works directly with the value stored at the memory location to which **ch** points. If the function does anything to this value, the change will be permanent because the value is the original and not a copy.

The next example includes a function with two parameters, one a pointer and one a regular variable. This function updates a balance by the amount specified in the non-pointer argument.

```
#include <stdio.h>

main ()
{
        double bal = 1000.0, amt1 = 200.0, amt2 = -600.0;
        void   update_balance ( double *, double);

        printf ( "Starting conditions\n");
        printf ( "balance = %10.2lf; amt1 = %10.2lf; amt2 = %10.2lf\n",
                bal, amt1, amt2);

        update_balance ( &bal, amt1);
        printf ( "\n\nAfter adding amt1\n");
        printf ( "balance = %10.2lf; amt1 = %10.2lf; amt2 = %10.2lf\n",
                bal, amt1, amt2);

        update_balance ( &bal, amt2);
        printf ( "\n\nAfter adding amt2\n");
        printf ( "balance = %10.2lf; amt1 = %10.2lf; amt2 = %10.2lf\n",
                bal, amt1, amt2);
}


void update_balance ( double *current, double amt)
{
        *current += amt;
        amt = 0.0;              /* not needed; just to show scope boundary */
}
```

This program produces the following output:

```
Starting conditions
balance =      1000.00; amt1 =      200.00; amt2 =      -600.00


After adding amt1
balance =      1200.00; amt1 =      200.00; amt2 =      -600.00


After adding amt2
balance =       600.00; amt1 =      200.00; amt2 =      -600.00
```

This program changes the value of **bal** by the amount specified in either **amt1** or **amt2**, then displays the result. Notice that the value of **bal** always comes back changed by the appropriate amount after a call to **update‑balance( )**. This is what passing a parameter by reference accomplishes.

The second arguments are unchanged, however, despite the fact that this parameter is explicitly changed in function **update‑balance( )**. This is because the contents of parameters passed by value are only copied, not used directly.

Pointer Arithmetic

One of the most unusual features of pointers in C is the ability to do arithmetic with pointers. Let's look at an example to see what pointer arithmetic might be.

```c
/* Program to illustrate pointer arithmetic */

main ()
{
        int i1 = 111, i2 = 222;
        int *i_ptr;

        printf ( "1) i1 = %d; &i1 = %u\n", i1, &i1);
        printf ( "2) i2 = %d; &i2 = %u\n\n", i2, &i2);

        i_ptr = &i2;            /* assign an address to the pointer */
        printf ( "3) i_ptr = %u; *i_ptr = %d\n\n", i_ptr, *i_ptr);

        i_ptr = i_ptr + 1;    /* add 1 to contents of the POINTER variable */
        printf ( "Adding 1 to POINTER variable\n");
        printf ( "4) i_ptr = %u; *i_ptr = %d\n\n", i_ptr, *i_ptr);

        *i_ptr = *i_ptr + 1;  /* add 1 to contents of the TARGET variable */
        printf ( "Adding 1 to TARGET value\n");
        printf ( "5) i_ptr = %u; *i_ptr = %d\n\n", i_ptr, *i_ptr);
}
```

This program produces the following output in a specific environment:

```
1) i1 = 111; &i1 = 4064
2) i2 = 222; &i2 = 4062

3) i_ptr = 4062; *i_ptr = 222

Adding 1 to POINTER variable
4) i_ptr = 4064; *i_ptr = 111

Adding 1 to TARGET value
5) i_ptr = 4064; *i_ptr = 112
```

This program shows what happens when changes are made to values in the pointer variable (that is, addresses stored in the pointer are altered) or to the values stored in the pointer's target variable.

The first two calls to **printf( )** display the addresses and values of the non-pointer variables used in the program. The third call displays information about **i_ptr** and its target value, after assigning the address of **i2** to **i_ptr** — that is, after making **i_ptr** point to **i2**.

Call 4 shows the results after adding 1 to **i_ptr**. Let's see how this addition works. First, note that the variable involved in the assignment statement (**i_ptr** = **i_ptr** + **1**) is a pointer, not a target variable. This means that, in the right operand, the program first adds 1 to an address, then assigns the resulting address to **i_ptr**.

It turns out that adding 1 to an address is different from ordinary addition. Adding 1 to the value stored in a pointer variable effectively sets the value to the next valid address value. Think of this as adding 1 *address unit* to the current address. The size of an address unit depends on the type of the target variable, as Table 10-1 shows.

For example, an **int** takes two bytes of memory, so an address unit for **int** also equals two bytes. If you check the values for **i_ptr** in calls 3 and 4 (that is, before and after the assignment under discussion), you'll see that the two addresses differ by two. So, in this case, adding 1 to a pointer value meant increasing the contents of **i_ptr** by two memory locations.

Similarly, suppose you had a pointer to **double**, and the current value of the pointer variable was 4000. Adding 1 to this pointer value (that is, to the address stored there) would give the pointer a new value of 4008 — because you're actually adding one address unit, or eight bytes. Subtracting 3 from this

Table 10-1. Address Unit Sizes in QuickC

Type	Size of Address Unit
char	1
int	2
float	4
double	8

address value would store the address 3984 because $4008 - (3 * 8) = 3984$.

Contrast this with the effects of the assignments between calls 4 and 5. This assignment involves target variables. There are no changes in address values because only **int** (rather than pointer) variables were involved. Therefore, this is an ordinary arithmetic expression. The value stored in the target variable is increased by the specified amount (here, 1). The resulting value is assigned to *i_ptr.

The compiler automatically determines the size of an address unit associated with a particular pointer variable, based on your definition of the pointer variable. This means that you can use pointer arithmetic to move from one integer address to the next without knowing the amount of space allocated for integers. This comes in handy for moving around in strings and other types of arrays.

The ability to do pointer arithmetic without taking into account the amount of storage allocated for a type is very helpful for transporting programs. To move a program from an implementation that allocates two bytes for **int** variables to a compiler that allocates four bytes, you just need to recompile the program. There is no need to change any expressions involving pointer arithmetic.

▶**REMEMBER** The size of an address unit in pointer arithmetic depends on the type of the target variable; the size is the same as the amount of space allocated to a variable of the target type.

The flexibility of pointer arithmetic also comes with a price, however. It's your responsibility to make sure the pointers point to the correct type of variable, *and* that the correct type is actually stored at the location you've put into the pointer variable using pointer arithmetic.

Make sure you move only to memory locations allocated for the function or program in which you're doing the pointer arithmetic. Also, make sure that when you try to read the contents of the target variable, the bit pattern will actually represent the type of value your program is expecting. For example, you don't want your program to read the first two bytes of a **double** stored at a location, expecting to find an **int** there.

Addition and subtraction are the only pointer arithmetic operations; no pointer multiplication or division is possible. Furthermore, you can only add whole number values to an address, or subtract a whole number from an address. Thus, you cannot increase an address by .5 address units. Finally, the numbers you add to an address should be "pure" numbers — that is, they should not be addresses.

▶ **REMEMBER**   The only valid pointer arithmetic operations are addition or subtraction of whole numbers to and from an address.

Study and modify the following program, which includes additional examples of pointer arithmetic and ordinary arithmetic involving target variables. Notice the use of parentheses in the increment before **printf( )** call 5—**(*d_ptr1)++**. Consider what would happen if the parentheses were left off:

```
/* Program to illustrate pointer arithmetic */

main ()
{
        double d1 = 111.11, d2 = 222.22, d3 = 333.33;
        double *d_ptr1, *d_ptr2;

        printf ( "1) &d1 = %u; &d2 = %u; &d3 = %u\n", &d1, &d2, &d3);
        printf ( "2) d1 = %lf; d2 = %lf; &d3 = %lf\n\n", d1, d2, d3);

        d_ptr1 = &d2;
        printf ( "3) d_ptr1 = &d2 \t :: d_ptr1 = %u; *d_ptr1 = %lf\n\n",
                d_ptr1, *d_ptr1);

        d_ptr1++;           /* increment POINTER value */
        printf ( "Incrementing the POINTER by 1\n");
        printf ( "4) d_ptr1++ \t\t :: d_ptr1 = %u; *d_ptr1 = %lf\n\n",
                d_ptr1, *d_ptr1);
```

```
        (*d_ptr1)++;        /* increment TARGET value */
        printf ( "Incrementing the TARGET by 1\n");
        printf ( "5) (*d_ptr1)++ \t\t :: d_ptr1 = %u; *d_ptr1 = %lf\n\n",
                d_ptr1, *d_ptr1);

        d_ptr2 = --d_ptr1 - 1;        /* decrement one lvale POINTER (d_ptr1),
                                         then decrement resulting rvalue by 1,
                                         then assign resulting address to lvalue
                                      */
        printf ( "Decrementing one POINTER by  2 and other POINTER by 1\n");
        printf ( "6) d_ptr2 = --d_ptr1 - 1 :: d_ptr1 = %u; *d_ptr1 = %lf\n",
                d_ptr1, *d_ptr1);
        printf ( "7) d_ptr2 = --d_ptr1 - 1 :: d_ptr2 = %u; *d_ptr2 = %lf\n",
                d_ptr2, *d_ptr2);

        *d_ptr2 = *d_ptr1 + 7; /* add 7 to TARGET value, assign to lvalue */
        printf ( "\nAdding 7 to TARGET then assigning to other TARGET\n");
        printf ( "8) *d_ptr2 = *d_ptr1 + 7 :: d_ptr1 = %u; *d_ptr1 = %lf\n",
                d_ptr1, *d_ptr1);
        printf ("9) *d_ptr2 = *d_ptr1 + 7 :: d_ptr2 = %u; *d_ptr2 = %lf\n\n",
                d_ptr2, *d_ptr2);

        printf ( "10) d1 = %lf; d2 = %lf; &d3 = %lf\n\n", d1, d2, d3);
}
```

You can use the following output from the program to check your conclusions:

```
1) &d1 = 5354; &d2 = 5346; &d3 = 5338
2) d1 = 111.110000; d2 = 222.220000; &d3 = 333.330000

3) d_ptr1 = &d2           :: d_ptr1 = 5346; *d_ptr1 = 222.220000

Incrementing the POINTER by 1
4) d_ptr1++               :: d_ptr1 = 5354; *d_ptr1 = 111.110000

Incrementing the TARGET by 1
5) (*d_ptr1)++            :: d_ptr1 = 5354; *d_ptr1 = 112.110000

Decrementing one POINTER by  2 and other POINTER by 1
6) d_ptr2 = --d_ptr1 - 1 :: d_ptr1 = 5346; *d_ptr1 = 222.220000
7) d_ptr2 = --d_ptr1 - 1 :: d_ptr2 = 5338; *d_ptr2 = 333.330000

Adding 7 to TARGET then assigning to other TARGET
8) *d_ptr2 = *d_ptr1 + 7 :: d_ptr1 = 5346; *d_ptr1 = 222.220000
9) *d_ptr2 = *d_ptr1 + 7 :: d_ptr2 = 5338; *d_ptr2 = 229.220000

10) d1 = 112.110000; d2 = 222.220000; &d3 = 229.220000
```

Miscellaneous Points

Pointers contain addresses. There is one special address, 0, that is used to indicate that the pointer is not pointing anywhere. QuickC and Microsoft C 5.0 both define the manifest constant **NULL** to represent this value.

This value is particularly handy for determining whether you are at the end of a list — that is, whether the last list pointer is not pointing anywhere. You can also use it to make sure a pointer has a valid target variable before doing something with this target. For example, the following test can be useful for avoiding unpredictable errors:

```
/* Program to test whether a pointer has a valid target to point to.
   Program illustrates use of NULL and of pointer values in logic tests
*/

#include <stdio.h>   /* contains definition of NULL */

main ()
{
        int i1 = 10, i2;
        int *i_ptr;

        i_ptr = &i1;
        if ( i_ptr != NULL)
                i2 = *i_ptr;
        else
                printf ( "Sorry, can't make that assignment.\n");
}
```

This program assigns the contents of a target variable only if that target variable exists. Notice the preprocessor command to read the contents of file **stdio.h**. This file contains the definition of **NULL** as 0 in QuickC and Microsoft C 5.0.

Pointer Pitfalls

Pointers can be powerful programming tools. They can also get you into trouble, if you're not careful. In this section, we'll look at a few of the most common dangers and errors involving pointers. You'll almost certainly find more on your own as you use pointers in your programs.

Pointer Aliases

Pointers refer indirectly to variables. When you read statements involving pointers, you won't necessarily know what they're referencing. This can make it difficult to determine exactly what's being changed in a program.

One common error that can be very difficult to track down arises if you have more than one way of accessing a particular memory location. Let's look at an example:

```
/* Program to illustrate aliasing and its effects. */
main ()
{
        int i1 = 11;
        int *i_ptr1, *i_ptr2;

        printf ( "address of i1 = %u; contents of i1 = %d\n\n", &i1, i1);
        i_ptr1 = &i1;      /* make i_ptr1 point to i1 */
        i_ptr2 = i_ptr1;   /* make i_ptr2 point to same place as i_ptr1 */

        *i_ptr2 = 37;      /* change value of i_ptr2's target value */
        printf ( "address of i1 = %u; contents of i1 = %d\n", &i1, i1);
        printf ( "contents of i_ptr1 = %u; contents of i_ptr2 = %u\n",
                 i_ptr1, i_ptr2);
}
```

This program produces the following output. Notice the contents of the two pointer variables, and compare this to the location of **i2**.

```
address of i1 = 4078; contents of i1 = 11

address of i1 = 4078; contents of i1 = 37
contents of i_ptr1 = 4078; contents of i_ptr2 = 4078
```

Notice that the value of **i1** is changed without any assignments involving **i1** as the left operand. The reason is that the storage allocated for **i1** actually has three names in the program. It is the target location for **i_ptr1**, for **i_ptr2**, and the location also goes under the direct name, **i1**. When a memory location has several names, these are *aliases* of each other.

Aliases can make it difficult to keep track of the changes to a memory location, since it is possible to change the contents of the location indirectly. For example, in our program, the contents of **i1** were changed by assigning a new value to one of the variable's aliases. Even in a ten-line program, it can be difficult to notice such a change; think how difficult it can be in a program several thousand lines long, involving lots of functions with parameters passed by reference.

When using pointers, try to keep as much control over references to particular memory locations as you can. Fortunately, this is usually possible.

For example, when passing pointers as parameters, you have control over the arguments. As long as you have only one name for the variable in the calling function, the only changes that can occur in this context will be inside the function, and those changes will be passed back out to the calling function in a controlled manner.

Misguided Pointers

Earlier we saw a listing involving pointer arithmetic. By adding to or subtracting from an address, we could move to the next memory location containing a variable of the target type. If you look back at that example, you'll see that the original pointer variable was set to point to the middle variable of three. Had the pointer been set to point to the first or the third, the pointer arithmetic might have produced a memory location that was either undefined or one that contains a value other than an **int**.

When you use pointer arithmetic, the compiler simply makes the adjustments required to move as far as your target type warrants. The compiler will not check to make sure that the new location contains a variable of the appropriate type.

▶**REMEMBER**   It is your responsibility to make sure that the memory location to which the pointer arithmetic brings your program contains the appropriate type of information.

Again, this problem can usually be avoided. Most situations that call for pointer arithmetic will involve arrays, which are essentially a collection of values of the same type occupying successive locations in memory. By knowing the dimensions of the array, you can easily make sure you are staying within bounds. We'll discuss arrays in the next chapter.

Summary

In this chapter, you've learned about pointers, a new type of data structure which contains memory addresses as its values. Pointers allow you to refer to memory locations indirectly. Pointers will be useful in many contexts. For now, the most important use of pointers is to pass information back from functions — by using pointers in a call by reference.

You also learned about the indirection and the address operators involved with pointers. These operators are inverses of each other: one returns the address of a variable, the other returns the variable corresponding to an address.

We also introduced pointer arithmetic, a means of moving around in address space. In the next chapter, we'll look at arrays and their relationship to pointers. Some of the uses of pointer arithmetic will become clearer then.

11

Arrays and Strings

Often, you'll need to work with multiple pieces of information that form a collection, or that somehow belong together. For example, suppose you had records of daily temperatures for a one month period. If you wanted to analyze this information in a program, you would need to allocate a memory location for each value.

You could define a separate variable for each temperature reading, naming them **temp1** through **temp31**. However, typing all this can get tedious. Fortunately, C's array concept provides an easier way to deal with such data collections.

Arrays Basics

In C, an *array* is an aggregate variable consisting of a collection of elements, each of the same type. The array identifier is the name given to the entire collection; individual elements are identified in terms of their location in the array.

To store daily temperature readings for a one month period, you could define an array as follows:

```
double daily_temp [ 31];
```

This definition creates a variable named **daily — temp**. The type specifier indicates that the variable contains information of type **double**. The square brackets containing the number 31 indicate that the variable is an *array* of **double** values containing 31 elements.

▶ **REMEMBER**   To define an array containing variables of a particular type, you need to specify the type (as in other variable definitions), give the array a name, and indicate the array's size within square brackets. The brackets indicate that the variable is an array.

When the variable **daily — temp** is defined, the compiler allocates enough contiguous storage for 31 variables of type **double**. The first array element has the lowest address in the array, and also represents the address of the entire array variable.

To access a particular element in the array, specify the array name followed by the subscript corresponding to the element's position in the array. In C, all arrays start with the subscript 0. Thus, the subscript values in the array **daily — temp[ ]** range from 0 to 30, *not* from 1 to 31. To refer to the tenth element, you would write **daily — temp[9]**, since the first element has index 0. You'll almost certainly forget this at least once in your programs, so try to do it as quickly as possible, so you can remember it after that.

Let's look at a sample program that uses arrays:

```
/* Program to show definition and use of array */
#define MAX_SIZE 11  /* array size */
main ()
{
```

```
      int running_sum = 0, count;
      int sums [ MAX_SIZE];                  /* MAX_SIZE element array of int */

      /* initialize array */
      for ( count = 0; count <= MAX_SIZE - 1; count++)
      {
              running_sum += count;
              sums [ count] = running_sum;      /* assign value to cell */
      }

      /* Display array contents */
      printf ( "Count\tSums [ Count]\n\n");
      for ( count = 0; count < MAX_SIZE; count++)
              printf ( "%3d :\t%5d\n", count, sums [ count]);
}
```

The following table is the output from the program:

Count	Sums [Count]
0 :	0
1 :	1
2 :	3
3 :	6
4 :	10
5 :	15
6 :	21
7 :	28
8 :	36
9 :	45
10 :	55

This program stores the running sum of integers between 0 and 10 in an array, then displays each cell of the array in a table. Let's see how the array cells are used and how the loops are set up in the program.

The array definition has the same form as the earlier example, except that a manifest constant is used to indicate the size. This is allowed, as long as the constant is replaced by a positive integral value. Notice that MAX—SIZE is 11—the array has 11 elements, not 10—even though the largest subscript is 10. Again, this is because the first cell has subscript 0.

The individual cells of the array are denoted by the array name followed by the subscript, or index, in square brackets. These brackets identify the variable as an array in a definition or declaration and identify a value as an array element when used in an expression.

The continuation conditions in the two **for** loops accomplish the same thing, but use different tests. The first test, count $<=$ MAX—SIZE minus 1, is more awkward, but makes explicit the fact that the last array element has a subscript one less than the array size. The second form of continuation condition is more convenient, but makes the relationship between array size and largest subscript value less explicit. Use whichever form you prefer. Just keep in mind that, in C, it's *your* responsibility to keep your program within the bounds of the array.

▶ **REMEMBER**   In C, all array subscripts begin with 0. The last array element has a subscript that is one less than the array size.

Arrays: Storage Classes and Initialization

Arrays are, in one sense, variables just like any other. You can define arrays as global or local, with static or automatic storage duration. The only restriction is that you cannot define arrays with register storage class.

Thus, the following are all valid array definitions, and declarations:

```
/* Program to show array definitions at different scope levels and with
    different storage classes.
*/
double  global_dbl [ 25];    /* 25 element array of double; global */
static int int_array [ 10];  /* 10 element array of int;
                                global, but hidden from linker.
                             */

main ()
{
        static double local_array [ 5];   /* local array; static storage */
        int another_array [ 12];          /* local array */

        printf ( "Hi, there\n");
}
```

The syntax for defining array variables is similar to that for defining other types of variables. This is also true if you include storage class specifiers in the definition.

Array declarations and definitions are different. Once you've defined an array, including an array size, you can declare it in other places. You don't have to specify the array size in *declarations,* because the compiler allocates storage at definition time. At declaration time, when no storage is allocated, the compiler isn't interested in the array size because it's your responsibility to stay within the array's bounds.

We've seen that it's possible to initialize variables when defining them. Is this possible with arrays? Yes and no. You can initialize arrays with static lifetime (that is, global arrays and those with storage class **static**); you *cannot* initialize arrays with automatic lifetime (e.g., arrays declared *within* a function).

To initialize an array at definition time, you need to specify the values for the cells, after giving the array name and dimensions. The values are written within curly braces, with individual values separated by commas. Your initialization may extend over multiple lines, but you may not split an individual value between lines.

For example, the following definition initializes the cells in the array, **days — in — month[ ]** to the appropriate values. The definition could be made globally (in which case the array would be hidden from the linker) or locally (in which case the storage for the array would last beyond the function in which the array was defined).

```
static int days_in_month [ 12] = {31, 28, 31, 30, 31, 30,
                                   31, 31, 30, 31, 30, 31};
```

If you don't initialize an array that has a static lifetime, C initializes the elements to zero by default. The contents of a local, automatic array are undefined until you store something in the cells.

One exception to the rule that array size must be specified when you define the array is when you initialize an array with static lifetime at definition time. For example, the following is a valid definition for the **days — in — month[ ]** array:

```
static int days_in_month [] = {31, 28, 31, 30, 31, 30,
                               31, 31, 30, 31, 30, 31};
```

Here, the compiler counts the number of initial values (12) and takes this number as the size of the array. However, it is not considered good practice to define arrays without specifying the size explicitly at definition time.

Arrays and Pointers

The implementation of arrays in C is strongly tied to pointers. In many ways, array indexing simplifies pointer arithmetic for the programmer. In C, the name of an array is a pointer to the first element in the array. Unlike other pointers we've seen so far, however, you *cannot* change the value of the array pointer. Once defined, an array's location is fixed, just like that of any other variable. Consider these examples:

```
/* Program to show similarities between pointers and arrays. */

#define MAX_SIZE 11
#define OFFSET   100

main ()
{
        int entry [ MAX_SIZE];
        int count, *i_ptr;

        /* initialize array */
        for ( count = 0; count < MAX_SIZE; count++)
        {
                entry [ count] = count + OFFSET;
        }
        i_ptr = entry;   /* make pointer point to array */
        printf ( "&entry [ 0] = %u; i_ptr = %u; entry = %u\n",
                &entry [ 0], i_ptr, entry);
        printf ( "entry [ 0] = %d; *i_ptr = %d; *entry = %d\n",
                entry [ 0], *i_ptr, *entry);
}
```

In the following program output, notice the types displayed for each of the parameters to the **printf( )** calls, as well as the values printed:

```
&entry [ 0] = 4012; i_ptr = 4012; entry = 4012
entry [ 0] = 100; *i_ptr = 100; *entry = 100
```

This program initializes an array of **int** values. Then, **i_ptr**, a pointer to **int**, is assigned a value that turns out to be the starting address of the array. The program then displays information about the variables involved.

Notice three of the values displayed are addresses, and that they are all the same location. The value of **entry** is, as we said, the address of the first element of the array, which is equivalent to **&entry[0]**. Thus, we could just as well have initialized **i_ptr** as follows:

```
i_ptr = &entry [ 0];
```

Notice that **entry** is an address, but **entry[0]** is an **int**. In fact, **entry** is simply a label for the address of the first array element. You cannot change the value of **entry** or ask for *its* address because **entry** doesn't have one. If you do ask for the address of **entry** (that is, for **&entry**) in the program, you get a compiler warning, that the compiler is ignoring the **&** operator for the array.

After compiling, you would get the same output as in the program above. If you want to display the address of the array, you need to ask for **&entry[0]**, the address of the first element, or simply for **entry**, which amounts to the same thing.

You can, however, ask for the target of this pointer, that is, for the *value* of the first array element. The indirection operator, *, will return the variable located at the address specified by its operand. Thus, *entry returns the first array element. Since the address stored in i‒ptr is the same as the value of entry, asking for *i‒ptr also returns the first array element. Because entry[0] is not an address, you don't need the indirection operator with this variable.

▶REMEMBER   The name of an array without subscript brackets is equivalent to the address of the first element in the array. Asking for the array name has the same effect as asking for the address of the first array element. Whereas the array name is a pointer constant, the individual elements of the array (such as entry[5], in our example) are variables of the base type of the array (int, in our example).

Accessing Individual Array Elements

Suppose you wanted to use the value of an individual element in the array. We already saw how to do this, in the previous section. To use the value of the fifth element in an array, such as entry, you simply ask for entry[4].

In this section, we're going to look more closely at how your program gets the element you want. Let's modify the previous program, to see what happens when we access individual elements.

```
/* Program to illustrate how to access individual cells, or elements,
   in an array. Program uses both array indexing and pointer arithmetic.
*/

#define MAX_SIZE 11
#define OFFSET   100

main ()
{
        int entry [ MAX_SIZE];
        int count, *i_ptr;

        for ( count = 0; count < MAX_SIZE; count++)
        {
                entry [ count] = count + OFFSET;
        }

        i_ptr = entry;
        printf ( "entry = %u\n", entry);

        printf ( "&entry [ 4] = %u; i_ptr + 4 = %u; entry + 4 = %u\n",
                &entry [ 4], i_ptr + 4, entry + 4);

        printf ( "entry [ 4] = %d; *(i_ptr + 4) = %d; *(entry + 4) = %d\n",
                entry [ 4], *(i_ptr + 4), *(entry + 4));
}
```

This program produces the following output:

```
entry = 4044
&entry [ 4] = 4052; i_ptr + 4 = 4052; entry + 4 = 4052
entry [ 4] = 104; *(i_ptr + 4) = 104; *(entry + 4) = 104
```

The program displays the same information as the previous program, but for the fifth element rather than the first. The program also demonstrates the essential similarity of pointers and arrays. We can access arbitrary array elements using either array syntax (subscripts) or pointer arithmetic and indirection. Let's study the program and its output.

The second line of the output displays the address of the fifth array element, showing three different ways to specify this location. The first, **&entry[4]**, is the most straightforward and the easiest to interpret. The other two explicitly use pointer arithmetic. Recall that adding 4 to an address means adding four address units, where the size of an address unit depends on the base type of the variable.

Thus, the 4 in this context equals 4 * 2 (bytes per **int**), or 8, bytes. The value of **entry** (4044) is the address of the first array element, **entry[0]**. Therefore, an offset of 8 bytes from this yields the location of the fifth element. QuickC actually uses pointer arithmetic to access array elements. Essentially, using array indexing is really a convenience for the programmer.

The third output line shows three different methods of writing the value of the fifth array element. Specifying the cell's name, **entry[4]**, is most straightforward. The other two methods use the indirection operator to return the contents of the target variable at the specified location. Notice the use of the parentheses around the pointer arithmetic. These are necessary because the indirection operator has higher precedence than addition. (Compare the *(i _ ptr + 4) with the *i _ ptr + 4 in the second output line.)

We've seen that you can use pointer arithmetic instead of array indexing to get information from an array. Let's look at one more version of this program. Notice how the pointer variable **i _ ptr** is used.

```
/* Program to illustrate use of pointer as an array. */
#define MAX_SIZE 11
#define OFFSET   100

main ()
{
        int entry [ MAX_SIZE];
        int count, *i_ptr;
```

```
for ( count = 0; count < MAX_SIZE; count++)
{
        entry [ count] = count + OFFSET;
}

i_ptr = entry;       /* make pointer point to array */
printf ( "entry = %u\n", entry);

/* display information about entry notation */
printf ( "&entry [ 8] = %u; entry + 8 = %u; ",
        &entry [ 8], entry + 8);

printf ( "entry [ 8] = %d; *(entry + 8) = %d\n",
        entry [ 8], *(entry + 8));

/* display information about i_ptr notation */
printf ( "&i_ptr [ 8] = %u; i_ptr + 8 = %u; ",
        &i_ptr [ 8], i_ptr + 8);

printf ( "i_ptr [ 8] = %d; *(i_ptr + 8) = %d\n",
        i_ptr [ 8], *(i_ptr + 8));
}
```

This program produces the following output:

```
entry = 4092
&entry [ 8] = 4108; entry + 8 = 4108; entry [ 8] = 108; *(entry + 8) = 108
&i_ptr [ 8] = 4108; i_ptr + 8 = 4108; i_ptr [ 8] = 108; *(i_ptr + 8) = 108
```

This example uses array indexing with variables defined as pointers. In many instances, array and pointer syntaxes are interchangeable. Notice that the individual "array" elements indexed using **i⎯ptr** are ordinary variables. Thus, used in this way, the pointer behaves just like an array identifier.

Differences Between Arrays and Pointers

There are some important differences between arrays and pointers. When you declare an array of a particular type, the compiler allocates enough consecutive memory to store the entire array. (This is the reason for specifying the array size when you define an array.)

The first array element has the lowest address allocated, and each subsequent array element is stored in the next available memory location. Thus, defining a ten-element array of **int** guarantees you memory for ten **int** variables in succession. You can safely access the eighth element in the array. In a sense, when you define an array, you get storage for the individual elements, and you get a pointer *constant* thrown in. The compiler does not allocate any storage for a pointer variable.

On the other hand, when you define a pointer, the compiler *only* allocates the storage for the pointer variable, not for a target value. Even if you have an appropriate target value to begin with, it's still your responsibility to make sure you'll have the appropriate variables at locations computed using pointer arithmetic. Suppose you define a pointer to **int** — **ptr**, for example — and make it point to an **int**. Syntactically, you can then access the memory location **ptr[7]**, and the compiler will not complain.

Just as for pointer arithmetic, it's your responsibility to keep from accessing array elements that are out of bounds. Using an array definition when you want to access variables in a collection is safer, because you can always check the array index to determine whether you're still within the permitted range of values.

Another important difference between the array **entry** and the pointer **i— ptr** is that you can change the value of **i— ptr**, whereas **entry** is a constant. Until you feel confident using pointers, you're better off using array definitions for collections of variables, and using pointer definitions for accessing individual variables.

Because of the way in which the QuickC and the Microsoft C 5.0 compilers do their work, there is no real difference in the speed at which you can do array indexing as opposed to pointer arithmetic, although generally, pointer arithmetic is faster.

Array Parameters

You can pass arrays as parameters to functions. When you do this, you're actually passing the contents of a pointer to the first array element. Thus, arrays are passed by reference, although the array's address is passed by value. The function does not make a copy of the array contents. Let's look at an example:

```
/* Program to show how to pass arrays as parameters to functions. */

#define MAX_SIZE 11
#define OFFSET    100
```

```
main ()
{
        int entry [ MAX_SIZE];
        int count, *i_ptr;
        void times_two ( int [], int);

        for ( count = 0; count < MAX_SIZE; count++)
        {
                entry [ count] = count + OFFSET;
        }

        times_two ( entry, MAX_SIZE);

        printf ( "Count\tEntry [ Count]\n\n");
        for ( count = 0; count < MAX_SIZE; count++)
                printf ( "%3d :\t%5d\n", count, entry [ count]);
}


/* Function to multiply specified elements in an array by 2.
   Note array declaration in function declarator.
*/

void times_two ( int vals [], int array_size)
{
        int count;

        for ( count = 0; count < array_size; count++)
                vals [ count] *= 2;
}
```

This program produces the following table as output:

Count	Entry [Count]
0 :	200
1 :	202
2 :	204
3 :	206
4 :	208
5 :	210
6 :	212
7 :	214
8 :	216
9 :	218
10 :	220

The program initializes an 11-element array of type **int** with consecutive values from 100 to 110. The program then calls a function, **times _ two( )**, which doubles the value of each cell in the array. Finally, the program displays the resulting array in a table.

In examining function calls involving arrays, notice the function prototype declared in **main( )**. The prototype informs the compiler that function **times _ two( )** does not return a value, but takes two parameters, an array of **int** and an **int**. The array is indicated by using the square brackets. Thus, **int[ ]** specifies an array of **int**, just as **int *** indicated a pointer to **int**. Since arrays and pointers are equivalent, we could just as easily have used the pointer to **int** in the prototype. That is, the following would have been an equally valid prototype:

```
void twice_two ( int *, int);
```

Notice that the function declaration did not specify the size of the array. This was not necessary because the compiler won't allocate any space for the array in the function. Rather, the compiler will reference the actual memory location containing the array (call by reference). Generally, you'll pass in a separate parameter that tells the function how many elements to process, as we've done in this program. In other cases, the function may look for a particular value in the array, and will stop when this value is encountered. See the next section's discussion about strings.

In the function call, we used the array name, **entry**, as the first argument. Again, since only a pointer is being passed, we could also have used **&entry[0]**.

Note that in the definition of **times — two( )**, no size is specified for the array parameter. That information is passed in as a separate parameter, and the value is used to tell the function when to stop rather than how much storage to allocate. The only storage allocated for the array is enough space to store the pointer value. Everything else is done in the actual storage allocated for the array in **main( )**.

We could have specified an array size in the function declarator. But, since the compiler does no range checking, this would have had no effect. As in the prototype, we also could have declared the parameter as a pointer, rather than an array. Develop the habits that best suit your programming needs and style. In this book, we'll use pointers mainly for individual variables, and array definitions when a collection of values is under consideration.

▶**REMEMBER**   Because an array name is actually a reference to the starting address of the array, passing an array as an argument to a function is always a pass by reference. Any changes are made to the original array. Because the compiler doesn't have to allocate space to store a copy of the array, you don't have to specify the size of the array. Let's look at another example of a function involving an array parameter, the function will compute the arithmetic mean, or average of the array values passed in.

```
/* Program to show use of arrays as parameters. */

#define MAX_SIZE 100

main ()
{
        int entry [ MAX_SIZE], count;
        int rand ( void);                /* generates random integers */
        double  mean ( int [], int);  /* computes mean of array elements */
        double  average;

        /* initialize array with random integers */
        for ( count = 0; count < MAX_SIZE; count++)
                entry [ count] = rand ();

        average = mean ( entry, MAX_SIZE);
        printf ( "Nr of cases = %d; mean = %10.5lf\n", MAX_SIZE, average);
}

double mean ( int vals [8], int array_size)
{
        int     count;
        double running_sum= 0.0;

        for ( count = 0; count < array_size; count++)
                running_sum += vals [ count];
        return ( running_sum / array_size);
}
```

This program calls **rand( )** to generate 100 pseudo-random integers, which are stored in an array of **int**, **entry**[ ]. **main( )** then passes this array to **mean( )**, which computes the average value of these 100 numbers and returns this information. The array is not changed inside **mean( )**, although it could be. The values in the array are needed to compute the mean.

In the following more complex example, see how the program carries out the same general task—generating pseudo-random integers, and computing the mean of the integers generated. A major difference between the programs is that this program relies much more on "specialist" functions to do the work. The program also breaks up the task into a series of small tasks before computing intermediate results, then combines these into a final answer.

```
/* More specialized program than previous one to show use of arrays
   as parameters.
*/

#define MAX_SIZE 100
#define MAX_SAMPLES 30

main ()
{
        int entry [ MAX_SIZE];
        double sampling [ MAX_SAMPLES];
        int count;
        double  int_mean ( int [], int);
```

```
        double   dbl_mean ( double [], int);
        void get_rand ( int [], int);   /* generates array of random ints */
        double   average;

        /* generate repeated samples of random integers;
           each time through the loop fills and processes the array once
        */
        for ( count = 0; count < MAX_SAMPLES; count++)
        {
                get_rand ( entry, MAX_SIZE);
                sampling [ count] = int_mean ( entry, MAX_SIZE);

                /* display mean of the curent sampling */
                if ( count % 5 == 4)
                        printf ( "%10.5lf\n", sampling [ count]);
                else
                        printf ( "%10.5lf      ", sampling [ count]);
        }

        average = dbl_mean ( sampling, MAX_SAMPLES);
        printf ( "Nr of cases = %d; mean = %10.5lf\n",
                MAX_SAMPLES * MAX_SIZE, average);
}


/* fill an array with random integers */
void get_rand ( int entry [], int nr_of_vals)
{
        int count, rand ( void);

        for ( count = 0; count < nr_of_vals; count++)
                entry [ count] = rand ();
}


/* compute mean of an array of integers */
double int_mean ( int vals [], int array_size)
{
        int     count;

        double running_sum= 0.0;

        for ( count = 0; count < array_size; count++)
                running_sum += vals [ count];
        return ( running_sum / array_size);
}


/* compute mean of an array of double */
double dbl_mean ( double vals [], int array_size)
{
        int     count;
        double running_sum= 0.0;

        for ( count = 0; count < array_size; count++)
                running_sum += vals [ count];
        return ( running_sum / array_size);
}
```

A sample run of this program produces the following output:

```
16213.48000     15999.79000     17099.69000     16190.17000     16003.85000
15941.38000     17343.95000     15697.17000     17572.45000     15909.62000
17151.91000     16154.44000     16638.04000     15390.97000     16531.69000
15009.45000     15655.08000     15814.97000     15919.03000     17141.60000
17750.73000     17441.25000     16996.10000     17330.57000     16731.65000
15918.98000     14991.80000     16477.40000     16908.15000     16868.38000
Nr of cases = 3000; mean = 16426.45800
```

This program generates 30 times as many random numbers in groups of 100 as the previous one. Thus, this program essentially represents 30 copies of the previous program.

After 100 values have been generated, the program computes the mean for these values, and stores this result in the array, **sampling[ ]**. Once all 30 groups of values have been generated and their mean computed, the program calls **dbl＿mean( )** to compute the grand mean of all the values.

Let's look at the major points concerning this program. First, we have two arrays, one to store the random integers as they're generated **(entry[ ])**, and the other to store the means for each group of 100 integers **(sampling[ ])**.

The program has given the task of generating the random integers to a function, **get＿rand( )**, which is passed a pointer to the first element in an array of integers and a value indicating the number of integers to generate. The array elements are changed by **get＿rand( )**.

Notice that the program uses two different functions for computing means. The **int＿mean( )** function works with an array of **int** values; the **dbl＿mean( )** function works with the array of means computed during the program's execution. Since array indexing is done using pointers, the function decides where the next element is on the basis of the size of a single element. Since arrays of **int** and arrays of **double** have different element sizes, they must be handled by different functions.

A final, minor, point concerns the last call to **printf( )**. Notice the expression MAX＿SAMPLES * MAX＿SIZE as an argument. Based on our discussion of the preprocessor and of **printf( )**, you should realize that this is valid and should be able to determine what the result is.

Strings

Strings are an important part of any program. You can use them to write messages to the user, to read text files, and generally to make interactions with users go smoothly. In this section, we'll look at how strings are represented and used in C.

Note that the QuickC Run-Time library includes functions for doing many things with strings, including reading and writing them, comparing them, and appending one string to another. We will discuss some of these functions in this section.

In C, a string is an array of characters terminated by a null character, ' **\0** '.

There is no distinct type, **string**, although the **printf( )** and **scanf( )** functions do recognize a placeholder, %s, for displaying and reading strings. When you define a string, you need to make the array large enough to include a null character. For example, to store the word "hello" you would need an array of *at least* six characters, as the following illustration shows:

0	1	2	3	4	5
h	e	l	l	l	\0

As you read through the QuickC or the Microsoft C 5.0 documentation, you may see the term, "ASCIIZ string." This term simply refers to a character string with a zero byte at the end. C strings, therefore, are ASCIIZ strings.

Let's look at a sample program that illustrates some features of strings.

```
/* Program to show string definition and initialization */

#define MAX_STRING 50

/* define string array and initialize to string constant */
char word [ MAX_STRING] = "hello, there!";

main ()
{
        int   index;
        int   strlen ( char []);

        /* print string, each character on separate line */
        for ( index = 0; word [ index] != '\0'; index++)
                printf ( "%2d : %c\n", index, word [ index]);

        printf ( "LENGTH, not counting \\0 == %d\n", strlen ( word));
}
```

This program produces the following output:

```
 0 : h
 1 : e
 2 : l
 3 : l
 4 : o
 5 : ,
 6 :
 7 : t
 8 : h
 9 : e
10 : r
11 : e
12 : !
LENGTH, not counting \0 == 13
```

The program writes each character of the string, **word[ ]**, on a separate line. Then the program writes the total number of characters, *excluding the null character,* in **word[ ]**.

The string used, **word[ ]**, is defined as a global array of **char**. Note first that the technique for initializing a string is different from the array initialization we saw earlier. This method — initializing the array with a string constant — is allowed only with arrays of **char**. This is equivalent to, but much more convenient than

```
char word [ MAX_STRING] = {'h', 'e', 'l', 'l', 'o', ',', ' ', 't', 'h', 'e','
                'r', 'e', '!'};
```

This "initialization by assignment" situation is one of the only places where an array name can appear on the left side of an assignment statement. Ordinarily, you cannot assign a value to the array name, since this name is a label for a constant value.

Notice that **word** was defined as an array of 50 characters, but the program only wrote 13 (characters 0 through 12). Strings can be shorter than the space allocated. The length of a string is determined by the position of the null character marking the end of the string. Allocating too much space for your string is not a problem. You must, however, make sure you've allocated *enough* space to hold the longest string you expect to store in the array.

▶**REMEMBER**   Make sure you've allocated *enough* space to hold the longest string you expect to store in the array, including the null character.

Notice that the **for** loop in the program ends, even though a null character is not included at the end of the string constant. The compiler automatically adds the '\0' character to the end of string constants, so it isn't needed in your initialization.

The function **strlen( )** is a predefined Run-Time library function that returns the number of characters in the string argument, without including the null character. Thus, **strlen( )** returns the number of characters that you have put into the string, although the actual number of characters in that string is one more than the value reported by **strlen( )**.

▶**REMEMBER** You don't need to include the null character (' \0') in string constants — the compiler will add the character for you.

Let's look at another example:

```
/* Program to illustrate use of gets() to read strings */

#include <stdio.h>
#define MAX_STRING 50

main ()
{
        int   index;
        int   strlen ( char []); /* library function, return string length */
        char wd_read [ MAX_STRING];

        printf ( "Enter a string please.\n");
        gets ( wd_read);          /* read a string from stdin */
        printf ( "%s\n", wd_read);
        printf ( "LENGTH, not counting \\0 == %d\n", strlen ( wd_read));
}
```

This program prompts you for a string, reads your input, then displays the string and tells you how long it is. This time, the character array, **wd ‑ read[ ]**, is defined as a local variable. The Run-Time library function, **gets( )**, is used to read the value for **wd ‑ read[ ]**. This function is declared in the file, **stdio.h**, and returns a string value.

Functions such as **gets( )** allow you to read information into string variables. You can write this information, using the **%s** placeholder when calling **printf( )**. This placeholder tells the function to expect an array of characters, either a string variable or a constant.

Because the string array name is a pointer constant, you cannot really use it as the left operand of an assignment statement — except when initializing a character array of static lifetime. Thus, the library routines for handling strings are especially handy because they let you read variable values into your strings.

You can also build your own strings, character by character, by using a routine such as the macro, **getchar( )**, in a loop — reading characters until a predetermined end of input character is entered. Usually, the loop will end when a newline character (' \n') is read. The following program illustrates this method for building a string:

```
/* Program showing how to build a string, character by character. */

#include <stdio.h>
#define MAX_STRING 50
#define NULL_CHAR '\0'        /* end of string marker in C */
main ()
{
        int  index;
        int  strlen ( char []);
        char wd_read [ MAX_STRING];

        printf ( "Enter a string please.\n");

        for ( index = 0; (wd_read [ index] = getchar ()) != '\n'; index++)
                ;           /* do nothing; all work done in for expression */

        wd_read [ index] = NULL_CHAR;  /* terminate string properly */

        printf ( "%s\n", wd_read);
        printf ( "LENGTH, not counting \\0 == %d\n", strlen ( wd_read));
}
```

This program reads characters up to, but not including, a newline character, since the loop stops when this character is encountered. Each character read is added to the string, **wd▬read[ ]**. Notice that if you build the string yourself, you may need to add the **NULL▬CHAR ('\0')** yourself. (Many C programs use the predefined manifest constant, NULL, to indicate the end of the string. Because this chapter is our first discussion of strings, we've used NULL▬ CHAR to emphasize that a special character ends the string.)

Notice the parentheses around **(wd▬read [index] = getchar( ))** in the continuation condition of the preceding program. These parentheses are important, since they ensure that the assignment to **wd▬read[index]** is made before the comparison with '**\n**'. Without the parentheses, the higher precedence of the inequality operator would dominate, causing the comparison, **getchar( )** != '**\n**', to be made first. This would return a true as long as the character read was not a newline character. This nonzero value would then be assigned to **wd▬read[index]**. This is not what you want, so be careful about using parentheses in such situations.

There's yet another way to handle strings in C, based on the fact that a string can be considered a pointer to **char**. The following program illustrates this, and also shows a situation where arrays and pointers differ:

```
/* Program showing how to define and initialize string as pointer to char */

#include <stdio.h>
#define MAX_STRING 50
#define NULL_CHAR '\0'        /* end of string character in C */
main ()
{
```

```
int  index;
char wd_read [ MAX_STRING];
/* define string as pointer to char;
    initialize by pointing to first char of string constant
*/
char *str_ptr = "hello";

printf ( "%s\n", str_ptr);
printf ( "Enter a string please.\n");

/* read string, character by character */
for ( index = 0; (wd_read [ index] = getchar ()) != '\n'; index++)
                :
wd_read [ index] = NULL_CHAR;    /* terminate string properly */
printf ( "%s\n", wd_read);
printf ( "LENGTH, not counting \\0 == %d\n", strlen ( wd_read));
printf ( "Assigning string I read to my str_ptr\n");
str_ptr = wd_read;        /* point str_ptr at a different string */
printf ( "str_ptr = %s\n", str_ptr);
}
```

For an input of "How do you do?" this program produces the following output:

```
hello
Enter a string please.
How do you do?
How do you do?
LENGTH, not counting \0 == 14
Assigning string I read to my str_ptr
str_ptr = How do you do?
```

Let's look carefully at this program. We've already seen the definition of **wd — read[ ]** and its use in the previous program. The **str — ptr** variable is new, however. This is defined as a pointer to **char**. In practice, this definition amounts to a definition of a string, with some differences from the definition of **wd — read[ ]**, however.

Note first that the pointer definition allocates space for a pointer variable, whereas the array definition only does so for the array elements (since the array name refers to the address of the first element).

Second, we could initialize the pointer variable, even though it is local with an automatic lifetime. (Recall that arrays can only be initialized if they have static lifetimes.) Any pointer variable can be initialized, however. In this case, the initialization essentially stores the string constant in memory and makes **str — ptr** point to the location of the first character in the string constant.

Notice the format of the **printf( )** call. In the string argument, we specified that it was to write a string **(%s)**. The function takes this as an instruction to go to the variable specified, and to start displaying characters until a

NULL—CHAR is encountered. Since the compiler automatically adds a NULL—CHAR to a string constant, the function writes "hello" when called.

Next, notice the assignment statement, **str—ptr** = **wd—read**. We've seen that we can't have an array name on the left side of an assignment statement. We can have a pointer name there, however, since this is a variable, not a constant. The assignment statement makes **str—ptr** point to the start of the array, **wd—read[ ]**. That is, the assignment makes the two names refer to the same string. The "hello" string is lost at this point, since its starting location, which had been stored in **str—ptr**, is overwritten. The contents are still in memory; they're just inaccessible after the assignment.

To convince yourself of this, run the following program, which adds a second character pointer **(str—ptr2)** to preserve the address of the "hello" before **str—ptr** has its contents changed.

```
/* Program to show use of pointer assignments with strings */

#include <stdio.h>
#define MAX_STRING 50
#define NULL_CHAR '\0'
main ()
{
        int  index;
        char wd_read [ MAX_STRING];
        char *str_ptr = "hello";
        char *str_ptr2;

        printf ( "%s\n", str_ptr);
        printf ( "Enter a string please.\n");

        /* build string, character by character */
        for ( index = 0; (wd_read [ index] = getchar ()) != '\n'; index++)

        wd_read [ index] = NULL_CHAR;  /* terminate string properly */

        printf ( "%s\n", wd_read);
        printf ( "LENGTH, not counting \\0 == %d\n", strlen ( wd_read));
        str_ptr2 = str_ptr;       /* to keep pinting at "hello" */

        printf ( "Assigning string I read to my str_ptr\n");
        str_ptr = wd_read;        /* str_ptr now points elsewhere */
        printf ( "str_ptr = %s\n", str_ptr);
        printf ( "str_ptr2 = %s\n", str_ptr2);
}
```

String Library Functions

Let's look briefly at some of the library functions available for handling strings in QuickC and Microsoft C 5.0. We'll just be able to scratch the surface here. You should look through the Run-Time library documentation for more information about these functions as well as others that are provided.

gets( ) and puts( )   We've already used **gets( )**, which lets you read a string from the standard input, **stdin**. This function takes a string argument, into which it places the string read. Note that **gets( )** substitutes a NULL—CHAR for the newline character the ends the input string, making the string conform to C's requirements.

As you might have guessed, there's an output counterpart to **gets( )**. The **puts( )** function writes a string to the standard output, **stdout**. This function takes a string argument, and returns an **int**, representing the last character written. Also, **puts( )** replaces the NULL—CHAR at the end of the string with a newline character (**' \n'**) when writing the string. Thus, if all goes well, this should always be the character returned by the function.

The following program illustrates the use of these two functions:

```
/* Program to show use of gets() and puts() functions */

#include <stdio.h>
#define MAX_STRING 50
#define NULL_CHAR '\0'
main ()
{
        int  outcome;
        char wd_read [ MAX_STRING];
        int puts ( char *);

        printf ( "Enter a string please.\n");
        gets ( wd_read);
        printf ( "string = %s\n", wd_read);

        printf ( "Using puts() : ");
        outcome = puts ( wd_read);
        printf ( "value returned by puts() = %d", outcome);
}
```

For an input of "turkey trot," this program produces the following output:

```
Enter a string please.
turkey trot
string = turkey trot
Using puts() : turkey trot
value returned by puts() = 10
```

strcmp( ) and strncmp( )

These two functions are used to compare the *lexicographic* ordering of two strings. (A lexicographic ordering is one based on the position of the characters in the character set used. For QuickC, this would refer to ordering based on the ASCII character set.) The functions return either a negative, zero, or positive value depending on the relative ordering of the two strings compared.

These functions are case sensitive. Both functions require valid strings — that is, strings terminated by a NULL_CHAR.

The **strcmp( )** function takes two string arguments. We'll call these arguments **string1** and **string2**, respectively. If **string1** comes earlier in a lexicographic ordering than **string2**, the function returns a negative value; if the two strings are identical, the function returns zero. Finally, if the first string is "greater than" the second (comes later in an ordering), the function returns a positive value.

strncmp( ) takes three arguments. The first two are strings, just as for **strcmp( )**. The third is an integer that specifies the number of characters to compare. This function does the same thing as **strcmp( )**, and returns the same range of values, but can be used to compare just portions of strings.

The following program illustrates the use of these functions:

```
/* Program to show use of strcmp() and strncmp() functions */

#include <stdio.h>
#define MAX_STRING 50
#define NULL_CHAR '\0'

main ()
{
        int  outcome;
        char wd1 [ MAX_STRING];
        char wd2 [ MAX_STRING];
        int  strcmp ( char *, char *);
        int  strncmp ( char *, char *, int);

        printf ( "Enter a string please.\n");
        gets ( wd1);
        printf ( "Enter another string please.\n");
        gets ( wd2);

        printf ( "string 1 = %s\n", wd1);
        printf ( "string 2 = %s\n", wd2);

        outcome = strcmp ( wd1, wd2);
        printf ( "value returned by strcmp() = %d\n", outcome);

        outcome = strncmp ( wd1, wd2, 5);
        printf ( "value returned by strncmp() using 5 chars = %d\n",
                outcome);
}
```

For inputs of "hello here" and "hello there," this program produces the following output.

```
Enter a string please.
hello here
Enter another string please.
hello there
string 1 = hello here
string 2 = hello there
value returned by strcmp() = -1
value returned by strncmp() using 5 chars = 0
```

When comparing just the first five characters, notice that the two strings are identical, so that **strncmp( )** returns 0. (Warning: if you're using **strcmp( )** as a test in a selection or loop construct, keep in mind that the function returns 0 — interpreted as false in C — when two strings are identical. If you *want* them to be identical, you need to make the appropriate adjustments in your test.)

For inputs of "hello" and "Hello," this program produces the following output:

```
Enter a string please.
hello
Enter another string please.
Hello
string 1 = hello
string 2 = Hello
value returned by strcmp() = 1
value returned by strncmp() using 5 chars = 1
```

Both versions of the function return 1; since the lowercase *h* comes later than the uppercase *H* in the ASCII character set, "hello" is greater than "Hello."

strcat( ) and strncat( )

These two functions add one string to the end of another. Each function takes two string arguments (**string1** and **string2**, for example). The functions add some or all of **string2** to the end of **string1**. When doing their work, these functions remove the NULL—CHAR at the end of **string1**, and put a new NULL—CHAR at the end of the expanded string. Thus, **string1** (the first argument) will come back changed from these function calls.

▶**REMEMBER**   You must make sure that you've allocated enough space for **string1** to store the characters being added.

The **strcat( )** function adds the entire second argument, **string2**, to the end of the first string. **strncat( )** takes three arguments — two strings (like **strcat( )**), and an integer specifying the number of characters from **string2** to add to the end of **string1**.

The following program illustrates the use of these functions:

```
/* Program to show use of strcat() and strncmp() functions */

#include <stdio.h>
#define MAX_STRING 50
#define NULL_CHAR '\0'

main ()
{
        int   outcome;
        int   strlen ( char *);
        char wd1 [ MAX_STRING];
        char wd2 [ MAX_STRING];

        printf ( "Enter a string please. (No longer than 25 characters) \n");
        gets ( wd1);
        printf ( "Enter another string please.\n");
        gets ( wd2);
        printf ( "string 1 = %s\n", wd1);
        printf ( "string 2 = %s\n", wd2);

        strcat ( wd1, wd2);
        printf ( "string built by strcat() = %s\n", wd1);
        printf ( "Length of new string = %d\n", strlen ( wd1));

        strncat ( wd1, wd2, 5);
        printf ( "string built by strncat() using 5 chars = %s\n", wd1);
}
```

This program produces the following output when "first" and "second" are entered as the strings:

```
Enter a string please. (No longer than 25 characters)
first
Enter another string please.
second
string 1 = first
string 2 = second
string built by strcat() = firstsecond
Length of new string = 11
string built by strncat() using 5 chars = firstsecondsecon
```

Notice the last line of the output. Since we added **wd2** to **wd1** using **strcat( )**, wd1 was changed. Therefore, the first argument to **strncat( )** is not the same as the **wd1** passed to **strcat( )**.

strcpy( ) and strncpy( )

While the **strcat( )** and **strncat( )** functions added one string to the *end* of another, **strcpy( )** and **strncpy( )** copy one string *over* another. The functions take two string arguments, **string1** and **string2**, and copy **string2** over **string1**. Thus, the original **string1** is overwritten when the second string is copied. Notice that the second argument is being copied over the first.

▶**REMEMBER**   It's *your* responsibility to make sure that you've allocated enough space for **string1** to fit all the characters being copied.

The **strcpy( )** function copies all of **string2**, including the NULL—CHAR that terminates the string, over **string1**. Whatever had been stored in **string1** is overwritten.

The **strncpy( )** function takes the same two string arguments, as well as a third, integer, argument. The integer specifies the number of characters of **string2** to copy into **string1**. Use this function carefully. If the number of characters to be copied is greater than the length of **string2**, the function will simply pad **string1** with NULL—CHAR characters. On the other hand, if you are copying *fewer* characters than **string2** contains, the function *will not* terminate the new **string1** with NULL—CHAR.

▶**REMEMBER**   If you're using **strncpy( )** to copy fewer characters than are contained in **string2**, *you* must terminate the new **string1** with a NULL—CHAR. The function will not do so.

The following program illustrates the use of **strcpy( )** and **strncpy( )**:

```
/* Program to illustrate the use of strcpy() and strncpy() functions */

#include <stdio.h>
#define MAX_STRING 50
#define NULL_CHAR '\0'

main ()
{
        int  outcome;
        int  strlen ( char *);
        char wd1 [ MAX_STRING];
        char wd2 [ MAX_STRING];

        printf ( "Enter a string please. (No longer than 25 characters) \n");
        gets ( wd1);
        printf ( "Enter another string please.\n");
        gets ( wd2);
        printf ( "string 1 = %s\n", wd1);
        printf ( "string 2 = %s\n", wd2);
```

```
strcpy ( wd1, wd2);
printf ( "string created by strcat() = %s\n", wd1);
printf ( "Length of new string = %d\n", strlen ( wd1));

strncpy ( wd1, wd2, 5);
wd1 [ 5] = NULL_CHAR;      /* terminate string properly */
printf ( "string created by strncpy() using 5 chars = %s\n", wd1);
}
```

For inputs of "abcdefghijklm" and "nopqrstuvwxyz," this program produces the following output:

```
Enter a string please. (No longer than 25 characters)
abcdefghijklm
Enter another string please.
nopqrstuvwxyz
string 1 = abcdefghijklm
string 2 = nopqrstuvwxyz
string created by strcat() = nopqrstuvwxyz
Length of new string = 13
string created by strncpy() using 5 chars = nopqr
```

Miscellaneous String Functions

QuickC and Microsoft C 5.0 include many other functions for dealing with strings. Check the documentation for more information. Among the functions you may want to study are those that convert information from one type to another. For example, **itoa( )** converts the digits of an integer variable to a null terminated string; **atoi( )** works in the other direction—converting a string into an integer. There are several of these functions, and they can be useful in various contexts.

Many string handling functions are also provided in C libraries available from various sources. For example, *The C Library,* by Kris Jamsa (Osborne/McGraw-Hill, 1985) includes 18 functions for manipulating strings. Studying the source code in such libraries can help you become more comfortable with C and can provide you with new insights into different ways of doing things.

Multidimensional Arrays

C allows you to define two-, three-, and even higher dimensional arrays. A two-dimensional array is essentially an array, each of whose elements is itself an array. Consider the following example:

```
/* Program showing how to define and use multidimensional arrays */

#define MAX_ROWS 4
#define MAX_COLS 3

main ()
{
        /* define 2-dimensional array,
            with MAX_ROWS rows and MAX_COLS columns
        */
        int matrix [ MAX_ROWS] [MAX_COLS];
        int    row, col;

        for ( row = 0; row < MAX_ROWS; row++)            /* for each row */
        {
                for ( col = 0; col < MAX_COLS; col++)    /* for each column */
                        matrix [ row] [ col] = 10 * row + col;
        }

        for ( row = 0; row < MAX_ROWS; row++)            /* for each row */
        {
                for ( col = 0; col < MAX_COLS; col++)    /* for each column */
                        printf ( "Row %d, Col %d : %d\n",
                                row, col, matrix [ row] [ col]);
        }
}
```

This program produces the following output:

```
Row 0, Col 0 :  0
Row 0, Col 1 :  1
Row 0, Col 2 :  2
Row 1, Col 0 : 10
Row 1, Col 1 : 11
Row 1, Col 2 : 12
Row 2, Col 0 : 20
Row 2, Col 1 : 21
Row 2, Col 2 : 22
Row 3, Col 0 : 30
Row 3, Col 1 : 31
Row 3, Col 2 : 32
```

The program initializes a 12-cell array of **int**, then displays the contents of the array. Let's see how this array definition works. Notice that the identifier has two sets of square brackets, one for each dimension in the array. The definition works as follows. Define a three-element array of **int**. In a one-dimensional form, this definition would be something like this:

```
#define MAX-COLS 3
int three_array [ MAX_COLS];
```

The second dimension is a four-element array, each of whose elements is such a three-element array—that is, a **three ⎯ array[ ]**. In C, arrays are row oriented. The two-dimensional array has four rows (each row is an element in the four-element array). Each of these rows has three columns. Each row thus consists of a three-element array. The following illustration shows the layout of the matrix in the preceding program:

```
          Col 0   Col 1   Col 2
Row 0       0       1       2
Row 1      10      11      12
Row 2      20      21      22
Row 3      30      31      32
```

When you do array indexing, the rightmost dimension changes most quickly. For example, **matrix[2][1] = 21;** the next value (reading from right to left in the illustration), is **matrix[2][2] = 22;** then (reading from top down in the illustration) **matrix[3][0] = 30.** Thus, the indexes change the way you would read the cells of the matrix: matrix [0][0], matrix [0][1], matrix [0][2], matrix [1][0], . . ., matrix [3][1], matrix [3][2].

Let's look at another example, this time in a program that passes a two-dimensional array to a function.

```c
/* Program showing how to pass 2-dimensional arrays as parameters. */

#define MAX_ROWS 4
#define MAX_COLS 3

/* multiply array elements by 2 */
void times_two ( int mat[][MAX_COLS], int row, int col)
{
        int r_index, c_index;

        for ( r_index = 0; r_index < row; r_index++)
        {
                for ( c_index = 0; c_index < col; c_index++)
                        mat [ r_index] [ c_index] *= 2;
        }
}

main ()
{
        int    matrix [ MAX_ROWS] [MAX_COLS];
        int    row, col;
        void   times_two ( int [][ MAX_COLS], int, int);

        /* initialize matrix array */
        for ( row = 0; row < MAX_ROWS; row++)          /* for each row */
        {
                for ( col = 0; col < MAX_COLS; col++)   /* for each column */
                        matrix [ row] [ col] = 10 * row + col;
        }

        times_two ( matrix, MAX_ROWS, MAX_COLS);

        /* display array */
        for ( row = 0; row < MAX_ROWS; row++)          /* for each row */
        {
                for ( col = 0; col < MAX_COLS; col++)   /* for each column */
                        printf ( "Row %d, Col %d : %d\n",
                                row, col, matrix [ row] [ col]);
        }
}
```

This program produces the following output:

```
Row 0, Col 0 : 0
Row 0, Col 1 : 2
Row 0, Col 2 : 4
Row 1, Col 0 : 20
Row 1, Col 1 : 22
Row 1, Col 2 : 24
Row 2, Col 0 : 40
Row 2, Col 1 : 42
Row 2, Col 2 : 44
Row 3, Col 0 : 60
Row 3, Col 1 : 62
Row 3, Col 2 : 64
```

This program creates the same two-dimensional array as the previous program does. Then this array is passed to a function that multiplies every element in the array by two. Finally the resulting array is displayed.

There are some important differences in the way one- and two-dimensional array parameters are handled. Let's look first at the definition of the function **times_two( )**.

In the parameter declarations, the *second* dimension of the array is specified. It turns out that the compiler needs to know the size of any array dimension beyond the first.

To see why this is so, remember that an array is simply a consecutive collection of elements, all of the same type. When indexing an array, the program simply uses pointer arithmetic to move to the appropriate cell. But to do pointer arithmetic, the compiler needs to know the amount of storage required by an element of the base type.

In a one-dimensional array, every element is a simple type (or a structured type, which we'll cover later), whose size is known. Therefore, the compiler knows how many bytes to skip when moving to the next valid address for that type. The compiler knows how far to move for each address unit in a one-dimensional array. Since it's your responsibility to stay within the array bounds, the compiler also doesn't care where the last array element is. So, in a one-dimensional array, you can leave out the array size in the parameter declaration.

In a two or higher dimensional array, each element is another array in itself. The compiler has no way of knowing how large one of these arrays is, unless you tell it. If you had declared the parameter in the preceding program as **mat[ ][ ]**, and then asked for **mat[1][0]**, the compiler would not know where the second row of mat started, because it hadn't been told the size of each row. If the compiler is told that each row is a three-element array, it will know how to do the arithmetic for the indexing.

▶**REMEMBER**   When multidimensional arrays are declared as parameters in a function, you must specify the size of all dimensions other than the first.

The prototype declaration for **times two( )** in **main( )** also includes the size of the second dimension. The compiler issues a warning if the size of the second array dimension is not included in the prototype. Thus, the program will compile with the following declaration:

```
void  times_two ( int [][], int, int);
```

However, the compiler will then let you know that there's a discrepancy between the prototype and the function declaration. Giving the compiler the information needed for such checking is a major advantage of using prototypes.

Multidimensional Arrays and Pointers

Let's look briefly at how indexing works in multidimensional arrays. This should provide an additional perspective on such arrays, and should also give you a chance to practice your pointer arithmetic.

As in the one-dimensional case, the array name, **matrix**, is a label for the address of the first element. That is, **matrix** is equivalent to **&matrix[0][0]**. In an earlier section, we saw that we could do pointer arithmetic with arrays. Back then, we found that *(entry + 1)* returned the second element in the array.

What is *(matrix + 1)*? Using the reasoning in the one-dimensional case, this is the second array element. But matrix is an array of arrays. That would mean that *(matrix + 1)* was the name of an array. The following program shows that this, indeed, is the case:

```
/* Program to show names for certain elements of 2-dimensional array */

#define MAX_ROWS 4
#define MAX_COLS 3

main ()
{
        int    matrix [ MAX_ROWS] [MAX_COLS];
        int    row, col;

        /* initalize array */
        for ( row = 0; row < MAX_ROWS; row++)          /* for each row */
        {
                for ( col = 0; col < MAX_COLS; col++)   /* for each column */
```

```
                        matrix [ row] [ col] = 10 * row + col;
    }

    printf ( "*(matrix + 1), the second array element = %d\n",
            *(matrix + 1));

    for ( row = 0; row < MAX_ROWS; row++)              /* for each row */
    {
            for ( col = 0; col < MAX_COLS; col++)   /* for each column */
                    printf ( "Row %d, Col %d : %2d at location %5d\n",
                        row, col, matrix [ row] [ col],
                        &matrix [ row] [ col]);
    }
}
```

The program produces the following output:

```
*(matrix + 1), the second array element = 4016
Row 0, Col 0 :  0 at location  4010
Row 0, Col 1 :  1 at location  4012
Row 0, Col 2 :  2 at location  4014
Row 1, Col 0 : 10 at location  4016
Row 1, Col 1 : 11 at location  4018
Row 1, Col 2 : 12 at location  4020
Row 2, Col 0 : 20 at location  4022
Row 2, Col 1 : 21 at location  4024
Row 2, Col 2 : 22 at location  4026
Row 3, Col 0 : 30 at location  4028
Row 3, Col 1 : 31 at location  4030
Row 3, Col 2 : 32 at location  4032
```

Notice that the value is an address, rather than a cell value, because an array name refers to the location of the first element of an array. Thus, ***(matrix + 1)** is equivalent to **matrix [1]**, which is how you would refer to the second row (i.e., the second array) in **matrix**. Notice that the name, **matrix[1]**, does *not* include an address operator. Recall that (in the case of one-dimensional arrays) the address operator was ignored when applied to an array name, since the name is simply a constant and does not have an address of its own.

If, in the one-dimensional case, **entry[3]** was equivalent to ***(entry + 3)**, how would you represent **matrix[2][1]**? Well, to get to the third row of matrix, you would write ***(matrix + 2)**. Once there, all that is needed is to compute the offset for the second element in that row—that is, the element with the index 1. Extending the rule for the one-dimensional arrays, the element should be ***(*(matrix + 2) + 1)**. The following program will show you whether that's correct:

```
/* Program to provide more information about specific elements of a
   2-dimensional array, and to show use of pointers to access / name
   these elements.
*/
```

```
#define MAX_ROWS 4
#define MAX_COLS 3

main ()
{
        int    matrix [ MAX_ROWS] [ MAX_COLS];
        int    row, col;

        /* initialize array */
        for ( row = 0; row < MAX_ROWS; row++)              /* for each row */
        {
                for ( col = 0; col < MAX_COLS; col++)    /* for each column */
                        matrix [ row] [ col] = 10 * row + col;
        }

        printf ( "*(*(matrix + 2) + 1) = %d\n",
                *(*(matrix + 2) + 1));

        for ( row = 0; row < MAX_ROWS; row++)              /* for each row */
        {
                for ( col = 0; col < MAX_COLS; col++)    /* for each column */
                        printf ( "Row %d, Col %d : %2d at location %5d\n",
                                row, col, matrix [ row] [ col],
                                &matrix [ row] [ col]);
        }
}
```

To test your understanding of the rules for creating arrays of higher dimensions, try answering the questions we've raised in this section for the array defined in the following program. In particular, consider what ***(hyper __ matrix + 1)** is, and how you would compute **hyper __ matrix[1][1][1]**, using pointer arithmetic. Also, try to determine the array name of the second element in **hyper __ matrix[1]**.

```
/* Program in which to exercise your understanding of 3-dimensional arrays */

#define MAX_DIM1 3
#define MAX_DIM2 2
#define MAX_DIM3 2

main ()
{
        int    hyper_matrix [ MAX_DIM1] [ MAX_DIM2] [ MAX_DIM3];
        int    dim1, dim2, dim3;

        /* initialize hyper_matrix --- 3-dimensional array */
        for ( dim1 = 0; dim1 < MAX_DIM1; dim1++) /* for each matrix */
        {
                /* initialize matrix --- 2-dimensional array */
                for ( dim2 = 0; dim2 < MAX_DIM2; dim2++) /* for each row */
                {
                        /* initialize row --- 1-dimensional array */
                        for (dim3 = 0; dim3 < MAX_DIM3; dim3++) /* for col */
                                hyper_matrix [ dim1] [ dim2] [dim3] =
                                        100 * dim1 + 10 * dim2 + dim3;
                }
        }
```

```
        /* display hyper_matrix */
        for ( dim1 = 0; dim1 < MAX_DIM1; dim1++) /* for each matrix */
        {
                /* display matrix */
                for ( dim2 = 0; dim2 < MAX_DIM2; dim2++) /* for each row */
                {
                        /* display row */
                        for (dim3 = 0; dim3 < MAX_DIM3; dim3++) /* for col */
                        {
                                printf ( "dim1 %d, dim2 %d, dim3 %d :",
                                        dim1, dim2, dim3);
                                printf ( " %3d at location %5d\n",
                                        hyper_matrix [dim1][dim2][dim3],
                                        &hyper_matrix [dim1][dim2][dim3]);
                        }
                }
        }
}
```

Pointer Arrays

You can define arrays of just about any type, including pointers. The following example of an array of pointers will provide the first example of more complex definitions:

```
/* Program to illustrate definition and use of pointer arrays */

#define MAX_SIZE 5

main ()
{
        int i1 = 1, i2 = 2, i3 = 3, i4 = 4, i5 = 5;
        int *ptr_array [ MAX_SIZE];  /* array of pointers to int */
        int index;

        /* initialize pointers */
        ptr_array [ 0] = &i1;
        ptr_array [ 1] = &i2;
        ptr_array [ 2] = &i3;
        ptr_array [ 3] = &i4;
        ptr_array [ 4] = &i5;

        printf ( "index\t&ptr_array []\tptr_array []\t*ptr_array[]\n\n");

        /* display information about pointers and targets */
        for ( index = 0; index < MAX_SIZE; index++)
        {
                printf ( "%d\t%u\t\t%u\t\t%d\n", index, &ptr_array [ index],
                        ptr_array [ index], *ptr_array [ index]);
        }

        /* display information about individual variables */
        printf ( "\n\n&i1 = %u; i1 = %d\n", &i1, i1);
        printf ( "&i2 = %u; i2 = %d\n", &i2, i2);
        printf ( "&i3 = %u; i3 = %d\n", &i3, i3);
        printf ( "&i4 = %u; i4 = %d\n", &i4, i4);
        printf ( "&i5 = %u; i5 = %d\n", &i5, i5);
}
```

This program produces the following output:

```
index   &ptr_array []    ptr_array []     *ptr_array[]
0       4104             4100             1
1       4106             4098             2
2       4108             4096             3
3       4110             4094             4
4       4112             4092             5

&i1 = 4100; i1 = 1
&i2 = 4098; i2 = 2
&i3 = 4096; i3 = 3
&i4 = 4094; i4 = 4
&i5 = 4092; i5 = 5
```

This program initializes an array of five pointers to **int**, making each array element point to one of five integers. Then the program displays various types of information about the array elements and the variables involved.

First, notice that the definition of the array includes both the indirection indicator (∗) and the brackets characteristic of an array ([ ]). The ∗ indicates the pointer, whereas the [ ] indicates the array. What determines that this is an array of pointers, rather than a pointer to an array?

Although we haven't discussed it as such, it turns out that the [ ] array indicator is actually an operator in C. This *array subscript operator* has higher precedence than the indirection operator. Therefore, the definition is interpreted as an array of type "pointer to **int**." You can use parentheses to define a pointer to an array, as the following definition illustrates:

```
#define MAX_SIZE 5
int (*array_ptr) [ MAX_SIZE]; /* pointer to 5 element array of int */
```

As we encounter more complex definitions and declarations, we'll learn some rules of thumb for interpreting such expressions.

▶**REMEMBER**   The array subscript operator ([]) has higher precedence than the indirection operator (∗).

Let's look at the output of the sample program. Because it's an array, the array name, **ptr▁array**, is equivalent to the location of the first element, that is, to **&ptr▁array[0]**.

As in other one-dimensional arrays, an array element contains a variable of the base type. In this case, **ptr__array[0]** contains a *pointer*. Thus, writing the value of this cell will not give us an **int**. Rather, we get an address. To find the value stored at the pointer's target value, we need to apply the indirection operator. So, we need to look at ***ptr__array[0]** for the value of the variable to which the first array element is pointing. The target value for this pointer happens to be **i1**, whose value is 1. If you look at the output, you will see that the address of **i1** — **&i1** — matches the contents of **ptr__array[0]**, as you would expect if this pointer were pointing to **i1**. Similarly, the *value* of **i1** matches ***ptr__array[0]**.

String Arrays

Recall that a string is just an array of characters, and can also be defined as a pointer to character. Just as you can define an array of pointers to **int**, you can define an array of strings. The following program shows how to define an array of strings and how to write each element of the array:

```
/* Program to illustrate definition and use of array of strings */

#define MAX_SIZE 5

/* define and initialize string array */
char *prompts [ MAX_SIZE] = { "Hello there",
                              "Hello again",
                              "This is prompts [ 2]",
                              "This is the next prompt",
                              "And this is the last one"};


main ()
{
        int index, outcome;
        int puts ( char *);

        /* display each string in the array */
        for ( index = 0; index < MAX_SIZE; index++)
                outcome = puts ( prompts [ index]);
}
```

This program produces the following output:

```
Hello there
Hello again
This is prompts [ 2]
This is the next prompt
And this is the last one
```

Notice that the array is global. That way, we were able to initialize it with several string constants. This is common in programs that need to display messages or labels at various points in the program. By collecting the messages or prompts in one place, it's easier to change them, if necessary, or even to adapt the array for different programs. We'll find a use for such arrays in later programs.

Finally, the following program combines many of the concepts presented in this chapter, by performing a simple sort on the strings pointed to by the array, **prompts[ ]**:

```
/* Program to sort an array of strings, using a bubble sort algorithm. */
#include <string.h>

#define MAX_SIZE 5

/* define and initialize string array */
char *prompts [ MAX_SIZE] = { "Hello there",
                              "Hello again",
                              "This is prompts [ 2]",
                              "This is the next prompt",
                              "And this is the last one"};

main ()
{
        int index, outcome;
        int puts ( char *);
        void bbl_sort ( char *[], int);

        /* display each string in the array */
        for ( index = 0; index < MAX_SIZE; index++)
                outcome = puts ( prompts [ index]);

        /* sort the strings in the array */
        bbl_sort ( prompts, MAX_SIZE);

        printf ( "*******\n");
        /* display each string in the sorted array */
        for ( index = 0; index < MAX_SIZE; index++)
                outcome = puts ( prompts [ index]);

}


/* void bbl_sort ( char *strs [], int size)
   Sort an array of strings by letting the "largest" remaining string
   work its way to the top of the array on each pass.
*/

void bbl_sort ( char *strs [], int size)
{
        char *temp;           /* for exchanging pointers */
        int  low, hi, top;    /* for looping through array */

        top = size;      /* highest element that will need to be compared */
        while ( top > 0)
        {
```

```
            for ( low = 0, hi = 1; hi < top; low++, hi++)
            {
                    /* if strs [ low] > strs [ hi], exchange them */
                    if ( (strcmp (strs [ low], strs [ hi])) > 0)
                    {
                            temp = strs [ low];
                            strs [ low] = strs [ hi];
                            strs [ hi] = temp;
                    }
            }   /* END for hi < top */
            top--;              /* another string has been placed. */
      } /* END while top > 0 */
} /* END bbl_sort () */
```

This program produces the following output:

```
Hello there
Hello again
This is prompts [ 2]
This is the next prompt
And this is the last one
*******
And this is the last one
Hello again
Hello there
This is prompts [ 2]
This is the next prompt
```

The basic strategy behind a bubble sort is to compare successive values of the array, while moving the larger value of each comparison toward the end of the array. This value is involved in the next comparison, etc. After one pass through the array, the largest value is at the top of the array, allowing the program to ignore the top element the next time through the array. The second time through, the second largest value moves to the second highest array position. Each time through the array, another value is put into place.

Let's look at the first few passes through the array. The first time through the array, the function will look at each array element (**top** == MAX __SIZE). The first comparison will switch "Hello there" and "Hello again" so that **prompts[1]** will now point to "Hello there." The next comparison ("Hello there" with "This is prompts [2]") produces no changes. The next comparison ("This is prompts [2]" with "This is the next prompt") also makes no changes. The next comparison switches "And this is the last one" with "This is the next prompt." After this pass, the highest array element points to the largest string.

The next time through the array, the function only needs to look at four strings (**top--**). This pass exchanges only "And this is the last one" with "This is the next prompt" on the last comparison.

Summary

In this chapter, we've covered lots of material. We've looked at arrays and their relationship to pointers, learning how to define arrays of one or more dimensions, how to access individual elements in an array, and even how to use arrays to accomplish some of the same tasks as pointers.

We've also looked at a particularly useful class of arrays, namely, strings. Although these arrays of characters have many of the same properties as other arrays, they also have their own unique features. In particular, the use of pointers to define string variables is much more common than using pointers to mimic other types of arrays. The QuickC Run-Time library provides numerous functions for handling strings.

In the next chapter, we'll have more to say about functions, and we'll try to consolidate the things we've learned so far. In the process, we'll add to the function collection that we've been building in our programs.

12

More on Functions
and More Functions

This chapter contains several miscellaneous topics that add some minor points about functions and provide an opportunity to collect some of the functions we've developed so far. You'll learn about functions that return pointers, and we'll look at some error handling techniques. You'll also find some new functions to add to your collection. Finally, the chapter provides a brief introduction to recursion, a powerful programming technique in which functions can call themselves.

Functions Returning Pointers

You've seen how to define functions that return the simple data types we've discussed so far. In C, functions can also return *pointers* to simple and complex data types. For example, the following program uses the **build—str( )** function to combine three other strings into a new sentence. This function returns the address of a string (pointer to **char**) containing the new sentence.

```
/* Program to build a string out of three other strings.
   Program illustrates use of functions returning a pointer to char.
*/

#define MAX_STR 80

main ()
{
        char *subject = "The cow ";
        char *verb = "jumped over ";
        char *object = "the moon";
        char *sentence;
        char *build_str( char *, char *, char *);

        sentence = build_str ( subject, verb, object);
        printf ( "sentence: %s\n", sentence);
        printf ( "subject: %s\n", subject);
}

char *build_str ( char first [], char second [], char third [])
{
        char t1 [ MAX_STR], t2 [ MAX_STR], t3 [ MAX_STR];
        int   count, l1, l2;

        /* note use of strcpy(), rather than simple assignment */
        strcpy ( t1, first);
        strcpy ( t2, second);
        strcpy ( t3, third);

        /* add t2 only if there's enough room in t1 */
        if ( ( l1 = strlen ( t1)) + ( l2 = strlen ( t2)) < MAX_STR)
                strcat ( t1, t2);
        /* add t3 only if there's enough room in t1 */
        if ( ( l1 = strlen ( t1)) + ( l2 = strlen ( t3)) < MAX_STR)
                strcat ( t1, t3);
        return ( t1);            /* other strings have been added to t1 */
}
```

The program produces the following output:

```
sentence: The cow jumped over the moon
subject: The cow
```

This program writes "The cow jumped over the moon" and the value of **subject** to the screen. Let's look at the program.

The **main( )** function calls **build—str( )** with three strings (defined as pointers to **char**, so they could be initialized) as arguments. The **build—str( )** function makes a longer string by combining the three string parameters. The function returns a pointer to the first character of the resulting string.

Look at the function definition for **build—str( )**. Just as you would use **char** to specify the return type for a function returning a character, you use **char *** when defining a function that returns a *pointer* to a character. Remember that, in definitions, the indirection indicator tells you the type involved is a pointer to the base type rather than an ordinary variable of that type.

The function prototype for **build—str( )** in **main( )** also uses the * to declare the function as returning a pointer to **char**. Concerning the prototype, we can ask the same kind of question we asked when defining an array of pointers: why doesn't this syntax indicate a pointer to a function returning a **char**?

The answer takes the same form as for the earlier question. The parentheses represent an operator in C. The *function call operator,* ( ), has higher precedence than the indirection operator. The precedence of the function call operator is the same as the precedence of the array subscripting operator, [ ], the highest precedence of any operator. (Incidentally, it *is* possible to have pointers to functions, but they're too advanced for this book. You may want to explore such pointers on your own.)

Let's look at another example, involving integers this time:

```
/* Program to illustrate use of function returning a pointer to int */

main ()
{
        int result;
        int *get_value (char *);

        result = *(get_value ( "value to return?"));
        printf ( "%d\n", result);
}

int *get_value ( char *message)
{
        int value;

        printf ( "%s ", message);
        scanf ( "%d", &value);
        return ( &value);
}
```

This program writes the target value for the pointer returned by **get—value( )**. The indirection operator in the assignment to **result** tells the program to get the value directly, in this case, and assign this value to **result**. By using the indirection operator (thus getting a value right away), the program ensures that an **int** value is stored in **result**, and that this value will be accessible even if the **get_value( )** function is called again.

Returned Pointer Pitfalls

If you're using functions that return pointers to something, be careful of what you're returning and of what happens at the locations to which the functions return. The function returns an address. That address may have been allocated and assigned a value in a local environment (such as in the function). The variable to which the returned pointer is assigned will thus be pointing to a reusable address.

In the previous program, we used a function that returned a pointer to **int**. Rather than assigning the result to another pointer, we used the indirection operator to read the value directly. In this section, you'll see what happens if you work with the pointers instead.

The next program assigns the pointer returned by **get_value( )** to another pointer. Notice what happens when **get_value( )** is called a second time with a different assignment statement. The contents of **rptr**'s target value, ***rptr**, are changed without an explicit assignment.

The storage allocated for **value**, whose address is assigned to **rptr**, is local, and it will probably be reused the next time the function is called. Because **rptr** was pointing to the area of memory used to store information local to **get_value( )**, the contents of its target location can be changed by a call to **get_value( )**. Here is the program:

```
/* Program to illustrate consequences of returning an address to a pointer,
   then reusing the address.
*/

main ()
{
        int result, result2, *rptr;
        int *get_value (char *);

        rptr = get_value ( "value to return?");

        /* This assignment will change the value of *rptr,
           since the contents of the location stored in rptr will change.
        */
        result2 = *(get_value ( "value to return?"));

        printf ( "\n*rptr = %d; rptr = %u\n", *rptr, rptr);
        printf ( "result2 = %d; &result2 = %u\n", result2, &result2);
}
```

```
int *get_value ( char *message)
{
        int value;

        printf ( "%s ", message);
        scanf ( "%d", &value);
        printf ( "value = %d; &value = %u\n", value, &value);
        return ( &value);
}
```

The following listing represents a typical session:

```
value to return? 38
value = 38; &value = 4356
value to return? 94
value = 94; &value = 4356

*rptr = 94; rptr = 4356
result2 = 94; &result2 = 4368
```

Notice that the value of ***rptr** changes after the second call to **get_value( )**, without any assignments involving ***rptr**. You'll see why if you look at the address stored in **rptr** and the storage used for the local variable **value**.

In this case, the same memory location has two names, or aliases. We saw earlier that aliasing could get you into trouble. In a situation such as the one in the preceding program, aliasing may be more difficult to detect because the names occur at two different levels of scope.

▶ **REMEMBER**   Be careful of aliasing, particularly of referring to the same location in two different scopes. Your program may make unwanted changes in the aliased memory location, and these changes may go unnoticed.

String Pitfalls

String handling can also get tricky in C, because of subtle differences among the variety of ways you can define and manipulate strings. In this section, we'll look at some programs that illustrate common errors to be avoided.

In an earlier program, we defined three character arrays in function **build_str( )**, and *copied* (not assigned) the parameter strings into these arrays. The actual string building was done using the local copies of the strings. The following program shows what happens if the function works directly with the parameter strings.

```
/* Program to illustrate consequences of working directly with parameters
   passed by reference.
*/

#define MAX_STR 80

main ()
{
        char *subject = "The cow ";
        char *verb = "jumped over ";
        char *object = "the moon";
        char *sentence;
        char *bad_build_str( char *, char *, char *);

        sentence = build_str ( subject, verb, object);
        printf ( "sentence: %s\n", sentence);
        printf ( "subject: %s\n", subject);
}

/* This function does not make copies of the string contents.
   The function works directly with the original strings (because the
   parameters are pointers).
*/
char *bad_build_str ( char *first, char *second, char *third)
{
        int l1, l2;

        if ( ( l1 = strlen ( first)) + ( l2 = strlen ( second)) < MAX_STR)
                strcat ( first, second);
        if ( ( l1 = strlen ( first)) + ( l2 = strlen ( third)) < MAX_STR)
                strcat ( first, third);
        return ( first);
}
```

The program produces the following output:

```
sentence: The cow jumped over the moon
subject: The cow jumped over the moon
```

Notice that the value of subject has been changed by the function call because **strcpy( )** changes the value of its first argument. The following version of **build_str( )** won't work properly either, for a similar, but subtler, reason. String assignments, such as **t1 = first**, merely store an address; these assignments do not transfer string contents. Therefore, the assignment just creates an alias for the parameter string. When **strcat( )** does its work, the parameter string is changed, as in the previous example, as is shown below.

```
char *bad_build_str ( char *first, char *second, char *third)
{
        int l1, l2;
        char *t1, *t2, *t3;

        t1 = first;
        t2 = second;
        t3 = third;
        if ( ( l1 = strlen ( t1)) + ( l2 = strlen ( t2)) < MAX_STR)
                strcat ( t1, t2);
        if ( ( l1 = strlen ( t1)) + ( l2 = strlen ( t3)) < MAX_STR)
                strcat ( t1, t3);
        return ( t1);
}
```

The assignment just stored an address; the assignment *does not* make a copy of the string contents. Therefore, any changes made to **t1** are also made to **subject**, since the two names are aliases for the same memory location.

The library function, **strcpy( )**, *does* make an actual copy of the string. This means any changes made in **t1** are confined to the function's duration and scope. That's why the first program in this chapter worked without changing the parameter variable.

▶**CAUTION**   Be careful when using string handling functions. Such functions may change one or more of their string arguments. Make sure you work with copies of any argument strings whose original value you'll need.

The following program creates random sentences by building longer strings out of shorter components. The program also addresses other string pitfalls related to string storage allocation.

```
/* Program to generate random sentences built out of components.
   Program illustrates importance of copying string contents, rather than
   merely transferring addresses.
*/

#define MAX_STR 80
#define MAX_ENTRY 5

char *subj [ MAX_ENTRY] = { "The bull ", "The cow ",  "The robin ",
                            "The train ", "The wind "};
char *vb [ MAX_ENTRY] = { "broke ", "jumped over ", "ate ", "arrived at ",
                          "bent "};
char *obj [ MAX_ENTRY] = { "the window", "the moon", "the worm",
                           "the station", "the trees"};

main ()
{
        char *temp;
        char subject [ MAX_STR];
        char verb [ MAX_STR];
        char object [ MAX_STR];
        char sentence [ MAX_STR];
        char *build_str( char *, char *, char *);
        char *get_random_str ( char *[], int);
        int  index;

        for ( index = 1; index <= 15; index++)
        {
                temp = get_random_str ( subj, MAX_ENTRY);
                strcpy ( subject, temp);

                temp = get_random_str ( vb, MAX_ENTRY);
                strcpy ( verb, temp);

                temp = get_random_str ( obj, MAX_ENTRY);
                strcpy ( object, temp);

                temp = build_str ( subject, verb, object);
                strcpy ( sentence, temp);
                printf ( "%s\n", sentence);
        }
}
```

```
char *build_str ( char first [], char second [], char third [])
{
        char t1 [ MAX_STR], t2 [ MAX_STR], *t3;
        int  count, l1, l2;

        strcpy ( t1, first);
        strcpy ( t2, second);
        strcpy ( t3, third);
        if ( ( l1 = strlen ( t1)) + ( l2 = strlen ( t2)) < MAX_STR)
                strcat ( t1, t2);
        if ( ( l1 = strlen ( t1)) + ( l2 = strlen ( t3)) < MAX_STR)
                strcat ( t1, t3);
        return ( t1);
}

char *get_random_str ( char *strings [], int array_size)
{
        int  rand();
        int  element, index;
        char chosen_str [ MAX_STR];

        element = rand () % array_size;
        strcpy ( chosen_str, strings [ element]);
        return ( chosen_str);
}
```

This program produced the following output:

```
The cow ate the trees
The bull bent the trees
The train arrived at the worm
The wind broke the window
The cow ate the moon
The cow broke the worm
The robin jumped over the moon
The wind ate the station
The robin ate the moon
The cow arrived at the window
The robin jumped over the moon
The train bent the worm
The robin bent the window
The wind arrived at the moon
The robin arrived at the station
```

This program generates random sentences, created by selecting components from different string arrays. The program works as follows:

The function **main( )** calls **get‐random‐str( )** three times to get three random sentence elements: a subject, verb, and object. Then, **main( )** calls **build‐str( )** with these elements as arguments. Finally, the program displays the resulting sentence.

Look at the string definitions in **main( )**. We've defined five strings: four as arrays of characters. one as a pointer to character. The program allocates storage for the arrays, so we are guaranteed enough space to store the values assigned. The pointer variable, **temp**, is used to assign values to the string. This value is then copied into the appropriate array.

Notice how **temp** is used. First, we assign the pointer returned by the function **get_random_str( )** or by **build_str( )** to **temp**. Then we *copy* the string to which **temp** is pointing to a different string. Why did we use such a roundabout way of getting the strings we wanted? Why not return the new string directly to the appropriate string?

You cannot have an array name on the left side of any assignment statement other than an initialization at definition time. To get around this problem, you need to define the variables as pointers to **char** instead of as character arrays. The drawback there is that you're not allocating any memory for a string.

The second reason is subtler, and explains why simply using pointers to **char** won't do the trick. Suppose we did define **subject**, **verb**, **object**, and **sentence** as pointers to characters (**char** *) instead of as arrays of **char**. Suppose also that the program returned the strings resulting from the function calls directly to these strings.

When **get_random_str( )** returns its result, the function is returning an address: the contents of a *local* pointer variable. The storage referred to is local storage. Suppose this variable points to address location 4000. The function return means that the variable on the left side, **subject**, now contains the same address as the local variable. The program has not made a second copy of the string whose contents start at location 4000; rather, the program has merely made a second variable point to the same copy of the string.

After the first call to **get_random_str( )**, things may still be all right, but the next call to **get_random_str( )** will almost certainly upset things. When the program puts the environment for **get_random_str( )** into memory, there is a good chance that roughly the same areas of memory will be used as in the previous call — since memory for a function's local environment is given back when a function finishes executing, the program generally uses the next available memory when executing a function call, and all variables and formal parameters in the functions are local. This means the storage allocated for the parameters can be reused when the function ends.

When **get _ random _ str( )** is called a second time, there is a good chance that the storage around location 4000 will be used again, quite possibly to store a new string. As a result, the memory to which **subject** is pointing is being changed by the second function call. Results will be incorrect after all three components have been determined using **get _ random _ str( )**.

By passing the result to a pointer variable, then making a copy of the string to which the pointer is pointing, you avoid this difficulty. **strcpy( )**

creates a second version of the string so the program can safely write over the first version.

▶**CAUTION**   Be very careful if a function is returning a pointer to a local variable. The contents of the memory for that variable may change without the recipient of the function **return** knowing it.

Error Handling and stderr

Earlier, we found that some files were opened automatically when a C program started, and were closed automatically when the program finished. We discussed **stdin** and **stdout** at that time: these two files are used by **scanf( )** and **printf( )**, respectively. Ordinarily, **stdin** refers to the keyboard and **stdout** refers to the screen.

Another useful, but less frequently used, file can also be opened automatically when a program starts. The file **stderr** is generally used to display error messages. By default, this file is the screen in DOS. If you tell your program to read the **stdio.h** file, **stderr** is opened for you, and will be closed when the program ends. Do not try to open and close this file yourself.

Although both **stderr** and **stdout** refer to the screen by default, there is an important difference between them. You can easily use the DOS redirection operators (> and >>) to redirect **stdout**, to a disk file, for example. Ordinary redirection has no effect on **stderr**. It remains associated with the screen, even if **stdout** has been associated with a disk file.

This means you can have your program write its normal output to a file, but have it display any error messages to the screen. Thus, you get the advantages of error reporting without cluttering up the output file. The following program shows how to write error messages to **stderr**:

```
/* Program to show use of stderr and fprintf() */

#include <stdio.h>
#define MAX_COUNT 20

main ()
{
        int count;
```

```
for ( count = 1; count <= MAX_COUNT; count++)
{
        printf ( "%3d: %10.5lf\n",
                count, (count - 1.0) / ( count + 1.0));
        if (!(count % 3))
                fprintf ( stderr, "%3d is divisible by 3\n", count);
}
}
```

This program produces the following output:

```
  1:      0.00000
  2:      0.33333
  3:      0.50000
  3 is divisible by 3
  4:      0.60000
  5:      0.66667
  6:      0.71429
  6 is divisible by 3
  7:      0.75000
  8:      0.77778
  9:      0.80000
  9 is divisible by 3
 10:      0.81818
 11:      0.83333
 12:      0.84615
 12 is divisible by 3
 13:      0.85714
 14:      0.86667
 15:      0.87500
 15 is divisible by 3
 16:      0.88235
 17:      0.88889
 18:      0.89474
 18 is divisible by 3
 19:      0.90000
 20:      0.90476
```

The program counts from 1 to 20, and displays an appropriate fraction at each value. The program also checks whether the current value is divisible by 3, in which case the program writes a message to **stderr**.

Notice in the output that everything seems to be written to the same place. There is no distinction between **stderr** and **stdout** because the default for each is the screen. In the next example, we'll redirect **stdout** to a file.

First, let's look at this program. Notice the preprocessor command to include the contents of file **stdio.h**. This file contains the definitions needed for QuickC to recognize your reference to **stderr**. Although you don't need to open or close **stderr**, the status of this file is different from **stdin** and **stdout**. The latter two files are known to QuickC immediately, whereas **stderr** must first be defined for the compiler.

The **stderr** file is used with **fprintf( )**, a version of **printf( )** for which you can specify a file to which the function is to write. In this case, we've specified **stderr**. Note the order of the parameters.

Notice the condition in the **if** statement. By asking for the negation of the expression, **count % 3**, we get a nonzero value whenever this expression *is* zero. That is, the condition is true whenever **count** is divisible by 3.

Watching an if Statement with QuickC   To see this more explicitly, run this program in debugging mode: at the same time, you'll see more clearly how the flow of control changes when the condition in an **if** statement becomes true. To see this, do the following:

1. Start QuickC with the file containing the previous program.

2. Type CTRL-D, then **C**, to clear any breakpoints currently set in the file.

3. Type CTRL-D, then **L**, to clear any watch variables set in the file.

4. Type CTRL-R , then **C**, to get to the compiler options.

5. If you don't have debug set to on, type **D** to set this option to on. Then press ENTER to compile the program.

6. Type CTRL-D , then press ENTER , to indicate that you want to add a watch variable, and enter **count** as the watch variable.

7. Move the cursor to the line containing the condition for the **if** statement.

8. Type CTRL-D , then **B**, to set a breakpoint at this line.

9. Move the cursor to the *next* line, containing the call to **fprintf( )**.

10. Type CTRL-D, then **B**, to set a breakpoint at this line.

11. Type CTRL-R, then press ENTER , to start the program.

12. Step through the program using the F5 key. Notice that the program stops at the second breakpoint line (**fprintf( )**) only when **count** is a multiple of 3 — that is, only when the condition evaluates to nonzero. Any time the condition fails, the second breakpoint line is bypassed.

To see the difference between **stderr** and **stdout**, run the program (which we'll call **errdemo**) using redirection. To do this, type

```
errdemo > demo.out
```

This command assumes that the program is called **errdemo.exe**. Substitute whatever name you've given the program. Running the program this way redirects any output to **stdout** to the file, **demo.out**. You can look at **demo.out** with your text editor. To see it, type

```
qc demo.out
```

or whatever the appropriate command would be for the text editor you're using. If you run the program and then look at the file, you'll see the following:

```
 1:    0.00000
 2:    0.33333
 3:    0.50000
 4:    0.60000
 5:    0.66667
 6:    0.71429
 7:    0.75000
 8:    0.77778
 9:    0.80000
10:    0.81818
11:    0.83333
12:    0.84615
13:    0.85714
14:    0.86667
15:    0.87500
16:    0.88235
17:    0.88889
18:    0.89474
19:    0.90000
20:    0.90476
```

On the screen, you should have seen this:

```
 3 is divisible by 3
 6 is divisible by 3
 9 is divisible by 3
12 is divisible by 3
15 is divisible by 3
18 is divisible by 3
```

By redirecting **stdout** you changed this file from its default while leaving **stderr** alone. When the program ran, the two streams were sent to their respective targets.

▶**REMEMBER**   To use **stderr**, you need to include the contents of the file **stdio.h**. Do *not* try to open and close **stderr** yourself.

exit( )

C provides two functions for leaving programs earlier than anticipated. The program will do some cleaning up before terminating. It can also pass along information to the operating system about the reasons for program termination.

The **exit( )** function allows a graceful exit from a program. If you need to end a program immediately, you can use this function. It closes any open output files and flushes any buffers before ending the program. This allows you to keep whatever the program had created up to that point.

The following program illustrates the use of the **exit( )** function:

```
/* Program to illustrate use of exit() */

#include <stdio.h>
#define MAX_COUNT 20

main ()
{
        int count;

        for ( count = 1; count <= MAX_COUNT; count++)
        {
                printf ( "%3d: %10.5lf\n",
                        count, (count - 1.0) / ( count + 1.0));
                if (!(count % 13))
                {
                        fprintf ( stderr, "Ending program\n");
                        exit ( 1);
                }
        }
}
```

This program produces the following output:

```
 1:    0.00000
 2:    0.33333
 3:    0.50000
 4:    0.60000
 5:    0.66667
 6:    0.71429
 7:    0.75000
 8:    0.77778
 9:    0.80000
10:    0.81818
11:    0.83333
12:    0.84615
13:    0.85714
Ending program
```

The program counts and displays values until it reaches a number divisible by 13, at which point the program terminates with the error message.

Notice the argument, 0, passed to **exit( )**. This **int** parameter represents the "terminating status" of the program. A status of 0 generally means normal termination. Other return codes will represent different conditions. Check your DOS documentation for information about these return codes. This return value can be used by the DOS batch command, IF ERRORLEVEL, as shown in the following example, which assumes the preceding program is named test13:

```
echo off
test13
if errorlevel 1 goto early
echo program terminated normally
goto done
:early
echo program terminated early
echo on
:done
```

The other function for leaving a program is ▬ **exit( )**. This function is just like **exit( )**, except that ▬ **exit( )** *does not* close files and flush buffers before ending the program.

You've now learned four different ways of breaking out of a program or program portion: **break**, **continue**, **exit( )**, and **return**. Table 12-1 reviews the conditions under which each of these is appropriate.

Table 12-1.   Four Ways of Breaking Out of a C Program or Program Portion

Method	Use	Effect
break	**for** or **while** loop, **switch**	Break out of block
continue	**for** or **while** loop	Begin next iteration of loop
exit( )	anywhere	Terminate program
return( )	function	Leave function, return to calling function

Adding to Your Function Collection

Throughout the book, we've used various functions to illustrate concepts in C. Some of these functions can be generally useful and are worth considering for inclusion in function libraries. In this section, we'll gather some of these functions, and we'll introduce two programs that provide additional functions.

This segment gives you more exposure to C code and to some of the concepts the code illustrates, and also provides you with some usable tools for writing your own programs. Many functions require one or more of the library functions gathered in **qcstuff.qlb**, which we built to make these functions available to the QuickC compiler. This library, which is described in Appendix B, is only needed for QuickC; you don't need the library when compiling under Microsoft C 5.0. If you're using a different compiler, you may need to build a comparable library.

Already Defined Functions

We've defined several functions that can be useful in various situations. In this section, we'll look at a few of these.

non＿zero( ) and safe＿division( )   The functions **non＿zero( )** and **safe＿division( )** help make programs a bit more robust, by avoiding certain situations that will cause problems in a program. Both functions are used in the finance program later in the chapter.

non＿zero( ) takes one argument, a **double**, and returns TRUE if the argument differs from zero by more than a predetermined amount. Otherwise, the function returns FALSE.

safe＿division( ) takes two arguments, both **double**, and returns the quotient of the first argument divided by the second. The function checks whether the denominator (the second argument) is zero. If so, the function returns a predetermined extreme value.

swap＿int( ) and swap＿dbl( )   These functions swap the contents of the two arguments passed between them. The changed values are passed back to the calling function because the parameters for these functions are pointers. In the case of **swap＿int( )** the parameters are pointers to **int**; the parameters are pointers to **double** in the case of **swap＿dbl( )**.

zero＿one＿rand( )   This function takes no arguments, and returns a random **double** between 0.0 and 1.0 inclusive. Such a function can be useful for creating simulations or for generating sample table values. This function may be used in conjunction with a function that fills such a table with random values. The latter function would be passed an array of **double**, and would fill this array with random values.

dbl＿mean( ) and int＿mean( )   These two functions compute the average, or mean, of an array of values. Each function takes two arguments — an array of the appropriate type and an **int** specifying the number of values to generate — and returns a **double** whose value is the average of the array elements.

These functions, along with the functions for generating random values, form the beginnings of a statistics toolbox. For example, functions could be added to compute the standard deviation of arrays of values or to generate random samples with desired characteristics.

String Functions

In this section, we'll describe a few functions for handling strings and we'll look at a program that will let you exercise the functions. First, we'll summarize the purpose and usage of each of the functions. Then we'll look at the program that lets you loop and test whichever string function you want.

delete( )   This function deletes a specified number of characters from a string. The function takes three parameters: the string in which to make the deletion, the starting position of the deletion, and the number of characters to delete. Note that the starting position is in terms of counting position in the string, *not* in terms of the array subscripting for the string. Thus, to delete the first five characters of the string **str**, you would call **delete( )** as follows:

```
delete ( str, 1, 5);        /* delete first 5 characters from str */
```

Notice that the function call uses 1 rather than 0 as the second argument. You are likely to count characters in a string to determine when to start deleting. Since it's more natural for us to count from 1 than from 0, the **delete( )** function uses counting numbers instead of array indexes.

reverse—str( )   This function reverses the string passed in as a parameter. There is a library function, **strrev( )**, that does the same thing. However, this function illustrates a common strategy when doing such things as reversing or comparing corresponding elements on opposite sides of a midpoint. The strategy is to work from both ends toward the middle, stopping when the middle is bypassed.

reverse—str( ) takes one parameter—the string to be reversed. The following call illustrates the use of this function:

```
reverse_str ( str);        /* reverse string str */
```

clean—of—char( )   This function removes all occurrences of a specified character from a string. The function simply copies the string onto itself, leaving out any occurrences of the character to be filtered in the process. The function takes two parameters: the string to clean and the character to remove. The following call would tell a program to remove all occurrences of the letter *y* from the string **str**:

```
clean_of_char ( str, 'y');        /* remove all y's from str */
```

char—pos( )   This function returns the array subscript of the first time a specified character appears in the string. This function takes two parameters and returns an **int**. The parameters are the string to search and the character to seek. The function returns the *array subscript* of the first occurrence of the character in the string. If the character is not contained in the string, the function returns -1.

Note that the position returned by this function is an array index — unlike the starting position specified for **delete( )**, which is a counting value. Thus, the following call would return 0:

```
/* assume result has been defined as an int */
result = char_pos ( "hello there", 'h');
```

You might use the value returned by **char—pos( )** as an array index; in that case, returning the subscript value is an advantage.

remove—wd( )   This function removes the first word in a string and returns this word. The function takes one string parameter and returns a string. The parameter is the string from which a word is to be removed, and the returned value is the word removed from the string. A word is any sequence of characters followed by a blank.

If the string contains no blanks, then the entire string is returned as the word, and the string is reduced to an empty string. The function deletes any leading blanks in the string before removing a word. Such a function can be useful if you want to change the line breaks in a text file — for example, if you need to print in smaller or wider margins.

The following call would assign the string "why," to **word** and would remove this string from **sentence**, leaving that string with the value, "hello there."

```
/* assume sentence has the value "why, hello there."
   assume word has been defined as a pointer to char.
*/
word = remove_wd ( sentence);        /* word now == "why,"
                                        sentence now == "hello there.'
                                     */
```

A Program to Exercise the String Functions   The program that follows includes the source code for the functions described above. The program also includes additional routines for testing the string handling functions. Try running the program and trying out the functions, to get a feel for what they do.

There are several things worth noting about this program. First, notice the global array of strings, **menu[ ]**. This contains the messages displayed for the menu options. You can tailor this menu to different programs, as we'll see later in the chapter.

The **show __ menu( )** function displays the desired menu and prompts the user for a selection. The **show __ menu( )** function takes two parameters: an array of strings and the number of menu items currently initialized. This function can be used, without modification, by any program containing the appropriate type of menu. The only thing you need to change is the menu itself.

The **main( )** function contains one long **switch** construct. Each case in the **switch** corresponds to a menu selection. Each selection lets you test a different string function. The appropriate actions are specified for each selection. This **switch** construct is inside a loop that continues until the user wants to quit. Again, this strategy can be adapted for different programs. The only changes required are in the actions corresponding to each **switch** case, and the value displayed at the end of the **switch**. The program follows.

```
/* Program to exercise string functions. */
#define NULL_CHAR       '\0'        /* end of string character */
#define MAX_STR         80          /* maximum string length */
#define MAX_MENU        10          /* maximum # of menu selections */
#define BLANK_CHAR      ' '

/* menu for the selections possible with this program */
char *menu [ MAX_MENU] = { "0) Quit", "1) Delete", "2) Reverse", "3) Clean",
                           "4) Char_Pos", "5) Remove_Word"};


/* void show_menu ( char *menu [], int menu_size)

    Display the specified menu, which is an array of strings.
    menu_size indicates the number of strings in the menu.
    Function also prompts user for a choice.
    CALLS : printf ()
    GLOBALS : MAX_MENU
    PARAMETERS :
            char *menu [] : array of strings, containing menu.
            int menu_size : number of items in menu.
    USAGE: show_menu ( str_array, nr_entries);
*/

void show_menu ( char *menu [], int menu_size)
{
        int count;

        printf ( "\n\n");

        /* if programmer claims menu has more than maximum allowed items,
           bring the value into line.
        */
        if ( menu_size > MAX_MENU)
                menu_size = MAX_MENU;

        /* display the individual strings in the array */
        for ( count = 0; count < menu_size; count++)
                printf ( "%s\n", menu [ count]);

        printf ( "\n\n");

        /* prompt user */
        printf ( "Your choice? (%d to %d) ", 0, MAX_MENU - 1);
}


main ()
{
        void reverse_str ( char *);
        void clean_str ( char *, int);
        void delete ( char *, int, int);
        void show_menu ( char*[], int);
        char *remove_wd ( char *);
        char *temp_str, new_word [ MAX_STR];
        int char_pos ( char *, int);
        char test_str [ MAX_STR];
        char char_str [ MAX_STR];
        int to_clean, start, how_many, selection, result;

        printf ( "String? ");
        gets ( test_str);
        /* repeat this loop until user wants to quit */
        do
        {
                show_menu ( menu, 6);
                scanf ( "%d", &selection);

                /* switch on user's menu selection */
                switch ( selection)
                {
```

```
                        default:
                                break;
                        case 1:                             /* delete */
                                printf ( "Start? ");
                                scanf ( "%d", &start);
                                printf ( "How many? ");
                                scanf ( "%d", &how_many);
                                delete ( test_str, start, how_many);
                                break;
                        case 2:                             /* reverse_str */
                                reverse_str ( test_str);
                                break;
                        case 3:                             /* clean_str */
                                printf ( "Char? ");
                                scanf ( "%s", char_str);
                                to_clean = char_str [ 0];
                                clean_str ( test_str, to_clean);
                                break;
                        case 4:                             /* char_pos */
                                printf ( "Char? ");
                                scanf ( "%s", char_str);
                                to_clean = char_str [ 0];
                                result = char_pos ( test_str, to_clean);
                                printf ( "%d\n", result);
                                break;
                        case 5:                             /* remove_wd */
                                temp_str = remove_wd ( test_str);
                                strcpy ( new_word, temp_str);
                                printf ( "%s\n", new_word);
                                break;
                }
                printf ( "%s\n", test_str);
        }
        while ( selection != 0);
}



/* void reverse_str ( char *str)

   Reverse the string passed in as a parameter.
   CALLS : strlen()
   GLOBALS :
   PARAMETERS :
           char *str : string to be reversed.
   USAGE : reverse_str ( str);
   Basic strategy have two counters, one (up) running from start to end of
   string, the other (down) running from end to front of string.
   Each time through the loop, swap the two characters at the positions
   indexed by the two counters. When the counters pass each other
   (that is, when up becomes greater than down), the job is done and the
   loop ends.
*/

void reverse_str ( char *str)
{
        int temp,       /* to hold character during swap */
            up,     /* index, up : left --> right in string */
            down;   /* index, down : right -> left in string */

        /* swap first with last, second with second to last, etc., until
           middle of string is reached.
        */
        for ( up = 0, down = strlen ( str) - 1; up < down; up++, down--)
        {
                temp = str [ up];
                str [ up] = str [ down];
                str [ down] = temp;
        }
}
```

```
/* void clean_str ( char *str, int ch)

    Remove all occurrences of a specified character from a string.
    CALLS :
    GLOBALS : NULL_CHAR;
    PARAMETERS:
            char *str : string form which to remove character occurrences;
            int  ch : character to remove from string.
    USAGE : clean_str ( str, ch);
*/

void clean_str ( char *str, int ch)
{
        int old, new;    /* array indexes for old and new version of string */

        /* Keep two separate counters:
                new for the characters being added to new version of string;
                old for character in old string currently being examined.
            Old is incremented each time through loop;
            new is incremented only when a character passes the filter
            and is added to the new version of the string.
        */
        for ( new = 0, old = 0; str [ old] != NULL_CHAR; old++)
        {
                /* if character is OK, add it to new string,
                    and increment counter for new string.
                */
                if ( str [ old] != ch)
                        str [ new++] = str [ old];
        }
        str [ new] = NULL_CHAR;        /* terminate string properly */
}


/* void delete ( char *str, int start, int how_many)

    Delete a specified number of characters from a string,
    beginning at a specified position in the string.
    NOTE: The starting position refers to the actual position of the
          characater in the string, NOT in the array.
          Thus, the first starting position in the string is 1 NOT 0.

    CALLS : strlen()
    GLOBAL : NULL_CHAR
    PARAMETERS :
            char *str : string from which characters are to be deleted;
            int start : position (NOT array subscript index) of first
                        character to delete;
            int how_many : number of characters to delete.
    USAGE : delete ( str, 2, 27);
*/

void delete ( char *str, int start, int how_many)
{
        int index1, index2;

        /* if starting position is an invalid value, start with 1 */
        if ( start < 1)
                start = 1;
        /* if # of chars to delete would go past end of string,
            just delete to end of string.
        */
        if ( start + how_many - 1 > strlen ( str))
                how_many = strlen ( str) + 1 - start;

        /* leave all characters before start position alone;
            begin changing characters at character (start - 1),
            (because arrays begin at index 0)
            begin moving new characters from position (start + how_many - 1);
```

```
            substitute the characters indexed by index2 for those indexed by
            index1.
            continue until the end of the string has been reached.
        */
        for ( index1 = start - 1, index2 = start + how_many - 1;
                str [ index2] != NULL_CHAR; index1++, index2++)
        {
                str [ index1] = str [ index2];
        }
        str [ index1] = NULL_CHAR;    /* terminate the string properly */
}




/* int char_pos ( char *str, int ch)

    Return the array subscript corresponding to the first occurrence of the
    specified character in the string.
    If the character does not occur in the string, the function returns -1.
    CALLS :
    GLOBALS : NULL_CHAR;
    PARAMETERS :
            char *str : string to search for occurrence of character.
            int  ch : character to seek in str.
    RETURN : int representing array subscript of 1st occurrence of ch in str.
    USAGE : where = char_pos ( str, ch);

*/

int char_pos ( char *str, int ch)
{
        int index;

        /* The function only searches, continuing until either
           the character is found OR end of string is reached.
        */
        for ( index = 0;
            ( str [ index] != ch) && ( str [ index] != NULL_CHAR);
            index++)
                ;

        /* if end of string (i.e., character NOT found), return -1,
           else return subscript (index value) at which character was found.
        */
        if (str [ index] == NULL_CHAR)
                return ( -1);
        else
                return ( index);
}




/* char *remove_wd ( char *str)

    Remove the first word from a string; a word is any sequence of characters
    followed by a blank. Strip this word from the string being processed.
    If no blanks are found in the specified string, the entire string is
    returned as the word.
    CALLS : char_pos(), delete(), strcpy()
    GLOBALS : BLANK_CHAR, MAX_STR, NULL_CHAR
    PARAMETERS :
            char *str : string from which to remove a word.
    RETURN : string containing first word found in str.
    USAGE : new_word_str = remove_wd ( str);
*/

char *remove_wd ( char *str)
{
```

```
int index, where;
int char_pos ( char *, int);
char temp [ MAX_STR];

/* remove any leading blanks from string */
while ( !char_pos ( str, BLANK_CHAR))
       delete ( str, 1, 1);

/* find position of first blank in string.
   If a blank is found, copy everything up to (but not including)
   the blank into temp, then delete everything up to (and including
   blank) from the string.
   If no blank is found, return entire string as the new word,
   then empty the original string.
*/
where = char_pos ( str, BLANK_CHAR);
if ( where >= 0)
{
       /* copy word into temp */
       for ( index = 0; index < where; index++)
             temp [ index] = str [ index];
       temp [ index] = NULL_CHAR;      /* terminate temp properly */
       delete ( str, 1, where + 1);   /* remove word from str */
}
else
{
       strcpy ( temp, str);          /* copy str to temp */
       str [ 0] = NULL_CHAR;         /* set str to empty string */
}
return (temp);
}
```

Finance-Oriented Functions

In this section we'll introduce a few functions for computing some values commonly encountered in financial contexts, such as banking, borrowing, or saving. After the discussion of the individual functions, you'll again find a program that lets you exercise the finance functions. You'll see how to adapt the menu array and the **switch** construct for this new group of functions. You'll also find additional general purpose functions that can be used in other programs.

compound＿interest( )   This function returns the interest on a starting principal (such as an initial deposit), given the principal, frequency of compounding, and annual interest rate. For example, for a principal of $1000, invested at 8% interest, compounded quarterly for 3 years, the function returns $268.24 as the interest earned.

The function takes four arguments, all **double**—*principal, annual interest rate, frequency of compounding,* and *number of years*—and returns the resulting interest as a double. The following call illustrates the usage for **compound＿interest( )**.

```
/* assume result, princ, interest, freq, and yrs are all double */
result = compound_interest ( princ, interest, freq, yrs);
```

monthly_mortgage( )   This function computes monthly mortgage payments when mortgage amount, annual interest rate, and total number of monthly payments are specified. For example, for a mortgage of $80,000, at 9.5% interest amortized for 420 months (35 years), the monthly mortgage payment is $657.29.

The function takes three **double** arguments — *mortgage, annual interest, and number of monthly payments* — and returns a **double** specifying the size of the required monthly payment. The following call illustrates the usage for **monthly_ mortgage( )**:

```
/* assume result, mortgage, interest, payments are all double */
result = monthly_mortgage ( mortgage, interest, payments);
```

annuity( )   This function computes the size of an annuity when the annual interest rate, annual deposit, and number of years are specified. For example, for an interest rate of 8.5%, with $300 deposited annually for 21 years, the function returns $16,046.72.

The function takes three **double** arguments — *annual deposit, annual interest rate, and number of years* — and returns the annuity size as a **double**. The following call illustrates the usage for **annuity( )**:

```
/* assume result, deposit, interest, yrs are all double */
result = annuity ( deposit, interest, yrs);
```

annuity_deposit( )   This function computes the annual deposit required to reached a desired annuity when the desired annuity, annual interest rate, and number of years are specified. For example, for a desired $10,000 after 14 years at 8.5% interest, you must deposit $398.42 annually, according to the function.

The function takes three **double** arguments — *desired annuity, annual interest rate, and number of years* — and returns the required annual deposit as a **double**. The following call illustrates the usage for **annuity_deposit( )**:

```
/* assume result, goal, interest, yrs are all double */
result = annuity_deposit ( goal, interest, yrs);
```

A Program to Exercise the Finance Functions   The following program includes the source code for the functions described above. The program also includes additional functions useful for testing the finance functions. Try running the program and trying out the functions to get a feel for what they do.

There are several things worth noting about the program. First, notice again the global array of strings, **menu[ ]**. This contains the messages displayed for the menu options. It was easy to initialize **menu[ ]** to the selections required for the finance functions.

Again, the **main( )** function contains one long **switch** construct. Each case in the **switch** corresponds to a menu selection. Each selection lets you test a different finance function. The appropriate actions are specified for each selection. The **switch** shell and the loop within which the shell is found are the same as in the string testing program. The only differences are the actions carried out when a specific **switch** case arises.

This program makes use of some of the functions we've built during the earlier chapters, such as **non — zero( )** and **safe — division( )**. There is also a new function, **get — dbl( )**, which takes a string parameter and returns a **double**. The string will usually be a prompt of some sort.

The include files **float.h** and **math.h** contain definitions used by library functions such as **pow( )**.

```
/* Program to exercise finance functions */

#include <float.h>
#include <math.h>
#define MAX_MENU 10
#define TOLERANCE      1.0e-7    /* acceptable difference or error */
#define INVALID_VAL  -99999.999  /* val to return for invalid double */
#define FALSE          0
#define TRUE           1


/* array with menu selections for this program */
char *menu [ MAX_MENU] = { "0) Quit", "1) Monthly Mortgage",
                           "2) Compound Interest", "3) Annuity",
                           "4) Annuity Deposit"};

/* void show_menu ( char *menu [], int menu_size)

    Display the specified menu, which is an array of strings.
    menu_size indicates the number of strings in the menu.
    Function also prompts user for a choice.
    CALLS : printf ()
    GLOBALS : MAX_MENU
    PARAMETERS :
            char *menu [] : array of strings, containing menu.
            int menu_size : number of items in menu.
    USAGE : show_menu ( menu_array, Nr_of_entries);
*/

void show_menu ( char *menu [], int menu_size)
{
```

```
        int count;

        printf ( "\n\n");

        /* if programmer claims menu has more than maximum allowed items,
           bring the value into line.
        */
        if ( menu_size > MAX_MENU)
                menu_size = MAX_MENU;

        /* display the individual strings in the array */
        for ( count = 0; count < menu_size; count++)
                printf ( "%s\n", menu [ count]);

        printf ( "\n\n");

        /* prompt user */
        printf ( "Your choice? (%d to %d) ", 0, MAX_MENU - 1);
}

/* double get_dbl ( char *message)

   Prompt user with message, read and return a double.
   If the read was unsuccessful, returns INVALID_VAL.
*/

double get_dbl ( char *message)
{
        double   val;         /* slot to store value read */
        int      args_read;   /* number of values read successfully */

        printf ( "%s ", message);
        args_read = scanf ( "%lf", &val);
        if ( args_read)                   /* if at least one value was read */
                return ( val);
        else
                return ( INVALID_VAL);
}


/* double safe_division ( double numer, double denom)

   Divide num by denom, checking for division by zero before doing so.
   Return quotient or a default value ( INVALID_VAL) on division by zero.
*/

double safe_division ( double numer, double denom)
{
        int non_zero ( double);

        if ( non_zero ( denom))
                return ( numer / denom);
        else
                return ( INVALID_VAL);
}


/* int non_zero ( double val)

   Return true if val differs from zero by more than a predefined amount.
*/

int non_zero ( double val)
{
```

```
            if ( (( val - 0.0) > TOLERANCE) || ((val - 0.0) < -TOLERANCE))
                    return ( TRUE);
            else
                    return ( FALSE);
}



main ()
{
        double  monthly_mortgage ( double, double, double);
        double  compound_interest ( double, double, double, double);
        double  amortization ( double, double, double, double);
        double  annuity ( double, double, double);
        double  annuity_deposit ( double, double, double);
        double  get_dbl ( char *);
        int     get_int ( char *);
        void    show_menu ( char *[], int);

        double princ, interest, months, result, freq, yrs;
        int selection;

        do
        {
                show_menu ( menu, 5);
                scanf ( "%d", &selection);
                switch ( selection)
                {
                        default:
                                break;
                        case 0:
                                break;
                        case 1:
                                princ = get_dbl ( "Mortgage? ");
                                interest = get_dbl ( "Interest? ");
                                months = get_dbl ( "Months? ");
                                result = monthly_mortgage ( princ, interest,
                                                            months);
                                break;
                        case 2:
                                princ = get_dbl ( "Principal? ");
                                interest = get_dbl ( "Interest? ");
                                freq = get_dbl ( "Frequency? ");
                                yrs = get_dbl ( "Years? ");
                                result = compound_interest ( princ, interest,
                                                             freq, yrs);
                                break;
                        case 3:
                                princ = get_dbl ( "Annual Deposit? ");
                                interest = get_dbl ( "Interest? ");
                                yrs = get_dbl ( "Years? ");
                                result = annuity ( princ, interest, yrs);
                                break;
                        case 4:
                                princ = get_dbl ( "Desired Annuity? ");
                                interest = get_dbl ( "Interest? ");
                                yrs = get_dbl ( "Years? ");
                                result = annuity_deposit ( princ, interest,
                                                           yrs);
                                break;
                }
                printf ( "%10.2lf\n", result);
        }
        while ( selection != 0);
}



/* double monthly_mortgage ( double mortgage, double interest, double months)
```

```
        Compute monthly mortgage payment, given annual interest rate and
        total number of monthly payments.
        Formula: mortgage * ( numer / denom),
        where numer = (interest / 12) * term;
        where denom = term - 1;
        where term = (1 + interest / 12) ^ months.

        CALLS : pow(), safe_division()
        GLOBALS :
        PARAMETERS :
                double mortgage : total mortgage
                double interest : annual interest rate
                double months : total months of mortgage
        RETURN : monthly mortgage payments.
        USAGE : payment = monthly_mortgage ( mortgage, interest, months)
*/

double monthly_mortgage ( double mortgage, double interest, double months)
{
        double pow ( double, double);
        double safe_division ( double, double);
        double result, numer, denom, term;

        /* if person enters 25 instead of .25 for 25%, convert to fraction */
        if ( interest > 1.0)
                interest /= 100.0;

        /* compute intermediate terms in equation */
        term = pow ( 1 + interest / 12.0, months);
        numer = (interest / 12.0) * term;
        denom = term - 1;

        /* compute monthly mortgage */
        result = safe_division ( numer, denom);
        return ( mortgage * result);
}



/* double compound_interest ( double principal, double interest,
                              double frequency, double years)

   Compute compound interest on a principal, given: the principal,
   annual interest rate, frequency of compounding, and number of years.
   Formula: principal * term ^ (freq * yrs),
   where term = 1 + interest / freq;

   CALLS : pow(), safe_division()
   GLOBALS :
   PARAMETERS :
           double principal : starting amount
           double interest : annual interest rate
           double frequency : frequency of compounding / year
           double years : number of years
   RETURNS : amount of interest
   USAGE : result = compound_interest ( princ, interest, frequency, years);
*/

double compound_interest ( double principal, double interest,
                           double frequency, double years)
{
        double result, term;          /* term used for intermediate values */
        double pow ( double, double);
        double safe_division ( double, double);

        /* if person enters 25 instead of .25 for 25%, convert to fraction */
        if ( interest > 1.0)
                interest /= 100.0;

        /* compute intermediate terms */
```

```
          term = 1 + safe_division ( interest, frequency);
          result = pow ( term, frequency * years);

          return ( principal * result - principal);
}


/* double annuity ( double deposit, double interest, double years)

   Computes amount of an annuity, given: annual deposit,
   annual interest, years.
   Formula: deposit * term / interest
   where term = (1 + interest) ^ years - 1;

   CALLS : pow(), safe_division()
   GLOBALS :
   PARAMETERS :
          double deposit : initial deposit
          double interest : annual interest rate
          double years : number of years building annuity
   RETURN : annuity amount.
   USAGE : annuity_amt = annuity ( deposit, interest, years);
*/

double annuity ( double deposit, double interest, double years)
{
          double result, term;
          double pow ( double, double);
          double safe_division ( double, double);

          /* if person enters 25 instead of .25 for 25%, convert to fraction */
          if ( interest > 1.0)
                    interest /= 100.0;
          term = 1 + interest;
          result = pow ( term, years) - 1;
          return ( deposit * result / interest);
}


/* double annuity_deposit ( double total, double interest, double years)

   Computes annual deposit required to get a specified annuity, given:
   desired total, annual interest, years.
   Formula: total  * interest / term
   where term = (1 + interest) ^ years - 1;

   CALLS : pow(), safe_division()
   GLOBALS :
   PARAMETERS :
          double total : desired annuity
          double interest : annual interest rate
          double years : number of years building annuity
   RETURN : annual deposit required to reach desired annuity
   USAGE : deposit = annuity_deposit ( total, interest, years);
*/

double annuity_deposit ( double total, double interest, double years)
{
          double result, term;
          double pow ( double, double);
          double safe_division ( double, double);
          /* if person enters 25 instead of .25 for 25%, convert to fraction */
          if ( interest > 1.0)
                    interest /= 100.0;

          /* compute intermediate terms */
          term = 1 + interest;
          result = pow ( term, years) - 1;
          return ( total * interest / result);
}
```

Using Debugging to Check Intermediate Values

Several of the functions in this section compute intermediate values on the way to returning the desired value. Sometimes it can be helpful to check these intermediate values, so you can follow the solution more easily, or because you need to show your work.

Rather than embedding **printf( )** commands throughout your source code, you can use QuickC's debugging facility to watch the variables associated with these intermediate values. For example, to check the values of **term** and **result** in **annuity_deposit( )**, you just need to compile the program with the Debug option on, add **term** and **result** as watch variables, and set breakpoints at the lines assigning values to these variables. Then step through the program, noting the values of **term** and **result** at the appropriate times.

Recursion

Earlier, you learned about the flow of control when a program is executing and when functions are called. Essentially, when **main( )** (or any function) calls another function (let's say, **specialist( )**), execution of **main( )** is suspended temporarily while **specialist( )** executes. When **specialist( )** finishes, control returns to **main( )**.

Now, suppose that **specialist( )**, itself, calls a third function (let's call it **superspecialist( )**). Execution of **specialist( )** pauses while **superspecialist( )** does its work. Thus, while **superspecialist( )** executes, there are two other functions temporarily on hold in our example. If the program terminates normally, these suspended functions will eventually be completed.

A recursive function is, in some ways, the ultimate specialist. It calls *itself* to do part of its task. This means that one version of the function is put on hold, while a different version is activated.

A recursive function takes a task. If the task is simple enough to be solved right away—that is, if there is nothing left to do—the function solves it and returns control to the calling function. On the other hand, if there is still work to be done, the function calls a copy of itself to work on a slightly easier version of the function. This continues until one of the calls occurs with a simple enough version of the problem.

Let's look at a few examples. The first example simply counts to the desired number, displaying some information about where the program is in the recursion. The recursive function, **count( )**, checks whether the parameter is 1, in which case the function displays the value of its parameter. If the parameter is not 1, the function calls itself with an argument one less than the parameter that was passed to it. Thus, if **count( )** is called with a parameter other than 1, versions of **count( )** will be put on hold, while other versions work on a simpler task. Eventually, the parameter passed to a version of **count( )** will be 1, at which point the function can display its value and return control to the function that called it. Here is our first example:

```
/* Program to count recursively, and also to write information about
    current level of recursion.
   Program illustrates recursive function call.
*/

#include <stdio.h>

int level;

void count ( int val)
{
        /* Write some information about the level of recursion. */
        printf ( "Starting count, level %3d; val == %3d\n", ++level, val);

        /* the actual recursion occurs if the condition is true.
           Otherwise, control simply passes to the next statement.
        */
        if ( val > 1)
                count ( val - 1);

        /* Main task line for function count().
           After a return from another call to count(), control returns
           to this point.
        */
        printf ( "\t\t\t\t**** Displaying val: %3d\n", val);

        /* Write some more information about the level of recursion. */
        printf ( "Leaving count, level %3d; val == %3d\n", level--, val);
}

main ()
{
        void count ( int);
        int  how_high;

        printf ( "Count to what value? ");
        scanf ( "%d", &how_high);
        level = 0;
        count ( how_high);
}
```

For an input of 4 for **how — high**, the program produces the following output:

```
Count to what value? 4
Starting count, level   1; val ==    4
Starting count, level   2; val ==    3
Starting count, level   3; val ==    2
Starting count, level   4; val ==    1
                              **** Displaying val:    1
Leaving count, level    4; val ==    1
                              **** Displaying val:    2
Leaving count, level    3; val ==    2
```

```
                                    **** Displaying val:    3
    Leaving count, level    2; val ==    3
                                    **** Displaying val:    4
    Leaving count, level    1; val ==    4
```

This program counts to the desired number, but also displays some administrative information to help us see what happens in recursive calls. Let's look at the output first, to see how the recursion process works.

The program begins executing in **main( )**. This function calls **count( )** with an argument of 4. At this point, **main( )** is on hold, and **count(4)** begins executing.

The function **count(4)** displays information about level of recursion. The function then checks whether it can do its work — that is, whether its parameter has value 1. Since 4 != 1, the function calls **count( )** with an argument of 3. At this point, **main( )** *and* **count(4)** are on hold, and **count(3)** begins executing. Notice, **count(4)** *has not yet done its main task,* which is writing the "displaying" line.

Just as its calling routine did, **count(3)** displays information about level of recursion. The function then checks whether it can do its work — that is, whether *its* parameter has value 1. Since 3 != 1, the function calls **count( )** with an argument of 2. At this point, **main( )**, **count(4)**, *and* **count(3)** are on hold, and **count(2)** begins executing.

Just as the two previous calls to **count( )** did, **count(2)** displays information about level of recursion. The function then checks whether it can do its work — that is, whether its parameter has value 1. Since 2 != 1, the function calls **count( )** with an argument of 1. At this point, **main( )**, **count(4)**, **count(3)**, and **count(2)** are on hold, and **count(1)** begins executing.

The function **count(1)** displays its information about recursion level. This time, however, the test condition for the **if** statement fails. Control thus passes to the next statement *in the same function,* which turns out to be the call to **printf( )** for officially displaying the value of **val**. Before leaving, **count(1)** writes some additional information about level of recursion. Control then transfers back to its calling function, namely **count(2)**.

Notice that the *last* version of **count( )** called was the first version to do any work. One feature of recursive function calls is that the last version called is the first one to do its work. The last one called is, therefore, also the first one to *finish* its work. You can see this in the output from the program.

The function **count(1)** writes the recursion level (4) when the function starts. The function then displays its value for **val**, namely, 1. Finally, the function writes its recursion level as the function finishes.

When control transfers back to **count(2)**, this function continues executing at the next statement — namely, *its* call to **printf( )** to display the value of **val**. Notice that the value written this time is 2. You would expect this, since this value was passed in as a parameter, and since the parameters are merely being passed by value (rather than by reference) in the function. This means that, while **count(1)** was executing, there were 4 versions of **val** allocated — one for each call to **count( )**. The versions do not interfere with each other, since each version has a scope local to the function itself, and since different calls to the same function are essentially different functions.

After **count(2)** writes its value and its recursion level information, the function transfers control back to its caller. Notice that **count(2)** was the second to last function called and is the second function finished. The same process is repeated for **count(3)** and for **count(4)**. Again, notice that **count(4)**, the first function called, is the *last* to finish.

▶**REMEMBER**   In recursive function calls, the function versions finish their work in the reverse order in which the functions were called; the first version of the function called is the last to finish and the last to be called is the first to finish.

Before we look at another example, let's look at the unembellished form of the recursive function in the preceding program:

```
/* Unembellished version of recursive count () function */

void count ( int val)
{
        /* the actual recursion occurs if the condition is true.
           Otherwise, control simply passes to the next statement.
        */
        if ( val > 1)
                count ( val - 1);

        /* Main task line for function count().
           After a return from another call to count(), control returns
           to this point.
        */
        printf ( "\t\t\t\t**** Displaying val: %3d\n", val);
}
```

Without the statements that write information about the recursion level, this function turns out to be very simple. A recursive function must include the following types of statements:

1. The statements needed to carry out the task of the function. In the preceding function, this would be the call to **printf( )**.

2. A test to determine whether the function can avoid calling itself again—that is, to determine whether the function can simply do its work and terminate. In the preceding function, this is the **if** statement testing whether (**val** > 1).

3. A statement that calls the function itself. This call *must* be made with parameter values that will eventually make the test condition take on a value that will bypass the recursive call. In the preceding function, this is accomplished by calling the function with arguments that approach the termination value of 1.

The function *must* test whether a recursive call is necessary before making such a call. If you write your function so that the function calls itself first, then tests whether it's all right to stop, the function will never terminate. Thus, the following version of the recursive function will never terminate:

```
/* Incorrect recursive function */

/* NOTE:   DO NOT USE THIS VERSION OF THE RECURSIVE FUNCTION.
   This version will terminate in a run-time error.
*/

void count ( int val)
{
        /* The recursion occurs first in this version.
           The function will keep calling itself, so that no version
           of the function will ever get to test whether it can stop.
           The program will eventually terminate with a run-time error.
        */
        count ( val - 1);
        if ( val > 1)
                printf ( "\t\t\t\t**** Displaying val: %3d\n", val);
}
```

Similarly, the following version of the function is incorrect because the value of **val** used in each call is moving *away* from the termination value of 1. This version will also end in a run-time error.

```
/* Incorrect recursive function */

/* NOTE:   DO NOT USE THIS VERSION OF THE RECURSIVE FUNCTION.
   This version will terminate in a run-time error.
*/

void count ( int val)
{
        if ( val > 1)
                count ( val + 1);  /* val increases, so it won't terminate */
```

```
                    /* Main task line for function count().
                       After a return from another call to count(), control returns
                       to this point.
                    */
                    printf ( "\t\t\t\t**** Displaying val: %3d\n", val);
           }
```

▶**REMEMBER**   A recursive function must always test whether it can stop *before* calling another version of itself. If a recursive call is made, the parameters in some call should eventually have values that will make further recursive calls unnecessary.

The following program calls a function, **recurse — reverse( )**, to print the reversed form of a string:

```
/* Program to reverse a string and display it.
   Program uses a recursive function to reverse and display the line.
*/

#include <stdio.h>
#define NULL_CHAR '\0'
#define MAX_STR    80

/* reverse a line, and display it backwards. */
void recurse_reverse ( char *str)
{
        /* If the next character is NULL_CHAR, do nothing.
           Note that the condition increments the pointer value,
           so the "new" string is actually one character shorter.
           Thus, if the original string was "hello",
           the new string would be "ello".
           NOTE: the test condition increments the current position
           in str BEFORE testing. Thus, the version of str passed in the
           recursive call starts one character into the string.
           For example, if str == "hello", the argument to the recursive
           call == "ello".
        */
        if ( *(++str) != NULL_CHAR)
                recurse_reverse ( str);

        /* NOTE: The  current position of str is decremented BEFORE writing.
           This is because the if test had incremented the position before
           the recursive call. This decrement essentially restores str to
           the value it is supposed to have in the current version of the
           function.
           For example, if the value of str == "hello" coming into the
           function, then this version of the function is responsible for
           writing the 'h' NOT the 'e'.
        */
        printf ( "%c", *(--str));
}

main()
{
        void recurse_reverse ( char *);
        char curr_str [ MAX_STR];

        printf ( "? ");
        gets ( curr_str);
        printf ( "%s\n", curr_str);
        recurse_reverse ( curr_str);
}
```

The function works by checking whether it is positioned before the null character. If so, the function writes the current character. If not, the function moves forward one character in the string and calls itself with the shortened version of the string. Each successive call to **recurse—reverse( )** works with a shorter string. Eventually, the function must be called with a single character string. The following illustration summarizes the calls and the values of ***(++str)** and ***(−−str)** after each call:

| | | Inside called function | |
Calling function	Called function	*(++str)	*(--str)
main ()	recurse_reverse (hello)	e	h
recurse_reverse (hello)	recurse_reverse (ello)	l	e
recurse_reverse (ello)	recurse_reverse (llo)	l	l
recurse_reverse (llo)	recurse_reverse (lo)	o	l
recurse_reverse (lo)	recurse_reverse (o)	\0	o

Costs of Recursion

Recursive functions can make your code much more compact and easy to read, but not necessarily more efficient. In fact, sometimes recursive versions of a function can be very inefficient. In this section, we'll look briefly at an example of a recursive function that becomes more inefficient as the values used increase. If you don't feel comfortable with the numbers used here, don't worry. The main point is to give you an idea of how the number of recursive calls can grow. The example also shows that you can make more than one recursive call in a function.

The following program uses a recursive function to compute a Fibonacci number. Fibonacci numbers are elements in a mathematical series that seem to occur in all sorts of situations. The definition of a Fibonacci number is simple but recursive.

The first two Fibonacci numbers, **fib(1)** and **fib(2)**, are defined as 1. Subsequent Fibonacci numbers are formed by adding the two preceding Fibonacci numbers. Thus, **fib(3)** == **fib(2)** + **fib(1)** == 1 + 1 == 2. Table 12-2 lists the first few Fibonacci numbers.

The following program computes the desired Fibonacci number. The program starts to become quite inefficient after about the twentieth Fibonacci number.

Table 12-2.   Fibonacci Numbers

Number	Value	Source
fib(1)	1	definition
fib(2)	1	definition
fib(3)	2	fib(1) + fib(2)
fib(4)	3	fib(2) + fib(3)
fib(5)	5	fib(3) + fib(4)
fib(6)	8	fib(4) + fib(5)
fib(7)	13	fib(5) + fib(6)
fib(8)	21	fib(6) + fib(7)

```
/* Program to compute a specified Fibonacci number.
   Program also illustrates recursion.
*/

#include <stdio.h>
#include <math.h>

long fib ( int x)
{
        if ( x > 2)
                return ( fib ( x - 1) + fib ( x - 2));
        else
                return ( 1);
}


main ()
{
        long fib (int), fibans;
        int seed;

        printf ( "Number? ");
        scanf ( "%d", &seed);
        fibans = fib ( seed);
        printf ( " fib (%2d) == %ld\n", seed, fibans);
}
```

This function computes the specified Fibonacci number. Notice the structure of the recursive function, **fib( )**. Before making a recursive call, the function tests whether it can stop. If so, a specific value (1) is returned, and the function returns control to the calling function. If not, the function calls itself *twice*. This is valid but less common.

The Fibonacci number **fib(4)** is the sum of **fib(2)** and **fib(3)**. But **fib(3)** is itself the sum of **fib(2)** and **fib(1)**. If you don't keep track of the two preceding Fibonacci numbers, you need to do lots of work each time one of the higher Fibonacci numbers is computed.

The following program records each call to the **fib( )** function. Otherwise, it is identical to the preceding program.

```
/* Program to compute a specified Fibonacci number,
   and also to keep track of the number of recursive calls.
   Program also illustrates recursion.
*/

#include <stdio.h>
#include <math.h>

long nrcalls = 0;

long fib ( int x)
{
        nrcalls += 1;
        if ( x > 2)
                return ( fib ( x - 1) + fib ( x - 2));
        else
                return ( 1);
}


main ()
{
        long fib (int), fibans;
        int seed;

        printf ( "Number? ");
        scanf ( "%d", &seed);
        fibans = fib ( seed);
        printf ( " fib (%7d) == %ld;       ", seed, fibans);
        printf ( "%7ld calls to fib()\n", nrcalls);
}
```

The program produces the following outputs for selected Fibonacci numbers:

```
Number?  fib (10) ==        55;        109 calls to fib()
Number?  fib (20) ==      6765;      13529 calls to fib()
Number?  fib (30) ==    832040;    1664079 calls to fib()
```

Notice that the number of calls gets unacceptably high for even a relatively small value of **seed**.

It is always possible to accomplish a task in a nonrecursive way. The trade-offs are efficiency of coding and efficiency of execution. For example, the following version of the **fib( )** function will compute Fibonacci numbers nonrecursively:

```
/* Non-recursive version of Fibonacci function. */

long fib ( int x)
{
        long f1 = 1,      /* fib ( n - 1) */
             f2 = 1,      /* fib ( n - 2) */
```

```
        curr_fib;      /* current value of fib () */
int index;

if ( x > 2)
{
        /* cases 1 and 2 are handled by the else */
        for ( index = 3; index <= x; index++)
        {
                curr_fib = f1 + f2;
                /* as index increases, f1 becomes f2, and
                   curr_fib becomes f1.
                */
                f2 = f1;
                f1 = curr_fib;
        }
        return ( curr_fib);
}
else
        return ( 1);
}
```

In this section, we've only been able to introduce some of the main concepts associated with recursion. We'll see more examples in Chapter 17. You may want to consult other sources. *The C Library,* by Kris Jamsa (Osborne/McGraw-Hill, 1985) has a chapter on recursion, and includes numerous additional examples.

Summary

In this chapter you learned more about functions, and learned some procedures for error handling. The chapter also provided some additional examples of C source code, including two short programs for exercising some specialized but useful functions.

In the next chapter, you'll learn about a variant of the **main( )** function that includes parameters. You'll learn how to write programs that allow you to specify options on the command line when invoking the program. In the process, you'll get another exercise program you can add to or adapt to your needs.

13

Command Line Arguments

Under many operating systems, including DOS, you start a program simply by typing the program's name. Thus, to start QuickC, you can type

```
qc
```

and press RETURN. At that point, the QuickC environment will start up, placing you in a file named **untitled.c**.

You can also start up QuickC with various options, including a file name. For example, suppose you wanted to edit, then compile the contents of the string exercising program from the previous chapter. Suppose this program was in a file named **str.c**.

The following command line will start QuickC and will immediately put you in the **str.c** file, ready for editing:

```
qc str
```

Let's assume you had the finance exercising program in a file named **finance.c**; some of its functions should be taken from the Quick library, **qcstuff.qlb**. You could use the following command line to invoke QuickC, tell the compiler to refer to the **qcstuff.qlb** Quick library, and tell the compiler that you want to work with the file **finance.c**.

```
qc /lqcstuff finance
```

So, we've seen three different ways to call up the QuickC program. Each invocation puts you into a somewhat different mode. These three ways represent only a small fraction of the options you can specify when invoking the program. QuickC is a very flexible program, capable of operating in different ways.

This chapter will discuss how to give your programs the same kind of flexibility.

main( ) as Program and as Function

You've seen that C programs start executing at the function **main( )**. If a program terminates normally, the program ends when **main( )** has finished executing. In a sense, **main( )** *is* the program. On the other hand, because the **main( )** function can be put anywhere in the program, it doesn't really look any different from other functions. In this sense **main( )** is just an ordinary function.

Functions, as you know, can have parameters. You can define a **main( )** function with parameters. However, C restricts **main( )** in the number and types of parameters it can have, as we'll see.

If you define **main( )** with parameters, you are essentially passing parameters to the program, since **main( )** will start executing. Thus, the **qc str** command invokes the QuickC program with the name of a file as a parameter.

What Are Command Line Arguments?

When you interact with the operating system, you are generally giving commands of one sort or another. We've already seen that typing a program's name amounts to giving a command to run the program. A line containing such a command is called a *command line*.

As the examples above and your own experience should demonstrate, you can specify more than just a program name on a command line. Such additional terms on a command line are known as *command line arguments*. Command line arguments are separated by blank spaces. Thus, **str** was a command line argument for the **qc** command; **/lqcstuff** and **finance** were command line arguments for **qc** in another example.

You may have been using command line arguments all along, perhaps without even knowing that you were doing so. All of the following examples include command line arguments:

```
A> copy finance.c b:
A> diskcopy a: b:
A> type finance.c
A> cat file1 file2 file3 file4
A> tex ch13
A> qc /lqcstuff /b
```

The first of these copies the file **finance.c** from the current directory to the same name on a disk in drive B. In addition to the program name (**copy**), there are two command line arguments (**finance.c** and **b:**). The second command, **diskcopy**, also has two command line arguments (**a:** and **b:**). The next example has only one argument in addition to the program name. The following example actually has four command line arguments, besides the program; this command displays the contents of each of the four files on the screen. Finally, the last example invokes QuickC, using the **qcstuff.qlb** Quick library, and running the program on a monchrome monitor.

Eventually, you will learn to write your C programs so that you pass the programs such command line arguments. This is a powerful facility that allows you to build flexible programs.

Command Line Arguments in DOS

Before looking at how to implement command line arguments in your C programs, let's look at a few examples of command line arguments with some DOS commands. If you're familiar with DOS, these examples may give you a better insight into how DOS works. If you're new to DOS, you can read these examples for information about how the programs work.

The echo Command

The DOS **echo** command displays messages on the screen. You'll generally use **echo** in batch files (files consisting of DOS command sequences), to provide certain messages as the commands in the file are being carried out. The following batch file (let's call it **showecho.bat**) provides an example:

```
echo This line and the same line without the echo will be written
```

If you type **showecho** or **showecho.bat** at the DOS prompt line (let's say, **A>**), the following will appear on the screen:

```
A> echo This line and the same line without the echo will be written
This line and the same line without the echo will be written
```

You can also use **echo** in other ways, and we'll look at these different uses of **echo** to find out how the command works.

echo with No Arguments   If you type **echo** at the DOS prompt, the following message will appear on your screen:

```
ECHO is on
```

This tells you that DOS is in its default mode, which echoes (or displays) whatever you type and whatever DOS has to say to you.

When you type **echo** by itself, DOS checks whether or not the default mode is to echo input and other information. Thus, if DOS finds no command line arguments for the **echo** command, the response is to tell you whether the echo mode is on or off.

echo with On or Off   If you type **echo on** or **echo off** at the DOS prompt, or if you include one of these command lines in a batch file, DOS will change its setting for the **echo** mode to the specified value. Thus, if DOS reads either "on" or "off" as the first command line argument, the **echo** mode is set to the specified value.

echo with a String   If you type **echo** followed by an ordinary string at the DOS prompt, two lines (such as those in the first **echo** example) will be displayed on your screen. Thus, if DOS sees a sequence of characters, not starting with either "on" or "off," the remainder of the command line is interpreted as something to be displayed. (There are certain characters that will make **echo** do additional processing, but we won't get into them here.)

Depending on how you give the **echo** command, DOS will take different actions, and will interpret the contents of the command line differently. You don't need to worry about how DOS does this. Essentially, DOS checks a certain area of memory for anything you might have typed on the command line. Based on what, if anything, it finds there, the **echo** command does what you've asked.

The dir Command

The **dir** command gives you a listing of files and directories. You can ask for such a listing by simply typing **dir**, or you can include command line arguments to elaborate your request.

dir with No Arguments   If you just type **dir**, DOS will list the files and directories contained in your current directory. DOS interprets the absence of command line arguments as an instruction to display the contents of the directory in which you are currently working, and to use the default directory display mode.

Thus, typing **dir** at a DOS prompt produced the following listing:

```
Volume in drive C has no label
Directory of  C:\BK\SRC

.              <DIR>          5-13-87    2:34p
..             <DIR>          5-13-87    2:34p
TXDETAB  EXE         9590     7-20-87    3:26p
STRINGS  H             90     5-13-87    1:30p
CH10           <DIR>          7-13-87   12:20a
CH11           <DIR>          7-14-87   12:56a
CH9            <DIR>          7-08-87    9:00a
PROGINFO H            494     5-21-87   12:04a
DETEX    EXE         9776     7-01-87   10:51a
WFMACS   H           1757     6-05-87    6:52p
WFTIME   H           1433     7-08-87    9:46a
WFPREP   H            902     7-08-87   12:56a
CH13           <DIR>          7-09-87    4:17p
CH14           <DIR>          7-14-87    1:29p
CH12           <DIR>          7-08-87    3:05p
CH15           <DIR>          7-16-87    4:19p
       16 File(s)    1890304 bytes free
```

The default display mode is to provide various types of information about the entries in the listing, such as the file's size, and the date and time when the file was last modified. Entries identified as <DIR> are directories contained within the current directory (C:\BK\SRC).

dir with a File Specification   You may want a listing of only certain types of files in a directory. For example, to get a listing of the header files in the current directory, type **dir *.h** at the DOS prompt. The * is a wildcard character, which tells DOS to accept any name in that position. The command tells DOS to list all files in the current directory that end in **.h**. Invoking **dir** with this command line argument would produce a listing such as the following:

```
Volume in drive C has no label
Directory of  C:\BK\SRC

STRINGS  H             90     5-13-87    1:30p
PROGINFO H            494     5-21-87   12:04a
WFMACS   H           1757     6-05-87    6:52p
WFTIME   H           1433     7-08-87    9:46a
WFPREP   H            902     7-08-87   12:56a
        5 File(s)    1886208 bytes free
```

Including a file specification as a command line argument provides a selective listing of a directory. DOS understands various types of file specifications. Consult your DOS documentation for more information.

dir with Switches   You can also control the way in which the contents of a directory are displayed. DOS allows switches to specify certain processing options. Switches usually begin with a predefined character (/ in DOS and — in UNIX), and are used to tell a command or program what options you want to use when invoking the command.

The DOS **dir** command can understand two switches, /**p** and /**w**. The /**p** switch tells DOS to fill the screen with directory entries, then to pause until the user presses a key. The following command line leaves the partial directory listing below it on the screen:

```
C:\BK\SRC> dir ch12 /p
      .           <DIR>       7-08-87   3:05p
      ..          <DIR>       7-08-87   3:05p
      1     C       1390      7-20-87   3:27p
      2     C        211      7-20-87   3:27p
      3     C        554      7-20-87   3:27p
      4     C        978      7-20-87   3:28p
      5     C        306      7-20-87   3:28p
      6     C       1170      7-20-87   3:28p
      7     C        231      7-20-87   3:28p
      8     C        568      7-20-87   3:28p
      9     C       2378      7-20-87   3:28p
     10     C        568      7-20-87   3:28p
     11     C        565      7-20-87   3:28p
     12     C        628      7-20-87   3:29p
     13     C        175      7-20-87   3:29p
     14     C        168      7-20-87   3:29p
     15     C        489      7-20-87   3:29p
     16     C        293      7-20-87   3:29p
     17     C        643      7-20-87   3:29p
     18     C        392      7-20-87   3:29p
     19     C        295      7-20-87   3:55p
     20     C        225      7-20-87   3:29p
     21     C        209      7-20-87   3:29p
Strike a key when ready . . .
```

This command line tells DOS to display the contents of the directory **ch12**, contained in the current directory. The /**p** switch tells DOS to pause when the screen is filled, until the user presses a key.

After a key is pressed, the remainder of the listing is displayed.

DOS looks for a / in the command line arguments. If the line contains such a character, DOS checks the character after it and acts according to the interpretation it gives that character. A switch can be a separate command line argument, or it can be at the end of a command line argument. Thus, the following command — which leaves no space between the directory name and the switch — would have the same effect as the command in the previous example:

```
C:\BK\SRC> dir ch12/p
```

The /**w** option tells DOS to list only the file names and extensions, writing five names on each line displayed. Using a /**w** switch in the previous example would produce the following listing:

```
C:\BK\SRC> dir ch12/p/w

Volume in drive C has no label
Directory of   C:\BK\SRC\CH12

.                 . .              1        C     2        C     3        C
4         C       5        C       6        C     7        C     8        C
9         C       10       C       11       C     12       C     13       C
14        C       15       C       16       C     17       C     18       C
19        C       20       C       21       C     22       C     23       C
24        C       25       C       26       C     27       C     28       C
29        C       30       C       31       C     32       C     33       C
34        C       35       C       36       C     37       C     38       C
39        C       40       C
          42 File(s)      1882112 bytes free
```

In this case, the /**p** switch has no effect, since the listing is not long enough to fill the screen. Notice that DOS processes *each* switch included on a command line.

Switches are a commonly used technique for letting users control the way a program is to work. You will come across switches in many contexts, and will probably find yourself using them in your own programs.

Arguments to main( )

The basic strategy for writing a C program capable of handling command line arguments is to pass the arguments to **main( )** as strings. Once inside, it will become the program's responsibility to interpret the arguments appropriately. Let's look at an example. Assume that the following program is in a file named **argdemo.c**:

```c
/* Program to illustrate use of parameters with main() */

main ( int argc, char *argv [])
{
        if ( argc > 1)        /* if there is a command line argument */
        {
                printf ( "At start of program, argc == %d\n\n", argc);
```

```
                    /* write the appropriate strings from the argv array */
                    while ( argc-- > 1)
                            printf ( "argc == %d: argv [ %d] == %s\n",
                                      argc, argc, argv [ argc ]);
            }
    }
```

If the executable version of this program were named **argdemo.exe**, the following command line would produce the output below it in the listing. The command line includes a program name and five command line arguments.

```
argdemo you? are How there. Hello

At start of program, argc == 6

argc == 5: argv [ 5] == Hello
argc == 4: argv [ 4] == there.
argc == 3: argv [ 3] == How
argc == 2: argv [ 2] == are
argc == 1: argv [ 1] == you?
```

The program displays information about **argc** and strings from **argv[ ]**. In particular, the program displays the starting value of **argc** (6), and then five strings. The parameters to **main( )** are an **int**, and an array of strings.

Notice that the strings in **argv[ ]** match the command line arguments to **argdemo**. This suggests that there is a relationship between the strings in **argv[ ]** and the command line arguments. Notice also that these are written in the reverse order from the way they were entered on the command line. This is to be expected, since the program counts downwards.

Strings in **argv[ ]** correspond to command line arguments. Furthermore, a string's subscript in **argv[ ]** corresponds to the argument's position on the command line. Thus, the string to which **argv[1]** points is the first command line argument.

According to the Draft Proposed ANSI Standard, **argv[1]** is guaranteed to be the first command line argument after the program name, if this argument is present. Subsequent strings correspond to subsequent command line arguments. Thus, if your program has four arguments, then **argv[1]** through **argv[4]** will point to the strings corresponding to the parameters.

Recall that **argc** was one larger than the number of parameters, since **argc** represents the number of command line arguments *plus* the program name. Note that **argv[argc]** has a null pointer, according to the Draft Proposed ANSI Standard. That is, the command line argument array, **argv[ ]** has an empty string after the last argument string. This makes it possible to check cleanly whether you've processed all the arguments.

The following listing illustrates this, using a variant of the preceding program:

```
/* Program to illustrate use of parameters with main() */

main ( int argc, char *argv [])
{
        int  index = 0;

        if ( argc > 1)         /* if there is a command line argument */
        {
                printf ( "At start of program, argc == %d\n\n", argc);

                /* write the appropriate strings from the argv array;
                   stop when the empty string is reached.
                */
                while ( strlen (argv [ ++index]) > 0)
                        printf ( "index == %d: argv [ %d] == %s\n",
                                 index, index, argv [ index ]);
        }
}
```

The following command line produces the output shown below the command line:

```
argdemo2 Hello there. How are you?

At start of program, argc == 6

argc == 1: argv [ 1] == Hello
argc == 2: argv [ 2] == there.
argc == 3: argv [ 3] == How
argc == 4: argv [ 4] == are
argc == 5: argv [ 5] == you?
```

This program writes the command line arguments, but writes them in the order the arguments were entered on the command line. Internally, the program moves forward in **argv[ ]**—that is, toward higher subscripts.

Notice the continuation condition for the **while** loop. The loop stops after the last command line argument has been written—when the empty string that indicates the end of the **argv[ ]** array is encountered.

Incidentally, the parameter names, **argc** and **argv[ ]**, are just conventional identifiers used for arguments to **main( )**. The names derive from *arg*ument *c*ount and *arg*ument *v*alues, respectively. You can, of course, name them anything you want.

Elements **1** through **argc** − **1** in **argv[ ]** correspond to the command line arguments. What about **argv[0]**? That depends on the operating system in which you're working. In some environments (including DOS 3.0 or later), the first string in the **argv[ ]** array contains the program's name. This is not the case with earlier versions of DOS.

▶**REMEMBER**   Strings in **argv[1]** through **argv[argc − 1]** correspond to command line arguments. In most implementations, **argv[0]** points to the program name.

Using Parameters to main( )

Let's look more closely at what you've just seen. You can define the **main( )** function with either zero or two parameters. If you define the function with two parameters, one must be an **int** and the second must be an array of strings (array of pointers to **char**).

In this context, each word on the command line is treated as a separate string, thus becoming a separate command line argument. Blanks separate words from each other. The **int** parameter specifies the number of words on the command line, including the program name. This value will always be at least 1, because 0 points to the program name.

Although you can have only two parameters to **main( )**, you can have virtually any number of command line arguments. This is because one of the arguments is an array that can be of variable size. The actual number of command line arguments supported is always operating system dependent.

The fact that the array elements must be strings is not a real limitation, as some examples will show. You can enter numerical values on the command line, read them as strings, then convert them to numerical form. The following program illustrates this:

```
/* Program to illustrate use of parameters with main()
   and use of conversion function atof().
*/

#include <stdlib.h>    /* for atof() */

main ( int argc, char *argv [])
{
        double fahr_to_cent ( double);
        double cent_to_fahr (double);
        double temperature, result;
        double atof ( const char *);

        if ( argc == 3)    /* if there's a 3 element command line argument */
        {
```

```
            temperature = atof ( argv [ 2]);
            if ( argv [ 1][0] == 'f')
            {
                    result = fahr_to_cent ( temperature);
                    printf ( "%6.2lf F == %6.2lf C\n",
                            temperature, result);
            }
            else
            {
                    result = cent_to_fahr ( temperature);
                    printf ( "%6.2lf C == %6.2lf F\n",
                            temperature, result);
            }
        } /* if 2 command line arguments */
        else
                printf ( "Usage : temp <'f' | 'c'> <temperature>\n");
}


double fahr_to_cent ( double fahr)
{
        return ( ( fahr - 32.0) * (5.0 / 9.0));
}

double cent_to_fahr ( double cent)
{
        return ( ( cent * (9.0 / 5.0)) + 32.0);
}
```

For each of the following calls to the program **temp**, the program produces the outputs below them:

```
temp f 98.6
 98.60 F ==   37.00 C

temp c 100
100.00 C == 212.00 F

temp f
Usage : temp <'f' or 'c'> <temperature>
```

This program reads the command line arguments as strings, just as in the earlier examples. The program then calls the QuickC library function, **atof( )**. This function converts a string argument to a floating point type, and returns this as a **double**. Thus, the function lets you read numerical information into your programs. The **stdlib.h** header file is needed to make **atof( )** usable in your programs.

Notice how we referred to the first letter in **argv[1]**: as element 0 in this array, or **argv[1][0]**.

Learning About Functions in QuickC   One of QuickC's handiest facilities is its on-line help with C and with the available library functions. Use this facility to find out about **atof( )**. To get on-line information about the library function **atof( )**:

1. Press the F1 key to get the Help dialog box.

2. Press **K** to get the C keywords list.

3. Use the arrow keys to move the cursor downward, and select the Data Conversion label from the list.

4. Select **atof( )**. Notice that there are other functions, with similar names: **atoi( )**, **atol( )**.

5. Press RETURN.

The top part of the screen will contain information about the function, including any header files required, a prototype for the function, and a brief summary of its purpose.

Notice the prototype for the function,

```
double atof ( const char *<string>);
```

contains the keyword **const** before the declaration for the string parameter. This keyword is a *type specifier,* and indicates that the **lvalue** associated with the specifier cannot be modified. In this case, the **const** specifier makes the parameter that is being declared a constant. This arrangement protects against undesirable changes to the parameter that might surprise the calling function.

You can use the **const** specifier in conjunction with other type specifiers (such as **int**, **double**), in definitions or declarations. The following two definitions are equivalent:

```
const   int    val;
const   val;
```

If you define a **const** variable without specifying a type, the variable is assumed to be of type **int**.

By looking at QuickC's on-line help, you can also find other functions related to the one you're inquiring about. For example, in searching for help about **atof( )**, you will come across **atoi( )** and **atol( )**, which convert strings to **int** and **long**, respectively.

Another Example Involving Conversions   Let's look at a more complex example, where the number of command line arguments may vary drastically

each time you run the program. The following program uses one of the
functions mentioned in the last chapter, **int — mean( )**:

```
/* Program to illustrate use of parameters with main()
   and use of conversion function atoi().
*/

#include <stdlib.h>    /* for atoi() */
#define MAX_SIZE 30

main ( int argc, char *argv [])
{
        double int_mean ( int [], int);
        double result;
        int atoi ( const char *);
        int index = 0;
        int values [ MAX_SIZE];

        while ( strlen ( argv [ ++index]) != 0)
                values [ index - 1] = atoi ( argv [ index]);
        if (index > 1)
                result = int_mean ( values, --index);
        else
                result = 0.0;
        printf ( "mean == %10.5lf, # of values == %2d\n", result, index);
}

/* compute mean of an array of integers */
double int_mean ( int vals [], int array_size)
{
        int     count;
        double running_sum= 0.0;

        for ( count = 0; count < array_size; count++)
                running_sum += vals [ count];
        return ( running_sum / array_size);
}
```

This program computes the mean of a collection of **int** values which have
been entered on the command line. In this program, you can enter up to 30
values. In DOS, there is a limit to the number of *characters* a command line
can have (127 bytes). This will indirectly determine how many arguments you
can pass to a program. If you think this restriction may cause problems in your
programs, check the documentation for your operating system to find out
more about the command line, and the possibility of increasing its size.

A Program to Exercise Command
Line Arguments

The following program lets you convert from any of several units to another.
The program also illustrates the use of parameters to **main( )**. The program
checks the number of command line arguments, and acts accordingly.

To run the program, **convert.exe**, you can simply type the program name or you can pass up to two command line arguments—a starting unit and a starting value. If you enter both a starting unit and a value, the program immediately computes the answer for you. If you enter just a starting unit (one command line argument), the program asks you for a value. If you simply type the program name, with no arguments, the program prompts you for both a conversion and a value.

The program uses include files, to make it somewhat easier to read and to indicate more clearly the portions of the program that are related to each other. The functions for converting between units are read in from file **units.c**. Some general utilities used in this program are in a file named **utils.c**. The header files (those with the **.h** extension) are read in so that certain functions will work properly. The following listing contains only the main program file; the listing does not include the source for the conversion functions.

The main program action occurs in two **switch** statements. The one in **main( )** acts on the basis of the number of command line arguments. The second **switch** statement, in **handle__all__values( )**, acts on the basis of the conversion requested by the user.

```
/* Program to convert values from one unit to another.
   User provides a unit, using either the full name of the
   unit or a common abbreviation;
   user also provides a value to convert.
   Program returns the corresponding value in the new unit.
   USAGE : convert {<starting unit>} {<value>}
            where both arguments are optional, but
            a value must be preceded by a starting unit.
   Program also illustrates use of parameters with main()
*/

#include <stdio.h>
#include <math.h>          /* needed for atof() */
#include "units.c"         /* contains unit conversion functions */
#include "utils.c"         /* contains miscellaneous utility functions */

#define INVALID_VAL -99999.999
#define MAX_STRING  80
#define MAX_UNITS   30
#define NULL_CHAR   '\0'

/* array of strings containing the valid names and abbreviations for
   units recognized by the program.
   NOTE: Add new names to the end of the array, since the function
   calls are based on the position of a name in the array.
*/
char *units [ MAX_UNITS] = {"cel", "centig", "centim", "cm", "fahr",
                 "gm", "gram", "in", "kg", "kilog",
                 "kilom", "km", "lb", "pou", "liter",
                 "mi", "ou", "oz", "qt", "quart"};

char start_units [ MAX_STRING];      /* abbreviation for starting units */
char end_units [ MAX_STRING];        /* abbreviation for ending units */

main ( int argc, char *argv [])
{
        void   make_str_lower ( char *);
```

```
        double get_dbl ( char *);
        double handle_all_values (int, double);
        int    what_case ( char *, char*[], int);
        int    conversion;
        double answer, value;
        char   which_unit [ MAX_STRING];

        /* handle 0, 1, or 2 command line arguments, in cases 1, 2, 3 */
        switch ( argc)
        {
                case 1 :  /* 0 command line arguments; just program name */
                          /* go into complete prompt mode */
                          /* get starting unit */
                          printf ( "Convert from what unit? ");
                          gets ( which_unit);
                          make_str_lower ( which_unit);

                          /* get starting value */
                          value = get_dbl ( "Value? ");

                          /* determine the conversion desired */
                          conversion = what_case ( which_unit, units, 20);

                          /* compute the result */
                          answer = handle_all_values ( conversion, value);
                          break;
                case 2 :   /* 1 command line argument; just starting unit */
                          /* got conversion, but no value; prompt for value */
                          /* get starting value */
                          value = get_dbl ( "Value? ");

                          /* prepare argument for checking */
                          make_str_lower ( argv [ 1]);

                          /* determine the conversion desired */
                          conversion = what_case ( argv [ 1], units, 20);

                          /* compute the result */
                          answer = handle_all_values ( conversion, value);
                          break;
                case 3 :  /* 2 command line arguments */
                          /* got conversion and value */

                          /* prepare argument for checking */
                          make_str_lower ( argv [ 1]);

                          /* convert argument to a double */
                          value = atof ( argv[ 2]);

                          /* determine the conversion desired */
                          conversion = what_case ( argv [ 1], units, 20);
                          /* compute the result */
                          answer = handle_all_values ( conversion, value);
                          break;
                default :
                          break;
        }
        printf ( "%10.5lf %s == %10.5lf %s\n",
                 value, start_units, answer, end_units);
}   /* END main() */


/* int what_case ( char *str, char *table [], int how_many)
   Determine what conversion is being asked for.
*/
```

```
int what_case ( char *str, char *table [], int how_many)
{
        int index;

        for ( index = 0; ( str_pos ( str, table [ index]) != 0) &&
                          ( index < how_many); index++)
                ;                               /* do nothing */
        if ( index >= how_many)                 /* if no match was found */
                return ( -1);
        else
                return ( index);
} /* END what_case() */


/* void assign_units ( char *start, char *finish)
   Store the appropriate units in the globals start_unit and end_unit
*/

void assign_units ( char *start, char *finish)
{
        strcpy ( start_units, start);
        strcpy ( end_units, finish);
}



/* double handle_all_values (int conversion, double value)
   call the required conversion function and return the conversion
*/

double handle_all_values (int conversion, double value)
{
        /* function prototypes */
        double cent_to_fahr ( double), fahr_to_cent ( double);
        double cm_to_inch ( double),   inch_to_cm ( double);
        double gm_to_oz ( double),     oz_to_gm ( double);
        double kg_to_lb ( double),     lb_to_kg ( double);
        double km_to_mi ( double),     mi_to_km ( double);
        double qt_to_liter ( double),  liter_to_qt ( double);
        void   assign_units ( char *, char *);

        double result;

        /* switch on conversion selected */
        switch ( conversion)
        {
                default:
                        printf ( "I don't recognize that unit. ");
                        printf ( "Leaving program.\n");
                        exit (0);
                case 0 :
                case 1 :
                        assign_units ( "C", "F");
                        result = cent_to_fahr ( value);
                        break;
                case 2 :
                case 3 :
                        assign_units ( "cm", "in");
                        result = cm_to_inch ( value);
                        break;
                case 4 :
                        assign_units ( "F", "C");
                        result = fahr_to_cent ( value);
                        break;
                case 5 :
                case 6 :
                        assign_units ( "gm", "oz");
```

```
                      result = gm_to_oz ( value);
                      break;
              case 7 :
                      assign_units ( "in", "cm");
                      result = inch_to_cm ( value);
                      break;
              case 8 :
              case 9 :
                      assign_units ( "kg", "lb");
                      result = kg_to_lb ( value);
                      break;
              case 10 :
              case 11 :
                      assign_units ( "km", "mi");
                      result = km_to_mi ( value);
                      break;
              case 12 :
              case 13 :
                      assign_units ( "lb", "kg");
                      result = lb_to_kg ( value);
                      break;
              case 14 :
                      assign_units ( "liter", "qt");
                      result = liter_to_qt ( value);
                      break;
              case 15 :
                      assign_units ( "mi", "km");
                      result = mi_to_km ( value);
                      break;
              case 16 :
              case 17 :
                      assign_units ( "oz", "gm");
                      result = oz_to_gm ( value);
                      break;
              case 18 :
              case 19 :
                      assign_units ( "qt", "liter");
                      result = qt_to_liter ( value);
                      break;
      }
      return ( result);
} /* END handle_all_values() */
```

The function **what — case( )** determines the array position of the conversion requested by the user. The array contains the abbreviations or names for the units allowed. For example, array positions 0 or 1 correspond to a centigrade to Fahrenheit conversion, since "cel" and "centig" are both accepted as indicating centigrade as a starting unit. The function simply searches the array until it reaches the end or finds the element with which the string, **str**, begins.

The **assign — units( )** function serves to elaborate for the output. This function puts the appropriate information into the **start — units** and **end — units** strings.

The bulk of the work is done in **handle — all — values( )**. This function looks intimidating but is actually quite simple, being nothing but a very long **switch** statement. You can easily add to this function if you add new conversion functions. Notice that the **default** case does not end with a **break**, unlike all the other cases, since the **exit( )** terminates the program anyway.

To complete our discussion, let us consider the contents of the two function files read in at the start of the conversion program. The following listing contains the functions from **utils.c**:

```
/* include file containing some miscellaneous utilities used in the
     unit conversion program.
*/

#include <ctype.h>       /* needed for tolower() macro */

/* int str_pos ( char str [], char substr [])
    returns the subscript value of the first occurrence of substr inside str.
    Returns -1 if substr is not found in str.
*/

int str_pos ( char str [], char substr [])
{
        int start, current, sub_current;

        /* see whether substr begins at each value of start */
        for ( start = 0; str [ start] != NULL_CHAR; start++)
                /* compare substr with str, from position start in
                    str onwards. Stop as soon as a mismatch is found
                    or the end of substr is reached.
                */
                for ( current = start, sub_current = 0;
                        str [ current] == substr [ sub_current];
                        current++, sub_current++)
                        ;

        /* if entire substr was found in str, return current value of
            start as position.
        */
        if ( substr [ sub_current] == NULL_CHAR)
                return ( start);
        else
                /* if substr was not found */
                return ( -1);
}  /* END str_pos() */



/* void make_str_lower ( char *str)
    convert a string to lower case characters
*/

void make_str_lower ( char *str)
{
        int index;

        for ( index = 0; str [ index] != NULL_CHAR; index++)
                str [ index] = tolower ( str [ index]);
}
```

```
/* double get_dbl ( char *message)
   Prompt for and read a double.
*/


double get_dbl ( char *message)
{
        double   val;         /* slot to store value read */
        int      args_read;   /* number of values read successfully */

        printf ( "%s ", message);
        args_read = scanf ( "%lf", &val);
        if ( args_read)                  /* if at least one value was read */
                return ( val);
        else
                return ( INVALID_VAL);
}
```

This file contains three general purpose functions that are useful for the conversion program. The **make—str—lower( )** function converts a string to all lowercase characters. This is important for the conversion program, since the array containing the units uses only lowercase characters. The header file, **ctype.h**, is needed for the **tolower( )** macro. This file is actually a nested include file, since the **utils.c** file is read into **convert.c**.

The **str—pos( )** function returns the array subscript corresponding to the first occurrence of **substr** in **str**. If **substr** is not found in **str**, the function returns −1.

Let's look at the algorithm used in this function. The basic strategy is to move through **str** from left to right, one character at a time. Starting with each character, the next step is to check whether **substr** is in **str**, beginning at the current starting character (**start**). To do this the function compares successive characters of **substr** with successive characters of **str** until the function reaches the end of **substr** or until there is a mismatch. If the end of **substr** is reached without a mismatch, then the position to be returned is the value of the current starting character.

The next listing contains the functions in **units.c**. These are all very simple functions—single line formulas. Nonetheless, they can be useful.

```
/* Include file containing various functions for converting between units.
   Currently used by program CONVERT.C
*/

double cent_to_fahr ( double cent)
{
        return ( ( cent * (9.0 / 5.0)) + 32.0);
}

double cm_to_inch ( double cm)
{
```

```
#define INCH_PER_CM  0.3937

        return ( cm * INCH_PER_CM);
}

double fahr_to_cent ( double fahr)
{
        return ( ( fahr - 32.0) * (5.0 / 9.0));
}

double gm_to_oz ( double grams)
{
#define OZ_PER_GRAM 0.03527396

        return ( grams * OZ_PER_GRAM);
}

double inch_to_cm ( double inch)
{
#define CM_PER_INCH  2.540005

        return ( inch * CM_PER_INCH);
}

double kg_to_lb ( double kg)
{
#define LB_PER_KG 2.20462

        return ( kg * LB_PER_KG);
}

double km_to_mi ( double km)
{
#define MI_PER_KM 0.62137

        return ( km * MI_PER_KM);
}

double lb_to_kg ( double lb)
{
#define KG_PER_LB  0.45359

        return ( lb * KG_PER_LB);
}

double liter_to_qt ( double liter)
{
#define QT_PER_LITER  1.05668

        return ( liter * QT_PER_LITER);
}

double mi_to_km ( double mi)
{
#define KM_PER_MI  1.609347

        return ( mi * KM_PER_MI);
}

double oz_to_gm ( double oz)
{
#define GRAM_PER_OZ 28.349527

        return ( oz * GRAM_PER_OZ);
}

double qt_to_liter ( double qt)
{
#define LITER_PER_QT 0.94636

        return ( qt * LITER_PER_QT);
}
```

The program is designed to make it easy to add new conversion functions. To do so, you simply need to add new values to the **units[ ]** array, and add new cases to the **switch** in **handle — all — values( )**.

Summary

In this chapter you learned about a means of making your C programs more flexible. By defining the main function to accept arguments, you make it possible to call the program with command line arguments, thereby making it easy to do things quickly with the program.

One of the most common uses of command line arguments is to specify files to read and write. In the next chapter, you'll find out how to create and open files, and how to use command line arguments to tell your program what files to use.

14

Files and Memory

So far, all our programs have involved just the standard input and output sources, **stdin**, **stdout**, and **stderr**. In the previous chapter, you learned how to pass arguments to a C program. You should now be able to handle files conveniently in C programs.

In this chapter, you'll learn how to create, use, and close files. We'll also look at some Run-Time library functions for working with files, and simple programs for manipulating files, such as removing blank lines.

Memory is the second major topic of the chapter. We'll look at why you would want to get additional memory while the program is running, how to get the memory when you need it, and how to use it when you have it.

Files

Earlier, you learned that a stream is essentially a sequence of characters. In most cases, this stream will be interpreted as a sequence of *text* characters, although sometimes the stream is treated as binary data. In text streams, some of the characters may play special roles, such as indicating the end of a line or the end of the stream. You also found that the standard files automatically available to your program were closely related to streams. In this section, you'll learn to define and use your own files.

From your perspective as programmer, files in C are pointers. When you create or open a file in a C program, you get a pointer to a variable of type FILE. This is a data type that contains information about a stream, such as its location, size, your current position in the stream, and so on. FILE is defined in **stdio.h**, so you need to include this header file in any program that involves files.

Let's look at a very simple example, useful only for demonstrating how to define a file. (If, by some coincidence, you have a file named **zqzqzqzq** on your disk, change its name temporarily or change the string argument to **fopen( )** to a name that doesn't match one of your disk files.)

```
/* Program to open and close a file. */

#include <stdio.h>

main ()
{
        FILE *file_ptr;                          /* 1 */
        FILE *fopen ( char *, char *);           /* 2 */

        file_ptr = fopen ("zqzqzqzq", "w");      /* 3 */
        if ( file_ptr != NULL)                   /* 4 */
                fclose ( file_ptr);              /* 5 */
}
```

If you compile and run this program, you will find a file named **zqzqzqzq** in your directory. The program defines a file, opens the file and immediately closes it, if possible. Let's look at the statements that do each of these things.

Line 1 defines a pointer to type FILE. Remember, FILE contains information about a stream. In C, this pointer is used to refer to a file. Line 2 contains the function prototype for **fopen( )**. This is a function that returns a pointer to FILE. The function takes two string arguments. In most implementations, this function declaration is included in **stdio.h**, so you would not need the declaration in your functions. In subsequent listings, we'll assume the function is declared in **stdio.h**.

In line 3, the program opens a new file. The library function, **fopen( )** (which is declared in **stdio.h**), associates the variable name, **file _ ptr**, with a text stream. If saved properly, this stream will become a file on your disk. In addition to returning a pointer to information about a stream, **fopen( )** fills in some of this information.

The first argument to **fopen( )** is a string that specifies the name to use for the disk file. When saved, the stream associated with **file _ ptr** will be a file named **zqzqzqzq** on your disk. The second argument tells **fopen( )** how you want to use this file. In this case, you are telling the program that you want to be able to write to this file.

If, for some reason, **fopen( )** cannot open a file, the function returns a null pointer. This indicates that no suitable target location could be found. The example just shows the syntax for calling **fopen( )**. Ordinarily, you'll check for an unsuccessful outcome when you first try to open a file, as in the next example. In the current program, line 4 checks for a null pointer.

If a file was opened — that is, if the pointer returned by **fopen( )** pointed somewhere — line 5 closes the file. The function **fclose( )** takes a file as its argument, and saves the file's contents to disk. This preserves anything written to the file. Nothing was written in the program, so the file, **zqzqzqzq**, contains zero bytes, as you'll see if you do a directory listing. You can remove this file from your disk, since we won't use it again.

What You Can Do to a File

In C, you can do the following things to a file:

- Open an existing file, for reading (**r**)

- Create a new file for writing (**w**)

- Add to an existing file (**a**)

- Open an existing file for both reading and writing, starting at the beginning of the file (**r+**)

- Create a new file for both reading and writing (**w+**)

- Open an existing file for both reading and writing, starting at the last place anything was changed in the file (**a+**)

The second argument to **fopen( )** specifies one of these things.

If you want to read information from a file that you've already created, use **r** when opening the file. This argument assumes that the file already exists. That is, **fopen( )** checks your disk for the file specified in the first argument to **fopen( )**, and returns a pointer to this file. If the function can't find the file, **fopen( )** returns a null pointer. You are not allowed to write to a file opened with the **r** option.

If you want to create a new file, into which you'll write information, use **w** as the argument to **fopen( )**. If you already have a disk file with the specified name, you'll lose the existing disk file. The **w** option always creates a new file. You can't read from such a file; you can only write to it.

If you'd like to write to an existing file, use **a** as the argument to **fopen( )**. This option tells the function to try to open an existing file for writing. If the function is able to do this, it moves you to the current end of the file and starts writing from that point. If the file you specified doesn't exist, the function creates a new file with that name. You can only write to such a file.

Sometimes, you may need to read from and write to the same file. You can enhance the preceding options to tell the function you want to be able to do both.

Use **r+** if you want to start at the beginning of an existing file, so you can read and write your way through it. As with **r**, this option tells **fopen( )** to look for an existing file, and return a pointer to it. However, the **r+** option lets you both read from and write to the file, once it is opened.

Use **w+** to create a new file that you'll be able to read from and write to, as needed. As with W, this option will destroy any existing file with the name you specify.

Finally, use **a+** to add to the file (starting at the current position in the file), while being able to read from or write to it. The current position is the last place at which anything was read from or written to the file.

▶**REMEMBER**   To open a file, use **fopen( )**, with two arguments. The first argument is the name of the disk file to be saved. The second argument specifies what you want to do with the file.

To close a file, use **fclose( )**, with the file pointer as its argument.

A Simple Notepad Program

The following program is a very simple note-taker. It provides another example of how to define and use files. The program is small, but contains important information. Study it carefully.

```c
/* Program to write text entered at the keyboard into a file.
   Program illustrates use of files in C.
*/

#include <stdio.h>

#define MAX_STR 100

main ( int argc, char *argv [])
{
        FILE *notes;                    /* essentially, the file you defined */
        char curr_str [ MAX_STR];       /* text entered at keyboard */
        int  line_count = 0;            /* # lines written */

        if ( argc < 2)                  /* if user didn't specify a file name */
            printf ( "Usage:: note <file name>\n");
        else    /* if argc >= 2 */
        {
            /* try to create a file, for writing to.
               If unable to create file, you get a NULL pointer back.
            */
            if ( ( notes = fopen ( argv [ 1], "w")) != NULL)
            {
                /* prompt for and get string */
                printf ( ": ");
                gets ( curr_str);

                /* stop when user enters an empty line */
                while ( strlen ( curr_str) != 0)
                {
                    /* write string to the file you created */
                    fprintf ( notes, "%d: %s\n",
                                ++line_count, curr_str);

                    /* prompt for and get string */
                    printf ( ": ");
                    gets ( curr_str);
                } /* END while no empty string */

                fclose ( notes);  /* close file to save your work */

                printf ( "%3d lines written\n", line_count);
            }                           /* END file writing activity */

            else                        /* if unable to open file */
                printf ( "Couldn't open file\n");
        }       /* END else (if argc >= 2) */
} /* END main() */
```

Suppose you had a compiled version of this program in a file called **note.exe**, and you started the program with the command line that follows.

```
note 7.10
```

The program will create a file that will be saved to disk as file **7.10**. Each line you entered while the program was running will be written to file **7.10**. When you finish your note-taking by entering a blank line, the program will close the disk file. Look at the contents of the file with your editor or by using the DOS TYPE command.

First, let's look at the major portions of the program. The body of **main( )** consists of an **if** statement and its alternative. If the program does not find a file name as a command line argument — if there is only one element in **argv[ ]** — you see a "usage" message. The real work occurs if you *have* specified a file to be opened.

The **else** construct also contains an **if** statement. If the log file was successfully created, the program reads your input and writes it to the log file. If the program is unable to open a file — that is, if the call to **fopen( )** returns a null pointer — the program displays an error message.

The pointer variable **notes** is used to refer to the file, and is defined the same way as **file ＿ ptr** was in the earlier program. Similarly, the call to **fclose( )** has the same format as in the earlier example.

The call to **fopen( )** is made in a different context than in the first example. This syntax for using **fopen( )** is common in C programs. The main work of creating a file is done in the assignment statement. This time, however, the assignment is made within a test for the **if** statement. If the returned pointer is NULL, the file could not be created, the condition would be false, and the **else** portion of the selection construct would be executed. (Remember that **argv[ ]** contains strings, so the first parameter to **fopen( )** is valid.)

The other statement involving files is the call to **fprintf( )**. Recall that we used this function when discussing **stderr**. The function works just like **printf( )**, except that you can specify the file to which it writes. This program writes to **notes**, the program's name for disk file **7.10**.

A Simple File Reader Program

While the **note** program writes simple files, the following program reads them:

```
/* Program to read text from a file.
   Program illustrates use of files, and some file functions in C.
*/

#include <stdio.h>
```

```
#define MAX_STR 100

main ( int argc, char *argv [])
{
        FILE *notes;                    /* essentially, the file you defined */
        char curr_str [ MAX_STR];       /* text entered at keyboard */

        if ( argc != 2)                 /* if user didn't specify a file name */
                printf ( "Usage:: note <file name>\n");
        else
        {
                /* try to open a file, for reading.
                   If unable to open file, you get a NULL pointer back.
                */
                if ( ( notes = fopen ( argv [ 1], "r")) != NULL)
                {
                        /* stop when a NULL pointer is returned. */
                        while ( fgets ( curr_str, MAX_STR, notes))
                                /* display string */
                                printf ( "%s\n", curr_str);

                        if ( feof ( notes))
                                printf ( "\n\n End of file reached.\n");
                        fclose ( notes);  /* close file */
                }                          /* END file reading activity */
                else                       /* if unable to open file */
                        printf ( "Couldn't open file\n");
        }       /* END else (if argc == 2) */
} /* END main() */
```

This program, called **reader**, opens the file specified in a command line argument (stored in **argv[1]**) and reads from this file, line by line, until an error is encountered or the end of the file is reached. The program displays each line as it's read from the file.

The only difference between the calls to **fopen( )** in **note** and in **reader** is in the option specifying what you want to do with the file. In this case, the **r** option says you want to read from the beginning of the file.

This program introduces two new functions, **fgets( )** and **feof( )**. The **fgets( )** function is for reading strings from a file. It is similar to the **gets( )** function you've seen already. There are some important differences between the two functions, however. The functions differ in the number of parameters they take, and in how they handle the newline character.

Notice that **fgets( )** takes three parameters, whereas **gets( )** takes only one. The first parameter to **fgets( )** specifies the string to be read. The second parameter specifies the maximum number of characters to be read. The third parameter specifies the file from which to read the string.

In the call to **fgets( )** in **reader**, the function reads characters from the specified file (**notes**), and builds a string (**curr ‗ str**) from these characters. The function keeps adding to **curr ‗ str** until it reads a newline character or until **MAX ‗ STR − 1** characters have been read. After it has finished reading, the function adds a ' \0' to terminate the string properly. Notice that the maximum number of characters the function reads is one less than the function call specifies. This is because the function needs to add the null character at the end of the string.

Recall that **gets( )** replaces the newline character with a null character. On the other hand, **fgets( )** keeps the newline character *and* adds a null character. Because of this, the output from this program is double spaced. One newline character is contained at the end of the string read, and another is at the end of the string argument to **printf( )**.

Notice how **fgets( )** is being used in the continuation condition for the **while** loop in **reader**. If the end of the file has been reached, the function returns an empty, or null, string. This is just a null character, 0, which evaluates to false in C. Thus, the continuation condition tests whether an empty string has been read.

A Note About Function Returns   If you check the documentation for **fgets( )** or for **gets( )**, you'll find that these functions have a return type, **char ***. Ordinarily, when you call a function in C, you'll assign its returned value to a variable of the appropriate type. In that case, the function call will be on the right of an assignment statement, and the variable to which the returned value is being assigned will be the left operand.

Sometimes, however, you may want to call the function in order to accomplish a task or to get information back through one of the parameters. In that case, you needn't use an assignment statement; just call the function with the appropriate parameters. We've generally been doing this when using **printf( )** and **scanf( )**. Recall that these functions actually do return values — the number of characters printed, and the number of arguments processed, respectively. However, we've been using these functions just to display or read information, and haven't made use of the returned value. For this reason, the calls to these functions have not been assignment statements.

Similarly, we've been using **gets( )** and **fgets( )** without making use of their returned values because we've gotten the desired strings through the parameters. However, unless the function is defined as returning **void**, it always returns the appropriate type of value — whether or not your program uses this value.

In the previous listing, we've implicitly made use of this property of C functions by using the value returned by **fgets( )** — looking for an empty string in the continuation condition for the **while** loop. Thus, when the **fgets( )**

function cannot read a proper string—because the end of the file has been reached or because of another error—the function returns an empty string. If the function returns a null string, then the function's "value" can also be interpreted as false.

feof( ) and ferror( )   When the **fgets( )** function returns a null pointer, your program has no way of knowing whether this value was returned because of a normal end of file or because of an error. Your program's actions may depend on the answer to this question. The **feof( )** macro tells you whether the end of file was encountered.

This macro takes one argument, a pointer to the file, or stream, you want to check. The macro returns 0 if the current file position is *not* the end of the file, and a nonzero value if the end of the file has been reached.

There's also a macro available for asking explicitly whether an error occurred. An error might occur, for example, if you open a file just for reading (using the R option), and then try to write into the file. The **ferror( )** macro also takes a file pointer as an argument, and returns a nonzero (true) value if an error has occurred while reading or writing the file.

A Program to Remove Blank Lines from a File

The following program removes blank lines from a file, then writes the remaining lines to a new file. The program opens and closes both files, **in** for reading and **out** for writing.

```
/* Program to remove blank lines from a file.
   A "blank" line contains only a newline, \n, or other whitespace,
   such as a tab, \t.
   USAGE :: deline <infile> <outfile>
*/

#include <string.h>
#include <stdio.h>

#define FALSE 0
#define TRUE  1
#define MAX_LINE 100

main ( int argc, char *argv [])
/* argc : Number of command line words    */
/* argv [] : Pointers to command line words */
{
        FILE *in;                       /* File used for input      */
        FILE *out;                      /* File used for output     */
```

```
int  nr_lines = 0;            /* nr of lines written */
int  discard_lines = 0;       /* nr of lines discarded */
char *test_str, curr_str [ MAX_LINE];

if (argc < 3)
{                   /* Check if enough arguments        */
        fprintf(stderr,"BLANK LINE removal utility\n");
        fprintf(stderr,"Usage: deline in_filename out_filename\n");
        exit(1);
}

if ((in = fopen(argv[1],"r")) == NULL)
{
        fprintf(stderr,"Can't open source file:       %s\n",argv[1]);
        exit(1);
}

if ((out = fopen(argv[2],"w")) == NULL)
{
        fprintf(stderr,"Can't open target file:       %s\n",argv[2]);
        exit(1);
}

/* main work of the program is done here */
while ( (test_str = fgets ( curr_str, MAX_LINE, in)) != NULL)
{
        /* if the line contains any material, write line to new file
                (otherwise, discard line)
        */
        if ( just_wspace_str ( curr_str) == 0)
        {
                fputs ( curr_str, out);
                nr_lines++;

                }
                else     /* if the string was just whitespace */
                        discard_lines++;
        }

        /* Report on activity */
        printf ( "\n\n%s  ---->   %s\n\n", argv [ 1], argv [ 2]);

        printf ( "%5d lines written; %5d lines discarded\n",
                nr_lines, discard_lines);
        fclose(in);
        fclose(out);
}


/* Returns true if the entire string has just whitespace characters. */
int just_wspace_str ( char *the_str)
{
        int  index;
        int  just_wspace_char ( char);

        for ( index = 0; just_wspace_char ( the_str [ index]);
                index++)
        {
                ;
        }
        if ( index >= strlen ( the_str))
                return ( TRUE);
        else
                return ( FALSE);
}


/* returns TRUE if character is a whitespace or end of string character. */
int just_wspace_char ( char the_char)
{
```

```
        switch ( the_char)
        {
                case ' ':
                case '\n':
                case '\r':
                case '\t':
                case '\0':
                        return ( TRUE);
                        break;
                default:
                        return ( FALSE);
                        break;
        }
}
```

This program opens the first file specified, and reads its contents line by line. Each line is examined to determine whether it contains anything other than whitespace characters. If so, the line is written to the second file; otherwise, the line is discarded, and is not written to the file.

Notice the commands for opening the two files. They are similar to the commands in the earlier examples, and are just the standard way of opening a file. You've seen **fprintf( )** for writing material to a file. You've also seen **puts( )** for writing a string to **stdout**.

The **fputs( )** function writes a string to the specified file. The function takes two parameters, the string and the file, and it returns the last character written as an integer. The function does *not* copy the terminating null character to the file.

The section of the program responsible for deciding whether to write a line to the new file uses the specialist functions, **just_wspace_char( )** and **just_wspace_str( )**. These functions return a nonzero **int** if the string or character they have been processing contains anything other than a whitespace character. Notice the use of **just_wspace_char( )** in the continuation condition of **just_wspace_str( )**.

A Program to Replace Tabs with Spaces

Let's look at one more program involving files. This one replaces any occurrences of the tab character ('\t') with the appropriate number of spaces:

```
/* Program to replace tabs with spaces in a file, and to write
   detabbed information to a new file.
*/

#include <stdio.h>
```

```
#define FALSE 0
#define TRUE  1
#define CZ    '\032'          /* Ctrl-Z */
#define TABSKIP  8

main(int argc, char *argv [])
{
        FILE *in;                       /* File used for input       */
        FILE *out;                      /* File used for output      */
        int ch_read, index;

        printf ("%d\n", argc);

        if (argc < 3)                   /* Check if enough arguments      */
        {
                fprintf(stderr,"TAB removal utility\n");
                fprintf(stderr,"Usage:   detab in_filename out_filename\n");
                exit(1);
        }

        if ((in = fopen(argv[1],"r")) == NULL)
        {
                fprintf(stderr,"Can't open source file:      %s\n",argv[1]);
                exit(1);
        }

        if ((out = fopen(argv[2],"w")) == NULL)
        {
                fprintf(stderr,"Can't open target file:      %s\n",argv[2]);
                exit(1);
        }

        /* detabbing process starts here */
        index = 1;

        /* read contents of in file character by character, to find tabs */
        while ( ( ch_read = getc ( in)) != EOF)
        {
                switch ( ch_read)
                {
                        case '\t' :      /* tab character */
                                do      /* put spaces until next tabstop */
                                {
                                        putc ( ' ', out);
                                        index++;
                                }
                                while ((index % TABSKIP) != 1);

                                break;
                        case '\r':       /* return */
                        case '\n':       /* newline */
                                putc ( ch_read, out);
                                index = 1;
                                break;
                        /* to strip out Ctrl-Zs that may be there
                           at end of file;
                        */
                        case CZ:
                                break;
                        default     :
                                putc ( ch_read, out);
                                index++;
                                break;
                }   /* switch */
        }   /* while */
        fclose(in);
        fclose(out);
}
```

This program replaces any tab character encountered in a file with the number of blanks needed to get to the next tabstop. The program then writes the resulting string to a new file. To do its work, the program reads character by character from **in**, the source file, and writes character by character to **out**, the detabbed file. The program uses the character handling macros you learned about in Chapter 5, **putc( )** and **getc( )**.

The CZ case in the **switch** construct is designed to deal with text editors that pad out files with Control-Z characters. The detabbing program just ignores these characters, and does not write them to the detabbed file.

Overview of File Manipulation

Although you'll use files often in your programs, the number of things you'll actually do with files is quite small. Before you can do anything with files you've defined, you must open them, using the **fopen( )** function. This function gives you a pointer to a FILE.

Depending on what you intend to do with the file, you'll use either the input routines—**getc( )**, **fgets( )**—or the output routines—**putc( )**, **fputs( )**, **fprintf( )**—or both.

If anything goes wrong, you can use the **feof( )** and **ferror( )** macros, to determine what actions to take. Finally, you'll need to close the file, using the **fclose( )** function. This ensures that files are properly terminated and saved.

Dynamic Memory Allocation

When you define variables in a program or function, the compiler allocates storage space for these variables. The amount of storage allocated for these variables is predetermined and fixed. This allocation strategy is called *static storage,* since you allocate the memory once, in advance, and then leave it alone. Static storage works well if you know in advance the amount of storage you'll need.

However, sometimes your memory requirements may vary drastically. For example, suppose you had a program to compute the mean of a collection of numbers read from a file. Sometimes the file might contain only a few values, and sometimes it might contain several hundred. You could define an array large enough to hold the largest number of values expected. This would use up lots of memory each time you ran the program, but would probably be acceptable if you only had one such array.

On the other hand, suppose you had several arrays you needed to manipulate, each with a range of possible sizes. In such a situation it won't be practical, and may not even be possible, to allocate enough storage for the largest possible size of each. For example, suppose you had 10,000 bytes of available memory, and you had five arrays, in each of which you might need to store as many as 400 **double** values. For each of these, you would need 3,200 (400 values * 8 bytes per **double**) bytes. The 16,000 bytes required exceeds what you have available. So you won't be able to define all five of these arrays — even if you'll never need all the space in each of the arrays at the same time.

What you really need to be able to do for each array is get enough memory to store the number of values you'll need to read for that particular run of the program. For example, suppose you had 400, 200, 100, 100, and 200 values for the 5 arrays. Using space efficiently means you would need 3,200 + 1,600 + 800 + 800 + 1,600 = 8,000 bytes, which is under the 10,000 byte limit. With a means of allocating the required storage when you need it, you would be able to run this program.

The solution is a technique called *dynamic memory allocation,* which allows you to allocate memory as you need it. For a situation such as the above, a dynamic storage allocation strategy would grab enough memory to hold 400 **double** values, then 200, then 100, and so on. C implementations include functions for allocating memory in this manner. Before we look at some examples, you need to find out about another operator, for converting information from one type to another.

C's Cast Operator

So far, you've seen that the C compiler can convert information from one type to another to evaluate an expression. Sometimes you'll want to force such conversions.

For example, suppose you have a **double** variable, which you need to display in integer format. You can't simply include an **int** placeholder and pass **printf( )** a **double** argument. The outcome will not be correct, as the following program and output show. One way to solve the problem is to assign the **double** to an **int** variable, then pass this variable as the parameter to **printf( )**. This is effective, but very roundabout.

The C *cast operator* — **( )** — lets you make such conversions much more directly. The following example illustrates the use of this operator, and shows the differences when using or not using the operator:

```
main ()
{
        double d1 = 10;

        printf ( "as int: %5d\n", d1);
        printf ( "as (int) %5d\n", (int) d1);
}
```

This program produces the following output. Notice that the first line is incorrect:

```
as int:     0
as (int)    10
```

This program tries to write the contents of a **double** variable as an **int**. The first time, the **double** is passed directly, and an incorrect result is written. The second time, the **double** is first converted to **int** by using the cast operator — in this case, **(int)** — to copy the value to an integer internally, so that the proper result could be displayed.

To use the cast operator with an expression, simply precede the expression with the type to which you want to cast the expression. This "target type" must be in parentheses, because these parentheses represent the cast operator. The cast operator is a unary operator. As such, it has very high precedence — at the same level as the address, indirection, and **sizeof( )** operators. For example, to convert the result of evaluating **7.0 ∗ test ─ val** to integer, you would write:

```
(int) (7.0 * test_val)
```

Recall that the unary operators associate right to left. This means that if you have multiple unary operators in succession, they are applied from right to left. For example, what will be displayed in the following?

```
main ()
{
        int i1 = 10, i2 = 10;
```

```
            printf ( "as (double) %10.5lf\n", (double) - ++i1);
            printf ( "as (double) %10.5lf\n", (double) - --i2);
    }
```

This program writes the values −11 and −9 in **double** format. Let's see how the program arrives at these values. The first call to **printf( )** builds its argument as follows, by applying the unary operators from right to left.

1. Increment **i1** before using (→ **11**).

2. Apply unary negation operator to the new value of **i1** (→ −**11**).

3. Convert this value to a **double**.

The second call works in a similar manner, except that the value of **i2** after step 1 above == 9, rather than 11.

Why is the call to **printf( )** in the following program invalid? If you're not sure, compile the program to see the error message.

```
/* Program to test your command of the unary operators. */
main ()
{
        int i1 = 10;
        printf ( "as (double) %10.5lf\n", (double) ++ -i1);
}
```

▶**REMEMBER**   To apply the cast operator to an expression, put the type to which you wish to convert the expression inside parentheses, then put this operator to the left of the expression you want to convert. For example, to cast **x * y** to **double**, type **(double) (x*y)**.

Note that **(double) x * y** would produce a different intermediate result, since the cast operator has higher precedence than multiplication. Only the **x** would be cast to **double**. The final outcome, in this case, would still be the same, however.

Syntactically, you can convert an expression to either integral or floating point types, or to a pointer type. Thus, the following assignment is a valid conversion—converting the value of **i1** from an ordinary integer to an address.

```
/* assume i_ptr is a pointer to int; i1 = 4000;

i_ptr = (int *)i1;
```

Applying the cast operator produces only values, not variables. That is, the cast operator never returns an **lvalue**. The operator simply returns a temporary value of the appropriate type, for use in an expression. The program can assign this temporary value to a variable, if necessary.

In the next section we'll see why converting to a pointer variable can be useful.

The Strategy of Dynamic Memory Allocation

The strategy for dynamic storage allocation is to define a pointer to the appropriate type, then allocate the desired amount of contiguous storage and make the pointer variable point to the first cell in this storage. (Contiguous storage is storage in consecutive address spaces.) Once allocated, you can move through the values you've read by using pointer arithmetic or array subscripting. The following program shows how to allocate such storage:

```
/* Program to allocate storage for an array of elements,
   and to display the contents.
   Program illustrates use of malloc().
*/

#include <stdlib.h>
#define MAX_SIZE 10

main ()
{
        int     int_array [ MAX_SIZE];
        int     *int_ptr, index;

        for ( index = 0; index < MAX_SIZE; index++)
                int_array [ index] = index;

        int_ptr = (int *) malloc ( MAX_SIZE * sizeof ( int));

        if ( int_ptr)
        {
                for ( index = 0; index < MAX_SIZE; index++)
                        *(int_ptr + index) = int_array [ index];

                for ( index = 0; index < MAX_SIZE; index++)
                {
                        printf ( "%2d: &int_array [ index] == %u; ",
                                index, &int_array [ index]);
```

```
                              printf ( "int_array [ index] == %2d\n",
                                      int_array [ index]);
                     }

                     printf ( "\n\n");
                     for ( index = 0; index < MAX_SIZE; index++)
                     {
                              printf ( "%2d: int_ptr + index == %u; ",
                                      index, int_ptr + index);
                              printf ( "*(int_ptr + index) == %2d\n",
                                      *(int_ptr + index));
                     }
             }    /* END if storage was allocated */
     }
```

On a sample run, this program produces the following output:

```
0: &int_array [ index] == 4076; int_array [ index] == 0
1: &int_array [ index] == 4078; int_array [ index] == 1
2: &int_array [ index] == 4080; int_array [ index] == 2
3: &int_array [ index] == 4082; int_array [ index] == 3
4: &int_array [ index] == 4084; int_array [ index] == 4
5: &int_array [ index] == 4086; int_array [ index] == 5
6: &int_array [ index] == 4088; int_array [ index] == 6
7: &int_array [ index] == 4090; int_array [ index] == 7
8: &int_array [ index] == 4092; int_array [ index] == 8
9: &int_array [ index] == 4094; int_array [ index] == 9


0: int_ptr + index == 4306; *(int_ptr + index) == 0
1: int_ptr + index == 4308; *(int_ptr + index) == 1
2: int_ptr + index == 4310; *(int_ptr + index) == 2
3: int_ptr + index == 4312; *(int_ptr + index) == 3
4: int_ptr + index == 4314; *(int_ptr + index) == 4
5: int_ptr + index == 4316; *(int_ptr + index) == 5
6: int_ptr + index == 4318; *(int_ptr + index) == 6
7: int_ptr + index == 4320; *(int_ptr + index) == 7
8: int_ptr + index == 4322; *(int_ptr + index) == 8
9: int_ptr + index == 4324; *(int_ptr + index) == 9
```

This program initializes an array of **int**, then calls the function **malloc( )** to allocate space for as many integers as are contained in the array. The starting address of this allocated memory is assigned to the pointer variable, **int_ptr**. The contents of the array elements are assigned to the successive storage locations in the memory allocated by the call to **malloc( )**.

The program then displays the contents and addresses of the array cells and of the MAX_SIZE integers stored in consecutive integer slots starting at location 4306 (the first cell allocated by the call to **malloc( )**).

The dynamic memory allocation takes place in the statement that assigns an address as the value of **int_ptr**. Notice that the right operand of the assignment statement involves a cast operator. The **malloc( )** function actually returns a pointer to an unspecified type. The cast operator makes the compiler interpret the returned value as a pointer to **int**. In this way, the appropriate amount of storage is allocated, so that integer pointer arithmetic will work.

The call to **malloc( )** returns enough space to store a MAX __ SIZE element array of **int**. In addition to ensuring that the space is available, the use of **malloc( )** also guarantees that the storage is in consecutive memory locations. The advantage is that there is no need to define a huge array at the beginning of the program or function.

More on malloc( )   Before we look at another example, let's look a bit more closely at **malloc( )**. If you look at the documentation for **malloc( )**, you'll see that the function is defined as returning a pointer to **void**, **void ***. You'll also see that its parameter is a variable of type **size __ t**.

The argument to **malloc( )** represents the number of bytes of storage requested. The identifier **size __ t** is simply a **typedef** for **unsigned int**, as you'll see if you look in the file **stdlib.h**. This type is intended to represent values of the sort the **sizeof( )** operator returns. Making the argument unsigned increases the range of values you can pass. This can be useful if you need to allocate very large amounts of storage.

The return type, **void ***, is really a placeholder that makes **malloc( )** usable with any variable types. The Draft Proposed ANSI Standard says that a pointer to **void** may be converted to a pointer to any type. In our program, the conversion was to a pointer to **int**, so that each address unit is two bytes. Had we cast the result from **malloc( )** to pointer to **double**, the size of each address unit would have been eight bytes.

The **malloc( )** function returns a null pointer if it cannot allocate the amount of storage your call requested. It is always a good idea to check that the storage was actually allocated, as in the next example.

Using malloc( )

The following program generates a specified number of random numbers, then writes these to a file:

```
/* Program to allocate storage for specified number of int values,
   then to generate random integers to store in these cells.
   Program illustrates use of dynamic memory allocation and
   command line arguments.
*/

#include <stdlib.h>
```

```
#include <stdio.h>
#define MAX_SIZE 200

main ( int argc, char *argv [])
{
        int     *int_ptr, index;
        int     rand ( void), val, curr_rand;
        FILE    *fp;

        if ( argc < 3)
                printf ( "Usage: getrand <# values> <file name>\n");
        else
        {
                /* convert the first command line argument to a number */
                val = atoi ( argv [ 1]);

                /* if the user wants too many values */
                if ( val > MAX_SIZE)
                {
                        printf ( "Too many values. Max = %d\n", MAX_SIZE);
                        exit (0);
                }
                else       /* if program can handle requested # of values */
                {

                        /* allocate storage for requested # of integers */
                        int_ptr = (int *) malloc ( val * sizeof ( int));

                        if ( int_ptr != NULL)
                                for ( index = 0; index < val; index++)
                                        *(int_ptr + index) = rand ();
                        else       /* is storage could not be allocated */
                        {
                                printf ( "Couldn't allocate storage.\n");
                                exit (1);
                        }

                        /* try to create a file for writing. */
                        if ( ( fp = fopen ( argv [ 2], "w")) != NULL)
                        {
                                /* write array to file */
                                for ( index = 0; index < val; index++)
                                {
                                        /* write 5 values per line */
                                        if ( ( index % 5) == 4)

                                        fprintf ( fp, "%10d\n",
                                                *(int_ptr + index));
                                else
                                        fprintf ( fp, "%10d",
                                                *(int_ptr + index));
                                }
                                fclose ( fp);   /* close file when done */
                        } /* END if file was opened */
                        else            /* if file can't be opened. */
                                printf ( "File could not be opened\n");
                } /* END if have a valid number of values */
}       /* END if have the correct number of arguments */
```

Suppose this program is stored in a file named **getrand.exe**. The following command line would write the contents below it to the file called **randout**:

```
getrand 100 randout

       41    18467     6334    26500    19169
    15724    11478    29358    26962    24464
     5705    28145    23281    16827     9961
      491     2995    11942     4827     5436
    32391    14604     3902      153      292
    12382    17421    18716    19718    19895
     5447    21726    14771    11538     1869
    19912    25667    26299    17035     9894
    28703    23811    31322    30333    17673
     4664    15141     7711    28253     6868
    25547    27644    32662    32757    20037
    12859     8723     9741    27529      778
    12316     3035    22190     1842      288
    30106     9040     8942    19264    22648
    27446    23805    15890     6729    24370
    15350    15006    31101    24393     3548
    19629    12623    24084    19954    18756
    11840     4966     7376    13931    26308
    16944    32439    24626    11323     5537
    21538    16118     2082    22929    16541
```

The file **randout** is an ordinary text file that you can modify or edit with your text editor.

The program allocates space for an array of **int** to hold the number of values specified as the second command line argument. Then the program generates the appropriate number of random integers, assigning these values to the successive locations allocated with the **malloc( )** call. The use of pointer arithmetic makes sure the assignments are made to the appropriate storage locations. Note that the indirection operator is used, since the program is actually moving values, rather than addresses, around. The **atoi( )** function converts a string to an **int**, just as the **atof( )** function we saw earlier converted from string to **double**.

The following program reads a specified number of values from a file. The values read are stored in memory allocated to hold values of the appropriate type.

```
/* Program to read a specified number of values from a file,
   storing these in memory allocated for the purpose.
   Program illustrates dynamic memory allocation and reading from files.
*/

#include <stdlib.h>
#include <stdio.h>
#define MAX_SIZE 200

main ( int argc, char *argv [])
{
        int     *int_ptr, index;
        int     rand ( void), val;
        FILE    *fp;
```

```
if ( argc < 3)
        printf ( "Usage: readvals <# values> <file name>\n");
else
{
        /* find the number in the first command line argument */
        val = atoi ( argv [ 1]);

        if ( val > MAX_SIZE)
        {
                printf ( "Too many values. Max = %d\n", MAX_SIZE);
                exit (0);
        }
        else
        {
                /* allocate the space, if possible */
                int_ptr = (int *) malloc ( val * sizeof ( int));

                /* if unable to allocate storage, exit program */
                if ( int_ptr == NULL)
                {
                        printf ( "Couldn't allocate space.\n");
                        exit (1);
                }

                /* if file could be opened, read from the file;
                   continuation condition says stop if either:
                   1. enough (val) values have been read, OR
                   2. as many values as possible have been read
                      from the file --- for example, because
                      the end of the file has been reached.
                */
                if ( ( fp = fopen ( argv [ 2], "r")) != NULL)
                {
                        for ( index = 0;
                                (index < val) &&
                                (fscanf ( fp, "%d",
                                        int_ptr + index) > 0);
                                index++)
                                ;               /* do nothing */
                        fclose ( fp);
                }

                val = index;  /* in case not all values were read */

                /* display the values read */
                for ( index = 0; index < val; index++)
                {
                        /* display 5 values per line */
                        if ( (index % 5 ) == 4)
                                printf ( "%10d\n",
                                        *(int_ptr + index));
                        else
                                printf ( "%10d",
                                        *(int_ptr + index));
                } /* END if file was opened */
        } /* END if have a valid number of values */
} /* End if have the correct number of arguments */
}
```

With the preceding program stored in a file named **readval.exe** and the data in the **randout** file created in an earlier example, the following function call would produce the output below it:

```
readval 23 randout
          41     18467      6334     26500     19169
       15724     11478     29358     26962     24464
        5705     28145     23281     16827      9961
         491      2995     11942      4827      5436
       32391     14604      3902
```

This program allocates space for the desired number of **int** values. If successful, the program opens the file from which to read its information. The program then reads as many values as requested from the file, or as many values as possible, if the file ends before the requested number of values could be read. Finally, the program displays the values read.

The storage is allocated with a call to **malloc( )**, which returns enough contiguous memory to store the desired number of **int** values. Again, it is important to check that the memory has actually been allocated — that is, that the function call has not returned a null pointer.

The input from the file is done using the **fscanf( )** function. This function works like **scanf( )**, but lets you specify the file from which the function is to read its information. The other components of **fscanf( )** — the string argument containing placeholders, and one additional argument for each placeholder — are the same as for **scanf( )**.

The **fscanf( )** function returns the number of arguments successfully read and assigned, or the function returns a predefined value, EOF, if the end of file is reached before the function has finished its work. EOF is a manifest constant defined in **stdio.h**, and is usually defined as (-1).

Notice how **fscanf( )** is used in the continuation condition. The condition fails (evaluates to false) if either of the following things happens:

- **index** becomes equal to **val**, in which case the desired number of values has been read.

- **fscanf( )** returns a value less than 1 — either 0 or EOF. In this case, something has gone wrong or the end of the file has been reached and the desired number of values could not be read.

Notice also the arguments for **fscanf( )**. Recall that **scanf( )** required addresses as its arguments so that it could store the values directly in the specified locations. When we first discussed **scanf( )**, this requirement may have seemed somewhat arbitrary. Now that we've covered pointers and passing parameters by reference, this use of addresses should be clear.

In this program, **int﹍ptr** is a pointer variable, so passing its value as a parameter to **fscanf( )** means that an address is being passed in, as required. Because **int﹍ptr** is a pointer, offsets (such as those involving **index**) are interpreted in terms of address units. Thus, **int﹍ptr + 2** refers to an *address* 4 bytes higher than the address contained in **int﹍ptr**.

calloc( )

The **malloc( )** function simply gets you the number of bytes you want, and leaves it up to you to partition those bytes and to assign values to them. There is a related function, **calloc( )**, that also returns a pointer to an area of contiguous storage. The **calloc( )** function works in a slightly more structured manner, and it even initializes the memory returned.

The **calloc( )** function takes two arguments—the number of elements and the size of each element—and returns a pointer to **void**, which your program should cast to a pointer of the appropriate type. Essentially, **calloc( )** returns a pointer to the first element of an array that has as many elements as you requested in the first argument to the function, or a null pointer if the function cannot allocate the desired amount of storage. The **calloc( )** function initializes each element allocated to 0.

Usage for **calloc( )** is the same as for **malloc( )**. Thus, the following would allocate storage for a 200 element array of **double** and would make **dbl﹍ptr** point to the first element of this array. Each element in this array would be initialized to 0.0:

```
/* assume the following definition :  double *dbl_ptr;
dbl_ptr = (double *) calloc ( 200, sizeof ( double));
```

Getting More Memory Later

It may happen that you allocate a specified amount of space for information, and then find that you need more space. It's generally not desirable to store information in two separate data structures, when it really belongs together.

C provides the **realloc( )** function for dealing with situations such as this. This function lets you add to an existing collection of contiguous storage, or gets you a new, larger section of contiguous storage. The function takes two arguments — a pointer to the existing storage collection, and the new size (in bytes) — and returns a pointer to **void**. This pointer references the first element of a contiguous area of memory having the desired size.

The following program illustrates the use of **realloc( )**:

```
/* Program to illustrate use of realloc() to modify amount of
   storage allocated dynamically.
*/

#include <stdlib.h>
#include <stdio.h>

main ()
{
        double d1, *dbl_ptr;

        /* get room for 150 double values */
        dbl_ptr = (double *) calloc ( 150, sizeof ( double));

        if ( dbl_ptr != NULL)
        {
                /* display starting and ending addresses */
                printf ( "&dbl_ptr [ 0] == %u; &dbl_ptr [ 149] == %u\n",
                        &dbl_ptr [ 0], &dbl_ptr [ 149]);

                /* expand the storage to room for 200 double values */
                dbl_ptr = (double *) realloc ( dbl_ptr, 200);

                if ( dbl_ptr != NULL)
                        /* display starting and ending addresses */
                        printf ( "&dbl_ptr [ 0] == %u; ",
                                &dbl_ptr [ 0]);
                        printf ( "&dbl_ptr [ 199] == %u\n",
                                &dbl_ptr [ 199]);
        }   /* END if not a null ptr */
        else
                printf ( "null pointer\n");
}
```

On a sample run, the program produces the following output:

```
&dbl_ptr [ 0] == 4292; &dbl_ptr [ 149] == 5484
&dbl_ptr [ 0] == 4292; &dbl_ptr [ 199] == 5884
```

This program first allocates storage for an array of 150 **double** elements, and writes the addresses of the first and last elements in this array. Then the program tries to reallocate storage for a 200 element array of the same type. Finally, the program writes the addresses of the first and last elements in this array.

The intent when using **realloc( )** is to expand the original array to a larger size. Data from the original array should not be lost. When **realloc( )** does its work, it will simply return the same starting address if enough contiguous storage is available immediately after the last cell of the original array, as in this example.

If this is not possible, **realloc( )** will try to find the storage for a large enough array elsewhere. If successful in this search, the function will then transfer the contents of the original array to the new location, and will release the storage that had been allocated for the original array. In the second case **realloc( )** moves the array into a new, bigger location.

In the previous program, the function was able to simply allocate the 50 additional **double** storage spaces immediately after the original array. In other situations, this may not be possible because the storage right after the original array is being used. In that case, the function moves the array's contents to a new location. Because the original array may be moved, you should not count on the value of the pointer parameter being the same before and after the call to **realloc( )**.

The **realloc( )** function can be useful, but you must use it carefully. Like other storage allocation functions, **realloc( )** returns a null pointer if it is unable to allocate the desired storage. In this case, however, a null pointer means that your original storage has been lost.

▶**REMEMBER**   Be careful when using **realloc( )**. You can lose your original data if something goes wrong. Always test the value of the pointer **realloc( )** returns.

Giving Storage Back

So far, you've seen three ways of obtaining storage space and reserving it for use in a program. In this section, you'll learn about a way of returning storage to the program for reuse.

Suppose you had a program that needed to manipulate as many as five large arrays, but that your available memory could only fit four of these arrays at any one time. The **free( )** function lets you "deallocate" storage. This makes the storage available for use at another point in the program.

To deallocate storage, call the **free( )** function with a pointer parameter. In the function definition, this parameter is a pointer to **void**, for which you can substitute a pointer to the appropriate type. The pointer *must* refer to storage allocated with either the **malloc( )**, **calloc( )**, or **realloc( )** functions. The **free( )** function does not return any value. Using **free( )** with a pointer allocated by other means causes an undefined result, and is likely to cause storage errors.

▶**REMEMBER**   You can only use **free( )** to deallocate storage allocated with **malloc( )**, **calloc( )**, **realloc( )**, or similar Run-Time library functions.

With this function, you can get around certain storage limitations, if you can discard data after you've processed it. For example, if you can only fit four of the five large arrays mentioned earlier, you might do the following:

1. Use **malloc( )** or **calloc( )** to allocate storage for up to four of the arrays.

2. When you've finished with one of these arrays, use **free( )** to deallocate the storage.

3. Use **malloc( )** or **calloc( )** to allocate storage for any remaining arrays.

Determining Available Storage

Sometimes it's useful to know how much storage is available for use. For example, suppose you want to expand an array of **double** by 100 values. If you knew that there were fewer than 800 bytes of available storage, you could save yourself the grief of possibly losing your data (because **realloc( )** returned a null pointer) by not even calling the **realloc( )** function.

QuickC (and Microsoft C v5.0) provide a function for determining the amount of storage available. The **_memavl( )** function returns an **unsigned** (actually a **size_t**) value indicating the number of bytes of storage available.

The following program lets you see how the available storage changes as the amount of storage allocated varies. In some cases, the program is unable to allocate the storage, in which case the return from **_memavl( )** remains unchanged.

```
/* Program to show use of _memavl() for determining available storage */

#include <stdlib.h>
#include <stdio.h>
#include <malloc.h>
#define MAX_TRIALS  10

main ()
{
        double   d1, *dbl_ptr, *dbl_ptr2;
        unsigned memory;
        int      rand (), index, how_many;

        for ( index = 0; index < MAX_TRIALS; index++)
        {
                /* determine amount of available storage */
                memory = _memavl ();
                printf ( "_memavl = %u\n", memory);
```

```
        /* get a random size to allocate */
        how_many = rand();

        /* allocate storage */
        dbl_ptr = (double *) calloc (how_many / 2, sizeof (double));

        /* now how much storage is available? */
        memory = _memavl ();
        printf ( "after getting %5d doubles, _memavl = %u\n\n",
                 how_many / 2, memory);

        /* deallocate storage, to start afresh */
        free ( dbl_ptr);
    }
}
```

The following listing contains a sample run of this program.

```
_memavl = 61286
after getting    20 doubles, _memavl = 61122

_memavl = 61286
after getting 9233 doubles, _memavl = 61286

_memavl = 61286
after getting 3137 doubles, _memavl = 35948

_memavl = 61286
after getting 13250 doubles, _memavl = 61286

_memavl = 61286
after getting 9584 doubles, _memavl = 61286

_memavl = 61286
after getting 7862 doubles, _memavl = 61286

_memavl = 61286
after getting 5739 doubles, _memavl = 15372

_memavl = 61286
after getting 14679 doubles, _memavl = 61286

_memavl = 61286
after getting 13481 doubles, _memavl = 61286

_memavl = 61286
after getting 12232 doubles, _memavl = 61286
```

This program displays the available storage before and after allocating storage for a random number of **double** (8 byte) values. The random value is divided by two because so many of the random values were too large for storage to be allocated (which happens at about 7,600). After each cycle, the storage allocated is given back for reuse, by means of the **free( )** function.

Notice that sometimes no storage seems to be allocated. These cases ask for too much storage, in which case **malloc( )** returns a null pointer and allocates no space.

Dynamic Allocation Pitfalls

There are certain common errors to watch out for when dealing with dynamic memory allocation. These errors concern errant or lost pointers and unavailable space.

First, do not lose access to your starting value. This means you should always have a way of getting to the first element of the array to use as an origin for pointer arithmetic.

Second, don't change the value of a pointer to a collection of data. You'll lose your real data, and may damage your environment when you try to write to the new (and unknown) data area.

Finally, your program should always make sure it has gotten the storage it requested. Don't assume you have the storage and begin writing to it. You may overwrite important information by mistake.

Uses of Dynamic Storage Allocation

A major advantage of dynamic storage allocation is that you need to allocate only the storage required to do the job. The examples we've looked at generally involve arrays of values, with some way of finding out how large the array needs to be. Using the storage allocation functions guarantees that the amount requested will be available, if a non-null pointer is returned.

Dynamic allocation can also be useful for string handling because you can get storage for a new string or for a temporary string while needed. This is much safer than relying on pointers to **char**, which may overwrite other data if you're not careful. By assigning the pointer to the first cell of an array of character that **malloc( )** allocates, you ensure that the storage for the string is available and can be used safely.

A third major use of dynamic storage allocation comes in programs that involve data structures such as trees and linked lists. You'll learn about the data structures used to build trees and lists in Chapter 16.

Summary

In this chapter you learned how to open and use files, including how to read from and write to them. File handling is particularly convenient if you use command line arguments, since that makes it much easier to specify the files with which the program should work.

You also learned how to allocate and deallocate storage dynamically, as needed while running a program. This capability is handy for certain types of data structures whose size will not be determined until the program is actually running.

In the next chapter, we'll cover some miscellaneous topics and operators for manipulating individual bits in variables.

15

Bit and Other Operators

The first chapter claimed that C lets you manipulate data at the level of individual bits. In this chapter, you'll find out how this is done. In addition, you'll encounter a new operator.

Bitwise Operators

A *bit* is a single binary digit, a 0 or 1. In C, integral data types are stored as a sequence of bits occupying an allocated amount of storage. Thus, in QuickC, an **int** is a sequence of 16 bits, while a **long int** is a sequence of 32 bits. The operators for manipulating bits apply to integral types only. (Floating point variables are also stored as bit sequences. However, for these types, different parts of the bit patterns serve different functions — fraction and exponent, for example. Therefore, the bitwise operators do not apply to floating point types.)

Bit Patterns

Before discussing the bitwise operators themselves, let's look at some examples of numbers represented in binary form. The following program generates bit patterns for specified numbers. To get some practice working with binary representations, play with this program.

```
/* Program to display the binary representation of 16-bit integers.
   Program illustrates binary representations.
*/
#include <stdlib.h>
#define NULL_CHAR '\0'
#define MAX_STR   80

main ()
{
        int     value;
        int     make_bin_str ( char *, int);
        char    curr_str [ MAX_STR];
        char    val_str [ MAX_STR];  /* value to convert, read as string */

        printf ( "? ");
        gets ( val_str);
        value = atoi ( val_str);

        do
        {
                printf ( "%d : ", value);
                if ( make_bin_str ( curr_str, value))
                        printf ( "%s\n", curr_str);
                else
                        printf ( "string not built correctly:: %s\n",
                                curr_str);

                printf ( "? ");
                gets ( val_str);
                value = atoi ( val_str);
        }
        while ( value != 0);
}
```

```
/* build a string consisting of binary digits, based on value passed in */
int  make_bin_str ( char *str, int value)
{
#define MAX_PWR  32768L           /* largest bit in an unsigned 16 bit int */

        unsigned     index;
        int          outcome, bin_place = 0;

        for ( index = MAX_PWR; index > 0; index /= 2)
        {
                outcome = (int) ( value / index);
                if ( (outcome == 1) || (outcome == -1))
                        str [ bin_place++] = '1';
                else
                        str [ bin_place++] = '0';

                value %= index;
        }

        str [ bin_place] = NULL_CHAR;

        if ( bin_place == 16)    /* if 16 bits were processed : 0 -- 15 */
                return ( 1);
        else
                return ( 0);
}
```

This program produced the following sample session:

```
? 0
0 : 0000000000000000
? 2
2 : 0000000000000010
? -2
-2 : 1111111111111110
? 10
10 : 0000000000001010
? -10
-10 : 1111111111110110
? 1024
1024 : 0000010000000000
? -1024
-1024 : 1111110000000000
? 32767
32767 : 0111111111111111
? -32767
-32767 : 1000000000000001
? 0
```

The program uses **gets( )** to read a string, then converts this input to an **int**. The 16-bit pattern for this value is returned in a string by **make _ bin _ str( )**. The program displays this string.

Converting internally from a string to the desired type is a safer way of getting input than using **scanf( )**, because **scanf( )** can get confused if it encounters the wrong type of information, such as a string, when it expects a numerical value.

The **make ‒ bin ‒ str( )** function works with a **long** MAX ‒ PWR value to avoid difficulties with the leftmost bit, the sign bit on regular **int** variables.

Note that in the program you can only get the bit pattern for 0 if this is the first binary representation you ask for. After the first time through the loop, the program checks at the bottom of the **do-while** loop, so the bit pattern for 0 is never computed again.

Although the bitwise operators have the same kinds of names as the logical operators — AND, OR, NOT — there are some important differences between them. The logical operators work with entire expressions, and always return a value that can be interpreted as true or false. The bitwise operators, on the other hand, work with each individual bit of their operands. The results can be any integral number within the allowable range. Thus, the logical operators return logical values, whereas the bitwise operators return numbers having the appropriate bit patterns.

The Bitwise Complement Operator

You may want to reverse a bit pattern by turning every 1 bit to 0, and every 0 bit to 1. For example, 1010101010101010 would become 0101010101010101. C's *bitwise complement,* or *negation operator,* ~, performs such a reversal. This operator, which is sometimes known as the *one's complement operator,* converts every 0 to 1 and every 1 to 0. The following program illustrates the bitwise complement operator at work:

```
/* Program to display the binary representation of 16-bit integers,
   and the bitwise negation of the specified integers..
   Program illustrates binary representations and bitwise negation operator.
*/
#include <stdlib.h>
#define NULL_CHAR '\0'
#define MAX_STR   80
```

```
main ()
{
        int     value;
        int     make_bin_str ( char *, int);
        char    curr_str [ MAX_STR];
        char    val_str [ MAX_STR];  /* value to convert, read as string */

        printf ( "? ");
        gets ( val_str);
        value = atoi ( val_str);

        do
        {
                printf ( "%d : ", value);
                if ( make_bin_str ( curr_str, value))
                        printf ( "%s\n", curr_str);
                else
                        printf ( "string not built correctly:: %s\n",
                                curr_str);

                /* now apply the bitwise negation operator. */
                printf ( "~ == %d : ", ~value);
                if ( make_bin_str ( curr_str, ~value))
                        printf ( "%s\n", curr_str);
                else
                        printf ( "string not built correctly:: %s\n",
                                curr_str);

                printf ( "? ");
                gets ( val_str);
                value = atoi ( val_str);
        }
        while ( value != 0);
}


/* build a string consisting of binary digits, based on value passed in */
int  make_bin_str ( char *str, int value)
{
#define MAX_PWR  32768L            /* largest bit in an unsigned 16 bit int */

        unsigned    index;
        int         outcome, bin_place = 0;
        for ( index = MAX_PWR; index > 0; index /= 2)
        {
                outcome = (int) ( value / index);
                if ( (outcome == 1) || (outcome == -1))
                        str [ bin_place++] = '1';
                else
                        str [ bin_place++] = '0';

                value %= index;
        }

        str [ bin_place] = NULL_CHAR;

        if ( bin_place == 16)   /* if 16 bits were processed : 0 -- 15 */
                return ( 1);
        else
                return ( 0);

}
```

A sample session with this program produced the following listing:

```
? 0
0 : 0000000000000000
~ == -1 : 1111111111111111
? 1
1 : 0000000000000001
~ == -2 : 1111111111111110
? -1
-1 : 1111111111111111
~ == 0 : 0000000000000000
? 2
2 : 0000000000000010
~ == -3 : 1111111111111101
? -2
-2 : 1111111111111110
~ == 1 : 0000000000000001
? 32767
32767 : 0111111111111111
~ == -32768 : 1000000000000000
? -32767
-32767 : 1000000000000001
~ == 32766 : 0111111111111110
? -32768
-32768 : 1000000000000000
~ == 32767 : 0111111111111111
? 0
```

This program does the same things as the previous program and, in addition, it computes and displays the binary representation of the bitwise negation of each value.

Notice that the bitwise complement, or negation, of a number is *not* the same as the arithmetic negation. Thus, ~5 (1111 1111 1111 1010) does not represent the same number as −5 (1111 1111 1111 1011). However, both the arithmetic and bitwise negation operators produce a positive number from a negative one, and vice versa.

The Bitwise AND Operator

The *bitwise AND operator*, &, combines the bit patterns of its two operands. If corresponding bits on *both* operands are 1, then the same bit in the outcome will be 1; otherwise the bit will be 0 in the outcome. For example, 1000000000000001 & 1010101010101010 would produce 1000000000000000, since only the leftmost bit is 1 in both operands.

Essentially, the bitwise AND operator multiplies corresponding bits from each operand, and puts this product in the corresponding position in the result. The only possible products are 0 —from 0 ∗ 0, 0 ∗ 1, 1 ∗ 0 —and 1 —from 1 ∗ 1. Thus, the bitwise AND operator returns a 1 in a specific position only if both elements used to compute the bit are 1.

The results of such an operator can often be shown in a truth table. For the bitwise AND operator, combining bits from left and right operands, the truth table is shown in the following illustration:

left bit	right bit	result bit (left & right bit)
0	0	0
0	1	0
1	0	0
1	1	1

Notice that the symbol for the bitwise AND operator is the same as the symbol for the address operator, and is very similar to the symbol for the logical AND operator. The address and bitwise OR operators are generally used in very different contexts, so you will probably not confuse these two.

On the other hand, the logical and bitwise operators can be used in very similar situations. You are very likely to use one when you intend to use the other, so be careful to catch it when you do. To minimize the probability of such an error, get into the habit of mentally checking any expression involving either logical or arithmetic operators. If your expression is supposed to evaluate to a true or a false, then you need the logical operators, which reduce an entire expression to a zero or nonzero value. If, however, your expression is supposed to evaluate to a usable number, then you probably want bitwise operators, which work with each bit separately but return a numerical value at the end.

Masks   A very common use of the bitwise AND operator is to mask off certain parts of a number. For example, suppose you want to quickly discard any portion of a number above 255 (that is, you want to keep only the rightmost byte of the number). The **mask( )** function in the following program would let you do this.

```
/* Program to display the binary representation of 16-bit integers,
   and the bitwise AND operator in masking.
   Program illustrates binary representations and bitwise AND operator.
*/
#include <stdlib.h>
#define NULL_CHAR '\0'
#define MAX_STR    80

main ()
{
        int     value;
```

```
        int     make_bin_str ( char *, int);
        int     mask ( int, int);
        int     masked_val;
        char    curr_str [ MAX_STR];
        char    val_str [ MAX_STR];   /* value to convert, read as string */
        void    put_nibble ( char *);

        printf ( "\n? ");
        gets ( val_str);
        value = atoi ( val_str);

        do
        {
                printf ( "%d : ", value);
                if ( make_bin_str ( curr_str, value))
                        put_nibble ( curr_str);
                else
                        printf ( "string not built correctly:: %s\n",
                                curr_str);


                /* now apply the bitwise AND operator. */
                masked_val = mask ( value, OxFF);
                printf ( "\nvalue & %X == %d : ", OxFF, masked_val);
                if ( make_bin_str ( curr_str, masked_val))
                        put_nibble ( curr_str);
                else
                        printf ( "string not built correctly:: %s\n",
                                curr_str);

                printf ( "\n? ");
                gets ( val_str);
                value = atoi ( val_str);
        }
        while ( value != 0);
}


/* build a string consisting of binary digits, based on value passed in */
int  make_bin_str ( char *str, int value)
{

#define MAX_PWR  32768L          /* largest bit in an unsigned 16 bit int */

        unsigned    index;
        int         outcome, bin_place = 0;

        for ( index = MAX_PWR; index > 0; index /= 2)
        {
                outcome = (int) ( value / index);
                if ( ( outcome == 1) || (outcome == -1))
                        str [ bin_place++] = '1';
                else
                        str [ bin_place++] = '0';

                value %= index;
        }

        str [ bin_place] = NULL_CHAR;

        if ( bin_place == 16)    /* if 16 bits were processed : 0 -- 15 */
                return ( 1);
        else
                return ( 0);
}
```

```
/* mask off the specified bit patterns */
int mask ( int value, int the_mask)
{
        return ( value & the_mask);
}


/* write a string in groups of 4 characters,
   with each group separated by a space.
   Useful for writing bit patterns --- grouping the bits into
   groups of 4 makes it easy to determine hexadecimal digits.
*/
void put_nibble ( char *str)
{
        int  index;

        for ( index = 0; str [ index] != NULL_CHAR; index++)
        {
                if ( ( index % 4) == 3)
                        printf ( "%c ", str [ index]);
                else
                        printf ( "%c", str [ index]);
        }
}
```

For a sample session, this program produces the following output:

```
? 0
0 : 0000 0000 0000 0000
value & FF == 0 : 0000 0000 0000 0000
? 256
256 : 0000 0001 0000 0000
value & FF == 0 : 0000 0000 0000 0000
? 1023
1023 : 0000 0011 1111 1111
value & FF == 255 : 0000 0000 1111 1111
? 1001
1001 : 0000 0011 1110 1001
value & FF == 233 : 0000 0000 1110 1001
? 0
```

This program displays the bit pattern for the number you enter, and displays the bit pattern of the number resulting when you mask this number with the number 0xFF, which has all 1's in its rightmost byte and all 0's in the rest of the number. The bit patterns are displayed in groups of 4 bits, sometimes known as a *nibble*.

The only differences betwen this **main( )** function and the previous one are the calls to **put _ nibble( )** instead of **printf( )**, and the activity involving **masked _ value**. This program has two new functions to do the work: **mask( )** and **put _ nibble( )**.

The **mask( )** function returns the result of applying a bitwise AND operator to its two parameters. Notice that the parameter is specified in hexadecimal (prefixed by **0x**). While not necessary, this is common, because it is often much easier to determine what bits are 1 by looking at the hexadecimal representation. Remember, each hexadecimal digit represents 4 binary bits, or one nibble. Thus, the value **0xFF** represents the bit pattern 0000 0000 1111 1111.

Similarly, the value **0xAF** represents the bit pattern 0000 0000 1010 1111. This bit pattern is much easier to determine from the hexadecimal representation than from its decimal value, 175.

The function **put—nibble( )** writes characters to the screen in groups of four. This function will usually be passed a string representing binary digits. The function makes it much easier for you to read a binary number than if all 16 bits are written together. You can determine the hexadecimal representation of the number more easily from the output of **put—nibble( )**.

If **0xFF** masks off everything but the rightmost byte of a number, how would you mask off *just* the rightmost byte? You can accomplish this by substituting the following assignment for the one in the preceding program, and changing **0xFF** to ~**0xFF** wherever you find it.

```
masked_val = mask ( value, ~0xFF);
```

For a session with the same input as for the previous program, the new version of the program would produce the following output:

```
? 0
0 : 0000 0000 0000 0000
value & FF00 == 0 : 0000 0000 0000 0000
? 256
256 : 0000 0001 0000 0000
value & FF00 == 256 : 0000 0001 0000 0000
? 1023
1023 : 0000 0011 1111 1111
value & FF00 == 768 : 0000 0011 0000 0000
? 1001
1001 : 0000 0011 1110 1001
value & FF00 == 768 : 0000 0011 0000 0000
? 0
```

The only difference between the two programs is in the value used to mask—**0xFF** in one case, and its one's complement (~**0xFF**) in the other. How would you use masks to distinguish even from odd numbers?

The Bitwise OR Operator

The *bitwise OR operator*, |, takes two operands and returns a value whose bit pattern contains 1 wherever the corresponding bits of the left *or* the right operand, or of both operands, are 1. The only zero bits in the result of a bitwise OR operation come in places where both operands have 0 bits. For example, 1101010101010101 | 1010101010101010 would produce 1111111111111111, since one or the other operand has 1's in each place in the result.

In essence, the bitwise OR operator works like a loose form of *addition* on bits. Just as the bitwise AND operator multiplied corresponding bits from the left and right operands, so the bitwise OR operator adds corresponding bits. This addition differs from ordinary addition, however. First, there are no carries from one bit position to another. Second, $1 + 1 == 1$ in this addition. The truth table for the bitwise OR operator provides the same results, as shown here.

left bit	right bit	result bit (left | right bit)
0	0	0
0	1	1
1	0	1
1	1	1

Essentially, the bitwise OR operator is used to turn bits on. For example, suppose you want to break a territory up into multiple regions, and you would like your data analyses to use whatever regions are specified. Bitwise operators can be useful for recording and manipulating such information, as the following program indicates:

```
/* Program to illustrate bitwise OR operator. */

#define NORTH  0x1     /* 0000 0000 0000 0001 */
#define NNE    0x2     /* 0000 0000 0000 0010 */
#define NE     0x4     /* 0000 0000 0000 0100 */
#define ENE    0x8     /* 0000 0000 0000 1000 */
#define EAST   0x10    /* 0000 0000 0001 0000 */
#define ESE    0x20    /* 0000 0000 0010 0000 */
#define SE     0x40    /* 0000 0000 0100 0000 */
#define SSE    0x80    /* 0000 0000 1000 0000 */
#define SOUTH  0x100   /* 0000 0001 0000 0000 */
#define SSW    0x200   /* 0000 0010 0000 0000 */
#define SW     0x400   /* 0000 0100 0000 0000 */
```

```
#define WSW     0x800    /* 0000 1000 0000 0000 */
#define WEST    0x1000   /* 0001 0000 0000 0000 */
#define WNW     0x2000   /* 0010 0000 0000 0000 */
#define NW      0x4000   /* 0100 0000 0000 0000 */
#define NNW     0x8000   /* 1000 0000 0000 0001 */


main ()
{
        int  terr1, terr2, terr3, terr4;

        /* Assign regions to territories */
        terr1 = NORTH | NNE | NE | ENE; /* terr1 == 0000 0000 0000 1111 */
        terr2 = EAST | ESE | SE | SSE;  /* terr2 == 0000 0000 1111 0000 */
        terr3 = SOUTH | SSW | SW | WSW; /* terr3 == 0000 1111 0000 0000 */
        terr4 = WEST | WNW | NW | NNW;  /* terr4 == 1111 0000 0000 0000 */

        /* Make sure none of the territories overlap */
        if ( terr1 & terr2)
                printf ( "1 and 2 overlap\n");
        if ( terr1 & terr3)
                printf ( "1 and 3 overlap\n");
        if ( terr1 & terr4)
                printf ( "1 and 4 overlap\n");
        if ( terr2 & terr3)
                printf ( "2 and 3 overlap\n");
        if ( terr2 & terr4)
                printf ( "2 and 4 overlap\n");
        if ( terr3 & terr4)
                printf ( "3 and 4 overlap\n");

        /* consolidate terr1 and terr2, and drop NORTH and EAST regions */
        printf ( "terr1 == %x;  terr2 == %x\n", terr1, terr2);

        terr1 = (terr1 | terr2) & ~NORTH & ~EAST;

        printf ( "After rearranging territories, ");
        printf ( "terr1 == %x;  terr2 == %x\n", terr1, terr2);
}
```

This program produces the following output:

```
terr1 == f;  terr2 == f0
After rearranging territories,
terr1 == ee;  terr2 == f0
```

This program defines several territories, each of which includes several regions. The program displays certain regions, modifies them, then displays the new regions. This is one way of using the bitwise OR operator — to group things, or to create a summary of the properties that some piece of information is supposed to have.

Let's look carefully at this program. First, notice the large number of manifest constants, each corresponding to a region. The substitution text for the constants consists of different powers of 2 from 0 through 15. These are "pure" powers of two, so that each of these constants has a different bit pattern.

The regions have been defined in a way that will keep them from overlapping; that is, no two regions have a 1 bit in the same place. This makes it possible to use the bitwise OR operator to specify a combination of regions, all of which can be treated together. This combination of bit patterns results in a number that is useful not for its value, but for its bit pattern. The binary representation of the resulting number has a 1 in each bit position that corresponds to one of the regions out of which the number was built, and has 0 in all the other bit positions.

Thus, the first assignment statement makes **terr1** consist of the following regions: NORTH, NNE, NE, ENE. The bit pattern for **terr1** would therefore consist of 0000 0000 0000 1111.

Once you've created the new value for **terr1** and other territories, you can ask such questions as whether a given region is in a particular territory. The following expression would determine whether WEST was in **terr2**:

```
/* assume my_val has been defined as int */
my_val = terr2 & WEST;
```

If the bit corresponding to WEST is *not* on in **terr2**, the expression on the right side will be 0, since that expression could contain a number with a 1 bit only if **terr2** had the WEST bit turned on.

Look at the last assignment to **terr1** in the program, in which the territories are rearranged. To combine territories, you can simply "add" the numbers representing the two territories. This creates a new territory whose bit pattern is the "sum" (bitwise OR) of the original territories.

A complication arises because the statement also redefines the territory by removing some regions. Recall that the bitwise AND operator can be used to mask particular values, effectively removing them from the number. To create a mask to remove a specific bit, use a number with that bit set to 0, and with the remaining bits set to 1. The easiest way to do this in our example is to take the bitwise complement of the region. Thus, the mask to *remove* NORTH would have the bit pattern, 1111 1111 1111 1110.

The bitwise AND operator can then be used to remove the region. The following illustration carries out the operations in the assignment statement, showing the resulting bit patterns along the way:

```
  0000 0000 0000 1111   (terr1)           ==  0xF
| 0000 0000 1111 0000   (terr2)           ==  0xF0
---------------------------------------------------
  0000 0000 1111 1111   (terr1 | terr2) == 0xFF

  0000 0000 1111 1111   (terr1 | terr2)              ==  0xFF
& 1111 1111 1111 1110   (~NORTH)                     ==  0xFFFE
-----------------------------------------------------------------
  0000 0000 1111 1110   (terr1 | terr2) & ~NORTH ==   0xFE

  0000 0000 1111 1110   (terr1 | terr2) & ~NORTH             ==  0xFE
& 1111 1111 1110 1111   (~EAST)                              ==  0xFFEF
--------------------------------------------------------------------------
  0000 0000 1110 1110   (terr1 | terr2) & ~NORTH & ~EAST ==   0xEE
```

Notice the parentheses in the right operand. These are necessary because of the precedences of the operators involved. The three bitwise operators considered so far follow the general rules for precedence. Bitwise negation, being a unary operator, has the highest precedence of the three. Its precedence is the same as for the other unary operators we've seen, such as **sizeof( )**, *, !, and the unary minus operator (−).

Of the three, the bitwise AND operator has the next highest precedence. Recall that operators for multiplication have higher precedence than those for addition. Thus, arithmetic multiplication has precedence over addition, and logical multiplication (&&) has precedence over logical addition (‖). Here too, bitwise multiplication (&) has precedence over bitwise addition (|).

In relation to other operators, the binary bitwise operators are just above the logical operators. This places the bitwise operators lower than the arithmetic operators, and just below the relational and equality operators. See the table at the end of this chapter for a summary of the operators and their precedence.

Had you left out the parentheses, the AND operators would have been applied first. That is, **terr2 &** ~NORTH would have been evaluated. Then the result of this evaluation would have been ANDed with ~EAST. Finally, this result would have been the right operand for the bitwise OR operator.

Use the technique from the previous illustration to determine what the result would be if the parentheses were left off. Then test your answer by modifying the program in which the assignment occurred.

The bitwise XOR operator

The *bitwise XOR operator* (^) shares properties with the other bitwise operators. The XOR (for eXclusive OR) operator, fits somewhere between the bitwise AND and bitwise OR operators. It combines corresponding bits in its left and right operands, returning 0 if the two bits have the same values, and returning 1 if the two bits have different values. That is, the XOR operator returns a 1 when *either* the left bit is 1 *or* the right bit is 1, *but not both*. Whereas the bitwise OR operator includes the cases where both bits are 1, the XOR operator excludes the cases where both bits are 1. For example, 1101010101010101 ^ 1010101010101010 would produce 0111111111111111. This is almost identical to the result for the OR operator, except that the leftmost bit in this result is 0, because both operands had a 1 in this position.

The truth table for the bitwise XOR operator is shown in the following illustration:

left bit	right bit	result bit (left ^ right bit)
0	0	0
0	1	1
1	0	1
1	1	0

The bitwise XOR operator can be convenient. However, its work can also be done by combining the other bitwise operators appropriately. Remember, the XOR operator essentially says, "left or right bit, but not both left and right bits." This amounts to saying **(left | right) & ~ (left & right)**. The following program illustrates the use of the bitwise XOR operator, and also shows this equivalence:

```
/* Program to illustrate bitwise XOR operator. */

#define NORTH  0x1    /* 0000 0000 0000 0001 */
#define NNE    0x2    /* 0000 0000 0000 0010 */
#define NE     0x4    /* 0000 0000 0000 0100 */
#define ENE    0x8    /* 0000 0000 0000 1000 */
#define EAST   0x10   /* 0000 0000 0001 0000 */
#define ESE    0x20   /* 0000 0000 0010 0000 */
#define SE     0x40   /* 0000 0000 0100 0000 */
#define SSE    0x80   /* 0000 0000 1000 0000 */
```

```
#define SOUTH    0x100    /* 0000 0001 0000 0000 */
#define SSW      0x200    /* 0000 0010 0000 0000 */
#define SW       0x400    /* 0000 0100 0000 0000 */
#define WSW      0x800    /* 0000 1000 0000 0000 */
#define WEST     0x1000   /* 0001 0000 0000 0000 */
#define WNW      0x2000   /* 0010 0000 0000 0000 */
#define NW       0x4000   /* 0100 0000 0000 0000 */
#define NNW      0x8000   /* 1000 0000 0000 0001 */


main ()
{
        int  terr1, terr2, terr3, terr4;

        /* Assign regions to territories */
        terr1 = NORTH | NNE | NE | ENE;
        terr2 = EAST | ESE | SE | SSE;
        terr3 = SOUTH | SSW | SW | WSW | WEST;
        terr4 = WEST | WNW | NW | NNW | SOUTH;

        printf ( "terr3 ^ terr4 == %x\n", terr3 ^ terr4);
        printf ( "(terr3 | terr4) & ~(terr3 & terr4) == %x\n",
               (terr3 | terr4) & ~(terr3 & terr4));
}
```

This program produces the following output:

```
terr3 ^ terr4 == ee00
(terr3 | terr4) & ~(terr3 & terr4) == ee00
```

Toggling   The XOR operator is particularly useful for toggling bits — that is, for turning a bit on when it is off, or turning it off when it is on. Toggling *always* changes the current value.

Using the territory example, suppose that a given region can either have someone working in it or not. One of the actions you may want a program to carry out is to mark whether a region is being worked, and to update this value as required. The following program shows how you can toggle this information for a particular region:

```
/* Program to illustrate bitwise XOR operator for toggling values. */

#define NORTH    0x1     /* 0000 0000 0000 0001 */
#define NNE      0x2     /* 0000 0000 0000 0010 */
#define NE       0x4     /* 0000 0000 0000 0100 */
#define ENE      0x8     /* 0000 0000 0000 1000 */
#define EAST     0x10    /* 0000 0000 0001 0000 */
#define ESE      0x20    /* 0000 0000 0010 0000 */
#define SE       0x40    /* 0000 0000 0100 0000 */
#define SSE      0x80    /* 0000 0000 1000 0000 */
#define SOUTH    0x100   /* 0000 0001 0000 0000 */
```

```
#define SSW     0x200    /* 0000 0010 0000 0000 */
#define SW      0x400    /* 0000 0100 0000 0000 */
#define WSW     0x800    /* 0000 1000 0000 0000 */
#define WEST    0x1000   /* 0001 0000 0000 0000 */
#define WNW     0x2000   /* 0010 0000 0000 0000 */
#define NW      0x4000   /* 0100 0000 0000 0000 */
#define NNW     0x8000   /* 1000 0000 0000 0001 */

main ()
{
        int  terr1, terr2, terr3, terr4;
        void toggle_val ( int *, int);

        /* Assign regions to territories */
        terr1 = NORTH | NNE | NE | ENE;
        terr2 = EAST | ESE | SE | SSE;
        terr3 = SOUTH | SSW | SW | WSW | WEST;
        terr4 = WEST | WNW | NW | NNW | SOUTH;

        printf ( "terr1 == %x\n", terr1);
        toggle_val ( &terr1, NORTH);
        printf ( "After toggling NORTH, terr1 == %x\n", terr1);
        toggle_val ( &terr1, NORTH);
        printf ( "After toggling NORTH again, terr1 == %x\n", terr1);
}

/* Toggle the specified bits in val.
   Note use of compound assignment operator with bitwise XOR.
*/
void toggle_val ( int *val, int bits)
{
        *val ^= bits;
}
```

This program produces the following output:

```
terr1 == f
After toggling NORTH, terr1 == e
After toggling NORTH again, terr1 == f
```

After **terr1** is initialized, the NORTH bit is 1 in **terr1**. The first call to **toggle—val( )** turns this bit off. Because NORTH is the rightmost bit, this decreases the value of **terr1** by 1, as indicated in the value after toggling. The second call to **toggle—val( )** turns the NORTH bit back on. Because no other changes were made to **terr1** between calls to **toggle—val( )**, the second call simply restored the variable to its original value. Two consecutive calls to **toggle—val( )**, with the same arguments, will always restore the variable to its original value.

Notice the definition of **toggle—val( )**. This uses a compound assignment statement, ^=, involving the XOR operator. The assignment in **toggle—bit( )** is equivalent to the following:

```
*val = *val ^ bits;
```

Any of the binary operators can be used in compound assignment statements, which have the same low precedence as all the other assignment statements. The XOR operator, on the other hand, has a precedence between that of the bitwise AND operator and that of the bitwise OR operator. This is reasonable considering the fact that this operator seems to share properties with each of these other operators.

Let's look at one more example, to illustrate that you can toggle on multiple bits at a time.

```
/* Program to illustrate bitwise XOR operator for toggling values. */

#define ODD_FLIP   0xAAAA        /* 1010 1010 1010 1010 */
#define EVEN_FLIP  0x5555        /* 0101 0101 0101 0101 */

main ()
{
        int  i1 = 32767, i2 = 32767;
        void toggle_val ( int *, int);

        printf ( "i1 == %x; i2 == %x\n", i1, i2);
        toggle_val ( &i1, ODD_FLIP);
        toggle_val ( &i2, EVEN_FLIP);
        printf ( "i1 odd == %x; i2 even == %x\n", i1, i2);
}


/* Toggle the specified bits in val. */
void toggle_val ( int *val, int bits)
{
        *val ^= bits;
}
```

This program produces the following output:

```
i1 == 7fff; i2 == 7fff
i1 odd == d555; i2 even == 2aaa
```

This program simply flips the even numbered bits in one number and the odd numbered bits in a second number. Toggling is a very common type of program change. For example, many printers have controls that simply toggle between on and off. Keeping various printer settings in distinct bits on a variable can be a compact way of storing the information, just as changing settings by making bitwise changes to the variables can be an efficient way of controlling the printer.

Shift Operators

C also provides operators for simply shifting a sequence of bits to the left or right by a specified number of positions. When bits are shifted to the left, the bits at the left end are "pushed off" the variable and discarded. Positions being vacated (that is, postions to the right, in this case) are filled in with zeros as the shifting process occurs.

The *left shift operator* ($<<$) lets you carry out such bit moves. The following program illustrates the use of the left shift operator.

```
/* Program to illustrate use of left shift operator. */

#include <stdlib.h>
#define NULL_CHAR '\0'
#define MAX_STR    80

main ()
{
        int     value;
        int     make_bin_str ( char *, int);
        int     shifted_val, shift_amt;
        char    curr_str [ MAX_STR];
        char    val_str [ MAX_STR];  /* value to convert, read as string */
        void    put_nibble ( char *);

        /* get value to shift and amount to shift */
        printf ( "\n? ");
        gets ( val_str);
        value = atoi ( val_str);
        printf ( "Shift by? ");
        gets ( val_str);
        shift_amt = atoi ( val_str);

        /* bring shift_amt within valid bounds */
        shift_amt = bound_int ( shift_amt, 0, 15);

        do
        {
                printf ( "%d : ", value);
                if ( make_bin_str ( curr_str, value))
                        put_nibble ( curr_str);
                else
                        printf ( "string not built correctly:: %s\n",
                                 curr_str);

                /* now apply the left shift operator. */
                shifted_val = value << shift_amt;
                printf ( "\nvalue << %d == %d : ", shift_amt, shifted_val);
                if ( make_bin_str ( curr_str, shifted_val))
                        put_nibble ( curr_str);
```

```
                        else
                                printf ( "string not built correctly:: %s\n",
                                        curr_str);

                        /* get value to shift and amount to shift */
                        printf ( "\n\n? ");
                        gets ( val_str);
                        value = atoi ( val_str);
                        if ( value != 0)       /* stop if 0 entered */
                        {
                                printf ( "Shift by? ");
                                gets ( val_str);
                                shift_amt = atoi ( val_str);
                                shift_amt = bound_int ( shift_amt, 0, 15);
                        }
                }
        while ( value != 0);
}


/* build a string consisting of binary digits, based on value passed in */
int  make_bin_str ( char *str, int value)
{
#define MAX_PWR  32768L          /* largest bit in an unsigned 16 bit int */

        unsigned    index;
        int         outcome, bin_place = 0;

        for ( index = MAX_PWR; index > 0; index /= 2)
        {
                outcome = (int) ( value / index);
                if ( (outcome == 1) || (outcome == -1))
                        str [ bin_place++] = '1';
                else
                        str [ bin_place++] = '0';

                value %= index;
        }

        str [ bin_place] = NULL_CHAR;

        if ( bin_place == 16)   /* if 16 bits were processed : 0 -- 15 */
                return ( 1);
        else
                return ( 0);
}


/* write a string, in groups of four letters */
void put_nibble ( char *str)
{
        int  index;

        for ( index = 0; str [ index] != NULL_CHAR; index++)
        {
                if ( ( index % 4) == 3)
                        printf ( "%c ", str [ index]);
                else
                        printf ( "%c", str [ index]);
        }
}


/* bring an integer value between the specified bounds */
int bound_int ( int val, int lower, int upper)
{
        if ( val < lower)
                return ( lower);
        else if ( val > upper)
                return ( upper);
        else
                return ( val);
}
```

A sample session with this program produces the following:

```
? 100
Shift by? 5
100 : 0000 0000 0110 0100
value << 5 == 3200 : 0000 1100 1000 0000

? 16
Shift by? 5
16 : 0000 0000 0001 0000
value << 5 == 512 : 0000 0010 0000 0000

? 2000
Shift by? 8
2000 : 0000 0111 1101 0000
value << 8 == -12288 : 1101 0000 0000 0000

? 2000
Shift by? -5
2000 : 0000 0111 1101 0000
value << 0 == 2000 : 0000 0111 1101 0000

? 0
```

This program lets you specify the value you want to change and the number of places you want to shift the value to the left. The program then carries out the left shift, and displays the results.

The **main( )** function has been changed somewhat from earlier versions of the program to present the left shift operator. In addition, the function **bound_int( )** has been added to make sure the program doesn't try to shift by more than the allowable amounts. This function brings any values entered for **shift_amt** within the range 0 through 15.

When the left shift operator is applied, the bits on the left simply disappear as they are overwritten by the bits coming from the right. As the positions on the right are vacated, those bits are replaced by 0. The following version of the program makes this even clearer. The middle part of **main( )** has been changed from the previous program—to loop through the left shift process, one place at a time.

```
/* Program to illustrate use of left shift operator, step by step. */
#include <stdlib.h>
#define NULL_CHAR '\0'
#define MAX_STR   80

main ()
{
        int     value, index;
        int     make_bin_str ( char *, int);
        int     shifted_val, shift_amt;
        char    curr_str [ MAX_STR];
        char    val_str [ MAX_STR];   /* value to convert, read as string */
        void    put_nibble ( char *);

        printf ( "\n? ");
        gets ( val_str);
        value = atoi ( val_str);
        printf ( "Shift by? ");
```

```
gets ( val_str);
shift_amt = atoi ( val_str);
shift_amt = bound_int ( shift_amt, 0, 15);

do
{
        printf ( "%d : ", value);
        if ( make_bin_str ( curr_str, value))
                put_nibble ( curr_str);
        else
                printf ( "string not built correctly:: %s\n",
                        curr_str);

        /* because will need to shift one place at a time in loop */
        shifted_val = value;

        /* now apply left shift operator, one place at a time */
        for ( index = 1; index <= shift_amt; index++)
        {
                shifted_val <<= 1;
                printf ( "\nvalue << %d == %d : ",
                        index, shifted_val);
                if ( make_bin_str ( curr_str, shifted_val))
                        put_nibble ( curr_str);
                else
                        printf ( "string not built correctly:: %s\n",
                                curr_str);
        }

        printf ( "\n\n? ");
        gets ( val_str);
        value = atoi ( val_str);
        if ( value != 0)
        {
                        printf ( "Shift by? ");
                        gets ( val_str);
                        shift_amt = atoi ( val_str);
                        shift_amt = bound_int ( shift_amt, 0, 15);
        }
}
while ( value != 0);
}


/* build a string consisting of binary digits, based on value passed in */
int  make_bin_str ( char *str, int value)
{
#define MAX_PWR  32768L          /* largest bit in an unsigned 16 bit int */

        unsigned     index;
        int          outcome, bin_place = 0;

        for ( index = MAX_PWR; index > 0; index /= 2)
        {
                outcome = (int) ( value / index);
                if ( (outcome == 1) || (outcome == -1))
                        str [ bin_place++] = '1';
                else
                        str [ bin_place++] = '0';

                value %= index;
        }

        str [ bin_place] = NULL_CHAR;

        if ( bin_place == 16)   /* if 16 bits were processed : 0 -- 15 */
                return ( 1);
        else
                return ( 0);
}


/* mask off the specified bit patterns */
int mask ( int value, int the_mask)
{
```

```
        return ( value & the_mask);
}


/* write a string, in groups of four letters */
void put_nibble ( char *str)
{
        int  index;

        for ( index = 0; str [ index] != NULL_CHAR; index++)
        {
                if ( ( index % 4) == 3)
                        printf ( "%c ", str [ index]);
                else
                        printf ( "%c", str [ index]);
        }
}


/* bring an integer value between the specified bounds */
int bound_int ( int val, int lower, int upper)
{

        if ( val < lower)
                return ( lower);
        else if ( val > upper)
                return ( upper);
        else
                return ( val);

}
```

For an input of 127 as the value and 6 as the number of places to shift, the program produces the following output:

```
127 : 0000 0000 0111 1111
value << 1 == 254 : 0000 0000 1111 1110
value << 2 == 508 : 0000 0001 1111 1100
value << 3 == 1016 : 0000 0011 1111 1000
value << 4 == 2032 : 0000 0111 1111 0000
value << 5 == 4064 : 0000 1111 1110 0000
value << 6 == 8128 : 0001 1111 1100 0000
```

In this version of the program, you can literally see the bits marching across the number.

▶**REMEMBER**   When the left shift operator ($<<$) is applied, the bit pattern is always filled in with 0's on the right.

There is also a *right shift operator* ($>>$) that moves bits towards the right end of the number. Bits at the right end disappear as they are overwritten by the new bits. The bits at the left end are not necessarilyfilled in with zeros, however. The action taken at the left of a number to which the right shift operator is being applied is implementation dependent.

Logical and Arithmetic Shifts   There are two strategies that can be used when filling in bits at the left end of a number to which the right shift operator is being applied. A *logical shift* always fills in these bits with 0. An arithmetic shift may fill them in with 0 or 1, depending on the value and type of the variable being shifted.

If the variable is an **unsigned int**, the bits are always filled in with 0. On the other hand, if the variable is a **signed int**, the bits are filled in with whatever value was currently stored in the sign bit.

Testing the Right Shift   You can take advantage of QuickC's integrated environment to experiment quickly and easily with the way the implementation handles right shifts. The following program currently defines the variable **shifted—val** as an **unsigned int**.

```
/* Program to illustrate use of shift operators. */

#include <stdlib.h>
#define NULL_CHAR '\0'
#define MAX_STR    80

main ()
{
        int     value, index;
        int     make_bin_str ( char *, int);
        unsigned    shifted_val;
        int     shift_amt;
        char    curr_str [ MAX_STR];
        char    val_str [ MAX_STR];  /* value to convert, read as string */
        void    put_nibble ( char *);

        printf ( "\n? ");
        gets ( val_str);
        value = atoi ( val_str);
        printf ( "Shift by? ");
        gets ( val_str);
        shift_amt = atoi ( val_str);
        shift_amt = bound_int ( shift_amt, 0, 15);

        do
        {
                printf ( "%d : ", value);
                if ( make_bin_str ( curr_str, value))
                        put_nibble ( curr_str);
                else
                        printf ( "string not built correctly:: %s\n",
                                curr_str);

                shifted_val = value;

                /* now apply the left shift operator. */
                for ( index = 1; index <= shift_amt; index++)
                {
                        shifted_val >>= 1;
```

```
                    printf ( "\nvalue >> %d == %d : ",
                            index, shifted_val);
                    if ( make_bin_str ( curr_str, shifted_val))
                            put_nibble ( curr_str);
                    else
                            printf ( "string not built correctly:: %s\n",
                                    curr_str);
            }

            printf ( "\n\n? ");
            gets ( val_str);
            value = atoi ( val_str);
            if ( value != 0)
            {
                    printf ( "Shift by? ");
                    gets ( val_str);
                    shift_amt = atoi ( val_str);
                    shift_amt = bound_int ( shift_amt, 0, 15);
            }
    }
    while ( value != 0);
}


/* build a string consisting of binary digits, based on value passed in */
int  make_bin_str ( char *str, int value)
{
#define MAX_PWR  32768L            /* largest bit in an unsigned 16 bit int */

    unsigned    index;
    int         outcome, bin_place = 0;

    for ( index = MAX_PWR; index > 0; index /= 2)
    {
            outcome = (int) ( value / index);
            if ( (outcome == 1) || (outcome == -1))
                    str [ bin_place++] = '1';
            else
                    str [ bin_place++] = '0';

            value %= index;
    }

    str [ bin_place] = NULL_CHAR;

    if ( bin_place == 16)    /* if 16 bits were processed : 0 -- 15 */
            return ( 1);
    else
            return ( 0);

    /* write a string, in groups of four letters */
    void put_nibble ( char *str)
    {
            int   index;
```

```
        for ( index = 0; str [ index] != NULL_CHAR; index++)
        {
                if ( ( index % 4) == 3)
                        printf ( "%c ", str [ index]);
                else
                        printf ( "%c", str [ index]);
        }
}


/* bring an integer value between the specified bounds */
int bound_int ( int val, int lower, int upper)
{
        if ( val < lower)
                return ( lower);
        else if ( val > upper)
                return ( upper);
        else
                return ( val);
}
```

Start up QuickC with this program as your working file by selecting the Start option in the Run menu. Try tracing 35 and −35, for example. When you've finished running the program, QuickC will put you back in the program source file. Change the type of **shifted_val** to **int** and start the program again using the same values as before. Notice the difference in the bit patterns that result.

QuickC uses an arithmetic shift, so that signed numbers get shifted by filling in the left bits with whatever value was stored in the sign bit.

▶ **CAUTION** Be careful when using the right shift operator. If your implementation uses an arithmetic shift (as does QuickC), then the left bits may sometimes fill with 1 and sometimes with 0.

Another way of seeing the differences between signed and unsigned values when applying the right shift operator is to perform the same operations on two different variables, one an **int** and the other an **unsigned int**. Add the following three lines to the preceding program:

```
int  shifted_int_val;  /* add to variable definitions in main() */
shifted_int_val = value;  /* add after shifted_val = value; */
shifted_int_val >>= 1;    /* add after shifted_val >>= 1; */
```

Try the following to see how QuickC handles signed and unsigned variables when right shifting:

1. Start up QuickC with this revised program as your working file.

2. Clear all breakpoints and watch variables.

3. Compile the program with the Debug option on.

4. Add the following watch variables:

   shifted＿val,x
   shifted＿int＿val,x
   index

5. Set a breakpoint at the first call to **printf( )** after the right shifts in the **for** loop.

6. Step through this program, comparing the values of **shifted＿val** and **shifted＿int＿val** as the right shift proceeds.

Because the bitwise shift operators have a precedence just below the arithmetic addition operators, and just above the relational operators, the shift operators have a higher precedence than the other binary bitwise operators.

▶**REMEMBER**   The precedence of the bitwise shift operators is between the precedences of the arithmetic operators and the relational operators.

Shift Operators and Powers of Two

As you probably know, the easiest way to multiply a number by 10 is to add a 0 at the right end of the number. To multiply by 100, add two zeros, and so on. For example, $35 * 10 == 350$, $35 * 100 = 3,500$, $35 * 1000 = 35,000$. To multiply by a power of ten, you move the number over one digit to the left, and add a zero in the one's position.

Similarly, there is a direct relationship between the left shift operator and multiplication by powers of two. Shifting a value's bits left by one place amounts to multiplying by 2; shifting by 2 bits amounts to multiplying by 4, and so forth.

The following listing shows this relationship:

```
/* Program to illustrate relationship between left shift operator
   and multiplication by two.
*/

#include <stdio.h>
#include <stdlib.h>
#define MAX_SHIFT 12
#define MAX_STR   80
#define NULL_CHAR '\0'

main ()
{
        unsigned value, index, shift;
        char   *info, bit_str [ MAX_STR];
        int    make_bin_str ( char *, int);
        void   put_nibble ( char *);

        printf ( "Value to shift? ");
        gets ( info);
        value = atoi ( info);

        for ( index = 0; index < MAX_SHIFT; index++)
        {
                shift = value << index;
                printf ( "%2u:  %5u -- ", index, shift);
                if ( make_bin_str ( bit_str, shift))
                        put_nibble ( bit_str);
                /* else do nothing */
                printf ( "\n");
        }
}


/* build a string consisting of binary digits, based on value passed in */
int  make_bin_str ( char *str, int value)
{
#define MAX_PWR  32768L          /* largest bit in an unsigned 16 bit int */

        unsigned    index;
        int         outcome, bin_place = 0;

        for ( index = MAX_PWR; index > 0; index /= 2)
        {
                outcome = (int) ( value / index);
                if ( (outcome == 1) || (outcome == -1))
                        str [ bin_place++] = '1';
                else
                        str [ bin_place++] = '0';

                value %= index;
        }

        str [ bin_place] = NULL_CHAR;

        if ( bin_place == 16)   /* if 16 bits were processed : 0 -- 15 */
                return ( 1);
        else
                return ( 0);
}


/* write a string in groups of 4 characters,
   with each group separated by a space.
   Useful for writing bit patterns --- grouping the bits into
   groups of 4 makes it easy to determine hexadecimal digits.
*/
void put_nibble ( char *str)
{
```

```
        int  index;

        for ( index = 0; str [ index] != NULL_CHAR; index++)
        {
                if ( ( index % 4) == 3)
                        printf ( "%c ", str [ index]);
                else
                        printf ( "%c", str [ index]);
        }
}
```

This program produces the following bit shift values for a starting value of 5:

```
Value to shift? 5
  0:     5 -- 0000 0000 0000 0101
  1:    10 -- 0000 0000 0000 1010
  2:    20 -- 0000 0000 0001 0100
  3:    40 -- 0000 0000 0010 1000
  4:    80 -- 0000 0000 0101 0000
  5:   160 -- 0000 0000 1010 0000
  6:   320 -- 0000 0001 0100 0000
  7:   640 -- 0000 0010 1000 0000
  8:  1280 -- 0000 0101 0000 0000
  9:  2560 -- 0000 1010 0000 0000
 10:  5120 -- 0001 0100 0000 0000
 11: 10240 -- 0010 1000 0000 0000
```

Just as multiplying by powers of ten amounts to placing a 0 at the right side of a number in base 10, so multiplying by powers of two amounts to placing a 0 at the right side of a number in base 2. The left shift operator accomplishes this.

The range of values for which left shifts will produce a valid result depends on the bit pattern of the number you want to shift. When the leftmost 1 drops off the "edge" of the number, the results are no longer accurate. Thus, in the preceding output, you could left shift two more times — 13 bits in all, for a value of 40960. After that, the result would be incorrect.

Similarly, applying the right shift operator to a value amounts to *dividing* the number by 2 for every shift — assuming that you are using unsigned values, or that your compiler uses a logical shift operator. For example, shifting the bit pattern of 4096 to the right by 3 bits amounts to dividing by 8, and gives a result of 512.

The following program shows this process:

```
/* Program to illustrate relationship between right shift operator
   and multiplication by two.
*/

#include <stdio.h>
#include <stdlib.h>
#define MAX_SHIFT 12
#define MAX_STR   80
#define NULL_CHAR '\0'
```

```
main ()
{
        unsigned value, index, shift;
        char  *info, bit_str [ MAX_STR];
        int   make_bin_str ( char *, int);
        void  put_nibble ( char *);

        printf ( "Value to shift? ");
        gets ( info);
        value = atoi ( info);

        for ( index = 0; index < MAX_SHIFT; index++)
        {
                shift = value >> index;
                printf ( "%2u:  %5u -- ", index, shift);
                if ( make_bin_str ( bit_str, shift))
                        put_nibble ( bit_str);
                /* else do nothing */
                printf ( "\n");
        }
}


/* build a string consisting of binary digits, based on value passed in */
int  make_bin_str ( char *str, int value)
{
#define MAX_PWR  32768L         /* largest bit in an unsigned 16 bit int */

        unsigned     index;
        int          outcome, bin_place = 0;

        for ( index = MAX_PWR; index > 0; index /= 2)
        {
                outcome = (int) ( value / index);
                if ( (outcome == 1) || (outcome == -1))
                        str [ bin_place++] = '1';
                else
                        str [ bin_place++] = '0';

                value %= index;
        }

        str [ bin_place] = NULL_CHAR;

        if ( bin_place == 16)   /* if 16 bits were processed : 0 -- 15 */
                return ( 1);
        else
                return ( 0);
}


/* write a string in groups of 4 characters,
   with each group separated by a space.
   Useful for writing bit patterns --- grouping the bits into
   groups of 4 makes it easy to determine hexadecimal digits.
*/
void put_nibble ( char *str)
{
        int  index;

        for ( index = 0; str [ index] != NULL_CHAR; index++)
        {
                if ( ( index % 4) == 3)
                        printf ( "%c ", str [ index]);
```

```
            else
                        printf ( "%c", str [ index]);
        }
    }
```

This program produces the following output:

```
Value to shift? 40960
   0:   40960 -- 1010 0000 0000 0000
   1:   20480 -- 0101 0000 0000 0000
   2:   10240 -- 0010 1000 0000 0000
   3:    5120 -- 0001 0100 0000 0000
   4:    2560 -- 0000 1010 0000 0000
   5:    1280 -- 0000 0101 0000 0000
   6:     640 -- 0000 0010 1000 0000
   7:     320 -- 0000 0001 0100 0000
   8:     160 -- 0000 0000 1010 0000
   9:      80 -- 0000 0000 0101 0000
  10:      40 -- 0000 0000 0010 1000
  11:      20 -- 0000 0000 0001 0100
```

The Conditional Operator

Another operator that we haven't yet discussed is the *conditional operator*. This operator is useful in situations where you may want your program to do one of two things in a particular situation.

For example, suppose you want your program to assign the absolute value of a number. The following code would accomplish this, by assigning the absolute value of **x** to **z**.

```
if ( x < 0)
        z = -x;
else
        z = x;
```

C's conditional operator lets you do the same thing in a single assignment statement. The preceding **if** construct is equivalent to the following statement, which uses the conditional operator:

```
z = (x < 0) ? -x : x;
```

Consider the components of the conditional operator, which consists of *three* operands and the operator. The following illustration shows the structure of the conditional operator, and identifies the elements:

```
Structure of Conditional Operator:

        condition ? alternative1 : alternative2

     condition
             alternative1
                   alternative2
                     |
  z = (x < 0) ?  -x  :  x;
                \   /
               operator
```

The conditional operator takes three operands. The first is an expression that evaluates to true or false. If the condition is true, the second operand is used; otherwise, the third operand is used.

Since the **?:** operator has precedence just above that of the assignment operators, we don't need parentheses in the above statement.

The conditional operator is often used in defining macros for the preprocessor. The following are some examples:

```
#define ABS_VAL(x)        ( (x) >= 0) ? (x) : ( 0 - (x))

#define MAX2(x,y)         ( (x) > (y)) ? (x) : (y)
#define MAX3(x,y,z)       ( (x) > (y)) ? MAX2(x,z) : MAX2(y,z)

#define MIN2(x,y)         ( (x) > (y)) ? (y) : (x)
#define MIN3(x,y,z)       ( (x) > (y)) ? MIN2(y,z) : MIN2(x,z)

#define PR_NICE(v,w,x,y,z)  ( ( ((v) % (w)) == (x)) ? (y) : (z))
```

The last macro can be used to display information with a specified number of entries per line. So far, we've been using an **if** statement to accomplish this. The following program illustrates the use of the macros:

```
/* Program to illustrate use of conditional operator */

#include <stdlib.h>
#define MAX_VALS  150

#define MAX2(x,y)         ( (x) > (y)) ? (x) : (y)
#define MAX3(x,y,z)       ( (x) > (y)) ? MAX2(x,z) : MAX2(y,z)

#define MIN2(x,y)         ( (x) > (y)) ? (y) : (x)
#define MIN3(x,y,z)       ( (x) > (y)) ? MIN2(y,z) : MIN2(x,z)

#define PR_NICE(v,w,x,y,z)  ( ((v) % (w)) == (x)) ? (y) : (z)
```

```
main ()
{
        int rand (void);
        int array [ MAX_VALS];
        int index;

        for ( index = 0; index < MAX_VALS; index++)
                array [ index] = rand();

        for ( index = 0; index < MAX_VALS -3; index++)
        {
                printf ( "%7d",
                        MIN3 ( array [ index], array [ index + 1],
                               array [ index + 2]));
                PR_NICE ( index, 10, 9, printf ( "\n"), printf ( ""));
        }
}
```

This program produces the following output:

```
   41    6334    6334   15724   11478   11478   11478   24464    5705    5705
 5705   16827    9961     491     491     491    2995    4827    4827    5436
 3902     153     153     153     292   12382   17421   18716    5447    5447
 5447   11538    1869    1869    1869   19912   17035    9894    9894    9894
23811   23811   17673    4664    4664    4664    7711    6868    6868    6868
25547   27644   20037   12859    8723    8723    8723     778     778     778
 3035    1842     288     288     288    8942    8942    8942   19264   22648
15890    6729    6729    6729   15006   15006   15006    3548    3548    3548
12623   12623   18756   11840    4966    4966    4966    7376   13931   16944
16944   11323    5537    5537    5537    2082    2082    2082    4833    4833
 4639    4639    4639    9930    9930    2306    2306    2306    5021    5021
 5021   19072    6270    5829    5829    5829    5097    5097    5097   13290
 9161    9161    9161   18636   22355   15574    4031    4031    4031    1150
 1150    1150   13966    3430    3430    3430   18007   11337   11337   11337
12287   10383   10383    8909    8909    8909    9758
```

This program generates 100 random integers. Then it writes the smallest of successive groups of three integers. The MIN3( ) macro decides which value to write. The PR—NICE( ) macro makes sure that just ten values are written on a line.

Notice that you can put expressions that are quite complex into the conditional operator. The only restriction is that the condition expression needs to evaluate to true or false.

Let's look at one more example. This program also generates 100 random integers. This time, however, the program keeps only the portion of the number within the range 0 through 255; that is, the program keeps only the far-right byte of the number.

```
/* Program to illustrate use of conditional operator */

#include <stdlib.h>
#define MAX_VALS   150

#define MAX2(x,y)            ( (x) > (y)) ? (x) : (y)
```

```
#define MAX3(x,y,z)          ( (x) > (y)) ? MAX2(x,z) : MAX2(y,z)

#define MIN2(x,y)            ( (x) > (y)) ? (y) : (x)
#define MIN3(x,y,z)          ( (x) > (y)) ? MIN2(y,z) : MIN2(x,z)

#define PR_NICE(v,w,x,y,z)  ( ((v) % (w)) == (x)) ? (y) : (z)


main ()
{
        int rand (void);
        int array [ MAX_VALS], val;
        int index;


        for ( index = 0; index < MAX_VALS; index++)
                array [ index] = rand();

        for ( index = 0; index < MAX_VALS; index++)
        {
                val = array [ index];
                val = ( (val >= 0) && ( val <= 255)) ? val : val & 255;
                printf ( "%7d", val);
                PR_NICE ( index, 10, 9, printf ( "\n"), printf ( ""));
        }
}
```

This program produces the following output:

41	35	190	132	225	108	214	174	82	144
73	241	241	187	233	235	179	166	219	60
135	12	62	153	36	94	13	28	6	183
71	222	179	18	77	200	67	187	139	166
31	3	90	125	9	56	37	31	93	212
203	252	150	245	69	59	19	13	137	10
28	219	174	50	32	154	80	238	64	120
54	253	18	73	50	246	158	125	73	220
173	79	20	242	68	64	102	208	107	196
48	183	50	59	161	34	246	34	145	157
225	139	31	218	176	202	153	2	185	114
157	73	44	128	126	197	153	213	233	128
178	234	201	204	83	191	103	214	191	20
214	126	45	220	142	102	131	239	87	73
97	255	105	143	97	205	209	30	157	156

Table 15-1.   Precedence Hierarchy for C Operators

Operator	Comments
( ) [ ]	function and array operators
! ~ & = * (cast) + − sizeof( ) ++ −−	unary operators
* / %	arithmetic (multiplication)
+ −	arithmetic (addition)
<< >>	shift operators
< <= > >=	relational operators
== !=	equality operators
&	bitwise AND
^	bitwise XOR
|	bitwise OR
&&	logical multiplication
||	logical addition
?:	conditional operator
= += −= *= /= %= &= ^= |= <<= >>=	assignment operators
,	comma operator

Summary

This chapter covered some miscellaneous operators. In particular, it examined the bitwise operators, which can be very useful for situations involving collections of objects or for systems programs, which often have to manipulate individual bits.

You have also learned about the conditional operator, which allows you to select between two alternatives in a compact manner. This operator can be used to write very powerful macros.

We've covered just about all the operators there are in C. Table 5-1 summarizes these operators and their precedences.

16

Structures, Unions, and Other Types

So far, the data types you've seen have contained only one type of information. Even arrays, which contain multiple elements, store only one type of information. Sometimes, however, it's convenient to group different types of information together — either because the information is logically related or because the items are all components of a larger unit. In this chapter, you'll learn about the **structure** and **union** data types, which allow you to group different types of information together in one variable. You'll also learn about the bit fields available in structures. Finally, you'll find out about enumerated data types, which are available in many implementations, but won't become an official part of C until the Draft Proposed ANSI Standard is adopted.

Structures

Suppose you want to represent information about a day's weather in January. To record the average temperature and average windspeed for the day, you could use C's structure type to store the data so that the two items are grouped together.

A *structure* is an aggregate variable that consists of several components, or *members*. Members can be of different types. In the weather structure example, you might want to use two members, **temp** and **wind**, to record the information. The following listing specifies a structure named **weather**, having two members, or components, **temp** and **wind**. In this case, both members are of type **double**. Note that the members of a structure are stored in consecutive storage locations.

```
struct weather {
        double temp;
        double wind;
};
```

This declaration merely creates a structure description, or template, based on the members specified; it *does not* allocate any storage for such a structure. Let's look at the components of this template. The declaration begins with the keyword **struct**, which identifies what follows as a structure. The word **weather** is the *tag,* or *tag name,* of the structure being created.

The material between the matching left and right curly braces represents the structure's members. Each of these members is declared as if it were a variable of the specified type. Thus, **temp** and **wind** are both specified as being of type **double**. The right brace ends the declared structure, and the semicolon ends the declaration statement. The following illustration shows the components of a structure declaration:

If you think of **struct weather** together as specifying the variable's name, then, to define a variable of this type, you could enter the following:

```
struct weather {
        double temp;
        double wind;
};

main()
{
        struct weather  today;

        /* main function body here */
}
```

The preceding listing describes a global structure named **weather**. A local variable of that type is defined in **main( )**. The definition contains the keyword, **struct**, the tag name associated with the structure (**weather**), and an identifier for the variable itself (**today**).

Let's look at a few more structure declarations and definitions. In mathematics, complex numbers are aggregates with two components: a real part and an imaginary part. The following listing creates a local complex number structure, **complex**, and, at the same time, defines two variables of this type, **comp1** and **comp2**:

```
main ()
{
        struct complex {
                double re, im;
        } comp1, comp2;

        /* code here */
}
```

This structure has the tag name **complex**, and has two members, **re** and **im**. Both members are of type **double**. Notice that you can allocate storage for structure variables at the same time you create the structure itself. In this listing, only function **main( )** would know about the structure of type **complex**. The storage allocated for the two variables of this type would also be local to **main( )**.

The following example specifies a more elaborate structure, which contains various types of information about an adult, including name, age, and income. The example also defines an array of such structures:

```
#define MAX_NAME 25
#define MAX_PERSONS  10

struct person {
        char    first, last [ MAX_NAME];
        int     age;
        double income;
};

main ()
{
        struct person  sample [ MAX_PERSONS];

        /* code here */
}
```

The **person** structure declared here has four members — a **char(first)**, a string (**last[]**), an **int (age)**, and a **double (income)**.

The preceding listing also defines an array of type **person** which contains MAX—PERSONS elements of this structure. Each element in this array refers to an entire structure. That is, each array element contains first initial (a **char** variable) and last name, age, and income information. Thus, **sample[0]** refers to the first person in the array, and **sample[9]** would refer to the last person. The following listing shows you how much storage each array element takes up:

```
#define MAX_NAME     25
#define MAX_PERSONS  10

struct person {
        char    first, last [ MAX_NAME];
        int     age;
        double income;
};

main ()
{
        struct person  sample [ MAX_PERSONS];
        int     index;

        printf ( "Each person requires %d bytes\n", sizeof ( sample [ 0]));
}
```

If you compile and run this program, you'll find that a **person** structure requires 36 bytes of storage — 1 byte for the person's initial (**char**), 25 bytes for the last name (**char []**), 2 bytes for **age (int)**, and 8 bytes for **income (double)**. Notice the use of the **sizeof( )** operator with a structure as an argument here. How would you determine the amount of storage allocated for the entire array, **sample[]**?

In this example, the structure template is global, so any function in the program could have variables of structure type **person**. The storage allocated for **sample[]** is local, however.

Accessing Structure Members

Once you've allocated space for a structure, by defining a variable of the appropriate type you can use the *structure member operator* (**.**) to access individual members of the structure. This operator takes two operands. The left operand is the name of a variable of the structure's type and the right operand is a member within that structure. The result of applying the operator is the specified structure element itself, or its value—depending on the context. In the following program, the structure member operator identifies the members to which specific values will be assigned. This structure member operator is sometimes called the *dot operator,* to distinguish it from another member operator that you'll learn about later in this chapter. The dot operator is in the highest category of precedence, along with the array subscripting and the function call operators.

```
/* Program to show how to access a structure member */

struct weather {
        double temp;
        double wind;
};

main()
{
        struct weather  today;

        today.temp = 84.5;
        today.wind = 10.1;
        printf ( "Temp == %10.2lf; wind == %10.2lf\n",
                today.temp, today.wind);
}
```

In this program, **today.temp** is assigned the value 84.5, and **today.wind** is assigned the value 10.1. Notice that no space has been left between the variable name, operator, and member identifier. This is common programming practice, but is not required. Thus, the following assignment statement would also be valid, although it is rarely seen:

```
today . wind = 10.1;
```

The following program uses the **sample[]** array defined in a previous example to get information about five persons from the user, and then to display this information.

```
/* Program to read  and display contents of an array of structures */

#include <stdio.h>
#include <stdlib.h>
```

```
#define MAX_NAME     25
#define MAX_PERSONS  5
#define MAX_STR      80

struct person {
        char    first, last [ MAX_NAME];
        int     age;
        double  income;
};

main ()
{
        struct person  sample [ MAX_PERSONS];
        int     index;
        char    info [ MAX_STR];  /* used to read info for conversion */

        /* get information about each structure in the array */
        for ( index = 0; index < MAX_PERSONS; index++)
        {
                printf ( "First initial? ");
                gets ( info);
                sample [ index].first = info [ 0];

                printf ( "Last name? ");
                gets ( sample [ index].last);

                printf ( "Age? ");
                gets ( info);
                sample [ index].age = atoi ( info);

                printf ( "Income? ");
                gets ( info);
                sample [ index].income = atof ( info);
        }

        /* display information about each structure in the array */
        for ( index = 0; index < MAX_PERSONS; index++)
        {
                printf ( "%c. %s: age == %3d; income == $%6.2lf\n",
                        sample [ index].first, sample [ index].last,
                        sample [ index].age, sample [ index].income);
        }
}
```

This program prompts the user for values for each of the **person** elements in the **sample[]** array. Notice the use of **gets( )**, in conjunction with a conversion function (**atoi( )** or **atof( )**, in this case), to read the information. This is often safer than using **scanf( )**, which is sensitive to entries of the wrong type. The **info[]** string is used solely for the purpose of getting the strings for conversion, so it can be used for each entry.

Rules for Structures

A structure declaration will have three elements:

1. The keyword, **struct**

2. A tag name for the structure being created

3. A member list

Tag Names   The tag name specifies the identifier for the structure. Once it has been created, you can think of the structure as being of type **struct <tag name>**, although it will be easier to speak simply of type **<tag name>**. In our earlier examples, tag names included: **person**, **complex**, and **weather**.

You can refer to the structure as a unit by using its tag. For this reason, you can assign an entire structure to another, *provided the structures have the same members*. Thus, the following assignments are all valid:

```
/* Program to illustrate assignments using structures ---
       assigning individual members and entire structures.
*/

struct card {
        char suit;
        int  val;
};

main ()
{
        struct card hand [ 5];

        /* assign  values to individual members */
        hand [ 0].suit = 'c';
        hand [ 0].val = 0;

        hand [ 1].suit = 'd';
        hand [ 1].val = 1;

        hand [ 2].suit = 'h';
        hand [ 2].val = 2;

        hand [ 3].suit = 's';
        hand [ 3].val = 3;

        hand [ 4].suit = 's';
        hand [ 4].val = 4;

        /* assign entire structures at once */
        hand [ 0] = hand [ 1];
        hand [ 1] = hand [ 2];
        hand [ 2] = hand [ 3];
        hand [ 3] = hand [ 4];

        /* display structure contents */
        printf ( "\n\nHand [ 0]: suit == %c, val == %u\n",
                hand [ 0].suit, hand [ 0].val);
        printf ( "Hand [ 1]: suit == %c, val == %u\n",
                hand [ 1].suit, hand [ 1].val);
        printf ( "Hand [ 2]: suit == %c, val == %u\n",
                hand [ 2].suit, hand [ 2].val);
        printf ( "Hand [ 3]: suit == %c, val == %u\n",
                hand [ 3].suit, hand [ 3].val);
        printf ( "Hand [ 4]: suit == %c, val == %u\n",
                hand [ 4].suit, hand [ 4].val);
}
```

This program produces the following output:

```
Hand [ 0]: suit == d, val == 1
Hand [ 1]: suit == h, val == 2
Hand [ 2]: suit == s, val == 3
Hand [ 3]: suit == s, val == 4
Hand [ 4]: suit == s, val == 4
```

Assigning an entire structure to another one has the same effect as assigning each of the structure's members one at a time.

Member Lists and Nested Structures   The member list is essentially a variable declaration list. You simply specify the type and an identifier for each member of the structure. Members can be of any type, including another structure, with two restrictions:

1. You can't put a storage class specifier before a member.

2. A structure can't be a member of itself. You can, however, have a pointer to the structure as a member.

For example, the following are all valid structure templates. Notice that they're also definitions.

```
/* The following structure has members: ed.major, ed.degree, ed.gpa */
struct education {
        char    major [ MAX_EDUC];
        char    degree [ MAX_EDUC];
        double  gpa;
} ed;

/* The following structure has members:
   stu.id, stu.yr_grad, stu.school.major, stu.school.degree, stu.school.gpa
*/
struct student {
        struct education school;
        char    id [ MAX_EDUC];
        int     yr_grad;
} stu;

/* The following structure has members:
   pers.first, pers.last, pers.learning.id, per.learning.yr_grad,
   pers.learning.school.major, pers.learning.school.degree,
   pers.learning.school.gpa
*/
struct person {
        char    first;
        char    last [ MAX_NAME];
        int     age;
        double  income;
        struct student learning;
} pers;
```

The preceding listing shows examples of nested structures, that is, structures declared within other structures. Notice how the naming process works.

When you want to access a member of a structure, use the structure member operator. For example, you would use this operator when you access **pers.first**, **pers.last**, and so on. You would use the same operator to access the **learning** member: **pers.learning**.

Once you've accessed **pers.learning**, you can access any of *its* members, since **pers.learning** is a structure. To access its members, use the dot operator. For example, **pers.learning.id** and **pers.learning.yr—grad** are valid members. Again, you can access **school** in the same way: **pers.learning.school**.

Once you've accessed that, you can access its members as follows: **pers.learning.school.major**, **pers.learning.school.degree**, and **pers.learning.school.gpa**. The access rules for nested structures can get long-winded, but they are straightforward.

Structures and Addresses   Structures are aggregate variables, like arrays. Unlike arrays, however, the structure's tag refers to a variable rather than to a pointer. However, you *can* ask C for the address of a structure. This address is the same as the location of the structure's first member. The following program shows how the addresses of structures and their members are related:

```
/* Program to provide information about storage for structures. */

struct card {
        char suit;
        int  val;
};

main ()
{
        struct card hand [ 5];

        /* assign values to individual members */
        hand [ 0].suit = 'c';
        hand [ 0].val = 0;

        hand [ 1].suit = 'd';
        hand [ 1].val = 1;

        hand [ 2].suit = 'h';
        hand [ 2].val = 2;

        hand [ 3].suit = 's';
```

```
        hand [ 3].val = 3;

        hand [ 4].suit = 's';
        hand [ 4].val = 4;

        /* assign entire structures */
        hand [ 0] = hand [ 1];
        hand [ 1] = hand [ 2];
        hand [ 2] = hand [ 3];
        hand [ 3] = hand [ 4];

        /* display storage required for entire structure */
        printf ( "A card requires %d bytes\n", sizeof ( struct card));

        /* display atructure contents */
        printf ( "\n\nHand [ 0]: suit == %c, val == %u\n",
                hand [ 0].suit, hand [ 0].val);
        printf ( "Hand [ 1]: suit == %c, val == %u\n",
                hand [ 1].suit, hand [ 1].val);
        printf ( "Hand [ 2]: suit == %c, val == %u\n",
                hand [ 2].suit, hand [ 2].val);
        printf ( "Hand [ 3]: suit == %c, val == %u\n",
                hand [ 3].suit, hand [ 3].val);
        printf ( "Hand [ 4]: suit == %c, val == %u\n",
                hand [ 4].suit, hand [ 4].val);

        /* display location information */
        printf ( "\n\nHand [ 0]: & == %u, &suit == %u, &val == %u\n",
                &hand [ 0], &hand [ 0].suit, &hand [ 0].val);
        printf ( "Hand [ 1]: & == %u, &suit == %u, &val == %u\n",
                &hand [ 1], &hand [ 1].suit, &hand [ 1].val);
        printf ( "Hand [ 2]: & == %u, &suit == %u, &val == %u\n",
                &hand [ 2], &hand [ 2].suit, &hand [ 2].val);
        printf ( "Hand [ 3]: & == %u, &suit == %u, &val == %u\n",
                &hand [ 3], &hand [ 3].suit, &hand [ 3].val);
        printf ( "Hand [ 4]: & == %u, &suit == %u, &val == %u\n",
                &hand [ 4], &hand [ 4].suit, &hand [ 4].val);
}
```

This program produces the following output:

```
A card requires 4 bytes

Hand [ 0]: suit == d, val == 1
Hand [ 1]: suit == h, val == 2
Hand [ 2]: suit == s, val == 3
Hand [ 3]: suit == s, val == 4
Hand [ 4]: suit == s, val == 4


Hand [ 0]: & == 4364, &suit == 4364, &val == 4366
Hand [ 1]: & == 4368, &suit == 4368, &val == 4370
Hand [ 2]: & == 4372, &suit == 4372, &val == 4374
Hand [ 3]: & == 4376, &suit == 4376, &val == 4378
Hand [ 4]: & == 4380, &suit == 4380, &val == 4382
```

This program displays the values and addresses of five cards. Notice that the locations of a structure's members are consecutive. The C compiler guarantees this. Similarly, the compiler guarantees that successive array elements, which are structures in this case, have consecutive addresses.

Structures as Function Parameters   You can pass structures as parameters to functions. The prototypes and declarators follow the same general rules as for storage class specifiers. That is, to declare a structure as a parameter, you need to put **struct** before the name of the structure. The following program shows how to pass structures as parameters:

```
/* Program to get and display various information about education,
   students, and persons.
   Program illustrates use of nested structures and structures as parameters
   to functions.
*/

#include <stdio.h>
#include <stdlib.h>

#define MAX_STR     80
#define MAX_NAME    25
#define MAX_EDUC    15

struct education {
        char    major [ MAX_EDUC];
        char    degree [ MAX_EDUC];
        double gpa;
};

struct student {
        struct education school;
        char    id [ MAX_EDUC];
        int     yr_grad;
};

struct person {
        char    first;
        char    last [ MAX_NAME];
        int     age;
        double income;
        struct student learning;
};

main ()
{
        struct education ed;
        struct student    stu;
        struct person     pers;
        char    info [ MAX_STR];
        void    show_ed ( struct education);   /* show education structure */
        void    show_stu ( struct student);    /* show student structure */
        void    show_pers ( struct person);    /* show person structure */

        /* Get information for education structure. */
        printf ( "Major? ");
        gets ( ed.major);
        printf ( "Degree? ");
        gets ( ed.degree);
```

```
        printf ( "GPA? ");
        gets ( info);
        ed.gpa = atof ( info);

        /* Display values for structure's members */
        show_ed ( ed);

        /* Get information for student structure. */
        printf ( "Student ID? ");
        gets ( stu.id);
        printf ( "Graduated what year? ");
        gets ( info);
        stu.yr_grad = atoi ( info);
        stu.school = ed;

        /* Display values for structure's members */
        show_stu ( stu);

        /* Get information for person structure. */
        printf ( "First initial? ");
        gets ( info);
        pers.first = info [ 0];
        printf ( "Last name? ");
        gets ( pers.last);
        printf ( "Age? ");
        gets ( info);
        pers.age = atoi ( info);
        printf ( "Income? ");
        gets ( info);
        pers.income = atof ( info);
        pers.learning = stu;

        /* Display values for structure's members */
        show_pers ( pers);
}

/* Display values of education structure.
   Illustrates function declarator for structure parameters.
*/
void show_ed ( struct education edu)
{
        printf ( "%s, %s, %6.2lf\n", edu.major, edu.degree, edu.gpa);
}

/* Display values of student structure, including education structure */
void show_stu ( struct student stdnt)
{
        void show_ed ( struct education);

        printf ( "%s, %5d\n", stdnt.id, stdnt.yr_grad);
        show_ed ( stdnt.school);
}

/* Display values of person structure,
   including values of student structure
*/
void show_pers ( struct person pers)
{
        void show_stu ( struct student);

        printf ( "%c. %s, age %3d, income == $%6.2lf\n",
                pers.first, pers.last, pers.age, pers.income);
        show_stu ( pers.learning);
}
```

This program produces the following session:

```
Major? cs
Degree? bs
GPA? 3.85
cs, bs,   3.85
Student ID? 1234567890
Graduated what year? 1954
1234567890,  1954
cs, bs,   3.85
First initial? q
Last name? werty
Age? 57
Income? 63500
q. werty, age  57, income == $63500.00
1234567890,  1954
cs, bs,   3.85
```

Notice the function prototypes. You must include the keyword, **struct**, in the prototype and in the function declarator.

Because structures are ordinary variables, you are just passing a copy of the structure when you use the structure as an argument in a function call. In other words, unless you take special actions, structures are passed by value.

Functions Returning Structures   In the Draft Proposed ANSI Standard, C functions can also return structures. The following program uses a function that returns a structure after doing its work:

```
/* Program to illustrate functions returning structures. */

#include <stdio.h>
#include <stdlib.h>
#include <math.h>   /* for sqrt() */

#define MAX_STR    80

struct weather {
        double temp, wind;
};

struct chill {
        struct weather weath;
        double windchill;
};

/* Compute the windchill factor for the given temp and wind values */
struct chill get_chill ( struct weather today)
{
        double num1, num2;
        struct chill wch;

        num1 = 10.45 + 6.68 * sqrt ( today.wind) - 0.447 * today.wind;
        num2 = 457 - 5 * today.temp;
        wch.windchill = 91.4 - (num1 * num2 / 110);
```

```
        wch.weath.temp = today.temp;
        wch.weath.wind = today.wind;
        return ( wch);
}


main ()
{
        struct weather todays_weather;
        struct chill todays_chill;
        char    info [ MAX_STR];
        struct chill get_chill ( struct weather);

        printf ( "Temperature? ");
        gets ( info);
        todays_weather.temp = atol ( info);

        printf ( "Wind? ");
        gets ( info);
        todays_weather.wind = atol ( info);
        todays_chill = get_chill ( todays_weather);

        printf ( "Temp == %6.2lf, wind == %6.2lf, windchill == %6.2lf\n",
                todays_chill.weath.temp,
                todays_chill.weath.wind,
                todays_chill.windchill);
}
```

This program computes the windchill factor, or index, when given a temperature (in degrees Fahrenheit) and a wind speed (in miles per hour). The windchill index is the temperature with no wind at which you would feel as cold as you do in the given wind and temperature combination. For example, when the temperature is 0° Fahrenheit and the wind is blowing at 20 mph, the temperature seems as if it's almost −39° F. The program produces the following sessions:

```
Temperature? -10
Wind Speed? 10
Temp == -10.00, wind ==  10.00, windchill == -33.52

Temperature? -10
Wind Speed? 20
Temp == -10.00, wind ==  20.00, windchill == -53.25

Temperature? 0
Wind Speed? 10
Temp ==   0.00, wind ==  10.00, windchill == -21.20

Temperature? 0
Wind Speed? 20
Temp ==   0.00, wind ==  20.00, windchill == -38.90

Temperature? 10
Wind Speed? 10
Temp ==  10.00, wind ==  10.00, windchill ==  -8.80

Temperature? 10
Wind Speed? 20
Temp ==  10.00, wind ==  20.00, windchill == -24.72
```

Pointers to Structures

As you learned earlier, structures are ordinary variables, not pointers. If you pass a structure as an argument, you are passing by value, *not* by reference. The contents of the structure are not changed by the function called, because only a copy of the structure is passed.

To change a structure directly within another function, you need to pass the address of the structure, and declare a parameter that is a pointer to the structure. The following program shows this:

```c
/* Program to illustrate use of structure pointers as parameters. */

#include <stdio.h>
#include <stdlib.h>
#include <math.h>    /* for sqrt() */

#define MAX_STR    80

struct weather {
        double temp, wind;
};

struct chill {
        struct weather weath;
        double windchill;
};


/* Compute the windchill factor for the given temp and wind values */
struct chill get_chill ( struct weather today)
{
        double num1, num2;
        struct chill wch;

        num1 = 10.45 + 6.68 * sqrt ( today.wind) - 0.447 * today.wind;
        num2 = 457 - 5 * today.temp;
        wch.windchill = 91.4 - (num1 * num2 / 110);
        wch.weath.temp = today.temp;
        wch.weath.wind = today.wind;
        return ( wch);
}


main ()
{
        struct weather todays_weather;
        struct chill todays_chill;
        char    info [ MAX_STR];
        struct chill get_chill ( struct weather);
        void    get_temp ( struct weather *);
        void    get_wind ( struct weather *);

        get_temp ( &todays_chill.weath);
        get_wind ( &todays_chill.weath);
        todays_chill = get_chill ( todays_chill.weath);

        printf ( "Temp == %6.21f, wind == %6.21f, windchill == %6.21f\n",
                todays_chill.weath.temp,
                todays_chill.weath.wind,
```

```
                    todays_chill.windchill);
}

/* Get temperature from user.
   Illustrates passing pointers to structures.
*/
void get_temp ( struct weather *w_ptr)
{
        printf ( "Temperature? ");
        gets ( info);
        (*w_ptr).temp = atol ( info);
}

/* Get wind from user.
   Illustrates passing pointers to structures.
*/
void get_wind ( struct weather *w_ptr)
{
        printf ( "Wind Speed? ");
        gets ( info);
        (*w_ptr).wind = atol ( info);
}
```

Notice the use of the address operator when passing the structure. This ensures that the function will work directly in the structure's storage.

The syntax for specifying a pointer to a structure is straightforward. You simply use the indirection indicator to specify that the variable is a pointer rather than a structure. Notice also the declarations in the function prototypes in **main( )** and the parameter declarations in **get_temp( )** and **get_wind( )**.

The parentheses around the pointer names in functions **get_temp( )** and **get_wind( )** are necessary, because the structure member operator (.) has higher precedence than the indirection operator (*). You will rarely see this notation used, however, because C provides another operator that accomplishes the same thing, but is simpler to write: the *arrow operator.*

A Structure Member Operator for Pointers   If your programs require the use of structures, you may very well find yourself working with pointers to structures. It would quickly become tedious to use parentheses around the indirection operator whenever you wanted to access a structure member, so as always, C provides an easier way of doing things — another structure member operator (—>), for accessing structure members indirectly via pointers. This operator is sometimes known as the arrow operator, to distinguish it from the dot operator used for accessing structure members directly. Use the arrow operator when you need to access a member in a function to which a pointer to structure is pointing.

The arrow operator, —>, takes two operands, and returns the value of the structure member accessed or this member as an **lvalue**, depending on the context in which the operator is used. The right operand is a member of the appropriate type of structure. This operand is thus the same as for the dot operator. The left operand is the structure pointer that references the structure whose member you want to access. The following version of **get—temp( )** uses the arrow operator. This version is equivalent to the function used in the preceding program. The only difference is in the operators used in the last lines.

```
/* Get temperature from user.
   Illustrates passing pointers to structures.
*/
void get_temp ( struct weather *w_ptr)
{
        printf ( "Temperature? ");
        gets ( info);
        w_ptr->temp = atol ( info);
}
```

The left operand here is a pointer, namely, the node referencing the structure whose member you want to access. For the dot operator, the left operand is a target structure, rather than a pointer.

Most C programs use the arrow operator when pointers to structures are involved. The precedence of the arrow operator is the same as that of the dot operator, the highest precedence of any operator in C.

Structure Arrays and Structure Pointer Arrays

There is an important difference between an array of structures and an array of pointers to structures. This difference is easy to see if you need to sort a collection of structures based on one of the members. Let's look at two versions of a program that illustrate this difference.

The following program sorts an array of structures based on the **gpa** member of the structure:

```
/* Program to "sort" an array of structures ---
   based on value of gpa members.
   Program exchanges only the gpa members, not the entire structures ---
   because an array of structures has been used.
*/
```

```c
#include <stdio.h>
#include <stdlib.h>

#define MAX_EDUC  15
#define MAX_ELEM  5
#define MAX_STR   80

struct ed {
        char   major [ MAX_EDUC];
        double gpa;
} struct_array1 [ MAX_ELEM];

/* get values for members of an ed structure */
void get_struct ( struct ed *stuff)
{
        char info [ MAX_STR];

        printf ( "Major? ");
        gets ( stuff->major);

        printf ( "GPA? ");
        gets ( info);
        stuff->gpa = atof ( info);
}

main()
{
        void get_struct ( struct ed *);
        void bbl_sort ( struct ed [], int);
        void show_struct ( struct ed);
        int  index;

        /* initialize structure array */
        for ( index = 0; index < MAX_ELEM; index++)
                get_struct ( &struct_array1 [ index]);

        /* display values of structures in array */
        for ( index = 0; index < MAX_ELEM; index++)
        {
                printf ( "%d: ", index);
                show_struct ( struct_array1 [ index]);
        }

        /* sort structures */
        bbl_sort ( struct_array1, MAX_ELEM);


        /* display values of structures in sorted array */
        printf ( "\n\nAfter sorting array of structures\n");
        for ( index = 0; index < MAX_ELEM; index++)
        {
                printf ( "%d: ", index);
                show_struct ( struct_array1 [ index]);
        }
}


/* void bbl_sort ( struct ed stru [], int size)
   Sort an array of structures by letting the "largest" remaining structure
   work its way to the top of the array on each pass.
*/

void bbl_sort ( struct ed stru [], int size)
{
        double temp;            /* for exchanging pointers */
        int  low, hi, top;      /* for looping through array */
```

```
        top = size;       /* highest element that will need to be compared */
        while ( top > 0)
        {
                for ( low = 0, hi = 1; hi < top; low++, hi++)
                {
                        /* if stru [ low].gpa > stru [ hi].gpa, exchange */
                        if ( stru [ low].gpa >  stru [ hi].gpa)
                        {
                                /* NOTE: only the gpa members are being
                                   swapped.
                                */
                                temp = stru [ low].gpa;
                                stru [ low].gpa = stru [ hi].gpa;
                                stru [ hi].gpa = temp;
                        }
                }   /* END for hi < top */
                top--;            /* another string has been placed. */
        }  /* END while top > 0 */
}  /* END bbl_sort () */

/* display contents of an ed structure */
void show_struct ( struct ed stru)
{
        printf ( "%s major, gpa == %6.2lf\n", stru.major, stru.gpa);
}
```

In a sample session, this program produces the following:

```
Major? astron
GPA? 3.5
Major? bio
GPA? 2.7
Major? chem
GPA? 3.7
Major? math
GPA? 3.65
Major? psych
GPA? 3.4
0: astron major, gpa ==    3.50
1: bio major, gpa ==    2.70
2: chem major, gpa ==    3.70
3: math major, gpa ==    3.65
4: psych major, gpa ==    3.40


After sorting array of structures
0: astron major, gpa ==    2.70
1: bio major, gpa ==    3.40
2: chem major, gpa ==    3.50
3: math major, gpa ==    3.65
4: psych major, gpa ==    3.70
```

This program is supposed to sort structures based on the values of the **gpa** member in each of the structures. Unfortunately, the result is not what you want; the sorting function has simply exchanged the **gpa** members in the structures it compared.

To sort properly, it is easier to use an array of pointers to structures. The sorting routine would then exchange pointers and actually change the order in which the structures are referenced. The following program accomplishes this, and illustrates the use of structure pointer arrays:

```
/* Program to sort an array of structures ---
   based on the value of the gpa members.
   Program uses structure pointers, so the structures themselves
   are reordered.
*/

#include <stdio.h>
#include <stdlib.h>

#define MAX_EDUC  15
#define MAX_ELEM  5
#define MAX_STR   80

struct ed {
        char    major [ MAX_EDUC];
        double  gpa;
} struct_array [ MAX_ELEM],     /* array of structures */
  *ptr_array [ MAX_ELEM];       /* array of pointers to structures */

void get_struct ( struct ed *stuff)
{
        char info [ MAX_STR];

        printf ( "Major? ");
        gets ( stuff->major);
        printf ( "GPA? ");
        gets ( info);
        stuff->gpa = atof ( info);

}

main()
{
        void get_struct ( struct ed *);
        void bbl_sort_ptr ( struct ed *[], int);
        void show_struct ( struct ed);
        int  index;

        /* initialize structure array */
        for ( index = 0; index < MAX_ELEM; index++)
                get_struct ( &struct_array [ index]);

        /* make pointers reference the structure array elements */
        for ( index = 0; index < MAX_ELEM; index++)
                ptr_array [ index] = &struct_array [ index];

        /* display the structures referenced by the pointers */
        for ( index = 0; index < MAX_ELEM; index++)
        {
                printf ( "%d: ", index);
                show_struct ( *ptr_array [ index]);
        }

        /* sort the structures referenced by the pointers */
        bbl_sort_ptr ( ptr_array, MAX_ELEM);

        /* display the sorted structures. */
        printf ( "\n\nAfter sorting array of pointer to structures\n");
        for ( index = 0; index < MAX_ELEM; index++)
        {
```

```
                        printf ( "%d: ", index);
                        show_struct ( *ptr_array [ index]);
                }

        }


/* void bbl_sort_ptr ( struct ed *stru [], int size)
   Sort an array of structure pointers by letting the "largest" remaining
   structure work its way to the top of the array on each pass.
*/

void bbl_sort_ptr ( struct ed *stru [], int size)
{
        struct ed *temp;      /* for exchanging pointers */
        int  low, hi, top;    /* for looping through array */

        top = size;       /* highest element that will need to be compared */
        while ( top > 0)
        {
                for ( low = 0, hi = 1; hi < top; low++, hi++)
                {
                        /* if *stru [ low].gpa > *stru [ hi].gpa, exchange */
                        if ( stru [ low]->gpa > stru [ hi]->gpa)
                        {
                                temp = stru [ low];
                                stru [ low] = stru [ hi];
                                stru [ hi] = temp;
                        }
                }   /* END for hi < top */
                top--;                  /* another string has been placed. */
        }  /* END while top > 0 */
}  /* END bbl_sort_ptr () */


/* display contents of an ed structure */
void show_struct ( struct ed stru)
{
        printf ( "%s major, gpa == %6.2lf\n", stru.major, stru.gpa);
}
```

This program produces the following, for a session with the same responses as in the previous example:

```
Major? astron
GPA? 3.5
Major? bio
GPA? 2.7
Major? chem
GPA? 3.7
Major? math
GPA? 3.65
Major? psych
GPA? 3.4
0: astron major, gpa ==    3.50
1: bio major, gpa ==    2.70
2: chem major, gpa ==    3.70
3: math major, gpa ==    3.65
4: psych major, gpa ==    3.40
```

```
After sorting array of pointer to structures
0: bio major, gpa ==    2.70
1: psych major, gpa ==   3.40
2: astron major, gpa ==    3.50
3: math major, gpa ==   3.65
4: chem major, gpa ==    3.70
```

This program sorts the structures properly. The entire structure is moved by making a different pointer reference the structure.

Notice that the arrow operator is only used for the comparison in the test condition, in function **bbl—sort—ptr( )**. After the comparison has been made, addresses, not structure members, are transferred. On the other hand, when showing the array, you need to use the indirection operator to get the actual structure, because the array element is a pointer. *Inside* the **show—struct( )** function, the arrow operator is not needed, because the entire structure, rather than a pointer to the structure, has been passed.

In this program, the information was first read into a static array of structures. Then the locations of these structures were assigned to the structure pointers in **ptr—array[]** in order to allocate storage for the structures. In the next section, you'll learn how to allocate storage dynamically for structures.

When using multiple structures in a program, think carefully about what you want to do with these structures. The answer to this question may determine whether it makes more sense to work with an array of structures or with an array of pointers to structures.

Self-Referential Structures

Often, a program will use multiple elements of the same type, where the number of elements needed is determined at run time. A dynamic storage allocation strategy is advisable here. Structures are essential in such situations. Look at the following template:

```
/* A structure that points to another structure like itself. */
struct lnode {
        double data;
        struct lnode *next;
};
```

This structure has two members. The **data** member contains the actual information to be stored in the node. The **next** member is a pointer to another **lnode**. Such nodes can be used to make arbitrarily long chains of structures, linked together by the **next** members of each **lnode**.

Such chains of structures are called *linked lists*. The first **lnode** in a linked list is often referenced by a pointer to **lnode** — that is, an ordinary pointer, not a structure member. This pointer will reference an **lnode**, whose **next** member may, in turn, reference another **lnode**. The list may contain as many **lnode** elements as your implementation can handle. The **next** member of the last **lnode** in the list should be a null pointer.

The following program includes functions for adding an **lnode** to a linked list. You can add the element to the front or back of the list, or at the position corresponding to the relative position of the new structure's **data** member in the existing list.

```
/* Program to build and display linked lists */

#include <stdio.h>
#include <stdlib.h>
#include <malloc.h>

#define MAX_STR    80
#define FALSE       0
#define TRUE        1
#define TOLERANCE 1e-7

/* Node for a linked list.
   Two members: data, and a pointer to another node like this one.
*/
struct lnode {
        double   data;
        struct  lnode *next;      /* pointer to another lnode */
};

/* allocate space for and initialize a structure; return pointer to it */
struct lnode *get_node ( struct lnode *item)
{
        void *malloc ( size_t);

        /* allocate enough space to store an lnode */
        item = (struct lnode *) malloc ( sizeof ( struct lnode));

        /* if allocated, initialize the structure */
        if (item != NULL)
        {
                item->next = NULL;
                item->data = 0.0;
        }
        else
                printf ( "Nothing allocated\n");
```

```
        return ( item);          /* return the pointer */
}

/* add the structure pointed at by new to the front of the list pointed
   at by list.
*/
struct lnode * front_of_list ( struct lnode *new, struct lnode *list)
{
        new->next = list;
        list = new;
        return (list);
}

/* add lnode to which new points to end of list to which list points. */
struct lnode *back_of_list ( struct lnode *new, struct lnode *list)
{
        if ( list == NULL)
        {
                list = new;
                return ( list);
        }
        else
        {
                /* return results of most recent search. */
                list->next = back_of_list ( new, list->next);
                return ( list);
        }
}

/* add lnode to list at position corresponding to data member's
   relative position
*/
struct lnode *middle_of_list ( struct lnode *new, struct lnode *list)
{
        if ( list == NULL)
        {
                list = new;
                return ( list);
        }
        else if ( list->data >= new->data)
        {
                new->next = list;
                list = new;
                return ( list);
        }
        else
        {
                /* return results of most recent search. */
                list->next = middle_of_list ( new, list->next);
                return ( list);
        }
}


/* display contents of the list */
void show_list ( struct lnode *list)
{
        if ( list != NULL)
        {
                printf ( "%6.2lf\n", list->data);
                if ( list->next != NULL)
                        show_list ( list->next);
        }
}


main ()
{
        struct lnode *front_of_list ( struct lnode *, struct lnode *);
        struct lnode *back_of_list ( struct lnode *, struct lnode *);
        struct lnode *middle_of_list ( struct lnode *, struct lnode *);
```

```
struct lnode *get_node ( struct lnode *);
void    show_list ( struct lnode *);

struct lnode *temp, *root = NULL;
char    info [ MAX_STR];
int     selection;
int     done = FALSE;
int     non_zero ( double);
printf ( "Add to 1) front; 2) middle; or 3) back of list? ");
gets (info);
selection = atoi ( info);

temp = get_node ( temp);
while ( (temp != NULL) && ( !done))
{
        printf ( "Data? ");
        gets ( info);
        temp->data = atof (info);
        if ( non_zero ( temp->data))
        {
                switch ( selection)
                {
                        case 1:
                                root = front_of_list ( temp, root);
                                break;
                        case 2:
                                root = middle_of_list ( temp, root);
                                break;
                        default:
                                root = back_of_list ( temp, root);
                                break;
                }   /* END switch */
        }   /* END if data is nonzero */
        else
                done = TRUE;

        temp = get_node (temp);
}

        if ( root != NULL)
                show_list ( root);
}


/* return true if val differs from zero by more than a predefined amount. */
int non_zero ( double val)
{
        if ( (( val - 0.0) > TOLERANCE) || ((val - 0.0) < -TOLERANCE))
                return ( TRUE);
        else
                return ( FALSE);
}
```

This program produced the following three sessions, when instructed to add to the front, middle, and back of the list, respectively:

```
Add to 1) front; 2) middle; or 3) back of list? 1
Data? 2
Data? 7
Data? 3
Data? 8
Data? 0
    8.00
    3.00
    7.00
    2.00
```

```
Add to 1) front; 2) middle; or 3) back of list? 2
Data? 2
Data? 7
Data? 3
Data? 8
Data? 0
   2.00
   3.00
   7.00
   8.00

Add to 1) front; 2) middle; or 3) back of list? 3
Data? 2
Data? 7
Data? 3
Data? 8
Data? 0
   2.00
   7.00
   3.00
   8.00
```

The program lets you build lists using three different insertion methods. The following illustration shows the sequence of steps for adding to the front of the list. The names in parentheses are the names that correspond to **root** and **temp**, respectively, in the **front—of—list( )** function.

The basic strategy in **front—of—list( )** is to make the **next** member of the **new** structure point to the beginning of the list — that is, to the same place as **list**. Once this is accomplished, the contents of **list** are modified to point to the same **lnode** as **new**. Thus, the list is built as follows: 2, then 7, 2, then 3, 7, 2, then 8, 3, 7, 2. The process is illustrated here:

```
Add nodes to front of list

/* get data for first lnode */

root → NULL

temp → [ 2 | ] → NULL


/* pass root and temp to front_of_list() */
(list) → NULL

(new) → [ 2 | ] → NULL


/* new->next = list;
   make the new node's next member point to the same place as list
*/

(list) → NULL

(new) → [ 2 | ]
```

```
/* list = new;
   new and list both point to the same lnode
*/

(list)→[ 2 | ]→   NULL

(new)
```

```
/* back to main() */

root →[ 2 | ]→   NULL

temp
```

```
/* get next lnode */

root →[ 2 | ]→   NULL

temp →[ 7 | ]→   NULL
```

```
/* pass root and temp to front_of_list() */

(list)→[ 2 | ]→   NULL

(new) →[ 7 | ]→   NULL
```

```
/* new->next = list;
   make new node's next member point to the same lnode as list
*/

(list)→[ 2 | ]→   NULL

(new)→[ 7 | ]
```

```
/* list = new;
   make list point to same lnode as new
*/

(list)→[ 7 | ]→ [ 2 | ]→   NULL

(new)
```

```
/* back to main */

root →[ 7 | ]→ [ 2 | ]→   NULL

temp
```

```
/* get next structure */

root →[ 7 | ]→ [ 2 | ]→   NULL

temp →[ 3 | ]→   NULL
```

```
/* etc. */
(list)→[7|+]→[2|+]  NULL
(new)→[3|+]  NULL


/* new->next = list
(list)→[7|+]→[2|+]  NULL
(new)→[3|]


/* list = new */
(list)→[3|+]→[7|+]→[2|+]  NULL
(new)


root→[3|+]→[7|+]→[2|+]  NULL
temp


root→[3|+]→[7|+]→[2|+]  NULL
temp→[8|+]  NULL


(list)→[3|+]→[7|+]→[2|+]  NULL
(new)→[8|]


/* new->next = list */
(list)→[3|+]→[7|+]→[2|+]  NULL
(new)→[8|]


/* list = new */
(list)→[8|+]→[3|+]→[7|+]→[2|+]  NULL
(new)


root→[8|+]→[3|+]→[7|+]→[2|+]  NULL
temp
```

The next illustration provides a similar map of the assignments when adding new structures in their "size places" in the list. The basic strategy in **middle_of_list( )** is as follows:

```
Add in middle of list
/* get first structure */
root --> NULL
temp -->[ 2 | ]-> NULL


/* pass root and temp to middle_of_list() */
(list)-->NULL
(new) -[ 2 | ]-> NULL


/* list = new;
   make list point to same node as new, since list is empty
*/
(list)-[ 2 | ]-> NULL
(new)


/* back to main */
root -->[ 2 | ]-> NULL
temp


/* get new structure and information */
root -->[ 2 | ]-> NULL
temp -->[ 7 | ]-> NULL


/* pass root and temp to middle_of_list() */
(list)-[ 2 | ]-> NULL
(new) -->[ 7 | ]-> NULL


/* list->next = middle_of_list ( new, list->next);
   since 7 > 2, can't add new structure yet;
   call middle_of_list() with the list starting at list->next ---
   that is, with the (empty) list right after the lnode containing 2.
*/
```

```
(list)→ NULL
(new)→[7|→]  NULL
```

```
/* list = new;
   make list point to same node as new, since list is empty
*/
```

```
(list)→[7|→]  NULL
(new)↗
```

```
/* returning to the calling function, and to the longer list */
```

```
(list)→[2|→] [7|→]  NULL
(new)↗
```

```
/* back to main */
```

```
root →[2|→] [7|→]  NULL
temp ↗
```

```
/* get new structure and information */
```

```
root →[2|→] [7|→]  NULL
temp →[3|→]  NULL
```

```
/* pass root and temp to middle_of_list () */
```

```
(list)→[2|→] [7|→]  NULL
(new)→[3|→]  NULL
```

```
/* list->next = middle_of_list ( new, list->next);
   since 3 > 2, can't add new structure yet;
   call middle_of_list() with the list starting at list->next ---
   that is, with the (one element) list right after the lnode containing 2.
*/
```

```
(list)→[7|→]  NULL
(new)→[3|→]  NULL
```

```
/* new->next = list;
   make new structure's next member point to same lnode as list.
*/
```

```
(list)→[7|→]  NULL
(new)→[3|]
```

```
/* list = new;
   insert the new structure before the start of the shortened list,
   since 3 < 7
*/
```

(list)→[3|→]→[7|→]→   NULL
(new)↗

```
/* returning to the calling function, and to the longer list */
```

(list)→[2|→]→[3|→]→[7|→]→   NULL
(new)↗

```
/* back to main */
```

root →[2|→]→[3|→]→[7|→]→   NULL
temp ↗

```
/* get new structure and information */
```

root →[2|→]→[3|→]→[7|→]→   NULL
temp →[8|→]→   NULL

```
/* pass root and temp to middle_of_list() */
```

(list)→[2|→]→[3|→]→[7|→]→   NULL
(new) →[8|→]→   NULL

```
/* list->next = middle_of_list ( new, list->next);
   since 8 > 2, can't add new structure yet;
   call middle_of_list() with the list starting at list->next ---
   that is, with the (two element) list right after the lnode containing 2.
*/
```

(list)→[3|→]→[7|→]→   NULL
(new) →[8|→]→   NULL

```
/* list->next = middle_of_list ( new, list->next);
   since 8 > 3, can't add new structure yet;
   call middle_of_list() with the list starting at list->next ---
   that is, with the (one element) list right after the lnode containing 3
*/
```

(list)→[7|→]→   NULL
(new) →[8|→]→   NULL

```
/* list->next = middle_of_list ( new, list->next);
   since 8 > 7, can't add new structure yet;
```

```
        call middle_of_list() with the list starting at list->next ---
        that is, with the (empty) list right after the lnode containing 7.
*/

(list)──NULL

(new)──▶ 8  ─▶ NULL


/* list = new;
     make list point to same node as new, since list is empty
*/

(list)──8  ─▶   NULL

(new)


/* return ( list);
returning to the calling function, and to the longer list
*/

(list)──7  ─▶ 8  ─▶   NULL

(new)


/* return ( list);
returning to the calling function, and to the longer list
*/

(list) ──▶ 3  ─▶ 7  ─▶ 8  ─▶   NULL

(new) ─────────────────


/* return ( list);
     returning to the calling function, and to the longer list
*/

(list)──2  ─▶ 3  ─▶ 7  ─▶ 8  ─▶ NULL

(new) ─────────────────


/* back to main() */

root ──▶ 2  ─▶ 3  ─▶ 7  ─▶ 8  ─▶ NULL

temp ────────────────────
```

If the end of the **list** has been reached, make **list** point to the same **lnode** as **new**, and return this value. Otherwise, the function will need to do some more processing. If the function is not at the end of the list, then **list—>data** exists (since **list** is pointing to an **lnode**). If the **data** member of **list** is greater than the **data** member of **new**, the new structure should be inserted just before the **lnode** to which **list** is pointing. Once accomplished, the value of **list** is changed to point to the **lnode** referenced by **new**. The new address stored in **list** is returned to the calling function.

If **list** is pointing to something, but the **data** member of this **lnode** is *less than* the **new—>data**, then the function must keep searching for the proper place to insert the **lnode** to which **new** points. The function accomplishes this by calling itself with a shortened version of the list — namely, one starting with the **lnode** referenced by **list—>next**. The idea is that, if **list—>data** is still too small, the **data** member of the next **lnode** in the list may be larger.

When the recursive call returns with the modified list referenced by **list—>next**, the new structure has been inserted at the appropriate point. The current version of the function can then return its value, **list,** to the calling function. Once that's done, the various versions of the function will return the appropriate values to *their* calling functions.

There are several important points to notice about the program under discussion. First, each **lnode** is allocated as it's needed. The **get—node( )** function is responsible for getting this storage, initializing the structure, if possible, and returning a pointer to the storage allocated. By calling the function **get—node( )** only when you need another **lnode**, you can minimize the storage required to run your program.

A second point concerns the returns from the list-building functions. Notice that the same variable is used twice in expressions involving a list-building function — once as the **lvalue** to which a returned pointer is assigned, and once as argument to the function. Let's see why this is necessary. The following program shows why this returned value is needed in this particular situation.

```
/* Program to add to the front of a linked list, and to display
   information about the locations where things are occurring.
   Program helps illustrate importance of return values for certain
   functions.
*/

#include <stdio.h>
#include <stdlib.h>
#include <malloc.h>

#define MAX_STR    80
#define FALSE       0
#define TRUE        1
#define TOLERANCE 1e-7

/* Node for a linked list.
   Two members: data, and a pointer to another node like this one.
*/
struct lnode {
        double  data;
        struct  lnode *next;     /* pointer to another lnode */
};

/* allocate space for and initialize a structure; return pointer to it */
struct lnode *get_node ( struct lnode *item)
{
```

```
        void *malloc ( size_t);

        /* allocate enough space to store an lnode */
        item = (struct lnode *) malloc ( sizeof ( struct lnode));

        /* if allocated, initialize the structure */
        if (item != NULL)
        {
                item->next = NULL;
                item->data = 0.0;
        }
        else
                printf ( "Nothing allocated\n");
        return ( item);               /* return the pointer */
}
/* add the structure pointed at by new to the front of the list pointed
   at by list.
*/
struct lnode * front_of_list ( struct lnode *new, struct lnode *list)
{
        printf ( "FRONT: &list == %u; list == %u; ", &list, list);
        printf ( "&new == %u; new == %u\n", &new, new);
        new->next = list;
        list = new;
        printf ( "front: &list == %u; list == %u; ", &list, list);
        printf ( "&new == %u; new == %u\n", &new, new);
        return (list);
}


/* display contents of the list */
void show_list ( struct lnode *list)
{
        if ( list != NULL)
        {
                printf ( "%6.2lf\n", list->data);
                if ( list->next != NULL)
                        show_list ( list->next);
        }
}


main ()
{
        struct lnode *front_of_list ( struct lnode *, struct lnode *);

        struct lnode *get_node ( struct lnode *);
        void    show_list ( struct lnode *);

        struct lnode *temp, *root = NULL;
        char    info [ MAX_STR];
        int     selection;
        int     done = FALSE;
        int     non_zero ( double);

        temp = get_node ( temp);
        while ( (temp != NULL) && ( !done))
        {
                printf ( "\n\nData? ");
                gets ( info);
                temp->data = atof (info);
                if ( non_zero ( temp->data))
                {
                        printf ( "MAIN: &root == %u; root == %u; ",
                                &root, root);
                        printf ( "&temp == %u; temp == %u\n", &temp, temp);
```

```
                        root = front_of_list ( temp, root);
                        printf ( "main: &root == %u; root == %u; ",
                                    &root, root);
                        printf ( "&temp == %u; temp == %u\n", &temp, temp);
                }
                else
                        done = TRUE;

                temp = get_node (temp);
        }

        if ( root != NULL)
                show_list ( root);
}


/* return true if val differs from zero by more than a predefined amount. */
int non_zero ( double val)
{
        if ( (( val - 0.0) > TOLERANCE) || ((val - 0.0) < -TOLERANCE))
                return ( TRUE);
        else
                return ( FALSE);
}
```

When run with the same data as in our previous example, this program produces the following.

```
Data? 2
MAIN: &root == 4972; root == 0; &temp == 4974; temp == 5182
FRONT: &list == 4882; list == 0; &new == 4880; new == 5182
front: &list == 4882; list == 5182; &new == 4880; new == 5182
main: &root == 4972; root == 5182; &temp == 4974; temp == 5182


Data? 7
MAIN: &root == 4972; root == 5182; &temp == 4974; temp == 5194
FRONT: &list == 4882; list == 5182; &new == 4880; new == 5194
front: &list == 4882; list == 5194; &new == 4880; new == 5194
main: &root == 4972; root == 5194; &temp == 4974; temp == 5194


Data? 3
MAIN: &root == 4972; root == 5194; &temp == 4974; temp == 5206
FRONT: &list == 4882; list == 5194; &new == 4880; new == 5206
front: &list == 4882; list == 5206; &new == 4880; new == 5206
main: &root == 4972; root == 5206; &temp == 4974; temp == 5206


Data? 8
MAIN: &root == 4972; root == 5206; &temp == 4974; temp == 5218
FRONT: &list == 4882; list == 5206; &new == 4880; new == 5218
front: &list == 4882; list == 5218; &new == 4880; new == 5218
main: &root == 4972; root == 5218; &temp == 4974; temp == 5218


Data? 0
  8.00
  3.00
  7.00
  2.00
```

Let's see how this program does its work. The goal of each call to

front—of—list( ) is to add a new **lnode** to the front of the list. This means that **root** will point at a new **lnode** after each call to **front—of—list( )**. More specifically, this means that the contents of storage location 4972 (the location at which **root**'s value is stored) should be different after each call to **front—of—list( )**.

Let's look at the output within **front—of—list( )** to see whether this can happen. First, notice the address and contents of **list**, the parameter corresponding to **root** in the function. This variable has the same contents as **root**, but this address is stored at a different location, because all that has been passed to the function is a *copy* of the address stored in **root** — that is, stored at location 4972. The address of **root** itself (4972) has not been passed.

Because the value passed is an address, you can make changes in the variable located at that address. For example, after making **list** point to the same place as **new**, you could make changes in ∗**list**, the variable at which **list** is pointing. Because ∗**list** is an alias for ∗**root**, these changes would remain after you left the function.

However, you *cannot* change the contents of **root** itself, even though you can change the address stored in **list**. This is because **root** and **list** are not aliases. By returning the desired address from the function, and assigning this address directly to **root** in the calling function, you make **root** point to a new **lnode** after the function call. (You could also have accomplished this by passing a pointer to a pointer to structure, **struct lnode** ∗∗, but that's another topic altogether.)

Bit-Fields

Sometimes it's convenient to have different bits in an **int** represent different settings or options. You saw examples of this in Chapter 15, when you assigned regions to territories in some programs, and learned to define manifest constants to represent mutually exclusive regions. These constants were all powers of two, so that exactly one bit was one in any constant.

C also lets you declare and manipulate a variable number of bits as a member in a structure. Such a member is called a *bit-field*. A bit-field is a collection of adjacent bits, usually in an **int**. Bit-fields give you easy access to storage areas smaller than a byte, and let you refer to these areas by name.

Bit-fields are particularly useful in programs that need to keep track of settings or options that are in effect — such as driver programs (for controlling things like printers or screens) and operating systems.

Suppose you have a program that needs to keep track of the settings on a printer. In particular, let's assume the program needs to maintain information about the following:

1. Current font (16 possibilities)

2. Boldface (on / off)

3. Italic (on / off)

4. Font size (3 values)

5. Single spacing (on / off)

6. Emulation mode (10 possibilities)

7. Print quality (4 modes)

8. Paper dimensions (6 possibilities)

You could define each of these as a separate variable. In that case, each would take up at least one byte, and more likely two bytes because it would be more convenient to represent most of them as integers rather than characters. That means you might use as many as 16 bytes to store this information.

Bit-fields let you represent all of these variables in two bytes. The following program shows you how.

```
/* Program to illustrate declaration and use of bit fields */

#include <stdio.h>
#include <stdlib.h>

/* This structure consists of two bytes.
   The number following each unsigned declaration represents the number of
   bits to be allocated for that structure member.
*/
struct printer {
        unsigned font : 4;
        unsigned bold : 1;
        unsigned italic : 1;
        unsigned size : 2;
        unsigned single_space : 1;
        unsigned emulation : 4;
        unsigned quality : 2;
        unsigned paper : 3;
};
```

```
main ()
{
        struct printer laser;

        /* assign values to individual members. */
        laser.font = 8;
        laser.bold = 0;
        laser.italic = 1;
        laser.size = 2;
        laser.single_space = 0;
        laser.emulation = 0;
        laser.quality = 0;
        laser.paper = 0;

        /* Display values of the bit-fields */
        printf ( "font == %u; bold == %u; italic == %u; size == %u\n",
                laser.font, laser.bold, laser.italic, laser.size);
        printf ("spacing == %u; emulation == %u; ",
                laser.single_space, laser.emulation);
        printf ( "quality == %u; paper == %u\n",
                laser.quality, laser.paper);

        /* assign an out of range value to a member */
        laser.font = 17;

        /* Display the result. Did it affect the next member? */
        printf ( "\n\nAfter giving font too high a value (17)\n");
        printf ( "font == %u; bold == %u; italic == %u; size == %u\n",
                laser.font, laser.bold, laser.italic, laser.size);
        printf ( "spacing == %u; emulation == %u; ",
                laser.single_space, laser.emulation);
        printf ( "quality == %u; paper == %u\n",
                laser.quality, laser.paper);
}
```

This program produces the following output:

```
font == 8; bold == 0; italic == 1; size == 2
spacing == 0; emulation == 0; quality == 0; paper == 0


After giving font too high a value (17)
font == 1; bold == 0; italic == 1; size == 2
spacing == 0; emulation == 0; quality == 0; paper == 0
```

The preceding program declares a structure whose members are all bit-fields. Each member declaration includes the base type of the member (**unsigned**, in this case), an identifier for the member, and the number of bits to be allocated for the member.

▶ **REMEMBER**   Bit-fields can only be declared within a structure. When declaring a bit-field in a structure, you must provide a base type for the member, an identifier, and the number of bits to be allocated for the field.

When you declare bit-fields, the compiler stores the members in adjacent bits, subject to some constraints. That is, the compiler does not start each member on a new byte or word boundary. For example, in the preceding program, four bits were allocated for **fonts**. The next bit was allocated for **bold**, and the next bit for **italic**. Then two bits were allocated for **size**. At this point, only one byte of storage had been used.

The next byte was allocated for **single_space**, and the four after that for **emulation**. Notice that four bits were allocated for this member, since ten values cannot be stored in three bits. This means that several possible values in this bit-field will be unused. The two bits following were allocated for **quality**. So far, 15 bits of storage have been allocated.

The next field requires three bits. If the compiler continues allocating storage consecutively, this variable would straddle two words of memory. Not all compilers will do this. QuickC and Microsoft C 5.0, for example, will store **paper** completely in the next word. Check your compiler to see how bit-fields are handled when they cross word boundaries.

You can also use padding to control how the compiler handles fields that cross word boundaries. You can pad the storage allocation in a structure by declaring a nameless bit-field. If you specify just a type and the number of bits, the compiler will skip the specified number of bits. The special width, 0, tells the compiler to pad to the next boundary appropriate to the variable type. For example, the following version of the **printer** declaration would assure that **paper** did not straddle a word boundary, regardless of how the compiler would handle this situation by default:

```
/* This structure consists of two bytes.
   The number following each unsigned declaration represents the number of
   bits to be allocated for that structure member.
   The nameless member --- before paper --- pads the structure to a
   word boundary, before allocating storage for paper.
*/
struct printer {
        unsigned font : 4;
        unsigned bold : 1;
        unsigned italic : 1;
        unsigned size : 2;
        unsigned single_space : 1;
        unsigned emulation : 4;
        unsigned quality : 2;
        unsigned : 0;                   /* pads to end of word */
        unsigned paper : 3;
};
```

The Draft Proposed ANSI Standard says that bit-fields can be declared as having **int**, **unsigned int**, or **signed int** types. If you declare a bit-field as being signed, the action taken if you assign an out-of-range value is implementation dependent. In QuickC and Microsoft C 5.0, the value is treated as if it were unsigned, for purposes of computing the overflow. In the preceding program, the effect of assigning too large a value to **font** was confined to that bit-field. The overflow did not affect the **bold** member.

In addition to the base types allowed in the Draft Proposed ANSI Standard, QuickC and Microsoft C 5.0 also allow you to declare bit-fields of type **char** and **long**—either signed or unsigned. If you declare a bit-field as a **long**, and then pad the structure, the padding will extend to the next **long** address boundary. Thus, in QuickC the following structure would take 14 bytes, 12 for the three **long** variables, and 2 for the **int**.

```
struct size_test {
        long one : 6;
        long : 0;   /* pad to first long boundary --- 4 bytes */
        long two : 5;
        long : 0;   /* pad to second long boundary */
        long three : 3;
        int  not_a_field;
};
```

The two nameless members each pad the structure to the next **long** address boundary. The first one pads 26 bits (32 bits allocated for **long**, less the 6 bits for **one**). The second one pads 27 bits. The compiler pads to the end of the third **long**, ensuring that structure members that are not bit-fields will be aligned at the proper address boundaries. You can have both bit-field and other members in the same structure.

Restrictions on Bit-Fields

While bit-fields can be convenient for certain types of tasks, there are several restrictions and implementation dependencies associated with them. Because of these restrictions, you should be very careful about making assumptions concerning the particular locations at which you will find specific fields.

Some implementations allocate storage to bit-fields from left to right (high-order to low-order bit), while others allocate them in the reverse direction. This can be a crucial difference if you're reading data generated by a program.

Bit-field locations are not accessible, so you can't apply the address operator, **&**, to a bit-field. This means that you can't have arrays of bit-fields (since arrays are actually pointers) or pointers to bit-fields. Nor can functions return bit-fields.

Unions

Unions are aggregate types that have members, like structures. Unlike structures, however, unions may hold different types of information at different times. That is, the same variable may be used to store different members at different times. For example, the union variable, **number**, defined below may contain an **int** at some times, a **double** at other times, and a complex number on other occasions. At any one time, however, only one of these types is stored in the union variable.

```
struct complex {
        double  re, im;
};

union value {
        int     int_val;
        double dbl_val;
        struct complex comp_val;
} number;
```

This data structure can store the value for either an **int**, *or* a **double**, *or* a **struct complex** variable at any one time. The union cannot have more than one member present at any given time. Rather, the union has a certain amount of space allocated, and this space can contain information that may be interpreted in any of three ways, depending on context.

The following program makes clear that the members of a union occupy the same storage:

```
/* Program to display amount and location of storage allocated to
   a union.
*/

#include <stdio.h>
#include <stdlib.h>

/* create a template for a complex number */
struct complex {
        double  re, im;
};

/* create a template whose storage can be interpreted in any of three
   ways at a given time --- depending on context.
*/
union value {
        int     int_val;
        double dbl_val;
```

```
        struct complex comp_val;
};

main ()
{
        union value number;

        printf ( "Size of entire union == %d\n", sizeof ( union value));

        printf ( "Size of int member == %d\n", sizeof ( number.int_val));
        printf ( "Size of double member == %d\n", sizeof ( number.dbl_val));
        printf ( "Size of complex union member == %d\n",
                sizeof ( number.comp_val));
        printf ( "Size of complex re == %d\n",
                sizeof ( number.comp_val.re));
        printf ( "Size of complex im == %d\n",
                sizeof ( number.comp_val.im));

        printf ( "\n\n&number == %u\n", &number);
        printf ( "&number.int_val == %u\n", &number.int_val);
        printf ( "&number.dbl_val == %u\n", &number.dbl_val);
        printf ( "&number.comp_val == %u\n", &number.comp_val);
        printf ( "&number.comp_val.re == %u\n", &number.comp_val.re);
        printf ( "&number.comp_val.im == %u\n", &number.comp_val.im);
}
```

This program produces the following output:

```
Size of entire union == 16
Size of int member == 2
Size of double member == 8
Size of complex union member == 16
Size of complex re == 8
Size of complex im == 8


&number == 4256
&number.int_val == 4256
&number.dbl_val == 4256
&number.comp_val == 4256
&number.comp_val.re == 4256
&number.comp_val.im == 4264
```

Let's look closely at this program to see how to create unions, and how to store them. The declaration for a union has the same format as for a structure. It begins with a keyword, **union** here, followed by a tag name for the union. The tag name is followed by type declarations of the same sort as in structure declarations. These declarations are surrounded by left and right curly braces.

Union members can be of any type, except the union being declared and bit-fields. You can have pointers to a union of the type being declared.

In this case, we have three different types declared, with one of these being a structure. In a structure, these three different types would coexist. In a union, however, only one can be represented at a time. The compiler allocates enough storage for the largest union member declared. In our example, this means 16 bytes, since the **complex** is the largest union member. The program displays this value as the size of the structure. If you're storing an **int**, the compiler would use only two of the bytes.

The storage allocated for the union will be interpreted differently, depending on the union member being accessed. Storage for all members will start at the same location, as the program shows. This means that the union members overwrite each other. You are responsible for making sure your program asks for the kind of information that was last stored there. If you overlook this, you'll get erroneous results.

Unions of Structures

A very common use of unions is to store either of several structures, depending on the context. For example, the following declarations would let you record information about either a book or a journal article:

```
#include <stdio.h>

#define MAX_SMALL 40

struct book {
        char author [ MAX_SMALL];
        char title [ MAX_SMALL];
};

struct article {
        char author [ MAX_SMALL];
        char title [ MAX_SMALL];
        char journal [ MAX_SMALL];
};

union entry {
        struct book bk;
        struct article art;
};
```

With these declarations, you could build entries for a data base, where some entries would be for books and some for articles. In the next chapter, you'll learn how to use some unions declared in QuickC and Microsoft C 5.0 to access DOS functions, such as getting the system time.

Enumeration Types

C lets you provide names for values that certain variables can take on. For example, suppose you wanted to create a template for a deck of cards. It would be convenient to have meaningful names for the individual cards. C's enumeration type gives you this capability. The enumeration type will officially become part of the C language when the Draft Proposed ANSI Standard is adopted. This type is already available in many implementations, so you'll probably run across programs that use it.

The following declaration shows how to define a deck of cards:

```
#define MAX_CARDS  52

enum suits { clubs, diamonds, hearts, spades};

enum face { ace, two, three, four, five, six, seven, eight, nine,
            ten, jack, queen, king};

struct card {
        enum suits suit;
        enum face  value;
} deck [ MAX_CARDS];
```

When you create an **enum** type, you are specifying names for the range of values a variable of that type can have. Thus, in the example, variables of **enum** type **suits** can take on the named values **clubs**, **diamonds**, **hearts**, or **spades**. Similarly, variables of **enum** type **faces** can take on any named values in the list between **ace** and **king**, inclusive. Enumerations are really nothing more than names for integer constants that represent specified values. They are useful for specifying actions in a more memorable way, however.

When you declare an enumeration type, you specify a set of names to use when referring to particular values such variables could take on. Internally, the compiler numbers elements in order, starting from 0. Thus, the values **clubs** through **spades** would correspond to the numerical values 0 through 3; the values **ace** through **king** would correspond to 0 through 12. You worry about the names, the compiler will take care of the values.

You can use these enumeration values in expressions wherever an **int** value is allowed. When the compiler sees such a value in your program, it substitutes the value it has associated with the name into the expression.

Although, by default, the compiler starts numbering **enum** values from 0, you can override the default by simply associating a new number with an identifier. The following program illustrates this:

```
/* Program to display a playing card.
   Program also illustrates use of enum type, and how to override the
   default values assigned to the enum type values
*/

#define MAX_CARDS  52
#define MAX_SUIT    4
#define MAX_FACE   13

enum suits { clubs, diamonds, hearts, spades};

enum faces { ace = 1, two, three, four, five, six, seven, eight, nine,
             ten, jack, queen, king};
struct card {
        enum suits suit;
        enum faces value;
} deck [ MAX_CARDS];

main ()
{
        int  rand ( void);
        enum suits  suit_val, face_val;

        /* get and display face value. rand() returns 0 -- 12, so add 1 */
        face_val = rand () % MAX_FACE + 1;
        switch ( face_val)
        {
                case ace:
                        printf ( "A ");
                        break;
                case jack:
                        printf ( "J ");
                        break;
                case queen:
                        printf ( "Q ");
                        break;
                case king:
                        printf ( "K ");
                        break;
                default:
                        printf ( "%d ", face_val);
        }

        /* get and display suit value */
        suit_val = rand () % MAX_SUIT;
        switch ( suit_val)
        {
                case clubs:
                        printf ( "clubs");
                        break;
                case diamonds:
                        printf ( "diamonds");
                        break;
                case hearts:
                        printf ( "hearts");
                        break;
                case spades:
                        printf ( "spades");
                        break;
        }
}
```

In this program, the values associated with **faces** variables range from 1 through 13, rather than from 0 through 12. This is because the first value was set to 1, overriding the compiler's default of 0.

You can specify any integer value, positive or negative, for an **enum** value name. The compiler will associate subsequent names in the list with successive values, starting with the value you specified. The following declaration shows an example of this.

```
enum example { a, b, c, d, e = -2, f, g, h, i = -4, j, k, l, m,
               n = 14, o, p, q, r, s, t = 0, u, v, w, x, y, = 0};
```

In this declaration, the following values can be found:

Value	Names
-4	i
-3	j
-2	e, k
-1	f, l
0	a, g, m, t, z
1	b, h, u
2	c, v
3	d, w
4	x
5	y
14	n
15	o
16	p
17	q
18	r
19	s

The first few names, **a** through **d**, use the compiler's default values. Since **e** is specified to be -2, the counting for subsequent names continues from this value. This means **f** is -1, **g** is 0, and so on. The name **i** is specified as representing -4, which starts the counting from this value.

Notice that several names can be associated with the same value. Notice also that you can start renumbering from any point, and that numbering will continue from that value until you specify a new renumbering or until the end of the list.

Summary

Congratulations, you've done it! You've mastered all the fundamental topics in the C language. This chapter has covered the last major topics — the structure and union aggregate types and the "new" enumerated type.

Many of the concepts covered in this chapter (such as self-referential structures and linked lists) are fundamental to writing certain types of programs. You may want to explore other data structures (such as trees), which you can build using self-referential structures.

You should now be ready to write programs to do just about anything you want. In the next chapter you'll learn more about some of the functions available to you in the QuickC Run-Time library. You'll also find some additional functions for specialized tasks, such as checking the time or date on the system.

17

QuickC Library Functions

This chapter provides more tools and information for your C programming. In it, you'll find brief discussions of some of the more commonly used Run-Time library functions. You'll also find useful functions for doing things such as getting the time and date, determining elapsed time, and using DOS commands in your programs. Although it presents a great deal of information, this chapter should be enjoyable and helpful — especially if you take time to play with the programs.

The discussions tell you whether a given function is built into QuickC. If it is, you can use the function anywhere in your program without declaring the function or including any header files. If a function is not built into QuickC, you may simply need to include the header file in which the function is declared. Or, the function may be included in the Quick library, **qcstuff.qlb**, used for some of the programs in this book. If it is, you need to use the **/l** option with **qcstuff** as argument when calling QuickC, as shown in the following command line:

```
qc /lqcstuff myprog
```

The discussion of the library functions is organized around some of the major header files provided with QuickC and Microsoft C 5.0. The contents of many of these files are specified in the Draft Proposed ANSI Standard. Some files are "extras," provided to make certain types of functions (such as those that work directly with the operating system) easier to write. The Microsoft Run-Time library contains over 200 functions, and QuickC includes over 30 header files that you can use. We'll only be able to cover a small portion of these. Check your Run-Time library documentation for more information about the functions presented here, and for additional functions not discussed here.

stdio.h

This header file contains definitions for manifest constants, macros, and new types—for stream input/output activity. Many of the functions we've been using rely on this header file for definitions and other information. The **stdio.h** file includes definitions of NULL as 0 or 0L, to represent a null pointer, and of EOF, the value to be returned when the end of a file has been reached or an error has occurred.

You've already seen many of the functions declared in this header file. The I/O functions supported include: **fclose( )**, **fgetc( )**, **fgetchar( )**, **fgets( )**, **fopen**, **fprintf( )**, **fputc( )**, **fputchar( )**, **fputs( )**, **fscanf( )**, **gets( )**, **printf( )**, **puts( )**, and **scanf( )**. All of these are built into QuickC except **fgetchar( )** and **fputchar( )**, which are in the **qcstuff.qlb** Quick library. In addition, you've seen the following macros: **feof**, **ferror**, **getc( )**, **getchar( )**, **putc( )**, and **putchar( )**.

The Familiar Functions

Because the following functions are discussed elsewhere in this book, they are described only briefly here.

int fclose (FILE *f—ptr)   This function closes the specified file. Before closing, the buffers associated with the file are flushed and written to the file. If the file is successfully closed, **fclose( )** returns 0. The function returns EOF if there is an error.

feof (FILE *f—ptr)   This macro determines whether the end of the file has been reached. The macro returns a 0 if the end-of-file has not been reached, and a nonzero value if the end-of-file has been reached.

ferror (FILE *f—ptr)   This macro determines whether an error has occurred in relation to the specified file. Such errors can occur if you try to read from a file that has been opened for writing. The macro returns a 0 if *no error* has occurred, and a nonzero value if an error has occurred. The error indicator remains set until you use **clearerr( )** (discussed later) to reset the indicator, close the file, or move back to the beginning of the file.

int fgetc (FILE *f—ptr)
int fgetchar (void)   These two functions read one character at a time, and return each character as an **int**. The functions return EOF if an error occurred. The **fgetchar( )** function reads from **stdin**, and **fgetc( )** reads from a specified file.

char *fgets (char *str, int size, FILE *f—ptr)   This function reads a string from the specified file, and returns this string. The string's maximum length is specified by **size**. Newlines are included in the string read, and the function terminates the string with a null character. The function returns the string read if successful, or a null pointer if unsuccessful.

FILE *fopen (char *name, char *mode)   This function opens a file and returns a pointer to the stream associated with this file. The function also associates a disk file, called **name**, with the stream. The **mode** parameter specifies how the file is to be used. The function returns a file pointer if successful, or a null pointer if unsuccessful.

int fprintf (FILE *f—ptr, const char *str, . . .)   This function works just like **printf( )** except that **fprintf( )** writes to the file specified by **f—ptr**. The function has the same string argument as **printf( )**, and can contain optional arguments of types specified in the string argument. In addition, **fprintf( )** takes a file pointer as its first argument and returns the number of characters printed.

int fputc (char ch, FILE ∗f__ptr)
int fputchar (char ch)   These two functions write one character at a time, and return the character written as an **int**. They return EOF if an error occurs. Note that **fputchar( )** writes to **stdout**, and **fputc( )** writes to the file specified by **f__ptr**.

int fputs (char ∗str, FILE ∗f__ptr)   This function writes the character string, **str**, to the specified file. The function copies the entire string *except* for the terminating null character. The function returns the last character written as an **int**, as is common in C. The returned character will be a newline character, if the string was read using **fgets( )**. Unlike **puts( )**, **fputs( )** does *not* add a newline character before writing the string. The **fputs( )** function returns 0 if **str** is empty, and EOF if there is an error.

int fscanf (FILE ∗f__ptr, const char ∗str, . . .)   This function reads from the specified file the types of information indicated in the string argument. This function works like **scanf( )**, except that the source for **fscanf( )** is a specified file, rather than **stdin**. The function contains additional arguments specifying *addresses* for storing the input read. The function returns the number of items that were read and assigned, or EOF if the end-of-file has been reached. A return value of 0 indicates that an error has occurred, since no items are assigned.

int getc (FILE ∗f__ptr)
int getchar (void)   These are the macro versions of **fgetc( )** and **fgetchar( )**, respectively.

char ∗gets (char ∗str)   This function reads a string from **stdin** and returns this string in a modified form. The newline character read is replaced by a null character, which terminates the string returned. If the function is unsuccessful at reading a string, it returns a null pointer.

int printf (char ∗str, . . .)   This function displays the specified information on **stdout**. It contains at least a string argument, which may contain place-holders indicating other arguments to be written. If **str** contains such place-holders, the function will contain additional arguments consisting of the variables or values corresponding to the placeholders. This function returns the number of characters written.

int putc (FILE *f—ptr)
int putchar (void)   These are the macro versions of **fputc( )** and **fputchar( )**, respectively.

int puts (const char *str)   This function writes a string to **stdout**, replacing the null character that terminates **str** with a newline character. The function returns the last character written (usually the newline character), or EOF if there is an error.

int scanf (const char *str, . . .)   This function reads the types of information indicated in the string argument. It must include additional arguments corresponding to any placeholders in the string arguments. These additional arguments must be addresses so that the information can be assigned directly to these locations. The function returns either the number of items that were read *and* assigned, or EOF if the end-of-file has been reached. A return value of 0 indicates that an error has occurred, since no fields have been assigned.

New Functions

The following functions have not appeared in the programs so far, but you may want to use them in your programs.

void clearerr(FILE *f—ptr)   When a file access returns an end-of-file or an error, an indicator is set — to warn that file access is not going smoothly. You need to clear this indicator when the error has been fixed or is no longer of consequence and can be ignored.

The **clearerr( )** function lets you reset the error indicator when you wish. This function takes a file reference as its argument and simply changes the file's error indicator.

The following call resets the error indicator for the file referenced by **f—ptr.**

```
/* Assume f_ptr has been defined as FILE *f_ptr. */

clearerr ( f_ptr);
```

int fcloseall (void)   This function closes any open streams, or files, except those opened by the system—that is, except **stdin**, **stderr**, **stdout**, and so on. The function returns the number of files closed successfully, or EOF if there is an error. The following listing shows how to call **fcloseall( )**.

```
nr_closed = fcloseall ();
```

FILE *freopen(const char *new_name, const char mode, FILE *f_ptr)
This function closes the file referenced by **f_ptr**, and reassigns this stream to a new file. Such a capability can be very useful if you need to write the output of a standard stream, such as **stderr**, to a disk file.

For example, you could use the following call to **freopen( )** to send the messages going to **stderr** to a disk file named **error.tex** instead.

```
new_f_ptr = freopen ( "error.tex", "w+", stderr);
```

This function call effectively accomplishes two things: it opens a file and it redirects the output of a stream to this file. The variable **new_f_ptr** references the newly opened file, which is associated with the disk file **error.tex**. The effect of the **w+** option is to create a new file that can be read from and written to. Note that **freopen( )** is not built into QuickC. To access the function, you need to include the **stdio.h** file at the top of your program. If you intend to compile and run your program within the QuickC environment, you need to add **freopen( )** to a Quick library, as described in Appendix B.

void perror (const char *str)   This function writes a specified error message to **stderr**. You pass the message to the function, as a string argument. In addition, **perror( )** prints a system error message appropriate for the nature of the error encountered.

For example, if you want to delete a file using a C function, but no file with the specified name is found, the following line at the appropriate point in your program will write the message below it to **stderr**.

```
perror ( "Deletion unsuccessful");
/* output from preceding statement */
Deletion unsuccessful: No such file or directory
```

The **perror( )** function is often used after errors are detected using the **ferror( )** or **feof( )** macros. Call **perror( )** immediately after the error has occurred.

Otherwise, subsequent errors will overwrite the error you wanted to report. Note that **perror( )** is not built into QuickC.

The "Deletion unsuccessful" message (passed as argument to **perror( )**) is stored in the appropriate header file. The "No such file or directory" message is an internal one associated with the error type encountered when attempting to delete the file.

int remove (const char ∗name)   This function removes the disk file specified in the **name** parameter. If successful, the function returns 0; if not successful, the function returns −1. The function does not give you a chance to change your mind. So before calling this function make sure your program is not about to remove a file you want to keep.

The following statement would delete the disk file **zzzzgone.bye**.

```
remove ( "zzzzgone.bye");
```

void rewind (FILE ∗f__ptr)   Every file has a pointer associated with it. This pointer indicates the current position in the file. Generally, the next action will occur at this position. Thus, if the file position pointer is at the second element in the file, the next read process would read this element into the program. The file position pointer would then move to the third element. If your program writes to the file at this point, it will overwrite the third element, and the file position pointer will move to the fourth element. (These actions assume that your program has been opened in a mode that allows the actions, and that the specified elements exist.)

The **rewind( )** function moves the file position pointer to the beginning of the file. The function also clears any end-of-file or error indicators. It does not return a value. The following would move the file position pointer to the beginning of the file referenced by **f__fptr**:

```
rewind ( f_ptr);
```

A Program to Exercise the I/O Functions

The following program shows how these functions work. The program, which basically reads and writes files, uses each of the functions you've just read about.

The program first redirects the **stderr** stream to the file referenced by **err—ptr**, which is written to disk as **zzzztest.log**. (In the unlikely event that you have such a file, please change the name of your file or the file name in the program before you compile it.)

```
/* Program to exercise some of the functions declared in stdio.h */

#include <stdio.h>
#include <stdlib.h>

#define MAX_STR    80
#define MAX_ENTRY  50

main()
{
        void show_error_file ( FILE *);
        void get_src_file ( FILE *);
        void build_new_file ( FILE *);
        void test_new_file ( FILE *);

        int outcome, nr_closed;
        FILE *err_ptr, *f_ptr, *src;

        /* reassign stderr to err_ptr --- aka zzzztest.log */
        err_ptr = freopen( "zzzztest.log", "w+", stderr);

        /* open and read source file, if possible */
        src = fopen ( "zzzztest.src", "r");
        if ( src != NULL)
        {
                /* read and display contents of src */
                get_src_file ( src);
                fclose ( src);

                /* remove disk file associated with src */
                printf ( "Removing current version of source file");
                remove ( "zzzztest.src");
        }
        else    /* if source file could not be opened */
        {
                perror ( "Source file not opened");
                printf ( "Creating a source file for next time.\n");

                /* try to create new version of the source file */
                f_ptr = fopen ( "zzzztest.src", "w+");
                if ( f_ptr)
                {
                        /* generate a new source file */
                        build_new_file ( f_ptr);

                        /* test newly created file, by displaying a line */
                        printf ( "zzzztest.src created. Test line below.\n");
                        test_new_file ( f_ptr);

                        fclose ( f_ptr);
                }   /* END if successfully created new file */
                else
                        perror ( "Could not create a new ztestsrc");
        }   /* END if could NOT open source */

        /* display contents of file to which error output was written */
        show_error_file ( err_ptr);

        /* close any files still open */
        nr_closed = fcloseall();
        printf ( "%d files closed\n", nr_closed);
}
```

```
/* display contents of error file */
void show_error_file ( FILE *e_ptr)
{
        char *info, line [ MAX_STR];

        printf ( "\n\nContents of error file:\n");
        rewind ( e_ptr);               /* move to beginning of file */
        while ( ( info = fgets ( line, MAX_STR, e_ptr)) != NULL)
                printf ( "%s\n", line);
}



/* display first line of newly created file. */
void test_new_file ( FILE *f_ptr)
{
        char *info, line [ MAX_STR];

        rewind ( f_ptr);          /* move to beginning of file */
        if ( ( info = fgets ( line, MAX_STR, f_ptr)) != NULL)
                printf ( "%s\n", line);
        else                      /* if unable to read from file */
        {
                perror ( "Couldn't read. Clearing error.");
                clearerr ( f_ptr);
        }
}



/* create a new source file */
void build_new_file ( FILE *f_ptr)
{
        int index, value;

        /* generate MAX_ENTRY random values, write them to file, 5 / line */
        for ( index = 0; index < MAX_ENTRY; index++)
        {
                value = rand();
                if ( (index % 5) == 4)
                        fprintf ( f_ptr, "%10d\n", value);
                else
                        fprintf ( f_ptr, "%10d", value);
        }
}



/* read each line of source file as a string,
   get a number from the string --- which discards 4 numbers on the line
   --- and display the number.
*/
void get_src_file ( FILE *src)

{
        char *info, line [ MAX_STR];
        int   value;

        while ( ( info = fgets ( line, MAX_STR, src)) != NULL)
        {
                value = atoi ( line);
                printf ( "%d\n", value);
        }

        /* report on why the reading process ended */
        if ( feof ( src))
                perror ( "End of source file reached");
        else if ( ferror ( src))
                perror ( "Error in source file");
        /* else do nothing */
}
```

This program will run in either of two different ways, depending on the files that exist when the program executes. If the program is run when you do not have a file named **zzzztest.src** in your current directory, it will create such a file and produce the following output:

```
zzzztest.src created. Test line follows
         41      18467       6334       26500        19169


Contents of error file:
Source file not opened: No such file or directory

0 files closed
```

This creates a source file for next time. The complete contents of the **zzzztest.src** file that has been created are shown here:

```
   41      18467       6334      26500      19169
15724      11478      29358      26962      24464
 5705      28145      23281      16827       9961
  491       2995      11942       4827       5436
32391      14604       3902        153        292
12382      17421      18716      19718      19895
 5447      21726      14771      11538       1869
19912      25667      26299      17035       9894
28703      23811      31322      30333      17673
 4664      15141       7711      28253       6868
```

In this version—where there is no source file to be read—the program creates a source file by generating MAX_ENTRY random integers and writing these to a file, **zzzztest.src**, created for this purpose. Five values are written on each line of the file.

The program displays the first line of the newly created file to verify that the file has been written. Notice that when the file line is read as a string, all five entries are displayed. The program also displays the error messages that were written to **zzzztest.err**.

The next time the program is run, the file **zzzztest.src** will exist, so the program will be able to open and read it. After doing so, the program will use **remove()** to delete the source file, so that the program will have to create this file when you run the program again. Thus, when the program begins executing the second time, you will have a file named **zzzztest.src** on your disk; when the program finishes, this file will be gone.

The following listing shows the output from this version of the program:

```
41
15724
5705
491
32391
12382
5447
19912
28703
4664
Removing current version of source file

Contents of error file:
End of source file reached: Error 0

0 files closed
```

This version displays ten numbers, then writes various items, including the contents of the error file. Notice that the program only displays ten numbers, even though the file contains fifty. This is because of the way **atoi( )** works.

The program reads the entire line (with five values) as a string. Note that **atoi( )** processes from the beginning of the string until it has built a number. In our example, the number built will be the first number on the line. Once a number has been returned, the rest of the string is discarded, and the program reads the next line of the file. When the string is discarded, the remaining four numbers on the line are also discarded. (To get around this, you could use the **remove__wd( )** function defined in Chapter 12.)

The "Error 0" in **perror( )** indicates that no error was encountered.

stdlib.h

This header file contains declarations for several commonly used functions, including the conversion functions such as **atoi( )**, the **rand( )** function, and the dynamic storage allocation functions, such as **malloc( )**. (The allocation functions are also defined in the header file **malloc.h**.) In addition, **stdlib.h** contains the declaration for **errno**, a global variable whose value is set by various functions to a number representing a specific error.

Familiar Functions

We've used several of the functions declared in **stdlib.h** in example programs. Of these, the most useful have been the conversion functions and the pseudo-random integer generating function, **rand( )**.

int abs (int val)   This function returns the absolute value of an **int**, **val**. If **val** is negative, the function returns −**val**, otherwise the function simply returns **val**. The **abs( )** function is not built into QuickC.

double atof (const char *str)
int atoi (const char *str)
long atol (const char *str)   These functions convert the string, **str**, to a number of the appropriate type, and return this number. The string is assumed to contain characters that could be read as numerical input. The function builds a number until it encounters a character it does not recognize as belonging to the desired type of number. The functions return the value built, or 0 if no number could be built.

void *calloc (size__t nr__elems, size__t bytes__per__elem)   This function allocates enough storage to hold an array containing **nr__elems** elements, each of which is a data structure that requires **bytes__per__elem** bytes of storage. In short, **calloc( )** allocates **nr__elems** * **bytes__per__elem** bytes of storage. The function returns a pointer to the beginning of that storage. This pointer should be cast to the appropriate type of variable. The function returns a null pointer if the space could not be allocated.

void exit (int outcome)   This function ends the program, closing any open files before terminating. The **outcome** value indicates the conditions under which the program ended. Usually, an **outcome** of 0 indicates a normal termination, and a nonzero **outcome** indicates an error condition on termination. This **outcome** information is accessible to other programs, and also to DOS batch files, as you saw in Chapter 12.

void free (void *buff)   This function deallocates the specified area of memory. This area *must* have been allocated using **calloc( )** or **malloc( )**. Note that **buff** points to the beginning of the storage that will be released.

void *malloc (size__t nr__bytes)   This function allocates the specified amount of storage, and returns a pointer to the beginning of the storage allocated. As with **calloc( )**, the function returns a pointer to void, which should be cast to the desired type. If the function cannot allocate the storage, it returns a null pointer.

int rand (void)   This function returns a pseudorandom integer within the range of values allowed by an **int**, 0 to 32767 in QuickC and Microsoft C 5.0. Note that **rand( )** is not built into QuickC.

void *realloc (void *buff, size—t size)   This function lets you change the size of a block of memory previously allocated with **calloc()** or **malloc( )**. The contents of **buff** are unchanged up to the original size of **buff**. The function returns a pointer to the new location of **buff** if **buff** was moved, or to the current location if the additional storage was available right after the end of **buff**. The function returns a null pointer if the additional storage cannot be allocated.

New Functions

The following functions are also declared in **stdlib.h**, and may be useful for your programming tasks.

div—t div (int numerator, int denominator)   This function returns a structure containing the results of using integer division to divide **numerator** by **denominator**. Two items of information are returned: the whole number quotient and whole number remainder. The returned type, **div—t** is a **typedef** that specifies a structure containing two **int** members, **quot** and **rem**, for storing the quotient and remainder, respectively. Look at the **stdlib.h** file to see the exact definition.

Essentially, **div( )** returns the results of applying both integer division and the modulus operator to **numerator**. Be aware that **div( )** is not predefined in QuickC. The following statement would assign the structure returned by **div( )** to the **div—t** variable, **outcome**.

```
/* assume num and denom are int variables,
   and outcome is a div_t
*/

outcome = div ( num, denom);
```

char *getenv (const char *str)   This function reads environment information stored by the operating system. You can set various environment variables when using your computer. In DOS, these include **path**, **lib**, **include**, and others.

Calling **getenv( )** with an environment variable name tells the function to check the system's environment table to determine the current value of the specified environment. The function returns a pointer to the string associated with the environment, or a null pointer if the environment variable is not defined at the time or if the variable name is not one the system recognizes. The following call would assign the contents of the **include** environment string to **whats_included**.

```
/* assume whats_included is a string variable */

whats_included = getenv ( "INCLUDE");   /* upper case needed */

whats_included = getenv ( "include");    /* produces different result */
```

In this function, the case of the string argument does make a difference. The program will give two different results for the two calls. Try the two versions of the call on your machine.

char *itoa (int nr, char *str, int radix)   This function converts an integer value to a string, returning the resulting string. The value you want converted is the first argument, **nr**; the second argument is **str**, the string built (and eventually returned). The third argument, **radix**, is the number base you want the function to use when building the string. This base can be any value between 2 and 36.

The following statements would convert the value −2300 to strings containing binary, octal, decimal, and hexadecimal forms of the number, respectively:

```
/* Program to illustrate use of itoa() function */

#include <stdlib.h>
#define MAX_STR   80

main()
{
        char *result, temp [ MAX_STR];

        result = itoa ( -2300, temp, 2);
        printf ( "base 2 : %s\n", result);
        result = itoa ( -2300, temp, 8);
        printf ( "base 8 : %s\n", result);
        result = itoa ( -2300, temp, 10);
        printf ( "base 10 : %s\n", result);
        result = itoa ( -2300, temp, 16);
        printf ( "base 16 : %s\n", result);
}
```

This program produces the following output:

```
base 2  : 1111011100000100
base 8  : 173404
base 10 : -2300
base 16 : f704
```

Notice that only the base ten representation still has a minus sign in the resulting string. For other bases, the number is handled as if it were unsigned, and the bit pattern for the number is merely converted. You can see this if you look at the bit pattern from the binary representation and then translate these bits into hexadecimal digits: 1111 == F; 0111 == 7; 0000 === 0; 0100 == 4.

You need to make sure that the second argument is a string for which enough storage has been allocated to build a value up to 17 bytes long — 16 bytes for the **int** and 1 byte for the null terminator.

long labs (long val)   This function returns the absolute value of a **long** argument. It is used in the same way as **abs( )**, but with **long** variables instead of **int**. The **labs( )** function is not built into QuickC.

ldiv__t ldiv (long int numerator, long int denominator)   This function returns a structure containing the results of using **long** integer division to divide **numerator** by **denominator**. Two values are returned: the whole number quotient and the whole number remainder. The returned type, **ldiv__t** is a **typedef** that specifies a structure containing two **long int** members, **quot** and **rem**, for storing the quotient and remainder, respectively. Look at the **stdlib.h** file to see the exact definition.

Essentially, **ldiv( )** returns the results of applying both integer division and the modulus operator to **numerator**. Note that **ldiv( )** is not predefined in QuickC. The following statement would assign the structure returned by **ldiv( )** to the **ldiv__t** variable, **l__outcome**. This function is not built into QuickC.

```
/* assume num and denom are long int variables,
   and l_outcome is a ldiv_t
*/

l_outcome = ldiv ( num, denom);
```

char *ltoa (long nr, char *str, int radix)   This function converts a long integer value to a string. The resulting string is returned. The value you want converted is the first argument, **nr**; the second argument is **str**, the string built (and eventually returned). The third argument, **radix**, is the number base in which you want the function to represent the value. This base can be any value between 2 and 36.

The following statements would convert the value −2300L to strings containing binary, octal, decimal, and hexadecimal forms of the number, respectively:

```
/* Program to illustrate use of ltoa() */

#include <stdlib.h>
#define MAX_STR    80

main()
{
        char *result, temp [ MAX_STR];

        result = ltoa ( -2300L, temp, 2);
        printf ( "base 2 : %s\n", result);
        result = ltoa ( -2300L, temp, 8);
        printf ( "base 8 : %s\n", result);
        result = ltoa ( -2300L, temp, 10);
        printf ( "base 10 : %s\n", result);
        result = ltoa ( -2300L, temp, 16);
        printf ( "base 16 : %s\n", result);
}
```

This program produces the following output:

```
base 2 : 11111111111111111111011100000100
base 8 : 37777773404
base 10 : -2300
base 16 : fffff704
```

Notice that, as with the **itoa( )** function for **int** arguments, only the base ten representation still has a minus sign in the resulting string. For other bases, the number is handled as if it were unsigned, and the bit pattern for the number is merely converted. You can see this if you look at the bit pattern from the binary representation and translate these bits into hexadecimal digits.

Compare this output with that for the integer version of −2300. You need to make sure that the second argument is a string for which enough storage has been allocated to build a value up to 33 bytes long — 32 bytes for the **long int** and 1 byte for the null terminator.

int system (const char *str)   This function passes the string argument to the operating system command interpreter, which takes this string as an ordinary command line. Thus, the effect of a call to **system( )** with a DOS command can be the same as if you had typed the string at a regular DOS prompt outside your program.

If you call the function with a null pointer, the function returns a nonzero value if the DOS command processor is present, and 0 if the command processor cannot be found. Otherwise, if you pass a nonempty string, the function returns 0 if the string is successfully executed, and −1 if there is an error. Check your documentation for a discussion of the types of error this function can report.

The following instruction in a program would do a directory listing while your program was running, and would redirect this listing to a file named **syslist.zzz**:

```
/* assume result is an int */
result = system ( "dir > syslist.zzz");
```

The **system( )** function is not built into QuickC.

Exercising the stdlib.h Functions

The following program illustrates the use of the functions that are declared in **stdlib.h** and described in this section:

```
/* Program to exercise some of the functions declared in stdlib.h */
#include <stdio.h>
#include <stdlib.h>
#define MAX_STR   80

main()
{
        void show_system ( void);
        void show_itoa ( void);
        void show_ltoa ( void);
        void show_div ( void);
        void show_ldiv ( void);
        void show_setenv ( void);

        show_setenv ();
        system ( "pause");
        show_system ();
        system ( "pause");
        show_itoa ();
        show_ltoa ();
        show_div ();
        show_ldiv ();

}


void show_itoa ()
{
        char   *info, *result, temp [ MAX_STR];
        int    value, radix;
```

```
        printf ( "itoa : Value to convert? (0 to stop) ");
        info = gets ( temp);
        value = atoi ( info);
        while ( value)
        {
                do
                {
                        printf ( "Base? ");
                        info = gets ( temp);
                        radix = atoi ( info);
                }
                while ( ( radix < 2) || ( radix > 36));

                result = itoa ( value, temp, radix);
                printf ( "value == %5d; base == %2d; result == %s\n",
                        value, radix, result);

                printf ( "itoa : Value to convert? (0 to stop) ");
                info = gets ( temp);
                value = atoi ( info);
        }
}


void show_ltoa ()
{
        char    *info, *result, temp [ MAX_STR];
        int     radix;
        long int value;

        printf ( "ltoa : Value to convert? (0 to stop) ");
        info = gets ( temp);
        value = atol ( info);
        while ( value)
        {
                do
                {
                        printf ( "Base? ");
                        info = gets ( temp);
                        radix = atoi ( info);
                }
                while ( ( radix < 2) || ( radix > 36));

                result = ltoa ( value, temp, radix);
                printf ( "value == %5ld; base == %2d; result == %s\n",
                        value, radix, result);

                printf ( "ltoa : Value to convert? (0 to stop) ");
                info = gets ( temp);
                value = atol ( info);
        }
}


void show_div ()
{
        char    *info, temp [ MAX_STR];
        div_t   results;
        int     numer, denom;

        printf ( "div : Numerator? (0 to stop) ");
        info = gets ( temp);
        numer = atoi ( info);
        while ( numer)
        {
                do
```

```
                  {
                          printf ( "Denominator? ");
                          info = gets ( temp);
                          denom = atoi ( info);
                  }
                  while ( denom == 0);

                  results = div ( numer, denom);
                  printf ( "numer == %5d; denom == %5d; ", numer, denom);
                  printf ( "quotient == %5d; remainder == %5d\n",
                          results.quot, results.rem);

                  printf ( "Numerator? (0 to stop) ");
                  info = gets ( temp);
                  numer = atoi ( info);
          }
  }

void show_ldiv ()
{
          char       *info, temp [ MAX_STR];
          ldiv_t     results;
          long int   numer, denom;

          printf ( "ldiv : Numerator? (0 to stop) ");
          info = gets ( temp);
          numer = atol ( info);
          while ( numer)
          {
                  do
                  {
                          printf ( "Denominator? ");
                          info = gets ( temp);
                          denom = atol ( info);
                  }
                  while ( denom == 0);

                  results = ldiv ( numer, denom);
                  printf ( "numer == %10ld; denom == %10ld\n", numer, denom);
                  printf ( "quotient == %10ld; remainder == %10ld\n",
                          results.quot, results.rem);

                  printf ( "Numerator? (0 to stop) ");
                  info = gets ( temp);
                  numer = atol ( info);
          }
  }

void show_system()
{
          char *str1 = "dir /p";

          printf ( "Calling system with : %s\n", str1);
          system ( "pause");
          system ( str1);
  }

void show_setenv ()
{
          char *whats_included;

          printf ( "setenv :\n");
          whats_included = getenv ( "INCLUDE");
          printf ( "include == %s\n", whats_included);
          whats_included = getenv ( "PATH");
          printf ( "path == %s\n", whats_included);
  }
```

This program produced the following session:

```
setenv :
include == \qc\inc;\c\inc
path == \;\QC\BIN;\C\BIN;\BIN;\BIN\BAT;\USRBIN;\UXBIN;\TEX;..;\SH\BT;
Strike a key when ready . . .
Calling system with : dir /p
Strike a key when ready . . .

  Volume in drive C has no label
  Directory of  C:\BK\SRC

.             <DIR>        5-13-87    2:34p
..            <DIR>        5-13-87    2:34p
TXDETAB EXE    9590        7-27-87    4:52p
STRINGS H        90        5-13-87    1:30p
SLIB    EXE   19608        7-27-87    9:52p
SLIBOUT         202        7-27-87    9:54p
PROGINFO H      494        5-21-87   12:04a
DETEX   EXE    9776        7-01-87   10:51a
WFMACS  H      1757        6-05-87    6:52p
WFTIME  H      1433        7-08-87    9:46a
WFPREP  H       902        7-08-87   12:56a
CH14          <DIR>        7-14-87    1:29p
CH15          <DIR>        7-16-87    4:19p
CH16          <DIR>        7-23-87    3:55p
      14 File(s)    2975744 bytes free
Strike a key when ready . . .
itoa : Value to convert? (0 to stop) -5
Base? 3
value ==      -5; base ==   3; result == 10022220002
itoa : Value to convert? (0 to stop) -5
Base? 10
value ==      -5; base ==  10; result == -5
itoa : Value to convert? (0 to stop) -5
Base? 16
value ==      -5; base ==  16; result == fffb
itoa : Value to convert? (0 to stop) 0
ltoa : Value to convert? (0 to stop) -5
Base? 3
value ==      -5; base ==   3; result == 102002022201221111122
ltoa : Value to convert? (0 to stop) -5
Base? 10
value ==      -5; base ==  10; result == -5
ltoa : Value to convert? (0 to stop) -5
Base? 16
value ==      -5; base ==  16; result == fffffffb
ltoa : Value to convert? (0 to stop) 0
div : Numerator? (0 to stop) -57
Denominator? 23
numer ==      -57; denom ==      23; quotient ==      -2; remainder ==      -11
Numerator? (0 to stop) 0
ldiv : Numerator? (0 to stop) -57
Denominator? 23
numer ==          -57; denom ==          23
quotient ==          -2; remainder ==          -11
Numerator? (0 to stop) 0
```

Let's look at some of the functions in this program. The **show__setenv( )** function checks the current path and the directories that your programs will search for **include** files. The calls to **system( )** invoke the DOS **pause** command, which waits for the user to press a key before proceeding.

The **show__system( )** function provides a directory listing, and also uses **system( )** to pause. The **/p** switch tells DOS to pause after each screenful, which is unnecessary in the example but convenient if you have many files in a directory.

The other functions exercise the functions for converting **int** and **long** variables. Notice that **itoa( )** and **ltoa( )** retain the minus sign only for base ten values. Notice also that the same number produces different strings for the **int** and the **long** values. This is because the sign bit creates a very large number in bases other than ten.

The results are identical for both **int** and **long** variables when computing integral division structures (**div__t** and **ldiv__t**).

string.h

This header file contains declarations for the string handling functions described in Chapter 11. In addition, the file contains declarations for several functions useful for handling arbitrary data stored in memory.

Familiar Functions

Before moving on to some new functions, let's look briefly at the functions described in Chapter 11.

char *strcat (char *str1, const char *str2)
char *strncat (char *str1, const char *str2, size__t nr)   These functions append one string (**str2**) to the end of the other string (**str1**). Note that **strcat( )** appends the entire **str2**, whereas **strncat( )** appends only the specified **nr** of characters. The function removes and adds terminating null characters at the appropriate places, before returning the newly built string.

int strcmp(const char *str1, const char *str2)
int strncmp (const char *str1, const char *str2, size__t nr)   These functions compare the two strings passed as arguments. The **strcmp( )** function compares the entire strings, whereas **strncmp( )** compares only the specified **nr**

of characters. The functions return -1 if **str1** $<$ **str2**, 0 if the strings are equal, and 1 if **str1** $>$ **str2**.

char *strcpy (char *str1, const char *str2)
char *strncpy (char *str1, const char *str2, size__t nr)   These functions copy one string (**str2**) into another (**str1**). The **strcpy( )** function copies the entire **str2**, whereas **strncpy( )** copies only the first **nr** characters. The functions return the newly created string.

If you instruct **strncpy( )** to copy less than all of **str2**, you will need to terminate the newly built string, since the function will not do so automatically.

size__t strlen (const char *str)   This function returns the number of characters in the specified string. The value returned does not include the terminating null character in its count.

New Functions

The next group of functions (those whose names begin with **mem**) are useful for moving data around in memory. Rather than working only with strings, the functions can manipulate arbitrary data types. Some of the functions are **mem** counterparts to some of the string handling functions briefly described earlier.

void *memchr (const void *target, int ch, size__t nr)   This function searches **target** for any occurrence of **ch**. It will search up to **nr** bytes or until it finds **ch**, whichever comes first. Note that **target** is declared as a pointer to **void**, which you can cast to a different type of pointer. The **memchr( )** function returns a pointer to the location of **ch** in **target**, or a null pointer if **ch** is not found in the first **nr** bytes of **target**.

The following statement returns a pointer to **int**, after searching the first **nr** bytes of **int__buff[ ]** for the character with ASCII value 37.

```
/* Assume int_ptr has been defined as (int *),
   and that int_buff[] is an array of int.
*/

int_ptr = memchr ( int_buff, 37, nr);
```

int memcmp (const void *buffer1, const void *buffer2, size＿t nr)   This
is a comparison function, like **strcmp( )**; **memcmp( )** compares the first **nr** bytes
of the two buffers. The function returns −1 if **buffer1** is less than **buffer2**, 0 if
the two buffers are equal, and 1 if **buffer1** exceeds **buffer2**. You can cast the
buffers to the type of pointers you need in your program. The following listing
shows how to call **memcmp( )**.

```
/* assume buffer1 and buffer2 have been defined as pointers to int,
   and result has been defined as an int.
*/

result = memcmp ( buffer1, buffer2, nr);
```

void *memcpy (void *target, const void *src, size＿t nr)   This function
copies the first **nr** bytes of **src** to **target**, and returns a pointer to the target
buffer. Be very careful using this function if the two buffers overlap. For
example, suppose **src** starts at address 4000 and **target** starts at address 4050. If
you want to copy 100 bytes of **src** to **target**, the compiler may overwrite the
contents of **src** starting at location 4050 before copying them to **target**. The
next function described, **memmove( )**, is better suited for transfers involving
overlapping storage sections.

The following listing copies **nr** bytes from **src** to **target** and returns a
pointer to the resulting buffer:

```
/* assume target, src, and result have been defined as pointers to int. */

result = memcpy ( target, src, nr);
```

void *memmove (void *target, const void *src, size＿t nr)   This function
also copies the specified number of bytes from **src** to **target**. Unlike **memcpy( )**,
however, **memmove( )** moves overlapping bytes before writing over them. The
function returns a pointer to the target buffer.

The following call moves **nr** bytes from **src** to **target**:

```
/* assume target, src, and result have been defined as pointers to int. */
result = memmove ( target, src, nr);
```

void *memset (void *target, int ch, size__t nr)   This function copies **ch** into the first **nr** bytes of **target**, and returns a pointer to this target buffer. The following call puts 'w' into the first 50 bytes of **target**. The **memmove( )** function is not built into QuickC.

```
/* Assume target and result have been defined as pointer to char. */
result = memset ( target, 'w', 50);
```

char *strchr (const char *str, int ch)   This function searches for the first occurrence of the character, **ch**, in **str**, and returns a pointer to the first occurrence of **ch** in **str**, or a null pointer if **ch** is not found.
    The following listing finds the first 'a' in **str**:

```
/* Assume str is a pointer to char, and result is an int */
result = strchr ( str, 'a');
```

char *strdup (const char *str)   This function makes a duplicate of **str**, and returns a pointer to this duplicate. If the function can't allocate storage for a copy of the string, the function returns a null pointer. Otherwise, the function returns a pointer to the newly allocated space containing the string.
    The following call assigns a duplicate of "hello there" to the string, **message**:

```
/* Assume message is a string */
message = strdup ( "hello there");
```

char *strlwr (char *str)   This function converts any uppercase characters in **str** to lowercase, then returns a pointer to the resulting string. The following listing converts "HELLO THERE" to lowercase, returning "hello there."

```
/* Assume lower is a string */
lower = strlwr ( "HELLO THERE");
```

char *strpbrk (const char *str1, const char *str2)   This function looks for the first occurrence, in **str1**, of *any* character from **str2**. If one is found, the function returns a pointer to this character — which effectively returns the rest of the string. If no matching character is found, the function returns a null pointer.

The following listing searches for any character from "hello" that appears in "California." The value of **str** will be "lifornia" after the function call.

```
/* Assume str is a string */
str = strpbrk ( "California", "hello");
```

char *strrchr (const char *str, int ch)   This function looks for the *last* occurrence of the character **ch** in **str**, and returns a pointer to this character, if it is found. If the character is not found in the string, the function returns a null pointer.

The following listing finds the last 'l' in "Walla Walla," and returns a pointer to this character. In the example, this would result in the string "la" after the call.

```
/* Assum str is a string */
str = strrchr ( "Walla Walla", 'l');
```

char *strrev (char *str)   This function reverses the characters in **str** (except for the null terminator) and returns a pointer to the reversed string. The following listing shows how to call **strrev( )**. You also have **reverse __ str( )** in your function collection from earlier.

```
/* Assume str is a string */
str = strrev ( "Walla Walla");
```

char *strset (char *str, int ch)   This function fills **str** with the character **ch**, except for the null terminator, which the function leaves as is. The **strset( )** function returns a pointer to the newly initialized string.

The following listing shows how to call this function:

```
/* Assume str is a string */
str = strset ( str, 'w');
```

char *strstr (const char *str1, const char *str2)   This function looks for the first occurrence in **str1** of **str2**, and returns a pointer to the beginning of this first occurrence. If **str2** is not found in **str1**, the function returns a null pointer.

The following listing looks for "law" in "Wallawalla" and returns a pointer to the beginning of its appearance.

```
/* Assume str is a string */
str = strstr ( "Wallawalla", "law");
```

char *strupr (char *str)   This function converts any lowercase characters in **str** to uppercase, and then returns a pointer to the resulting string. The following listing converts "hello there" to uppercase, returning "HELLO THERE."

```
/* Assume upper is a string */

upper = strupr ( "hello there");
```

Exercising the Functions

The following program lets you exercise the functions discussed in this section:

```
/* Program to exercise some of the functions declared in string.h */

#include <string.h>
#include <stdlib.h>
#include <stdio.h>

#define MAX_STR    80
#define MAX_NR     80
#define MAX_MENU   15
#define NULL_CHAR  '\0'

int  buff [ 80];
char cbuff [ 80];

void wait ();   /* function to let pause until user presses a key */

/* array with menu selections for this program */
char *menu [ MAX_MENU] = { "0) Quit", "1) memchr",
                           "2) memcmp", "3) memcpy",
                           "4) memmove", "5) memset",
                           "6) strchr", "7) strdup",
                           "8) strlwr", "9) strpbrk",
                           "10) strrchr", "11) strrev",
                           "12) strset", "13) strstr",
                           "14) strupr"};

void wait ()
{
        system ( "pause");
}


/* void show_menu ( char *menu [], int menu_size)

    Display the specified menu, which is an array of strings.
    menu_size indicates the number of strings in the menu.
    Function also prompts user for a choice.
    CALLS : printf ()
    GLOBALS : MAX_MENU
```

```
    PARAMETERS :
           char *menu [] : array of strings, containing menu.
           int menu_size : number of items in menu.
    USAGE : show_menu ( menu_array, Nr_of_entries);
*/

void show_menu ( char *menu [], int menu_size)
{
        int count;

        printf ( "\n\n");

        /* if programmer claims menu has more than maximum allowed items,

            bring the value into line.
        */
        if ( menu_size > MAX_MENU)
                menu_size = MAX_MENU;

        /* display the individual strings in the array */
        for ( count = 0; count < menu_size; count++)
                printf ( "%s\n", menu [ count]);

        printf ( "\n\n");

        /* prompt user */
        printf ( "Your choice? (%d to %d) ", 0, MAX_MENU - 1);
}



main ()
{
        void show_menu ( char *[], int);
        void show_memchr ( void);
        void show_memcmp ( void);
        void show_memcpy ( void);
        void show_memmove ( void);
        void show_memset ( void);
        void show_strchr ( void);
        void show_strdup ( void);
        void show_strlwr ( void);
        void show_strpbrk ( void);
        void show_strrchr ( void);
        void show_strrev ( void);
        void show_strset ( void);
        void show_strstr ( void);
        void show_strupr ( void);
        char info [ MAX_STR];
        int selection;

        do
        {
                show_menu ( menu, MAX_MENU);
                gets ( info);
                selection = atoi ( info);
                switch ( selection)
                {
                        default:
                                break;
                        case 0:
                                break;
                        case 1:
                                show_memchr ();
                                break;
                        case 2:
                                show_memcmp ();
                                break;
```

```
                              case 3:
                                      show_memcpy ();
                                      break;
                              case 4:
                                      show_memmove ();
                                      break;
                              case 5:
                                      show_memset ();
                                      break;

                              case 6:
                                      show_strchr ();
                                      break;
                              case 7:
                                      show_strdup ();
                                      break;
                              case 8:
                                      show_strlwr ();
                                      break;
                              case 9:
                                      show_strpbrk ();
                                      break;
                              case 10:
                                      show_strrchr ();
                                      break;
                              case 11:
                                      show_strrev ();
                                      break;
                              case 12:
                                      show_strset ();
                                      break;
                              case 13:
                                      show_strstr ();
                                      break;
                              case 14:
                                      show_strupr ();
                                      break;
                      }
              }
          while ( selection != 0);
}


void show_memchr ()
{
        int  index, i_byte;
        int  *result, src [ MAX_NR];
        char *cresult;
        char csrc [ MAX_STR], info [ MAX_STR];
        char ch;
        int  rand ( void);

        printf ( "Testing with numbers first\n");
        for ( index = 0; index < MAX_STR; index ++)
                src [ index] = rand ();
        printf ( "Byte to find? ");
        gets ( info);
        i_byte = atoi ( info) & 0xff;
        result = memchr ( src, i_byte, MAX_NR);
        if ( result == NULL)
                printf ( "no %d found\n", i_byte);
        else
        {
                printf ( "%d found; return value = %d\n", i_byte, *result);
        }
        for ( index = 0; index < 10; index++)
                printf ( "%7d as bytes: high == %7d; low == %7d\n",
                        src [ index], src [ index] & 0xff00,
                        src [ index] & 0xff);
```

```
        printf ( "\n\nString to search? ");
        gets ( csrc);
        printf ( "Character to find? ");
        gets ( info);
        ch = info [ O];
        cresult = memchr ( csrc, ch, 80);
        if ( cresult == NULL)
                printf ( "no %c found\n", ch);
        else
        {
                printf ( " %c found; return value = %s\n", ch, cresult);
        }
        for ( index = 0; (index < 15) && ( csrc [ index] != NULL_CHAR);
                index++)
                printf ( "%4c", csrc [ index]);
        printf ( "\n");
        wait ();
}


void show_memcmp ()
{
        char    str1 [ MAX_STR], str2 [ MAX_STR];
        int     result;

        printf ( "String 1? ");
        gets ( str1);
        printf ( "String 2? ");
        gets ( str2);
        result = memcmp ( str1, str2, strlen ( str1));
        printf ( "For %d bytes: result = %d\n", strlen ( str1), result);
        wait ();
}


void show_memcpy ()
{
        char str1 [ MAX_STR], *str2, *result, temp [ MAX_STR];

        printf ( "String? (At least 20 characters, please) ");
        gets ( str1);
        if ( strlen ( str1) < 20)
        {
                printf ( "substituting abcdefghijklmnopqrstuvwxyz\n");
                strcpy ( str1, "abcdefghijklmnopqrstuvwxyz");
        }
        strcpy ( temp, str1);
        str2 = str1 + 10;
        printf ( "str2 == %s\n", str2);
        result = memcpy ( str2, str1, strlen (str2));
        printf ( "After copying to overlapping string: %s\n", result);
        /* str1 = temp;
        printf ( "restored str2 == %s\n", str2); */
        result = memcpy ( str2, temp, strlen (str2));
        printf ( "After copying to NON-overlapping string: %s\n", result);
        wait ();
}


void show_memmove ()
{
        char str1 [ MAX_STR], *str2, *result, temp [ MAX_STR];

        printf ( "String? (At least 20 characters, please) ");
        gets ( str1);
        if ( strlen ( str1) < 20)
        {
```

```
                printf ( "substituting abcdefghijklmnopqrstuvwxyz\n");
                strcpy ( str1, "abcdefghijklmnopqrstuvwxyz");
        }
        strcpy ( temp, str1);
        str2 = str1 + 10;
        printf ( "str2 == %s\n", str2);
        result = memmove ( str2, str1, strlen (str2));
        printf ("After copying to overlapping string: %s\n", result);
        result = memmove ( str2, temp, strlen (str2));
        printf ("After copying to NON-overlapping string: %s\n", result);
        wait ();
}


void show_memset ()
{
        char    str [ MAX_STR], info [ MAX_STR], ch, *result;

        printf ( "String to initialize? ");
        gets ( str);
        printf ( "Initialization character? ");
        gets ( info);
        ch = info [ 0];
        result = memset ( str, ch, strlen ( str) - 1);
        printf ( "When initializing %d bytes, result = %s\n",
                strlen ( str) - 1, result);
        wait ();
}


void show_strchr ()
{
        char    str1 [ MAX_STR], info [ MAX_STR], ch, *result;

        printf ( "String to search? ");
        gets ( str1);
        printf ( "Character to find? ");
        gets ( info);
        ch = info [ 0];
        result = strchr ( str1, ch);
        printf ( "For first occurrence, result = %s\n", result);
        wait ();
}


void show_strdup ()
{
        char    str1 [ MAX_STR], *result;

        printf ( "String to duplicate? ");
        gets ( str1);
        result = strdup ( str1);
        printf ( "result = %s\n", result);
        wait ();
}


void show_strlwr ()
{
        char    str1 [ MAX_STR], *result;
        printf ( "String to convert to lower case? ");
        gets ( str1);
        result = strlwr ( str1);
        printf ( "result = %s\n", result);
        wait ();
}
```

```
void show_strpbrk ()
{
        char    str1 [ MAX_STR], str2 [ MAX_STR], *result;

        printf ( "String to search? ");
        gets ( str1);
        printf ( "String to compare? ");
        gets ( str2);
        result = strpbrk ( str1, str2);
        printf ( "result = %s\n", result);
        wait ();
}


void show_strrchr ()
{
        char    str1 [ MAX_STR], info [ MAX_STR], ch, *result;

        printf ( "String to search? ");
        gets (str1);
        printf ( "Character to find? ");
        gets ( info);
        ch = info [ 0];
        result = strrchr ( str1, ch);
        printf ( "result = %s\n", result);
        wait ();
}


void show_strrev ()
{
        char    str1 [ MAX_STR], *result;

        printf ( "String to reverse? ");
        gets ( str1);
        result = strrev ( str1);
        printf ( "result = %s\n", result);
        wait ();
}


void show_strset ()
{
        char    str [ MAX_STR], info [ MAX_STR], ch, *result;

        printf ( "String to initialize? ");
        gets ( str);
        printf ( "Initialization character? ");
        gets ( info);
        ch = info [ 0];
        result = strset ( str, ch);
        printf ( "Initialized result = %s\n", result);
        wait ();
}



void show_strstr ()
{
        char    str1 [ MAX_STR], str2 [ MAX_STR], *result;

        printf ( "String to search? ");
        gets ( str1);
        printf ( "String to find? ");
        gets ( str2);
        result = strstr ( str1, str2);
```

```
        printf ( "result = %s\n", result);
        wait ();
}

void show_strupr ()
{
        char    str1 [ MAX_STR], *result;

        printf ( "String to convert to upper case? ");
        gets ( str1);
        result = strupr ( str1);
        printf ( "result = %s\n", result);
        wait ();
}
```

The best way to become comfortable with the way these functions work is to play with this program, trying various values for each of the available functions to see the results.

The session with **memchr( )** may need a word or two of explanation. This function lets you look for a particular byte in an array of pseudorandom **int** values (generated using **rand( )**), and then in a string. To emphasize the fact that **memchr( )** works with bytes rather than 16-bit **int** values, the program displays the array values in two ways: as a regular **int** (all 16 bits at a time) and by displaying the high and low bytes, which must add up to the 16-bit value. Remember that **memchr( )** compares the specified byte against the two bytes that make up each array element, not against the entire array element.

ctype.h

This file contains information about several character handling routines, which can make string handling and parsing easier. The routines generally serve to determine whether the character passed to the routine is of a particular type. In QuickC and in Microsoft C 5.0, these routines are defined as macros rather than functions.

The format and returns for most of these routines are similar. The routines return a nonzero value if the specified character meets the conditions tested by the routines, and a 0 otherwise. All these routines take an **int** argument and return an **int**.

Table 17-1 summarizes the routines, and includes the conditions the **int** argument must meet for each routine to return a nonzero value.

Table 17-1.   Character Type Routines

Routine	Condition	Example
isalnum( )	alphanumeric	'A' - 'Z', 'a' - 'z', or '0' - '9'
isalpha( )	letter	'A' - 'Z', 'a' - 'z'
isascii( )	ASCII character	value between **0x00** and **0x7F**
iscntrl( )	control character	value between **0x00** and **0x1F** or **0x7F**
isdigit( )	digit	'0' - '9'
isgraph( )	printable character (except space)	**0x21 - 0x7E**
islower( )	lowercase	'a' - 'z'
isprint( )	printable character (including space)	**0x21 - 0x7E**
ispunct( )	punctuation character	isgraph( ) && !isalnum( )
isspace( )	whitespace character	**0x09 - 0x0D** or **0x20**
isupper( )	uppercase character	'A' - 'Z'
isxdigit( )	hexadecimal digit	'0' - '9', 'A' - 'F', 'a' - 'f'

Most of these routines test conditions with which you're probably familiar. For example, **isalnum( )** tests whether the character passed is an ordinary letter or a digit. The **ispunct( )** routine tests whether a character is printable, but is not an alphanumeric character or a space. This routine would return true for characters such as % and #. The **isascii( )** routine is not specified in the Draft Proposed ANSI Standard, although it is included in most C implementations. This routine returns true if the **int** argument has a value between 0 and 127.

Conversion Routines

Some additional routines included in **ctype.h** convert an argument from one form to another. The most common conversions are from lowercase to uppercase, and vice versa.

The **tolower( )** routine converts an uppercase character to lowercase. If the character is not uppercase to begin with, the routine leaves the character untouched. The **toupper( )** routine converts a lowercase character to uppercase, and leaves other characters untouched.

Both **toupper( )** and **tolower( )** are defined as macros in **ctype.h**, but they are also declared as functions in **stdio.h**. You are probably better off using the function versions of these routines, because the macros can cause certain side effects.

If you are going to use the **isXXX** macros defined in **ctype.h**, but wish to use the **tolower( )** and **toupper( )** functions built into QuickC, you need to use the #**undef** preprocessor directive to undefine the macros. The next program will provide an example of how to do this.

In addition to these two conversion functions, Microsoft has included a **toascii( )** function in QuickC and Microsoft C 5.0. This function takes an **int** argument and returns an **int** containing only the seven rightmost bits of the number—that is, an **int** with a value in the ASCII range of **0x00** to **0x7F**. Essentially, this function masks the argument with **0x7F**, that is, **argument & 0x7F**.

▶**CAUTION**   The **toascii( )** function is not specified in the Draft Proposed ANSI Standard; using this function will make your programs less transportable.

Exercising the Character Routines

The following program lets you explore the behavior of these character routines, and also shows how to undefine **tolower( )** and **toupper( )**.

```
/* Program for exercising the character checking macros and functions */

#include <stdio.h>
#include <ctype.h>

/* undefine the toupper and tolower macros, so that the functions
   declared in stdio.h will be used instead.
*/
#ifdef toupper
#undef toupper
#endif

#ifdef tolower
#undef tolower
#endif

#define MAX_STR   80
#define MAX_MENU  16
```

```
/* array with menu selections for this program */
char *menu [ MAX_MENU] = { "0) Quit", "1) isalnum",
                          "2) isalpha", "3) isascii",
                          "4) iscntrl", "5) isdigit",
                          "6) isgraph", "7) islower",
                          "8) isprint", "9) ispunct",
                          "10) isspace", "11) isupper",
                          "12) isxdigit", "13) toascii",
                          "14) tolower", "15) toupper"};


/* void show_menu ( char *menu [], int menu_size)

   Display the specified menu, which is an array of strings.
   menu_size indicates the number of strings in the menu.
   Function also prompts user for a choice.
   CALLS : printf ()
   GLOBALS : MAX_MENU
   PARAMETERS :
           char *menu [] : array of strings, containing menu.
           int menu_size : number of items in menu.
   USAGE : show_menu ( menu_array, Nr_of_entries);
*/

void show_menu ( char *menu [], int menu_size)
{
        int count;

        printf ( "\n\n");

        /* if programmer claims menu has more than maximum allowed items,
           bring the value into line.
        */
        if ( menu_size > MAX_MENU)
                menu_size = MAX_MENU;

        /* display·the individual strings in the array */
        for ( count = 0; count < menu_size; count++)
                printf ( "%s\n", menu [ count]);

        printf ( "\n\n");

        /* prompt user */
        printf ( "Your choice? (%d to %d) ", 0, MAX_MENU - 1);
}


main ()
{
        void report ( int);
        int  ch, selection, result;
        char info [ MAX_STR];

        do
        {
                selection = 0;
                show_menu ( menu, MAX_MENU);
                gets ( info);
                selection = atoi ( info);
                if ( ( selection > 0) && ( selection < MAX_MENU))
                {
                        printf ( "Character to test (enter int value)? ");
                        gets ( info);
                        ch = atoi ( info);
                }
                switch ( selection)
                {
                        default:
                                break;
```

```
case 0:
        break;
case 1:
        result = isalnum ( ch);
        report ( result);
        break;
case 2:
        result = isalpha ( ch);
        report ( result);
        break;
case 3:
        result = isascii ( ch);
        report ( result);
        break;
case 4:
        result = iscntrl ( ch);
        report ( result);
        break;
case 5:
        result = isdigit ( ch);
        report ( result);
        break;
case 6:
        result = isgraph ( ch);
        report ( result);
        break;
case 7:
        result = islower ( ch);
        report ( result);
        break;
case 8:
        result = isprint ( ch);
        report ( result);
        break;
case 9:
        result = ispunct ( ch);
        report ( result);
        break;
case 10:
        result = isspace ( ch);
        report ( result);
        break;
case 11:
        result = isupper ( ch);
        report ( result);
        break;
case 12:
        result = isxdigit ( ch);
        report ( result);
        break;
case 13:
        result = toascii ( ch);
        printf ( "%c\n", result);
        break;
case 14:
        result =  tolower ( ch);
        printf ( "%c\n", result);
        break;
case 15:
        result =  toupper ( ch);
        printf ( "%c\n", result);
        break;
        }
}
while ( selection != 0);
```

```
        }

        void report ( int val)
        {
                if ( val == 0)
                        printf ( "False\n");
                else
                        printf ( "True\n");
        }
```

dos.h

This file, which is not part of the Draft Proposed ANSI Standard, provides information and data structures for taking advantage of some of the services DOS can provide. In this file, QuickC and Microsoft C v5.0 provide a REGS union type that you can use to access the machine registers in your computer. You can access entire (16-bit) registers at one time, or you can access the individual bytes of a register. This union is used when you want to call DOS or the BIOS (Basic Input Output System) to perform a particular task.

In addition to this union declaration, **dos.h** also contains the function declarations you need to access the registers. In this section, you'll learn about one of these functions, and how you can use it to get various types of information from DOS.

Background

You don't really need to know the details of how things operate internally when you ask the operating system to do something. A few words about how the hardware and software interact to provide DOS services might be helpful, however.

Registers   Machines based on the Intel 8086 family of processors (including the 8088, 80286, and so on) do much of their work in machine registers of various sorts. These registers are 16 bits wide, and are used to store various pieces of information while a program runs. When a program is run, much of the action either takes place in these registers or is controlled by values stored in them.

Four general-purpose registers, known as AX, BX, CX, and DX, respectively, are used by the function we'll be using. You can access an entire register at once, or you can access the high and low-order bytes of the register separately. When you are accessing an entire register, you refer to AX, BX, and so on. When you are accessing individual bytes, you refer to the AH (high-order byte) and the AL (low-order byte) of AX, for example. Look at the declaration of the REGS union in **dos.h**, to see how these elements are used as union members.

Interrupts   An interrupt is essentially a signal from the program (or from elsewhere) to the CPU. When an interrupt is made, the current activity stops temporarily, while the new task is carried out. Each interrupt has a numerical code associated with it. This identifies the interrupt for the hardware, which then finds the code required to carry out the task specified by the interrupt.

There are two general ways of interrupting DOS via software. The first uses a function call to pass an interrupt number to the operating system. The number passed corresponds to the interrupt requested. For example, software interrupt 0x25 is a request to do an absolute disk read — that is, to read a particular section of the disk, regardless of whether this section is part of a file or not.

The other way to interrupt DOS is to call a special software interrupt, 0x21, which provides access to additional DOS services. This interrupt is sometimes known as the *function dispatcher,* since its job is to access the appropriate DOS service. To use interrupt 0x21, you need to pass another value, which corresponds to the DOS service that you want. For example, DOS service 0x36 tells you the amount of free disk space, and service 0x30 returns the DOS version number. The requested service number must be placed in a particular register before you call interrupt 0x21.

The examples we'll look at can all be accomplished using interrupt 0x21. Therefore, we'll discuss only the library function that gives you access to this interrupt. For more information on DOS interrupts and DOS services, consult more specialized books, such as Kris Jamsa's *DOS: The Complete Reference* (Osborne/McGraw-Hill, 1987) or Ray Duncan's *Advanced MS DOS* (Microsoft Press, 1986).

int intdos(union REGS *inreg, union REGS *outreg)   This function initiates a DOS software interrupt, 0x21, to request a specified operating system service. Before you call **intdos( )**, you need to put a value corresponding to the desired service in one of the members of the **inreg** union. You may also have to provide other information, depending on the service requested. In all cases, this information should be stored in the appropriate union member, *before* calling **intdos( )**. Note that **intdos( )** returns the value in register AX *after* the requested DOS service has done its work. Let's look at an example, to see how this works.

Determining Available Disk Space   The following program tells you how much storage space is available on the default drive of your computer. The function **get — free — space( )** calls **intdos( )** for software interrupt 0x21 and requests DOS service 0x36, which ascertains free disk space.

```
/* Program to determine available disk space.
   Program also illustrates use of DOS interrupts.
*/

#include <stdio.h>
#include <dos.h>

union REGS inreg, outreg;

main ()
{
        long get_free_space ( void);
        long result;

        result = get_free_space ();
        printf ( "%ld total bytes free\n", result);
}


long get_free_space ()
{
        long    sectors, clusters, bytes, clusters_per_drive;
        long    total_free, disk_capacity;

        /* prepare inreg with the required information.
           The AH byte contains the DOS service requested;
           the DL byte contains the drive about which you want information
        */
        inreg.h.ah = 0x36;      /* to ask for DOS service 0x36 */
        inreg.h.dl = 0x0;       /* to ask for current drive */

        /* Call the DOS interrupt 0x21, using intdos */
        intdos ( &inreg, &outreg);    /* to use interrupt 0x21 */
```

```
        /* results are stored in the registers.
           Total available space can be computed from:
           Sectors per cluster * Bytes per sector * Available Clusters
        */
        sectors = outreg.x.ax;       /* sectors per cluster returned in AX */
        clusters = outreg.x.bx;      /* available clusters returned in BX */
        bytes = outreg.x.cx;         /* bytes per sector returned in CX */

        /* The following number is not needed to compute FREE space.
           It is useful for computing disk capacity, however.
        */
        clusters_per_drive = outreg.x.dx;   /* clusters on drive in DX */

        printf ( "sectors == %d\n", sectors);
        printf ( "clusters == %d\n", clusters);
        printf ( "bytes == %d\n", bytes);
        printf ( "clusters_per_drive == %d\n", clusters_per_drive);
        total_free = bytes * sectors * clusters;
        disk_capacity = bytes * sectors * clusters_per_drive;
        printf ( "Total disk capacity == %ld\n", disk_capacity);
        printf ( "Total bytes free == %ld\n", total_free);
        return ( total_free);
}
```

This program produces the following output:

```
sectors == 4
clusters == 1204
bytes == 512
clusters_per_drive == 16318
Total disk capacity == 33419264
Total bytes free == 2465792
2465792 total bytes free
```

Once the DOS service has been performed, the data needed to compute available disk space are returned in members of the union **outreg**. The number of sectors per cluster is returned in the AX member; the number of free clusters is returned in BX; the number of bytes per sector is returned in CX; and the total number of clusters on the disk is returned in DX. (See your DOS documentation, or Jamsa's *DOS: The Complete Reference,* for more information about how disks are organized into sectors and clusters.)

Notice that bytes were manipulated before calling **intdos( )**, whereas entire register values are returned. This is not uncommon when dealing with DOS interrupts and services. Generally, the number of the DOS service requested will be stored in AH, the high-order byte of AX. Additional information needed by a particular service may be stored in other bytes.

Getting Date and Time   The following program adds three new functions to the preceding program. Two of these use DOS services to do their work; the third, **how_long( )** is used to compute the time elapsed between any starting and finishing points.

```
/* Program to get current date
   and to time how long it takes to do this 1000 times.
   Program also illustrates use of DOS interrupts.
*/

#include <stdio.h>
#include <dos.h>

union REGS inreg, outreg;

main ()
{
        long    get_free_space ( void);
        long    result;
        double get_time ( void);
        double how_long ( double, double);
        void    get_date ( int *, int *, int *);
        double start, finish;
        int     index, month, day, year;

        start = get_time ();
        for ( index = 0; index < 1000; index++)
        {
                get_date ( &month, &day, &year);
        }
        finish = get_time ();
        printf ( "%d / %d / %d\n", month, day, year);
        printf ( "%10.2lf seconds elapsed\n", how_long ( start, finish));
}


long get_free_space ()
{
        long    sectors, clusters, bytes, clusters_per_drive;
        long    total_free, disk_capacity;

        /* prepare inreg with the required information.
           The AH byte contains the DOS service requested;
           the DL byte contains the drive about which you want information
        */
        inreg.h.ah = 0x36;      /* to ask for DOS service 0x36 */
        inreg.h.dl = 0x0;       /* to ask for current drive */

        /* Call the DOS interrupt 0x21, using intdos */
        intdos ( &inreg, &outreg);      /* to use interrupt 0x21 */

        /* results are stored in the registers.
           Total available space can be computed from:
           Sectors per cluster * Bytes per sector * Available Clusters
        */
        sectors = outreg.x.ax;      /* sectors per cluster returned in AX */
        clusters = outreg.x.bx;     /* available clusters returned in BX */

        bytes = outreg.x.cx;        /* bytes per sector returned in CX */

        /* The following number is not needed to compute FREE space.
           It is useful for computing disk capacity, however.
        */
        clusters_per_drive = outreg.x.dx;   /* clusters on drive in DX */

        printf ( "sectors == %d\n", sectors);
        printf ( "clusters == %d\n", clusters);
        printf ( "bytes == %d\n", bytes);
        printf ( "clusters_per_drive == %d\n", clusters_per_drive);
        total_free = bytes * sectors * clusters;
        disk_capacity = bytes * sectors * clusters_per_drive;
        printf ( "Total disk capacity == %ld\n", disk_capacity);
        printf ( "Total bytes free == %ld\n", total_free);
        return ( total_free);
```

```
/* function to get current date, and to pass information back
   in three pieces : month, date, year.
   Notice that month and date are stored in bytes, whereas year
   is stored in a 16 bit register value.
*/
void get_date ( int *month, int *day, int *year)
{
        /* Ask for DOS service 0x2a */
        inreg.h.ah = 0x2a;

        /* Call DOS interrupt 0x21 */
        intdos ( &inreg, &outreg);

        *month = outreg.h.dh;   /* current month returned in DH (byte) */
        *day = outreg.h.dl;     /* current day returned in DL (byte) */
        *year = outreg.x.cx;    /* current year returned in CX (register) */
}



/* Function to get the number of seconds elapsed since midnight on the
   system clock.
*/
double get_time ()
{
        unsigned int hrs, mins, secs, hundredths;

        /* Request DOS service 0x2c */
        inreg.h.ah = 0x2c;

        /* Call interrupt 0x21 with the appropriate unions */
        intdos ( &inreg, &outreg);

        hrs = outreg.h.ch;      /* hours elapsed returned in CH */
        mins = outreg.h.cl;     /* minutes elapsed returned in CL */
        secs = outreg.h.dh;     /* seconds elapsed returned in DH */
        hundredths = outreg.h.dl; /* 1/100's seconds returned in DL */

        /* Total elapsed time (in seconds) =
           3600 (secs / hr)  * hrs +
           60 ( secs / min) * mins +
           1 ( secs / sec) * secs +
           .01 ( secs per 1/100th sec) * hundredths.
        */
        return ( (double) hrs * 3600.0 + (double) mins * 60.0 +
                 (double) secs + (double) hundredths / 100.0);
}



/* Function to compute the number of seconds elapsed between
   start and finish
*/
double how_long ( double start, double finish)
{
#define FULL_DAY 86400.0  /* seconds in a 24 hr day */

        /* start == first elapsed time measurment;
           finish == second elapsed time measurement.
           If start > finish then the time must have passed midnight
           between start and finish of process.
           In that case, a formula adjustment is necessary.
        */
        if ( start > finish)
                return ( FULL_DAY - start + finish);
        else
                return ( finish - start);
}
```

The function **get — date( )** is used to determine the current date on your machine. The DOS service to provide this information is number 0x2a. The service returns the information in three pieces, corresponding to month, day, and year. Notice that month and day are returned in bytes, whereas the year is returned in an entire 16-bit value. (This service also returns the day of the week in numerical form. This information is returned in AL, with Sunday == 0, and so on. You can modify the function so that it also provides this information to your program.)

The **get — time( )** function uses DOS service 0x2c to get information about the amount of time elapsed on the system clock since midnight. This amount is reported in units ranging from hours down to hundredths of a second. Again, each of these data is returned in a different byte: hours in CH, minutes in CL, seconds in DH, and hundredths of a second in DL.

To time something in your program, call **get — time( )** before starting the portion of the program that you want to time. This call assigns the amount of time elapsed up to the time the program portion begins. When the timed portion is finished, call **get — time( )** again. The difference between the values returned by the two calls to **get — time( )** represents the amount of time the program portion took, provided you were not running this program around midnight.

If your first time reading is before midnight and your second reading is after midnight, the results will be incorrect if you simply subtract one value from the other, because elapsed time starts from 0 again at midnight. The **how — long( )** function returns the amount of time elapsed between two calls to **get—time( )**, and corrects the computations for the cases where you cross the midnight boundary.

The program uses these three functions to determine how long it takes to call DOS for the current date 1,000 times.

Cautions When Using DOS Interrupts

Be careful when using DOS interrupts, especially if you are using interrupts or services that will actually change something on the disk. Before you use services that will reset the current date or write to particular parts of a disk, make certain that you understand exactly how the interrupt or service works, that you know exactly what values you want to change, and exactly what new values you want. You can get into lots of trouble if you are sloppy here. Again, the references mentioned earlier can provide more details about the interrupts and services.

io.h

This file, which is not specified in the Draft Proposed ANSI Standard, contains definitions and declarations for doing lower-level input and output, and file handling.

Familiar Functions

You've already learned about one of the functions declared in **io.h**: the **remove( )** function, which deletes the specified file from disk. The function takes a string argument, which specifies the file's disk name, and returns 0 if the file has been removed, or a negative value if it has not been removed.

New Functions

The following functions provide additional ways to use and change files:

int access (char *file—name, int mode)   This function determines whether the specified file, **file—name**, exists and whether the file can be accessed in the mode specified. The function returns 0 if the file can be accessed in the specified mode, and −1 otherwise.

File modes refer to the manner in which you can interact with the file. The most common modes are *read only, write only,* and *read and write*. In DOS all files can be read, so effectively there are only two modes: read only or read and write. You also can tell the **access( )** function simply to check whether the file exists.

The following listing shows how to call **access( )**:

```
/* Assume result is an int */
result = access ( "myfile.tex", 00);  /* just test for existence */
```

The **mode** argument can take the following values: 0x00 (check for existence only), 0x02 (check for write permission), 0x04 (check for read permission), or 0x06 (check for read and write permission).

int chmod(char *file＿name, int mode)   This function changes the file access setting associated with a particular file. For example, the function lets you make a read only file out of one that you could previously read and write. The function does *not* open the file; it only changes the file's status in the disk's directory.

As noted in the previous function, there are essentially three modes for interacting with a file: read only, write only, and read and write. The **chmod( )** function lets you specify a new setting for the file you pass as the first argument. The possible values are represented by manifest constants: S＿IWRITE, S＿IREAD, or S＿IREAD|S＿IWRITE. In DOS, the first and third are equivalent, since all DOS files have read permission.

The following statement shows how to call **chmod( )**:

```
/* Assume result is an int */
result = chmod ( "myfile.tex", S_IWRITE);
```

This statement will modify the status of **myfile.tex** so that it will be possible to write to the disk file with that name. Note that **chmod( )** returns 0 if the change was successful, and −1 if there was an error.

int rename (const char *old, const char *new)   This function lets you rename an existing disk file or directory, from **old** to **new**. The two arguments are strings that specify the file name, including any necessary path information. The function returns 0 if the name change is successful, and a nonzero value if there is an error. The **rename( )** function is not built into QuickC.

There are some restrictions on this function. First, **old** *must* exist, and **new** must *not* exist. If a file with the same name as **new** exists, the function will return an error value. Another restriction is that you can't transfer files from one drive to another. For example, you could not use this function to transfer a file from drive B: to drive A:.

The following listing illustrates the use of **rename( )**. The statement would effectively move the file **17.5** from the **\bk \src** directory to the **\bk** directory.

```
/* assume result is an int */
result = rename ( "\bk\src\17.5", "\bk\17.5");
```

Exercising Some of the io.h Functions

The following program shows how some of the functions declared in **io.h** work. The program checks whether a file named **zzzztest.io** exists. If not, the program creates such a file, opening it as write enabled. The program then changes the access mode to make this file read only. Notice that one consequence of this is that the DOS command to delete the file fails, as it does in the calls to **system( )**. The "Access denied" message comes from DOS.

Notice the way **access( )** is used in the tests. You are always looking for the negation of the value returned. This is because **access( )** returns a 0 if the outcome is as you expected. So, you need to make this 0 true, which you can do by negating it.

```c
/* Program to illustrate use of some functions declared in io.h */

#include <stdio.h>
#include <sys\types.h>      /* needed for chmod () */
#include <sys\stat.h>       /* needed for chmod () */
#include <io.h>
#include <stdlib.h>

main ()
{
        FILE *f_ptr;
        /* chmod ( "zzzztest.io2", S_IWRITE);
        exit ( 0); */

        if ( !access ( "zzzztest.io", 0x00))
                printf ( "File already exists.\n");
        else
        {
                f_ptr = fopen ( "zzzztest.io", "w");
                printf ( "File opened as write enabled.\n");
                fprintf ( f_ptr, "Hello there");
        }

        fcloseall();

        if ( !access ( "zzzztest.io", 0x02))
        {
                chmod ( "zzzztest.io", S_IREAD);
                printf ( "File changed to read only\n");
        }
        else
                printf ( "File is already read only.\n");

        printf ( "Trying to delete zzzztest.io, a read only file.\n");
        system ( "del zzzztest.io");

        printf ( "Renaming zzzztest.io to zzzztest.io2.\n");
        rename ( "zzzztest.io", "zzzztest.io2");
        printf ( "Trying to delete zzzztest.io2, a read only file.\n");
```

```
        system ( "del zzzztest.io2");
        if ( !access ( "zzzztest.io2", 0x04))
        {
                chmod ( "zzzztest.io2", S_IWRITE);
                printf ( "File changed to read / write\n");
        }

        if ( !access ( "zzzztest.io2", 0x00))
                printf ( "New file is in directory.\n");
        else
        {
        printf ( "New File NOT in directory, checking old name.\n");
                if ( !access ( "zzzztest.io", 0x00))
                        printf ( "Old file is in current directory.\n");
                else
                        printf ( "Old file NOT in directory, either.\n");
        }
    }
```

This program produces the following output:

```
File already exists.
File is already read only.
Trying to delete zzzztest.io, a read only file.
Access denied
Renaming zzzztest.io to zzzztest.io2.
Trying to delete zzzztest.io2, a read only file.
Access denied
File changed to read / write
New file is in directory.
```

Notice the preprocessor directives to include **sys\types.h** and **sys\stat.h**. These are needed for the second argument to **chmod( )**, because elements of S__IREAD, and so on are defined in these files.

You should remove the **zzzztest.io2** file, since we won't be using it anymore.

math.h

This file contains the declarations for many functions useful for mathematical work. The file also includes a structure declaration for **complex** numbers. The math functions are not built into QuickC.

Familiar Functions

You've seen a few of the functions declared in **math.h** in some of the example programs.

abs( )

labs( )   These functions compute the absolute value of an **int** and a **long**, respectively. Recall that the absolute value is the positive form of a number. Thus, **abs(5) == 5**, and **abs(−5) == 5**, as well.

pow( )   This function takes two arguments, raises the first argument to the power specified by the second argument, and returns the result as a **double.**

sqrt( )   This function returns the square root of the value passed in. The argument to **sqrt( )** must be 0 or greater. If you pass the function a negative value, the function will return 0 and will set **errno** to the appropriate error value.

New Functions

The following math functions represent only a few of the functions declared in the **math.h** header file:

double acos (double value)
double asin (double value)
double atan (double value)   These functions return the angle corresponding to the **value** passed to the function. For example, **acos(−1)** would return the angle whose cosine was −1. This angle is 180°, or π in radian measures. Saying that the arcos of (−1) is π means that the cosine of π equals −1.

The **acos( )** function can only handle arguments between −1 and 1, inclusive. This means the function will return values between 0 and π inclusive. If the argument is outside this range, the function returns a 0, sets the value of **errno** (a global variable containing a code for the last error encountered), and prints an error message to **stderr**.

Note that **asin( )** also handles only arguments between −1 and 1. In this case, the function returns a value between $-\pi/2$ and $\pi/2$. The **asin( )** function behaves just like **acos( )** in the case of an invalid argument.

The **atan( )** function returns a value between $-\pi/2$ and $\pi/2$, which corresponds to the angle whose tangent is the argument **value**.

The following program illustrates the use of these functions:

```
/* Program to illustrate use of inverse trigonometric functions */

#include <stdio.h>
#include <math.h>

#define INCREMENT    0.1

main ()
{
        double counter;

        printf ( "Value\t\tACos ()\t\tAsin ()\t\tATan ()\n");
        for ( counter = -1; counter <= 1; counter += INCREMENT)

                /* display acos, asin and atan for each value */
                printf ( "%5.3lf\t\t%5.3lf\t\t%5.3lf\t\t%5.3lf\n",
                        counter, acos ( counter), asin ( counter),
                        atan ( counter));
}
```

This program produces the following output:

Value	ACos ()	Asin ()	ATan ()
-1.000	3.142	-1.571	-0.785
-0.900	2.691	-1.120	-0.733
-0.800	2.498	-0.927	-0.675
-0.700	2.346	-0.775	-0.611
-0.600	2.214	-0.644	-0.540
-0.500	2.094	-0.524	-0.464
-0.400	1.982	-0.412	-0.381
-0.300	1.875	-0.305	-0.291
-0.200	1.772	-0.201	-0.197
-0.100	1.671	-0.100	-0.100
-0.000	1.571	-0.000	-0.000
0.100	1.471	0.100	0.100
0.200	1.369	0.201	0.197
0.300	1.266	0.305	0.291
0.400	1.159	0.412	0.381
0.500	1.047	0.524	0.464
0.600	0.927	0.644	0.540
0.700	0.795	0.775	0.611
0.800	0.644	0.927	0.675
0.900	0.451	1.120	0.733
1.000	0.000	1.571	0.785

double ceil (double value)
double floor (double value)   The **ceil( )** function returns the smallest integer value that is greater than or equal to **value**. The **floor( )** function returns the largest integer less than or equal to **value**.

The following program illustrates the use of **ceil( )** and **floor( )**. Notice what the *ceiling* and the *floor* of a negative number are.

```
/* Program to illustrate  ceil() and floor() functions */

#include <stdio.h>
#include <math.h>

#define MAX_STR    80
#define TOLERANCE 1e-7
#define TRUE       1
#define FALSE      0

main ()
{
        double cresult, fresult, val;
        int    non_zero ( double);
        char   str [ MAX_STR];

        printf ( "Value? (0 to stop) ");
        gets ( str);
        val = atof ( str);
        while ( non_zero ( val))
        {
                cresult = ceil ( val);
                fresult = floor ( val);
                printf ( "Ceiling == %10.2lf; floor == %10.2lf\n",
                        cresult, fresult);
                printf ( "Value? (0 to stop) ");
                gets ( str);
                val = atof ( str);
        }
}

/* return true if val differs from zero by more than a predefined amount. */
int non_zero ( double val)
{
        if ( (( val - 0.0) > TOLERANCE) || ((val - 0.0) < -TOLERANCE))
                return ( TRUE);
        else
                return ( FALSE);
}
```

The program produces the following session:

```
Value? (0 to stop) 3.50
Ceiling ==       4.00; floor ==       3.00
Value? (0 to stop) -3.50
Ceiling ==      -3.00; floor ==      -4.00
Value? (0 to stop) 0
```

double cos (double angle)
double sin (double angle)
double tan (double angle)   These functions return the sine, cosine, and tangent, respectively, of the specified angle. The specified angle is in radians. If the **angle** argument is large, the returned value may lose precision.

The following program illustrates the use of these functions:

```
/* Program to illustrate use of trigonometric functions */

#include <stdio.h>
#include <math.h>

#define INCREMENT   0.1

main ()
{
        double counter;

        printf ( "Value\t\tCos ()\t\tsin ()\t\tTan ()\n");
        for ( counter = -1; counter <= 1; counter += INCREMENT)

                /* display acos, asin and atan for each value */
                printf ( "%5.3lf\t\t%5.3lf\t\t%5.3lf\t\t%5.3lf\n",
                        counter, cos ( counter), sin ( counter),
                        tan ( counter));
}
```

This program produces the following output:

Value	Cos ()	Sin ()	Tan ()
-1.000	0.540	-0.841	-1.557
-0.900	0.622	-0.783	-1.260
-0.800	0.697	-0.717	-1.030
-0.700	0.765	-0.644	-0.842
-0.600	0.825	-0.565	-0.684
-0.500	0.878	-0.479	-0.546
-0.400	0.921	-0.389	-0.423
-0.300	0.955	-0.296	-0.309
-0.200	0.980	-0.199	-0.203
-0.100	0.995	-0.100	-0.100
-0.000	1.000	-0.000	-0.000
0.100	0.995	0.100	0.100
0.200	0.980	0.199	0.203
0.300	0.955	0.296	0.309
0.400	0.921	0.389	0.423
0.500	0.878	0.479	0.546
0.600	0.825	0.565	0.684
0.700	0.765	0.644	0.842
0.800	0.697	0.717	1.030
0.900	0.622	0.783	1.260
1.000	0.540	0.841	1.557

Other Files

Several other header files are included in your QuickC package. These include declarations for dozens of additional functions available in QuickC. It simply isn't possible to discuss them all here. You should look through the Run-Time library documentation on your own, however. You could save yourself a lot of work if you find a function that does what you want to do in your program.

Summary

This chapter has provided a brief discussion of some of the header files that come with your QuickC package, and of some of the functions, data types, and constants declared in these files. With this information, you're all set to explore C more thoroughly on your own. Happy programming!

ASCII CODES*

Table A-1 lists the ASCII codes for characters.

Table A-1. ASCII Character Codes

DEC	OCTAL	HEX	ASCII	DEC	OCTAL	HEX	ASCII
0	000	00	NUL	18	022	12	DC2
1	001	01	SOH	19	023	13	DC3
2	002	02	STX	20	024	14	DC4
3	003	03	ETX	21	025	15	NAK
4	004	04	EOT	22	026	16	SYN
5	005	05	ENQ	23	027	17	ETB
6	006	06	ACK	24	030	18	CAN
7	007	07	BEL	25	031	19	EM
8	010	08	BS	26	032	1A	SUB
9	011	09	HT	27	033	1B	ESC
10	012	0A	LF	28	034	1C	FS
11	013	0B	VT	29	035	1D	GS
12	014	0C	FF	30	036	1E	RS
13	015	0D	CR	31	037	1F	US
14	016	0E	SO	32	040	20	SPACE
15	017	0F	SI	33	041	21	!
16	020	10	DLE	34	042	22	"
17	021	11	DC1	35	043	23	#

*Reprinted from *The C Library* by Kris Jamsa, (Osborne/McGraw-Hill, 1985).

Table A-1.   ASCII Character Codes (*continued*)

DEC	OCTAL	HEX	ASCII	DEC	OCTAL	HEX	ASCII
36	044	24	$	82	122	52	R
37	045	25	%	83	123	53	S
38	046	26	&	84	124	54	T
39	047	27	'	85	125	55	U
40	050	28	(	86	126	56	V
41	051	29	)	87	127	57	W
42	052	2A	*	88	130	58	X
43	053	2B	+	89	131	59	Y
44	054	2C	,	90	132	5A	Z
45	055	2D	—	91	133	5B	[
46	056	2E	.	92	134	5C	\
47	057	2F	/	93	135	5D	]
48	060	30	0	94	136	5E	^
49	061	31	1	95	137	5F	—
50	062	32	2	96	140	60	'
51	063	33	3	97	141	61	a
52	064	34	4	98	142	62	b
53	065	35	5	99	143	63	c
54	066	36	6	100	144	64	d
55	067	37	7	101	145	65	e
56	070	38	8	102	146	66	f
57	071	39	9	103	147	67	g
58	072	3A	:	104	150	68	h
59	073	3B	;	105	151	69	i
60	074	3C	<	106	152	6A	j
61	075	3D	=	107	153	6B	k
62	076	3E	>	108	154	6C	l
63	077	3F	?	109	155	6D	m
64	100	40	@	110	156	6E	n
65	101	41	A	111	157	6F	o
66	102	42	B	112	160	70	p
67	103	43	C	113	161	71	q
68	104	44	D	114	162	72	r
69	105	45	E	115	163	73	s
70	106	46	F	116	164	74	t
71	107	47	G	117	165	75	u
72	110	48	H	118	166	76	v
73	111	49	I	119	167	77	w
74	112	4A	J	120	170	78	x
75	113	4B	K	121	171	79	y
76	114	4C	L	122	172	7A	z
77	115	4D	M	123	173	7B	{
78	116	4E	N	124	174	7C		
79	117	4F	O	125	175	7D	}
80	120	50	P	126	176	7E	~
81	121	51	Q	127	177	7F	DEL

*Reprinted from *The C Library* by Kris Jamsa, (Osborne/McGraw-Hill, 1985).

B

Building Libraries in QuickC

One of C's most important features is the ease with which it allows you to build and use *function libraries*, precompiled collections of functions that you can use in you programs. The advantage of using such libraries, as opposed to having the source code for the library functions in your program, is in the time saved because the compiler doesn't have to compile the functions every time you make changes to your program.

QuickC is particularly flexible in the way it lets you work with libraries. You can build two types of libraries in QuickC. The first type, *Quick libraries,* are built for use when you want to run your program *inside* the QuickC environment, as opposed to building an executable version of your program.

That is, Quick libraries are used when you want to compile your program to memory while inside QuickC, and then run the program. Quick libraries have the extension **.qlb**. You don't need to use a Quick library if you plan to compile the function to executable code each time — that is, if you're going to create an **.exe** file whenever you compile. Quick libraries can only be used with QuickC.

The second type of library is a *stand-alone library,* which contains precompiled functions that can be linked into your program when you're building an executable version. Such libraries generally have the extension **.lib**. Stand-alone libraries have the same format as the libraries included with QuickC or Microsoft C 5.0.

In this appendix, you'll learn how to build both types of libraries. You'll build a Quick library containing Run-Time library functions that are used in our example programs, but that are not built into QuickC. Chapter 6 of the *QuickC Programmer's Guide* contains a table of the functions built into QuickC. As you'll notice, several of the functions we've used — including **rand( )**, **pow( )**, and **fgetc( )** — are not built into QuickC. In the next section, you'll see how to build a Quick library file, **qcstuff.qlb**, that contains these functions. (This library has been mentioned in earlier chapters.) You must build the **qcstuff.qlb** library yourself; it is not part of QuickC.

You'll also learn how to build a stand-alone library, and how to link this library into your programs. We'll only be looking at a small number of the possibilities here; read the discussion in your *QuickC Programmer's Guide* for details.

Building Quick Libraries

We'll look at the steps involved in building a Quick library by developing one that includes the functions used in the example programs for this book.

To create a Quick library for a program or programs, you need to do three things:

1. Create a source file that includes calls to the functions you want to include in the Quick library.

2. Compile and link this source file to create a compiled version of the file with the extension **.qlb**.

3. Load the Quick library when you want to run your program within QuickC.

Creating the Source File

The source file you create just needs a **main( )** function that contains calls to each of the functions you want. The following listing represents the source file used to build a file, **qcstuff.qlb**, usable for compiling the programs in Chapters 1 through 16 within the QuickC environment.

```
/* Source file containing calls to the functions needed for
   example program in Chapter 1 -- 16.
   File is eventually compiled and linked to create qcstuff.qlb.
*/

#include <math.h>
#include <stdio.h>

main ()
{
        char ch;
        double dbl1, dbl2;

        rand();
        srand();
        fgetchar();
        fputchar( ch);
        _ftol();
        pow ( dbl1, dbl2);
        sqrt ( dbl1);
}
```

As you can see, the format for this file is simple. The entire "program" consists of calls to the desired functions. The program does nothing with the results of these function calls.

The basic strategy is to get QuickC to link the desired functions into a file that really does nothing with them. The resulting object file is then transformed into a **.qlb** file having the format required for QuickC to be able to use these functions when you compile and run your program within QuickC.

Compiling and Linking
to a .qlb File

Once you've created your source file, you need to create a Quick library from it. The following line contains a batch file you can use to build the file **qcstuff.qlb**.

```
qcl /AM \qc\lib\quicklib %1.c /Fe%1.qlb /link /Q
```

Let's look at the elements in this rather long command line. The first "word" on the line, **qcl**, lets you compile and link files outside of the QuickC environment. The **qcl** program, which is included with QuickC, compiles and (if you wish) links the specified files without bringing you into the QuickC window environment.

The /AM specifies that a medium memory model is to be used. This memory model is necessary for a Quick library. Compiler and linker options are case-sensitive in QuickC and in Microsoft C 5.0, partly because of the large number of options available.

▶**REMEMBER**   Quick libraries *must* use a medium memory model.

The purpose of **\qc \inc \quicklib** is to tell the **qcl** program where the **quicklib.obj** file is to be found. The **quicklib.obj** file is needed for building Quick libraries. If you set up your QuickC files using the default directories, you only need to specify **quicklib** here — that is, you don't need to specify an entire path.

The next word (**%1.c**) specifies the file to be compiled. The **%1** is a placeholder in this batch file, just as it would be in a **printf( )** string argument. When you call this batch file, you need to specify **qcstuff** as a command line argument. You could just as well write **qcstuff** instead of **%1** in this file, thereby making the batch file capable of building just the one Quick library, **qcstuff.qlb**. The **.c** extension is necessary when specifying a file name here.

The /**Fe%1.qlb** specifies that the "run" file is to have the same name as your source file (the name substituted for **%1**), and the extension **.qlb**. Ordinarily, when you compile a file to become a stand-alone program, the resulting file will have the extension **.exe**, since this is the extension DOS expects. However, in this case, you don't want DOS to deal with the file; you want QuickC to run it. QuickC expects the **.qlb** extension.

The /**link** command invokes the linker, and the /**Q** option tells it to create a Quick library out of the compiled file. This Quick library file will have the format appropriate for use by QuickC.

You can accomplish the same thing with a two-step process. The following listing shows the two command lines needed:

```
qcl /c /AM qcstuff.c
link \qc\lib\quicklib.obj + qcstuff.obj, qcstuf.qlb, , /Q;
```

The first line invokes the **qcl** program as in the earlier example. The /**c** option specifies that you just want to compile, not to link. The /**AM** option again specifies the medium memory model, and the **qcstuff.c** tells **qcl** what file you want to compile.

The second command line invokes the linker. The lengthy expression, **\qc \libquicklib.obj** + **qcstuff.obj**, tells the linker what compiled files to link together. Such files will generally have the extension **.obj**, but they may also be stand-alone libraries — that is, **.lib** files.

The **qcstuff.qlb** argument specifies the "run" file you want the linker to create, just as in the one-line version. Notice that linker parameters, or fields, are separated by commas. This tells the linker where one type of information, or set of parameters (object files, for example) stops and the next type (run files, for example) starts.

Two commas with nothing between them indicate that the linker can use its default values for that field. In this case, the space between **qcstuff.qlb,** and the next comma indicates that the linker can use its default names for a file know as the *map* file, which the linker can create. (Such a file contains information about where in the module the segments of a program are to be found. For most purposes, you won't need this file.) By default, in this case, the linker would write this information to **qcstuff.map**.

You could also specify additional libraries for the linker to search for routines needed in other modules. In our case, there were no other libraries that needed to be searched. Ordinarily, the linker would prompt for additional libraries if none were specified. The semicolon suppresses this prompt.

Finally, the /**Q** option tells the linker to create a Quick library. Linker options can be included just about anywhere on the command line.

The commands in the previous listing produce three files in addition to the **qcstuff.c** file that started it all: **qcstuff.obj** (created by the compiler), **qcstuff.map**, and **qcstuff.qlb** (created by the linker). The following pair of command lines would have accomplished the same thing, except that no **.map** file would be built.

```
qcl /c /AM qcstuff.c
link /Q \qc\lib\quicklib.obj + qcstuff.obj, qcstuf.qlb;
```

Notice that the /**Q** option has been moved to an earlier part of the line. This makes no difference, but the semicolon immediately after the name of the run file is important. This tells the linker not to worry about the remaining two fields: map file and additional libraries. The result is that no **.map** file is created and the linker doesn't ask about whether to search additional library files.

Loading the Quick Library

Once you've created your Quick library, you're ready to use it in any programs that rely on more than the functions built into QuickC. To start QuickC with your Quick library loaded, use the **/l** option, followed by the name of the Quick library file, as in the following command line. This line will let you compile the file **srcfile** to memory, once you're in QuickC, even though this program uses more than the built-in QuickC functions.

```
qc /lqcstuff srcfile
```

Building Stand-alone Libraries

You can use the Microsoft Library Manager, **lib**, to build stand-alone libraries. Such libraries consist of compiled routines that can be added to any program you're building and can be used in the program. Once they are in compiled form, the compiler need not process these routines each time you compile a program that uses them.

For example, the following listing collects some of the more generally applicable functions we've defined in this book. We'll build a library containing these functions; you can link this library when you build any program that uses them.

```
/* File containing commonly used functions.
   File is used to illustrate how to build a stand-alone library.
*/

#include <stdio.h>
#include <dos.h>

#define NULL_CHAR     '\0'
#define FALSE         0
#define TRUE          1
#define TOLERANCE     1e-12
#define INVALID_VAL   -99999.999
```

```
/* double get_time ()
   Returns the number of seconds elapsed on system clock since midnight.
   NOTE : Assumes <dos.h> (Microsoft) or equivalent.
   USAGE : time_elapsed = get_time ();
*/
double get_time ()
{
        double hrs, mins, secs, hundredths;
        union  REGS inregs, outregs;

        /* Request DOS service 0x2c */
        inregs.h.ah = 0x2c;

        /* call interrupt 0x21 with DOS service request # 0x2c */
        intdos ( &inregs, &outregs);

        hrs = (double) outregs.h.ch;        /* hrs elapsed returned in CH */
        mins = (double) outregs.h.cl;       /* mins elapsed returned in CL */
        secs = (double) outregs.h.dh;       /* secs elapsed returned in DH */
        hundredths = (double) outregs.h.dl; /* 1/100's secs returned in DL */

        /* Total elapsed time (in seconds) =
            3600 (secs / hr)  * hrs +
            60 ( secs / min) * mins +
            1 ( secs / sec) * secs +
            .01 ( secs per 1/100th sec) * hundredths.
        */
        return ( hrs * 3600.0 + mins * 60.0 + secs + hundredths / 100.0);
}


/* double how_long ( double start, double finish)
   Returns the time elapsed between finish and start.
   Routine compensates for tasks that started before and finished
   after midnight.
   USAGE :  time_required = how_long ( start, finish);
*/
double how_long ( double start, double finish)

{
#define FULL_DAY 86400.0  /* seconds in a 24 hr day */

        /* start == first elapsed time measurement;
           finish == second elapsed time measurement.
           If start > finish then the time must have passed midnight
           between start and finish of process.
           In that case, a formula adjustment is necessary.
        */
        if ( start > finish)
                return ( FULL_DAY - start + finish);
        else
                return ( finish - start);
}


/* void make_str_lower ( char *str)
   Convert a string to lowercase characters
   USAGE :  make_str_lower ( my_str);
*/
void make_str_lower ( char *str)
{
        int index;

        for ( index = 0; str [ index] != NULL_CHAR; index++)
                str [ index] = tolower ( str [ index]);
}


/* void make_str_upper ( char *str)
```

```
    Convert a string to uppercase characters
    USAGE :  make_str_upper ( my_str);
*/
void make_str_upper ( char *str)
{
        int index;

        for ( index = 0; str [ index] != NULL_CHAR; index++)
                str [ index] = toupper ( str [ index]);
}


/* int non_zero ( double val)
    Return true if val differs from zero by more than a predefined amount.
    USAGE : test_result = non_zero ( val_to_test);
*/
int non_zero ( double val)
{
        if ( (( val - 0.0) > TOLERANCE) || ((val - 0.0) < -TOLERANCE))
                return ( TRUE);
        else
                return ( FALSE);
}


/* double safe_division ( double numer, double denom)
    Divide num by denom, checking for division by zero before doing so.
    Return quotient or a default value ( INVALID_VAL) on division by zero.
    USAGE : quotient = safe_division ( num, den);
*/
double safe_division ( double numer, double denom)
{
        int non_zero ( double);

        if ( non_zero ( denom))
                return ( numer / denom);
        else
                return ( INVALID_VAL);
}


/* void swap_dbl ( double *first, double *second)
    Exchange the values stored in *first and *second.
    USAGE : swap_dbl ( first, second);
*/
void swap_dbl ( double *first, double *second)
{
        double temp;          /* to store one of the values during swap */

        temp = *first;
        *first = *second;
        *second = temp;
}


/* void swap_int ( int *first, int *second)
    Exchange the values stored in *first and *second.
    USAGE : swap_int ( first, second);
*/
void swap_int ( int *first, int *second)
{
        int temp;        /* to store one of the values during swap */

        temp = *first;
        *first = *second;
        *second = temp;
}
```

```
/* double zero_one_rand ()
   Returns a pseudorandom value between  0 and 1, inclusive.
   USAGE : pseudo = zero_one_rand ();
*/
double zero_one_rand ()
{
#define  MAX_VAL  32767.0        /* NOTE: defined as floating point type */
         int   rand ( void);     /* returns a pseudorandom integer */
         int   rand_result;

         rand_result = rand ();  /* get a pseudorandom integer */
         return ( rand_result / MAX_VAL);
}
```

To build a stand-alone library, you need to do two things:

1. Compile the source file(s) to an **.obj** file.

2. Build a **.lib** library file from this object file, using the library manager program, **lib**.

A batch file containing the following two command lines will let you build a stand-alone library file from a source file. In the discussion, assume the file containing the preceding listings is named **utils.c**.

```
qcl /c %1.c
lib %1.lib +%1.obj;
```

The first line invokes the **qcl** program to compile the source file specified in the command line argument when starting the batch file. In our case, this argument would be **utils**, without an extension (since the extension is added in the batch file). You would include this argument on your command line when you invoked the batch file.

The output from the first line would be a file named **utils.obj**. The second line in the batch file builds the stand-alone library. The first field specifies the name of a library file to be modified. If no file with this name exists, the library manager will create a new one, which is what we want in this case. The second field specifies that the library manager should add (+) the contents of the object file specified (in this case, **utils**) to the **.lib** file. The semicolon again indicates that the program should not look for additional fields or options. (See Chapter 10 of the *QuickC Programmer's Guide* for details on these additional fields.) The outcome from executing this command line is that a file named **utils.lib** is created.

Using a Stand-alone Library

Once the **utils.lib** file has been created, you can link it into any programs you want to build that use functions in this library. For example, suppose you had the following program, which uses several of the functions in **utils.lib**:

```
/* Program to generate pseudorandom values betwen 0 and 1, and
   to keep track of the current maximum ratio between successive values.
   Program also illustrates use of stand-alone library files.
*/

#include <stdio.h>
#define MAX_TRIALS 20
main ()
{
        double first, second, ratio, max_ratio = 0.0;
        double start, finish;
        double zero_one_rand ( void), get_time ( void);
        double how_long ( double, double);
        double safe_division ( double, double);
        int    index;

        start = get_time ();
        first = zero_one_rand ();
        for ( index = 1; index <= MAX_TRIALS; index++)
        {
                second = zero_one_rand ();
                ratio = safe_division ( first, second);
                printf ( "%10.4lf\n", ratio);
                if ( ratio > max_ratio)
                {
                        printf ( "old max == %10.4lf;  new max == %10.4lf\n",
                                max_ratio, ratio);
                        max_ratio = ratio;
                }
                ratio = safe_division ( second, first);
                printf ( "%10.4lf\n", ratio);
                if ( ratio > max_ratio)
                {
                        printf ( "old max == %10.4lf;  new max == %10.4lf\n",
                                max_ratio, ratio);
                        max_ratio = ratio;
                }
                first = second;
        }
        finish = get_time ();
        printf ( "%10.2lf seconds\n", how_long ( start, finish));
}
```

The following command line would let you compile this program, which we'll call **ratios.c**, linking in the **utils.lib** library while creating the executable file.

```
qcl ratios.c /Feratios1.exe· /link utils.lib;
```

This line says to compile the file **ratios.c**, ultimately writing the executable file, **ratios.exe**. The linking instructions specify that the library file, **utils.lib** is to be searched for any functions not found in the **ratios.obj** file or in the standard libraries.

The resulting **ratios.exe** file behaves just the same as if the program had been built out of a large source file containing the functions included in both **ratios.c** and in **utils.c**, or out of two source files compiled separately or compiled together by including an instruction to read the contents of **utils.c** while compiling **ratios.c** The difference is in the compilation time required. In this case, compiling just **ratios.c**, then linking in **utils.lib**, is almost 20% faster than working with the source files alone.

You can explore additional options and ways of using the linker on your own. One thing to notice is that we didn't include the /**AM** option. By default, QuickC compiles with a small memory mode. The resulting files are different than they would be if they had been compiled with a medium memory model. When you link in libraries, make sure the libraries and the source files are compiled under the same memory models.

Summary

In this appendix, we've looked at two ways to use precompiled files to make program development quicker and more convenient. Quick libraries let you compile and run your programs within QuickC, which has the advantages of speed and ease of modification. This means you can create, compile, and revise without ever leaving QuickC—one of the nicest features of the software.

Once you've got the program working the way you want it to, you can compile it to an executable file. During this process you'll often want to save time by linking in precompiled libraries that have been tested, and can now be used in any of your programs. This approach makes the compilation process faster, and also gives you flexibility for building modular programs. By collecting related functions in libraries and then linking these libraries into the programs you're building, you can make your programs smaller (since only the libraries for needed functions will be linked in) and also make your programming tools more widely usable.

C

QuickC Command Summary

This appendix summarizes the commands and options available in QuickC. In the commands, special notation is used in a few places.

The vertical bar, |, means "or," so that 0 | 1 means "0 or 1," as in the command to set warning levels for **qcl.exe**, for which any of the following would be valid:

```
qcl first /W0

qcl first /W1

qcl first /W2

qcl first /W3
```

Material between curly braces, {}, is optional, as in the command to add watch variables. This material may be repeated more than once. Both of the following would be valid watch variable selections:

```
val
val; even
```

Angle brackets, < and >, around material mean that you are to provide information of the sort specified between these brackets. Do not include the brackets in your text. For example, the first of the following calls to QuickC is valid, but the second call is not valid:

```
/* the following call is valid */
qc /lqcstuff
/* the following call is NOT valid */
qc /l<qcstuff>
```

Commands for Calling QuickC

Start the QuickC program   **qc**

You can use the following commands as command-line arguments when you invoke QuickC—that is, when you use the **qc** command.

Start QuickC in black-and-white mode   **/b**

```
qc /b
```

Start QuickC when using a color graphics adapter **/g**

```
qc /g
```

Use as many screen lines as possible, given the
display adapter being used   **/h**

```
qc /h
```

Load a Quick library for use when compiling to
memory   **/l**<*library name*>

```
qc /lqcstuff
```

Start QuickC with a source file as the working file <*file name*>

```
qc first
```

Useful Commands in the QuickC Environment

The following predefined keys are very convenient, especially in dire situations. The on-line help feature provides a brief listing of the QuickC commands. The exit command can get you out of many tough situations.

On-line help	F1
On-line help about a C keyword or Run-Time library function (assumes cursor is on keyword or function name)	SHIFT-F1
Exit from QuickC	ALT-F X

Editing Commands

The following commands are available while editing a file. Many of these commands accomplish the same thing as QuickC menu options, eliminating the need to call up a menu.

Movement Commands

Move up one line	UP ARROW or CTRL-E
Move down one line	DOWN ARROW or CTRL-X
Move right one character	RIGHT ARROW or CTRL-D
Move left one character	LEFT ARROW or CTRL-S

Move right one word	CTRL-RIGHT ARROW
	or
	CTRL-F
Move left one word	CTRL-LEFT ARROW
	or
	CTRL-A
Move to top of screen	CTRL-Q E
Move to bottom of screen	CTRL-Q X
Move to beginning of line	HOME
	or
	CTRL-Q S
Move to end of line	END
	or
	CTRL-Q D
Move to beginning of file	CTRL-HOME
	or
	CTRL-Q R
Move to end of file	CTRL-END
	or
	CTRL-Q C
Move to next error	SHIFT-F3
Move to previous error	SHIFT-F4
Scroll up one line	CTRL-W
Scroll down one line	CTRL-Z
Scroll up one screen, or window	PGUP
	or
	CTRL-R
Scroll down one screen, or window	PGDN
	or
	CTRL-C
Scroll left one window	CTRL-PGUP
Scroll right one window	CTRL-PGDN
Find text to be specified	CTRL-Q F
Find next occurrence of text just found	F3
Find selected text	CTRL-\
Find and change text to be specified	CTRL-Q A

The following command is available after CTRL-Q A has been specified:

Switch to **Change To** text box   ALT-T

Selection Commands

Select preceding character	SHIFT-LEFT ARROW
Select current character	SHIFT-RIGHT ARROW
Select preceding "word"	SHIFT-CTRL-LEFT ARROW
Select current "word"	SHIFT-CTRL-RIGHT ARROW
Select preceding line	SHIFT-UP ARROW
Select current line	SHIFT-DOWN ARROW
Select to beginning of file	SHIFT-CTRL-PGUP
Select to end of file	SHIFT-CTRL-PGDN

Insertion Commands

Insert text from Clipboard	SHIFT-INS
Insert line below current line	CTRL-B
Insert line above current line	CTRL-N
Insert line deleted using CTRL-Y	SHIFT-INS
Insert tab at current cursor position	TAB
	or
	CTRL-I
Copy selected text to Clipboard	CTRL-INS

Deletion Commands

Delete character at current cursor position	DEL
	or
	CTRL-G
Delete preceding character	BACKSPACE
	or
	CTRL-H
Delete to end of current word	CTRL-T
Delete current line	CTRL-Y
Delete to end of current line	CTRL-Q Y

Delete selected text without saving in Clipboard   DEL
Delete selected text, saving in Clipboard   SHIFT-DEL
Delete control character   CTRL-P<*character*>

Miscellaneous Commands

Toggle between overtype and insert modes   INS
                                                      or
                                                      CTRL-V
Mark section of text   CTRL-K 0 | 1 | 2 | 3
Jump to marked section of text   CTRL-Q 0 | 1 | 2 | 3
Find matching left brace   CTRL-{
Find matching left bracket   CTRL-[
Find matching left angle bracket   CTRL-<
Find matching left parenthesis   CTRL-(
Find matching right brace   CTRL-}
Find matching right bracket   CTRL-]
Find matching right angle bracket   CTRL->
Find matching right parenthesis   CTRL-)
Move to next tabstop   TAB
Move to previous tabstop   SHIFT-TAB

Menu Commands

This section summarizes the commands and options available through QuickC menus. These commands are grouped by menu.

Files Menu (ALT-F)

The File menu serves to create, open, and save files of various sorts. It also includes miscellaneous options for getting access to DOS and printing a file.

File Manipulation Commands

Create new file	ALT-F N
Open existing file	ALT-F O
Open file edited before current file	F2
	or
	ALT-F F
Merge specified file into work file at current cursor location	ALT-F M
Save current file	ALT-F S
Save current file under a new name, leaving original file intact	ALT-F A

Program List Commands

The following commands let you create, modify, and delete program list files, which contain the names of all the source files that make up a large program.

Create a program list for current file	ALT-F L
Edit program list for current file	ALT-F E

The following options and commands are available when either of the preceding options has been set. That is, the following assume either ALT-F L or ALT-F E.

File name for program list (**.mak**) file	*<file name>*

Once QuickC has created or opened the specified program list file, the following commands can be used:

File name to be added to program list	*<file name>*
Add file name to list, if not present, or remove name from list, if present	RETURN
Select Add/Remove option, if not currently selected	ALT-A
Clear program list	ALT-C
Save program list	ALT-S
Clear, or delete, program list for current file	ALT-F C

Miscellaneous File Commands

Print current file	ALT-F P
Suspend QuickC, exit temporarily to DOS shell	ALT-F D

Edit Menu (ALT-E)

This menu makes it possible to modify the contents of the working file and possibly of other files as well.

Clear, or delete, text; do not copy to Clipboard	DEL or ALT-E E
Cut, or delete, text; copy text to Clipboard	SHIFT-DEL or ALT-E T
Copy text to Clipboard; do not delete from file	CTRL-INS or ALT-E C
Paste text from Clipboard to Target (requires text in Clipboard)	SHIFT-INS or ALT-E P
Make working file read only	ALT-E R
Undo last action on current line	ALT-BACKSPACE or ALT-E U

View Menu (Alt-V)

This menu lets you see various files associated with your current program file. It also lets you change the way QuickC appears on your screen.

View a program source file (that is, a file on the program list)	ALT-V S
View an include file for the current program	ALT-V I
View display format options	ALT-V O

View output screen   F4
                                                    or
                                                    ALT-V T
Open/Close Error window   ALT-V E

Search Menu (ALT-S)

This menu lets you find and modify specified text, find the definition of a
function in the source file, and so on.

Find specified text   ALT-S F
Find and change specified text   ALT-S C

The following all work with the preceding options. Each of the
following options toggles:

Require self-standing word   ALT-W
Require uppercase or lowercase matching   ALT-M
Regular Expression   ALT-R

The following commands assume the ALT-S C option has been
specified:

Switch to **Change To** text box   ALT-T
Change all occurrences of specified text, with-
    out verifying   ALT-C
Set default action to skip current occurrence
    of text   S
Set default action to change current occur-
    rence of text   C

The following special characters are allowed in regular expressions,
and assume that ALT-R has been specified:

Match any single character appearing in
    specified position   .
Match one or more occurrences of the char-
    acter preceding *   <character>*
Treat the next character literally   \
Match if specified phrase appears at *end* of
    line   <text>$
Match if specified phrase appears at
    beginning of line   ^<text>

Match occurrence of any one of the characters between the brackets	[<*text*>]

The following are special characters that can be used within the square brackets:

To search for any ASCII values between those of the starting and ending characters, use "-"	[<*char*>-<*char*>]
To match any characters *except* those listed between the brackets, use '^' in regular expressions	[^<*text*>]
Repeat search for last text found	F3 or ALT-S R
Find marked, or selected, text	CTRL - \ or ALT-S S
Find function definition	ALT-S U
Find next error	SHIFT-F3 or ALT-S N
Find previous error	SHIFT-F4 or ALT-S P

Run menu (ALT-R)

This menu lets you compile and run your program, or continue running your program if it has been stopped for some reason.

Start compilation and execution	SHIFT-F5 or ALT-R S
Continue interrupted program execution	F5 or ALT-R N

Restart interrupted program execution at next
statement   ALT-R R
Set compile-time options   ALT-R C

Compile-time options include the following. All these options
assume ALT-R C has been selected.

Warning Levels (0 through 3)   UP ARROW
                                                 or
                                                 DOWN ARROW

The following five commands toggle:

Compile for subsequent debugging   D
Compile with pointer checks   P
Compile with stack checks   S
Allow Microsoft language extensions L
Optimize for speed   Z

The following four options for specifying output from compilation
process are mutually exclusive:

Compile to object file   O
Compile to memory   M
Compile to executable file   X
Syntax check only   Y

In the Compiler option dialog box, the following additional commands are allowed:

Search in additional paths for include   I
                                          or
                                          ALT-I
Specify definitions for current compilation   D
                                          or
                                          ALT-D

In the Compiler option dialog box, the following commands, in
addition to Cancel, are valid:

Build program   B
                                         or
                                         RETURN

| Compile file | C |
| Rebuild all | R |

| Set run-time options | ALT-R O |

The following options all assume ALT-R O has been selected:

Specify information to be passed to program on command line for use in programs just being compiled in memory	*<command line information>*
Specify memory to allocate for global and static program data (*near data*)	ALT-N
Specify amount of memory to allocate for local variables (stack)	ALT-S

Debug menu (ALT-D)

This menu lets you set up your program to watch changes in the variables of interest to you, and to step through the program to watch these values change.

The following options both toggle:

| Turn program tracing on/off | ALT-D T |
| Turn screen swapping on/off | ALT-D S |

The following options all assume the program has been compiled with the Debug compiler option turned on:

| Add one or more watch variables | ALT-D A |

The following assumes ALT-D A has been selected:

| Specify the watch variable(s) to be added | *<name>*{;*<name>*;} |

You can also specify the output format for the watch variables, using the following specifiers. These specifiers are included after the watch variable name, and are separated by a comma from this name.

Signed decimal integer	d
	or
	i
Unsigned decimal integer	u
Unsigned octal integer	o
Hexadecimal integer	x
Real number in floating point format	f
Real number in scientific notation format	e
Real number in either floating point or scientific notation format, whichever is more compact	g
Single character	c
String (characters up to first null character)	s
Delete the last watch variable set	SHIFT-F2
	or
	ALT-D E
Clear all watch variables currently set	ALT-D L
Toggle breakpoint on/off	F9
	or
	ALT-D B
Clear all breakpoints currently set	ALT-D C

The following keyboard commands will let you step through the program in the debugger:

Execute the next program statement, tracing execution through the function	F8
Execute the next program statement, tracing execution around the function	F10
Execute the program until it reaches the current cursor position	F7
Execute program to next breakpoint	F5
Display the current output screen	F4

Compiling and Linking Outside of QuickC

The following commands and options can be used with the **qcl.exe** program. Defaults are in parentheses. Case is important for many of these options.

Get help about **qcl** commands	/ help
Set warning level (/ W1)	/ W0 | 1 | 2 | 3
Compile only to object file; no linking (off)	/ c
Debug mode (off)	/ Zq *and* Zi *and* Zd
Pointer checks on (off)	/ Zr
Stack checks off (on)	/ Gs
Syntax check only (off)	/ Zs
Language extensions off (on)	/ Za
Optimize for speed / time (off)	/ Ot
Optimize loops (off)	/ Ol
Optimize for everything (off)	/ Ox
Specify directories to search for include files	/ I<*path name*>
Do not search usual places for include files (off)	/ X
Specify definitions for current program / run (none)	/ D<*definitions*>
Set stack size (0x400)	/ F <*hexadecimal value*>
Specify name of executable file to be created (same name as main source file, **.exe** extension)	/ Fe<*file name*>
Specify name of map file to be created (none)	/ Fm<*file name*>
Specify name of object file to be created (same name as main source file, **.obj** extension)	/ Fo<*file name*>
Specify language underlying function-calling and naming conventions used by program (for mixed-language programming)	/ Gc fortran | pascal | cdecl

Memory Models

The following commands let you specify the memory models and library iles to use:

Use small memory model — one 64K data segment, one 64K code segment (default for **qcl**)	/ AS
Use medium memory model — one 64K data segment, multiple 64K code segments (default for **qc**)	/ AM
Use compact memory model — multiple 64K data segments, one 64K code segment	/ AC
Use large memory model — multiple 64K data segments, multiple 64K code segments	/ AL
Specify size threshold for including data structure in a new data segment	/ Gt{<*number*>}
Emulate 8087 or 80287 for floating point math (default)	/ FPi
Generate code for an 8087 or 80287 for floating point math	/ FPi87
Use instruction set for 8086 (default)	/ G0
Use instruction set for 80286	/ G2
Pack structure members	/ Zp
Do not use the default library or libraries	/ Zl

Controlling the Preprocessor

The following commands let you use the preprocessor and also save files after the preprocessor has finished with them.

Preserve comments in source files (observe case of command)	/ C

Write preprocessed output to a disk file	/ P
Write preprocessed output to **stdout**	/ E
Write preprocessed output to disk file *and* **stdout**	/ EP
Undefine the specified predefined name	/ U *<name>*
Undefine all predefined names	/ u

Controlling the Linker

The following commands are available when linking files to build a program or library. Note that linker options are not case-sensitive. For the following commands, you don't necessarily have to write out the entire command. The capitalized characters are necessary; the lowercase characters can be omitted when referring to the option.

Get help about linker options	/ HElp
Pause for disk swap before writing **.exe** file	/ PAUse
Display information during linking	/ Information
Don't prompt if linker can't find a file	/ Batch
Do not search in default libraries	/ NODefaultlibrary-search
Create a map file	/ Map
Include line numbers in output file	/ LInenumbers
Prepare executable file for use with Codeview	/ COdeview
Do not ignore case	/ NOIgnorecase
Create a Quick library	/ Quicklib
Make executable file as small and accessible as possible	/ Exepack
Optimize use of far calls to functions	/ Farcalltranslation
Do not optimize use of far calls to functions	/ NOFarcall-translation
Pack contiguous program segments	/ PACkcode
Do not pack contiguous program segments	/ NOPackcode
Order program segments using Microsoft high-level language defaults	/ DOsseg

The following linker options let you control various values relating to the program being compiled.

Maximum number of program segments
(default == 128)   / SEgments: *<number>*
Maximum amount of space needed by
program in memory   / CParmaxalloc: *<number>*
Maximum stack size (in bytes)   / STack:*<number>*

D

Features of QuickC and Microsoft C 5.0

In this appendix we'll briefly mention some of the differences between the QuickC programming environment and the Microsoft C 5.0 compiler and auxiliary programs. Each compiler has strengths suited to particular parts of a software development project. Together, they offer a more powerful development tool than either provides alone.

Environment and Performance

In a certain sense, QuickC and the Microsoft C 5.0 compiler represent two different philosophies of programming environments. The QuickC environment makes the programming *task* easy, by collecting the most useful development tools in one program, and by providing fast and convenient compilation. The C 5.0 compiler makes the programming *product* (the resulting program) as fast and efficient as possible. That is, the emphasis in the C 5.0 compiler is on the program being built, rather than on the process of building it.

QuickC is an integrated environment that includes an editor, a compiler, and a debugger, all of which can communicate with each other. This means that the compiler can tell the editor the location of compilation errors in your program. Because you can switch among these three programs so easily, QuickC's environment is ideal for the initial writing and compilation of your program. If you wish, you can also use the QuickC compiler independently of the rest of the environment.

The QuickC compiler is fast, and can build a list of errors encountered during compilation. Because the compiler and editor can communicate, the compiler is an important tool for correcting errors during the earliest program development phases.

The C 5.0 compiler, on the other hand, is a stand-alone program, and cannot communicate with the editor. The compiler does provide error messages, including information about the file location at which the error was encountered. The C 5.0 compiler's major strength is its ability to generate code optimized for performance. Whereas the QuickC compiler, itself, works quickly, the C 5.0 compiler can do more to make *your program* run quickly.

Memory Models and Libraries

Very generally, the features and capabilities of the Microsoft C 5.0 compiler form a superset of QuickC's features with respect to the memory models that are supported and the initial configuration of the Run-Time library.

Memory Models

The C 5.0 compiler supports Small, Compact, Medium, Large, and Huge memory models; QuickC supports all but the Huge model. While both compilers support mixed memory models, the C 5.0 compiler also lets you specify a customized memory model, as described in the *User's Guide* for the compiler.

QuickC defaults to a Medium memory model; C 5.0 defaults to a Small memory model. However, both compilers make it easy to specify a different model when compiling.

The C 5.0 compiler gives you somewhat greater flexibility for naming and controlling the use of your program modules or segments, another helpful feature when you are fine-tuning your program's execution.

Libraries

Both compilers include run-time libraries containing the same functions, and both include a library of graphics functions (**graphics.lib**). In addition, each compiler includes a library unique to that compiler. QuickC comes with a graphics Quick library file (**graphics.qlb**), which you can tell QuickC to use if you want to compile programs that use graphics to memory. The C 5.0 compiler includes an alternate floating point library.

To handle floating point operations in QuickC, you would use a floating point library (such as **mlibfp.lib**) and either of two other libraries. One of these (**87.lib**) requires a math coprocessor, such as the 8087 or 80287; the other (**em.lib**) essentially emulates such a coprocessor to carry out floating point operations.

In C 5.0, you can use an alternate math library (such as **mlibfa.lib**) instead of the **mlibfp.lib** and **em.lib** combination. The alternate math library is much faster, but is less accurate, than the emulator library. Using the alternate library lets you build smaller and faster programs. To go along with the alternate library, the C 5.0 compiler also gives you more options for specifying how floating point operations are to be handled in the program being created.

QuickC lets you compile a program to memory and then run the program. This compilation process does not include a link phase, so the compiler does not automatically get access to QuickC's Run-Time library. This means that only functions built into QuickC and those defined in your program can be used when compiling to memory.

If you need to use Run-Time library functions but would still like to compile to memory, you can build a Quick library as we did in Appendix B. Such a library consists of the Run-Time library functions needed by your program. A compiler switch lets you tell QuickC to make use of this library when compiling to memory. Because of their special purpose and format, QuickC libraries can be used only with QuickC. You don't need the Quick library if you compile and link outside the QuickC environment.

Debugging

As mentioned, the QuickC development tools represent a subset of their C 5.0 counterparts. This is because the features and commands available with the CodeView debugger included with C 5.0 are a superset of those available in the QuickC debugger.

The CodeView debugger can evaluate expressions written in any of several languages, including C, BASIC, FORTRAN, and Pascal. CodeView can even work with files that contain both C and assembly source code, for example.

In addition, the expressions CodeView can handle are more extensive than those possible in the QuickC debugger. For example, CodeView can handle expressions involving arithmetic and logical operators, as well as the operators available for the QuickC debugger, which include the indirection operator (*), the structure member and structure pointer operators (. and ->, respectively), the array subscript operator ([]), and parentheses.

CodeView also lets you watch or change specific memory locations, and even look at the contents of machine registers, as the program executes. You can also access individual bytes or entire words at specific locations in Code-View. This makes it easier to do such things as compare two areas of memory. In fact, CodeView lets you compare two areas of memory with a single command; to accomplish the same thing in QuickC, you need to do things in a more roundabout way.

CodeView lets you watch multiple windows (for example, source code, registers, and variables) when compiling, and lets you set conditional break-points, or *watchpoints*. Watchpoints are breakpoints that become active when a particular expression becomes true. Thus, the program will skip the watch-point as if no breakpoint had been set there until the expression becomes true — at which point the breakpoint becomes active, stopping the program when execution reaches the watchpoint statement. CodeView also lets you search memory for specific values.

In short, CodeView lets you watch either variables, expressions, or memory locations. In some cases, you can even change values temporarily in memory to try things during the debugging session. CodeView provides a rich set of commands for making such changes while debugging. The QuickC debugger, on the other hand, lets you see fewer things, and only lets you set regular breakpoints. QuickC does let you set watch variables, however.

CodeView provides support for expanded memory, which enables you to debug programs that were once too large to debug. CodeView also lets you debug library modules.

Finally, CodeView lets you redirect a debugging session to a file. This can provide you with a record of the steps and responses you used to get to a certain state in the program, such as a bug. After making the appropriate modifications in the program, you can replicate your original session with the new version of the program to determine whether you've fixed the bug.

While the QuickC debugger is useful for most ordinary purposes involving moderately sized programs, CodeView provides considerably greater power and flexibility. As your C programs become more complex, you may find CodeView's additional capabilities useful.

Miscellaneous

You can use QuickC's program list facility to provide the information QuickC needs to produce a **.mak** file automatically. Such "make" files save time by making it possible to compile only those files that need to be recompiled.

The format of the **.mak** file produced by QuickC is the same as that required for the C 5.0 compiler to use the same information when compiling. This is useful when you want to move large programs up to the C 5.0 compiler for optimization.

QuickC's on-line help facility, accessible with the F1 function key, is much more extensive than the help available when using the / HELP switch in the C 5.0 compiler. QuickC provides command summaries for each of the QuickC components, as well as information about each of the Run-Time library functions. In contrast, the C 5.0 help facility provides information about the available compiler switches.

Similarities

While there are a number of differences between QuickC and C 5.0, the two compilers also have many similarities.

QuickC source and object files are completely compatible with the C 5.0 compiler. That means you won't have to change programs developed with QuickC, if you decide to optimize or recompile them under C 5.0.

If you tell the QuickC compiler to compile your program for use with a debugger, the compiler produces a file that is compatible with CodeView. This means you can debug your QuickC programs with CodeView, if you wish.

All of QuickC's compiler and linker switches are identical to the same options for the C 5.0 compiler.

Finally, both compilers use the same language definition, as you might expect, since they use the same *Language Reference* manual. Both compilers support most features of the Draft Proposed ANSI Standard language definition, and both include various language extensions. You can tell either compiler not to accept code using language extensions if you need to ensure portability of your program to non-Microsoft environments.

Trademarks

dBASE®	Ashton-Tate
dBASE III®	Ashton-Tate
DOS™	International Business Machines Corporation
Microsoft®	Microsoft Corporation
QuickC®	Microsoft Corporation
UNIX®	AT&T
WordStar®	MicroPro International Corporation

Index

#define, 119, 124
#else, 132
#endif, 133
#error, 134
#flag, 157
#if, 133
#ifdef, 132
#include, 123
#o, 157
#pragma, 134
#symbol, 121
#undef, 132
#X, 157
%E, 154
%f, 154
%g or %G, 154
%hd, 153
%hu, 153
%i, 153
%ld, 153
%lf, 154
%lx, 153
%u, 153

A
abs( ), 136, 516, 552
Absolute value. *See* abs( )
access( ), 548
acos( ), 552
Actual parameters, 127, 217-224
Add Watch option, 67
Address, 0 (Zero), 285
Address operator, 158-165
Address units, 281
Addresses
    allocating, 264
    pointers and, 273-274
    structures and, 465
Aliases, pointer, 286
And operator (&&), 170
annuity( ), 353
annuity_deposit( ), 353
ANSI Standard, 7
Arguments
    command line, 369-390
    passing bad, 227
    passing to main( ), 376-382

Arithmetic, pointer, 280-284
Arithmetic operators, 107-113
Array subscript operator, 323
Array subscripts, returning, 346
Arrays, 290-303
    multidimensional, 315-322
    passing as parameters, 298-303
    pointer, 322-326
    pointers and, 293-298
    string, 324-326
    structure, 473
ASCII table, 558
ASCIIZ strings, 304
asin( ), 552
Assignment operators, 140
    compound, 182-184
    including, 127
Assignment statements, 86
atan( ), 552
atof( ), 411, 516
atoi( ), 315, 411, 516
Auto storage class, 255
Automatic storage duration, 249

B
Binary
    logical operators, 170-171
    operators, 108
    representations, 422
Bit patterns, 422
Bit-fields, 492-496
Bitwise AND operator, 426-430
Bitwise complement operator, 424-426
Bitwise operators, 421-450
Bitwise OR operator, 431-434
Bitwise XOR, 435-438
Blank lines, removing, 399
Blanks, 161
Blocks. *See* Compound statements
Braces, finding matching, 54
Break and continue, 201-204
Break statement, 201-204

Breaking out of programs, 342-343
Breakpoints, setting, 30
Buffered input, 149
Bugs. *See* Debugging
Build Program option, 65

C
Call by reference. *See* Pass by reference
Call by value. *See* Pass by value
Calling QuickC, commands for, 572-573
calloc( ), 414, 516
case, 179
Case sensitivity, 83
Cast operator, 404-407
ceil( ), 553
Changing text, 60
char type, 89
Character
    constants, 104
    routines, 537-541
    strings, 303-315
Characters
    blank, tab, and newline, 161
    reading, 146-152
    special search, 59
    whitespace, 161
char__pos( ), 346
chmod( ), 549
clean__of__char( ), 346
clearerr( ), 509
Clipboard, copying text to the, 46-50
CodeView, 592-593
Comma operator, 200
Command line arguments, 369-390
Command line text box, 66
Command summary, 571-587
Commands
    cursor movement, 573-575
    deletion, 575
    editing, 573
    entering QuickC, 15
    executing DOS, 70

Commands, *continued*
    insertion, 575
    menu, 576-583
    QuickC, 38-72
    selection, 575
Comments, program, 75
Compile errors, 19
Compile option, 65
Compiler instructions, table of, 65
Compiling, 9-11, 61-66
    outside QuickC, 584
Compound assignment operators,
    182-184
Compound statements, 81, 168, 208
    defining variables within, 245-247
compound_interest( ), 352
Conditional actions, 167
Conditional operators, 451-455
Constants, 101-106
    manifest, 120, 124-127
Continuation condition, 187
Continue option, 61
Continue statement, 201-204
Control constructs, 167-204
Controlling C, 167-204
Conversion routines, 537-541
Copying text, 23
    commands for, 50
cos( ), 554
Creating files, 39-60
Creating programs in QuickC, 14-17
ctype.h, 536-537
Cursor movement
    commands, 573-575
    keystrokes, 41-45
Cut and paste, 46-50

D

Data types. *See* also Types
    operations on mixed, 110-113
    simple, 88-98
    summary of, 101

Date and time, 544
dbl_mean( ), 345
Debug Menu, 66-67
    commands, 582-583
Debug options, 63
    table of, 68
Debugger, using the QuickC, 247-249
Debugging, 28-38
    features in QuickC, 592
Decimal numbers, 103
Declaration and definition, differences
    between, 258
Decrement operator (−−), 184-186
Default keywords and labels, 179-180
Defining
    simple data types, 95
    variables, 84-88
delete( ), 345
Delete All Watch option, 67
Deleting text, 49-51
Deletion commands, 575
dir command, 373-376
Direct reference, 269
Disk space, determining available, 543
div( ), 517
Do-while loop, 191-192
DOS, going temporarily to, 70
DOS Shell option, 70
dos.h, 541-548
Double constants, 106
Double precision, 92-95
double type, 92-95, 158
Dynamic memory allocation, 403-420

E

echo command, 372
Edit Menu commands, 576
Editing
    commands, summary of, 573-576
    files, 39-60
    modes, 39
Else, missing, 176

End of line, 164
Enumeration types, 500-502
Equality operators, 137, 168-169
Error handling, 338-344
Errors
    compile, 19
    moving the cursor to, 45
Escape codes, 79
Exe Output option, 37
Executable files, 10
exit( ), 342-343, 516
Extern storage class, 257-258

F
fabs( ), 136
fclose( ), 393, 507
fcloseall( ), 510
Features
    C programming language, 2-3
    Microsoft C 5.0, 589-594
    QuickC, 589-594
feof( ), 399, 507
ferror( ), 399, 507
fgetc( ), 149-150, 507
fgetchar( ), 148-149, 507
fgets( ), 398, 507
Fibonacci numbers, 365
Field width, 154-156
File manipulation commands, 577
File menu, 53-54, 577
Files, 392-403
    creating and editing, 39-60
    executable, 10
    header, 8, 118, 143-144
    include, 143-144
    library, 10
    manipulating, 53-54
    moving around in, 40-45
    moving text between, 45
    object, 10
    overwriting, 54
    reading and writing, 145-166

Files, *continued*
    source, 8
    using dir command with, 374
    working with in QuickC, 14-27
Find options, 56-59
Flags, printf( ), 156
Float constants, 106
float type, 90-92
Floating point
    numbers, 90-95
    type operators, 107
    types, 154
floor( ), 553
fopen( ), 392, 507
For loop, 193-200
    omitting expressions from, 197
Formal parameters, 127, 217-224
fprintf( ), 157, 507
fputc( ), 150-152, 508
fputchar( ), 150-152, 508
fputs( ), 508
free( ), 416-417, 516
freopen( ), 510
fscanf( ), 413, 508
Function
    body, 208
    call operator, 331
    calls, 210
    declaration, 137
    declarator, 208
    heading, 208
    libraries, building, 559-569
    option, 67-68
Function parameters
    pointers as, 274-280
    using structures as, 467
Function prototypes, 227-238
Function returns, 213-217
Functions
    creating, 205-225
    defined in this book, 344-358
    finance oriented, 352-359

Functions, *continued*
    I/O, 506-511
    library, 135-140
    QuickC library, 505-556
    returning pointers with, 330-338
    returning structures, 469
    string, 309-315, 345-352

G
getc( ), 149-150, 508
getch( ), 137, 146, 152
getchar( ), 148-149
getche( ), 137, 152
getenv( ), 517
gets( ), 306, 310, 398, 508

H
Header files, 8, 118, 143-144
Help, on-line, 39, 573
Hexadecimal numbers, 102-104, 153
High-level language, 5

I
I/O, 145-166
    functions, 506-511
Identifiers, 81-84
    naming, 82
    using to refer to memory locations,
      239
If statements, 172-178
    dangling, 178
    watching, 340
If-else construct, 172-178
Include files, 143-144
Increment operator (++), 184-186
Indexing in multidimensional arrays, 319
Indirect reference, 269
Indirection operator, 269
Initialization during variable definition,
    87
Initializing arrays, 292
Input/output, 145-166
Insert mode, 39
Insertion commands, 575

int type, 89
    using in a program, 135
intdos( ), 543
Integer constants, 102-104
Integer type operators, 107
Integers, 89
Integral types, 153
Interrupts, DOS, 542, 547
int__mean( ), 345
io.h, 548-551
isalnum( ), 537
isalpha( ), 537
isascii( ), 537
iscntrl( ), 537
isdigit( ), 537
isgraph( ), 537
islower( ), 537
isprint( ), 537
ispunct( ), 537
isspace( ), 537
isupper( ), 537
isxdigit( ), 537
Iteration, 167
itoa( ), 315, 518-519

K
Keystrokes for cursor movement, 41-45
Keywords, 84
    list of, 85

L
labs( ), 136, 519, 552
Languages, properties of high- and low-
    level, 6
ldiv( ), 519
Left shift operator, 439
Lexicographic ordering, 310
Libraries,
    building stand-alone, 564
    Microsoft C 5.0, 591
    Quick, 559-569
Library files, 10

Library functions, 135-140
    creating, 205-225
    QuickC, 505-556
    string, 309-315
Lifetime, storage, 249-251
Linked lists, 479-492
Linker, controlling the, 585
Linking, 9-11
    outside QuickC, 584
Lists, linked, 479-492
Logical negation operator, 171
Logical operators, 170-172
Logical shift, 443
long (integer), 99
long int, 153
    using in a program, 135
Loops, 186-204
Low-level language, 5
Lvalues, 264-267

M
Macro body, 120
Macros, 120
    parameters with, 127-132
    predefined, 141-142
Main program, 4
main( ), 4, 75-76
    passing parameters to, 376-382
    using as program and as function, 370
malloc( ), 408-414, 516
Manifest constants, 120, 124-127
Mantissa, 91
Marking text, 45-52
Masks, bit, 427
Matching braces, finding, 54
math.h, 551-555
Matrices, 319
Member lists, 464
Members, structure, 458

memchr( ), 526
memcmp( ), 527
memcpy( ), 527
memmove( ), 527
Memory allocation, 403-420
    function declaration and, 137
Memory models, 585
    Microsoft C 5.0, 590
memset( ), 528
Menu commands, 576-583
Merge option, 49
Microsoft C 5.0, similarities to QuickC, 593
Mixed types, operations on, 110-113
Modifying programs in QuickC, 18-21
Modularity, 3
Modulus operator, 108
monthly__mortgage( ), 353
Movement commands, cursor, 573-575
Moving blocks of text, 23, 45-52
Multidimensional arrays, 315-322

N
Name length, maximum, 83
Naming rules in C, 82
Negation operator, 171
Negative numbers, 89
Nested structures, 464
Newline characters, 161
non__zero( ), 344
NULL, 285
NULL character, 307
Numbers, octal and hexadecimal, 102-104

O
Object files, 10
Objects, 264-267
Octal numbers, 102-104
On-line help, 39, 573
One's complement, 424

Open Last File option, 53
Open option, 53
Operator precedence, 109-110
Operators
    address, 158-165
    arithmetic, 107-113
    bitwise, 421-450
    compound assignment, 182-184
    conditional, 451-455
    equality, 137, 169-170
    evaluating, 273
    increment and decrement, 184-186
    logical, 170-172
    precedence of, 173
    relational, 168-169
    shift, 439-450
    unary, 160
Or operator (||), 170
Overflow conditions, 91
Overtype mode, 39

P
Parameters
    actual, 217-224
    array, 298-303
    formal, 217-224
    function prototype, 233
    macros with, 127-132
    passing by reference, 278
    passing by value, 219
    passing structures as, 467
    passing to main( ), 376-382
    scope and, 243-245
    using pointers as function, 274-280
Pass by value, 219, 244, 471
Pass by reference, 278
perror( ), 510
Placeholder types, printf( ), 113
Pointer aliases, 286
Pointer arithmetic, 280-284

Pointer arrays, 322-326
Pointer Check option, 63
Pointers, 263-288
    arrays and, 293-298
    misguided, 287
    multidimensional arrays and, 319
    returning with functions, 330-338
    structures and, 471
Portability, 3
Postfix test, 185
pow( ), 552
Powers of two, shift operators and, 447
Precedence, operator, 109-110, 173
Precision, specifying, 154-156
Prefix test, 185
Preprocessor, C, 119-135
    controlling the, 585
Print option, 70
printf( ), 76-79, 153-157, 508
    placeholder types for, 113-114
Program
    character routine, 538-541
    example of structure and features,
        116-117
    file reader, 396
    finance function, 353-358
    I/O function, 511-515
    io.h, 550
    linked list, 479-492
    math.h, 555
    notepad, 395
    replacing tabs and spaces, 401
    right shift operator, 444
    stand-alone library, 564
    stdlib.h, 521-525
    string function, 348-352
    string.h, 530-536
    structure pointer array, 476
    using command line arguments,
        382-390

Program, *continued*
    using predefined macros, 141-142
Program execution
    resuming, 61
    tracking, 28
Program list commands, 577
Program lists, 69-70
Program structure, C, 74-79, 115-119
Programming, example of C, 3-5
Programs
    compiling, 61
    creating in QuickC, 14-17
    debugging, 28-38
    exiting, 342-343
    modifying in QuickC, 18-21
    steps in creating C, 11
Prototypes, function, 227-238
putc( ), 150-152, 509
putch( ), 152
putchar( ), 150-152, 509
puts( ), 310, 509

Q
qcstuff.qlb, 560
Quick Libraries, 559-569

R
rand( ), 137, 214-215, 517
Reading and writing in C, 145-166
Real numbers, 90-95
realloc( ), 414-416, 517
Recursion, 359-368
Redirection operators, DOS, 338
References, direct and indirect, 269
Register storage class, 255-257
Registers, Intel processor, 541
Relational operators, 168-169
remove( ), 511
remove__wd( ), 346
rename( ), 549
Replace text, 56-59
Reserved words, 2

Return (end of input line), 164
Return statement (function), 213-217
Returned pointers, 330-338
reverse__str( ), 346
rewind( ), 511
Right shift operator, 443
Run Menu, 61-66
    commands, 580-582
Run-time option, 35-36, 66

S
safe__division( ), 344
scanf( ), 160-164, 413, 509
Scope, 239-248
Screen, initial Quick C, 16
Screen, scrolling the, 44-45
Scrolling commands, 44-45
Search Menu, 54-56
    commands, 579
Searching for functions, 67-68
Seed values, 31
Selection commands, 575
Selection construct, 167
Self-referential structures, 478-492
Shift operators, 439-450
short (integer), 99
short int, 153
short unsigned int, 153
signed char, 99
signed int, 99
Simple data types, 88-98
    summary of, 101
    variants on, 99-101
Simple statements, 80
sin( ), 554
Source file, 8
Spaces, replacing, 401
Special characters, using in search
    expressions, 59
sqrt( ), 552
Stack Check option, 64

Standards, C, 7
Start option, 61
Statements, 80-81. *See also* Compound
    assignment, 86
Static storage, 403
    class, 251-255
stderr, 338-344
stdin, 148
stdio.h, 148, 506-509
stdlib.h, 515-525
stdout, 151
    using in error handling, 338
Storage class specifiers, 251-260
Storage classes
    array, 292
    default, 259
Storage, determining available, 417
Storage duration, 249-251
    default, 259
strcat( ), 312-315, 525
strchr( ), 528
strcmp( ), 310-312, 525
strcopy( ), 314, 526
strdup( ), 528
String
    arguments, comparing, 310
    arrays, 324-326
    constants, 105
    library functions, 309-315
string.h, 525-536
Strings, 303-315
    problems with defining and
      manipulating, 333-338
    using dynamic memory allocation
      with, 419
strlen( ), 305, 526
strlwr( ), 528
strncat( ), 312-315, 525
strncmp( ), 310-312, 525
strncopy( ), 314, 526
strpbrk( ), 528

strrchr( ), 529
strrev( ), 346, 529
strset( ), 529
strstr( ), 529
Structure arrays, 473
Structure member operator, 461
Structure pointer arrays, 473
Structures, 458-492
    self-referential, 478-492
strupr( ), 529
Suppressing values, 164
swap_dbl( ), 344
swap_int( ), 344
Switch construct, 178-182
Switches, compiler, 65
Syntax Check option, 63
Syntax, non-prototype, 237
system( ), 519

T
Tab characters, 161
Tabs
    inserting, 52
    replacing, 401
Tag name, structure, 458, 463-464
tan( ), 554
Text
    changing, 60
    copying, 23
    copying to the Clipboard, 46-50
    deleting, 49-51
    finding and replacing, 56-59
    marking, 23
    marking and moving, 45-52
Text marking commands, 48
Type specifiers, 381
Typedef storage class, 260
Types
    enumeration, 500-502
    floating point, 153
    integral, 153

Types, *continued*
  operations on mixed, 110-113
  simple data, 88-98
  variable, 84

U
Unary negation operator, 171
Unary operators, 108, 160
  evaluating, 273
Undo commands, 51
ungetc( ), 149-150
ungetch( ), 146
Unions, 497-500
Unions of structures, 499
unsigned char, 99
unsigned int, 99
  using to display address values, 272

V
Values, 264-267
  checking intermediate, 359
  returned function, 213-217
  suppressing, 164
  variable, 158-165
Variable types, 84

Variables
  array, 290-303
  checking values of, 30
  declarations and definitions of, 258
  defining, 84-88
  defining within compound
    statements, 245-247
  duration of, 249-251
  global and local, 119, 250
  initializing during definition, 87
  local, 242
  looping, 189
  passing, 158-165
  pointer, 267-274
  returning pointers to local, 338
  watching values of, 67
View Menu commands, 576
Visibility, 239-248
void, 238, 409

W
Warning Levels, 62
While loop, 186-191
  components of, 188
Whitespace, 161

Z
zero_one_rand( ), 345

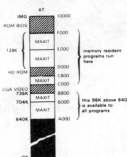
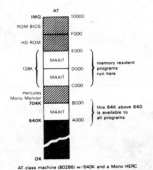